8 Practice Tests
for the SAT®

8 Practice Tests

for the SAT®

KAPLAN) PUBLISHING

New York

© 2018 by Kaplan, Inc.
Published by Kaplan Publishing, a division of Kaplan, Inc.
750 Third Avenue
New York, NY 10017

10   9   8   7   6   5   4   3   2   1

ISBN-13: 978-1-5062-3519-6

Kaplan Publishing print books are available at special quantity discounts to use for sales promotions, employee premiums, or educational purposes. For more information or to purchase books, please call the Simon & Schuster special sales department at 866-506-1949.

Table of Contents

Practice Makes Perfect vii

Practice Test One 1
Practice Test One Answers and Explanations 51
Practice Test Two 87
Practice Test Two Answers and Explanations 135
Practice Test Three 171
Practice Test Three Answers and Explanations 223
Practice Test Four 259
Practice Test Four Answers and Explanations 307
Practice Test Five 343
Practice Test Five Answers and Explanations 391
Practice Test Six 425
Practice Test Six Answers and Explanations 471
Practice Test Seven 505
Practice Test Seven Answers and Explanations 555
Practice Test Eight 591
Practice Test Eight Answers and Explanations 639

Practice Makes Perfect

Do not be scared of the SAT. Why? Because we know what's on the exam, and we know exactly how you should prepare for it. Kaplan has been teaching kids how to succeed on the SAT for more than 75 years—longer than anyone else, period.

This book contains 8 practice exams that mirror the SAT you will face on Test Day—more SAT practice than can be found between the covers of any other book. Practice is one of the keys to mastery, and these 8 exams give you plenty of practice to assess your strengths and weaknesses before you take the real thing.

Just as important as taking practice tests is understanding why you got a question right or wrong when you're done. The detailed answers and explanations that follow each practice test tell you the correct answers and explain how to get there.

Every practice question and answer explanation in this book is geared toward one thing—getting you more points on the actual SAT. So don't stress out over the SAT—Kaplan's got you covered.

HOW TO USE THIS BOOK

This book is filled with over 1,200 practice questions to help you master the SAT. Follow these steps to get the most out of these 8 practice tests:

1. Read about the SAT structure in the next section. This way, you'll know what to expect—not only as you work through the book but, more importantly, on Test Day.

2. Begin your practice! Buying this book has given you an advantage—after you've worked your way through the exams, the format and timing of the SAT will be second nature to you. All you will have to concentrate on is improving your skills in the areas that need work.

3. Keep track. Turn to the Score Tracker on page xvi, where you can track your score as you take each exam. Keep a record of your scores and watch how much you improve from test to test.

4. Assess your strengths and weaknesses. After you finish each test, carefully read the detailed explanations—pay attention to the questions you got wrong, but don't forget to read about the ones you got right. It's important to note your areas of strength as well as weakness. Take your own personal inventory of the skills you've mastered and the skills you need to work on.

5. Watch your scores improve! After you've made your way halfway through the book, compare your scores on Test 1 and Test 4. You've made progress, haven't you? See if your strengths and weaknesses have changed. Then work your way through the remaining tests, building skills and SAT competency along the way.

After making your way through these steps, we guarantee that you will have the test expertise and improved skills to tackle the SAT with confidence.

HOW THE SAT IS STRUCTURED

The SAT is 3 hours long, and 3 hours and 50 minutes if you take the optional Essay. It's primarily a multiple-choice exam, with an optional written essay and some grid-in math questions as the exceptions. It's divided into five sections: one Evidence-Based Reading, one Writing & Language, one Math without a calculator, one Math with a calculator, and one optional Essay.

Here is a breakdown of the test:

Structure of the SAT				
	Test	Content	Timing	Questions
Evidence-Based Reading and Writing	Reading Test	3,250 words total from 4 single passages and 1 paired set; 500-750 words per passage or paired set drawing from U.S. and World Literature, History/Social Studies, and Science. Two passages will include one or two informational graphics.	65 minutes	52 multiple-choice questions (10-11 per passage or passage set)
	Writing and Language Test	1,700 words total from 4 passages of 400-450 words each, drawing from Careers, History/Social Studies, Humanities, or Science. 1-2 passages will be Argumentative, 1-2 passages will be Informative/Explanatory, and 1 passage will be a Nonfiction Narrative.	35 minutes	44 multiple-choice questions (11 questions per passage)
Math	No-Calculator Section	Questions are drawn from the Heart of Algebra, Passport to Advanced Math, and Additional Topics in Math content areas. No Problem Solving or Data Analysis questions.	25 minutes	15 multiple-choice questions + 5 student-produced response questions = 20 total questions
	Calculator Section	Questions are drawn from the Heart of Algebra, Problem Solving and Data Analysis, Passport to Advanced Math, and Additional Topics in Math content areas.	55 minutes	30 multiple-choice questions + 8 student-produced response questions = 38 total questions
Essay (optional)		You will be asked to analyze a 650-750 word document and draft an essay. This essay question tests reading, analysis, and writing skills, and requires you to analyze a source document and explain how the author builds an argument.	50 minutes	1 prompt

HOW THE SAT IS SCORED

You gain one point for every question you answer correctly; you lose no points for answering a question wrong OR for leaving a question blank. This means you should ALWAYS answer EVERY question on the SAT—even if you have to guess.

Scoring information and conversion charts are found on pages xii–xv.

SAT TEST DATES

As a general rule, it's important to get one SAT score under your belt by the end of your junior year. This way, you know where you stand as you plan your college choices. Plus, it's likely that you'll improve your score by taking the exam again, because it will be familiar to you.

The SAT is administered on select Saturdays during the school year. Sunday testing is available for students who cannot take the Saturday test because of religious observances. The SAT exam is offered in January, March, May, June, October, November, and December of each year. Check the official College Board website at collegeboard.org for the most up-to-date test dates.

SAT REGISTRATION

Check the College Board website at www.collegeboard.org for complete information about registering for the SAT. Here are some important highlights:

- To register for the SAT by mail, you'll need to get an SAT Paper Registration Guide from your high school guidance counselor.
- You can register online at collegereadiness.collegeboard.org/sat/register. **Important:** Not all students are eligible to register online, so read the instructions and requirements carefully.
- Register early to secure the time you want at the test center of your choice and to avoid late registration fees.
- Students with disabilities can go to collegeboard.org/students-with-disabilities to read about how to apply for accommodations or call 212-713-8333 (TTY: (609) 882-4118) for more information.
- At press time, the fee for the SAT is $60 with the essay, and $46 without the essay in the United States. This price includes reports for you, your high school, and up to four colleges and scholarship programs. To get the most up-to-date information, please check collegereadiness.collegeboard.org/sat/register/fees.
- You will receive an admission ticket at least a week before the test. The ticket confirms your registration on a specified date, at a specified test center. Make sure to bring this, along with proper identification, to the test center. Some acceptable

forms of identification include photo IDs such as a driver's license, a school identification card, or a valid passport. (Unacceptable forms of identification include a
Social Security card, credit card, or birth certificate.)

- Your SAT scores will be available online approximately three weeks after the test.
- Remember to check with the College Board for all the latest information on the SAT. Every effort has been made to keep the information in this book as up-to-date as possible, but changes may occur after the book is published.
- Finally, bookmark the College Board's website: www.collegeboard.org.

ESSAY SCORING RUBRIC

Score	Reading	Analysis	Writing
4	• demonstrates **thorough comprehension** of the source text • shows an understanding of the text's central idea(s) and most important details and how they interrelate • is free of errors of fact or interpretation with regard to the text • makes skillful use of textual evidence	• offers an **insightful analysis** of the source text and demonstrates a **sophisticated understanding** of the analytical task • offers a thorough, well-considered evaluation of the author's use of evidence, reasoning, and/or stylistic and persuasive elements, and/or feature(s) of the student's own choosing • contains relevant, sufficient, and strategically chosen support for claim(s) or point(s) made • focuses consistently on those features of the text that are most relevant to addressing the task	• is **cohesive** and demonstrates a **highly effective use and command** of language • includes a precise central claim • includes a skillful introduction and conclusion; demonstrates a deliberate and highly effective progression of ideas both within paragraphs and throughout the essay • has a wide variety of sentence structures; demonstrates a consistent use of precise word choice; maintains a formal style and objective tone • shows a strong command of the conventions of standard written English and is free or virtually free of errors
3	• demonstrates **effective comprehension** of the source text • shows an understanding of the text's central idea(s) and important details • is free of substantive errors of fact and interpretation with regard to the text • makes appropriate use of textual evidence	• offers an **effective analysis** of the source text and demonstrates an **understanding** of the analytical task • competently evaluates the author's use of evidence, reasoning, and/or stylistic and persuasive elements, and/or feature(s) of the student's own choosing • contains relevant and sufficient support for claim(s) or point(s) made • focuses primarily on those features of the text that are most relevant to addressing the task	• is **mostly cohesive** and demonstrates **effective use and control** of language • includes a central claim or implicit controlling idea • includes an effective introduction and conclusion; demonstrates a clear progression of ideas both within paragraphs and throughout the essay • has variety in sentence structures; demonstrates some precise word choice; maintains a formal style and objective tone • shows a good control of the conventions of standard written English and is free of significant errors that detract from the quality of writing

Score	Reading	Analysis	Writing
2	• demonstrates **some comprehension** of the source text • shows an understanding of the text's central idea(s) but not of important details • may contain errors of fact and/or interpretation with regard to the text • makes limited and/or haphazard use of textual evidence	• offers **limited analysis** of the source text and demonstrates only **partial understanding** of the analytical task • identifies and attempts to describe the author's use of evidence, reasoning, and/or stylistic and persuasive elements, and/or feature(s) of the student's own choosing, but merely asserts rather than explains their importance • one or more aspects of analysis are unwarranted based on the text • contains little or not support for claim(s) or point(s) made • may lack a clear focus on those features of the text that are most relevant to addressing the task	• demonstrates **little or no cohesion** and **limited skill** in the use and control of language • may lack a clear central claim or controlling idea or may deviate from the claim or idea • may include an ineffective introduction and/or conclusion; may demonstrate some progression of ideas within paragraphs but not throughout • has limited variety in sentence structures; sentence structures may be repetitive; demonstrates general or vague word choice; word choice may be repetitive; may deviate noticeably from a formal style and objective tone • shows a limited control of the conventions of standard written English and contains errors that detract from the quality of writing and may impede understanding
1	• demonstrates **little or no comprehension** of the source text • fails to show an understanding of the text's central idea(s), and may include only details without reference to central idea(s) • may contain numerous errors of fact and/or interpretation with regard to the text • makes little or no use of textual evidence	• offers **little or no analysis or ineffective analysis** of the source text and demonstrates **little to no understanding** of the analytical task • identifies without explanation some aspects of the author's use of evidence, reasoning, and/or stylistic and persuasive elements, and/or feature(s) of the student's own choosing numerous aspects of analysis are unwarranted based on the text • contains little or no support for claim(s) or point(s) made, or support is largely irrelevant • may not focus on features of the text that are relevant to addressing the task • offers no discernible analysis (e.g., is largely or exclusively summary)	• demonstrates **little or no cohesion** and **inadequate skill** in the use and control of language • may lack a clear central claim or controlling idea • lacks a recognizable introduction and conclusion; does not have a discernible progression of ideas • lacks variety in sentence structures; sentence structures may be repetitive; demonstrates general and vague word choice; word choice may be poor or inaccurate; may lack a formal style and objective tone • shows a weak control of the conventions of standard written English and may contain numerous errors that undermine the quality of writing

Essay Rubric from College Board: collegereadiness.collegeboard.org/sat/scores/essay

CONVERT YOUR RAW SCORE TO A SCALED SCORE

For each subject area in the practice test, convert your raw score, or the number of questions you answered correctly, to a scaled score using the table below. To get your raw score for Evidence-Based Reading & Writing, add the total number of Reading questions you answered correctly to the total number of Writing questions you answered correctly; for Math, add the number of questions you answered correctly for the Math—No Calculator and Math—Calculator sections.

Evidence-Based Reading and Writing		Math	
TOTAL Raw Score	Scaled Score	Raw Score	Scaled Score
0	200	0	200
1	200	1	220
2	210	2	240
3	220	3	260
4	240	4	290
5	260	5	310
6	270	6	320
7	270	7	330
8	290	8	340
9	290	9	360
10	300	10	370
11	300	11	380
12	310	12	390
13	320	13	400
14	320	14	410
15	330	15	420
16	330	16	430
17	340	17	430
18	340	18	440
19	350	19	450
20	350	20	450
21	360	21	460
22	360	22	470
23	370	23	480
24	370	24	490
25	370	25	500
26	380	26	510
27	380	27	520
28	380	28	530
29	380	29	540
30	390	30	540
31	390	31	550
32	400	32	560
33	400	33	560
34	410	34	570
35	410	35	580
36	420	36	590
37	430	37	600
38	430	38	600
39	440	39	610
40	440	40	620
41	450	41	630
42	450	42	640
43	460	43	640

Evidence-Based Reading and Writing		Math	
TOTAL Raw Score	Scaled Score	Raw Score	Scaled Score
44	460	44	660
45	470	45	670
46	480	46	670
47	480	47	680
48	490	48	690
49	490	49	700
50	500	50	710
51	500	51	720
52	510	52	740
53	510	53	750
54	520	54	760
55	520	55	770
56	530	56	780
57	530	57	790
58	540	58	800
59	540		
60	550		
61	550		
62	560		
63	560		
64	570		
65	570		
66	580		
67	580		
68	590		
69	590		
70	600		
71	600		
72	610		
73	610		
74	610		
75	620		
76	620		
77	630		
78	630		
79	640		
80	640		
81	660		
82	660		
83	670		
84	680		
85	690		
86	700		
87	700		
88	710		
89	710		
90	730		
91	740		
92	750		
93	760		
94	780		
95	790		
96	800		

SCORE TRACKER

After you take each test, refer to the scoring conversion chart on the previous pages. Then translate your raw score into a scaled score of 200–800 for each section using the table that begins on page xiv. Write your results in the chart below. As you take more practice tests, watch as your scores in each section begin to go up!

	Math	Evidence-Based Reading and Writing	Total
Test 1			
Test 2			
Test 3			
Test 4			
Test 5			
Test 6			
Test 7			
Test 8			

Start your practice!

SAT PRACTICE TEST 1 ANSWER SHEET

Remove (or photocopy) this answer sheet and use it to complete the test. See the answer key following the test when finished.

Start with number 1 for each section. If a section has fewer questions than answer spaces, leave the extra spaces blank.

SECTION 1

1. A B C D
2. A B C D
3. A B C D
4. A B C D
5. A B C D
6. A B C D
7. A B C D
8. A B C D
9. A B C D
10. A B C D
11. A B C D
12. A B C D
13. A B C D
14. A B C D
15. A B C D
16. A B C D
17. A B C D
18. A B C D
19. A B C D
20. A B C D
21. A B C D
22. A B C D
23. A B C D
24. A B C D
25. A B C D
26. A B C D
27. A B C D
28. A B C D
29. A B C D
30. A B C D
31. A B C D
32. A B C D
33. A B C D
34. A B C D
35. A B C D
36. A B C D
37. A B C D
38. A B C D
39. A B C D
40. A B C D
41. A B C D
42. A B C D
43. A B C D
44. A B C D
45. A B C D
46. A B C D
47. A B C D
48. A B C D
49. A B C D
50. A B C D
51. A B C D
52. A B C D

correct in Section 1

incorrect in Section 1

SECTION 2

1. A B C D
2. A B C D
3. A B C D
4. A B C D
5. A B C D
6. A B C D
7. A B C D
8. A B C D
9. A B C D
10. A B C D
11. A B C D
12. A B C D
13. A B C D
14. A B C D
15. A B C D
16. A B C D
17. A B C D
18. A B C D
19. A B C D
20. A B C D
21. A B C D
22. A B C D
23. A B C D
24. A B C D
25. A B C D
26. A B C D
27. A B C D
28. A B C D
29. A B C D
30. A B C D
31. A B C D
32. A B C D
33. A B C D
34. A B C D
35. A B C D
36. A B C D
37. A B C D
38. A B C D
39. A B C D
40. A B C D
41. A B C D
42. A B C D
43. A B C D
44. A B C D

correct in Section 2

incorrect in Section 2

SECTION 3

1. Ⓐ Ⓑ Ⓒ Ⓓ
2. Ⓐ Ⓑ Ⓒ Ⓓ
3. Ⓐ Ⓑ Ⓒ Ⓓ
4. Ⓐ Ⓑ Ⓒ Ⓓ

5. Ⓐ Ⓑ Ⓒ Ⓓ
6. Ⓐ Ⓑ Ⓒ Ⓓ
7. Ⓐ Ⓑ Ⓒ Ⓓ
8. Ⓐ Ⓑ Ⓒ Ⓓ

9. Ⓐ Ⓑ Ⓒ Ⓓ
10. Ⓐ Ⓑ Ⓒ Ⓓ
11. Ⓐ Ⓑ Ⓒ Ⓓ
12. Ⓐ Ⓑ Ⓒ Ⓓ

13. Ⓐ Ⓑ Ⓒ Ⓓ
14. Ⓐ Ⓑ Ⓒ Ⓓ
15. Ⓐ Ⓑ Ⓒ Ⓓ

correct in Section 3

incorrect in Section 3

16. 17. 18. 19. 20.

SECTION 4

1. Ⓐ Ⓑ Ⓒ Ⓓ
2. Ⓐ Ⓑ Ⓒ Ⓓ
3. Ⓐ Ⓑ Ⓒ Ⓓ
4. Ⓐ Ⓑ Ⓒ Ⓓ
5. Ⓐ Ⓑ Ⓒ Ⓓ
6. Ⓐ Ⓑ Ⓒ Ⓓ
7. Ⓐ Ⓑ Ⓒ Ⓓ
8. Ⓐ Ⓑ Ⓒ Ⓓ

9. Ⓐ Ⓑ Ⓒ Ⓓ
10. Ⓐ Ⓑ Ⓒ Ⓓ
11. Ⓐ Ⓑ Ⓒ Ⓓ
12. Ⓐ Ⓑ Ⓒ Ⓓ
13. Ⓐ Ⓑ Ⓒ Ⓓ
14. Ⓐ Ⓑ Ⓒ Ⓓ
15. Ⓐ Ⓑ Ⓒ Ⓓ
16. Ⓐ Ⓑ Ⓒ Ⓓ

17. Ⓐ Ⓑ Ⓒ Ⓓ
18. Ⓐ Ⓑ Ⓒ Ⓓ
19. Ⓐ Ⓑ Ⓒ Ⓓ
20. Ⓐ Ⓑ Ⓒ Ⓓ
21. Ⓐ Ⓑ Ⓒ Ⓓ
22. Ⓐ Ⓑ Ⓒ Ⓓ
23. Ⓐ Ⓑ Ⓒ Ⓓ
24. Ⓐ Ⓑ Ⓒ Ⓓ

25. Ⓐ Ⓑ Ⓒ Ⓓ
26. Ⓐ Ⓑ Ⓒ Ⓓ
27. Ⓐ Ⓑ Ⓒ Ⓓ
28. Ⓐ Ⓑ Ⓒ Ⓓ
29. Ⓐ Ⓑ Ⓒ Ⓓ
30. Ⓐ Ⓑ Ⓒ Ⓓ

correct in Section 4

incorrect in Section 4

31. 32. 33. 34.
35. 36. 37. 38.

READING TEST

65 Minutes—52 Questions

This section corresponds to Section 1 of your answer sheet.

Directions: Read each passage or pair of passages, then answer the questions that follow. Choose your answers based on what the passage(s) and any accompanying graphics state or imply.

Questions 1-10 are based on the following passage.

This passage is adapted from *A Study in Scarlet*, Sir Arthur Conan Doyle's first story in his acclaimed Sherlock Holmes series. In this excerpt the narrator, Dr. Watson, observes Mr. Holmes, with whom he has recently entered into a shared housing arrangement, although he knows very little about this new room-mate as of yet.

As the weeks went by, my interest in him and my curiosity as to his aims in life gradually deepened and increased. His very person and appearance
Line were such as to strike the attention of the most
(5) casual observer. In height he was rather over six feet, and so excessively lean that he seemed to be considerably taller. His eyes were sharp and piercing, save during those intervals of torpor to which I have alluded; and his thin, hawk-like nose gave his
(10) whole expression an air of alertness and decision. His chin, too, had the prominence and squareness which mark the man of determination. His hands were invariably blotted with ink and stained with chemicals, yet he was possessed of extraordinary
(15) delicacy of touch, as I frequently had occasion to observe when I watched him manipulating his fragile philosophical instruments. . . .

He was not studying medicine. He had himself, in reply to a question, confirmed Stamford's[1]
(20) opinion upon that point. Neither did he appear to have pursued any course of reading which might fit him for a degree in science or any other recognized

portal which would give him an entrance into the learned world. Yet his zeal for certain studies
(25) was remarkable, and within eccentric limits his knowledge was so extraordinarily ample and minute that his observations have fairly astounded me. Surely no man would work so hard or attain such precise information unless he had some
(30) definite end in view. Desultory readers are seldom remarkable for the exactness of their learning. No man burdens his mind with small matters unless he has some very good reason for doing so.

His ignorance was as remarkable as his knowledge.
(35) Of contemporary literature, philosophy and politics he appeared to know next to nothing. Upon my quoting Thomas Carlyle,[2] he inquired in the naïvest way who he might be and what he had done. My surprise reached a climax, however, when I found
(40) incidentally that he was ignorant of the Copernican Theory and of the composition of the solar system. That any civilized human being in this nineteenth century should not be aware that the earth travelled round the sun appeared to be to me such an
(45) extraordinary fact that I could hardly realize it.

"You appear to be astonished," he said, smiling at my expression of surprise. "Now that I do know it I shall do my best to forget it."

"To forget it!"

(50) "You see," he explained, "I consider that a man's brain originally is like a little empty attic, and you have to stock it with such furniture as you choose. A fool takes in all the lumber of every sort that he comes across, so that the knowledge which might

[1]Stamford is the mutual acquaintance who introduced Dr. Watson to Mr. Holmes. In a previous scene he told Watson that Holmes was not a medical student.

[2]Thomas Carlyle was an influential writer and philosopher whose work was well known at the time of this novel's publication.

GO ON TO THE NEXT PAGE

(55) be useful to him gets crowded out, or at best is jumbled up with a lot of other things so that he has a difficulty in laying his hands upon it. Now the skillful workman is very careful indeed as to what he takes into his brain-attic. He will have

(60) nothing but the tools which may help him in doing his work, but of these he has a large assortment, and all in the most perfect order. It is a mistake to think that that little room has elastic walls and can distend to any extent. Depend upon it there comes

(65) a time when for every addition of knowledge you forget something that you knew before. It is of the highest importance, therefore, not to have useless facts elbowing out the useful ones."

"But the solar system!" I protested.

(70)   "What the deuce is it to me?"

1. According to the passage, as time passes, Watson finds Holmes

   A) increasingly intriguing.

   B) frequently irritating.

   C) somewhat snobby.

   D) occasionally generous.

2. As used in line 5, "casual" most nearly means

   A) impulsive.

   B) comfortable.

   C) relaxed.

   D) occasional.

3. As presented in the passage, Sherlock Holmes is best described as

   A) very secretive and hard to understand.

   B) an excellent companion to Watson.

   C) highly regarded by his peers.

   D) an unusual and extraordinary man.

4. As used in line 8, "torpor" most nearly means

   A) agitation.

   B) sluggishness.

   C) alertness.

   D) illness.

5. The passage most strongly suggests that which of the following is true of Holmes?

   A) He tried, but failed, to become a doctor.

   B) He was an excellent student at the university.

   C) He studies things he is passionate about.

   D) He is considered an expert in philosophy.

6. Which choice provides the best evidence for the answer to the previous question?

   A) Lines 12-17 ("His hands were . . . instruments")

   B) Lines 18-20 ("He was not . . . that point")

   C) Lines 24-28 ("Yet his . . . astounded me")

   D) Lines 28-30 ("Surely no man . . . in view")

7. The passage most strongly suggests that Holmes believes which of the following about learning?

   A) People should study broadly to know something about everything.

   B) Philosophy is not a valid field of study to pursue.

   C) The brain is limited in capacity, so you should prioritize what you learn.

   D) The Copernican Theory is unfounded and therefore should not be studied.

8. Which choice provides the best evidence for the answer to the previous question?

   A) Line 34 ("His ignorance . . . his knowledge")

   B) Lines 35-36 ("Of contemporary . . . nothing")

   C) Lines 42-45 ("That any . . . realize it")

   D) Lines 66-68 ("It is of the . . . ones")

GO ON TO THE NEXT PAGE ▷

9. The comparison of the brain to an attic mainly serves to

A) demonstrate Holmes's unique views on how a person should make use of knowledge.

B) illustrate Watson's combative nature.

C) provide an alternate explanation for why Holmes doesn't know about Copernicus.

D) resolve the conflict between Watson and Holmes.

10. The decision to tell the story from Watson's point of view suggests that the author

A) wants the reader to dislike Holmes.

B) needed a sympathetic narrator.

C) will focus the rest of the story on Watson's actions.

D) hopes the reader will share Watson's curiosity about Holmes.

Questions 11-20 are based on the following passage.

This passage is adapted from a speech given by President Woodrow Wilson to Congress on January 8, 1918. Here Wilson proposes a 14-point program for world peace. These 14 points became the basis for peace negotiations at the end of World War I.

It will be our wish and purpose that the processes of peace, when they are begun, shall be absolutely open and that they shall involve and
Line permit henceforth no secret understandings of any
(5) kind. The day of conquest and aggrandizement is gone by; so is also the day of secret covenants entered into in the interest of particular governments and likely at some unlooked-for moment to upset the peace of the world. It is this happy fact,
(10) now clear to the view of every public man whose thoughts do not still linger in an age that is dead and gone, which makes it possible for every nation whose purposes are consistent with justice and the peace of the world to avow now or at any other
(15) time the objects it has in view.

We entered this war because violations of right had occurred which touched us to the quick and made the life of our own people impossible unless they were corrected. . . . What we demand in this
(20) war, therefore, is nothing peculiar to ourselves. It is that the world be made fit and safe to live in; and particularly that it be made safe for every peace-loving nation which, like our own, wishes to live its own life, determine its own institutions, be assured
(25) of justice and fair dealing by the other peoples of the world. . . . The programme of the world's peace, therefore, is our programme; and that programme, the only possible programme, as we see it, is this:

I. Open covenants of peace . . . with no private
(30) international understandings of any kind but diplomacy shall proceed always frankly and in the public view.

II. Absolute freedom of navigation upon the seas . . . alike in peace and in war, except as
(35) the seas may be closed in whole or in part by international action for the enforcement of international covenants.

III. The removal, so far as possible, of all economic barriers and the establishment of
(40) an equality of trade conditions among all the nations consenting. . . .

IV. Adequate guarantees given and taken that national armaments will be reduced to the lowest point consistent with domestic safety.

(45) V. A free, open-minded, and absolutely impartial adjustment of all colonial claims. . . .

VI. The evacuation of all Russian territory and such a settlement of all questions affecting Russia as will secure the best and freest
(50) cooperation of the other nations of the world.

VII. Belgium . . . must be evacuated and restored, without any attempt to limit the sovereignty which she enjoys in common with all other free nations. . . .

(55) VIII. All French territory should be freed and the invaded portions restored. . . .

IX. A readjustment of the frontiers of Italy should be effected along clearly recognizable lines of nationality.

 GO ON TO THE NEXT PAGE

(60) X. The peoples of Austria-Hungary . . . should be accorded the freest opportunity to autonomous development.

XI. Rumania, Serbia, and Montenegro should be evacuated; occupied territories restored; *(65)* and Serbia accorded free and secure access to the sea. . . .

XII. The Turkish portion of the present Ottoman Empire should be assured a secure sovereignty, but the other nationalities *(70)* which are now under Turkish rule should be assured an undoubted security of life. . . .

XIII. An independent Polish state should be erected which should include the territories inhabited by indisputably Polish populations *(75)* . . . . [The state] should be assured a free and secure access to the sea. . . .

XIV. A general association of nations must be formed under specific covenants for the purpose of affording mutual guarantees *(80)* of political independence and territorial integrity to great and small states alike.

11. Based on the first two paragraphs, which choice best identifies Wilson's purpose in making this speech?

A) To build an international military and political alliance

B) To declare the sovereignty and independence of the United States

C) To outline ways to maintain peaceful relations in the world

D) To reform governments in aggressor nations bent on conquest

12. Which choice provides the best evidence for the answer to the previous question?

A) Lines 1-5 ("It will be . . . of any kind")

B) Lines 5-6 ("The day of . . . is gone by")

C) Lines 16-17 ("We entered . . . occurred")

D) Lines 26-27 ("The programme . . . is our programme")

13. As used in line 31, "frankly" most nearly means

A) in an honest manner.

B) in a blunt manner.

C) in an abrupt manner.

D) in an outspoken manner.

14. Based on the information in the passage, it can reasonably be inferred that in the past,

A) the United States avoided alliances.

B) some nations formed private pacts with one another.

C) wars usually involved only two nations.

D) the borders of France and Italy were not well-defined.

15. Which choice provides the best evidence for the answer to the previous question?

A) Lines 1-5 ("It will be . . . of any kind")

B) Lines 16-19 ("We entered . . . corrected")

C) Lines 55-59 ("All French . . . of nationality")

D) Lines 77-81 ("A general . . . states alike")

16. As used in line 44, "consistent" most nearly means

A) dependable.

B) continuing.

C) agreeable.

D) rigid.

17. In lines 45-46 ("A free . . . colonial claims"), Wilson argues that to preserve peace, nations must

A) engage in free, open, and fair trade with colonies.

B) give up all aspirations for territorial and economic expansion.

C) provide constitutional protections for colonies.

D) work to resolve conflicts originating from imperial conquests.

GO ON TO THE NEXT PAGE

18. Points VI through VIII serve as evidence to support which claim made by Wilson throughout the speech?

    A) Democratic nations ought to sign pacts of economic and political cooperation.

    B) During the war, aggressors damaged property that they should be required to repair.

    C) In the past, nations violated one another's territorial sovereignty.

    D) Current colonies are entitled to establish free and democratic governments.

19. Which of the following approaches to international relations is most similar to Wilson's approach?

    A) Economic sanctions against ideological enemies

    B) Joint efforts to mediate conflict among nations

    C) Nongovernmental organizations to regulate trade

    D) Unilateral military action against unfriendly regimes

20. Which choice best describes the developmental pattern of Wilson's argument?

    A) A statement and restatement of the argument

    B) A statement of the argument followed by specific examples

    C) Initial claims followed by counterclaims

    D) Specific examples leading to a concluding argument

Questions 21-31 are based on the following passages and supplementary material.

The following passages are concerned with meditation, particularly the practice of mindfulness. Passage 1 provides an overview of meditation, while Passage 2 focuses on a particular practitioner, Congressman Tim Ryan.

Passage 1

Meditation has been around for thousands of years, starting as a religious practice. Hindu scripture from around 1500 BCE describes meditating on
Line the divine, and art from this time period shows
(5) people sitting cross-legged and solitary in a garden. In China and India around the fifth century BCE, other forms of meditation developed. Several religions, including Taoism, Buddhism, Islam, and Christianity, have meditative rites. In 20th-century
(10) Europe and America, secular forms of meditation arrived from India. Rather than focusing on spiritual growth, secular meditation emphasizes stress reduction, relaxation, and self-improvement.

Although it still isn't exactly mainstream,
(15) many people practice meditation. Mindfulness meditation, in particular, has become more popular in recent years. The practice involves sitting comfortably, focusing on one's breathing, and bringing the mind's attention to the present.
(20) Concerns about the past or future are let go of. An individual can picture worries popping like a bubble or flitting away like a butterfly.

Mindfulness is about increasing awareness and practicing acceptance. To be present is to
(25) have sharpened attention, or to be in a state of heightened consciousness. Practitioners of mindfulness report having a better quality of experience, deeper engagement, and greater measure of fulfillment.

(30) There are also health benefits. According to the Mayo Clinic, "Meditation can give you a sense of calm, peace and balance that benefits your emotional well-being." Among the emotional benefits are reducing negative emotions, increased
(35) self-awareness, and stress management skills.

GO ON TO THE NEXT PAGE

Asthma, depression, and sleep disorders are all conditions worsened by stress. Several studies have shown that patients with these conditions benefit from meditation.

(40)   Dr. Robert Schneider, director of the Institute for Natural Medicine and Prevention, says, "I have been researching effects of meditation on health for thirty years and have found it has compelling benefits. The benefits of meditation are coming to
(45) be widely accepted by health professionals, business leaders, and the media. It is now time for the medical profession to catch up."

Passage 2

In 2008, hoping to relax from his stressful job, Congressman Tim Ryan took a weekend retreat
(50) where he first practiced mindfulness meditation. "I came out of it," he says, "with a whole new way of relating with what was going on in the world." Now Ryan is an advocate for the benefits of meditation on health, performance, and social aware-
(55) ness. In the busy and aggressive world of Washington politics, he's a voice for calm consideration.

Every week Ryan, a Democrat representing the 13th congressional district of Ohio, hosts a meditation session for his staff and any other
(60) members of Congress who want to join. Despite the fact that Republicans and Democrats are con- sidered politically opposed, Ryan believes that the benefits of meditation ought to appeal to members of both parties. Meditation promotes self-reliance
(65) and fiscal conservation because it's a health practice that can be self-sustained and doesn't require costly memberships or equipment.

In 2010, Ryan wrote the book *A Mindful Nation: How a Simple Practice Can Help Us Reduce Stress,*
(70) *Improve Performance, and Recapture the American Spirit,* in which he advocates increased mindful- ness in many disciplines and professions. After its publication, kindergarten classes in his Ohio district started using deep-breathing techniques;

(75) now teachers rave about their students' improved behavior. "Mental discipline, focus, self-reliance, deep listening—these are fundamental skills that are essential to kids' education," Ryan says. "We yell at kids to pay attention, but we never teach them
(80) *how* to pay attention."

Word seems to be spreading around Capitol Hill. "I've had members of Congress approach me and say, 'I want to learn more about this,'" Ryan says. "Between the fundraising, being away from fam-
(85) ily, (and) the environment of hyperpartisanship, Washington is really stressing people out."

Ryan supports legislation that puts meditation to good use for everyone. Among other bills, he has sponsored one to increase the holistic-medicine
(90) offerings of the Department of Veterans Affairs. "And I haven't met anyone in the country that isn't feeling a high level of anxiety right now, given the economy and what's going on in the world. So mindfulness is for everyone."

(95)   Mr. Ryan is quick to point out that mindfulness is not a religious practice, but rather a secular mental technique that can be effective regardless of spiritual beliefs. He compares it to his grandparents praying and to athletes working out until they feel
(100) "in the zone."

"Your mind and body sync up into a flow state, without a lot of mental chatter," Mr. Ryan says.

GO ON TO THE NEXT PAGE ▷

Improvements After Employee Meditation Program

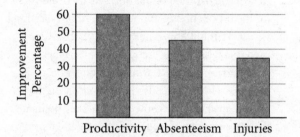

After the third year of its employee meditation program, a Detroit chemical plant reported these improvements.

21. The central idea of Passage 1 is that meditation and mindfulness

    A) were first practiced as religious rites.

    B) are becoming more accepted because of their benefits.

    C) are valuable tools for psychologists.

    D) help practitioners focus on their inner lives.

22. Passage 1 most strongly suggests that which of the following is true?

    A) Individuals who practice meditation are more likely to develop illness.

    B) Meditation helps people advance in their careers.

    C) Not many studies have been done on the results of daily meditation.

    D) Many medical professionals embrace the benefits of meditation.

23. Which choice provides the best evidence for the answer to the previous question?

    A) Lines 2-5 ("Hindu scripture . . . in a garden")

    B) Lines 15-17 ("Mindfulness meditation . . . in recent years")

    C) Lines 24-26 ("To be present . . . consciousness")

    D) Lines 30-33 ("According to . . . well-being")

24. As used in line 43, "compelling" most nearly means

    A) creative.

    B) judicial.

    C) persuasive.

    D) adaptable.

25. In Passage 2, what can be inferred about the author's point of view on meditation?

    A) The author is uncertain about its value.

    B) The author likes it but acknowledges its limits.

    C) The author appreciates its value.

    D) The author is devoted to it.

26. Passage 2 most strongly suggests that which of the following is true of Mr. Ryan?

    A) He acts on his beliefs.

    B) He is afraid to try new things.

    C) He likes to try new things.

    D) He is concerned about bipartisanship.

27. Which choice provides the best evidence for the answer to the previous question?

    A) Lines 48-50 ("In 2008 . . . mindfulness meditation")

    B) Lines 64-67 ("Meditation promotes . . . or equipment")

    C) Lines 88-90 ("Among other bills . . . Affairs")

    D) Lines 95-98 ("Mr. Ryan . . . spiritual beliefs")

28. As used in line 96, "secular" most nearly means

    A) nonreligious.

    B) serious.

    C) impersonal.

    D) pristine.

GO ON TO THE NEXT PAGE

29. In Passage 2, the author's use of the word "chatter" (line 102) implies that

    A) having an inner dialogue is a useful tool.

    B) people enjoy imagining themselves in various situations.

    C) meditation supporters talk about its surprises.

    D) much of what people think is relatively unimportant.

30. Both passages support which generalization about mindfulness meditation?

    A) It has become an acceptable way to show spirituality.

    B) It is making inroads into U.S. culture.

    C) It should be utilized in public institutions.

    D) It will soon be embraced by the American public.

31. Data in the graph provide most direct support for which claim from the passages?

    A) Meditation improves a person's focus and discipline.

    B) Children benefit from learning deep-breathing techniques.

    C) Meditation makes a person more generous.

    D) Health professionals are open to the idea of meditation being healthful.

Questions 32-42 are based on the following passage.

The following passage describes possible causes and impacts of colony collapse disorder, the mysterious disappearance of honey bee colonies.

Colony collapse disorder, sometimes referred to as CCD, is a phenomenon that has garnered much attention over the past few years from both *Line* the scientific community and the media alike. The
(5) disorder, which causes entire honey bee colonies to mysteriously disappear, is a major threat to both the environment and the economy. Honey bees are the world's natural pollinators, and are responsible for the production of about one-third of everything
(10) we eat. Without honey bees, produce that we're used to having in our diets, like apples, blueberries, strawberries, and nuts, would no longer be available. Honey bees also have an effect on the meat industry in the United States. They pollinate
(15) the various types of feed used by beef and dairy farmers. The services of the honey bee population are invaluable, and the survival of many different species depends on their well-being.

    When colony collapse disorder was first
(20) recognized, beekeepers and scientists assumed that a pathogen was to blame. For example, there are several known viruses and pests that can kill off entire hives of honey bees quickly and be extremely hard to prevent. Mites, fungus, and bacterial
(25) infections are all common killers. Because of how often they're seen in hives, farmers assumed that these common plights were responsible for colony collapse disorder. However, as time passed and the disorder was studied, researchers noticed some-
(30) thing odd. In many cases, there were simply no dead bees to discover. While common killers of the honey bee left telltale signs, colony collapse disor-der left nothing behind but empty hives.

    Scientists attributed the rapid disappearance of
(35) the bees to a form of altruistic behavior. When a bee gets sick, it flies away from the hive so as not to spread its illness to the other bees. It naturally prioritizes the overall health of the hive over its own. Although this behavior explained the bees'
(40) disappearing act, the cause of the disorder is yet to be understood and the list of possible explanations just keeps getting longer.

    One team of researchers hypothesized that fluctuations in the earth's magnetic field might
(45) be doing damage to the magnetoreceptors, or built-in homing devices, that bees use to find their way home to their hives after flying all day. Honey bees, as well as birds and fish, use the earth's magnetic field to identify their location. Sunspots,

GO ON TO THE NEXT PAGE

(50) which cause the strength of the earth's magnetic field to fluctuate, might be damaging the honey bee's biological tools.

While solar activity is outside the control of humans, another theory about the cause of colony (55) collapse disorder points to the human invention of pesticides. Pesticides, which are chemicals used to prevent pest infestation of crops on a large scale around the world, are often picked up by honey bees during their foraging and pollination flights. (60) Scientists have found that more than one pesticide can be found in the honey of one hive. They are currently studying the interaction of two or more pesticides, which travel into the hives and are stored by the bees in the pollen they use for protein.

(65) While the presence of one pesticide in a hive would certainly limit the life spans of bees and impair their navigational skills, it could be that it is the interaction of two or more pesticides that cause the entire colony to collapse. There are many ingredi-(70) ents in pesticides that are not regulated by world governments, and this leaves a lot of ground for bee scientists to cover when doing their research.

Research over time usually helps to narrow down the field of possible causes of a disorder, but in the (75) case of colony collapse disorder, scientists feel farther away than ever from finding the root cause and a cure. Many people around the world are taking up the cause of keeping honey bees alive by keeping bees in their backyards or on their roofs. Some (80) cities and towns have relaxed regulations on beekeeping in response to the honey bee population crisis. Hopefully, community initiatives and research can both help to save the world's honey bee population.

32. The primary purpose of the passage is to

A) show that honey bees require certain conditions in order to live.

B) instruct the reader on how to increase the number of honey bees.

C) explain the relationship between sunspots and colony collapse disorder.

D) alert the reader to the impending crisis of decreasing numbers of honey bees.

33. The author's point of view is most similar to

A) an advocate for honey bee survival.

B) an environmentalist concerned about toxic materials.

C) a naturalist who researches changes in animal populations.

D) a concerned citizen who hopes to raise honey bees.

34. The author uses the word "mysteriously" (line 6) to emphasize

A) that fluctuations of the earth's magnetic field are uncontrollable.

B) how little is known about why colony collapse occurs.

C) that the reason a bee leaves its hive when it is sick is unknown.

D) why researchers are studying the effect of pesticides on honey bees.

35. As used in line 27, "plights" most nearly means

A) causes.

B) promises.

C) intentions.

D) troubles.

36. The author uses the fact that no bees are found in a hive after a colony collapses to

A) examine the extent of damage to the honey bee population that has occurred.

B) emphasize the ways in which honey bees relate to human beings.

C) refute the possibility that pathogens are the reason for the collapse.

D) show that pesticides are not to blame for the decrease in the honey bee population.

GO ON TO THE NEXT PAGE

37. Which choice provides the best evidence for the answer to the previous question?

    A) Lines 4-7 ("The disorder . . . the economy")

    B) Lines 21-24 ("For example . . . to prevent")

    C) Lines 31-33 ("While common . . . empty hives")

    D) Lines 37-39 ("It naturally . . . its own")

38. As used in line 59, "foraging" most nearly means

    A) rejecting.

    B) offering.

    C) watching.

    D) searching.

39. The passage most strongly suggests that

    A) the author is cautiously optimistic about the future existence of the honey bee.

    B) the author thinks that scientists have not tried hard enough to find the reason for colony collapse.

    C) one team of scientists believes that they will have an answer to the problem of colony collapse very soon.

    D) scientists have ruled out the theory that pesticides are at fault for colony collapse.

40. Which choice provides the best evidence for the answer to the previous question?

    A) Lines 7-10 ("Honey bees . . . eat")

    B) Lines 25-28 ("Because of how . . . disorder")

    C) Lines 53-56 ("While solar . . . pesticides")

    D) Lines 82-83 ("Hopefully . . . population")

41. According to the passage, which of the following events has occurred in response to colony collapse disorder?

    A) Concerned citizens have fought to ban certain pesticides.

    B) Some towns have relaxed their regulations on beekeeping.

    C) Farmers have resorted to other means of pollinating their feed.

    D) Scientists are working to control the use of electromagnetic devices.

42. Based on information in the passage, which statement best describes the relationship between honey bees and human beings?

    A) Human beings depend on honey bees to keep the environment and economy healthy.

    B) Human beings depend on honey bees to keep the effects of sunspots to a minimum.

    C) Honey bees depend on human beings to provide them with food.

    D) Honey bees depend on human beings to protect them from solar flares.

Questions 43-52 are based on the following passage and supplementary materials.

The following passage describes the potential problems caused by debris that humans have left behind in space.

In the first days of space exploration, one concern was the possibility that astronauts or spacecraft might be hit by meteoroids. Scientists
Line calculated that this possibility was extremely
(5) small because meteoroids are rare. Astronauts and spacecraft, on the other hand, would almost certainly encounter micrometeorites, which are about the size of grains of dust and much more common.
However, in the 60 years since the beginning of
(10) space exploration, large quantities of human-made

GO ON TO THE NEXT PAGE ⇒

orbital debris have accumulated. Much of the debris consists of satellites that have stopped functioning or rocket booster sections that separated from the main spacecraft during a mission. Some of (15) the debris consists of items lost by astronauts, such as tools or space suit parts. Still, more of the debris is the result of collisions, such as when one satellite collides with another or with a large piece of debris.

NASA estimates there are millions of debris (20) particles that are too small to be tracked. These circle Earth at speeds up to 17,500 miles per hour, making even the smallest particles dangerous. One scientist calculated that a chip of paint hitting the window of a spacecraft at orbital speeds will hit (25) with the same amount of force as a bowling ball traveling at 60 mph. Such an impact occurred on the space shuttle *Challenger*'s second flight, chipping the windows and causing minor damage to the protective tiles on the spacecraft. While the damage (30) was not immediately dangerous, it led to the fear that any craft in orbit for long periods of time could accumulate enough damage to cease functioning.

Larger objects are even more dangerous, but they can be monitored and avoided. NASA tracks (35) about 500,000 pieces of debris larger than a marble, about 20,000 of which are larger than a softball. When NASA was still flying shuttle missions, it would often have to direct the shuttle to maneuver to avoid collisions with the larger debris. This could (40) usually be planned and accomplished in a few hours, but moving the International Space Station to avoid a collision takes up to 30 hours of advance notice.

Many satellites have the ability to adjust their (45) course slightly and can be remotely directed to avoid collisions with larger objects that would damage or destroy the satellites. NASA and the European Space Agency (ESA) have departments of scientists and engineers dedicated to cataloging, (50) modeling, and predicting the movements of space debris.

Some debris falls back to Earth, and most of it is burned up in the atmosphere. However, a large piece will survive long enough to get through (55) the atmosphere and crash. In 1979, the obsolete Skylab fell out of orbit, and much of it withstood

the trip through the atmosphere, crashing in the Australian outback. Space agencies also monitor debris to predict if and when any particular piece (60) might fall. Although they can issue warnings, there is currently nothing that can be done about pieces that might get through the atmosphere.

To avoid adding to the aggregation of debris, future satellites may need to be able to take (65) themselves out of orbit as their usefulness comes to an end. Until a way to remove these remains is implemented, however, those 500,000 pieces of large fragments, along with the millions of smaller pieces, will continue to orbit Earth.

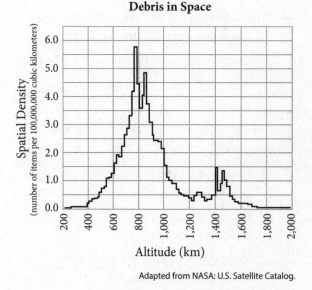

Debris in Space

Adapted from NASA: U.S. Satellite Catalog.

43. The passage is primarily concerned with the

A) unintended consequences of space exploration.

B) composition of the space debris that orbits Earth.

C) dangers posed by space debris created by humans.

D) causes and consequences of collisions in space.

GO ON TO THE NEXT PAGE ▷

44. Which choice provides the best evidence for the answer to the previous question?

    A) Lines 3-8 ("Scientists calculated . . . common")

    B) Lines 20-22 ("These circle . . . dangerous")

    C) Lines 33-34 ("Larger objects . . . avoided")

    D) Lines 44-47 ("Many satellites . . . satellites")

45. The second paragraph helps support the central idea of the passage by providing

    A) an explanation of why space debris left by humans is more dangerous than meteors.

    B) a summary of problems caused by old satellites and discarded equipment.

    C) a description of the types of human-made space debris that are causing problems.

    D) an argument for better tracking of the space debris that is orbiting Earth.

46. According to the passage, why does space debris created by humans pose a greater threat than meteoroids?

    A) Meteoroids are rare, while there are large quantities of space debris.

    B) Meteoroids are much smaller than most pieces of space debris.

    C) Space debris cannot be tracked and monitored, but meteoroids can.

    D) Space debris is only found in a narrow band around Earth.

47. Which of the following pieces of evidence most strengthens the author's central claim?

    A) An explanation of early concerns about space collisions in paragraph 1

    B) Information about how space debris is tracked in paragraph 5

    C) An example of space debris falling to Earth in paragraph 6

    D) The suggestion that obsolete satellites take themselves out of orbit in paragraph 7

48. As used in line 55, "obsolete" most nearly means

    A) displaced.

    B) redundant.

    C) excessive.

    D) outdated.

49. Based on information in the passage, which conclusion can reasonably be inferred?

    A) One way to prevent space debris from causing injuries on Earth is to warn people to avoid the predicted impact site.

    B) The smallest pieces of space debris can be removed by astronauts while they are working in space.

    C) Most space debris is not dangerous to space travelers because of its small size and relatively low speed.

    D) Pieces of space debris will become more of a problem as spacecraft travel farther into outer space.

GO ON TO THE NEXT PAGE

50. Which choice provides the best evidence for the answer to the previous question?

   A) Lines 19-22 ("NASA estimates . . . dangerous")

   B) Lines 33-34 ("Larger objects . . . avoided")

   C) Lines 34-36 ("NASA tracks . . . softball")

   D) Lines 60-62 ("Although . . . atmosphere")

51. As used in line 67, "implemented" most nearly means

   A) employed.

   B) investigated.

   C) prevented.

   D) appointed.

52. Based on the passage and the graphic, if NASA were to place a new satellite into orbit, which altitude range would pose the greatest danger?

   A) 500-700 kilometers

   B) 700-900 kilometers

   C) 1,400-1,600 kilometers

   D) 1,800-2,000 kilometers

WRITING AND LANGUAGE TEST

35 Minutes—44 Questions

This section corresponds to Section 2 of your answer sheet.

Directions: Each passage in this section is followed by several questions. Some questions will reference an underlined portion in the passage; others will ask you to consider a part of a passage or the passage as a whole. For each question, choose the answer that reflects the best use of grammar, punctuation, and style. If a passage or question is accompanied by a graphic, take the graphic into account in choosing your response(s). Some questions will have "NO CHANGE" as a possible response. Choose that answer if you think the best choice is to leave the sentence as written.

Questions 1-11 are based on the following passage.

A Sweet Discovery

[1] Like most chemists, a laboratory was where Constantin Fahlberg worked on his research. However, the discovery for which he is famous occurred not in the laboratory, but at supper.

1. A) NO CHANGE
   B) Like most chemists, Constantin Fahlberg worked on his research in a laboratory.
   C) Constantin Fahlberg worked on his research, like most chemists, in a laboratory.
   D) A laboratory, like most chemists, is where Constantin Fahlberg worked on his research.

[2] <u>Chemical compounds are derived from coal tar, which is what Fahlberg began working on as a research chemist in a laboratory at Johns Hopkins University in early 1878.</u> Coal tar was a by-product of steel manufacturing, and compounds derived [3] <u>from them</u> had been used as medicines and in dye formulations. Fahlberg, and others in the laboratory, were studying ways to add different chemicals to molecules found in coal tar to see if the new compounds formed had other useful properties.

One night in June, Fahlberg finished a long day of work; he had been so [4] <u>demanding</u> in his research that he forgot to eat lunch, so he hurried to his supper without stopping to wash his hands. He might have

2. A) NO CHANGE
    B) Johns Hopkins University is where Fahlberg began working as a research chemist in a laboratory, making chemical compounds derived from coal tar in early 1878.
    C) Coal tar creates chemical compounds. This is what Fahlberg began working on as a research chemist in a laboratory at Johns Hopkins University in early 1878.
    D) In early 1878, Fahlberg began working as a research chemist in a laboratory at Johns Hopkins University, making chemical compounds derived from coal tar.

3. A) NO CHANGE
    B) from it
    C) from these
    D) from him

4. A) NO CHANGE
    B) delayed
    C) engrossed
    D) excited

GO ON TO THE NEXT PAGE

considered hand washing unnecessary because he had not handled any toxic chemicals that day, or he might have just been so hungry he did not think about it. **5**

The bread tasted so sweet that Fahlberg thought he might have picked up some cake by mistake. He rinsed out his mouth with water and then patted his mustache dry with a napkin. He was surprised to find that the napkin tasted sweet as well. He took another sip of water and realized that the water now tasted sweet. **6** <u>The bread, napkin, and glass of water had something in common.</u> He then tasted his thumb, and it tasted sweeter than any candy he had ever had.

5. At this point, the writer wants to create an ideal transition to the next paragraph. Which choice most effectively accomplishes this goal?

A) Later, hand washing would become a critical protocol in the laboratory.

B) Thankfully, he didn't, or he never would have discovered what came next.

C) Fahlberg had not eaten any cake, or indeed anything sweet, that day.

D) Either way, he picked up his bread in his unwashed hands and took a bite.

6. A) NO CHANGE

B) Was there something that the bread, napkin, and glass of water had in common, he wondered?

C) In fact, everything Fahlberg touched seemed to taste sweeter than usual, which intrigued his scientific mind.

D) Fahlberg quickly realized that the one thing the bread, napkin, and glass of water had in common was that they had all touched his fingers.

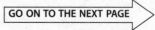

[1] Fahlberg rushed back into the lab and began to taste the contents of every beaker he had used that day. [2] Fortunately, he had not worked with anything poisonous or corrosive, or the story [7] may have a different ending. [3] [8] He had discovered saccharin, which he named for its intense sweetness. [4] He found a sweet-tasting mixture of chemicals and worked for weeks to isolate the sweet substance from the rest and to determine its chemical composition. [5] Although it is many times more sweet tasting than sugar, it cannot be used for energy by the body and therefore does not contribute to calories consumed or energy use. [6] Soon after Fahlberg started [9] making saccharin commercially in 1886, it became popular with people who needed to lose weight and with diabetic patients who needed to avoid sugar. [10] [11]

7. A) NO CHANGE
    B) would have had
    C) might have
    D) could have had

8. Which choice most clearly and effectively conveys the central idea of the paragraph?

    A) NO CHANGE
    B) The substance was saccharin, and it became known as an artificial sweetener.
    C) Instead, the substance was a harmless sweetener called saccharin.
    D) Interestingly, the substance was extremely sweet and would later be known as saccharin.

9. A) NO CHANGE
    B) inventing
    C) creating
    D) producing

10. To make this paragraph most logical, sentence 4 should be placed

    A) Where it is now
    B) Before sentence 1
    C) Before sentence 3
    D) Before sentence 6

GO ON TO THE NEXT PAGE

11. Which of the following sentences would provide the best conclusion for the passage?

A) Clearly, Constantin Fahlberg's legacy of research, along with his accidental discovery, continues to have lasting effects on society even today.

B) If Fahlberg had stopped to wash his hands that day, he might have continued his experiments on coal tar derivatives, never knowing that an important substance sat at the bottom of one of his laboratory beakers.

C) In addition to his discovery of saccharin, his work on coal tar proved that Constantin Fahlberg was a talented scientist whose work has applications in the present day, even though a number of new artificial sweeteners have been developed.

D) Fahlberg's discovery of saccharin is just one of the many examples of times when science was advanced through what some might call "a happy accident."

Questions 12-22 are based on the following passage.

René Descartes: The Father of Modern Philosophy

Throughout history, philosophy has shaped culture in pivotal ways. From the ancients to the postmoderns, great philosophers have spoken powerfully within [12] there respective contexts. For modern Western culture, one philosopher's formative impact surpassed his contemporaries: France's René Descartes. Called "the father of modern philosophy," Descartes crucially influenced Western perspectives on knowledge and rationality.

This 17th-century philosopher ushered Western thought through an era of great public doubt and upheaval and into the age of self-reliant rationalism. Political and religious tradition and authority—the [13] obvious premodern sources of truth and knowledge—were being questioned and rejected as new ideas identified potential inconsistencies. [14] Because foundations of truth seemed to be crumbling, Descartes's writings proposed an alternative foundation: individual reason.

12. A) NO CHANGE
    B) their
    C) its
    D) it's

13. A) NO CHANGE
    B) makeshift
    C) innovative
    D) reigning

14. A) NO CHANGE
    B) In a time when foundations of truth seemed to be crumbling, Descartes's writings proposed an alternative foundation: individual reason.
    C) Despite the fact that foundations of truth seemed to be crumbling, Descartes's writings proposed an alternative foundation: individual reason.
    D) Before foundations of truth seemed to be crumbling, Descartes's writings proposed an alternative foundation: individual reason.

GO ON TO THE NEXT PAGE

15 An expert in many fields, Descartes's work would on many levels serve to establish foundations for modern culture and science. **16** This emphasis on reason, as opposed to traditional or authoritative bases for certainty, would become the modern mechanism for determining truth and knowledge.

17 Modern culture would come to cherish this as an intellectual ideal. In his most famous project, Descartes sought certainty by mentally stripping away every layer of knowledge that was remotely possible to

15. A) NO CHANGE
     B) Expertise in many fields, Descartes created work that
     C) An expert in many fields, Descartes would create work that
     D) With his expertise in many fields, Descartes's work

16. At this point, the writer wants to add specific information that supports the central claim of the paragraph. Which choice provides the strongest support?
     A) Even so, his most impressive contribution was his advocacy for the individual's rationality.
     B) Unlike Descartes, other philosophers argued that reason alone could not provide the basis for knowledge.
     C) The idea known as "Cartesian dualism" posited that in the world there exists only mind and matter.
     D) His work on philosophy has proven to have more importance than his ideas about anatomy, many of which have since been disproven.

17. Which sentence should be added in front of sentence 1 to clarify the topic of the paragraph?
     A) Descartes's contributions to philosophy were seen as threatening to religion.
     B) Descartes focused his work on the pursuit of fact-based certainty.
     C) The foundation for the ideas of many other philosophers is Descartes's work.
     D) Descartes's ideas were rooted in his Jesuit training.

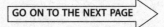 GO ON TO THE NEXT PAGE

doubt. Descartes arrived at his memorable
[18] conclusion, "I think, therefore I am," he could only be certain of the fact that he was thinking. [19] Building from there, he could work toward rational certainty in other areas of knowledge.

Emphasizing the importance of building knowledge on certain evidence, Descartes modeled a reversal of the reigning scientific processes (which typically worked backward from observation to explanation). Descartes founded the modern scientific method, in which research and study could be reliably conducted based on certain evidence. Scientific method, and the emphasis on human reason, would become standard elements of modern thought. Though reimagined by ensuing culture and philosophy, [20] these changes propelled by Descartes's initial contributions to that conversation.

18. A) NO CHANGE
    B) conclusion "I think, therefore I am" he could only be certain of the fact that he was thinking.
    C) conclusion, "I think, therefore I am" he could only be certain of the fact that he was thinking.
    D) conclusion, "I think, therefore I am." He could only be certain of the fact that he was thinking.

19. Which choice most logically follows the previous sentence and sets up the information that follows?
    A) This revelation came as a shock to many people.
    B) However, he believed that this certainty offered evidence to confirm his existence.
    C) Still, it was a place to start.
    D) This was a radical new way to think about thinking.

20. A) NO CHANGE
    B) these changes being propelled by
    C) these changes having been propelled by
    D) these changes were propelled by

GO ON TO THE NEXT PAGE ▷

[21] <u>Some people may argue that it is impossible to separate what Descartes accomplished from the things his contemporaries did.</u> Certainly, most scientists and philosophers influence and build from each other's work. But Descartes was the crucial voice in early modern dialogue. His expertise drew trusted readership, and his well-read ideas pointed culture down the road to modern understanding—a road paved with reason, modernism's great intellectual virtue. Shifts [22] <u>begun</u> by Descartes's work would influence the very structure of ideas and systems in the modern world, from research methods to public processes like government and health systems.

21. A) NO CHANGE
     B) Some may argue that it is impossible to separate Descartes's accomplishments from those of his contemporaries.
     C) Some people may argue that it is impossible to separate Descartes from his contemporaries.
     D) Some may argue that what Descartes accomplished is no different from what his contemporaries did.

22. A) NO CHANGE
     B) foreseen
     C) initiated
     D) evolved

Questions 23-33 are based on the following passage.

The Novel: Introspection to Escapism

Art is never [23] <u>immovable</u>, nor is it meant to be. A poem written today looks and sounds vastly different from a poem by Shakespeare, and a modern symphony no longer resembles one by Beethoven. So it is with the novel, that still relatively young member of the literary family (many consider *Don Quixote*, published in 1605, to be the first). The novel is evolving to reflect the [24] <u>changing world; for better</u> or for worse.

23. A) NO CHANGE
     B) sluggish
     C) static
     D) stationary

24. A) NO CHANGE
     B) changing world—for better
     C) changing world: for better
     D) changing world for better

 GO ON TO THE NEXT PAGE

[25] The novel, while well regarded, would never match the poem as the ideal form for conveying the struggles of humanity. A few quotations from acclaimed novelists of the past illustrate how [26] loftily the form was once regarded. G. K. Chesterton said, "A good novel tells us the truth about its hero; but a bad novel tells us the truth about its author." English writer Ford Madox Ford believed the novelist played an important role as a recorder of history. [27] Ford said of his friend Joseph Conrad, "We agreed that the novel is absolutely the only vehicle for the thought of our day."

It's not that over centuries writers of novels have shed these ambitions; novels today still address complexities and intricate social dynamics. [28] However, in recent decades, popular novels and their film adaptations have driven the novel market in a broader direction.

25. Which choice most effectively establishes the main topic of the paragraph?

A) NO CHANGE

B) The novel was once sacred ground, meant to capture and reveal universal truths, to depict society and all its ills, to explore and expound upon the human condition.

C) Both poetry and novels enjoyed a resurgence of popularity in the early 1900s due to the notoriety of many of the prominent authors of the day.

D) By the early 1900s, novels had evolved into something entirely different from the form Cervantes pioneered with *Don Quixote*.

26. A) NO CHANGE

B) broadly

C) haughtily

D) pretentiously

27. Which choice best improves the sentence?

A) Ford said of his friend, the novelist Joseph Conrad,

B) Ford said of his great friend, Joseph Conrad,

C) Ford said of Joseph Conrad,

D) Ford said of his friend, Joseph Conrad, a Pole who moved to Britain,

28. A) NO CHANGE

B) However: in recent decades,

C) However in recent decades,

D) In recent decades however;

GO ON TO THE NEXT PAGE ▷

[29] Novels are considered just another entertainment medium, which are now available on digital devices, one that ought to enthrall its passive reader and relieve him or her of the stress and tedium of life. The difficulties, challenges, and triumphs of real life are **[30]** less often the subject of popular novels; instead, escapist tales of fantastical lands and escapades are more popular. **[31]**

29. A) NO CHANGE
    B) Novels, which are now available on digital devices, are considered just another entertainment medium,
    C) Novels are considered just another entertainment medium, now available on digital devices,
    D) Novels, just another entertainment medium which are now available on digital devices

30. A) NO CHANGE
    B) less often the subject of popular novels instead, escapist tales of fantastical lands and escapades are more popular.
    C) less often the subject of popular novels, instead, escapist tales of fantastical lands and escapades are more popular.
    D) less often the subject of popular novels: instead, escapist tales of fantastical lands and escapades, are more popular.

31. At this point, the writer wants to add specific information that supports the ideas presented in the paragraph. Which choice provides the most relevant detail?

    A) Novels exploring deep social issues remain the most heavily decorated books come literary award season.
    B) Director James Cameron remarked recently about the "inherent difficulty" of adapting novels with fantasy themes.
    C) Writing in the *New Yorker* magazine in 2014, critic James Woods stated that readers now want novels that, like popcorn, are "easy to consume."
    D) The "slice of life" novel remains tremendously popular among books targeting younger readers.

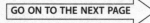 GO ON TO THE NEXT PAGE

It is rare today for a novelist to attempt to ask, "What does it mean?" Instead, **32** we strive to provide the reader with an answer to the question, "What happens next?"

"Publishers, readers, booksellers, even critics," critic James Woods wrote, "acclaim the novel that one can deliciously sink into, forget oneself in, the novel that returns us to the innocence of childhood or the dream of the cartoon, the novel of a thousand confections and no unwanted significance. What becomes harder to find, and lonelier to defend, is the idea of **33** the novel as—in Ford Madox Ford's words—a 'medium of profoundly serious investigation into the human case.'"

Questions 34-44 are based on the following passage and supplementary material.

Interning: A Bridge Between Classes and Careers

Kelli Blake, a chemical engineering major, recently **34** excepted a summer internship with BP, an international energy company, to gain career experience. Some argue against the value of internships, claiming they pay very little and can involve performing **35** boring tasks, yet Kelli feels her internship is critical to helping her discover whether engineering is right for her.

Kelli wants a real-world perspective on information she has gained in her classes. Her internship with a corporate leader is affording her the opportunity to apply her conceptual knowledge to tasks inside a major

32. A) NO CHANGE
    B) they strive
    C) it strives
    D) he or she strives

33. A) NO CHANGE
    B) the novel as, in Ford Madox Ford's words—a 'medium of profoundly serious investigation into the human case.'"
    C) the novel as, in Ford Madox Ford's words: a 'medium of profoundly serious investigation into the human case.'"
    D) the novel as, in Ford Madox Ford's words; a 'medium of profoundly serious investigation into the human case.'"

34. A) NO CHANGE
    B) accepted
    C) adopted
    D) adapted

35. A) NO CHANGE
    B) skilled
    C) menial
    D) challenging

GO ON TO THE NEXT PAGE

oil company. **36** During this internship, for example, Kelli is working on a glycol dehydration project; she will be using the classroom skills she learned from thermo-dynamics, organic chemistry, and more. She can later add this project to her résumé and portfolio, giving her an edge over other college graduates.

37 Offshore engineers have many rules and regula-tions. Helicopter underwater egress safety training is required of employees traveling to offshore facilities, so she will **38** stand out from other applicants by already being safety certified. "I have a new appreciation for the protocols followed by engineers at refineries," she states. Kelli believes that gaining new skills and showing she can apply her classroom knowledge to real situations will give her an advantage over her competition should she decide to join BP.

36. Which choice best supports the central idea of the paragraph?

A) NO CHANGE

B) Kelli can use the materials from her intern-ship in a professional-quality presentation; she can then deliver the presentation to her classmates when she returns to college after her internship.

C) In addition, Kelli is designing the next internship proposal for her classmates after she completes her own and graduates.

D) Kelli is hoping to formulate her project results as a professional published document to sell to BP.

37. Which choice provides the most appropriate introduction to the paragraph?

A) NO CHANGE

B) Kelli admires the engineers who administer the safety training.

C) The skills Kelli acquires can be applied to existing knowledge.

D) Kelli will also earn an underwater safety training certificate.

38. A) NO CHANGE

B) stand down

C) stand up

D) stand alone

Everyone has [39] their own reason for wanting to become an intern. Kelli has several other reasons behind her decision. [40] For example, Kelli wants to meet people to learn about the variety of careers available, from entry level to senior engineer. She will accomplish all of her intern goals [41] by working on technical projects, attend "lunch and learn" meetings, watching webinars, and shadow coworkers.

39. A) NO CHANGE
     B) your
     C) its
     D) his or her

40. A) NO CHANGE
     B) For example; Kelli wants to meet people to learn about the variety of careers available, from entry level to senior engineer.
     C) For example, Kelli wants to meet people—to learn about the variety of careers available, from entry level, to senior engineer.
     D) For example, Kelli wants to meet people to learn about the variety of careers available; from entry level to senior engineer.

41. A) NO CHANGE
     B) by working on technical projects, attending "lunch and learn" meetings, watching webinars, and shadowing coworkers.
     C) by working on technical projects, attend "lunch and learn" meetings, watch webinars, and shadow coworkers.
     D) by working on technical projects, attending "lunch and learn" meetings, watch webinars, and shadowing coworkers.

GO ON TO THE NEXT PAGE ⟶

What are some further benefits of internships? Besides gaining exposure in the field, Kelli is networking. The most important person to her now is her mentor, Dan, a senior engineer who can help her grow professionally by answering her questions. Gaining valuable contacts and **42** good role model. These are other reasons she has pursued this internship.

Kelli is now an acting member of a corporate team. She realizes she will be learning a lot about the industry and will benefit from adopting an entirely new vocabulary. She views her internship as an adventure, one in which engineering teams worldwide must work collaboratively and efficiently. **43** It is worth it to give up her summer, Kelli argues, because though she is losing her summer she is doing the job of an actual engineer through her internship. Moreover, she views the experience as one of the best ways to learn about her field and industry, which typically offers around **44** 35 internships per 1,000 hires.

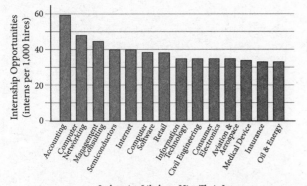

Industries Likely to Hire Their Interns

Adapted from Kurt Wagner, "Which Internships Really Pay Off?" ©2014 by Revere Digital LLC.

42. A) NO CHANGE
    B) a good role model, these are other reasons
    C) a good role model; are other reasons
    D) a good role model are other reasons

43. A) NO CHANGE
    B) It is worth giving up, Kelli argues, because though she is losing her summer, she is doing the job of an actual engineer through her internship.
    C) It is worth it to give up her summer, Kelli argues, because she is doing the job of an actual engineer through her internship.
    D) It is worth it to Kelli to give up her summer, because though summers are usually a time to relax, she argues, she is doing the job of an actual engineer through her internship.

44. Which choice most accurately and effectively represents the information in the graph and the passage?
    A) NO CHANGE
    B) 32 internships per 1,000 hires.
    C) 35 internships per 60 hires.
    D) 32 internships per 60 hires.

IF YOU FINISH BEFORE TIME IS CALLED, YOU MAY CHECK YOUR WORK ON THIS SECTION ONLY. DO NOT TURN TO ANY OTHER SECTION IN THE TEST.   **STOP**

MATH TEST

25 Minutes—20 Questions

NO-CALCULATOR SECTION

This section corresponds to Section 3 of your answer sheet.

Directions: For this section, solve each question and select the best answer choice. The available space on each page may be used for scratch work.

Notes:

1. Calculator use is NOT permitted.
2. All numbers used are real numbers, and all variables used represent real numbers, unless otherwise indicated.
3. Figures are drawn to scale and lie in a plane unless otherwise indicated.
4. Unless stated otherwise, the domain of any function f is assumed to be the set of all real numbers x, for which $f(x)$ is a real number.

Information:

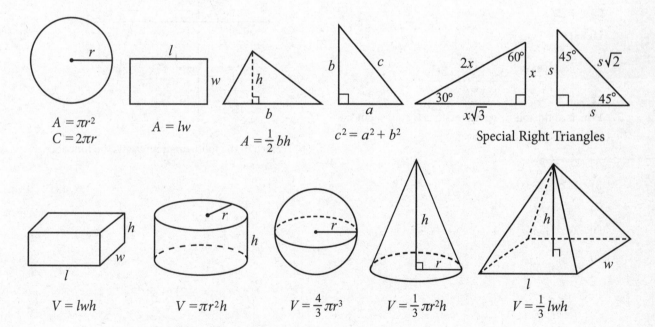

The sum of the degree measures of the angles in a triangle is 180.

The number of degrees of arc in a circle is 360.

The number of radians of arc in a circle is 2π.

GO ON TO THE NEXT PAGE

Fence Installation

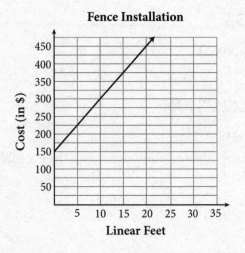

1. The graph shows the cost of installing a vinyl privacy fence. The company charges a flat installation fee plus a cost per linear foot of fencing. Based on the graph, how much does one linear foot of this particular vinyl fence cost?

    A) $5

    B) $15

    C) $75

    D) $150

$$\frac{24x^4 + 36x^3 - 12x^2}{12x^2}$$

2. Which of the following expressions is equivalent to the expression shown above?

    A) $2x^2 + 3x$

    B) $24x^4 + 36x^3$

    C) $2x^2 + 3x - 1$

    D) $24x^4 + 36x^3 - 1$

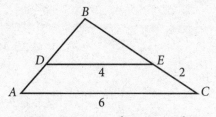

Note: Figure not drawn to scale.

3. In the figure shown, $\triangle ABC \sim \triangle DBE$. What is the length of $\overline{BE}$?

    A) 3.5

    B) 3.75

    C) 4

    D) 4.5

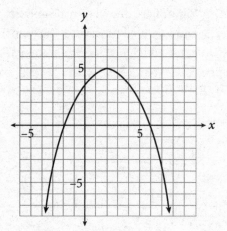

4. Which of the following represents the function shown?

    A) $f(x) = -\dfrac{1}{3}(x - 2)^2 + 5$

    B) $f(x) = -\dfrac{1}{3}(x + 2)^2 + 5$

    C) $f(x) = \dfrac{1}{3}(x + 2)^2 + 5$

    D) $f(x) = 3(x - 2)^2 + 5$

GO ON TO THE NEXT PAGE

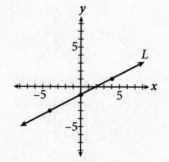

5. If line L shown here is reflected over the x-axis, what is the slope of the new line?

A) -2

B) $-\dfrac{1}{2}$

C) $\dfrac{1}{2}$

D) 2

6. If $p = 4x^3 + x - 2$, $q = x^2 - 1$, and $r = 3x - 5$, then what is $2p - (q + r)$?

A) $7x^3 - x + 2$

B) $8x^3 - x^2 - x + 2$

C) $8x^3 - x^2 - x - 10$

D) $8x^3 - x^2 + 5x - 8$

7. Which of the following are the roots of the equation $2x^2 + 4x - 3 = 0$?

A) $\dfrac{-2 \pm \sqrt{10}}{2}$

B) $-2 \pm \sqrt{5}$

C) $-1 \pm \sqrt{10}$

D) $-1 \pm 2\sqrt{10}$

8. If $g(x) = 3x - 5$ and $h(x) = \dfrac{7x + 10}{4}$, at what point does the graph of $g(x)$ intersect the graph of $h(x)$?

A) $(-2, -11)$

B) $(-2, 1)$

C) $(3, 4)$

D) $(6, 13)$

9. If $x = k^{-\frac{1}{3}}$, where $x > 0$ and $k > 0$, which of the following equations gives k in terms of x ?

A) $k = \dfrac{1}{x^3}$

B) $k = \dfrac{1}{\sqrt[3]{x}}$

C) $k = -\sqrt[3]{x}$

D) $k = -x^3$

$$4x - (10 - 2x) = c(3x - 5)$$

10. If the equation shown has infinitely many solutions, and c is a constant, what is the value of c ?

A) -2

B) $-\dfrac{2}{3}$

C) $\dfrac{2}{3}$

D) 2

11. If $0 < 1 - \dfrac{a}{3} \le \dfrac{1}{2}$, which of the following is not a possible value of a ?

A) 1.5

B) 2

C) 2.5

D) 3

GO ON TO THE NEXT PAGE

$$\begin{cases} y - \dfrac{2}{k}x \le 0 \\ \dfrac{1}{k}x - \dfrac{1}{2}y \le -1 \end{cases}$$

12. If the system of inequalities shown has no solution, what is the value of k ?

A) 1

B) 2

C) There is no value of k that results in no solution.

D) There are infinitely many values of k that result in no solution.

$$\frac{4x}{x-7} + \frac{2x}{2x-14} = \frac{70}{2(x-7)}$$

13. What value(s) of x satisfy the equation above?

A) 0

B) 7

C) No solution

D) Any value such that $x \ne 7$

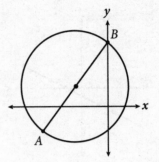

14. The circle shown is given by the equation $x^2 + y^2 + 6x - 4y = 12$. What is the shortest distance from A to B ?

A)   5

B)   10

C) $4\sqrt{3}$

D)   24

15. If g is a function defined over the set of all real numbers and $g(x - 1) = 3x^2 + 5x - 7$, then which of the following defines $g(x)$?

A) $g(x) = 3x^2 - x - 9$

B) $g(x) = 3x^2 + 5x + 1$

C) $g(x) = 3x^2 + 11x + 1$

D) $g(x) = 3x^2 + 11x - 6$

GO ON TO THE NEXT PAGE

Directions: For questions 16-20, enter your responses into the appropriate grid on your answer sheet, in accordance with the following:

1. You will receive credit only if the circles are filled in correctly, but you may write your answers in the boxes above each grid to help you fill in the circles accurately.

2. Don't mark more than one circle per column.

3. None of the questions with grid-in responses will have a negative solution.

4. Only grid in a single answer, even if there is more than one correct answer to a given question.

5. A **mixed number** must be gridded as a decimal or an improper fraction. For example, you would grid $7\frac{1}{2}$ as 7.5 or $\frac{15}{2}$.

   (Were you to grid it as $\boxed{7\ 1\ /\ 2}$, this response would be read as $\frac{71}{2}$.)

6. A **decimal** that has more digits than there are places on the grid may be either rounded or truncated, but every column in the grid must be filled in order to receive credit.

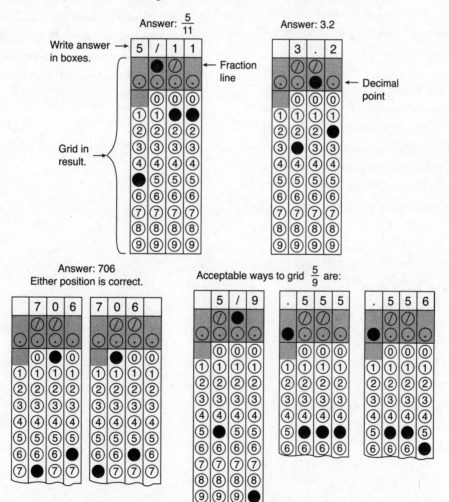

Answer: $\frac{5}{11}$

Write answer in boxes.

Fraction line

Grid in result.

Answer: 3.2

Decimal point

Answer: 706
Either position is correct.

Acceptable ways to grid $\frac{5}{9}$ are:

GO ON TO THE NEXT PAGE

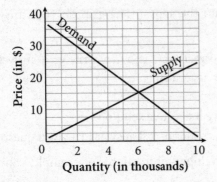

16. Retail businesses strive to price their products so that they sell as many as possible without losing money. Economic equilibrium is the price point at which the supply for a product is equal to the demand for that product. The graph above models this scenario. According to the graph, at what price in dollars will supply equal demand for this particular product?

17. Once an insect reaches its larval stage, its mass increases linearly for a short period of time and then slows down as it prepares to enter pupation. Suppose the larva of a certain species has an initial mass of 10 grams and grows linearly from $t = 0$ to $t = 48$ hours of its larval stage. If after 48 hours, the mass of the larva is 14 grams, what was its mass in grams at $t = 6$ hours ?

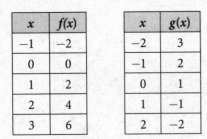

18. Several values for the functions $f(x)$ and $g(x)$ are shown in the tables. What is the value of $f(g(-1))$?

19. If $(4 + 3i)(1 - 2i) = a + bi$, then what is the value of a ? (Note that $i = \sqrt{-1}$.)

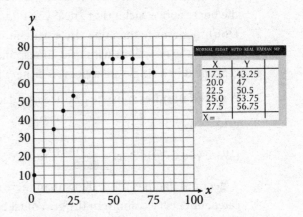

20. The maximum value of the data shown in the scatterplot occurs at $x = 56.25$. If the data is modeled using a quadratic regression and the model is an exact fit, then what is the y-value when $x = 90$?

MATH TEST

55 Minutes—38 Questions

CALCULATOR SECTION

This section corresponds to Section 4 of your answer sheet.

Directions: For this section, solve each question and select the best answer choice. The available space on each page may be used for scratch work.

Notes:

1. Calculator use is permitted.
2. All numbers used are real numbers, and all variables used represent real numbers, unless otherwise indicated.
3. Figures are drawn to scale and lie in a plane unless otherwise indicated.
4. Unless stated otherwise, the domain of any function f is assumed to be the set of all real numbers x, for which $f(x)$ is a real number.

Information:

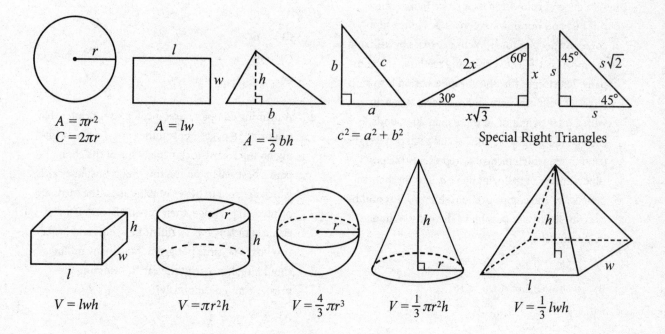

$A = \pi r^2$
$C = 2\pi r$

$A = lw$

$A = \frac{1}{2}bh$

$c^2 = a^2 + b^2$

Special Right Triangles

$V = lwh$

$V = \pi r^2 h$

$V = \frac{4}{3}\pi r^3$

$V = \frac{1}{3}\pi r^2 h$

$V = \frac{1}{3}lwh$

The sum of the degree measures of the angles in a triangle is 180.

The number of degrees of arc in a circle is 360.

The number of radians of arc in a circle is 2π.

GO ON TO THE NEXT PAGE

1. The U.S. Centers for Disease Control recommends that adults engage in 2.5 hours per week of vigorous exercise. A local health society conducts a survey to see if people are meeting this goal. They ask 100 people with gym memberships how many minutes of exercise they engage in per week. After analyzing the data, the health society finds that the average respondent exercises 142 minutes per week, but the margin of error was approximately 36 minutes. The society wants to lower this margin of error. Using which of the following samples instead would do so?

   A) 50 people with gym memberships

   B) 50 people randomly selected from the entire adult population

   C) 100 people with gym memberships, but from a variety of gyms

   D) 200 people randomly selected from the entire adult population

2. As a general rule, businesses strive to maximize revenue and minimize expenses. An office supply company decides to try to cut expenses by utilizing the most cost-effective shipping method. The company determines that the cheapest option is to ship boxes of ballpoint pens and mechanical pencils with a total weight of no more than 20 pounds. If each pencil weighs 0.2 ounces and each pen weighs 0.3 ounces, which inequality represents the possible number of ballpoint pens, b, and mechanical pencils, m, the company could ship in a box and be as cost-effective as possible? (There are 16 ounces in 1 pound.)

   A) $0.3b + 0.2m < 20 \times 16$

   B) $0.3b + 0.2m \leq 20 \times 16$

   C) $\dfrac{b}{0.3} + \dfrac{m}{0.2} < 20 \times 16$

   D) $\dfrac{b}{0.3} + \dfrac{m}{0.2} \leq 20 \times 16$

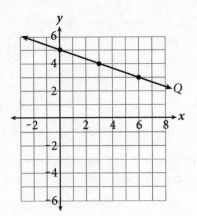

3. Where will line Q shown in the graph intersect the x-axis?

   A) 13

   B) 14

   C) 15

   D) 16

4. The function $f(x)$ is defined as $f(x) = 2g(x)$, where $g(x) = x + 5$. What is the value of $f(3)$?

   A) -4

   B) 6

   C) 8

   D) 16

5. A printing company uses a color laser printer that can print 18 pages per minute (ppm) when printing on thick cardstock paper. One of the company's best sellers on the Internet is business cards, which are sold in boxes of 225 cards. The cards are printed 10 per page, then cut and boxed. If a real estate company has 12 full-time agents and orders two boxes of cards per agent, how many minutes should it take to print the cards, assuming the printer runs continuously?

   A) 15

   B) 20

   C) 30

   D) 45

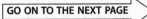 GO ON TO THE NEXT PAGE

6. If $0.002 \leq x \leq 0.2$ and $5 \leq y \leq 25$, what is the maximum value of $\dfrac{x}{y}$?

A) 0.04

B) 0.4

C) 4

D) 40

7. Following a study of children in the United States under three years old, the American Academy of Pediatrics stated that there is a positive correlation between the amount of time spent watching television and the likelihood of developing an attention deficit disorder. Which of the following is an appropriate conclusion to draw from this statement?

A) There is an association between television time and attention disorders for American children under three years old.

B) There is an association between television time and attention disorders for all children under three years old.

C) An increase in attention disorders is caused by an increase in television time for American children under three years old.

D) An increase in attention disorders is caused by an increase in television time for all children under three years old.

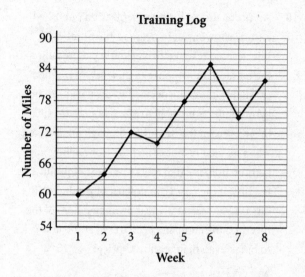

Training Log

8. A bicyclist is training for the Liège-Bastogne-Liège, one of Europe's oldest road bicycle races. The line graph above shows the number of miles she biked each week for eight weeks. According to the graph, what was the greatest change (in absolute value) in the weekly number of miles she biked between two consecutive weeks?

A) 7

B) 8

C) 9

D) 10

9. If a line that passes through the coordinates $(a - 1, 2a)$ and $(a, 6)$ has a slope of 5, what is the value of a ?

A) -2

B) $-\dfrac{1}{2}$

C) $\dfrac{1}{2}$

D) 2

GO ON TO THE NEXT PAGE

10. An occupational health organization published a study showing an increase in the number of injuries that resulted from elderly people falling in the bathtub. In response to this increase, a medical supply company decided to drop its price on bathtub lifts from $450 to $375, hoping to still break even on the lifts. The company breaks even when its total revenue (income from selling n bathtub lifts) is equal to its total cost of producing the lifts. If the cost C, in dollars, of producing the lifts is $C = 225n + 3,150$, how many more of the lifts does the company need to sell at the new price to break even than at the old price?

A) 7

B) 12

C) 14

D) 21

Questions 11 and 12 refer to the following information.

A zoo is building a penguin exhibit. It will consist of an underwater area and a land area. The land area is made of thick sheets of ice. An outline of the total space covered by the ice is shown below. A pipe 2 feet in diameter runs the full length of the exhibit under the ice. A substance known as ice-cold glycol continuously runs through the pipe to keep the ice frozen.

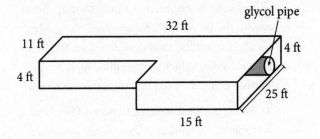

11. About how many cubic feet of water are needed to create the ice portion of the exhibit?

A) 1,850

B) 2,150

C) 2,450

D) 3,100

12. The zoo is planning to hire a company to fill the space with water. The company plans to use two 4-inch hoses that can each pump 60 gallons of water per minute. About how long should it take to fill the space? (There are 7.48 gallons of water in 1 cubic foot of ice.)

A) 1 hour

B) 1 hour, 30 minutes

C) 1 hour, 55 minutes

D) 2 hours, 15 minutes

GO ON TO THE NEXT PAGE

13. Which of the following quadratic equations has no solution?

    A) $0 = -2(x - 5)^2 + 3$

    B) $0 = -2(x - 5)(x + 3)$

    C) $0 = 2(x - 5)^2 + 3$

    D) $0 = 2(x + 5)(x + 3)$

Questions 14 and 15 refer to the following information.

Three airplanes depart from three different airports at 8:30 AM, all travelling to Chicago O'Hare International Airport (ORD). The distances the planes must travel are recorded in the following table. (Note: Assume all times provided are in Eastern Standard Time.)

From	Distance to Chicago (ORD)
Kansas City (MCI)	402
Boston (BOS)	864
Miami (MIA)	1,200

14. The plane traveling from Boston traveled at an average speed of 360 mph. The plane traveling from Kansas City arrived at 10:34 AM. How many minutes before the plane from Boston arrived did the plane from Kansas City arrive?

    A) 20

    B) 28

    C) 42

    D) 144

15. For the first $\frac{1}{4}$ of the trip, the plane from Miami flew through heavy winds and dense cloud cover at an average speed of 200 mph. For the remaining portion of the trip, the weather was ideal, and the plane flew at an average speed of 450 mph. Due to a backlog of planes at ORD, it was forced to circle overhead in a holding pattern for 25 minutes before landing. At what time did the plane from Miami land in Chicago?

    A) 12:00 PM

    B) 12:25 PM

    C) 12:50 PM

    D) 1:15 PM

16. If $h(t) = \sqrt{t^2 + 9}$ for all real values of t, which of the following is not in the range of $h(t)$?

    A) 1

    B) 3

    C) 9

    D) 10

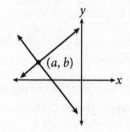

17. If (a, b) represents the solution to the system of equations shown in the graph and $a = -3b$, then which of the following could be the value of $a + b$?

    A) −9

    B) 0

    C) 3

    D) 6

GO ON TO THE NEXT PAGE

Thermostat A

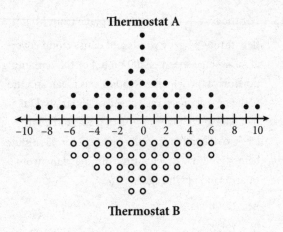

Thermostat B

18. A car manufacturer tested two types of thermostats to determine which one it wanted to use in a new model of car. The more consistently the thermostat engages the engine's cooling fan, the better the cooling system performs over the long run. The double dot plot above shows the test results, given the following conditions:

- Zero indicates that the cooling fan engaged at exactly the temperature at which the thermostat was set (the target temperature).

- Negative numbers indicate that the fan engaged below the target temperature.

- Positive numbers indicate that the fan engaged above the target temperature.

- The safe range for the fan to engage is 10 degrees above or below the target temperature.

Which of the following best states which thermostat the car manufacturer is likely to choose and why?

A) Thermostat A because the median of the data is 0, and the range is greater than that of Thermostat B

B) Thermostat B because the median of the data is 0, and the range is less than that of Thermostat A

C) Thermostat A because the mode of the data is 0, which indicates a more consistent thermostat

D) Thermostat B because the data is bimodal (has two modes), which indicates a more consistent thermostat

19. If p and q represent the zeros of a quadratic function and $p + q = -3$, which of the following could be the factored form of the function?

A) $f(x) = (x - 3)(x + 3)$

B) $f(x) = (x - 4)(x + 1)$

C) $f(x) = (x - 1)(x + 4)$

D) $f(x) = (x - 6)(x + 3)$

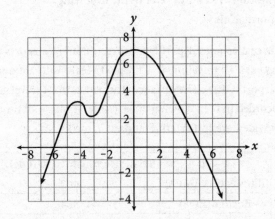

20. The figure above shows the graph of $p(x) - 4$. What is the value of $p(0)$?

A) 3

B) 4

C) 7

D) 11

GO ON TO THE NEXT PAGE

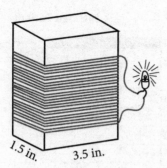

1.5 in.   3.5 in.

21. Geraldine is making a simple AC electric generator for a science project using copper wire, cardboard, a nail, and magnets. The first step in building the generator is wrapping the wire around a rectangular prism made from the cardboard and connecting it to a small lightbulb, as shown in the figure. If Geraldine has 18 feet of wire and needs to leave 3 inches on each end to connect to the lightbulb, how many times can she wrap the wire around the cardboard prism? (Note: 1 foot = 12 inches.)

A) 21

B) 28

C) 35

D) 42

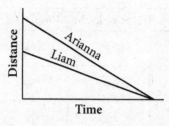

23. Arianna and her brother Liam both walk home from school each day, but they go to different schools. The figure shows their trip home on Monday. Based on the graph, which of the following statements is true?

A) It took Liam longer to walk home because his school is farther away.

B) It took Arianna longer to walk home because her school is farther away.

C) Arianna and Liam walked home at the same rate.

D) Arianna walked home at a faster rate than Liam.

24. If line L passes through the points $(-4, -8)$ and $(8, 1)$, which of the following points does line L not pass through?

A) $(0, -5)$

B) $(4, -1)$

C) $(12, 4)$

D) $(16, 7)$

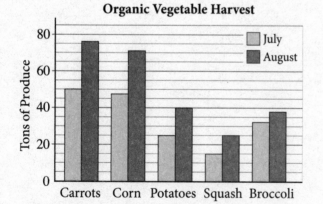

Organic Vegetable Harvest

22. The bar graph above shows the vegetable harvest, in tons, at an organic produce farm during July and August. Of the following, which best approximates the percent increase in the harvest of squash at this farm from July to August?

A) 67%

B) 60%

C) 53%

D) 40%

GO ON TO THE NEXT PAGE

	Unemployed	Employed	Totals
Female Degree	12	188	200
Female No Degree	44	156	200
Male Degree	23	177	200
Male No Degree	41	159	200
Totals	120	680	800

25. The table above shows the results of a sociological study identifying the number of males and females with and without college degrees who were unemployed or employed at the time of the study. If one person from the study is chosen at random, what is the probability that that person is an employed person with a college degree?

A) $\dfrac{73}{160}$

B) $\dfrac{10}{17}$

C) $\dfrac{17}{20}$

D) $\dfrac{73}{80}$

Infected Patient

26. Typically, when people contract an infectious disease, their immune system immediately begins to produce extra white blood cells to fight the disease. The scatterplot shows the white blood cells reproducing in an infected patient, along with several values found when modeling the data using a graphing calculator. According to this model, how many white blood cells per microliter of blood did the patient have before he contracted the disease?

A) 3,400

B) 8,500

C) 10,000

D) 13,600

27. A rodeo is building a circular arena. The arena will have a total area of 64π square yards and can either be left open for rodeo competitions or divided into 12 equal sections through the center for auctions. When holding auctions, the rodeo has an average of 4 bulls and 8 horses for sale. A bull cannot be placed in a section directly beside another section containing a bull, and all edges of these sections must be reinforced with strong steel to keep the bulls from getting out. Which of the following represents how much steel in yards the rodeo will need to reinforce the four bull sections?

A) 32π

B) 64π

C) $32 + \dfrac{16\pi}{3}$

D) $64 + \dfrac{16\pi}{3}$

28. Lena bought a saltwater fish tank that holds 400 gallons of water. She started filling the tank on Friday, but then stopped after putting only 70 gallons of water in the tank. On Saturday, she bought a bigger hose and began filling the tank again. It took her 1 hour and 50 minutes on Saturday to completely fill the tank. Which equation represents the number of gallons of water in the fish tank on Saturday, given the amount of time in minutes that Lena spent filling the tank?

A) $y = 3x + 70$

B) $y = 3x + 330$

C) $y = 70x + 330$

D) $y = 110x + 70$

29. A self-storage company has three sizes of storage units. The ratio of small to medium units is 3:5. The ratio of medium to large units is 3:2. The company analyzes its business model and current consumer demand and determines that it can benefit from utilizing larger economies of scale. In other words, it decides to grow its business based on current economic conditions and plans to build a second, larger self-storage building. The company's research indicates that the new market would benefit from having only two sizes of storage units, small and large, in the same ratio as its current facility. What ratio of small to large units should it use?

A) 1:1

B) 3:2

C) 5:3

D) 9:10

$$\frac{1}{x} + \frac{3}{x} = \frac{1}{7}$$

30. The equation shown above represents the following scenario: A chemical laboratory uses two air purifiers to clean the air of contaminants emitted while working with hazardous materials. One is an older model, and the other is a new model that is considerably more energy efficient. The new model can clean the air of contaminants three times as quickly as the older model. Working together, the two air purifiers can clean the air in the lab in 7 hours. Which of the following describes what the term $\dfrac{1}{x}$ in the equation represents?

A) The portion of the air the older model can clean in 1 hour

B) The portion of the air the new model can clean in 1 hour

C) The time it takes the older model to clean the air by itself

D) The time it takes the older model to clean $\dfrac{1}{7}$ of the air by itself

GO ON TO THE NEXT PAGE

Directions: For questions 31-38, enter your responses into the appropriate grid on your answer sheet, in accordance with the following:

1. You will receive credit only if the circles are filled in correctly, but you may write your answers in the boxes above each grid to help you fill in the circles accurately.

2. Don't mark more than one circle per column.

3. None of the questions with grid-in responses will have a negative solution.

4. Only grid in a single answer, even if there is more than one correct answer to a given question.

5. A **mixed number** must be gridded as a decimal or an improper fraction. For example, you would grid $7\frac{1}{2}$ as 7.5 or $\frac{15}{2}$.

   (Were you to grid it as $\boxed{7\ 1\ /\ 2}$, this response would be read as $\frac{71}{2}$.)

6. A **decimal** that has more digits than there are places on the grid may be either rounded or truncated, but every column in the grid must be filled in order to receive credit.

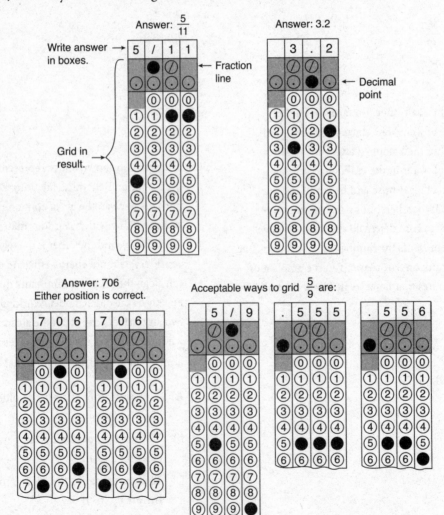

$$\frac{1}{3}(90x - 12) = \frac{1}{2}(8x + 10)$$

31. What is the solution to the equation shown?

32. If $n^{\frac{5}{2}} = 32$, what is the value of n?

33. When a thrift store gets used furniture in good condition to sell, it researches the original price and then marks the used piece down by 40% of that price. On the first day of each of the following months, the price is marked down an additional 15% until it is sold or it reaches 30% of its original price. Suppose the store gets a piece of used furniture on January 15th. If the piece of furniture costs $1,848 new, and it is sold on March 10th of the same year, what is the final selling price, not including tax? Round your answer to the nearest whole dollar.

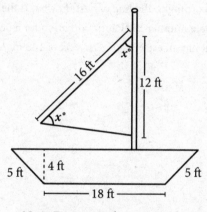

Note: Figure not drawn to scale.

34. Many sailboat manufacturers sell kits that include instructions and all the materials needed to build a simple sailboat. The figure shows the finished dimensions of a sailboat from such a kit. The instructions indicate that $\cos x° = b$, but do not give the value of b. What is the value of b?

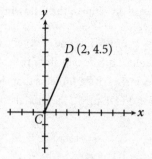

35. In the figure shown, line B (not shown) is parallel to $\overline{CD}$ and passes through the point $(0, -1)$. If line B also passes through the point $(2, y)$, what is the value of y?

36. Recycling of certain metals has been a common practice dating back to preindustrial times. For example, there is evidence of scrap bronze and silver being collected and melted down for reuse in a number of European countries. Today, there are recycling companies and even curbside collection bins for recycling. As a general rule, recycling companies pay for metals by weight. Suppose a person brings in 3 pounds of copper and receives $8.64, and 24 ounces of nickel and receives $10.08. If another person brings in equal weights of copper and nickel, what fractional portion of the money would he receive from the copper? (There are 16 ounces in 1 pound.)

GO ON TO THE NEXT PAGE ⟩

Questions 37 and 38 refer to the following information.

Body mass index, or BMI, is one of several measures used by doctors to determine a person's health as indicated by weight and height. Low-density lipoprotein, or LDL cholesterol, known as the "bad" cholesterol, is another health indicator and consists of fat proteins that clog arteries. Following are the results of a study showing the relationship between BMI and LDL for 12 individuals and the line of best fit for the data.

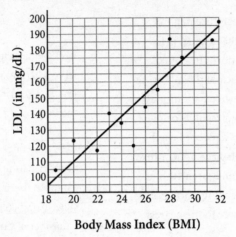

Body Mass Index (BMI)

37. How many of the 12 people have an actual LDL that differs by 10 or more mg/dL from the LDL predicted by the line of best fit?

38. According to the line of best fit, what is the closest whole number BMI approximation for a person that has an estimated LDL level of 140 mg/dL ?

ESSAY TEST

50 Minutes

You will be given a passage to read and asked to write an essay analyzing it. As you write, be sure to show that you have read the passage closely. You will be graded on how well you have understood the passage, how clear your analysis is, and how well you express your ideas.

Your essay must be written on the lines in your answer booklet. Anything you write outside the lined space in your answer booklet will not be read by the essay graders. Be sure to write or print in such a way that it will be legible to readers not familiar with your handwriting. Additionally, be sure to address the passage directly. An off-topic essay will not be graded.

As you read the passage, think about the author's use of

- evidence, such as statistics or other facts.

- logic to connect evidence to conclusions and to develop lines of reasoning.

- style, word choice, and appeals to emotion to make the argument more persuasive.

This passage deals with the issue of compensation for college athletes.

1   In the world of college sports, there is growing debate about whether student athletes should be awarded monetary compensation for their contribution to teams that garner millions of dollars for universities. Presently, the National Collegiate Athletics Association (NCAA), the governing body of college sports, doesn't allow it. Some hold this law as sacrosanct, saying it keeps college sports from becoming commercial and corrupting the experience of student athletes, who are in school, after all, for an education. But the reality is that we are past that point: college sports are big business, and the system that caps student salaries at zero is tantamount to wage fixing and collusion. If such practices happened in the investment market, universities would be fined by the FTC. In a labor market, they'd be shut down. Student athletes are being defrauded and taken advantage of.

2   So how much money is at stake? Basketball and football are the two main sports in question. Every year, the month of March becomes synonymous with a weeks-long basketball bracket that winnows down 64 teams to the single best. In football, a season of stadium-filling regular season games culminates in half a dozen lucrative "bowl games" sponsored by some of the biggest corporations in the world: FedEx, AT&T, and Mobil Oil.

3   For television networks, advertisers, universities, and local businesses where the events are held, these games are every bit as big as the NFL's Super Bowl and the NBA playoffs. In 2011, ESPN and Fox signed television rights deals worth $3 billion to the Pacific-12 conference. *Forbes* magazine reported that CBS and Turner Broadcasting make more than one billion dollars off the March Madness broadcasts, "thanks in part to a $700,000 advertising rate for a 30-second spot during the Final Four." One study put the value of a Texas A&M home game at $86 million for businesses in Brazos County, where A&M is located.

4   The dollar figures are indeed vast, and universities get their share. Here are two examples from schools with top football teams. According to the most recent federal data, the University of Texas football team netted a profit of $77.9 million in 2011-2012. Michigan made $61.6 million from football and $85.2 million in revenue.

GO ON TO THE NEXT PAGE →

5   Coaches, too, are a big part of the equation. Average salaries for major college football coaches have jumped more than 70 percent since 2006, to $1.64 million, according to *USA Today*. Nick Saban, head coach for Alabama, makes $7.3 million a year.

6   And yet, players take home no money. None. How can this be? Because, like unscrupulous tycoons from a Dickens novel, college presidents, athletic directors, and conference commissioners set their players' wages as low as they can get them—zero.

7   According to a recent study, if college football operated under the same revenue-sharing model as the NFL, each player on the Texas A&M squad would see a paycheck of about $225,000 per year.

8   All this talk of money might have you thinking that we should go back to square one and take the money out of college sports. But money is in college sports' DNA. It was conceived that way. It all grew out of the Morrill Land-Grant College Act of 1862. "As large public institutions spread into sparsely populated states, the competition for students grew fierce," says Allen Sack, a business professor at the University of New Haven. Football happened to be invented around that time, and schools took it up as a tool to draw students, and spectators, to campuses. The 1894 Harvard-Yale football game, for example, generated $119,000, according to the *New York Times*. That's nearly $3 million in today's dollars.

9   The historic justification for not paying players is that they are amateur student-athletes, and the value of their scholarships is payment enough. But the NCAA's own study shows that its scholarship limit leaves so-called "full" scholarship athletes with $3,000 to $5,000 in out-of-pocket expenses each year. The average shortfall is $3,200. Furthermore, most scholarships are revocable, so if an athlete doesn't perform well on the field, or is injured, he can, in a sense, lose that compensation. A student athlete devotes 40 hours a week on average towards sport; that's equivalent to a full-time job. Zero pay and immediate termination with no recourse? Those are labor conditions that any sensible workforce would unionize to change. But students are powerless to change. They are up against the NCAA, the Big 10 commission, university boards, and the almighty corporate dollar. Someone needs to become their advocate and get student athletes the compensation they deserve.

Write an essay that analyzes the author's approach in persuading his readers that athletes deserve fair compensation. Focus on specific features such as the ones listed in the box above the passage and explain how these features strengthen the author's argument. Your essay should discuss the most important rhetorical features of the passage.

Your essay should not focus on your own opinion of the author's conclusion, but rather on how the author persuades his readers.

ANSWER KEY
READING TEST

1. A	14. B	27. C	40. D
2. D	15. A	28. A	41. B
3. D	16. C	29. D	42. A
4. B	17. D	30. B	43. C
5. C	18. C	31. A	44. B
6. C	19. B	32. D	45. C
7. C	20. B	33. A	46. A
8. D	21. B	34. B	47. C
9. A	22. D	35. D	48. D
10. D	23. D	36. C	49. A
11. C	24. C	37. C	50. D
12. D	25. C	38. D	51. A
13. A	26. A	39. A	52. B

WRITING AND LANGUAGE TEST

1. B	12. B	23. C	34. B
2. D	13. D	24. B	35. C
3. B	14. B	25. B	36. A
4. C	15. C	26. A	37. D
5. D	16. A	27. A	38. A
6. D	17. B	28. A	39. D
7. B	18. D	29. B	40. A
8. A	19. B	30. A	41. B
9. D	20. D	31. C	42. D
10. C	21. B	32. D	43. C
11. B	22. C	33. A	44. B

MATH—NO CALCULATOR TEST

1. B	6. B	11. D	16. 15
2. C	7. A	12. D	17. 10.5 or 21/2
3. C	8. D	13. C	18. 4
4. A	9. A	14. B	19. 10
5. B	10. D	15. C	20. 50.5

MATH—CALCULATOR TEST

1. D	11. B	21. A	31. 9/26 or .346
2. B	12. D	22. A	32. 4
3. C	13. C	23. D	33. 801
4. D	14. A	24. B	34. 2/3 or .666 or .667
5. C	15. B	25. A	35. 3.5 or 7/2
6. A	16. A	26. B	36. 3/10
7. A	17. A	27. D	37. 3
8. D	18. B	28. A	38. 24
9. C	19. C	29. D	
10. A	20. D	30. A	

ANSWERS AND EXPLANATIONS

READING TEST

A Study in Scarlet

Suggested Passage Map notes:
¶1: W describes H
¶2: W stunned by H's deep knowledge of some subjects
¶3: W astonished by what H doesn't know
¶4: H: brain has only so much room, isn't interested in "useless facts"

1. A **Difficulty:** Easy

Category: Detail

Getting to the Answer: Eliminate answers that go against your understanding of the characters in the passage. The first paragraph explicitly states that Watson's curiosity about Holmes "gradually deepened and increased" (lines 2-3). Choice (A) is the correct answer.

2. D **Difficulty:** Medium

Category: Vocab-in-Context

Getting to the Answer: Predict a word that could be substituted for "casual" in context. Watson is explaining that Holmes's appearance is noticeable even to someone who hasn't seen him very often; therefore, (D) is correct.

3. D **Difficulty:** Easy

Category: Global

Getting to the Answer: The central idea in this passage should reflect the overall picture the author paints of Sherlock Holmes. The passage develops Holmes as an unusual and eccentric character. Watson marvels at Holmes's failure to pursue a typical path for an intelligent person, for example,

and describes in detail how Holmes' behavior and knowledge deviate from the ordinary. Choice (D) is the only answer choice that is directly supported by details in the passage.

4. B **Difficulty:** Medium

Category: Vocab-in-Context

Getting to the Answer: Use context clues to help you predict the meaning of the word as it is used in the sentence. In this sentence, the context clues provide a contrast to the target word. Watson says Holmes is usually "sharp" and "hawk-like" with great "alertness" except when he is in a period of "torpor" (lines 7-10). You can predict that the meaning of "torpor" will be something close to *the opposite of sharp and alert.* Choice (B) is the correct answer.

5. C **Difficulty:** Easy

Category: Inference

Getting to the Answer: Look for clues in the passage about how and why Holmes studies and learns. Watson notes that Holmes has not studied anything "which might fit him for a degree" (lines 21-22). This suggests that his learning is not motivated by something external, like a degree, but by his personal interests. Likewise, he has a "zeal" for particular subjects (line 24). Choice (C) reflects Holmes's motives for studying.

6. C **Difficulty:** Medium

Category: Command of Evidence

Getting to the Answer: Eliminate answer choices that don't explain why Holmes studies. A correct answer will allow you to make a logical guess as to Holmes's motives for studying. Choice (C) provides the best evidence by illustrating that Holmes pursues topics that he is passionate about rather than studying for external motivations.

7. C   Difficulty: Medium

Category: Inference

Getting to the Answer: Closely read Holmes's own statements for clues about his views. Holmes clearly suggests that the brain can only hold a limited amount of information, so one should prioritize the things that are most important. Therefore, (C) is the correct answer.

8. D   Difficulty: Easy

Category: Command of Evidence

Getting to the Answer: Reread each quote in the context of the passage. Find the one that supports the previous answer by giving evidence of Holmes's own ideas about learning. Of all the answer choices, Holmes's own statement about the necessity of prioritizing useful facts most directly supports the previous answer. Choice (D) is the correct answer.

9. A   Difficulty: Medium

Category: Rhetoric

Getting to the Answer: Consider what this figurative use of "attic" helps reveal about the character of Holmes. The author has Holmes compare the human brain to an attic to help illustrate Holmes's beliefs about useful facts versus those not worth learning. Choice (A) is the correct answer.

10. D   Difficulty: Medium

Category: Rhetoric

Getting to the Answer: Think about what insights the reader gains by having Watson narrate the story. The author is able to establish Holmes as an intriguing character by showing Watson's thoughts and reactions to Holmes. Presumably, readers will want to find out more about Holmes because the narrator depicts him as a fascinating person. Choice (D) fits this situation.

Woodrow Wilson Speech

Suggested Passage Map notes:

¶1: should be no secrets in peace process

¶2: war fought for justice; 14 pts for world peace

¶3: no secrets

¶4: freedom on the seas

¶5: equal trade

¶6: fewer weapons and armies worldwide

¶7: fair colonial land claims

¶8: Russia develop own gov't, Germans leave Russia

¶9: Germans leave Belgium, Belgium independent

¶10: France regain all territory

¶11: reestablish Italian borders

¶12: Austria-Hungary indep.

¶13: Serbia, Montenegro, Romania evacuated and indep.

¶14: Turkish people have own country

¶15: indep. Polish state

¶16: form League of Nations to protect indep.

11. C   Difficulty: Easy

Category: Rhetoric

Getting to the Answer: Examine the first two paragraphs. Try to paraphrase the reason Wilson gives for making the speech. In the first two paragraphs, Wilson anticipates the end of the war and alludes to the "processes of peace" (line 2). Although he refers to national sovereignty and conquest, he states that his purpose is to lay out a program for peace in the world, making (C) the correct answer.

12. D   Difficulty: Medium

Category: Command of Evidence

Getting to the Answer: Remember that the correct answer will provide information that directly relates to the answer to the previous question. The correct answer to the previous question concerns Wilson's plan to maintain peaceful relations in the world. Lines 26-27 read, "The programme of the world's peace, therefore, is our programme," making (D) the correct answer.

13. A   Difficulty: Medium

Category: Vocab-in-Context

Getting to the Answer: Predict a word that could substitute for "frankly" in context. In the list of points he presents, Wilson is defining actions and policies that will promote peace and open communication among nations. In this context, "frankly" suggests honesty, which makes (A) the correct answer.

14. B   Difficulty: Medium

Category: Inference

Getting to the Answer: Eliminate answer choices that cannot be inferred by the information provided in the passage. Calling for an end to "private international understandings" is one of Wilson's 14 points (lines 29-30). Therefore, it can be inferred that in the past, certain nations did indeed form "secret covenants" (line 6), or pacts, with one another. Choice (B) is correct.

15. A   Difficulty: Medium

Category: Command of Evidence

Getting to the Answer: The correct answer will reference a detail that provides evidence for the answer to the previous question. In the first paragraph of his speech, Wilson refers to "secret understandings" that cannot exist anymore if there is to be peace among nations. Therefore, (A) is correct.

16. C   Difficulty: Medium

Category: Vocab-in-Context

Getting to the Answer: Pretend the word is a blank in the sentence. Then predict what word could be substituted for the blank. The sentence states that "national armaments will be reduced to the lowest

point consistent with domestic safety" (lines 43–44). In this sense, Wilson aims to assure nations that they will still be able to protect themselves. Predict that armaments will be reduced to an extent agreeable with maintaining their own safety. (C) is the correct choice.

17. D   Difficulty: Hard

Category: Rhetoric

Getting to the Answer: Though the question is asking you about a specific line, it makes sense to choose an answer that is compatible with the broader context of the passage. In the excerpted line, Wilson identifies the "adjustment of all colonial claims" (line 46) as an item in his program for world peace. If his goal is to safeguard world peace, this must mean he believes conflicts resulting from colonization, itself an imperial pursuit, must be addressed. Choice (D) is correct.

18. C   Difficulty: Hard

Category: Rhetoric

Getting to the Answer: Locate the three points to which the question refers. Do not confuse them with other numbered points in the speech. Points VI through VIII refer to territorial sovereignty, evacuation of occupied lands, and restoration of lands. These points align with the claim that nations have violated one another's territorial sovereignty through invasion and occupation. This makes (C) the correct answer.

19. B   Difficulty: Hard

Category: Connections

Getting to the Answer: Be sure that the answer you choose reflects the ideology and positions expressed by Wilson in his speech. In the passage, Wilson expresses that he is in favor of international cooperation to promote and sustain global peace. Choice (B) is the correct answer because it describes an approach to international relations that is analogous to Wilson's.

20. B   Difficulty: Medium

Category: Rhetoric

Getting to the Answer: When asked a question involving the structure of a passage, consider the text as a whole. Often, the structure is visually noticeable. Wilson begins by stating his argument that countries must work together toward peace. He then follows up with specific examples (the 14 points) of how his ideas should be carried out. Choice (B) is the correct answer.

Paired Passages—Meditation

Suggested Passage Map notes:

Passage 1

¶1: history of meditation; secular meditation

¶2: describe mindfulness meditation

¶3: mindfulness → more fulfillment

¶4: health benefits

¶5: Dr. S – meditation good, drs should use it

Passage 2

¶1: Ryan uses mindfulness and sees many benefits

¶2: holds weekly bi-partisan meditation sessions

¶3: wrote book on mindfulness; improved attention

¶4: members of Congress getting interested

¶5: R supports legislation encouraging meditation

¶6: Ryan – not religious but secular

21. B   Difficulty: Medium

Category: Global

Getting to the Answer: Focus on the big picture rather than supporting details. Choice (B) correctly identifies the central idea in the passage. The other choices are based on misinformation or are details.

22. D   Difficulty: Hard

Category: Inference

Getting to the Answer: Keep the central idea of the passage in mind as you look for information in the passage about each of the choices. Determine which one can be inferred as true. The last two paragraphs of Passage 1 discuss "health benefits" of meditation (line 30), studies showing positive results of meditation, and a quote from a professional about meditation's advantages. This matches choice (D).

23. D   Difficulty: Medium

Category: Command of Evidence

Getting to the Answer: Avoid choices that do not provide direct evidence to support your answer to the previous question. Choice (D) supports the inference that some medical professionals accept meditation as beneficial.

24. C   Difficulty: Easy

Category: Vocab-in-Context

Getting to the Answer: Predict a word that could substitute for "compelling" in context. The context of the sentence suggests that meditation has great or convincing benefits. Therefore, (C) is correct.

25. C   Difficulty: Easy

Category: Inference

Getting to the Answer: Remember that you're analyzing the author's point of view on meditation, not Tim Ryan's view. Since the author makes statements such as calling Ryan a "voice for calm consideration," (line 56), the author must hold a positive view of meditation. However, there is little evidence that the author is devoted to meditation. Choice (C) correctly reflects the author's point of view.

26. A   Difficulty: Easy

Category: Inference

Getting to the Answer: Determine what can be inferred about Ryan's personality from what is stated in the passage. The passage contains numerous examples of Ryan putting his belief in the value of mindfulness into action. For instance, he hosts meditation sessions for his staff and supports legislation promoting meditation. Choice (A) is the correct answer.

27. C   Difficulty: Medium

Category: Command of Evidence

Getting to the Answer: Be careful of choices that do not provide direct evidence to support the inference about Ryan from the previous question. Choice (C) is correct. Mr. Ryan shows that he acts on what he believes by supporting legislation that encourages meditation, such as the bill supporting the increase in holistic medicine offered by the Department of Veterans Affairs.

28. A   Difficulty: Easy

Category: Vocab-in-Context

Getting to the Answer: Predict a word that is a synonym for "secular" in context. In the context of the sentence, "but rather" indicates that "secular" means the opposite of "religious," so (A) is the correct answer.

29. D   Difficulty: Easy

Category: Rhetoric

Getting to the Answer: Reread the sentence to determine what connotative meaning the author suggests through the use of "chatter." Since "chatter" in this sentence is contrasted with the "mind and body" syncing together, the word has a negative connotation that suggests background noise or frequent talk. Only (D) fits with this meaning.

30. B   Difficulty: Medium

Category: Synthesis

Getting to the Answer: Look for an answer that fits with the purposes of both passages. Avoid choices that are suggested by only one of the passages. Both passages discuss changing attitudes regarding the efficacy of mindfulness meditation: Passage 1 states it is becoming "more popular" (lines 16–17) and "widely accepted by health professionals" (line 45), while Passage 2 describes the impact of a politician who is promoting meditation. Only (B) reflects this.

31. A   Difficulty: Medium

Category: Synthesis

Getting to the Answer: Examine the graphic and the two passages to figure out which answer choice is supported by all three. The passages both discussed benefits of meditation. The graphic shows that workers were more productive and had fewer injuries after being in a meditation program. Choice (A) is the only one that relates to the information in the graphic.

Colony Collapse Disorder Passage

Suggested Passage Map notes:

¶1: CCD – all bees disappear; bees perform invaluable services

¶2: pathogens aren't the cause

¶3: altruism explains the disappearance but doesn't explain the cause

¶4: may be caused by fluctuation in earth's magnetic field

¶5: may be caused by pesticides

¶7: may be cause by pesticide combos

¶7: need more research; encourage more beekeeping, relax city rules

32. D   Difficulty: Hard

Category: Global

Getting to the Answer: Think of what the author wants the reader to learn about bees. This will help you figure out the passage's purpose. Choice (D) is the primary purpose of the passage. The author most wants the reader to know about colony collapse disorder.

33. A   Difficulty: Hard

Category: Connections

Getting to the Answer: Think back to the author's purpose that you explored in question 32. Consider what this purpose suggests about the author's point of view. The author seems knowledgeable about honey bees and very concerned about their loss. The author points out the many losses humans would have if bees were to disappear. Therefore, (A) is the correct answer.

34. B   Difficulty: Hard

Category: Rhetoric

Getting to the Answer: Notice that the word "mysteriously" appears toward the beginning of the passage, when the author is first introducing the topic. As the author introduces the topic of colony collapse disorder in the first paragraph, the word "mysterious" helps emphasize how puzzling the disorder truly is. Choice (B) is the correct answer.

35. D   Difficulty: Medium

Category: Vocab-in-Context

Getting to the Answer: Predict a word that is a synonym for "plights" in context. In the sentence, "common plights" refers to pests such as mites, fungus, and bacteria, which farmers commonly see in beehives. Predict a negative word. In this context, (D), "troubles" is the correct answer.

36. C   Difficulty: Hard

Category: Rhetoric

Getting to the Answer: Examine the part of the passage that discusses the lack of bees after a collapse. The author wants to stress the fact that research has shown that pathogens are not the reason for colony collapse. Choice (C) is the correct answer.

37. C   Difficulty: Medium

Category: Command of Evidence

Getting to the Answer: Be careful of choices that do not directly support your answer to the previous

question. In the context of its paragraph, lines 31-33 provide evidence to support the inference that the cause of colony collapse is not pathogens, since "common killers" such as pathogens would leave "telltale signs." Choice (C) is the correct answer.

38. D   Difficulty: Easy

Category: Vocab-in-Context

Getting to the Answer: Predict a word that could substitute for "foraging" in context. Predict an action that bees might perform during their "pollination flights," such as searching for flowers. The context of the sentence rules out all but (D), the correct answer.

39. A   Difficulty: Hard

Category: Inference

Getting to the Answer: Review your Passage Map and use the passage's central idea as a general prediction. Choice (A) is correct. Though the author laments the disappearance of honey bees and says how challenging it is to solve the problem, the last paragraph ends the passage on a cautiously optimistic note, particularly with the use of the word "hopefully" (line 82).

40. D   Difficulty: Medium

Category: Command of Evidence

Getting to the Answer: Be careful of choices that might support an incorrect answer in the previous question. Choice (D) is evidence that the author is cautiously optimistic about the future of the honey bee.

41. B   Difficulty: Medium

Category: Detail

Getting to the Answer: Watch out for answer choices that might sound plausible but are not explicitly stated in the passage. Choice (B) is correct; the last paragraph states that some towns and cities are relaxing their regulations about beekeeping "in response to the honey bee population crisis" (line 81).

42. A   Difficulty: Medium

Category: Connections

Getting to the Answer: Look for information in the passage that tells what honey bees and human beings do for each other. Paragraph 1 states that if honey bees disappear, people will not have certain foods; even the beef industry will be affected. Therefore, humans depend on the bees to keep the environment and economy healthy. Choice (A) is correct.

Space Debris Passage

Suggested Passage Map notes:

¶1: concern that spacecraft could be hit by micrometeorites

¶2: human-made debris in space; more likely than meteorites to hit spacecraft

¶3: small pieces are dangerous

¶4: larger pieces dangerous, but can be avoided

¶5: satellites can adjust course to avoid collision

¶6: some debris falls to earth; sci. can't stop it

¶7: in future, maybe spacecraft leave orbit when not used anymore

43. C   Difficulty: Medium

Category: Global

Getting to the Answer: Think about the idea that is developed throughout the passage. Avoid answers that refer only to supporting details. Choice (C) is the correct answer because all the information in the passage relates to the dangers posed by space debris created by humans.

44. B   Difficulty: Medium

Category: Command of Evidence

Getting to the Answer: Look at each quote from the passage and decide which most clearly supports the central idea. In paragraph 3, the author describes

how space debris created by humans is dangerous to spacecraft and the people inside of them. Choice (B) is the correct answer.

45. C   Difficulty: Medium

Category: Rhetoric

Getting to the Answer: Consider the central idea that you identified in question 43. Identify the central idea of paragraph 2. The passage is mostly about the dangers associated with human-made space debris. Paragraph 2 contains details about the types of human-made space debris orbiting Earth, thus providing support for the central idea. Choice (C) is the correct answer.

46. A   Difficulty: Medium

Category: Detail

Getting to the Answer: Reread the information about meteoroids at the beginning of the passage. Think about how this compares with the descriptions of space debris in the following paragraphs. The author states that although there were concerns about meteoroids in the early days of space travel, scientists concluded that the risk was small because meteoroids were rare. The author goes on to explain that space debris created by humans is a greater concern because it is so plentiful. Choice (A) is the correct answer.

47. C   Difficulty: Hard

Category: Rhetoric

Getting to the Answer: The author's central claim in the passage is that space debris left by humans is dangerous. Think about which of the answer choices most directly supports that claim. In paragraph 6, the author describes how Skylab fell to Earth. This example strengthens the claim, illustrating that the debris left in space can be dangerous even on Earth. Therefore, (C) is the correct answer.

48. D   Difficulty: Medium

Category: Vocab-in-Context

Getting to the Answer: Eliminate answers that are synonyms for "obsolete" but do not make sense in context. Since it was debris that fell out of space, Skylab was no longer in use. In this context, "obsolete" means "outdated," so (D) is the correct answer.

49. A   Difficulty: Hard

Category: Inference

Getting to the Answer: Eliminate answer choices that cannot be supported with information found in the passage. In paragraph 6, the author describes how space debris can be dangerous on Earth if a large enough piece gets through the atmosphere without burning up. It is logical, then, that (A) is the correct answer; warnings could help people avoid areas where impacts are predicted, thereby decreasing the chance of injury. The author explicitly states that agencies monitor debris to make predictions and issue warnings (lines 58–62).

50. D   Difficulty: Medium

Category: Command of Evidence

Getting to the Answer: Avoid answer choices that provide evidence for incorrect answers to the previous question. Choice (D) is the correct answer, because in lines 60–62, the author states that there is nothing to be done about space debris falling to Earth except to issue warnings.

51. A   Difficulty: Medium

Category: Vocab-in-Context

Getting to the Answer: Predict a word that is a synonym for "implemented" in context. Since the debris will remain in space unless a method of removal is "implemented," predict the word that means employed. In this context, (A) is the correct answer.

52. B   Difficulty: Hard

Category: Synthesis

Getting to the Answer: Make sure you understand the units and labels in the graphic before choosing an answer. The graphic shows that the highest

density of space debris occurs at an altitude just under 800 kilometers, posing the greatest risk of the dangers discussed in the passage. It is reasonable to conclude, therefore, that if NASA were to place a new satellite into orbit, the agency should choose to avoid the altitude range of 700–900 kilometers. Choice (B) is the correct answer.

WRITING AND LANGUAGE TEST

A Sweet Discovery

1. B   Difficulty: Medium

Category: Sentence Formation

Getting to the Answer: Determine the noun to which the modifier in this sentence is referring. Then check the noun's placement to make sure it is as close as possible to the modifier. The modifier is "like most chemists." Therefore, the noun it modifies should be a person. Choice (B) correctly rearranges the sentence so that "chemists" clearly refers to "Constantin Fahlberg."

2. D   Difficulty: Medium

Category: Development

Getting to the Answer: This is the topic sentence of the paragraph. Make sure that it focuses on the correct subject. The purpose of this sentence is to discuss Fahlberg and the circumstances in which he was working. Choice (D) correctly focuses the sentence on Fahlberg and flows well into the next sentence, which discusses the specifics of coal tar.

3. B   Difficulty: Easy

Category: Usage

Getting to the Answer: The pronoun should agree with the noun to which it refers. Identify this noun to determine the correct pronoun. The antecedent of the pronoun here is "coal tar," a singular, impersonal noun. Choice (B), "from it," is therefore the correct answer.

4. C   Difficulty: Easy

Category: Effective Language Use

Getting to the Answer: Predict what meaning the correct word should convey before choosing an answer. The sentence suggests that while working, Fahlberg was so "___" that he forgot to eat lunch. A word that means *focused on* or *preoccupied with* would be most appropriate. Choice (C), "engrossed," conveys this meaning successfully.

5. D   Difficulty: Hard

Category: Organization

Getting to the Answer: The passage is telling a story. Choose the answer that most effectively makes the transition between the paragraphs while maintaining a consistent tone with the rest of the story. The correct answer will relate to the sentences both before and after it. While answer B may intrigue readers, its tone is out of place when compared with that of the rest of the passage. Choice (D) is the correct answer. It provides a transition from the previous sentence and tells the next logical step in the story.

6. D   Difficulty: Hard

Category: Development

Getting to the Answer: The correct answer will clearly present the central idea of the paragraph. Identify the answer choice that presents the most important point about the scene being described. To be effective as a central idea, the sentence needs to sum up the supporting details in the paragraph and convey their meaning. Only (D) both explains what happened and describes why it was significant, which is the central idea of the paragraph.

7. B   Difficulty: Hard

Category: Usage

Getting to the Answer: Examine the context of the sentence. Notice that it's describing a potentially disastrous outcome if conditions had been different. Fortunately, he had not worked with anything poi-sonous or corrosive, or the story would have had a different ending. If Fahlberg had been working with poisonous or corrosive materials, there is no doubt that "the story" would have had a different—and terrible—ending. The word "might" is too conditional for this situation; therefore, (B), which includes the word "would," is the correct answer.

8. A   Difficulty: Hard

Category: Development

Getting to the Answer: Determine which option clearly states the most important information in this paragraph. The most important fact in this paragraph is that Fahlberg discovered a new substance accidentally. The rest of this paragraph provides details about this discovery. Therefore, the correct answer choice will state that Fahlberg made a discovery. Choice (A) makes this idea clear.

9. D   Difficulty: Easy

Category: Effective Language Use

Getting to the Answer: Look for clues in the rest of the sentence to determine which verb fits with the exact meaning of the sentence. The sentence states that Fahlberg is making the saccharin "commercially," or as part of a business. Choice (D), "producing," is correct, as it emphasizes the business nature of his work.

10. C   Difficulty: Medium

Category: Organization

Getting to the Answer: Try out each answer choice. What information seems confusing when not presented in the right order? Logically, Fahlberg should find the mixture of chemicals and work to isolate it before he names it and understands its significance. Therefore, (C) is the most logical place for sentence 4 and is the correct answer.

11. B   Difficulty: Hard

Category: Organization

Getting to the Answer: Specifically state in your own words what the passage is about. Then read the answer choices to see what fits best. The passage focuses on the specific moment of Fahlberg's discovery, including the significance of the discovery itself and its applications. Only (B) convincingly ties the sentence to the main ideas of the passage.

René Descartes: The Father of Modern Philosophy

12. B   Difficulty: Easy

Category: Usage

Getting to the Answer: A modifier should match its antecedent in number and gender. Also, be wary of words that sound alike but have different meanings and uses. As it stands, the sentence incorrectly uses the adverb "there." Since it refers to "great philosophers," the correct word is the possessive pronoun "their," which is often confused with "there." Choice (B) is the correct answer.

13. D   Difficulty: Hard

Category: Effective Language Use

Getting to the Answer: Read carefully to identify the context of the underlined word. Then, choose the word that best fits the context of the sentence. The underlined word modifies "premodern sources of truth and knowledge," which in turn refers to "political and religious tradition and authority." The context of the sentence indicates that these were powerful ideas that were being challenged by newer ideas. Choice (D), "reigning," conveys the idea that "political and religious tradition and authority" had monarch-like, or ruling, levels of power in people's lives.

14. B   Difficulty: Easy

Category: Effective Language Use

Getting to the Answer: Determine the relationship between the two parts of the underlined sentence, and then think about which answer choice best conveys this relationship. The sentence states that "foundations of truth seemed to be crumbling," and "Descartes's writings proposed an alternative foundation." The two ideas are connected to each other: Descartes's writings were a response to this "crumbling." Choice (B) is the answer that identifies this relationship.

15. C   Difficulty: Hard

Category: Sentence Formation

Getting to the Answer: Determine whether the modifying phrase in this sentence references the correct noun. If the modifier in this sentence is describing a person, then the noun that is described by the modifier should also be a person. Choice (C) correctly matches the modifier (beginning with "an expert") to the noun "Descartes," rather than the noun "work."

16. A   Difficulty: Hard

Category: Development

Getting to the Answer: Determine the central claim in the paragraph and then come back to the question. The central claim of the paragraph is that Descartes's work established the foundation for many modern ideas. The statement found in (A) provides information that best supports this claim and logically transitions to the following sentence. Choice (A) is correct.

17. B   Difficulty: Medium

Category: Development

Getting to the Answer: In your own words, identify what idea ties together the ideas presented in the rest of the paragraph. Sentence 1 states that "modern culture would come to cherish this." The question is, what is "this"? The rest of the paragraph goes into detail about Descartes's philosophical methods. Choice (B) identifies Descartes's general philosophical focus and is, therefore, the correct answer.

18. D   Difficulty: Medium

Category: Punctuation

Getting to the Answer: Identify whether the sentence consists of two independent clauses or an independent and a dependent clause. This will provide guidance for punctuating it. The sentence consists of two independent clauses ("Descartes arrived . . ." and "he could only be . . . "). Separating the independent clauses into two sentences is the best way to punctuate them. Choice (D) is the correct answer.

19. B   Difficulty: Hard

Category: Development

Getting to the Answer: Look for the answer choice that most clearly helps to develop the ideas in the surrounding sentences. The inserted sentence comes after a discussion of Descartes's only certainty—that he was thinking. The sentence that follows it explains that from this, he could build additional knowledge. The correct answer will develop the idea of certainty and how it can be used to acquire more knowledge. Choice (B) best conveys this information and therefore is the correct choice.

20. D   Difficulty: Medium

Category: Usage

Getting to the Answer: A grammatically correct sentence will include a verb whose form makes the sentence an independent clause. "Propelled by" needs the addition of an auxiliary verb for this sentence to stand alone. Inserting "were" before this phrase makes the sentence grammatically complete. Choice (D) is the correct answer.

21. B   Difficulty: Medium

Category: Effective Language Use

Getting to the Answer: Determine whether there is a way to make the sentence less wordy without changing its intended meaning. The sentence, especially in the context of the paragraph, seems to be saying that it's difficult to determine exactly what Descartes did versus what other people at the time did. Both answer choices C and D change the meaning of the sentence slightly to say either that Descartes himself could not be separated from his contemporaries or that what they did was identical. Choice (B) is correct, because it eliminates the wordiness of the sentence while maintaining its meaning.

22. C   Difficulty: Medium

Category: Effective Language Use

Getting to the Answer: Determine what role this verb has in the sentence. What is the precise nature of the action it is describing? The sentence is about how Descartes's work brought about shifts in thinking that critically influenced other developments. However, the word "begun," A, does not precisely convey the power with which this occurred. Choice (C), "initiated," conveys this meaning and is the correct answer.

The Novel: Introspection to Escapism

23. C   Difficulty: Medium

Category: Effective Language Use

Getting to the Answer: Reread the surrounding sentences to look for context clues. Then review the answer choices, paying attention to the meaning and nuance of each word. The passage tells us that art is constantly evolving and changing. The correct answer will represent the opposite of this meaning. The word "static" means that something does not change, so (C) is the correct answer.

24. B **Difficulty:** Medium

Category: Punctuation

Getting to the Answer: Read the sentence and determine whether the parts of the sentence on either side of the semicolon are independent clauses. If they are not, identify their function and choose the appropriate punctuation. "For better or worse" is not an independent clause; rather, it is a parenthetical element that adds an opinion to the main thrust of the sentence. Choice (B) is correct. It uses a dash to set off this additional information in the sentence.

25. B **Difficulty:** Medium

Category: Development

Getting to the Answer: To determine the main topic of a paragraph, identify important details and then summarize them in a sentence or two. Find a choice that matches your prediction. Avoid choices like A and C, which include details about poetry that are not in the paragraph. The details in this paragraph are about how the writers of the past viewed the novel as a vital way to record and comment on the human experience. Choice (B) captures this main topic.

26. A **Difficulty:** Medium

Category: Effective Language Use

Getting to the Answer: Read the surrounding sentences to get a sense of what the underlined word is meant to convey. Then review the answer choices to find the one that is closest to this meaning. The passage suggests that the novel was held in high regard. The correct answer needs to indicate high regard with a positive connotation. The word "loftily," (A), connotes both high regard and a positive view of the novel as a literary form.

27. A **Difficulty:** Medium

Category: Development

Getting to the Answer: Look for the answer choice that improves the sentence by adding important, relevant information. The paragraph is about the

opinions of acclaimed novelists. Choice (A) adds the information that Joseph Conrad was also a novelist.

28. A **Difficulty:** Medium

Category: Punctuation

Getting to the Answer: Identify the role of the underlined phrase; then use this information to determine the necessary punctuation. "However" is an introductory adverbial element that modifies the rest of the sentence. It should be followed by a comma. Choice (A) is correct.

29. B **Difficulty:** Medium

Category: Sentence Formation

Getting to the Answer: Check the placement of dependent clauses set off by commas. A dependent clause that modifies a noun in a sentence should be adjacent or as close as possible to the noun it is modifying. The dependent clause "which are now available on digital devices" modifies "novels," not "entertainment medium." It should be as close as possible to "novels," making (B) the correct answer.

30. A **Difficulty:** Medium

Category: Sentence Formation

Getting to the Answer: A compound sentence should be combined with a semicolon or a comma with a conjunction. Choice (A) is correct. This keeps the semicolon, which appropriately separates two related independent clauses.

31. C **Difficulty:** Hard

Category: Development

Getting to the Answer: Evaluate the paragraph for the central idea. Then review the answer choices to find the one that directly supports that idea. This paragraph discusses the change from novels that tackle serious social issues to books that are meant as light entertainment for mass consumption. Choice (C) is correct. It emphasizes that readers want novels to be "fun," providing a means of escape from their lives.

32. D   Difficulty: Medium

Category: Usage

Getting to the Answer: A pronoun needs to match its antecedent. Locate the antecedent of the pronoun and then predict an answer. The correct answer will match the antecedent in gender and number. The antecedent is "novelist," so the answer must be singular. Choice (D) is correct, as it matches the antecedent in number and appropriately identifies both gender options, since the antecedent did not specify gender.

33. A   Difficulty: Hard

Category: Punctuation

Getting to the Answer: Remember that dashes and parentheses act in similar ways. If the phrase is offering additional information before you get back to the main thrust of the sentence, then a dash is appropriate. A dash is an appropriate way to punctuate the phrase, so (A) is the correct choice.

Interning: A Bridge Between Classes and Careers

34. B   Difficulty: Easy

Category: Usage

Getting to the Answer: Read the entire paragraph to understand the context in which the underlined word appears. Be careful to distinguish between commonly confused words. The paragraph makes it clear that Kelli has started working at BP as a summer intern. The correct answer will convey this meaning. Choice A, "excepted," meaning "excluded from a group," is a word that is commonly confused with "accepted," which means "to have taken or received something." In this case, Kelli has taken the job offer with BP, making (B) the correct choice.

35. C   Difficulty: Medium

Category: Effective Language Use

Getting to the Answer: Read the entire sentence to

determine the context of the underlined word. The context implies that the tasks assigned to interns are low level and meaningless. Choices B, "skilled," and D, "challenging," suggest that the tasks are important, which does not match the context. Only (C) fits the tone and context of the paragraph and is more precise than "boring."

36. A   Difficulty: Hard

Category: Development

Getting to the Answer: Identify the central idea and then review the answer choices to find the one that best supports it. The paragraph is about the importance of gaining a real-world perspective on classroom knowledge. Choice (A) supports this central idea by showing how Kelli's internship will allow her to apply her classroom knowledge to the real world.

37. D   Difficulty: Hard

Category: Development

Getting to the Answer: Skim the paragraph to determine what content the sentences have in common. The paragraph discusses the safety training Kelli is required to complete and explains how this training will offer her an advantage over other job applicants. Choice (D) most effectively establishes the main topic of the paragraph; it introduces the type of certification Kelli will earn.

38. A   Difficulty: Medium

Category: Effective Language Use

Getting to the Answer: Analyze the sentence to determine which phrase best fits the context. Choice (A) is the correct answer. "Stand out" means that Kelli will clearly be noticed when compared with other applicants.

39. D   Difficulty: Medium

Category: Usage

Getting to the Answer: Examine the structure of the sentence and identify the pronoun or pronouns that match the antecedent. Use the word "everyone" in a simple sentence to determine if it's singular or plural: for example, "Everyone goes." "Everyone" is a singular pronoun referring to a person, so it requires a singular possessive pronoun. Using the plural "their" is accepted only in informal usage. Choice (D) is the correct answer because it correctly matches the antecedent in number and appropriately identifies both gender options, since the antecedent did not specify a gender.

40. A   Difficulty: Medium

Category: Punctuation

Getting to the Answer: Determine the need for punctuation within the sentence. "For" and "from" are both prepositions, a clue that both phrases are correctly set off with commas. Because both phrases are dependent on the remainder of the sentence, they are correctly connected with commas. Choice (A) is correct.

41. B   Difficulty: Easy

Category: Sentence Formation

Getting to the Answer: In a sentence with a series of actions, make sure all verbs or verb forms are parallel. Focusing on the action verbs, it becomes clear that they should all end in "-ing." Inconsistencies in this pattern result in a lack of parallel structure. Choice (B) is correct, as it uses the gerund form (nouns formed by adding "-ing" to verbs) of all four action verbs.

42. D   Difficulty: Medium

Category: Sentence Formation

Getting to the Answer: Identify the subject and predicate of each sentence to determine if it is a complete sentence or a fragment. As the sentences are written in A, the first one is an incomplete sentence, or fragment. Only (D) correctly and concisely combines the two to eliminate the fragment.

43. C   Difficulty: Medium

Category: Effective Language Use

Getting to the Answer: Often, when a sentence is long, it's a good idea to see if there are ways to edit out certain words or phrases to make the sentence more concise. Choice (C) is correct. By leaving out the phrase "though she is losing her summer," this answer choice conveys the intended meaning of the sentence with logical and concise language.

44. B   Difficulty: Medium

Category: Quantitative

Getting to the Answer: Make sure you understand the information conveyed by the graphic's labels before you attempt to choose the correct answer. The passage informs you that Kelli's chosen field is oil and energy, represented by the bar on the far right of the graphic. Choice (B) is the correct answer, as it matches the number of oil and energy interns per 1,000 hires noted on the *y*-axis.

MATH—NO CALCULATOR TEST

1. B   Difficulty: Easy

Category: Heart of Algebra / Linear Equations

Getting to the Answer: In a real-world scenario, the slope of a line represents a unit rate and the *y*-intercept represents a flat fee or a starting amount. The cost of one linear foot is the same as the unit rate (the cost per linear foot), which is represented by the slope of the line. Use the grid-lines and the axis labels to count the rise and the run from the *y*-intercept of the line (0, 150) to the next point that hits an intersection of two grid-lines. Pay careful attention to how the grid-lines are marked (by 5s on the *x*-axis and by 25s on the *y*-axis). The line rises 75 units and runs 5 units, so the slope is $\frac{75}{5} = 15$ dollars per linear foot of fence, which is (B). Note that you could also use the slope formula and two points from the graph to find the unit rate.

2. C   Difficulty: Easy

Category: Passport to Advanced Math / Exponents

Getting to the Answer: Don't be tempted—you can't simply cancel one term when a polynomial is divided by a monomial. Instead, find the greatest common factor of *both* the numerator and the denominator. Factor out the GCF from the numerator and from the denominator, and then you can cancel it. The GCF is $12x^2$.

$$\frac{24x^4 + 36x^3 - 12x^2}{12x^2}$$
$$= \frac{\cancel{12x^2}(2x^2 + 3x - 1)}{\cancel{12x^2}}$$
$$= 2x^2 + 3x - 1$$

This matches (C).

3. C   Difficulty: Easy

Category: Additional Topics in Math / Geometry

Getting to the Answer: Corresponding sides of similar triangles are proportional, so write a proportion (paying careful attention to the order of the sides) using the sides that you know and the side that you're looking for. Then, solve the proportion for the missing side.

Call the missing side x. Write a proportion using words first, and then fill in the lengths of the sides that you know:

$$\frac{\text{right side small}\triangle}{\text{base of small}\triangle} = \frac{\text{right side large}\triangle}{\text{base of large}\triangle}$$
$$\frac{x}{4} = \frac{2 + x}{6}$$
$$6x = 4(2 + x)$$
$$6x = 8 + 4x$$
$$2x = 8$$
$$x = 4$$

The length of $\overline{BE}$ is 4, so (C) is correct.

4. A   Difficulty: Easy

Category: Passport to Advanced Math / Quadratics

Getting to the Answer: Recognizing the different forms of a quadratic equation can save valuable time on Test Day. Each of the answer choices is given in vertex form, so start by matching the vertex of the parabola in the graph to the correct equation.

When a quadratic equation is written in vertex form, $y = a(x - h)^2 + k$, the vertex is (h, k). The vertex of the parabola in the graph is (2, 5); therefore, the equation should look like $y = a(x - 2)^2 + 5$. This means you can eliminate B and C. To choose between (A) and D, consider the value of a. The parabola in the graph opens downward, so a must be negative. This means (A) is correct.

5. B   Difficulty: Medium

Category: Heart of Algebra / Linear Equations

Getting to the Answer: You can approach this question conceptually or concretely. Drawing a quick sketch is most likely the safest approach. Line L shown in the graph rises from left to right, so it has a positive slope. Once reflected over the x-axis, it will fall from left to right, so the new line will have a negative slope. This means you can eliminate C and D. Now, draw a quick sketch of the reflected line on the coordinate plane in your test booklet and count the rise (or fall) and the run from one point to the next.

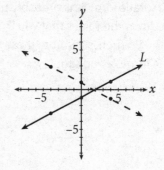

The reflected line falls 2 units and runs 4 units, so the slope is $-\frac{2}{4}$, which reduces to $-\frac{1}{2}$, making (B) the correct choice.

6. B **Difficulty:** Medium

Category: Passport to Advanced Math / Exponents

Getting to the Answer: To answer this question, you need to combine like terms, being careful to distribute negative signs where appropriate. Break the calculation into steps: Find 2p, find q + r, and then subtract the results. Arranging the terms in descending order will help keep them organized.

$$2p = 2(4x^3 + x - 2) = 8x^3 + 2x - 4$$
$$q + r = x^2 - 1 + 3x - 5 = x^2 + 3x - 6$$
$$2p - (q + r) = 8x^3 + 2x - 4 - (x^2 + 3x - 6)$$
$$= 8x^3 + 2x - 4 - x^2 - 3x + 6$$
$$= 8x^3 - x^2 + 2x - 3x - 4 + 6$$
$$= 8x^3 - x^2 - x + 2$$

This matches (B).

7. A **Difficulty:** Medium

Category: Passport to Advanced Math / Quadratics

Getting to the Answer: The roots of an equation are the same as its solutions. The answer choices contain radicals, which tells you that the equation can't be factored. Instead, either complete the square or solve the equation using the quadratic formula, whichever you are most comfortable using. The equation is already written in the form $y = ax^2 + bx + c$ and the coefficients are fairly small, so using the quadratic formula is probably the quickest method. Jot down the values that you'll need: $a = 2$, $b = 4$, and $c = -3$. Then, substitute these values into the quadratic formula and simplify:

$$x = \frac{-b \pm \sqrt{b^2 - 4ac}}{2a}$$
$$= \frac{-(4) \pm \sqrt{(4)^2 - 4(2)(-3)}}{2(2)}$$
$$= \frac{-4 \pm \sqrt{16 + 24}}{4}$$
$$= \frac{-4 \pm \sqrt{40}}{4}$$

This is not one of the answer choices, so simplify the radical. To do this, look for a perfect square that divides into 40 and take its square root.

$$x = \frac{-4 \pm \sqrt{4 \times 10}}{4}$$
$$= \frac{-4 \pm 2\sqrt{10}}{4}$$
$$= \frac{-2 \pm \sqrt{10}}{2}$$

Be careful—you can't simplify the answer any further because you cannot divide the square root of 10 by 2, so (A) is correct.

8. D **Difficulty:** Medium

Category: Heart of Algebra / Systems of Linear Equations

Getting to the Answer: Although this question asks where the *graphs* of the functions intersect, it is not necessary to actually graph them. Two graphs intersect at the point where they have the same x-value and the same y-value. The notations $g(x)$ and $h(x)$ can both be interpreted as "the y-value at a given value of x," so set $g(x)$ equal to $h(x)$ and solve for x. Then, if needed, plug this value into either function to find the corresponding y-value. Don't let the fraction intimidate you—you can write $g(x)$ as a fraction over 1 and use cross-multiplication.

$$\frac{3x - 5}{1} = \frac{7x + 10}{4}$$
$$4(3x - 5) = 7x + 10$$
$$12x - 20 = 7x + 10$$
$$5x = 30$$
$$x = 6$$

There is only one answer choice for which the x-coordinate is 6, (D), so the graphs of the functions will intersect at (6, 13).

9. A   Difficulty: Medium

Category: Passport to Advanced Math / Exponents

Getting to the Answer: When you write an equation *in terms of* a specific variable, you are simply solving the equation for that variable. In this question, you'll need to relate fractional exponents to radicals and understand how to use negative exponents. Be careful—you're not just rewriting the equation, you're solving it for k.

Raising a quantity to the one-third power is the same as taking its cube root. Applying a negative exponent to a quantity is the same as writing its reciprocal. Rewrite the equation using these properties and then solve for k using inverse operations. Note that the inverse of taking a cube root of a quantity is cubing the quantity.

$$x = k^{-\frac{1}{3}}$$
$$x = \frac{1}{\sqrt[3]{k}}$$
$$(x)^3 = \left(\frac{1}{\sqrt[3]{k}}\right)^3$$
$$x^3 = \frac{1}{k}$$
$$kx^3 = 1$$
$$k = \frac{1}{x^3}$$

Choice (A) is correct.

10. D   Difficulty: Medium

Category: Heart of Algebra / Linear Equations

Getting to the Answer: There are two variables and only one equation, so you can't actually solve the equation for c. Instead, recall that an equation has infinitely many solutions when the left side is identical to the right side. When this happens, everything cancels out and you get the equation $0 = 0$, which is always true.

Start by simplifying the left side of the equation. Don't forget to distribute the negative sign to both terms inside the parentheses.

$$4x - (10 - 2x) = c(3x - 5)$$
$$4x - 10 + 2x = c(3x - 5)$$
$$6x - 10 = c(3x - 5)$$

Next, quickly compare the left side of the equation to the right side. Rather than distributing the c, notice that if c were 2, then both sides of the equation would equal $6x - 10$, and it would have infinitely many solutions. Therefore, c is 2, which is (D).

11. D   Difficulty: Medium

Category: Heart of Algebra / Inequalities

Getting to the Answer: You don't need to separate this compound inequality into pieces. Just remember, whatever you do to one piece, you must do to all three pieces. Don't forget to flip the inequality symbols if you multiply or divide by a negative number. Here, the fractions make it look more complicated than it really is, so start by clearing the fractions by multiplying everything by the least common denominator, 6.

$$0 < 1 - \frac{a}{3} \le \frac{1}{2}$$
$$6(0) < 6\left(1 - \frac{a}{3}\right) \le 6\left(\frac{1}{2}\right)$$
$$0 < 6 - 2a \le 3$$
$$-6 < -2a \le -3$$
$$3 > a \ge \frac{3}{2}$$
$$1.5 \le a < 3$$

Now, read the inequality symbols carefully. The value of a is between 1.5 and 3, including 1.5, but *not* including 3, so (D) is the correct answer.

12. D   Difficulty: Hard

Category: Heart of Algebra / Inequalities

Getting to the Answer: The only way a system of inequalities can have no solution is if the graph consists of two parallel lines with shading in opposite directions so that there is no overlap.

Start by writing each equation in slope-intercept form to help you envision what the graphs will look like. You'll need to multiply the second equation by -2, so don't forget to flip the inequality symbol.

$$y - \frac{2}{k}x \le 0 \to y \le \frac{2}{k}x$$

$$\frac{1}{k}x - \frac{1}{2}y \le -1 \to -\frac{1}{2}y \le -\frac{1}{k}x - 1$$

$$\to y \ge \frac{2}{k}x + 2$$

Now, think about the graphs. The first equation has a slope of $\frac{2}{k}$, a y-intercept of 0, and is shaded below the line. The second equation also has a slope of $\frac{2}{k}$, but it has a y-intercept of 2 and is shaded above the line. This means that no matter what value of k is used (other than 0), the two lines are parallel and shaded in opposite directions, and thus there are infinitely many values of k that result in a system with no solution, (D).

13. C   Difficulty: Hard

Category: Passport to Advanced Math / Exponents

Getting to the Answer: When solving a rational equation, start by getting a common denominator. Then, you can set the numerators equal and solve for the variable. Don't forget, however: If the answer produces zero in any denominator, then it is not a valid answer. The denominators are almost the same

already; you just need to multiply the top and bottom of the first term by 2, factor the denominator of the second term, and you'll be ready to solve the equation.

$$\frac{2}{2}\left(\frac{4x}{x-7}\right) + \frac{2x}{2x-14} = \frac{70}{2(x-7)}$$

$$\frac{8x}{2(x-7)} + \frac{2x}{2(x-7)} = \frac{70}{2(x-7)}$$

Now that the denominators are all the same, you can solve the equation represented by the numerators.

$$8x + 2x = 70$$
$$10x = 70$$
$$x = 7$$

Be careful—this isn't the correct answer. Because there are variables in the denominator, you must check the solution to make sure it isn't extraneous, or in other words, doesn't cause a 0 in the denominator of any term. Here, if $x = 7$, then all of the denominators are zero (and division by zero is not possible), so the equation has no solution, (C).

14. B   Difficulty: Hard

Category: Additional Topics in Math / Geometry

Getting to the Answer: The shortest distance from A to B is through the center of the circle, along the diameter, which is twice the radius. When the equation of a circle is written in the form $(x - h)^2 + (y - k)^2 = r^2$, you can easily find the center and the radius of the circle. To find r, complete the square for the x terms and for the y terms. Start by reordering the terms. Then, take the coefficient of the x term and divide it by 2, square it, and add the result to the two terms with x variables. Do the same with the y term. Remember, you must also add these amounts to the other side of the equation. This creates a perfect square of x terms and y terms, and the equation will look more like a circle.

$$x^2 + y^2 + 6x - 4y = 12$$

$$x^2 + 6x + y^2 - 4y = 12$$

$$\left(x^2 + 6x + 9\right) + \left(y^2 - 4y + 4\right) = 12 + 9 + 4$$

$$(x + 3)^2 + (y - 2)^2 = 25$$

This means that the radius of the circle is $\sqrt{25} = 5$, so the diameter is 10, which is also the distance from A to B, making (B) correct. Note that you can do a quick check of your work by looking at the center; according to the equation, the center is $(-3, 2)$, which appears to match the location of the center on the graph.

15. C   Difficulty: Hard

Category: Passport to Advanced Math / Functions

Getting to the Answer: The key to answering this question is in having a conceptual understanding of function notation. Here, the input $(x - 1)$ has already been substituted and simplified in the given function. Your job is to determine what the function would have looked like had x been the input.

To keep things organized, let $u = x - 1$, the old input. This means $x = u + 1$. Substitute this into g and simplify:

$$g(x - 1) = 3x^2 + 5x - 7$$
$$g(u) = 3(u + 1)^2 + 5(u + 1) - 7$$
$$= 3(u^2 + 2u + 1) + 5u + 5 - 7$$
$$= 3u^2 + 6u + 3 + 5u + 5 - 7$$
$$= 3u^2 + 11u + 1$$

This means $g(u) = 3u^2 + 11u + 1$. When working with function notation, you evaluate the function by substituting a given input value for the variable in the parentheses. Here, if the input value is x, then $g(x) = 3x^2 + 11x + 1$, which matches (C).

16. 15   Difficulty: Easy

Category: Heart of Algebra / Systems of Linear Equations

Getting to the Answer: The equilibrium price occurs when the supply and demand are equal. Graphically, this means where the two lines intersect. The lines intersect at the point (6, 15). You can see from the axis labels that price is plotted along the y-axis, so the equilibrium price is $15.

17. 10.5 or 21/2   Difficulty: Medium

Category: Heart of Algebra / Linear Equations

Getting to the Answer: The key word in this question is *linear*. In a real-world scenario that involves a constant rate of change, you almost always need to find the slope and the initial amount so you can write an equation. The question states that the initial mass of the larva was 10 grams, so all you need to do is find the slope.

Write the information given in the question as ordered pairs (time, mass) so you can find the slope. At $t = 0$, the larva has a mass of 10 grams, so one pair is (0, 10). After 48 hours, the larva has a mass of 14 grams, so a second pair is (48, 14). Now, use the slope formula:

$$m = \frac{y_2 - y_1}{x_2 - x_1}$$
$$= \frac{14 - 10}{48 - 0}$$
$$= \frac{4}{48} = \frac{1}{12}$$

The equation is $y = \frac{1}{12}x + 10$, where y represents the mass of the larva after x hours. Substitute 6 for x to find the mass after 6 hours: $\frac{1}{12}(6) + 10 = \frac{6}{12} + 10 = 10.5$ grams.

18. 4   Difficulty: Medium

Category: Passport to Advanced Math / Functions

Getting to the Answer: The notation $f(g(x))$ indicates a composition of two functions which is read "f of g of x." It means that the output when x is substituted in $g(x)$ becomes the input for $f(x)$. Use the second table to find that $g(-1)$ is 2. This is your new input. Now, use the first table to find $f(2)$, which is 4.

19. 10   Difficulty: Medium

Category: Additional Topics in Math / Imaginary Numbers

Getting to the Answer: Multiply the two complex numbers just as you would two binomials (using FOIL). Then, combine like terms. The question tells you that $i = \sqrt{-1}$. If you square both sides of the equation, this is the same as $i^2 = -1$, which is a more useful fact.

$$\begin{aligned}(4 + 3i)(1 - 2i) &= 4(1 - 2i) + 3i(1 - 2i) \\ &= 4 - 8i + 3i - 6i^2 \\ &= 4 - 5i - 6(-1) \\ &= 4 - 5i + 6 \\ &= 10 - 5i\end{aligned}$$

The question asks for a in $a + bi$, so the correct answer is 10.

20. 50.5   Difficulty: Hard

Category: Passport to Advanced Math / Scatterplots

Getting to the Answer: This question requires a conceptual understanding of modeling data and properties of quadratic functions. Because the regression model fits the data exactly, you can use what you know about quadratic functions to answer the question.

The graph of a quadratic function is symmetric with respect to its axis of symmetry. The axis of symmetry occurs at the x-value of the vertex, which also happens to be where the maximum (or minimum) of the function occurs. The question tells you this value—it's $x = 56.25$. Because $x = 90$ is 33.75 (because $90 - 56.25 = 33.75$) units to the right of the axis of symmetry, you know that the y-value will be the same as the point that is 33.75 units to the left of the axis of symmetry. This occurs at $x = 56.25 - 33.75 = 22.5$. Read the y-value from the graphing calculator screenshot to find the answer, which is 50.5.

MATH—CALCULATOR TEST

1. D   Difficulty: Easy

Category: Problem Solving and Data Analysis / Statistics and Probability

Getting to the Answer: To reduce the margin of error, the society should use a larger sample size selected from a better representation of the population. The target population is *all* adults, not just those that have gym memberships. Using only adults with gym memberships is likely to skew the results because these respondents probably exercise considerably more than people who do not have gym memberships. This means (D) is correct.

2. B   Difficulty: Easy

Category: Heart of Algebra / Inequalities

Getting to the Answer: Think about this question conceptually. If the box cannot weigh *more than* 20 pounds (or 20×16 ounces), this means it can weigh *that much or less*, so the right half of the inequality you are looking for is $\leq 20 \times 16$. This means you can eliminate A and C based on the inequality symbol. A box is made up of ballpoint pens, b, and mechanical pencils, m. Each pen weighs 0.3 ounces, and each pencil weighs 0.2 ounces. The total weight of the box would be the number of pens, b, multiplied by their weight, 0.3, added to the number of pencils, m, multiplied by their weight, 0.2. So the inequality is $0.3b + 0.2m \leq 20 \times 16$, which matches (B).

3. C   Difficulty: Easy

Category: Heart of Algebra / Linear Equations

Getting to the Answer: Finding an *x*-intercept is easy when you know the equation of the line—it's the value of *x* when *y* is 0. Everything you need to write the equation is shown on the graph. The *y*-intercept is 5 and the line falls 1 unit and runs 3 units from one point to the next, so the slope is $-\frac{1}{3}$. This means the equation of the line, in slope-intercept form, is $y = -\frac{1}{3}x + 5$. Now, set the equation equal to zero and solve for *x*:

$$0 = -\frac{1}{3}x + 5$$
$$\frac{1}{3}x = 5$$
$$x = 15$$

Line *Q* will intercept the *x*-axis at 15, which is (C).

4. D   Difficulty: Easy

Category: Passport to Advanced Math / Functions

Getting to the Answer: When you see an expression such as *f*(*x*), it means to substitute the given value for *x* in the function's equation. When there is more than one function involved, pay careful attention to which function should be evaluated first. You are looking for the value of *f*(*x*) at *x* = 3. Because *f*(*x*) is defined in terms of *g*(*x*), evaluate *g*(3) first by substituting 3 for *x* in the expression *x* + 5.

$$g(3) = 3 + 5 = 8$$
$$f(3) = 2g(3) = 2(8) = 16$$

Choice (D) is correct.

5. C   Difficulty: Easy

Category: Problem Solving and Data Analysis / Rates, Ratios, Proportions, and Percentages

Getting to the Answer: Pay careful attention to the units. As you read the question, decide how and when you will need to convert units. In this problem,

work backward—you need to know how many pages of cards will be printed. To find this number, you first need to know how many cards will be printed. So, start with the number of agents (which tells you the number of boxes) and multiply by the number of cards per box:

$$12 \text{ agents} \times \frac{2 \text{ boxes}}{1 \text{ agent}} \times \frac{225 \text{ cards}}{1 \text{ box}} = 5{,}400 \text{ cards}$$

Next, use the information about *pages* to finish the calculations:

$$5{,}400 \text{ cards} \times \frac{1 \text{ page}}{10 \text{ cards}} \times \frac{1 \text{ minute}}{18 \text{ pages}} = 30 \text{ minutes}$$

This means (C) is correct.

6. A   Difficulty: Medium

Category: Heart of Algebra / Inequalities

Getting to the Answer: The question is asking about $\frac{x}{y}$, so think about how fractions work. Larger numerators result in larger values $\left(\frac{3}{2}\text{, for example, is greater than }\frac{1}{2}\right)$, and smaller denominators result in larger values $\left(\frac{1}{2}\text{, for example, is greater than }\frac{1}{4}\right)$. The largest possible value of $\frac{x}{y}$ is found by choosing the largest possible value for *x* and the smallest possible value for *y* which gives $\frac{0.2}{5} = 0.04$, or (A).

7. A   Difficulty: Medium

Category: Problem Solving and Data Analysis / Statistics and Probability

Getting to the Answer: Results from a study can only be generalized to the population from which the sample was taken. Also, keep in mind that positive correlations do not prove causation. The study was conducted by the American Academy of Pediatrics on children in the United States under three, so the sample is American children under three, which means conclusions can only be drawn about *this* population. Also, because correlations do not prove causation, the only conclusion that can be drawn is that there is an association between television time and attention disorders for American children under three years old, (A).

8. D   Difficulty: Medium

Category: Problem Solving and Data Analysis / Statistics and Probability

Getting to the Answer: The greatest change (in absolute value) in miles ridden per week could be an increase or a decrease. You don't have to worry about whether the change is positive or negative, so to keep things simple, always subtract the smaller number from the larger number. Make a list to show the changes in miles ridden per week between each pair of consecutive weeks. Save yourself some time by skipping weeks that clearly have smaller changes, such as between weeks 1 and 2 and between weeks 3 and 4.

Weeks 2-3: $72 - 64 = 8$

Weeks 4-5: $78 - 70 = 8$

Weeks 5-6: $85 - 78 = 7$

Weeks 6-7: $85 - 75 = 10$

Weeks 7-8: $82 - 75 = 7$

Of the differences, the greatest is from week 6 to week 7, which is a change of 10 miles, making (D) correct.

9. C   Difficulty: Medium

Category: Heart of Algebra / Linear Equations

Getting to the Answer: Given two points (even when the coordinates are variables), the slope of the line is $\frac{y_2 - y_1}{x_2 - x_1}$. You are given a numerical value for the slope and a pair of coordinate points with variables. To find the value of a, plug the points into the slope formula, and then solve for a:

$$\text{Slope} = \frac{y_2 - y_1}{x_2 - x_1}$$

$$5 = \frac{6 - 2a}{a - (a - 1)}$$

$$5 = \frac{6 - 2a}{1}$$

$$5 = 6 - 2a$$

$$-1 = -2a$$

$$\frac{1}{2} = a$$

Choice (C) is correct.

10. A   Difficulty: Hard

Category: Heart of Algebra / Systems of Linear Equations

Getting to the Answer: Questions about breaking even usually involve creating a system of equations (one for cost and one for revenue), setting the equations equal to each other, and solving for the variable. Create a system of equations at each price point using n for the number of bathtub lifts. Then solve each system. Note that the cost equation will be the same for both systems, and it is already given to you in the question.

$$\text{Old Price: } C = 225n + 3{,}150; R = 450n$$
$$C = R$$
$$225n + 3{,}150 = 450n$$
$$3{,}150 = 225n$$
$$14 = n$$

$$\text{New Price: } C = 225n + 3{,}150; R = 375n$$
$$C = R$$
$$225n + 3{,}150 = 375n$$
$$3{,}150 = 150n$$
$$21 = n$$

At the old price, the company needed to sell 14 lifts to break even. At the new price, it needs to sell 21 lifts, so it needs to sell $21 - 14 = 7$ more lifts at the new price to break even, which is (A).

11. B   Difficulty: Medium

Category: Additional Topics in Math / Geometry

Getting to the Answer: The amount of water needed to create the ice portion of the exhibit is another way of saying the *volume* of the ice. So, you need to find the volume of the entire space and then subtract the volume of the cylinder that runs through the ice. The volume of a rectangular prism is given by $V = l \times w \times h$, and the volume of a cylinder equals the area of its base times its height, or $\pi r^2 h$. To determine the volume of the ice, start by decomposing the figure into two rectangular prisms and adding their volumes. You can decompose the figure left to right or front to back. Front to back, it looks like the following figure:

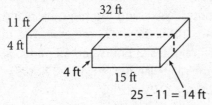

The prism in the back has a volume of $32 \times 11 \times 4 = 1{,}408$ cubic feet. The prism in the front has a length of 15 feet and a height of 4 feet, but the width is missing. Find the missing width by subtracting 11 from 25, which is 14 feet. So, the volume of the prism in the front is $15 \times 14 \times 4 = 840$ cubic feet. The total volume of the prisms is $1{,}408 + 840 = 2{,}248$ cubic feet. Be careful—that's not the answer. You still need to find the amount of space taken up by the glycol pipe and subtract it. The diameter of the pipe is 2 feet, so its radius is 1 foot, and the height (or the length in this question) is 32 feet, so the volume is $\pi(1)^2(32) \approx 100.53$ cubic feet. This means the amount of ice needed is $2{,}248 - 100.53 = 2{,}147.47$, or about 2,150 cubic feet, (B).

12. D   Difficulty: Medium

Category: Problem Solving and Data Analysis / Rates, Ratios, Proportions, and Percentages

Getting to the Answer: Let the units in this question guide you to the answer. You'll also need to use the answer you found in the previous question. The company will use two hoses, each of which pumps at a rate of 60 gallons per minute, so the rate is actually 120 gallons per minute. Convert the volume you found earlier from cubic feet to gallons, and then use the rate to find the time.

$$2{,}150 \text{ ft}^3 \times \frac{7.48 \text{ gal}}{1 \text{ ft}^3} \times \frac{1 \text{ min}}{120 \text{ gal}} = 134 \text{ minutes}$$

The answers are given in hours and minutes, so write 134 minutes as 2 hours and 14 minutes, or about 2 hours and 15 minutes, which is (D).

13. C   Difficulty: Medium

Category: Passport to Advanced Math / Quadratics

Getting to the Answer: The graph of every quadratic equation is a parabola, which may or may not cross the x-axis, depending on where its vertex is and which way it opens. Don't forget—if the equation is written in vertex form, $y = a(x - h)^2 + k$, then the vertex is (h, k), and the value of a tells you which way the parabola opens. The graph of an equation that has *no solution* does not cross the x-axis, so try to envision the graph of each of the answer choices. When a quadratic is written in factored form, the factors tell you the x-intercepts, which means every quadratic equation that can be written in factored form (over the set of real numbers) must have solutions. This means you can eliminate B and D. Now, imagine the graph of the equation in A: The vertex is (5, 3) and a is negative, so the parabola opens downward and consequently must cross the x-axis. This means you can eliminate A, and (C) must be correct. The graph of the equation in (C) has a vertex of (5, 3) and opens *up*, so it does not cross the x-axis and, therefore, has no solution.

You could also graph each of the answer choices in

your graphing calculator, but this is not the most time-efficient way to answer the question.

14. A   Difficulty: Medium

Category: Problem Solving and Data Analysis / Rates, Ratios, Proportions, and Percentages

Getting to the Answer: Questions that involve distance, rate, and time can almost always be solved using the formula Distance = rate × time. Use the speed, or rate, of the plane from Boston, 360 mph, and its distance from Chicago, 864 mi, to determine when it arrived. You don't know the time, so call it t.

$$\text{Distance} = \text{rate} \times \text{time}$$
$$864 = 360t$$
$$2.4 = t$$

This means it took 2.4 hours for the plane to arrive. This is more than 2 full hours, so multiply 2.4 by 60 to find the number of minutes it took: 60 × 2.4 = 144 minutes. Now determine how long it took the plane from Kansas City. It left at 8:30 AM and arrived at 10:34 AM, so it took 2 hours and 4 minutes, or 124 minutes. (As noted in the question, all times are Eastern, so time zone differences do not need to be considered.) This means the plane from Kansas City arrived 144 − 124 = 20 minutes before the plane from Boston, (A).

15. B   Difficulty: Hard

Category: Problem Solving and Data Analysis / Rates, Ratios, Proportions, and Percentages

Getting to the Answer: Break the question into short steps (first part of trip, second part of trip, circling overhead). To get started, you'll need to find the distance for each part of the trip—the question only tells you the total distance. Then, use the formula Distance = rate × time to find how long the plane flew at 200 mph and then how long it flew at 450 mph.

First part of trip: $\frac{1}{4} \times 1{,}200 = 300$ mi
$$300 = 200t$$
$$t = \frac{300}{200} = 1.5 \text{ hours}$$
$$1.5 \times 60 = 90 \text{ minutes}$$

Second part of trip: $\frac{3}{4} \times 1{,}200 = 900$ mi
$$900 = 450t$$
$$t = \frac{900}{450} = 2 \text{ hours}$$
$$2 \times 60 = 120 \text{ minutes}$$

This means the plane flew for a total of 90 + 120 = 210 minutes. Next, add the time the plane circled overhead: 210 + 25 = 235 minutes. The total trip took 235 minutes (3 hours and 55 minutes), which means the plane landed at 8:30 + 3 hours = 11:30 + 55 minutes = 12:25 PM, (B).

16. A   Difficulty: Medium

Category: Passport to Advanced Math / Functions

Getting to the Answer: The range of a function is the set of possible outputs, or y-values on a graph. For all real values of any number t, the value of t^2 cannot be negative. This means the smallest possible value of t^2 is 0 and, consequently, the smallest possible value of $h(t)$ is $h(0) = \sqrt{0^2 + 9} = \sqrt{9} = 3$. Thus, the number 1 is not in the range of the function, making (A) correct.

You could also graph the function in your graphing calculator and examine the possible y-values. The graph follows here:

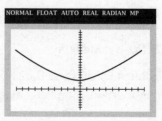

Notice that the lowest point on the graph is (0, 3), which tells you that the range of the function is $h(t) \geq 3$.

17. A   Difficulty: Medium

Category: Heart of Algebra / Systems of Linear Equations

Getting to the Answer: Graphically, the solution to a system of equations is the point or points where the graphs intersect. Whenever a graph with no grid-lines or axis labels is shown, you are usually interested primarily in the sign of the coordinates of a point, not the actual values. The graphs intersect in Quadrant 2 of the coordinate plane, so the x-value of the point of intersection (or a) is negative, and the y-value (or b) is positive. The question states that $a = -3b$, so you can eliminate B right away—the coordinates would have to be equal if their sum was 0. Now try Picking Numbers. Let $b = 1$, which means $a = -3$ and the sum of $a + b$ is -2, which is not one of the answer choices. Try another pair: If $b = 2$, then $a = -6$, and the sum is -4. This is still not one of the answer choices, but you should see a pattern—the x-coordinate will always overpower the y-coordinate, resulting in a negative sum, so the correct answer must be (A).

18. B   Difficulty: Medium

Category: Problem Solving and Data Analysis / Statistics and Probability

Getting to the Answer: When comparing two data sets for consistency, consider both the data center (mean or median) and the spread (standard deviation or range). Each set of data has a median of 0, and Thermostat A also has a mode of 0. Both of these measures indicate good test results. However, Thermostat A has a greater range of data. If the company chooses this thermostat, the cooling fan is likely to engage anywhere from –9 degrees below the target temperature to 10 degrees above the target temperature. Although this is within the safe temperature

range, it is not as consistent as Thermostat B, which engaged the fan within 6 degrees on either side of the target temperature. This means (B) is correct.

19. C   Difficulty: Medium

Category: Passport to Advanced Math / Quadratics

Getting to the Answer: When a quadratic function is written in factored form, you can find its zeros by setting each factor equal to 0 and solving for the variable. Each of the answer choices is written in factored form, so mentally solve each one by asking yourself what number would make each factor equal to 0. Then find the sum of the results:

Choice A: $3 + (-3) \neq -3$. Eliminate.

Choice B: $4 + (-1) \neq -3$. Eliminate.

Choice (C): $1 + (-4) = -3$, so (C) is correct.

Choice D: $6 + (-3) \neq -3$. Eliminate.

20. D   Difficulty: Hard

Category: Passport to Advanced Math / Functions

Getting to the Answer: A constant added or subtracted inside a function will shift the function left or right, while a constant added or subtracted from the outside will shift the function up or down. You're looking for the value of $p(0)$, but the graph shows $p(x) - 4$, which means the original graph has been shifted down 4 units. You'll need to find the y-value of the graph when $x = 0$, then add 4 to get back up to the original function. The graph passes through the point (0, 7), so $p(0) - 4 = 7$. Add 4 to both sides of the equation to get $p(0) = 7 + 4 = 11$, which is (D).

21. A   Difficulty: Medium

Category: Heart of Algebra / Linear Equations

Getting to the Answer: Sometimes writing an equation is the quickest route to answering a question. Assign a variable to the unknown, write the equation in words, and then translate from English into math. The unknown in this question is the number of times Geraldine can wrap the wire around the prism. Call this *n*. Now, write an equation in words: Total amount of wire equals distance around the prism times the number of wraps plus the extra on the ends. To fill in the numbers, you'll need to make a few calculations. Because the dimensions of the prism are given in inches, convert the amount of wire to inches as well: 18 ft = 18 ft × 12 in/ft = 216 inches. Next, figure out the distance around the prism using the picture. Don't forget, you have to go all the way around: 1.5 + 3.5 + 1.5 + 3.5 = 10 inches. Finally, read the question again to determine that the *extra on the ends* is 3 + 3 = 6 inches. Now you're ready to translate from English into math to write your equation, and then solve it.

$$216 = 10n + 6$$
$$210 = 10n$$
$$21 = n$$

Geraldine can wrap the wire around the prism 21 times, (A).

22. A   Difficulty: Medium

Category: Problem Solving and Data Analysis / Statistics and Probability

Getting to the Answer: To find a percent change (increase or decrease), use the percent change formula:

$$\text{Percent change} = \frac{\text{new amount} - \text{original amount}}{\text{original amount}}$$

The question asks about the increase from July to August, so the original amount is the July harvest of squash and the new amount is the August harvest. Read the graph's key and the axis labels carefully. Each grid-line represents 5 tons, so the July squash harvest was 15 tons and the August harvest was 25 tons. Substitute these numbers into the percent change formula and simplify:

$$\text{Percent change} = \frac{\text{new amount} - \text{original amount}}{\text{original amount}}$$
$$= \frac{25 - 15}{15}$$
$$= \frac{10}{15} \approx 0.667$$

This is equal to an increase of about 67%, which is (A).

23. D   Difficulty: Medium

Category: Problem Solving and Data Analysis / Rates, Ratios, Proportions, and Percentages

Getting to the Answer: Add reasonable numbers to the graph to help you answer the question. An example follows:

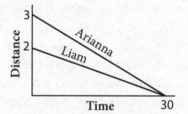

Use the numbers to help you evaluate each statement. It took Liam and Arianna each 30 minutes to walk home, so A and B are incorrect. Arianna walked 3 miles in 30 minutes, while Liam only walked 2 miles in 30 minutes; their rates are not the same, so C is also incorrect. This means (D) must be true. Arianna started out farther away than Liam, so she must have walked at a faster rate to arrive at home in the same amount of time.

24. B   Difficulty: Medium

Category: Heart of Algebra / Linear Equations

Getting to the Answer: The slopes between sets of points that lie on the same line are equal. You can find the slope between points using the slope formula or by looking for patterns. Before immediately jumping to the slope formula, take a peek at the answer choices—all the *x*-coordinates of the points are multiples of 4, so looking for a pattern is the quickest way to answer this question. It may help to put all the points in a table (including those given in the question stem), with the *x*-coordinates arranged from smallest to largest, and then see which point doesn't fit the pattern.

x	y
−4	−8
0	−5
4	−1
8	1
12	4
16	7

Notice that all the *x*-coordinates increase by 4, while most of the *y*-coordinates increase by 3. For the slope between each pair of points to be equal, the *y*-coordinate at *x* = 4 would need to be −2, not −1, so the point given in (B) does not lie on the line.

25. A   Difficulty: Medium

Category: Problem Solving and Data Analysis / Statistics and Probability

Getting to the Answer: Identify which pieces of information from the table you need. The question asks for the probability that a randomly chosen person from the study is employed and has a college degree, so you need the total of both females and males with college degrees who are employed compared to all the participants in the study. There are 188 employed females with a college degree and 177 employed males with a college degree for a total of 365 employed people with a college degree out of 800 participants, so the probability is $\frac{365}{800}$, which reduces to $\frac{73}{160}$, (A).

26. B   Difficulty: Medium

Category: Problem Solving and Data Analysis / Scatterplots

Getting to the Answer: Translate from English into math: The number of cells in the original sample means the value of the function at 0 hours, or *f*(0). The first *x*-value on the graph is 4, not 0, so

you'll need to use the values shown in the calculator screenshot to write an equation for the model. Notice that the *y*-values in the calculator screenshot double as the *x*-values increase by 1. This means that the model is an exponential growth function of the form $f(x) = f(0) \cdot 2^x$. Choose a point from the calculator screenshot such as (4, 136), substitute the values into the function, and solve for *f*(0):

$$136 = f(0) \cdot (2)^4$$
$$136 = f(0) \cdot 16$$
$$\frac{136}{16} = f(0)$$
$$8.5 = f(0)$$

The *y*-axis title tells you that the numbers are given in thousands, so there were 8,500 white blood cells per microliter in the original sample, (B).

You could also work backward from the calculator screenshot by dividing by 2 four times (from 4 hours to 3 hours, 3 hours to 2 hours, 2 hours to 1 hour, and 1 hour to before the patient contracted the disease). The result is $136 \div 2^4 = 136 \div 16 = 8.5$, which in thousands is 8,500, (B).

27. D   Difficulty: Hard

Category: Additional Topics in Math / Geometry

Getting to the Answer: Drawing a sketch is the key to answering this question. Your sketch might look like the one below.

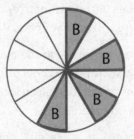

Notice that two radii and an arc form each section, so the amount of steel needed for one section is the length of the radius times 2, plus the length of the outer arc. Once you know this, you can simply multiply by 4.

You are given the total area, which means you can find the radius by substituting 64π for A in the area formula, $A = \pi r^2$.

$$64\pi = \pi r^2$$
$$64 = r^2$$
$$8 = r$$

For auctions, the arena is divided into 12 equal sections through the center, so divide 360 by 12 to find that the central angle measure for each section is $30°$. Now use the arc length formula:

$$\frac{n°}{360°} \times 2\pi r = \frac{30°}{360°} \times 2\pi(8)$$
$$= \frac{1}{12} \times 16\pi$$
$$= \frac{4\pi}{3}$$

The amount of steel needed for one section is $8 + 8 + \frac{4\pi}{3} = 16 + \frac{4\pi}{3}$, so the amount needed for all four sections is $4\left(16 + \frac{4\pi}{3}\right) = 64 + \frac{16\pi}{3}$, which is (D).

28. A   Difficulty: Hard

Category: Heart of Algebra / Linear Equations

Getting to the Answer: To write the equation of a line, you need two things—the starting amount (y-intercept) and the rate of change (slope). Substitute these values into slope-intercept form of a line ($y = mx + b$), and you have your equation.

The initial amount of water in the tank on Saturday is 70 gallons, so you already know b. To find m, you'll need to use the information given in the question to write two data points.

The amount of water in the tank *depends* on how long Lena has been filling it, so the number of gallons is the dependent variable and time is the independent variable. This tells you that the data points should be written in the form (time, gallons). At time = 0 on Saturday, the number of gallons is 70, so the data point is (0, 70). After 1 hour and 50 min-

utes, which is $60 + 50 = 110$ minutes, the tank is full (400 gallons), so another data point is (110, 400).

Now, use the slope formula to find that the rate of change is $\frac{400 - 70}{110 - 0} = \frac{330}{110} = 3$ gallons per minute. Substituting m and b into slope-intercept form results in the equation $y = 3x + 70$, so (A) is correct.

29. D   Difficulty: Hard

Category: Problem Solving and Data Analysis / Rates, Ratios, Proportions, and Percentages

Getting to the Answer: You need to find the ratio of small units to large units. You're given two ratios: small to medium and medium to large. Both of the given ratios contain medium size units, but the medium amounts (5 and 3) are not identical. To directly compare them, find a common multiple (15). Multiply each ratio by the factor that will make the number of medium units equal to 15.

small to medium: $(3:5) \times (3:3) = 9:15$

medium to large: $(3:2) \times (5:5) = 15:10$

Now that the number of medium units needed is the same in both ratios, you can merge the two ratios to compare small to large directly: 9:15:10. Therefore, the proper ratio of small units to large units is 9:10, which is (D).

30. A   Difficulty: Hard

Category: Passport to Advanced Math / Exponents

Getting to the Answer: Think of the rate given in the question in terms of the constant term you see on the right-hand side of the equation. Working together, the two air purifiers can clean the air in 7 hours. This is equivalent to saying that they can clean $\frac{1}{7}$ of the air in 1 hour. If $\frac{1}{7}$ is the portion of the air the two purifiers can clean *together* in 1 hour, then each term on the left side of the equation represents the portion that each purifier can clean *individually* in 1 hour. Because the new model is 3 times as fast as the older model, $\frac{3}{x}$ represents the portion of the air the new model can clean in 1 hour, and $\frac{1}{x}$ represents the portion of the air the older model can clean in 1 hour, which is (A).

31. 9/26 or .346   Difficulty: Easy

Category: Heart of Algebra / Linear Equations

Getting to the Answer: Distribute the fractions because the numbers inside each set of parentheses are evenly divisible by the denominators of the fractions by which they are being multiplied.

$$\frac{1}{3}(90x - 12) = \frac{1}{2}(8x + 10)$$
$$30x - 4 = 4x + 5$$
$$26x = 9$$
$$x = \frac{9}{26}$$

32. 4   Difficulty: Medium

Category: Passport to Advanced Math / Exponents

Getting to the Answer: When solving any type of equation, you should always think of inverse operations. The inverse of raising a quantity to the $\frac{5}{2}$ power is raising it to the $\frac{2}{5}$ power. Eliminate the exponent using inverse operations and then go from there.

$$n^{\frac{5}{2}} = 32$$
$$\left(n^{\frac{5}{2}}\right)^{\frac{2}{5}} = (32)^{\frac{2}{5}}$$
$$n = 32^{\frac{2}{5}}$$

Now, you have two choices—you can enter this value into your calculator as 32^(2/5) or you can evaluate the number using rules of exponents:

$$32^{\frac{2}{5}} = (\sqrt[5]{32})^2 = 2^2 = 4$$

33. 801   Difficulty: Hard

Category: Problem Solving and Data Analysis / Rates, Ratios, Proportions, and Percentages

Getting to the Answer: Draw a chart or diagram detailing the various price reductions for each 30-day period. You'll need to make several calculations, so don't round until the final answer.

Date	% of Most Recent Price	Resulting Price
Jan. 15	100 – 40% = 60%	$1,848 × 0.6 = $1,108.80
Feb. 1	100 – 15% = 85%	$1,108.80 × 0.85 = $942.48
March 1	100 – 15% = 85%	$942.48 × 0.85 = $801.108

You can stop here because the item was sold on March 10th. Before gridding in your answer, check that $801 is not less than 30% of the original price: 0.30 × $1,848 = $554.40. It's not, so the final selling price, rounded to the nearest whole dollar, was $801.

34. 2/3 or .666 or .667   Difficulty: Hard

Category: Additional Topics in Math / Trigonometry

Getting to the Answer: Two angles of the triangle have equal measures, so the triangle is isosceles, which means that drawing an altitude from the top to the base will bisect the base, resulting in two smaller right triangles as shown here:

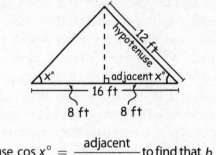

Now, use $\cos x° = \dfrac{\text{adjacent}}{\text{hypotenuse}}$ to find that $b = \dfrac{8}{12}$, which can be simplified to $\dfrac{2}{3}$.

35. 3.5 or 7/2   **Difficulty:** Hard

Category: Heart of Algebra / Linear Equations

Getting to the Answer: Remember that parallel lines have the same slope. Use the slope formula $m = \dfrac{y_2 - y_1}{x_2 - x_1}$ to find the slope of $\overline{CD}$. Because $\overline{CD}$ passes through the points (0, 0) and (2, 4.5), its slope is $\dfrac{4.5 - 0}{2 - 0} = 2.25$. Line B has the same slope and passes through (0, −1), so you can use the slope formula again to find the y-coordinate of the given point, (2, y).

$$2.25 = \frac{y - (-1)}{2 - 0}$$
$$2.25 = \frac{y + 1}{2}$$
$$4.5 = y + 1$$
$$3.5 = y$$

The y-coordinate of the point is 3.5.

36. 3/10 **Difficulty:** Hard

Category: Problem Solving and Data Analysis / Rates, Ratios, Proportions, and Percentages

Getting to the Answer: Whenever rates are given in different units, start by converting to the same units. In most cases, converting to the smaller unit avoids fractions and decimals. Start with nickel because the weight is already in ounces: $10.08 ÷ 24 = $0.42 per ounce. Now find the per-ounce rate for copper. There are 16 ounces in one pound, so three pounds is 48 ounces: $8.64 ÷ 48 = $0.18 per ounce. So, if a person were to bring in equal amounts of each, he would receive $0.18 per ounce of copper and $0.42 per ounce of nickel. To find the fractional portion he would receive from the copper, set up a comparison between the amount received for copper and the total amount received, $0.18 + $0.42 = $0.60. The portion of the total amount he receives from copper would be $\dfrac{0.18}{0.60}$, which reduces to $\dfrac{3}{10}$.

37. 3   **Difficulty:** Easy

Category: Problem Solving and Data Analysis / Scatterplots

Getting to the Answer: Each grid-line along the vertical axis represents 5 units, so look for points that are at least two grid-lines away from the line of best fit. The people who have BMIs of 20, 25, and 28 have LDLs that are 10 or more mg/dL greater than the LDLs predicted by the line of best fit. This represents 3 people.

38. 24   **Difficulty:** Medium

Category: Problem Solving and Data Analysis / Scatterplots

Getting to the Answer: A line of best fit serves as an approximation of data from which you can estimate an output for a given input (or vice versa). The key is in reading the axis labels carefully. To determine the requested BMI, find the LDL level of 140 (which is already reported in mg/dL) on the vertical axis. The question says "Based on the line of best fit," so trace over to the line (*not* to the closest data point) and then down to the corresponding value on the horizontal axis, which represents BMI. You should end up just slightly to the right of the 24 line. Be sure to follow directions. The closest whole number approximation is 24.

ESSAY TEST RUBRIC

The Essay Demonstrates ...

4—Advanced	• **(Reading)** A strong ability to comprehend the source text, including its central ideas and important details and how they interrelate; and effectively use evidence (quotations, paraphrases, or both) from the source text.
	• **(Analysis)** A strong ability to evaluate the author's use of evidence, reasoning, and/or stylistic and persuasive elements, and/or other features of the student's own choosing; make good use of relevant, sufficient, and strategically chosen support for the claims or points made in the student's essay; and focus consistently on features of the source text that are most relevant to addressing the task.
	• **(Writing)** A strong ability to provide a precise central claim; create an effective organization that includes an introduction and conclusion, as well as a clear progression of ideas; successfully employ a variety of sentence structures; use precise word choice; maintain a formal style and objective tone; and show command of the conventions of standard written English so that the essay is free of errors.
3—Proficient	• **(Reading)** Satisfactory ability to comprehend the source text, including its central ideas and important details and how they interrelate; and use evidence (quotations, paraphrases, or both) from the source text.
	• **(Analysis)** Satisfactory ability to evaluate the author's use of evidence, reasoning, and/or stylistic and persuasive elements, and/or other features of the student's own choosing; make use of relevant and sufficient support for the claims or points made in the student's essay; and focus primarily on features of the source text that are most relevant to addressing the task.
	• **(Writing)** Satisfactory ability to provide a central claim; create an organization that includes an introduction and conclusion, as well as a clear progression of ideas; employ a variety of sentence structures; use precise word choice; maintain an appropriate formal style and objective tone; and show control of the conventions of standard written English so that the essay is free of significant errors.

2—Partial	• **(Reading)** Limited ability to comprehend the source text, including its central ideas and important details and how they interrelate; and use evidence (quotations, paraphrases, or both) from the source text.
	• **(Analysis)** Limited ability to evaluate the author's use of evidence, reasoning, and/or stylistic and persuasive elements, and/or other features of the student's own choosing; make use of support for the claims or points made in the student's essay; and focus on relevant features of the source text.
	• **(Writing)** Limited ability to provide a central claim; create an effective organization for ideas; employ a variety of sentence structures; use precise word choice; maintain an appropriate style and tone; or show control of the conventions of standard written English, resulting in certain errors that detract from the quality of the writing.
1—Inadequate	• **(Reading)** Little or no ability to comprehend the source text or use evidence from the source text.
	• **(Analysis)** Little or no ability to evaluate the author's use of evidence, reasoning, and/or stylistic and persuasive elements; choose support for claims or points; or focus on relevant features of the source text.
	• **(Writing)** Little or no ability to provide a central claim, organization, or progression of ideas; employ a variety of sentence structures; use precise word choice; maintain an appropriate style and tone; or show control of the conventions of standard written English, resulting in numerous errors that undermine the quality of the writing.

SAMPLE ESSAY RESPONSE #1 (ADVANCED SCORE)

Anyone who watches NFL football every Sunday is most likely aware that the athletes on the field make a significant amount of money for their efforts. The NFL generates a lot of income from television contracts, corporate sponsors, and advertisers, and the teams themselves benefit from ticket and merchandise sales. The players in turn are paid market-appropriate salaries. Anyone who watches college football games on Saturday will see similar, if slightly younger athletes, yet how much are those players making? The author of this article correctly notes these players don't earn a salary, and that's something he would like to correct. His argument? College athletes deserve compensation for their work just like any other employee.

The author begins by detailing how much money corporations, athletic conferences, and universities make from advertising and sponsor revenue. The Pacific-12 conference, for example, "signed television rights deals worth $3 billion." Speaking of television, CBS and Turner Broadcasting made a lot of money as well—thirty seconds of commercial advertising during the Final Four cost $700,000. Schools with successful programs also do well. The article points out that the University of Texas football program netted $77.9 million in 2011–2012.

The author uses this evidence to portray corporations, athletic conferences, and universities as the "unscrupulous tycoons from a Dickens novel." Those familiar with Dickens can picture more than one wealthy character who doesn't care for the working poor left eking out miserable lives in relative poverty. And who are these working poor? Student athletes, of course! The author uses the Dickens metaphor to convince the reader that corporations, athletic conferences, and universities do not have the student athletes' interests at heart. He then pivots to how much the athletes make for their efforts on behalf of the "unscrupulous tycoons"—absolutely nothing.

How much is the average student scholarship worth? According to the author, most leave a few thousand dollars in yearly out-of-pocket expenses to the student in spite of an average "forty hours a week" dedicated to their sport. And if an athlete is unable to play due to injury, even that scholarship money can be revoked. The author uses this information to compare a student athlete with an employee who benefits from federal and state labor laws. The comparison is painfully clear and made even more so when the author points out that student athletes do not have the right to unionize.

Throughout his essay, the author has effectively painted a Dickensian picture in which student athletes literally sweat, strain, and toil under the watchful eye of their universities, while those in power rake in millions of dollars. The evidence presented convincingly leads the reader to one conclusion: that student athletes deserve to be compensated.

SAMPLE ESSAY RESPONSE #2 (PROFICIENT SCORE)

Anyone who watches NFL football Sunday knows that those players make a lot of money. They make so much money because the teams and the league make money from television and advertising. But what about college football players or other college athletes? They don't make any money at all. The author thinks that isn't right. He argues that student athletes should get paid for their work just like anyone else.

The author talks about how much money schools, conferences, and corporations make off of college sports. It's a lot of money. For example, a television deal was worth $3 billion for the Pacific-12 conference, and it cost $700,000 for a television commercial during the Final Four basketball tournament. The author includes this to make the point that other people make a lot of money, but student athletes don't. This helps the reader feel some sympathy for the players and supports the author's argument that they should be paid.

The author then turns to a comparison of student athletes and employees. Student athletes don't earn salaries. They do get a scholarship, but that still leaves many of them short of money to pay the bills. They work forty hours a week. If they are hurt, then they may lose their scholarship because they can't play. The author talks about this to compare how student athletes earn money with how typical employees earn money. Employees have legal rights, but student athletes don't really have any. This is a good comparison, and it makes the reader believe that student athletes should be paid like employees, which is the author's concluding point.

SAT PRACTICE TEST 2 ANSWER SHEET

Remove (or photocopy) this answer sheet and use it to complete the test. See the answer key following the test when finished.

Start with number 1 for each section. If a section has fewer questions than answer spaces, leave the extra spaces blank.

SECTION 1

1. Ⓐ Ⓑ Ⓒ Ⓓ	14. Ⓐ Ⓑ Ⓒ Ⓓ	27. Ⓐ Ⓑ Ⓒ Ⓓ	40. Ⓐ Ⓑ Ⓒ Ⓓ	
2. Ⓐ Ⓑ Ⓒ Ⓓ	15. Ⓐ Ⓑ Ⓒ Ⓓ	28. Ⓐ Ⓑ Ⓒ Ⓓ	41. Ⓐ Ⓑ Ⓒ Ⓓ	
3. Ⓐ Ⓑ Ⓒ Ⓓ	16. Ⓐ Ⓑ Ⓒ Ⓓ	29. Ⓐ Ⓑ Ⓒ Ⓓ	42. Ⓐ Ⓑ Ⓒ Ⓓ	# correct in Section 1
4. Ⓐ Ⓑ Ⓒ Ⓓ	17. Ⓐ Ⓑ Ⓒ Ⓓ	30. Ⓐ Ⓑ Ⓒ Ⓓ	43. Ⓐ Ⓑ Ⓒ Ⓓ	
5. Ⓐ Ⓑ Ⓒ Ⓓ	18. Ⓐ Ⓑ Ⓒ Ⓓ	31. Ⓐ Ⓑ Ⓒ Ⓓ	44. Ⓐ Ⓑ Ⓒ Ⓓ	
6. Ⓐ Ⓑ Ⓒ Ⓓ	19. Ⓐ Ⓑ Ⓒ Ⓓ	32. Ⓐ Ⓑ Ⓒ Ⓓ	45. Ⓐ Ⓑ Ⓒ Ⓓ	
7. Ⓐ Ⓑ Ⓒ Ⓓ	20. Ⓐ Ⓑ Ⓒ Ⓓ	33. Ⓐ Ⓑ Ⓒ Ⓓ	46. Ⓐ Ⓑ Ⓒ Ⓓ	# incorrect in Section 1
8. Ⓐ Ⓑ Ⓒ Ⓓ	21. Ⓐ Ⓑ Ⓒ Ⓓ	34. Ⓐ Ⓑ Ⓒ Ⓓ	47. Ⓐ Ⓑ Ⓒ Ⓓ	
9. Ⓐ Ⓑ Ⓒ Ⓓ	22. Ⓐ Ⓑ Ⓒ Ⓓ	35. Ⓐ Ⓑ Ⓒ Ⓓ	48. Ⓐ Ⓑ Ⓒ Ⓓ	
10. Ⓐ Ⓑ Ⓒ Ⓓ	23. Ⓐ Ⓑ Ⓒ Ⓓ	36. Ⓐ Ⓑ Ⓒ Ⓓ	49. Ⓐ Ⓑ Ⓒ Ⓓ	
11. Ⓐ Ⓑ Ⓒ Ⓓ	24. Ⓐ Ⓑ Ⓒ Ⓓ	37. Ⓐ Ⓑ Ⓒ Ⓓ	50. Ⓐ Ⓑ Ⓒ Ⓓ	
12. Ⓐ Ⓑ Ⓒ Ⓓ	25. Ⓐ Ⓑ Ⓒ Ⓓ	38. Ⓐ Ⓑ Ⓒ Ⓓ	51. Ⓐ Ⓑ Ⓒ Ⓓ	
13. Ⓐ Ⓑ Ⓒ Ⓓ	26. Ⓐ Ⓑ Ⓒ Ⓓ	39. Ⓐ Ⓑ Ⓒ Ⓓ	52. Ⓐ Ⓑ Ⓒ Ⓓ	

SECTION 2

1. Ⓐ Ⓑ Ⓒ Ⓓ	12. Ⓐ Ⓑ Ⓒ Ⓓ	23. Ⓐ Ⓑ Ⓒ Ⓓ	34. Ⓐ Ⓑ Ⓒ Ⓓ	
2. Ⓐ Ⓑ Ⓒ Ⓓ	13. Ⓐ Ⓑ Ⓒ Ⓓ	24. Ⓐ Ⓑ Ⓒ Ⓓ	35. Ⓐ Ⓑ Ⓒ Ⓓ	
3. Ⓐ Ⓑ Ⓒ Ⓓ	14. Ⓐ Ⓑ Ⓒ Ⓓ	25. Ⓐ Ⓑ Ⓒ Ⓓ	36. Ⓐ Ⓑ Ⓒ Ⓓ	# correct in Section 2
4. Ⓐ Ⓑ Ⓒ Ⓓ	15. Ⓐ Ⓑ Ⓒ Ⓓ	26. Ⓐ Ⓑ Ⓒ Ⓓ	37. Ⓐ Ⓑ Ⓒ Ⓓ	
5. Ⓐ Ⓑ Ⓒ Ⓓ	16. Ⓐ Ⓑ Ⓒ Ⓓ	27. Ⓐ Ⓑ Ⓒ Ⓓ	38. Ⓐ Ⓑ Ⓒ Ⓓ	
6. Ⓐ Ⓑ Ⓒ Ⓓ	17. Ⓐ Ⓑ Ⓒ Ⓓ	28. Ⓐ Ⓑ Ⓒ Ⓓ	39. Ⓐ Ⓑ Ⓒ Ⓓ	
7. Ⓐ Ⓑ Ⓒ Ⓓ	18. Ⓐ Ⓑ Ⓒ Ⓓ	29. Ⓐ Ⓑ Ⓒ Ⓓ	40. Ⓐ Ⓑ Ⓒ Ⓓ	# incorrect in Section 2
8. Ⓐ Ⓑ Ⓒ Ⓓ	19. Ⓐ Ⓑ Ⓒ Ⓓ	30. Ⓐ Ⓑ Ⓒ Ⓓ	41. Ⓐ Ⓑ Ⓒ Ⓓ	
9. Ⓐ Ⓑ Ⓒ Ⓓ	20. Ⓐ Ⓑ Ⓒ Ⓓ	31. Ⓐ Ⓑ Ⓒ Ⓓ	42. Ⓐ Ⓑ Ⓒ Ⓓ	
10. Ⓐ Ⓑ Ⓒ Ⓓ	21. Ⓐ Ⓑ Ⓒ Ⓓ	32. Ⓐ Ⓑ Ⓒ Ⓓ	43. Ⓐ Ⓑ Ⓒ Ⓓ	
11. Ⓐ Ⓑ Ⓒ Ⓓ	22. Ⓐ Ⓑ Ⓒ Ⓓ	33. Ⓐ Ⓑ Ⓒ Ⓓ	44. Ⓐ Ⓑ Ⓒ Ⓓ	

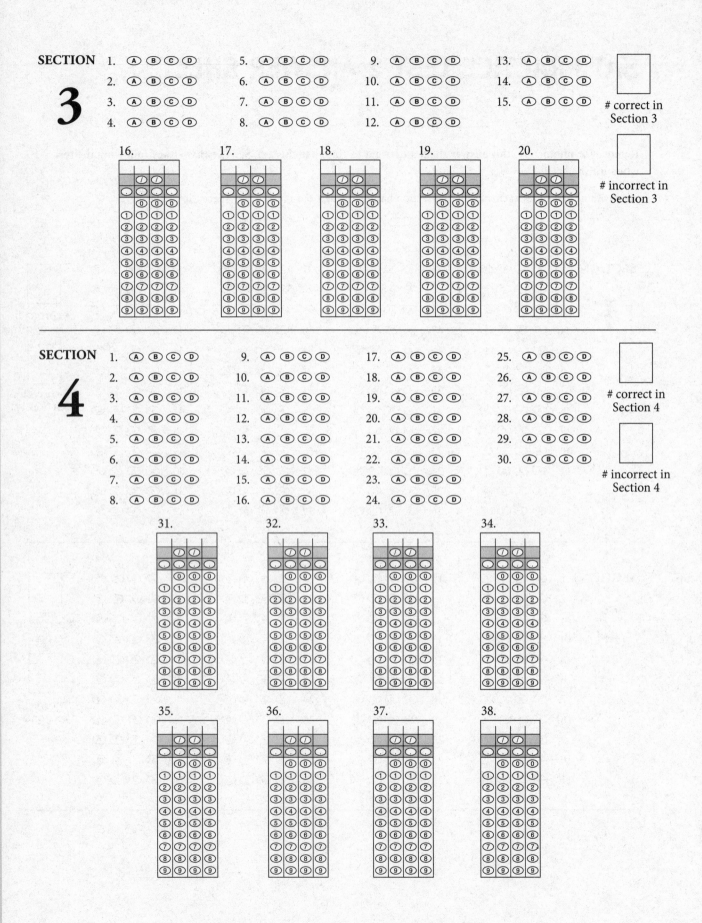

READING TEST

65 Minutes—52 Questions

This section corresponds to Section 1 of your answer sheet.

Directions: Read each passage or pair of passages, then answer the questions that follow. Choose your answers based on what the passage(s) and any accompanying graphics state or imply.

Questions 1-10 are based on the following passage.

The following passage is adapted from the nineteenth-century novel *Three Men in a Boat*. In this scene, George, William Samuel, Harris, Jerome, and a dog named Montmorency take a typical boating holiday of the time on a Thames River camping skiff. Jerome, the narrator, shares the story of how the journey with his friends began.

George had towed us up to Staines, and we had taken the boat from there, and it seemed that we were dragging fifty tons after us, and were walking
Line forty miles. It was half-past seven when we were
(5) through, and we all got in, and sculled up close to the left bank, looking out for a spot to haul up in.

We had originally intended to go on to Magna Carta Island, a sweetly pretty part of the river, where it winds through a soft, green valley, and to
(10) camp in one of the many picturesque inlets to be found round that tiny shore. But, somehow, we did not feel that we yearned for the picturesque nearly so much now as we had earlier in the day. A bit of water between a coal-barge and a gas-works would
(15) have quite satisfied us for that night. We did not want scenery. We wanted to have our supper and go to bed. However, we did pull up to the point— "Picnic Point," it is called—and dropped into a very pleasant nook under a great elm-tree, to the
(20) spreading roots of which we fastened the boat.

Then we thought we were going to have supper (we had dispensed with tea, so as to save time), but George said no; that we had better get the canvas up first, before it got quite dark, and while we could

(25) see what we were doing. Then, he said, all our work would be done, and we could sit down to eat with an easy mind.

That canvas wanted more putting up than I think any of us had bargained for. It looked so
(30) simple in the abstract. You took five iron arches, like gigantic croquet hoops, and fitted them up over the boat, and then stretched the canvas over them, and fastened it down: it would take quite ten minutes, we thought.

(35) That was an under-estimate.

We took up the hoops, and began to drop them into the sockets placed for them. You would not imagine this to be dangerous work; but, looking back now, the wonder to me is that any of us are
(40) alive to tell the tale. They were not hoops, they were demons. First they would not fit into their sockets at all, and we had to jump on them, and kick them, and hammer at them with the boat-hook; and, when they were in, it turned out that they were the
(45) wrong hoops for those particular sockets, and they had to come out again.

But they would not come out, until two of us had gone and struggled with them for five minutes, when they would jump up suddenly, and try and
(50) throw us into the water and drown us. They had hinges in the middle, and, when we were not look-ing, they nipped us with these hinges in delicate parts of the body; and, while we were wrestling with one side of the hoop, and endeavouring to
(55) persuade it to do its duty, the other side would come behind us in a cowardly manner, and hit us over the head.

GO ON TO THE NEXT PAGE

We got them fixed at last, and then all that was
to be done was to arrange the covering over them.
(60) George unrolled it, and fastened one end over the
nose of the boat. Harris stood in the middle to take
it from George and roll it on to me, and I kept by
the stern to receive it. It was a long time coming
down to me. George did his part all right, but it was
(65) new work to Harris, and he bungled it.

How he managed it I do not know, he could not
explain himself; but by some mysterious process or
other he succeeded, after ten minutes of superhuman effort, in getting himself completely rolled up
(70) in it. He was so firmly wrapped round and tucked
in and folded over, that he could not get out. He, of
course, made frantic struggles for freedom . . . and,
in doing so, knocked over George. . . .

1. According to the passage, the men change their
   minds about their destination because

   A) the weather is turning bad.

   B) they fear the location will be too crowded.

   C) they have lost interest in scenery.

   D) the supplies are running low.

2. As used in line 22, "dispensed with" most nearly
   means

   A) administered.

   B) distributed.

   C) served.

   D) skipped.

3. Based on paragraphs 1-3, it can reasonably be
   inferred that the men are

   A) thirsty and sore.

   B) tired and hungry.

   C) panicked and frantic.

   D) curious and content.

4. Which choice provides the best evidence for the
   answer to the previous question?

   A) Lines 1-4 ("George had . . . forty miles")

   B) Lines 13-15 ("A bit of water . . . for that
      night")

   C) Lines 16-17 ("We wanted . . . to bed")

   D) Lines 25-27 ("Then, he said, . . . easy mind")

5. What theme does the passage communicate
   through the experiences of its characters?

   A) It is important to plan in advance.

   B) Conflicts among friends should be avoided.

   C) False confidence can lead to difficulties.

   D) Every group benefits from a leader.

6. Based on information in the passage, it can reasonably be inferred that

   A) none of the men were experienced camper-
      boaters.

   B) the majority of the men were experienced
      camper-boaters.

   C) the narrator is the only one with camping-
      boating experience.

   D) George is the only one with camping-
      boating experience.

7. Which choice provides the best evidence for the
   answer to the previous question?

   A) Lines 23-25 ("we had better . . . doing")

   B) Lines 28-29 ("That canvas . . . bargained
      for")

   C) Lines 58-59 ("We got . . . over them")

   D) Lines 70-71 ("He was so . . . get out")

8. As used in line 30, "in the abstract" most nearly
   means

   A) in summary.

   B) in the directions.

   C) in the ideal.

   D) in theory.

GO ON TO THE NEXT PAGE

9. The author's main purpose of including the description of the hoops in paragraph 7 is to

    A) convey anger through the use of hyperbole.

    B) convey humor through the use of personification.

    C) convey severity through the use of understatement.

    D) convey confidence through the use of active verbs.

10. The tone of the passage is primarily one of

    A) fear and panic.

    B) comic reflection.

    C) arrogant frustration.

    D) mockery and disgust.

Questions 11-20 are based on the following passage.

The following passage is adapted from President John F. Kennedy's 1962 speech, which has come to be called "We Choose to Go to the Moon." Kennedy delivered the speech at Rice University in Texas.

We meet at a college noted for knowledge, in a city noted for progress, in a State noted for strength, and we stand in need of all three, for we
Line meet in an hour of change and challenge, in a dec-
(5) ade of hope and fear, in an age of both knowledge and ignorance. The greater our knowledge increases, the greater our ignorance unfolds. . . .

No man can fully grasp how far and how fast we have come, but condense, if you will, the 50,000
(10) years of man's recorded history in a time span of but a half-century. Stated in these terms, we know very little about the first forty years, except at the end of them advanced man had learned to use the skins of animals to cover them. Then about ten
(15) years ago, under this standard, man emerged from his caves to construct other kinds of shelter. Only five years ago man learned to write and use a cart with wheels. Christianity began less than two years ago. The printing press came this year, and then less
(20) than two months ago, during this whole fifty-year

span of human history, the steam engine provided a new source of power.

Newton explored the meaning of gravity. Last month electric lights and telephones and auto-
(25) mobiles and airplanes became available. Only last week did we develop penicillin and television and nuclear power, and now if America's new spacecraft succeeds in reaching Venus, we will have literally reached the stars before midnight tonight.

(30) This is a breathtaking pace, and such a pace cannot help but create new ills as it dispels old, new ignorance, new problems, new dangers. Surely the opening vistas of space promise high costs and hardships, as well as high reward.

(35) So it is not surprising that some would have us stay where we are a little longer to rest, to wait. But this city of Houston, this State of Texas, this country of the United States was not built by those who waited and rested and wished to look behind them.
(40) This country was conquered by those who moved forward—and so will space.

William Bradford, speaking in 1630 of the founding of the Plymouth Bay Colony, said that all great and honorable actions are accompanied with
(45) great difficulties, and both must be enterprised and overcome with answerable courage.

If this capsule history of our progress teaches us anything, it is that man, in his quest for knowledge and progress, is determined and cannot be
(50) deterred. The exploration of space will go ahead, whether we join in it or not, and it is one of the great adventures of all time. . . .

This generation does not intend to founder in the backwash of the coming age of space. We mean
(55) to be a part of it—we mean to lead it. For the eyes of the world now look into space, to the moon and to the planets beyond, and we have vowed that we shall not see it governed by a hostile flag of conquest, but by a banner of freedom and peace. We
(60) have vowed that we shall not see space filled with weapons of mass destruction, but with instruments of knowledge and understanding.

Yet the vows of this nation can only be fulfilled if we in this nation are first. . . . In short, our leader-

GO ON TO THE NEXT PAGE ▷

(65) ship in science and in industry, our hopes for peace and security, our obligations to ourselves as well as others, all require us to make this effort . . . to become the world's leading space-faring nation.

We set sail on this new sea because there is new
(70) knowledge to be gained, and new rights to be won, and they must be won and used for the progress of all people . . . .

There is no strife, no prejudice, no national conflict in outer space as yet. Its hazards are hostile to us
(75) all. Its conquest deserves the best of all mankind, and its opportunity for peaceful cooperation may never come again. But why, some say, the moon? Why choose this as our goal? And they may well ask why climb the highest mountain? Why, thirty-five years
(80) ago, fly the Atlantic? Why does Rice play Texas?[1]

We choose to go to the moon. We choose to go to the moon in this decade and do the other things, not because they are easy, but because they are hard, because that goal will serve to organize and
(85) measure the best of our energies and skills. . . .

[1]This is a college sports reference. Kennedy's audience (at Rice University) would have understood the University of Texas at Austin to be the challenging athletic opponent of Rice.

11. Which statement best describes Kennedy's purpose for giving this speech?

   A) To present a chronology of human achievements

   B) To explain the threat that other countries pose to the United States

   C) To encourage students to support the United States in the race to reach the moon

   D) To promote increased funding for NASA and space exploration

12. Which choice provides the best evidence for the answer to the previous question?

   A) Lines 8-11 ("No man . . . half-century")

   B) Lines 47-50 ("If this . . . deterred")

   C) Lines 50-52 ("The exploration . . . all time")

   D) Lines 81-85 ("We choose . . . skills")

13. As used in line 45, "enterprised" most nearly means

   A) undertaken.

   B) funded.

   C) promoted.

   D) determined.

14. What does Kennedy suggest about the motivations of other countries attempting to reach the moon?

   A) They wish to embarrass the United States by reaching the moon first.

   B) They are trying to advance technology for the good of humanity.

   C) They want to use the moon for hostile military actions.

   D) They lack the scientific knowledge to accomplish their goals.

15. Which choice provides the best evidence for the answer to the previous question?

   A) Lines 25-29 ("Only last . . . tonight")

   B) Lines 30-32 ("This is . . . new dangers")

   C) Lines 59-62 ("We have . . . understanding")

   D) Lines 69-72 ("We set . . . all people")

16. As used in line 53, "founder" most nearly means

   A) begin.

   B) innovate.

   C) dissolve.

   D) sink.

17. According to the passage, what does Kennedy say is true of progress?

   A) It creates new problems as it solves old ones.

   B) It was minimal until the invention of written language.

   C) It must be accomplished cooperatively with other countries.

   D) It leads to an increase in global hostilities.

GO ON TO THE NEXT PAGE →

18. The statement in lines 64-68 ("In short, . . . space-faring nation") supports the overall argument of the passage in its suggestion that

    A) the monetary rewards for space exploration are too great to pass up.

    B) the U.S. military will never use space for strategic operations.

    C) the United States is better equipped than other nations to ensure that space remains a peaceful frontier.

    D) the space race is an opportunity to solidify the position of the United States as a military superpower.

19. Based on the information in the passage, to what group can Kennedy's audience best be compared?

    A) Soldiers who were drafted for service and bravely served their country

    B) Farmers who have worked in the field for months and now see their harvest

    C) Students who are studying and preparing for graduation

    D) Pioneers who are about to embark on a difficult but important journey

20. Kennedy's main purpose of including paragraphs 2 and 3 was to

    A) persuade the audience to fund the race to the moon.

    B) frame space exploration as a logical next step in human progress.

    C) warn of the potential hazards of techno-logical advances.

    D) encourage audience members to be leaders of their generation.

Questions 21-31 are based on the following passages and supplementary material.

The following passages discuss the success of the Vikings, skilled sailors from modern Scandinavia who traveled throughout northern and central Europe in the 8th to 11th centuries.

Passage 1

At the end of the eighth century, the Scandinavi-ans known as the Vikings took to the seas, traveling to areas including Iceland, Greenland, England,

Line Ireland, France, and Russia, and even reaching the

(5) shores of America some 500 years before Colum-bus. The Vikings' innovations in shipbuilding were central to constructing their empire. They relied on the superior ships conjured in the minds of master shipwrights for travel and exploration. Us-

(10) ing vessels such as the longboat, these fascinating seafarers opened up new foreign connections. The great longboat itself attests to their outstanding maritime skills.

Viking travel was a mystery before archaeolo-

(15) gists discovered ships buried in the muck of Dan-ish fjords, but now ship reconstruction has pro-vided some answers. Viking ships were designed and built with uncommon ingenuity to serve the Vikings' purposes. The secret of the signature

(20) Viking ship is found in its unique construction. The invention of the longboat meant Vikings could travel vast distances over treacherous open water. In contrast to modern sailboats, the longboat was riveted together with enough spacing so that the

(25) boat was flexible. It could bend as it rode over waves instead of taking the full impact of a swell. Incred-ibly, simple tools such as axes, hammers, and scrap-ers were all that carpenters used to frame a ship.

Additionally, the sleek longboat was an exceed-

(30) ingly streamlined vessel. One kind of longboat could ride high by skimming the waves to swiftly transport a crew of about 30. This fast ship had a draft of as little as 20 inches, allowing navigation in extremely shallow water.

(35) While its shallow draft and ease of construction made the Viking longboat a superior seafaring ves-sel, the seamanship of the Norsemen was the most decisive factor in the success of their boats. For

GO ON TO THE NEXT PAGE ▷

example, Vikings navigated by looking at the sky (40) through a crystal, which was known as a sunstone. The composition of the crystal was recently identified as a transparent calcite common in Iceland.

The Vikings' outstanding talents in ship construction, coupled with their superlative skills (45) as navigators, greatly impacted Scandinavia. In turn, through their explorations, the Vikings influenced the rest of the world.

Passage 2

The Gokstad ship was excavated in 1880 and dates to around AD 890; discovery of this Viking (50) ship revealed innovations in construction. Aptly named "longboats," such ships were long and narrow and could travel on the open sea as well as along rivers. The Gokstad ship is considered the best preserved of the Viking longboats. It reveals (55) the technical achievements of the Vikings because the shape was different from the norm.

The Gokstad ship owes nothing to earlier boat designs, including those of the Egyptians and Romans. The longboat was developed specifically (60) for Arctic waters. Its shallow draft, plus its ability to change direction quickly, was a tremendous asset to the Vikings. The Gokstad ship is 78 feet long with two high, pointed ends. Constructed out of sturdy oak, it features a low freeboard[1] and is therefore (65) fast, the kind of ship used to carry Vikings on raids across the North Sea.

The ship has been restored to reveal the Gokstad's original shape. With holes for 16 oars along each side of the ship, the crew would have (70) numbered about 34, counting 32 oarsmen plus a steerman and lookout. Oars were typically 17 to 19 feet long, constructed of pine with a narrow blade that made each oar both efficient and lightweight. In addition, the Gokstad features a mast (75) near the center that carried a large rectangular sail.

The Gokstad is different from earlier boat designs in its planking, or framing out, as well; its carvel planking made the ship watertight. Carvel planking involves attaching wooden planks to a (80) frame and having the planks butt up edge to edge, providing support from the frame and forming a smooth surface.

Contrary to popular belief, the Vikings were not just warriors; they were also coastal farmers, fish- (85) ers, hunters, and craftsmen. Their lands were harsh, however, and increases in their population forced some men to search for other opportunities. Vikings, therefore, turned to trade and sea raiding. Their swift sailing ships, already perfect for coastal fishing, ena- (90) bled Vikings to attack ports and towns, making these seamen effective as both raiders and traders.

Truly, the Gokstad ship is representative of a great leap in seafaring, for this finest expression of technical achievement could serve many purposes. (95) In 1982, its swiftness and seaworthiness was proven when a copy, the *Hjemkomst,* journeyed from the United States to Norway.

[1]freeboard: the distance between the level of the water and the upper edge of the side of a boat

Partial Timeline of Viking History

ca. 795: Viking raid on Ireland begins.
ca. 844: Vikings invade Moorish Spain.
ca. 851: Viking raids on Wales take place.
ca. 860s: Vikings discover Iceland.
862: Vikings establish trade center of Novgorod, first important Russian city.
912: Vikings seize land in France; descendants become the Normans.
985: Vikings start settlement in Greenland.
1000: Leif Ericson reaches North America.
1066: Viking invasions end.

GO ON TO THE NEXT PAGE

21. The central idea of Passage 1 is that Vikings

    A) excelled at shipbuilding and navigation.

    B) had a passion for global exploration.

    C) helped map the known world of their time.

    D) led European peoples in technological innovation.

22. The first paragraph of Passage 1 most strongly suggests that which of the following is true?

    A) The Vikings depended on sea trade and fishing to survive.

    B) The Vikings expanded cultural interactions through seafaring.

    C) The Vikings relied on colonization to support a growing population.

    D) The Vikings sustained their economic development through sea raids.

23. Which choice provides the best evidence for the answer to the previous question?

    A) Lines 1-2 ("At the end . . . to the seas")

    B) Lines 7-9 ("They relied . . . exploration")

    C) Lines 9-11 ("Using vessels . . . connections")

    D) Lines 11-13 ("The great longboat . . . skills")

24. As used in line 30, "streamlined" most nearly means

    A) contoured.

    B) efficient.

    C) simplistic.

    D) slight.

25. The author of Passage 2 most likely chose to write about the Gokstad ship because it

    A) contradicts prevailing beliefs about modern shipbuilding.

    B) gives insight into various seafaring economic activities.

    C) stands out as a unique example of early shipbuilding.

    D) was a recent maritime archaeological discovery.

26. Passage 2 most strongly suggests that the Vikings

    A) adapted to their geography by moving often.

    B) became seafarers to spread their civilization.

    C) learned shipbuilding from other peoples.

    D) used raiding as a means of livelihood.

27. Which choice provides the best evidence for the answer to the previous question?

    A) Lines 57-59 ("The Gokstad . . . Romans")

    B) Lines 83-85 ("Contrary to . . . craftsmen")

    C) Lines 85-87 ("Their lands . . . opportunities")

    D) Lines 95-97 ("In 1982 . . . Norway")

28. As used in line 93, "expression" most nearly means

    A) adaptation.

    B) embodiment.

    C) sentiment.

    D) simplification.

29. The author of Passage 2 uses the phrase "a great leap" (lines 92-93) to emphasize

    A) the technological progress that Vikings made.

    B) the distance that Vikings traveled.

    C) the strong faith and traditions on which Vikings relied.

    D) the widespread influence of Viking culture.

30. Both passages support which generalization about the Vikings?

    A) Devoted to warfare, the Vikings built an empire that reshaped the map of Europe.

    B) Innovations in shipbuilding and navigation saved the Vikings from decline and extinction.

    C) The Vikings were noble warriors and farmers who sought to better understand the world.

    D) Through their seafaring skills and abilities, the Vikings expanded and changed the world.

GO ON TO THE NEXT PAGE

31. Which inference from the two passages is supported by the information in the timeline?

    A) The Vikings endeavored to relocate surplus population through colonization.

    B) The Vikings hoped to expand their cultural influence through economic exchange.

    C) The Vikings traveled extensively to launch sea raids and conduct trade.

    D) The Vikings were compelled to abandon their homelands because of scarcity.

Questions 32-42 are based on the following passage.

The following passage describes what scientists are learning from the discovery of specimens encased in amber from the carnivorous Roridulaceae plant family.

Fossil tree resin, commonly known as amber, has the ability to encase and preserve things for extensive periods of time. Researchers in Kaliningrad, Russia,
Line have recently discovered fossilized carnivorous
(5) plants for the first time. Encased in the variety of amber commonly found in the Baltic region, leaves from these rare and interesting plants have been preserved for what scientists estimate to be between 35 and 47 million years.
(10) Amber is often confused with sap because of its sticky, liquid form. It is chemically different, though, and hardens to such an extent that it can immaculately preserve what it encases. As a result, researchers often encounter insects and other
(15) animals preserved in amber for long periods of time. Considered a type of fossil, these findings are incredibly useful, as the animals found in amber are not usually found elsewhere in the fossil record. Plants, on the other hand, are rarely seen preserved
(20) this way. This new discovery, along with amber-encased animals, provides scientists with a more comprehensive view of life in earlier times.

The newly discovered plant fossils are also groundbreaking for two more specific reasons: They
(25) are the only fossilized carnivorous plant traps ever found, as well as the only fossilized evidence of the plant family Roridulaceae. The Roridulaceae plant has been seen only in seed form until now. While the seeds did offer scientists valuable information,
(30) the trapping mechanism of the plant's leaves was left to conjecture. In these newly discovered fossils, the leaves of the plants are fully intact and contain organic animal matter that had been captured in the leaves' tentacles when the plant was living.
(35) Geologists and botanists in Germany published these findings in the *Proceedings of the National Academy of Sciences*, noting that the leaves look similar to a genus of carnivorous plants called *Roridula*, which, until now, were considered
(40) endemic to Africa, where they still thrive. Unlike Venus flytraps, which are known to catch and dissolve insects using a digestive mechanism, all *Roridula* plants (and their newly discovered ancestor) absorb nutrients secondhand through
(45) a symbiotic relationship with an insect known as *Pameridea*. The *Pameridea* insect generates a greasy film, which allows it to live on *Roridula*'s leaves without being ensnared in the plant's tentacles. The insect then captures and digests its prey while still
(50) on the leaves of the plant, and then passes nutrients to the plant through its feces. This way of ingesting nutrients is the major link between this insect and the Roridulaceae family of plants.

The new fossil discovery in Russia completely
(55) challenges the conclusions that scientists had previously drawn about the paleobiogeography of the species. Roridulaceae was previously thought to originate from the prehistoric Pangaean supercontinent called Gondwana, which included
(60) modern-day Africa, South America, India, Antarctica, and Australia. However, recent findings suggest that the shared ancestors of these plant species had a much wider distribution. Researchers will need to continue to search for plant matter preserved in
(65) amber to fill in more of the blanks in the fossil record.

GO ON TO THE NEXT PAGE

32. The primary purpose of this passage is to

    A) explain how scientists use new technology to explore old findings.

    B) contrast the differences among various types of fossil tree resin.

    C) inform the reader about new plant fossils discovered in amber.

    D) encourage the reader to learn more about the plant fossil record.

33. Based on the information in the passage, the reader can infer that the author

    A) was part of the research team that discovered the new fossils.

    B) considers the discovery of the plant fossils in amber scientifically valuable.

    C) thinks the conclusions drawn by the scientists in Germany are flawed.

    D) does not expect scientists to find many more fossils in amber.

34. The author claims that animal fossils found in amber are important to scientists because they

    A) are samples of rare ancient life forms, though poorly preserved.

    B) contain remains of life forms not typically found in the fossil record.

    C) are easier to study than fossils found buried in rock formations.

    D) contain DNA that resembles various types of animals living today.

35. Which choice provides the best support for the answer to the previous question?

    A) Lines 5-9 ("Encased . . . million years")

    B) Lines 11-13 ("It is chemically . . . encases")

    C) Lines 16-18 ("Considered . . . record")

    D) Lines 23-27 ("The newly discovered . . . Roridulaceae")

36. As used in line 13, "immaculately" most nearly means

    A) correctly.

    B) innocently.

    C) perfectly.

    D) purely.

37. The author uses the phrase "rare and interesting" (line 7) to emphasize the importance of

    A) the discovery of the fossilized carnivorous plants.

    B) the study of paleontology and geology.

    C) the preservation of the existing fossil record.

    D) the continued exploration in the Baltic region.

38. It can most reasonably be inferred from the passage that

    A) scientists will begin to find *Roridula* plants in warm regions outside of Africa.

    B) future discoveries could change current theories about plant evolution.

    C) plants fossilized in amber can only be found in the Baltic region of Russia.

    D) the Venus flytrap is the only plant with a symbiotic relationship with insects.

39. Which choice provides the best evidence for the answer to the previous question?

    A) Lines 35-40 ("Geologists . . . thrive")

    B) Lines 43-46 ("all *Roridula . . . Pameridea*")

    C) Lines 54-57 ("The new fossil . . . species")

    D) Lines 57-63 ("Roridulaceae was . . . distribution")

GO ON TO THE NEXT PAGE ▷

40. According to the passage, the *Pameridea* insect is able to live on *Roridula*'s leaves without being eaten by the plant because

   A) the insect secretes a substance that prevents it from getting caught in the plant's tentacles.

   B) the plant does not need to eat the insect because it gets its energy from photosynthesis.

   C) the insect does not stay on the plant's leaves long enough to get caught in its sticky leaves.

   D) the plant only ingests insects that have already died and begun to decompose.

41. As used in line 40, "thrive" most nearly means

   A) advance.

   B) develop.

   C) flourish.

   D) succeed.

42. Which choice best describes how the discovery of the ancestor of the Roridulaceae plant changed scientists' thinking?

   A) They realized that the fossilized plants are more closely related to the Venus flytrap than previously thought.

   B) They realized that the fossilized plants did not have a symbiotic relationship with the *Pameridea* insect.

   C) They realized that the fossilized plants ingested insects directly rather than secondhand like modern *Roridula* plants.

   D) They realized that the Roridulaceae plant family was more widely distributed than previously believed.

Questions 43-52 are based on the following passage and supplementary material.

The following passage explains the cycles of sunspots that can be observed on the sun's surface, as well as how sunspots' resultant solar flares can impact the earth.

Sunspots are relatively cool areas on the surface of the sun, formed by changes in the sun's magnetic field. The sun's surface is very hot, approximately
Line 10,000°F, while the center of a sunspot is
(5) comparatively cool at about 6,000°F. Scientists do not know exactly what causes sunspots, but the magnetic field within a sunspot is about 100 times stronger than it is on the rest of the sun's surface. Normally, hot gases flow from the interior of the sun
(10) to the surface, maintaining the high temperature. Within a sunspot, however, the concentrated magnetic field inhibits the movement of the gases, causing the surface of the sunspot to cool.

Galileo and other astronomers started recording
(15) the sunspots they viewed through telescopes in the early 1600s, although sunspots had been observed and recorded without telescopes for over 2,000 years. When another astronomer, Samuel Schwabe, plotted the number of sunspots recorded each year,
(20) he found that the number increased and decreased in a cyclic pattern. Approximately every 11 years, the number of sunspots reaches a maximum. A graph of sunspots over the years has a fairly regular pattern of peaks and valleys, with about 11 years
(25) between peaks. Most recently, the sunspot cycle peaked around the middle of 2013, and it will reach its nadir around 2020.

Scientists use the 11-year cycle to predict solar flares, which cause changes in Earth's atmosphere.
(30) When two or more sunspots having magnetic fields with opposite directions are near each other, the magnetic fields can interact with plasma on the surface between the sunspots. The interaction between the fields sends a burst of plasma away
(35) from the surface, forming the solar flare. The flares quickly heat to several million degrees and release as much energy as several hundred million atomic bombs. Strong magnetic fields and x-rays travel from the flares to Earth, resulting in geomagnetic

GO ON TO THE NEXT PAGE ⟶

(40) storms. If these storms are strong enough, they have the potential to disrupt power and radio communications on Earth. Satellites are particularly susceptible to disruption by solar flares, thus causing interference with GPS, weather prediction,

(45) and mobile phone communication. A positive effect of these storms is that the increased energy and plasma particles interact with Earth's atmosphere, enhancing the auroras, also known as the Northern (and Southern) Lights.

(50)   Sunspots do not always follow the 11-year solar cycle; there was almost no sunspot activity between around 1645 and 1715. This minimum, which was named the Maunder Minimum after the husband and wife team who discovered patterns in the

(55) location of sunspots during the 11-year solar cycle, occurred during a period of lower-than-normal global temperatures known as the Little Ice Age. Scientists mostly agree that the lack of sunspot activity did not contribute very much, if at all, to

(60) the lowered temperatures.

     Sunspot activity has been decreasing during the last few cycles, and it is possible we will see another minimum in the next 20 years. The strength of the magnetic field in the sunspots also seems to

(65) be diminishing, which could be another sign of a minimum in our future. If we do experience a minimum, scientists will be able to learn more about the effect of sunspots on Earth's climate, in addition to learning more about the sun, its surface,

(70) and its magnetic fields.

Solar Cycle

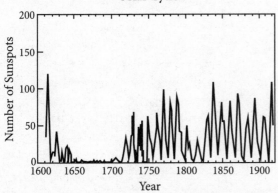

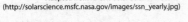

Adapted from NASA's Solar Science website
(http://solarscience.msfc.nasa.gov/images/ssn_yearly.jpg)

43. The passage is primarily concerned with

A) how solar activity can affect the climate on Earth.

B) the history of methods used by astronomers to study the sun.

C) scientists' current understanding of sunspots and solar flares.

D) the 11-year cycle of solar flare activity.

44. Which choice provides the best evidence for the answer to the previous question?

A) Lines 5-10 ("Scientists . . . high temperature")

B) Lines 14-18 ("Galileo . . . years")

C) Lines 50-52 ("Sunspots do not . . . 1715")

D) Lines 58-60 ("Scientists mostly agree . . . temperatures")

45. The author refers to the enhanced auroras resulting from solar flares mainly to

A) provide contrast with the negative effects of solar flares described.

B) illustrate the powerful effects of solar flares on Earth's atmosphere.

C) suggest that solar flares might cause more damage than previously believed.

D) give an example of how the solar flares affect Earth's climate.

46. According to the passage, which choice best describes what scientists currently understand about how solar flare activity affects the Earth?

A) Low solar flare activity can cause lower temperatures on Earth.

B) High solar flare activity can lead to disruptions of communication on Earth.

C) Low solar flare activity can cause an enhancement of the auroras on Earth.

D) High solar flare activity can lead to increased severe weather on Earth.

GO ON TO THE NEXT PAGE

47. Which of the following pieces of evidence would most strengthen the author's line of reasoning in the paragraph?

    A) Details added to paragraph 1 about features other than sunspots on the sun's surface and how they affect Earth

    B) Information added to paragraph 2 about how astronomers Galileo and Schwabe made their observations

    C) Examples in paragraph 3 of problems caused by disruption to communication caused by solar flares

    D) Examples in paragraph 5 of other periods in history during which the sun exhibited a decrease in observed sunspot activity

48. As used in line 34, "burst" most nearly means

    A) breach.

    B) eruption.

    C) force.

    D) fracture.

49. The passage most strongly suggests that which of the following statements is accurate?

    A) Although scientists have observed patterns in sunspot activity, it is not always possible to predict when sunspot activity will occur.

    B) Scientists will not be able to solve the mystery of what causes sunspots until technology allows astronauts to travel to the sun.

    C) Unless scientists find a way to control sunspot activity, radio and satellite communication on Earth will continue to be interrupted.

    D) The next minimum could interfere with weather prediction and cause drastic changes in the climate on Earth.

50. Which choice provides the best evidence for the answer to the previous question?

    A) Lines 18-21 ("When another . . . pattern")

    B) Lines 33-35 ("The interaction . . . flare")

    C) Lines 50-51 ("Sunspots . . . cycle")

    D) Lines 66-70 ("If we . . . fields")

51. As used in line 48, "enhancing" most nearly means

    A) developing.

    B) enlarging.

    C) improving.

    D) intensifying.

52. Which lines from the passage are best supported by the data presented in the graphic?

    A) Lines 14-16 ("Galileo . . . early 1600s")

    B) Lines 25-27 ("Most recently . . . 2020")

    C) Lines 51-52 ("there was . . . 1715")

    D) Lines 61-63 ("Sunspot activity . . . 20 years")

WRITING AND LANGUAGE TEST

35 Minutes—44 Questions

TThis section corresponds to Section 2 of your answer sheet.

Directions: Each passage in this section is followed by several questions. Some questions will reference an underlined portion in the passage; others will ask you to consider a part of a passage or the passage as a whole. For each question, choose the answer that reflects the best use of grammar, punctuation, and style. If a passage or question is accompanied by a graphic, take the graphic into account in choosing your response(s). Some questions will have "NO CHANGE" as a possible response. Choose that answer if you think the best choice is to leave the sentence as written.

Questions 1-11 are based on the following passage.

In Defense of *Don Quixote*

Before the holiday, the World Literature professor assigned the **1** classes' next novel, *Don Quixote*.

"Miguel de Cervantes Saavedra wrote *Quixote* in Spanish," he boomed over the end-of-class shuffle of notebooks and bags. "Find a good translation, start reading—and class?" **2** All motion stopped he had their attention. "Do more than read it; prepare to defend why you spent your holiday break reading a thousand pages of turn-of-the-seventeenth-century Spanish literature. Read the experts, check the data: Why does the book still matter?"

1. A) NO CHANGE
   B) class
   C) class's
   D) classes

2. A) NO CHANGE
   B) All motion stopped: he had
   C) All motion stopped, and had
   D) All motion stopped. Had

GO ON TO THE NEXT PAGE ▷

Class dismissed, the students entered break feeling uneasy at the prospect of this hefty early-modern novel, but each soon found in its pages a captivating story, beautiful and strange. **3** Clarified with paradoxes of sane and insane, tragic and comic, ideal and real, the novel surprised its newest set of readers with intellectual complexity as well as deeply human—and charmingly **4** adverse—characters.

As the students gradually finished their copies of *Quixote*, most felt the defense the professor had requested was somewhat unnecessary—it was a literary masterpiece. But research **5** will have been required, so they dutifully opened laptops and visited libraries.

For Monday's post-holiday class, students presented **6** its short defenses of *Quixote*. Most began with their personal appreciation of the novel and the enduring **7** triviality of questions it raised. Several students then mentioned scholars' praise for *Quixote*'s ideological impact on culture, challenging worldviews and highlighting ambiguities between reality and perception. *Quixote*, some noted, not only changed the literary imagination by expanding the possibilities of what a novel could intellectually accomplish, but also offered important early contributions to emerging discussions regarding psychology and women's rights.

3. A) NO CHANGE
   B) Deprived
   C) Peppered
   D) Littered

4. A) NO CHANGE
   B) averse
   C) bazaar
   D) bizarre

5. A) NO CHANGE
   B) is
   C) was
   D) will be

6. A) NO CHANGE
   B) it's
   C) their
   D) they're

7. A) NO CHANGE
   B) pertinence
   C) irrelevance
   D) inertia

To illustrate the book's importance, many students cited a famous 2002 survey of authors worldwide and the ensuing compilation of the world's "100 Best Books." This survey, students found, listed every qualifying "best" book at equal ranking, isolating only one as undeniably first: *Don Quixote*. **8**

After the last presentation was completed, the professor explained that **9** the university curriculum required students to read *Quixote* for World Literature. "Some call it the first great novel; many call it the greatest novel of all time, but superlatives aside, the true reason it's worth reading is somewhat indescribable, isn't it? **10** It changed you it moved you you were drawn to its beauty its ugliness or some confusion of the two. So it goes with great literature: The defense for its permanence is hidden in the piece itself."

8. Which sentence provides information that best supports the paragraph?

A) Most students also discovered that *Quixote* was second only to the Bible in its number of translations and publications across history, signifying its paramount global influence.

B) Students learned that around 100 well-known authors participated in the survey to identify the "most meaningful book of all time," organized by editors in Oslo, Norway.

C) Authors noted in the survey were few and far between but included Doris Lessing, Salman Rushdie, Chinua Achebe, and Toni Morrison.

D) The survey, although often cited by literary critics, has not been repeated since 2002.

9. Which choice most effectively establishes the main topic of the paragraph?

A) NO CHANGE

B) *Quixote* has touched the far reaches of the literary world.

C) He disagreed with experts regarding the literary value of *Quixote*.

D) He was pleased with the students' performance.

10. A) NO CHANGE

B) It changed you it moved you, you were drawn to its beauty, or its ugliness or some combination of the two.

C) It changed you it moved you, you were drawn to its beauty or its ugliness or some combination of the two.

D) It changed you; it moved you; you were drawn to its beauty, its ugliness, or some combination of the two.

GO ON TO THE NEXT PAGE ⟩

Opening [11] their books with a fondness like old friendship, the class began to discuss *Quixote* together.

Questions 12-22 are based on the following passage and supplementary material.

Women's Ingenuity

Until about 1840, only twenty-one patents for inventions were issued to women in the United States. [12] Yet by 1870, the number of patents granted to women had more than doubled. What spurred this increase of women as inventors?

[1]The secret lies partly in the stories of individual female inventors. [2] Some inventors—men and women—worked in teams, but many worked alone. [3] The most famous nineteenth-century female inventor became part of this patentee explosion. [4] She wasn't the first, but over her lifetime, Margaret Knight earned some twenty-six patents. [5] Her machine that made flat-bottomed paper bags is still in use. [13]

Knight spent her life working and inventing. As a child, she worked in the cotton mills and [14] many years later in her life, she was employed by the Columbia Paper Bag Company. While at the paper bag company, Knight perfected an idea for an automated machine that would cut, fold, and paste paper bags. [15] When a man

11. A) NO CHANGE
    B) there
    C) it's
    D) our

12. Which choice most accurately and effectively represents the information in the graph?
    A) NO CHANGE
    B) Yet by 1865, the number of patents granted to women had more than doubled.
    C) Yet by 1870, the number of patents granted to women had surpassed those granted to men.
    D) Yet by 1866, the number of patents granted to women had fallen short of the 1840 count.

13. Which sentence should be eliminated to improve the paragraph's focus?
    A) Sentence 1
    B) Sentence 2
    C) Sentence 3
    D) Sentence 5

14. A) NO CHANGE
    B) many years later on,
    C) years later,
    D) later on in her life,

15. A) NO CHANGE
    B) Despite the fact that
    C) Before
    D) Although

GO ON TO THE NEXT PAGE ▷

stole her idea, Knight fought for her rights. In the *Knight v. Annan* dispute of 1871, she won [16] an odd victory for women. The Patent Office eventually issued the patent to her. Knight's [17] alternate inventions included a rotary engine and a shoe-cutting machine.

In Knight's case, her profession helped her perceive the demand for an invention. [18] Knight's first invention was for a device that would stop machinery from injuring workers. Plus, she acquired the skills to become a trailblazer. During the Industrial Age, many women, like Knight, were able to secure jobs in [19] factories, this resulted in their higher labor market participation.

[20] The progress of feminism in the twentieth century that improved women's rights and provided greater

16. A) NO CHANGE
    B) an inconceivable
    C) a trivial
    D) a rare

17. A) NO CHANGE
    B) subsequent
    C) former
    D) ultimate

18. Which choice most effectively supports the claim made in the paragraph?

    A) NO CHANGE
    B) At least some of this can be attributed to her own qualities rather than social conditions.
    C) This is obvious when one considers the impressive rate of her creations.
    D) This was a quality few women had at the time, as it was considered unfeminine.

19. A) NO CHANGE
    B) factories, because this resulted
    C) factories; this resulted
    D) factories, but resulted

20. A) NO CHANGE
    B) The progress of feminism in the twentieth century, which
    C) The progress of feminism in the twentieth century,
    D) The progress of feminism in the twentieth century, it

GO ON TO THE NEXT PAGE

access to education, also contributed to women's ingenuity. By 1998, some ten percent of all patents issued were to American women. **21** Nevertheless, Dr. Carol B. Muller founder of a nonprofit that promotes women in science states, "Until women are fully represented in the fields of science and engineering, society is losing out on the talents of a vast number of potential contributors."

In the future, if women can attain more university research positions, graduate-level degrees in science and engineering, and leadership positions in high-tech companies, the result may well be more participation as patentees. **22**

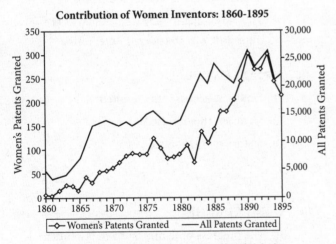

Contribution of Women Inventors: 1860-1895

Adapted from *The Democratization of Invention: Patents and Copyrights in American Economic Development, 1790-1920,* by B. Zorina Khan. Cambridge University Press, 2005.

21. A) NO CHANGE

B) Nevertheless, Dr. Carol B. Muller, founder of a nonprofit that promotes women in science states

C) Nevertheless Dr. Carol B. Muller, founder of a nonprofit that promotes women in science, states,

D) Nevertheless, Dr. Carol B. Muller, founder of a nonprofit that promotes women in science, states,

22. Which choice most effectively concludes the paragraph?

A) Given that we all benefit from new inventions that improve the quality of our lives, let us hope this becomes reality.

B) Recent social changes have had a positive impact on today's women inventors.

C) Unfortunately, women today are barely doing better than in Knight's day.

D) The patent system is alive and well in the twenty-first century, thanks to women trailblazers such as Margaret Knight.

GO ON TO THE NEXT PAGE

Questions 23-33 are based on the following passage.

Working from Home: Too Good to Be True?

It can be hard to break into your desired field, whether that's advertising, medicine, or technology. New graduates usually have to start at entry-level positions, where salaries are low. Meanwhile, the cost of rent can be **23** high, and if you live with your parents to save on rent, perhaps in the suburbs, then you might have a costly commute.

It may be tempting to take a position that promises high income for working at home. But don't be tempted. Many of these advertised "work-from-home" positions are outright scams. Of the 8,192 **24** compliants filed with Federal Trade Commission (FTC) in 2010 involving work-at-home business opportunities, the FTC estimates that only 1 in every 55 cases involved any real business. **25**

The scams come in many forms, but one thing they have in common is the promise of thousands of dollars per week, with no skills, experience, or degree required. That sounds too good to be true—precisely because it is. The other thing **26** it has in common is that they require a fee for the materials to get you started, everything from lists of phone numbers to registration with bogus agencies.

23. A) NO CHANGE
    B) high
    C) high:
    D) high—

24. A) NO CHANGE
    B) complaints
    C) compliments
    D) complements

25. At this point, the writer wants to add specific information that supports the main topic of the paragraph. Which choice provides the most relevant detail?

    A) Victims of scams should contact their local or state consumer affairs agency.
    B) Sadly, most cases are not covered by fraud protection policies offered by banks.
    C) Therefore, work-from-home opportunities have increased over the last decade.
    D) That means that 98 percent of the time, these "opportunities" are traps set to steal your cash.

26. A) NO CHANGE
    B) they have
    C) one has
    D) it have

GO ON TO THE NEXT PAGE

[27] Victims often find the paperwork difficult to complete. The [28] certification fee is supposed to get you marketing materials, software, and a training session. But once the company has your money, the training sessions are postponed indefinitely, and the materials never arrive. You don't earn a cent.

[29] Stuffing envelopes, assembling crafts, and entering data are all schemes that promise easy dollars for performing simple work. In each case, the company collects your setup fee and never provides any work. There is no service [30] department (with which to lodge complaints), and there are no refunds.

The lure of money is very powerful, but people entering the job market for the first time need to understand that earning a substantial income is something that comes from skill, education, and hard work. [31] They're are no shortcuts in life or in business, and anyone who thrills at the thought of getting something for nothing, or who loves the idea of working in pajamas, should learn that fast tracks to wealth are [32] a distortion.

27. Which choice provides the most effective topic sentence for this paragraph?
  A) NO CHANGE
  B) Training sessions are often long and tedious.
  C) One scam involves a fee to process insurance claims for doctors.
  D) Many people are naive enough to believe that fraud can't happen to them.

28. A) NO CHANGE
  B) registration
  C) conclusion
  D) termination

29. A) NO CHANGE
  B) Envelope stuffing, assembling crafts, and data entry
  C) Envelope stuffing, craft assembly, and entering data
  D) Stuffing envelopes, craft assembly, and entering data

30. A) NO CHANGE
  B) department—with which to lodge complaints,
  C) department with which to lodge complaints,
  D) department, with which to lodge complaints,

31. A) NO CHANGE
  B) They
  C) Their
  D) There

32. A) NO CHANGE
  B) an impression
  C) an illusion
  D) an apparition

GO ON TO THE NEXT PAGE

Besides, you'll get more satisfaction out of performing real work that uses real skills than you would stuffing envelopes. **33** Starting in a career field, building your experience and skills will earn you bigger dividends in the future. That's a guarantee that no work-from-home scam can match.

Questions 34-44 are based on the following passage and supplementary material.

Is Gluten-Free the Way to Be?

34 A lot of people suffer from celiac disease and find it hard to control the symptoms. Most of these people, however, are not doing so because of medical necessity. Gluten is not **35** an absolutely essential nutrient, so no one is harmed by following a gluten-free diet. In fact, it may be a good idea to try going gluten-free, as it may reveal some health issues that might have gone undiagnosed.

Studies indicate that about 1 percent of Americans have celiac disease, meaning that eating even **36** standard amounts of gluten will make them ill. Gluten is a protein composite found in **37** wheat, barley, rye—and a few other related grains, and it contains amino acid sequences that trigger immune responses in people with celiac disease. Tissues in the small intestine

33. A) NO CHANGE

   B) Just starting in a career field, building experience

   C) If starting in a career field, building your experience

   D) When starting in a career field, building your experience

34. Which choice provides the most appropriate introduction to the main topic of the paragraph?

   A) NO CHANGE

   B) Today, many people try different diets to see which ones they like the best.

   C) Gluten can cause gastric trouble if people who eat it are allergic to it.

   D) More and more people are trying to remove gluten from their diet.

35. A) NO CHANGE

   B) the very most essential,

   C) an essential nutrient,

   D) a very essential nutrient,

36. A) NO CHANGE

   B) nonexistent

   C) strong

   D) trace

37. A) NO CHANGE

   B) wheat, barley, rye, and a few other related grains,

   C) wheat barley, rye and a few other related grains,

   D) wheat, barley, rye, and, a few other related grains,

GO ON TO THE NEXT PAGE

react as if the protein belonged to a harmful virus or **38** bacteria. They become inflamed. This inflammation prevents nutrients from being properly absorbed in the small intestine, resulting in a variety of serious conditions. It also causes gas and bloating, cramps, and diarrhea or constipation.

Although a small percentage of Americans have celiac disease, a much higher percentage report that they try to eat a gluten-free diet or are trying to eat less gluten. **39** According to one survey, some 20 percent of people are trying to avoid or cut back on gluten. Why are so many people following, or trying to follow, a gluten-free diet if they have not been diagnosed with celiac disease? In some cases, they might feel better on the diet because they have celiac disease but have never been diagnosed. People who suspect they have celiac disease because a gluten-free diet made them feel better still need to get diagnosed, but they might never have suspected they had the disease if going gluten-free had not become so popular. **40** A recent study estimates that many Americans with celiac disease do not know they have it.

A lot of people who have been found not to have celiac disease still feel better when they follow a gluten-free diet. Researchers have carefully tested groups of these people, giving them a diet that omitted gluten and then adding gluten back into their diet in **41** pill form, some felt no difference when gluten was added back

38. Which choice most effectively combines the sentences at the underlined portion?

A) bacteria as they become inflamed.

B) bacteria and become inflamed.

C) bacteria, however they become inflamed.

D) bacteria; become inflamed.

39. Which choice offers an accurate interpretation of the data in the graph?

A) NO CHANGE

B) According to data gathered in 2012, a greater percentage of people were trying to cut back or avoid gluten than in previous years.

C) According to data gathered in 2011, about 25 percent of people were trying to cut back or avoid gluten in 2011.

D) According to one survey, more than 29 percent of people are trying to cut back or avoid gluten.

40. Which choice best supports the claim made in the previous sentence?

A) NO CHANGE

B) A recent study estimates that Americans do not always know they have celiac disease.

C) A recent study estimates that about 5 out of every 6 Americans with celiac disease do not know they have it.

D) A recent study estimates that a high percentage of Americans with celiac disease do not know they have it.

41. A) NO CHANGE

B) pill form. Some felt

C) pill form some felt

D) pill form consequently some felt

GO ON TO THE NEXT PAGE

into their diets. Some, 42 moreover, were affected by gluten, which suggests that there might be other health conditions related to gluten besides celiac disease. These conditions affect only a small percentage of people, so the conditions might not have been noticed and studied if gluten-free diets had not become so popular.

Although it will not necessarily improve the health of everyone who tries it, a gluten-free diet does no harm and definitely 43 benefiting more people than doctors and researchers originally 44 studied.

42. A) NO CHANGE
   B) in addition,
   C) however,
   D) besides,

43. A) NO CHANGE
   B) benefits
   C) is benefiting
   D) did benefit

44. A) NO CHANGE
   B) wanted
   C) tested
   D) suspected

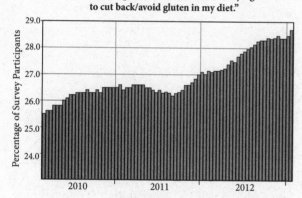

Positive Responses to Statement "I'm trying to cut back/avoid gluten in my diet."

Adapted from The NPD Group's consumer product research (www.npd.com).

MATH TEST

25 Minutes—20 Questions

NO-CALCULATOR SECTION

This section corresponds to Section 3 of your answer sheet.

Directions: For this section, solve each question and select the best answer choice. The available space on each page may be used for scratch work.

Notes:

1. Calculator use is NOT permitted.
2. All numbers used are real numbers, and all variables used represent real numbers, unless otherwise indicated.
3. Figures are drawn to scale and lie in a plane unless otherwise indicated.
4. Unless stated otherwise, the domain of any function f is assumed to be the set of all real numbers x, for which $f(x)$ is a real number.

Information:

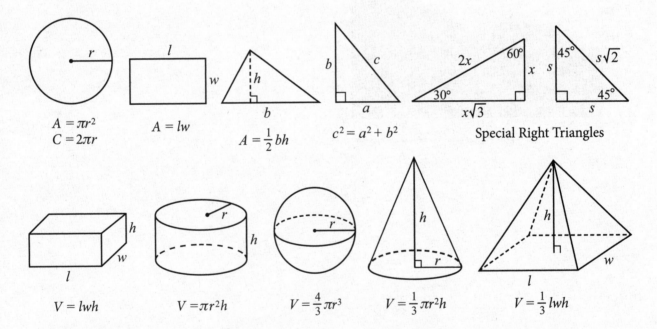

$A = \pi r^2$
$C = 2\pi r$

$A = lw$

$A = \frac{1}{2}bh$

$c^2 = a^2 + b^2$

Special Right Triangles

$V = lwh$

$V = \pi r^2 h$

$V = \frac{4}{3}\pi r^3$

$V = \frac{1}{3}\pi r^2 h$

$V = \frac{1}{3}lwh$

The sum of the degree measures of the angles in a triangle is 180.

The number of degrees of arc in a circle is 360.

The number of radians of arc in a circle is 2π.

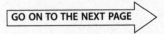
GO ON TO THE NEXT PAGE

Number of Runs	Total Number of People Who Have Ridden the Swings
2	28
3	42
5	70

1. The giant swings in an amusement park are run only when completely full to maintain a fairly even distribution of weight. The number of times the swings have been run, along with a cumulative rider count, is recorded in the table above. Based on the information, how many people will have ridden the giant swings when they have been run eight times?

   A)   98

   B)   112

   C)   140

   D)   224

2. Which of the following expressions is equivalent to $a^{\frac{2}{6}}$?

   A) $\sqrt[3]{a}$

   B) $\sqrt{3a}$

   C) $\dfrac{a}{3}$

   D) $\dfrac{2}{a^6}$

3. A publishing company ships books to schools, some of which are hardback textbooks and some of which are paperback workbooks. Each shipping box can hold a maximum of 20 textbooks or 64 workbooks. Each textbook takes up 192 cubic inches of space, and each workbook takes up 60 cubic inches of space. One box can hold a maximum of 3,840 cubic inches. The shipping department is packing a box containing both types of books. Which of the following systems of inequalities can the department use to determine how many textbooks, t, and workbooks, w, can be shipped in one box?

   A) $\begin{cases} t \le 20 \\ w \le 64 \\ 60t + 192w \le 3{,}840 \end{cases}$

   B) $\begin{cases} t \ge 20 \\ w \ge 64 \\ 192t + 60w \ge 3{,}840 \end{cases}$

   C) $\begin{cases} t \le 20 \\ w \le 64 \\ 192t + 60w \le 3{,}840 \end{cases}$

   D) $\begin{cases} t \le 192 \\ w \le 60 \\ 20t + 64w \le 3{,}840 \end{cases}$

4. A nutritionist is studying the effects of nutritional supplements on athletes. She uses the function $P_i(a)$ to represent the results of her study, where a represents the number of athletes who participated in the study, and P_i represents the number of athletes who experienced increased performance while using the supplements over a given period of time. Which of the following lists could represent a portion of the domain for the nutritionist's function?

   A) $\{...-100, -75, -50, -25, 0, 25, 50, 75, 100...\}$

   B) $\{-100, -75, -50, -25, 0, 25, 50, 75, 100\}$

   C) $\{0, 2.5, 5, 7.5, 10, 12.5, 15...\}$

   D) $\{0, 15, 30, 45, 60, 75...\}$

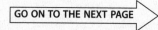
GO ON TO THE NEXT PAGE

5. Which of the following does not represent a linear relationship?

A)

x	−1	−4	−7	−10	−13
y	8	6	4	2	0

B)

x	−3	−1	1	3	5
y	5	3	1	−1	−3

C)

x	1	2	3	4	5
y	−5	−5	−5	−5	−5

D)

x	−2	−1	0	1	2
y	4	1	0	1	4

$$\begin{cases} Ax - 2y = 18 \\ Bx + 6y = 26 \end{cases}$$

6. If the graphs of the lines in the system of equations above intersect at $(4, -1)$, what is the value of $\dfrac{B}{A}$?

A) −3

B) $-\dfrac{1}{3}$

C) $\dfrac{1}{2}$

D) 2

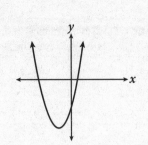

7. Which of the following equations could represent the graph in the figure shown above?

A) $y = x^2 - 4x - 4$

B) $y = x^2 + 4x - 4$

C) $y = x^2 - 8x + 16$

D) $y = x^2 + 8x + 16$

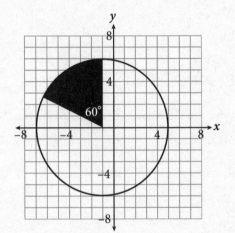

8. What is the area of the shaded sector of the circle shown in the figure above?

A) 2π

B) 6π

C) 12π

D) 36π

GO ON TO THE NEXT PAGE

9. Which of the following expressions has the same value as $\sqrt{0.25} \times \sqrt{2}$?

   A) $\dfrac{\sqrt{2}}{4}$

   B) $\dfrac{1}{2}$

   C) $\dfrac{\sqrt[4]{2}}{2}$

   D) $\dfrac{\sqrt{2}}{2}$

11. Given the polynomial $6x^4 + 2x^2 - 8x - c$, where c is a constant, for what value of c will $\dfrac{6x^4 + 2x^2 - 8x - c}{x + 2}$ have no remainder?

    A) -120

    B) -60

    C) 60

    D) 120

Wool-Polyester Blend Production

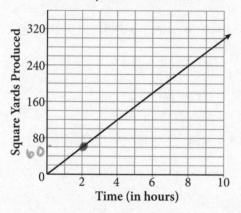

10. The figure above shows the rate at which a textile machine can produce a wool-polyester blend fabric. To produce a 100% polyester fabric, the same machine can produce 40 square yards per hour. Given that the company needs to fill an order for 2,400 square yards of each type of fabric, which of the following statements is true?

    A) It will take half as long to make the blended fabric as the 100% polyester fabric.

    B) It will take twice as long to make the blended fabric as the 100% polyester fabric.

    C) It will take 20 more hours to make the blended fabric than the 100% polyester fabric.

    D) It will take 20 fewer hours to make the blended fabric than the 100% polyester fabric.

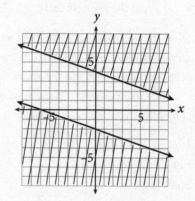

12. Which of the following systems of inequalities could be represented by the graph shown above?

    A) $\begin{cases} 3x - y \geq 4 \\ 3x - y \leq -2 \end{cases}$

    B) $\begin{cases} 3x + y \geq 4 \\ 3x + y \leq -2 \end{cases}$

    C) $\begin{cases} x - 3y \geq 12 \\ x - 3y \leq -6 \end{cases}$

    D) $\begin{cases} x + 3y \geq 12 \\ x + 3y \leq -6 \end{cases}$

GO ON TO THE NEXT PAGE

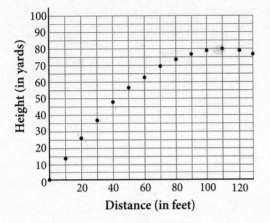

13. The figure above shows part of the parabolic path of a planned roller coaster hill. What is the sum, in feet, of the vertical height and the horizontal distance that the roller coaster will travel while on this particular hill? (Note: There are 3 feet in 1 yard.)

A) 220

B) 300

C) 460

D) 900

14. Which of the following expressions is equivalent to the complex number $\dfrac{2}{i + 6} + (2 + 5i)$? (Note that $\sqrt{-1} = i$.)

A) $\dfrac{32i + 9}{i + 6}$

B) $\dfrac{34i + 7}{i + 6}$

C) $\dfrac{32i + 19}{i + 6}$

D) $\dfrac{37i + 14}{i + 6}$

15. If $g(x) = 4x^2 - x + 5$, then what does $g(-2x)$ equal?

A) $16x^2 + 2x + 5$

B) $16x^2 - 2x + 5$

C) $-16x^2 + 2x + 5$

D) $-16x^2 - 2x + 5$

GO ON TO THE NEXT PAGE

Directions: For questions 16-20, enter your responses into the appropriate grid on your answer sheet, in accordance with the following:

1. You will receive credit only if the circles are filled in correctly, but you may write your answers in the boxes above each grid to help you fill in the circles accurately.

2. Don't mark more than one circle per column.

3. None of the questions with grid-in responses will have a negative solution.

4. Only grid in a single answer, even if there is more than one correct answer to a given question.

5. A **mixed number** must be gridded as a decimal or an improper fraction. For example, you would grid $7\frac{1}{2}$ as 7.5 or $\frac{15}{2}$.

    (Were you to grid it as $\begin{array}{|c|c|c|c|}\hline 7 & 1 & / & 2 \\\hline \end{array}$, this response would be read as $\frac{71}{2}$.)

6. A **decimal** that has more digits than there are places on the grid may be either rounded or truncated, but every column in the grid must be filled in order to receive credit.

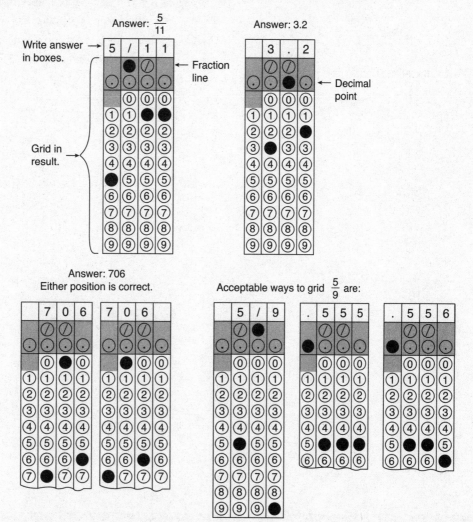

GO ON TO THE NEXT PAGE ⟶

16. If $0.2x + 1.8 = 3 - 0.6x$, what is the value of x ?

Equation 1	
x	y
5	-8
4	-5
3	-2
2	1

Equation 2	
x	y
-8	3
-6	4
-4	5
-2	6

17. The tables above represent data points for two linear equations. If the two equations form a system, what is the x-coordinate of the solution to that system?

$$18 - \frac{(3x)^{\frac{1}{2}}}{2} = 15$$

18. What value of x satisfies the equation above?

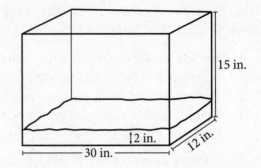

19. The figure above shows a fish tank with sand in the bottom. If the water level is to be 3 inches below the top, how many cubic inches of water are needed to fill the tank?

20. If $g(x) = 2x^3 - 5x^2 + 4x + 6$, and P is the point on the graph of $g(x)$ that has an x-coordinate of 1, then what is the y-coordinate of the corresponding point on the graph of $g(x - 3) + 4$?

MATH TEST

55 Minutes—38 Questions

CALCULATOR SECTION

This section corresponds to Section 4 of your answer sheet.

Directions: For this section, solve each question and select the best answer choice. The available space on each page may be used for scratch work.

Notes:

1. Calculator use is permitted.
2. All numbers used are real numbers, and all variables used represent real numbers, unless otherwise indicated.
3. Figures are drawn to scale and lie in a plane unless otherwise indicated.
4. Unless stated otherwise, the domain of any function f is assumed to be the set of all real numbers x, for which $f(x)$ is a real number.

Information:

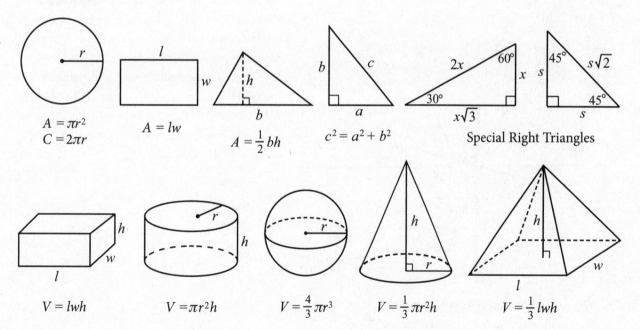

The sum of the degree measures of the angles in a triangle is 180.

The number of degrees of arc in a circle is 360.

The number of radians of arc in a circle is 2π.

GO ON TO THE NEXT PAGE ⇨

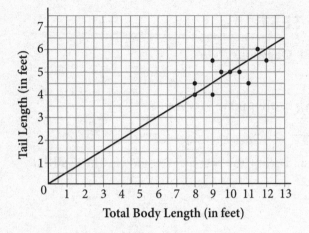

Total Body Length (in feet)

1. The Florida Department of Wildlife caught and tagged 10 adult female alligators as part of an effort to protect this endangered species. They took various measurements and readings related to body size and health. The total body length is plotted against the tail length in the scatterplot shown above, along with a line of best fit. Which of the following equations best models the data?

   A) $y = 0.5x$

   B) $y = 2x$

   C) $y = 0.4x + 1$

   D) $y = 0.6x - 1$

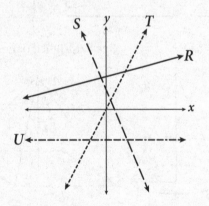

2. Which of the following lists correctly orders the lines in the figure above according to their slopes, from least to greatest?

   A) R, T, S, U

   B) S, U, R, T

   C) S, R, U, T

   D) U, S, R, T

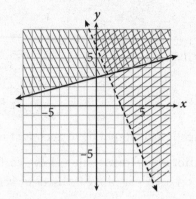

3. Which of the following is a solution to the system of inequalities shown in the figure above?

   A) $(-5, 2)$

   B) $(-2, 5)$

   C) $(2, 5)$

   D) $(5, 2)$

4. The American political system is largely a two-party system. In fact, only six candidates who were not associated with either the Republican or the Democratic Party have been elected governor in any state since 1990. In one such election, the ratio of votes received for the Independent candidate to the Democratic candidate to the Republican candidate was approximately 19:18:13. If 510,000 votes were cast in the election, how many more votes were cast for the Independent candidate than for the Republican candidate?

   A)   6,000

   B)   10,200

   C)   61,200

   D)   193,800

GO ON TO THE NEXT PAGE

Selection Method	Number of States
Election	22
Gubernatorial appointment	11
Legislative appointment	2
Missouri Plan	15

5. There are four ways in which state judges are selected for their positions. One is by election, another is appointment by the governor (usually with the confirmation by the state legislature), and a third is appointment by the state legislature. The final way is a hybrid of the last two, called the Missouri Plan, in which a nonpartisan legislative committee recommends a list of candidates and the governor chooses from this list. The table above shows the number of states that engage in each process for the highest court of the state, usually called the state Supreme Court. What percent of states select judges using the Missouri Plan?

    A) 17%

    B) 30%

    C) 33%

    D) 43%

6. A botanist collects and models some data and is able to determine that the number of germinated seeds of a certain plant is linearly correlated to the amount of rainfall during the previous month, according to the equation $s = 28.5r + 83$. In this equation, s is the number of seeds germinated, and r is the amount of rainfall in inches. In a certain geographic region that the botanist is studying, 197 seeds germinated. Approximately how many inches of rainfall did that area receive during the previous month?

    A) 3.1

    B) 4

    C) 7

    D) 9.8

7. A dendrologist (a botanist who studies trees exclusively) is examining the way in which a certain tree sheds its leaves. He tracks the number of leaves shed each day over the period of a month, starting when the first leaf is shed. He organizes the data in a scatterplot and sees that the data can be modeled using an exponential function. He determines the exponential model to be $f(x) = 6(1.92)^x$, where x is the number of days after the tree began to shed its leaves. What does the value 1.92 in the function tell the dendrologist?

    A) The number of leaves shed almost doubles each day.

    B) The number of leaves shed almost doubles every six days.

    C) The number of leaves left on the tree is reduced by about 92% each day.

    D) The number of leaves left on the tree is reduced by about 92% every six days.

GO ON TO THE NEXT PAGE ⟩

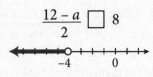

$$\frac{12 - a}{2} \;\square\; 8$$

8. Which inequality symbol would make the above statement true?

A) $\leq$

B) $\geq$

C) $<$

D) $>$

Price per Pencil	Projected Number of Units Sold
$0.20	150,000
$0.25	135,000
$0.30	120,000
$0.35	105,000
$0.40	90,000
$0.45	75,000

9. Generally, the price of an item is a good indicator of how many units of that item will be sold. The lower the price, the more units will be sold. A marketing department develops a table showing various price points and the projected number of units sold at that price point. Which of the following represents the linear relationship shown in the table, where x is the price and y is the number of units sold?

A) $y = 0.03x + 150,000$

B) $y = 300,000x + 75,000$

C) $y = -300,000x + 90,000$

D) $y = -300,000x + 210,000$

10. A mailing supply store sells small shipping boxes in packs of 8 or 20. If the store has 61 packs in stock totaling 800 small shipping boxes, how many packs have 20 boxes in them, assuming all the packs are full?

A) 26

B) 32

C) 35

D) 40

11. Given that $\sqrt{-1} = i$, which of the following is equivalent to the sum $i^{125} + i^{125}$?

A) i^{14}

B) i^{250}

C) $2i^{45}$

D) $2i^{250}$

$$-\frac{9}{2}x^{10} - \frac{3}{2}x^{9} + \frac{15}{2}x^{8}$$

12. Which of the following is equivalent to the expression above?

A) $-\frac{3}{2}x^{8}(3x^{2} + x - 5)$

B) $-\frac{1}{2}x^{8}(9x^{2} + 3x - 5)$

C) $\frac{3}{2}x^{8}(-3x^{2} + x + 5)$

D) $3x^{8}(-3x^{2} - x + 5)$

GO ON TO THE NEXT PAGE

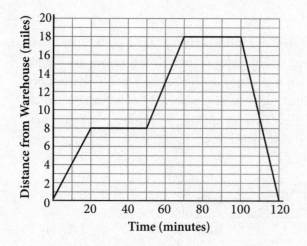

13. The graph above shows a delivery truck's distance from the company's warehouse over a two-hour period, during which time the delivery people made two deliveries and then returned to the warehouse. Based on the graph, which of the following statements could be true?

A) Each delivery took 30 minutes to complete, not including driving time.

B) The location of the second delivery was about 70 miles from the warehouse.

C) The truck traveled about 18 miles from the time it left the warehouse until it returned.

D) The second delivery was about 18 miles farther from the warehouse than the first delivery.

GO ON TO THE NEXT PAGE

Questions 14 and 15 refer to the following information.

Plants are capable of cross-pollinating with related but different plants. This creates a hybrid plant. Sometimes, a hybrid plant is superior to the two different plants from which it was derived. This is known as "hybrid vigor." Scientists can examine the DNA of a plant to see if it is a hybrid. This can be valuable information because if the plant appears superior, it would be beneficial to develop more of these hybrids. An agricultural scientist examines an orchard that has several types of apple trees and orange trees to see which ones are hybrids. Some of the information she collected is shown in the table below.

	Apple Trees	Orange Trees	Total
Hybrid			402
Non-hybrid		118	
Total			628

14. Based on the data, if 45% of the apple trees are not hybrids, how many apple trees are hybrids?

    A) 50

    B) 132

    C) 226

    D) 240

15. The scientist wants to study the orange trees to check for hybrid vigor. If she chooses one orange tree at random, what is the probability that it will be a hybrid?

    A) $\dfrac{59}{194}$

    B) $\dfrac{135}{314}$

    C) $\dfrac{97}{157}$

    D) $\dfrac{135}{194}$

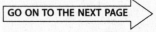

GO ON TO THE NEXT PAGE

$$\left(5x^4 - \frac{1}{4}x^3 + 3x\right) \div \frac{1}{2}x$$

16. What is the result of dividing the two expressions above?

   A) $\dfrac{5}{2}x^3 - \dfrac{1}{8}x^2 + \dfrac{3}{2}$

   B) $\dfrac{5}{2}x^3 - 2x^2 + \dfrac{3}{2}x$

   C) $10x^3 - \dfrac{1}{2}x^2 + 6$

   D) $10x^3 - \dfrac{1}{8}x^2 + 6x$

x	y
−1	7
0	5
1	3
2	1

17. If graphed, the ordered pairs in the table above would form a line. Where would this line intersect the x-axis?

   A) $-2\dfrac{1}{2}$

   B) $-\dfrac{1}{2}$

   C) $2\dfrac{1}{2}$

   D) 5

18. Mount Fuji in Japan was first climbed by a monk in 663 AD and subsequently became a Japanese religious site for hundreds of years. It is now a popular tourist site. When ascending the mountain, tourists drive part of the distance and climb the rest of the way. Suppose a tourist drove to an elevation of 2,390 meters and from that point climbed to the top of the mountain, and then descended back to the car taking the same route. If it took her a total of 7 hours to climb up and back down, and she climbed at an average rate of 264 vertical meters per hour going up and twice that going down, approximately how tall is Mount Fuji?

   A) 1,232 meters

   B) 2,464 meters

   C) 3,622 meters

   D) 3,776 meters

$$\begin{cases} y = 3x \\ -3x^2 + 2y^2 = 180 \end{cases}$$

19. If (x, y) is a solution to the system of equations above, what is the value of x^2?

   A) 12

   B) 20

   C) 60

   D) 144

20. If $M = 3x^2 + 9x - 4$ and $N = 5x^2 - 12$, then what is $2(M - N)$?

   A) $-2x^2 + 9x + 8$

   B) $-4x^2 + 18x - 32$

   C) $-4x^2 + 18x + 16$

   D) $8x^2 + 9x - 16$

GO ON TO THE NEXT PAGE

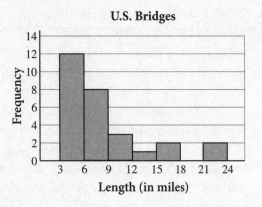

U.S. Bridges

Length (in miles)

21. The Lake Pontchartrain Causeway Bridge in Louisiana is the longest bridge in the United States, at 23.83 miles long. The histogram above shows the distribution of the lengths, in miles, of 28 of the longest bridges in the United States, including Lake Pontchartrain Causeway Bridge. Which of the following could be the median length of the 28 bridges represented in the histogram?

A) 5.9

B) 7.9

C) 9.2

D) 9.9

22. In the United States, the original full retirement age was 65. The retirement age has since been pushed to 66 and will soon move to 67, as life expectancies go up. The Social Security Administration periodically conducts studies regarding retirement age. One such study focused on whether or not retiring early lowers a person's life expectancy. The study found a weak positive correlation between retirement age and life expectancy. If data from the study were graphed in a scatterplot, which of the following statements would be true?

A) The slope of the line of best fit would be a large positive number.

B) The slope of the line of best fit would be a negative number close to 0.

C) The data points would follow, but not closely, an increasing line of best fit.

D) The data points would be closely gathered around an increasing line of best fit.

23. A student is doing a scale drawing of a woolly mammoth on a piece of poster board for her presentation on the last ice age. She was surprised to find that the woolly mammoth, reaching a height of only about 10 feet, 6 inches, was actually smaller than today's African elephant. Even more surprising is the fact that the woolly mammoth's tusks averaged 11.5 feet in length. If the student draws the mammoth 14 inches tall on her poster, approximately how many inches long should she make the tusks? (There are 12 inches in 1 foot.)

A) 12.78

B) 15.0

C) 15.33

D) 16.1

24. Johanna picked 3 pounds of strawberries at a "pick-your-own" patch. At this particular patch, the cost is $1.50 for the pail and $3.99 per pound of strawberries picked. If a linear equation is created to represent the situation and written in the form $y = mx + b$, which piece of the equation would the value 13.47 in this scenario most likely represent?

A) b

B) m

C) x

D) y

GO ON TO THE NEXT PAGE

25. In an effort to decrease reliance on fossil fuels, some energy producers have started to utilize renewable resources. One such power plant uses solar panels to create solar energy during the day and then shifts to natural gas at night or when there is cloud cover. One particularly bright morning, the company increases the amount of its power typically generated by solar panels by 60%. During a cloudy spell, it decreases the amount by 30%, and then when the sun comes back out, it increases the amount again by 75% before shutting the panels down for the night. What is the net percent increase of this company's reliance on solar panels during that day?

    A)   75%

    B)   96%

    C)   105%

    D)   165%

26. Zoos use various methods for determining how to feed different animals. Sometimes they use age, weight, or, usually in the case of snakes, length. If a snake that is 2 feet, 6 inches long receives 12 grams of frog mash per feeding, how many grams should a snake that is 1 meter in length get? (Use the approximate conversion 1 foot = 0.3 meters.)

    A)   5

    B)   13

    C)   14.5

    D)   16

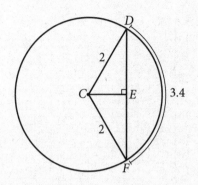

27. Which of the following gives the length of chord *DF* in the figure above?

    A) $2 \cos(1.7)$

    B) $2 \sin(1.7)$

    C) $4 \cos(0.85)$

    D) $4 \sin(0.85)$

28. If $y = 12 - x$ and $\dfrac{3y}{4} + 11 = \dfrac{-x}{2}$, what is the value of $\dfrac{x}{5} + \dfrac{y}{4}$?

    A) -1

    B) $\dfrac{19}{4}$

    C) $\dfrac{75}{4}$

    D)   33

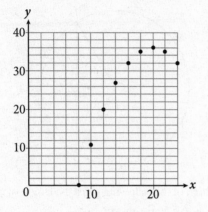

29. If a quadratic equation is used to model the data shown in the scatterplot above, and the model fits the data exactly, which of the following is a solution to the quadratic equation?

    A) 28

    B) 32

    C) 34

    D) 36

30. If h is a function defined over the set of all real numbers and $h(x - 4) = 6x^2 + 2x + 10$, then which of the following defines $h(x)$?

    A) $h(x) = 6x^2 - 2x + 114$

    B) $h(x) = 6x^2 - 46x + 98$

    C) $h(x) = 6x^2 + 2x + 98$

    D) $h(x) = 6x^2 + 50x + 114$

GO ON TO THE NEXT PAGE

Directions: For questions 31-38, enter your responses into the appropriate grid on your answer sheet, in accordance with the following:

1. You will receive credit only if the circles are filled in correctly, but you may write your answers in the boxes above each grid to help you fill in the circles accurately.

2. Don't mark more than one circle per column.

3. None of the questions with grid-in responses will have a negative solution.

4. Only grid in a single answer, even if there is more than one correct answer to a given question.

5. A **mixed number** must be gridded as a decimal or an improper fraction. For example, you would grid $7\frac{1}{2}$ as 7.5 or $\frac{15}{2}$.

   (Were you to grid it as ▦, this response would be read as $\frac{71}{2}$.)

6. A **decimal** that has more digits than there are places on the grid may be either rounded or truncated, but every column in the grid must be filled in order to receive credit.

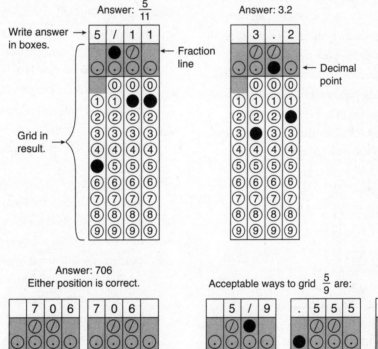

31. The Bar Exam is a test given in each state to determine whether or not a law school graduate is competent to practice law. The American Bar Association surveyed 3,000 law school graduates across the country who passed the bar exam in 2000. Of those surveyed, 720 were not practicing law in 2012. If 55,200 graduates passed the bar in 2000, about how many of them were practicing law in 2012, assuming the sample was a good representation of the population of law school graduates who passed the bar in 2000? Round to the nearest thousand and enter your answer in terms of thousands. (For example, enter 18,000 as 18.)

32. In recent years, car manufacturers have started producing hybrid vehicles, which run on both electricity and gasoline, resulting in a significantly higher gas mileage. Suppose the odometer of a hybrid car, which shows how many miles the car has traveled, reads 4,386 miles. If the car averages 48 miles to the gallon of gas and currently has 12 gallons in the tank, what should the odometer reading be when the tank is empty?

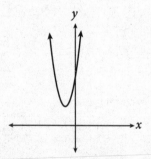

33. If the equation of the graph shown above is $y = 2(x + 3)^2 + 10$, what is the y-intercept of the graph?

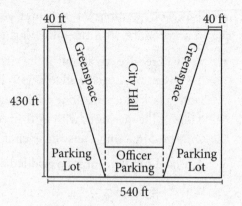

34. Many cities try to work "greenspaces" into their city planning because living plants help filter the city's air, reducing the effects of pollution. The figure above shows the plans for a new greenspace around City Hall, which will be created by converting portions of the existing parking lots. If the width of each parking lot is the same as the width of the City Hall building, how many thousands of square feet of greenspace will there be after the conversion? Round to the nearest thousand and enter your answer in terms of thousands. (For example, enter 14,000 as 14.)

35. Rasha volunteers at a charity that helps feed the homeless. He collects donations and then uses the money to buy food for care packages. This week, he collected $145. Each care package will include canned vegetables and bags of rice in the ratio 3:1. The cans cost $0.89 each, and the bags of rice cost $3.49 each. Using the given ratio, what is the maximum number of complete vegetable/rice care packages Rasha can make?

GO ON TO THE NEXT PAGE

36. A subway car on the New York City subway travels at an average speed of 17.4 miles per hour. Train cars on the Chicago L travel at an average speed that is 30% faster than that of the NYC subway. The DC Metro travels at an average speed that is 30% faster than that of the Chicago L. Marc rode the NYC subway from one stop to another and it took 6 minutes; Lizzie rode the Chicago L from one stop to another and it took 4.8 minutes; and Darius rode the DC Metro, which took 3.6 minutes between stops. How many miles did the person who traveled the shortest distance between stops travel? Round to the nearest tenth of a mile.

Questions 37 and 38 refer to the following information.

Mercury is a naturally occurring metal that can be harmful to humans. The current recommendation is for humans to take in no more than 0.1 microgram for every kilogram of their weight per day. Fish generally carry high levels of mercury, although certain fish have higher mercury content than others. Fish, however, are healthy sources of many other nutrients, so nutritionists recommend keeping them in the human diet. The figure shown here shows the average mercury content of several types of fish.

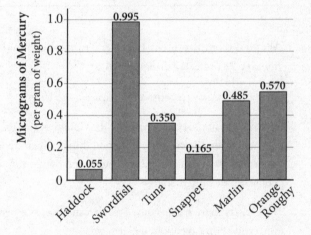

Average Mercury Content

37. If a person weighs 82 kilograms, how many grams of snapper can he safely consume per day? Round your answer to the nearest gram.

38. Suppose in a week, a person regularly eats one portion of each type of the fish shown in the bar graph, except the fish with the highest mercury content. What is this person's average daily mercury consumption, in micrograms, assuming a portion size of 100 grams? Round your answer to the nearest microgram.

ESSAY TEST

50 Minutes

You will be given a passage to read and asked to write an essay analyzing it. As you write, be sure to show that you have read the passage closely. You will be graded on how well you have understood the passage, how clear your analysis is, and how well you express your ideas.

Your essay must be written on the lines in your answer booklet. Anything you write outside the lined space in your answer booklet will not be read by the essay graders. Be sure to write or print in such a way that it will be legible to readers not familiar with your handwriting. Additionally, be sure to address the passage directly. An off-topic essay will not be graded.

As you read the passage, think about the author's use of

- evidence, such as statistics or other facts.

- logic to connect evidence to conclusions and to develop lines of reasoning.

- style, word choice, and appeals to emotion to make the argument more persuasive.

Adapted from President Harry S. Truman's Annual Message to the Congress on the State of the Union, January 7, 1948, Washington, DC.

1   We are here today to consider the state of the Union.

2   On this occasion, above all others, the Congress and the President should concentrate their attention, not upon party but upon the country; not upon things which divide us but upon those which bind us together—the enduring principles of our American system, and our common aspirations for the future welfare and security of the people of the United States.

3   The United States has become great because we, as a people, have been able to work together for great objectives even while differing about details....

4   The United States has always had a deep concern for human rights. Religious freedom, free speech, and freedom of thought are cherished realities in our land. Any denial of human rights is a denial of the basic beliefs of democracy and of our regard for the worth of each individual.

5   Today, however, some of our citizens are still denied equal opportunity for education, for jobs and economic advancement, and for the expression of their views at the polls. Most serious of all, some are denied equal protection under laws. Whether discrimination is based on race, or creed, or color, or land of origin, it is utterly contrary to American ideals of democracy.

6   The recent report of the President's Committee on Civil Rights points the way to corrective action by the federal government and by state and local governments. Because of the need for effective federal action, I shall send a special message to the Congress on this important subject....

GO ON TO THE NEXT PAGE

7   Our second goal is to protect and develop our human resources.

8   The safeguarding of the rights of our citizens must be accompanied by an equal regard for their opportunities for development and their protection from economic insecurity. In this Nation the ideals of freedom and equality can be given specific meaning in terms of health, education, social security, and housing.

9   Over the past twelve years we have erected a sound framework of Social Security legislation. Many millions of our citizens are now protected against the loss of income which can come with unemployment, old age, or the death of wage earners. Yet our system has gaps and inconsistencies; it is only half finished.

10 We should now extend unemployment compensation, old age benefits, and survivors' benefits to millions who are not now protected. We should also raise the level of benefits.

11 The greatest gap in our Social Security structure is the lack of adequate provision for the Nation's health. We are rightly proud of the high standards of medical care we know how to provide in the United States. The fact is, however, that most of our people cannot afford to pay for the care they need....

12 Another fundamental aim of our democracy is to provide an adequate education for every person.

13 Our educational systems face a financial crisis. It is deplorable that in a Nation as rich as ours there are millions of children who do not have adequate schoolhouses or enough teachers for a good elementary or secondary education. If there are educational inadequacies in any State, the whole Nation suffers. The Federal Government has a responsibility for providing financial aid to meet this crisis.

14 In addition, we must make possible greater equality of opportunity to all our citizens for education. Only by so doing can we insure that our citizens will be capable of understanding and sharing the responsibilities of democracy.

15 The Government's programs for health, education, and security are of such great importance to our democracy that we should now establish an executive department for their administration....

16 Our third goal is to conserve and use our natural resources so that they can contribute most effectively to the welfare of our people.

17 The resources given by nature to this country are rich and extensive. The material foundations of our growth and economic development are the bounty of our fields, the wealth of our mines and forests, and the energy of our waters. As a Nation, we are coming to appreciate more each day the close relationship between the conservation of these resources and the preservation of our national strength.

18 We are doing far less than we know how to do to make use of our resources without destroying them. Both the public and private use of these resources must have the primary objective of maintaining and increasing these basic supports for an expanding future.

GO ON TO THE NEXT PAGE ▷

Write an essay that analyzes the author's approach in persuading his readers that continued investment in the nation's collective welfare is based on the ideals of American democracy. Focus on specific features such as the ones listed in the box above the passage and explain how these features strengthen the author's argument. Your essay should discuss the most important rhetorical features of the passage.

Your essay should not focus on your own opinion of the author's conclusion, but rather on how the author persuades his readers.

ANSWER KEY
READING TEST

1. C	14. C	27. C	40. A
2. D	15. C	28. B	41. C
3. B	16. D	29. A	42. D
4. C	17. A	30. D	43. C
5. C	18. C	31. C	44. A
6. A	19. D	32. C	45. A
7. B	20. B	33. B	46. B
8. D	21. A	34. B	47. C
9. B	22. B	35. C	48. B
10. B	23. C	36. C	49. A
11. C	24. B	37. A	50. C
12. D	25. C	38. B	51. D
13. A	26. D	39. C	52. C

WRITING AND LANGUAGE TEST

1. C	12. A	23. A	34. D
2. B	13. B	24. B	35. C
3. C	14. C	25. D	36. D
4. D	15. A	26. B	37. B
5. C	16. D	27. C	38. B
6. C	17. B	28. B	39. B
7. B	18. A	29. A	40. C
8. A	19. C	30. C	41. B
9. B	20. B	31. D	42. C
10. D	21. D	32. C	43. B
11. A	22. A	33. D	44. D

MATH—NO CALCULATOR TEST

1. B	6. D	11. D	16. 3/2 or 1.5
2. A	7. B	12. D	17. 0
3. C	8. B	13. C	18. 12
4. D	9. D	14. A	19. 3600
5. D	10. C	15. A	20. 11

MATH—CALCULATOR TEST

1. A	11. C	21. B	31. 42
2. B	12. A	22. C	32. 4962
3. C	13. A	23. C	33. 28
4. C	14. B	24. D	34. 60
5. B	15. D	25. B	35. 23
6. B	16. C	26. D	36. 1.7
7. A	17. C	27. D	37. 50
8. D	18. C	28. A	38. 23
9. D	19. A	29. B	
10. A	20. C	30. D	

ANSWERS AND EXPLANATIONS

READING TEST

Three Men in a Boat

Suggested Passage Map notes:

¶1: everyone tired by the time "haul up" boat

¶2: moored not where they intended to but ok

¶3: hungry but first need to work on the boat

¶4: worked with hoops; took a long time

¶5: work hard and dangerous; used wrong hoops

¶6: hard to get wrong ones out

¶7: finally did but now need to cover them; Harris new at it, has trouble

¶8: Harris wrapped in cover; knocked over George when trying to get out

1. C   **Difficulty:** Easy

Category: Detail

Getting to the Answer: For some questions, like this one, the correct answer is stated directly in the passage. In lines 7-8, the narrator says that they "had originally intended to go on to Magna Carta Island." Later, however, they change their minds; the narrator says in lines 11-13 that "we did not feel that we yearned for the picturesque nearly so much now as we had earlier in the day." Choice (C) is the correct answer, as it reflects this idea.

2. D   **Difficulty:** Medium

Category: Vocab-in-Context

Getting to the Answer: Reread the paragraph and consider why the men are dispensing with tea. Then identify a synonym for this verb. The passage states that the men "dispensed with tea, so as to save time." Predict *foregoing*, or *skipping*, tea would result in saving time, so (D) is the correct answer.

3. B   **Difficulty:** Easy

Category: Inference

Getting to the Answer: Consider what the narrator states about the events of the day and how they have affected the men. The first three paragraphs establish that it has been a tiring but basically uneventful day. The men are essentially calm, but they want food and sleep. Choice (B) is the correct answer.

4. C   **Difficulty:** Medium

Category: Command of Evidence

Getting to the Answer: Carefully read the answer choices within the passage. Identify the sentence that best supports your answer to question 3. The men's thoughts are not on a difficult struggle ahead, but on basic needs like food and sleep. Choice (C) is correct.

5. C   **Difficulty:** Hard

Category: Global

Getting to the Answer: In your own words, describe what the narrator wants the reader to take away from the story. The passage is a comedy of errors, in which one minor difficulty piles on another. The whole situation is set in motion by the men's false belief that their task will be simple. Choice (C) best reflects this idea and is the correct answer.

6. A   **Difficulty:** Medium

Category: Inference

Getting to the Answer: When making an inference, remember that you must draw a logical conclusion based on details in the passage. Choice (A) is correct. Although George serves as an informal leader of the group, there is no indication that any of the men knew much about the tasks involved in camping or boating.

7. B   **Difficulty:** Hard

Category: Command of Evidence

Getting to the Answer: Reread your answer to the previous question. Identify the answer choice that most strongly supports your answer. The correct answer to question 6 concludes that none of the men knew much about camping or boating. Choice (B) supports this, as it indicates that the men did not anticipate what was going to happen with the canvas.

8. D   **Difficulty:** Medium

Category: Vocab-in-Context

Getting to the Answer: Without reading the answer choices, try to predict the meaning of "in the abstract" using context clues provided in the paragraph in which the phrase appears. Then compare your answer with the choices provided. The sentence reads "It looked so simple in the abstract" (lines 29-30), followed by a fairly straightforward description of how one would set up the canvas. Then everything goes wrong. In this context, predict "in the abstract" means *in theory*, as opposed to reality. Choice (D) is the correct answer.

9. B   **Difficulty:** Medium

Category: Rhetoric

Getting to the Answer: Reread the question stem and note that it's asking about the description of the hoops in paragraph 7. Decide what overall effect this description has on the reader. The description of the hoops makes use of extensive personification: "they would jump up suddenly, and try and throw us into the water and drown us" (lines 49-50), "when we were not looking, they nipped us with these hinges" (lines 51-52), and "while we were wrestling with one side of the hoop, and endeavouring to persuade it to do its duty, the other side would come behind us in a cowardly manner, and hit us over the head" (lines 53-57). In doing this, the author adds humor to the characters' predicament, implying that the hoops were capable of outsmarting the men. Choice (B) is the correct answer.

10. B   **Difficulty:** Hard

Category: Rhetoric

Getting to the Answer: Consider the emotional state of the narrator throughout the passage. With what attitude or feeling are events conveyed? Clues throughout the passage make it clear that the narrator is looking back and that there is no current fear, frustration, or disgust involved in recalling events. Instead, the tone is one of understated comic reflection at the foibles encountered by the group of friends. Therefore, (B) is the correct answer.

Kennedy Speech

Suggested Passage Map notes:

> ¶1: time of change and fear, knowledge and ignorance.
>
> ¶2: K collapses, 50,000 yrs of man's progress to 50 yrs
>
> ¶3: TV a week ago, spacecraft reach Venus before midnight?
>
> ¶4: very fast pace → problems and rewards
>
> ¶5: some want to stop but K says need to move on
>
> ¶6: Quotes Bradford: accomplishments have difficulties, must be courageous
>
> ¶7: progress can't be stopped, must join space exploration
>
> ¶8: lead exploration for freedom and peace
>
> ¶9: need to make big effort to lead
>
> ¶10: go into space for new knowledge and progress
>
> ¶11: why go to moon?
>
> ¶12: will show the best energies and skills

11. C   **Difficulty:** Easy

Category: Rhetoric

Getting to the Answer: Examine the language used in the speech. Consider the emotions Kennedy wants his audience to feel and why. Kennedy uses emotional and inspiring language so the audience of college students will understand the importance of reaching the moon. He does this in an attempt to gain support for the lunar mission. Choice (C) conveys this idea and is the correct answer.

12. D   Difficulty: Medium

Category: Command of Evidence

Getting to the Answer: Carefully review your answer to the previous question. Which answer choice best relates to the primary purpose of Kennedy's speech? Kennedy explains how important the space race is throughout his speech. He emphasizes the knowledge that can be gained, the prestige of being first, and the security reasons for prioritizing the race to the moon. He ends his speech by giving a final justification for supporting America's quest to reach the moon. Choice (D) is correct because it reiterates Kennedy's reasons that students should support the race to the moon.

13. A   Difficulty: Medium

Category: Vocab-in-Context

Getting to the Answer: Read the sentence for context clues about what Bradford thought must be done with "great difficulties." Bradford suggests that "great difficulties" (line 45) must be faced and overcome. The only answer choice that suggests facing the challenges is "undertaken." Choice (A) is the correct answer.

14. C   Difficulty: Hard

Category: Inference

Getting to the Answer: Follow Kennedy's rhetoric about world views on space exploration. What contrast does Kennedy draw between American goals and possible foreign goals? Kennedy remarks that the United States will not see a "hostile flag of conquest" placed on the moon (lines 58-59). He suggests that other countries may wish to act in a hostile manner and, therefore, Americans are obligated to prevent this by reaching the moon first. Choice (C) is the correct answer.

15. C   Difficulty: Easy

Category: Command of Evidence

Getting to the Answer: Carefully reread the part of the passage that addresses world views on the space race. Identify the specific claims it makes. Kennedy states that the world is looking to explore space. He goes on to say that the United States is obligated to prevent "weapons of mass destruction" (line 61) from being placed in space. Choice (C) is the correct answer because it suggests that other countries may have negative motives for lunar exploration.

16. D   Difficulty: Medium

Category: Vocab-in-Context

Getting to the Answer: Analyze the target sentence and the sentence that follows it, paying attention to the contrast between the two. Paraphrase what Kennedy is saying and predict a word that has the same meaning of "founder" in context. In these sentences, Kennedy contrasts "does not intend" (line 53) with "we mean to lead" (line 55) to state that the United States will not be left behind but will lead the world in space exploration. The meaning of "founder" must match the connotation of the phrase "backwash of the coming age" (line 54), conveying the notion of *capsizing* or *being left behind*. Choice (D) is the correct answer.

17. A   Difficulty: Easy

Category: Detail

Getting to the Answer: Search the passage for Kennedy's comments on the pace and effects of progress. What claims does he make? Kennedy comments on the "breathtaking pace" (line 30) of progress and states that this progress "cannot help but create new ills as it dispels old" (line 31). He encourages the race to the moon but cautions the audience to expect hardships and conflicts as part of these advances. Choice (A) is the correct answer.

18. C   Difficulty: Hard

Category: Rhetoric

Getting to the Answer: Reread the question stem. It's asking you to analyze how a particular statement functions in the overall argument presented by Kennedy. Choice (C) is correct. In the quoted sentence, Kennedy outlines the positive attributes he believes the United States has that make it the best nation to take the lead in space exploration, thus providing evidence to strengthen his claim.

19. D   Difficulty: Hard

Category: Connections

Getting to the Answer: Think about Kennedy's attempts to rally support from the group. What theme does he repeatedly return to when speaking about the space race? Kennedy frequently mentions that the race to the moon is necessary, but that it will be filled with hardship and challenges. He emphasizes a need to be first and lead the way, much like American colonists (lines 42-46) and aerial innovators (lines 79-80). Choice (D) is correct, as it expresses the idea of people leading the way on a difficult but necessary excursion.

20. B   Difficulty: Easy

Category: Rhetoric

Getting to the Answer: Reread your Passage Map and consider the paragraphs' relationship to the other paragraphs in the passage. These paragraphs offer a *capsule history* of human advances to set the stage for Kennedy's claim that space exploration is a natural extension of human progress. Choice (B) is the correct answer.

Paired Passages—Viking Longboats

Suggested Passage Map notes:

Passage 1

¶1: Vikings great sailors, Longboats

¶2: design of longboat allowed long journeys

¶3: boat also streamlined

¶4: great sailors and navigators

¶5: big impact on Scandinavia & rest of world

Passage 2

¶1: 1880: excavated V longboat Gokstad

¶2: details of design

¶3: details of oar holes, oars, how many people on boat

¶4: details about planking

¶5: harsh land → sea trade and raiding

¶6: Gokstad = big leap in seafaring

21. A   Difficulty: Easy

Category: Global

Getting to the Answer: Try to paraphrase the central idea of the passage in your own words. Then read each answer choice. The correct choice will most nearly match your idea. Passage 1 explores the shipbuilding abilities and the navigation skills of the Vikings. It discusses how these skills enabled the Vikings to travel, explore, and extend their civilization, but the central idea is that the Vikings had exceptional abilities in shipbuilding and navigation. The correct answer is (A).

22. B   Difficulty: Easy

Category: Inference

Getting to the Answer: Reread the introductory paragraph of Passage 1 and consider the implications suggested by the information provided. The correct answer will suggest an idea not directly stated but supported by the given information. In the first paragraph of Passage 1, the author suggests that the Vikings traveled far and wide, encountering other peoples and thereby engaging in cultural interactions. The concepts mentioned in the various answer choices, such as surviving via sea trade in A, supporting a growing population in C, and sustaining economic development through sea raids in D, are not supported in this paragraph. The correct answer is (B).

23. C **Difficulty:** Medium

Category: Command of Evidence

Getting to the Answer: Reread the answer to the previous question. The correct choice will provide evidence that directly supports, or even restates, that idea. Only (C) suggests the cultural interaction of the Vikings with other peoples through the phrase "opened up new foreign connections."

24. B **Difficulty:** Medium

Category: Vocab-in-Context

Getting to the Answer: Reread the sentence in which the word appears as well as the sentences that follow to get a sense for the meaning of the word in context. Before reviewing the answer choices, predict a definition in your own words. The correct answer will most nearly match your definition. The author explains that the ship was able to ride high, skim the waves, swiftly transport a large crew, and navigate shallow waters. Predict the implication is that the streamlined design affected the vessel's performance, making it more *efficient* in a variety of seafaring situations. Choice (B) is correct.

25. C **Difficulty:** Easy

Category: Rhetoric

Getting to the Answer: Determine the overarching topic of Passage 2. Then ask yourself why the author wrote specifically about the Gokstad ship in relation to that topic. The correct answer will explain why the Gokstad ship offers an interesting perspective on the broader topic. Choice (C) is correct. By focusing on the Gokstad ship, the author can illustrate the advanced technical abilities of the Viking shipbuilders.

26. D **Difficulty:** Medium

Category: Inference

Getting to the Answer: Look for information that relates to each answer choice. The correct answer will be supported by facts and opinions stated in the passage. In Passage 2, paragraph 5, the author puts the Viking raids in the context of other means of livelihood, such as farming, fishing, and so on. It is logical to infer that raiding was one more way of making a living. Choice (D) is correct.

27. C **Difficulty:** Easy

Category: Command of Evidence

Getting to the Answer: Consider what reasoning led you to select the answer choice to the previous question. Read the lines in each answer choice. The correct answer will support your reasoning. Only lines 85-87 ("Their lands...opportunities") explain the relationship between the geography and the economic needs of the Vikings and support the idea that the Vikings turned to sea raiding as an economic livelihood. Choice (C) is correct.

28. B **Difficulty:** Easy

Category: Vocab-in-Context

Getting to the Answer: Think about the different meanings of "expression." Read the sentence in which the word appears and predict which meaning of the word best applies to that usage. In the sentence, predict that the author uses "expression" to show that the Gokstad *embodies*, or *brings together*, the best of Viking technical achievements. Therefore, (B) is correct.

29. A **Difficulty:** Easy

Category: Rhetoric

Getting to the Answer: Think about the figurative, rather than literal, meaning of the phrase "a great leap." This will help you answer the question. The author applies the phrase to seafaring and goes on to reference the technical achievements of the Vikings. Thus, (A) is correct.

30. D **Difficulty:** Medium

Category: Synthesis

Getting to the Answer: In order to make a generalization based on two different sources, compare the ideas presented by each. Determine what ideas the two sources have in common. Both passages deal with the shipbuilding and navigation abilities of the Vikings, and both highlight how those abilities led to the expansion of Viking civilization beyond Scandinavia. This expansion had economic, social, and cultural impacts on other peoples. Therefore, (D) is correct.

31. C   Difficulty: Medium

Category: Synthesis

Getting to the Answer: Remember that the correct answer must synthesize information in both passages and in the timeline. Several events in the timeline describe places that the Vikings "raided," "invaded, "settled," and so on. The passages both suggest that the Vikings used their seafaring skills to travel throughout Europe and across the Atlantic. Passage 2 specifically cites trade and sea raids. Choice (C) is correct, as it connects several events described in the timeline with the ideas contained in both passages.

Plant Fossils Passage

Suggested Passage Map notes:

¶1: Russ. Scientists found fossils of carnivorous plants in amber

¶2: details of amber; rare & important to find plants in it

¶3: only carnivorous fossil plant ever found, has leaves

¶4: how it gets nutrients

¶5: changes theory of where Rorid. originated

32. C   Difficulty: Easy

Category: Rhetoric

Getting to the Answer: Consider which answer choice most accurately describes the purpose of the entire passage. Do not be distracted by choices that might sound appropriate but are not the best

statement of purpose. The author's purpose is to inform readers of new plant fossil discoveries. Choice (C) is the correct answer.

33. B   Difficulty: Easy

Category: Inference

Getting to the Answer: Consider the main points the author makes throughout the passage. The correct answer will be directly related to these points, even if it is not directly stated in the passage. Throughout the passage, the author uses words such as "groundbreaking" (line 24) and "incredibly useful" (line 17) to describe the discovery of the new plant fossils. This suggests that the author considers these discoveries valuable. Therefore, (B) is the correct answer.

34. B   Difficulty: Medium

Category: Rhetoric

Getting to the Answer: Use your Passage Map to locate the author's description of amber and its role in scientific research. This will help you choose the correct answer. The author explains that animal fossils found in amber are important because these animals are not typically found elsewhere in the fossil record. Choice (B) is the correct answer.

35. C   Difficulty: Medium

Category: Command of Evidence

Getting to the Answer: Locate each of the answer choices in the passage. The correct answer will provide direct support for the answer to the previous question. Choice (C) is the correct answer, as it reflects the correct statement of the author's claim in the previous question.

36. C   Difficulty: Easy

Category: Vocab-in-Context

Getting to the Answer: Predict a word to replace "immaculately" that makes the most sense in context and does not change the meaning of the sentence. Since the amber becomes extremely hard and therefore preserves creatures for "long periods of time" (lines 15-16), the life forms must be very well preserved. Predict that in this context "immaculately" most nearly means *perfectly*. Choice (C) is the correct answer.

37. A   Difficulty: Medium

Category: Rhetoric

Getting to the Answer: Consult your Passage Map note for paragraph 1. Identify the central idea of the paragraph and consider how the phrase "rare and interesting" supports the idea. The author's use of the phrase "rare and interesting" supports the claim that the discovery of the fossilized carnivorous plants is important. Therefore, (A) is the correct answer.

38. B   Difficulty: Medium

Category: Inference

Getting to the Answer: Remember that with an Inference question, the correct answer is not explicitly stated in the passage. You must draw a logical conclusion based on the information provided. Throughout the passage, and especially in the final paragraph, the author discusses how the discovery of these plants fossilized in amber has challenged conclusions previously drawn by scientists. It is reasonable to infer, therefore, that future discoveries could change current theories. Choice (B) is the correct answer.

39. C   Difficulty: Easy

Category: Command of Evidence

Getting to the Answer: Avoid answers that provide evidence for incorrect answers to the previous question. In paragraph 5, the author explains how the new discoveries challenge conclusions previously drawn by scientists. This is the best support for the answer to the previous question, making (C) the correct answer.

40. A   Difficulty: Easy

Category: Detail

Getting to the Answer: Use your Passage Map to locate the paragraph that describes how the *Pameridea* insect and *Roridula* plant interact. Choice (A) is the correct answer. In paragraph 4, the author explains that the *Pameridea* insect is able to live on the *Roridula* plant because the insect makes a "greasy film" (lines 46-47) that prevents it from getting trapped by the plant.

41. C   Difficulty: Easy

Category: Vocab-in-Context

Getting to the Answer: All of the answer choices are close in meaning. Therefore, it is important to predict a word that could substitute for "thrive" in context. The sentence states that the plant fossils resemble the *Roridula*, a kind of plant that currently thrives in Africa. If the plant is still in Africa today, predict it is *growing*. In this context, "thrive" means "flourish." Choice (C) is the correct answer.

42. D   Difficulty: Easy

Category: Connections

Getting to the Answer: Review the passage, looking for details about how scientists' understanding of the plant changed. Your Passage Map for the last paragraph should include information about how scientists' conclusions were challenged. The fact that the fossilized Roridulaceae were discovered in Russia made scientists realize that the plant family, originally thought only to be found in Africa, had a much wider distribution across the world. Therefore, (D) is the correct answer.

Sunspots Passage

Suggested Passage Map notes:

¶1: details of sunspots & magnetic field

¶2: Samuel Schwabe – sunspots on 11 yr cycle

¶3: details of sunspots & solar flares; effect of flares on earth and satellites

¶4: Maunder Minimum – almost no sunspots 1645-1715 during Little Ice Age

¶5: may have another minimum in 20 yrs; info about sun and Earth's climate

43. C   Difficulty: Medium

Category: Global

Getting to the Answer: Avoid answers like B and D that include details but do not describe the central idea. Throughout the passage, the author includes information related to what scientists know about sunspots and solar flares. Choice (C) is the correct answer.

44. A   Difficulty: Medium

Category: Command of Evidence

Getting to the Answer: Locate each answer choice in the passage and think about whether it provides support for the correct answer to the previous question. The passage is concerned with what scientists know about sunspots and solar flares. Lines 5-10 refer to what scientists do and do not currently understand about sunspots, so (A) is the correct answer.

45. A   Difficulty: Hard

Category: Rhetoric

Getting to the Answer: Consider how the details about the enhanced auroras relate to the central idea of the paragraph in which they are discussed. In paragraph 3, the author describes the negative effects of solar flares on Earth. In the last sentence, the author describes a positive effect, the enhanced auroras, to provide a contrast with these negative effects. Therefore, (A) is the correct answer.

46. B   Difficulty: Medium

Category: Inference

Getting to the Answer: Use your Passage Map to locate details about the consequences of solar flare

activity on Earth. In paragraph 3, the author explains that solar flares can cause disruption to satellites and radio transmissions used for communication. Choice (B) is the correct answer.

47. C   Difficulty: Hard

Category: Rhetoric

Getting to the Answer: Consider the central idea of each paragraph mentioned in the answer choices. The correct answer will improve the paragraph by providing solid support for the central idea. The author explains in paragraph 3 that solar flares can cause disruptions to satellites and other technologies used in communications. An example of how these disruptions affect people on Earth would strengthen this claim. Therefore, (C) is the correct answer.

48. B   Difficulty: Medium

Category: Vocab-in-Context

Getting to the Answer: Predict a word that could substitute for "burst" in context. In the context of plasma suddenly exploding from the sun's surface, the correct answer is (B), "eruption."

49. A   Difficulty: Medium

Category: Inference

Getting to the Answer: Look for clues in the passage that suggest which statement is most likely true. Make a logical inference based on these clues. Choice (A) is correct. For much of the passage, the author refers to an 11-year cycle for sunspots. However, the passage also states in paragraph 4 that sunspots do not always follow an 11-year cycle. It is reasonable to infer that it is not always possible to predict when sunspot activity will occur. Choice B is incorrect because travel to the sun is never mentioned in the passage. Choice C excludes other possible ways of preventing communication interference. Choice D is incorrect because the passage states scientists do not think sunspot activity significantly impacts temperature.

50. C   Difficulty: Medium

Category: Command of Evidence

Getting to the Answer: Locate each of the answer choices in the passage. Decide which one provides the best support for the answer to the previous question. In the previous question, the correct answer dealt with how sunspot activity is not always predictable. In paragraph 4, the author states that "sunspots do not always follow the 11-year solar cycle." This makes (C) the best evidence for the answer to the previous question.

51. D   Difficulty: Medium

Category: Vocab-in-Context

Getting to the Answer: Think about the context of the sentence in which the word appears. Predict a synonym for "enhancing" that provides the appropriate nuance of meaning in light of this context. The sentence in which "enhancing" appears discusses auroras, the unusual light displays that appear near the North and South Poles. In the context of solar flares having a "positive effect" on the light displays with "increased energy," predict "enhancing" means *intensifying*, choice (D).

52. C   Difficulty: Medium

Category: Synthesis

Getting to the Answer: Carefully examine the graphic to see which answer choice has a direct relationship with information provided in the graphic. Choice (C), which describes the lack of sunspot activity between 1645 and 1715, is clearly depicted in the graphic.

WRITING AND LANGUAGE TEST

In Defense of *Don Quixote*

1. C   Difficulty: Medium

Category: Punctuation

Getting to the Answer: Determine whether the choice should be singular or plural. Then ask yourself if the noun is meant to show possession and what, if any, punctuation is required. There is only one class being discussed, so a singular choice that shows ownership of the novel, (C), is correct.

2. B   Difficulty: Medium

Category: Sentence Formation

Getting to the Answer: Examine the underlined sentence and identify the subjects and verbs. Based on your findings, is the sentence grammatically correct? The sentence is a run-on, as it contains two separate independent clauses. Because the second part of the sentence provides an explanation for the first part, a colon is the correct punctuation to be added between the two clauses. Choice (B) is correct.

3. C   Difficulty: Medium

Category: Effective Language Use

Getting to the Answer: Look for context clues to establish how the word is used in the sentence. Then test each choice for appropriateness. The passage describes a novel filled with opposites. "Clarified" implies that the content of *Quixote* is made clear, but the paragraph describes the novel as being filled with contradictions. "Peppered" is used here as a verb meaning scattered throughout. Choice (C) is correct.

4. D   Difficulty: Hard

Category: Usage

Getting to the Answer: Make a prediction about the best meaning for the targeted word based on the content of the entire paragraph. Then test each answer choice against your prediction. The paragraph describes the novel as "beautiful and strange," so you can predict that the characters will likely exhibit one or both of these qualities. "Adverse" is an adjective indicating a sense of harm, which doesn't make sense in the context of this paragraph. "Averse" indicates a strong dislike of something. "Bazaar" is a

Middle Eastern marketplace, while "bizarre" means "strange." Therefore, (D) is correct.

5. C — Difficulty: Easy

Category: Usage

Getting to the Answer: Examine the verb forms used throughout the paragraph. Look for inappropriate shifts in verb tense in the sentence. Test each choice by comparing it with the surrounding verbs. "Will have been" is future perfect tense and is used to express action that will be completed in the future. "Was" is the only past-tense choice that matches the past-tense verbs in the paragraph: "finished," "felt," "opened," and "visited." Choice (C) is correct.

6. C — Difficulty: Easy

Category: Usage

Getting to the Answer: Be sure to correctly identify the pronoun's antecedent and whether it is singular or plural. The pronoun refers to "students," which is plural, so you can narrow down the choices to "their" and "they're." "They're" is a contraction meaning "they are." "Their" expresses possession, and the defenses that will be presented in class belong to the students. Choice (C) is correct.

7. B — Difficulty: Medium

Category: Effective Language Use

Getting to the Answer: As you examine the answer choices, apply your knowledge of roots, prefixes, and suffixes to determine meanings. Also, look for context clues in the paragraph. The use of the word "enduring" in the sentence is a clue that "triviality," as written in the passage, is not consistent with the sentence's meaning. "Pertinence" means "relevance," so (B) is correct.

8. A — Difficulty: Medium

Category: Development

Getting to the Answer: Closely examine the topic sentence and the supporting details to identify the central idea of the paragraph. What piece of information enhances this idea? The focus of the paragraph is the global importance of Cervantes's masterpiece. Choice (A) is the only option that adds supporting information regarding the significance of the novel rather than the structure of the survey.

9. B — Difficulty: Medium

Category: Development

Getting to the Answer: Identify the central idea of the paragraph by summarizing the details of the sentences that follow. The supporting sentences in this paragraph praise Cervantes's novel. Choice (B) is the only one that fits by claiming the novel has "touched the far reaches of the literary world."

10. D — Difficulty: Easy

Category: Punctuation

Getting to the Answer: Determine whether there are multiple elements of the sentence requiring punctuation to separate them from one another. Without punctuation, this sentence becomes a run-on. It has three distinct clauses that need to be separated by semicolons. In the last clause, "beauty," "ugliness," and "combination" are part of a series requiring commas to separate them. Choice (D) is correct.

11. A — Difficulty: Medium

Category: Usage

Getting to the Answer: Recall that a pronoun must agree with its antecedent in number and in gender. Examine the other words in the sentence to find context clues. A collective noun such as "class" may be either singular or plural. It is singular when it refers to the group as a unit and plural when it refers to the individual members of the group. Because the passage refers to how the members of the "class began to discuss Quixote together," the correct pronoun choice is "their." Choice (A) is correct.

Women's Ingenuity

12. A   Difficulty: Easy

Category: Quantitative

Getting to the Answer: When analyzing a graphic, study what is being represented by each axis. Then re-read the passage sentence you're being asked to connect to the graphic. Choice (A) is the correct answer. According to the graphic, it is accurate that by 1870, the number of patents granted to women had more than doubled from the 1840 count of just twenty-one.

13. B   Difficulty: Easy

Category: Development

Getting to the Answer: Carefully read the paragraph to determine what information is extraneous to the main idea of the paragraph. The paragraph is about the accomplishments of female inventors, with a particular focus on Margaret Knight. Sentence 2 diverges from this topic, making (B) the correct answer.

14. C   Difficulty: Medium

Category: Effective Language Use

Getting to the Answer: See whether any words can be eliminated from this phrase to make the sentence flow more smoothly. The phrase as it currently stands is wordy and redundant. Editing the phrase down to "years later" still conveys the intended meaning. Choice (C) is the correct answer.

15. A   Difficulty: Medium

Category: Organization

Getting to the Answer: The correct answer should make clear the relationship between the man's theft of Knight's idea and Knight's choice to fight for her rights. The transition word should demonstrate a sequence. As written, "when" accomplishes this. Choice (A) is, therefore, the correct answer.

16. D   Difficulty: Medium

Category: Effective Language Use

Getting to the Answer: Look for a word that makes the qualities of the "victory" clear to readers. It should also match the tone of the rest of the passage. The quality the sentence is trying to convey about Knight's victory is how unusual it was, given her gender and the time period. Therefore, both "rare" and "inconceivable" might fit the expected meaning, but only "rare" conveys the appropriate academic tone because "inconceivable" would be an exaggeration. Choice (D) is correct.

17. B   Difficulty: Medium

Category: Effective Language Use

Getting to the Answer: Consider the context of the entire paragraph and think about what the underlined word should convey. Then eliminate any incorrect choices. The paragraph is about Knight's inventions over her lifetime and is structured chronologically. Choice (B), "subsequent," is correct because it expresses that these inventions came later, which is the only meaning that can be directly inferred from the paragraph.

18. A   Difficulty: Medium

Category: Development

Getting to the Answer: Consider which answer choice describes a way in which Knight perceived— and met—a demand as claimed in the topic sentence. The first sentence states that Knight's profession "helped her perceive the demand for an invention." Choice (A) provides direct support for this claim, citing an invention that was inspired by Knight's workplace. The other choices provide opinions or unrelated details rather than concrete evidence. Choice (A) is correct.

19. C   Difficulty: Easy

Category: Sentence Formation

Getting to the Answer: Remember that a compound sentence must be joined either with a conjunction or with appropriate punctuation; a comma is not sufficient. As written, the sentence joins a compound sentence with a comma but no conjunction, resulting in a comma splice. Choice (C) is the correct answer; it correctly uses a semicolon to join the two clauses and maintains the meaning of the original sentence.

20. B   Difficulty: Medium

Category: Sentence Formation

Getting to the Answer: Be careful to note the relationship between the different parts of this sentence. Different types of clauses are joined in different ways. The part of the sentence that follows "The progress of feminism in the twentieth century" is a subordinate clause that describes the kind of progress achieved. It is nonrestrictive and should therefore be separated by commas and begin with "which." Therefore, (B) is the correct answer.

21. D   Difficulty: Medium

Category: Punctuation

Getting to the Answer: Remember that an appositive is a word or phrase that identifies or renames a noun that comes right before it; when an appositive adds extra information, it is set off with commas. The phrase that follows "Dr. Carol B. Muller" is an appositive and should be set off with commas. Therefore, (D) is the correct answer.

22. A   Difficulty: Hard

Category: Development

Getting to the Answer: Read the entire paragraph and then read each of the choices. Decide which one is a fitting conclusion for the rest of the information in the paragraph. Note that the question asks for an appropriate conclusion for the paragraph, not a conclusion for the passage as a whole. In the previous sentence, the author states that if women can attain educational and leadership opportunities in science and technology, more patents by women will result. It is consistent with the idea and tone of this sentence to conclude the paragraph with (A), a sentence that expresses hope for this to occur.

Working from Home: Too Good to Be True?

23. A   Difficulty: Medium

Category: Punctuation

Getting to the Answer: Decide whether the second part of the sentence indicates a sharp break in thought or is a continuation of the previous thought. Then, examine the answer choices to find the one with the correct punctuation. The sentence is a continuous thought. Because no sharp break in content exists, only a comma is needed, and no colon or dash separation is necessary. Choice (A) is correct.

24. B   Difficulty: Easy

Category: Usage

Getting to the Answer: Ask yourself how the word is used in the sentence; try substituting each choice in its place. Use the other words in the sentence to provide context clues. "Compliant" is an adjective meaning "obedient." "Complaint" is a noun expressing dissatisfaction. The paragraph depicts the negative aspects and false promises of work-from-home advertisers, so (B) is the correct answer.

25. D   Difficulty: Medium

Category: Development

Getting to the Answer: Closely examine the topic sentence and the supporting details; identify the central idea of the paragraph. The paragraph explains that most of these business opportunities give false promises. Choice (D) is the only option that adds supporting evidence, proving that most work-from-home opportunities are scams.

26. B   Difficulty: Easy

Category: Usage

Getting to the Answer: Identify the subject of the paragraph and determine its number; look for pronoun clues in the surrounding sentences. Determine whether the adjacent pronouns are singular or plural. A pronoun must agree in number with its antecedent. The antecedent, "scams," appears in the first sentence of the paragraph. The pronoun "they" is the only choice that is plural; therefore, (B) is correct.

27. C   Difficulty: Hard

Category: Development

Getting to the Answer: Based on the supporting sentences, identify the central idea of the paragraph. In other words, identify what the sentences have in common. All the sentences in this paragraph refer to the fees required and the loss of the investment, so (C) is correct.

28. B   Difficulty: Easy

Category: Effective Language Use

Getting to the Answer: Look for context clues to establish how the word is used in the sentence and consider the content of the entire paragraph. Then, test each choice for appropriateness. The passage describes the fees as being required before work can begin. "Certification" is a noun that means "a state of being certified or endorsed" and is inappropriate here. Choice (B), "registration," is a noun meaning "the act of enrolling in a program," so it is the correct choice.

29. A   Difficulty: Medium

Category: Sentence Formation

Getting to the Answer: Examine the grammatical forms used in the sentence. A sentence reads smoothly when the writer puts parallel ideas in the same grammatical form. For example, a series of nouns mixed with gerunds creates an awkward sentence. The gerunds "stuffing," "assembling," and "entering" express each activity in the same grammatical form. Choice (A) is correct.

30. C   Difficulty: Medium

Category: Punctuation

Getting to the Answer: Determine whether the underlined phrase is essential or nonessential to the meaning of the sentence. Essential elements should not be set off by punctuation; nonessential elements must be set off by punctuation. The phrase "with which to lodge complaints" is an essential element of the sentence because it is needed to explain the type of service department being described. No punctuation should be used, and the addition of parentheses or dashes complicates the sentence. Choice (C) is correct.

31. D   Difficulty: Easy

Category: Usage

Getting to the Answer: Test the choices individually. Look for other words in the sentence that might provide context clues. "They" is a pronoun, and "They're" is a contraction meaning "they are." "Their" expresses possession. None of these words makes sense in the context of the sentence. Choice (D), "There," is correct.

32. C   Difficulty: Easy

Category: Effective Language Use

Getting to the Answer: Examine the sentence in relation to other sentences in the paragraph; think about the content of the paragraph and the passage as you test each choice in the sentence. The paragraph warns against the false belief that it is possible to gain something from nothing. The noun "distortion," meaning "a warping of the truth," is incorrect because the "fast tracks to wealth" have not been "warped." Choice (C), "illusion," means "a false belief." It is more precise and is therefore correct.

33. D   Difficulty: Hard

Category: Sentence Formation

Getting to the Answer: Modifiers are words or phrases intended to make meanings more specific.

They are placed as near as possible to the words they modify. Misplaced or dangling modifiers make the writer's meaning difficult to comprehend. Try to identify the missing word or phrase that will make the sentence clear and sensible. "Starting in a career field" needs to be changed to an adverb clause by adding "When" so that it is clear how "you" will earn the dividends. Choice (D) is correct.

Is Gluten-Free the Way to Be?

34. D   Difficulty: Medium

Category: Development

Getting to the Answer: To find the central idea of a paragraph, read through it and get the general idea of the paragraph's focus. Then, summarize what seems to be the central idea. Select the choice that is the closest to your summary. This opening paragraph is mostly about people trying gluten-free diets. Choice (D) is therefore the correct answer.

35. C   Difficulty: Easy

Category: Effective Language Use

Getting to the Answer: Watch out for choices that are extremely wordy or that change the meaning of what is being communicated. It is better to be as direct and simple as possible. Choice (C) is the most concise and effective way of stating the information, so it is the correct answer.

36. D   Difficulty: Medium

Category: Effective Language Use

Getting to the Answer: Pretend the underlined word is a blank in the sentence. Predict what word could be substituted for the blank. Then, choose the word closest in meaning to your prediction. The word "even" helps you identify the correct answer choice. You might predict the word *little*, and "trace" would be a synonym for your choice. Choice (D) has the correct connotation and fits within the context of the sentence.

37. B   Difficulty: Easy

Category: Punctuation

Getting to the Answer: Study the words in a series, checking for the proper punctuation. Recall that lists of three or more items require commas after each item. Choice (B) has the correct punctuation.

38. B   Difficulty: Medium

Category: Effective Language Use

Getting to the Answer: Watch out for choices that may have incorrect transition words. The word "and" joins the sentences concisely and correctly. Choice (B) is correct.

39. B   Difficulty: Medium

Category: Quantitative

Getting to the Answer: The graphic gives specific information about how many of those people surveyed were trying to cut back or avoid gluten in their diet during specific years. Study the graphic in order to select the correct answer choice. Choice (B) accurately reflects the information in the graphic. None of the other choices presents a valid interpretation of the data.

40. C   Difficulty: Hard

Category: Development

Getting to the Answer: First, reread sentence 4 to identify the claim. Then, look for the answer choice that supports this claim with specific details. Sentence 4 claims that some people on a gluten-free diet feel better "because they have celiac disease but have never been diagnosed." Choice (C) best supports this claim because it provides specific numbers from a study about celiac disease.

41. B   Difficulty: Easy

Category: Sentence Formation

Getting to the Answer: Two complete thoughts should be two separate sentences. Be careful of inappropriate transition words. A period and a capital letter will divide the two complete thoughts correctly. Choice (B) is the correct answer.

42. C   Difficulty: Easy

Category: Organization

Getting to the Answer: Look for the relationship between this sentence and the previous one. This will help you choose the appropriate transition word. Choice (C) shows the relationship between the two sentences by emphasizing that, in contrast to the previous sentence, some people were affected by the gluten pill.

43. B   Difficulty: Easy

Category: Sentence Formation

Getting to the Answer: Verbs that have the same level of importance in a sentence must be in parallel form. Check to see if this is true here. Choice (B) is the correct answer. The verb "does" is in the singular present tense, and so is "benefits."

44. D   Difficulty: Easy

Category: Effective Language Use

Getting to the Answer: Use the context of the sentence to predict a word that fits best. Because doctors "originally" thought something different, predict they suspected there were fewer benefits. Choice (D) is correct.

MATH—NO CALCULATOR TEST

1. B   Difficulty: Easy

Category: Heart of Algebra / Linear Equations

Getting to the Answer: Determine from the table the number of people who ride the swings on a single run (the unit rate, or slope). If 28 people have ridden the swings after they have been run 2 times, this means $28 \div 2 = 14$ people ride the swings each time. Therefore, when the swings have been run 8 times,

$14 \times 8 = 112$ people will have ridden them, which is (B).

2. A   Difficulty: Easy

Category: Passport to Advanced Math / Exponents

Getting to the Answer: A variable with a fraction exponent can be written as a radical expression by writing the numerator of the fraction as the power of the radicand and the denominator as the degree (also called the index) of the root. For example, $x^{\frac{2}{3}} = \sqrt[3]{x^2}$. Start by reducing the fraction in the exponent: $\frac{2}{6} = \frac{1}{3}$. The variable a is being raised to the $\frac{1}{3}$ power, so rewrite the term as a radical expression with a 3 as the degree of the root and 1 as the power to which a is being raised.

$$a^{\frac{2}{6}} = a^{\frac{1}{3}} = \sqrt[3]{a^1} = \sqrt[3]{a}$$

Choice (A) is correct.

3. C   Difficulty: Easy

Category: Heart of Algebra / Inequalities

Getting to the Answer: The clue "holds a maximum" means it can hold exactly that much or less, so use the symbol ≤. This means you can eliminate B. The box can hold a maximum of 20 textbooks, so the first inequality is $t \le 20$. The box can hold a maximum of 64 workbooks, so the second inequality is $w \le 64$ (eliminate D). The third inequality deals with the size of each book. The box can fit t textbooks multiplied by the size of the textbook, 192 cubic inches, and w workbooks multiplied by the size of the workbook, 60 cubic inches. The box can fit a maximum of 3,840 cubic inches total, so the last inequality is $192t + 60w \le 3{,}840$. Together, the inequalities form the system in (C).

4. D   Difficulty: Medium

Category: Passport to Advanced Math / Functions

Getting to the Answer: The domain of a function represents the possible values of x, or the input values. In this function, x is represented by a, which is the number of athletes who participated in the study. Because there cannot be a negative number of athletes or a fraction of an athlete, the list in (D) is the only one that could represent a portion of the function's domain.

5. D **Difficulty:** Medium

Category: Heart of Algebra / Linear Equations

Getting to the Answer: Check to see whether the change in the y-values compared with the change in the x-values is constant for each pair of values. The table in (D) does not represent a linear relationship because the x-values change by $+1$ each time, while the y-values change by -3, then -1, then $+1$, then $+3$. A linear relationship has a constant rate of change, which means it is either always increasing or always decreasing by the same amount. This data clearly changes direction and is therefore not linear.

6. D **Difficulty:** Medium

Category: Heart of Algebra / Systems of Linear Equations

Getting to the Answer: If the graphs intersect at $(4, -1)$, then the solution to the system is $x = 4$ and $y = -1$. Substitute the values of x and y into each equation and solve for A and B. Then, divide B by A.

$$Ax - 2y = 18 \qquad Bx + 6y = 26$$
$$A(4) - 2(-1) = 18 \qquad B(4) + 6(-1) = 26$$
$$4A + 2 = 18 \qquad 4B - 6 = 26$$
$$4A = 16 \qquad 4B = 32$$
$$A = 4 \qquad B = 8$$

Therefore, $\dfrac{B}{A} = \dfrac{8}{4} = 2$, which is (D).

7. B **Difficulty:** Medium

Category: Passport to Advanced Math / Quadratics

Getting to the Answer: Factoring the quadratic equations could give you information about the x-intercepts, but upon inspection, A and (B) can't

be factored. As an alternate strategy, find the axis of symmetry using the formula $x = -\dfrac{b}{2a}$ (the quadratic formula without the radical part) to determine in which quadrant the vertex lies. You are looking for an equation whose graph has its vertex in the third quadrant. Choice (B) is correct because $x = -\dfrac{(4)}{2(1)} = -\dfrac{4}{2} = -2$, and when -2 is substituted into the equation $y = (-2)^2 + 4(-2) - 4 = -8$, it puts the vertex at $(-2, -8)$, which is in the third quadrant and matches the graph.

8. B **Difficulty:** Medium

Category: Additional Topics in Math / Geometry

Getting to the Answer: The area of a sector is equal to the area of the circle times the fraction of the circle represented by the sector. Start by finding the area of the whole circle: The diameter of the circle extends along the x-axis from -7 to 5, which is 12 units, which means the radius is 6. Substitute this into the area formula:

$$A = \pi r^2$$
$$A = \pi (6)^2$$
$$A = 36\pi$$

There are 360 degrees in a whole circle, so the fraction of the circle represented by the sector is $\dfrac{60}{360} = \dfrac{1}{6}$. The area of the sector is $\dfrac{1}{6} \times 36\pi = 6\pi$ square units, (B).

9. D **Difficulty:** Medium

Category: Passport to Advanced Math / Exponents

Getting to the Answer: Use the rules for radicals to simplify the product. Don't actually try to find the value of each answer choice. When two radical expressions with the same degree root are multiplied, you can multiply the numbers under the radicals, leaving the product inside. The root stays the same. Writing 0.25 as $\dfrac{1}{4}$ may make finding the product easier:

$$\sqrt{0.25} \times \sqrt{2} = \sqrt{\frac{1}{4} \times 2} = \sqrt{\frac{1}{2}} = \frac{1}{\sqrt{2}}$$

It's not proper to leave a radical in the denominator (and this is not one of the answer choices), so rewrite the expression by multiplying the top and bottom by $\sqrt{2}$ to get $\frac{1}{\sqrt{2}} \times \frac{\sqrt{2}}{\sqrt{2}} = \frac{\sqrt{2}}{2}$, which is (D).

10. C   Difficulty: Medium

Category: Heart of Algebra / Linear Equations

Getting to the Answer: Start by finding the rate at which the blended fabric is produced according to the graph. To do this, find the slope by picking two points and using the formula $m = \frac{y_2 - y_1}{x_2 - x_1}$. Pay careful attention to how the grid-lines are labeled. Using the points (0, 0) and (2, 60), the slope is $m = \frac{60 - 0}{2 - 0} = \frac{60}{2} = 30$, which means the machine produces 30 square yards of the blended fabric per hour. The question states that the machine can produce the 100% polyester fabric at a rate of 40 square yards per hour. Now, determine how long it would take the machine to produce 2,400 yards of each fabric:

Blended: 2,400 ÷ 30 = 80 hours

100% polyester: 2,400 ÷ 40 = 60 hours

This means it will take 20 more hours to make the blended fabric than the 100% polyester fabric, which matches (C).

11. D   Difficulty: Hard

Category: Passport to Advanced Math / Exponents

Getting to the Answer: Use long division to divide the two expressions. Don't forget to fill in 0 as a placeholder for the missing x^3 term.

$$\begin{array}{r} 6x^3 - 12x^2 + 26x - 60 \\ x + 2 \overline{\smash{\big)}\ 6x^4 + 0x^3 + 2x^2 - 8x - c} \\ \underline{-(6x^4 + 12x^3)} \\ -12x^3 + 2x^2 - 8x - c \\ \underline{-(-12x^3 - 24x^2)} \\ 26x^2 - 8x - c \\ \underline{-(26x^2 + 52x)} \\ -60x - c \\ \underline{-(-60x - 120)} \\ -c + 120 \end{array}$$

To make sure there is no remainder, c would have to be 120, (D).

12. D   Difficulty: Hard

Category: Heart of Algebra / Inequalities

Getting to the Answer: The system in the graph shows shading on opposite sides of two parallel lines, which means there is no solution to the system. This means you're looking for two equations with the same slope, different y-intercepts, and different inequality symbols. The equations are all given in standard form ($Ax + By = C$). It would be very time-intensive to convert all four systems to slope-intercept form, so look for ways to eliminate choices more quickly. Each line in the graph falls 1 unit and runs 3 units, so you need to find two lines that have a slope of $-\frac{1}{3}$. Use the trick $m = \frac{-A}{B}$ to quickly determine the slopes. The lines in A have a slope of $\frac{-3}{-1} = 3$, so eliminate A; the lines in B have a slope of $\frac{-3}{1} = -3$, so eliminate B; the lines in C have a slope of $\frac{-1}{-3} = \frac{1}{3}$, so eliminate C (pay attention to the sign). This means (D) must be correct. The lines in (D) have a slope of $\frac{-1}{3} = -\frac{1}{3}$, which matches the graph. You don't have to check the shading because none of the other slopes were a match.

13. C   **Difficulty:** Hard

Category: Passport to Advanced Math / Scatterplots

Getting to the Answer: The question asks for the sum of the vertical height and the horizontal distance that the roller coaster will travel above ground. The data points follow a parabolic (U-shaped) path, which means you can use properties of quadratic equations to find the solution. The vertical height is fairly straightforward—the vertex of the parabola is located at (110, 80), so the vertical height that the roller coaster reaches is 80 yards (notice the units). To find the horizontal distance, think about symmetry. Because the vertex occurs at a distance of 110 feet, the total horizontal distance that the roller coaster will travel is twice that, or 220 feet. Convert 80 yards to feet and add the result to 220 to arrive at the correct answer, $80 \times 3 = 240$ and $240 + 220 = 460$ feet.

14. A   **Difficulty:** Hard

Category: Additional Topics in Math / Imaginary Numbers

Getting to the Answer: Fractions with complex numbers are no different from any other fraction. You must find a common denominator before adding them. Find a common denominator by multiplying the second term by $i + 6$. You're given that $\sqrt{-1} = i$, but a more useful fact is that $i^2 = -1$, so be sure to make this substitution as you go. Once you have found the common denominator, you can simply add like terms.

$$\frac{2}{i + 6} + (2 + 5i) = \frac{2}{i + 6} + \frac{2 + 5i}{1}$$
$$= \frac{2}{i + 6} + \frac{2 + 5i}{1}\left(\frac{i + 6}{i + 6}\right)$$
$$= \frac{2}{i + 6} + \frac{2i + 12 + 5(-1) + 30i}{i + 6}$$
$$= \frac{2}{i + 6} + \frac{32i + 7}{i + 6}$$
$$= \frac{32i + 9}{i + 6}$$

This matches (A).

15. A   **Difficulty:** Medium

Category: Passport to Advanced Math / Functions

Getting to the Answer: Understanding function notation is the key to answering a question like this. For example, when you're given an equation written in function notation, $g(5)$ means to substitute 5 for each x in the equation and simplify. Similarly, $g(-2x)$ means to substitute $-2x$ for each x in the equation and simplify. Be very careful when squaring the negative term—it becomes positive.

$$g(x) = 4x^2 - x + 5$$
$$g(-2x) = 4(-2x)^2 - (-2x) + 5$$
$$= 4(-2x)(-2x) + 2x + 5$$
$$= 4(4x^2) + 2x + 5$$
$$= 16x^2 + 2x + 5$$

Choice (A) is correct.

16. 3/2 or 1.5   **Difficulty:** Easy

Category: Heart of Algebra / Linear Equations

Getting to the Answer: Multiply each term in the equation by 10 to move the decimal one place to the right, which eliminates all the decimals. Then, solve as usual:

$$10(0.2x + 1.8 = 3 - 0.6x)$$
$$2x + 18 = 30 - 6x$$
$$8x = 12$$
$$x = \frac{12}{8} = \frac{3}{2}$$

17. 0   **Difficulty:** Medium

Category: Heart of Algebra / Systems of Linear Equations

Getting to the Answer: The solution to the system is the point that both tables will have in common, but the tables, as given, do not share any points. You could use the data to write the equation of each line and then solve the system, but this would use up valuable time on Test Day. Instead, whenever data is presented in a table, look for patterns that can be extended.

In the table on the left, the x-values decrease by 1 each time and the y-values increase by 3. In the table on the right, the x-values increase by 2 each time and the y-values increase by 1. Use these patterns to continue the tables.

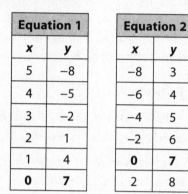

Equation 1	
x	**y**
5	−8
4	−5
3	−2
2	1
1	4
0	**7**

Equation 2	
x	**y**
−8	3
−6	4
−4	5
−2	6
0	**7**
2	8

The point (0, 7) satisfies both equations, so the x-coordinate of the solution to the system is 0.

18. 12   Difficulty: Medium

Category: Passport to Advanced Math / Exponents

Getting to the Answer: Solving an equation that has a fractional exponent can be very intimidating, so rewrite that part of the equation using a radical instead. Then, solve the equation the same way you would any other: Isolate the variable using inverse operations, one step at a time. After rewriting the equation using a radical, start by subtracting 18 from both sides. Next, multiply both sides of the equation by −2. Then, square both sides to remove the radical. Finally, divide both sides by 3.

$$18 - \frac{(3x)^{\frac{1}{2}}}{2} = 15$$

$$18 - \frac{\sqrt{3x}}{2} = 15$$

$$-\frac{\sqrt{3x}}{2} = -3$$

$$\sqrt{3x} = 6$$

$$3x = 36$$

$$x = 12$$

19. 3600   Difficulty: Medium

Category: Additional Topics in Math / Geometry

Getting to the Answer: Determine the dimensions of the tank in which there will be water. Then, use the formula for finding the volume of a rectangular prism: Volume = length × width × height. The tank is 30 inches long, 15 inches tall, and 12 inches wide. The sand and the space left at the top of the tank do not affect the length or the width, only the height of the water. There are 2 inches of sand in the bottom and 3 inches of space left at the top, which means the height of the water is 15 − 2 − 3 = 10 inches. Use the formula Volume = l × w × h = 30 × 12 × 10. To multiply the numbers without a calculator, multiply 3 × 1 × 12 = 36 and then add two zeros to get 3,600 cubic inches of water.

20. 11   Difficulty: Hard

Category: Passport to Advanced Math / Functions

Getting to the Answer: This question is, for the most part, conceptual. Start by finding the y-coordinate of P in the original equation. Then, perform the transformation on the coordinates (rather than the function) to save yourself valuable time. Substitute 1 for x in the original equation. Graphically, the resulting value of g(1) is the y-coordinate of the point.

$$g(x) = 2x^3 - 5x^2 + 4x + 6$$

$$= 2(1)^3 - 5(1)^2 + 4(1) + 6$$

$$= 2 - 5 + 4 + 6$$

$$= 7$$

The point on the graph of $g(x)$ is (1, 7). Now, the question asks for the y-coordinate of the corresponding point on the transformed graph. When performing transformations, the operations grouped with the x are performed on the x-coordinate, and the operations *not* grouped with the x are performed on the y-coordinate. So, add 4 to 7 to find that the y-coordinate of the point on the transformed graph is 11.

MATH—CALCULATOR TEST

1. A   Difficulty: Easy

Category: Problem Solving and Data Analysis / Scatterplots

Getting to the Answer: You're looking for the equation that best matches the line drawn through the data points. The best-fit line begins at the origin, which means the y-intercept is 0 (the b in the equation $y = mx + b$), so you can eliminate C and D. Now, find the slope of the line. Between (0, 0) and (8, 4), the line rises 4 units and runs 8 units, so the slope is $\frac{4}{8} = \frac{1}{2}$, which is equivalent to 0.5. This means (A) is correct.

2. B   Difficulty: Easy

Category: Heart of Algebra / Linear Equations

Getting to the Answer: A horizontal line has a slope of 0. Lines that slant downward from left to right have a negative slope, and lines that slant upward from left to right have a positive slope. Only one line has a negative slope, S, so it should come first in the list. This means you can eliminate A and D. Next comes the horizontal line with a slope of 0, which is line U. You can now eliminate C, which means (B) must be correct. To confirm (which isn't absolutely necessary), there are two lines with positive slopes: R and T. Line T has a steeper slant than line R, which means line T has a greater slope; therefore, the correct ordering is S, U, R, T.

3. C   Difficulty: Easy

Category: Heart of Algebra / Inequalities

Getting to the Answer: Algebraically, the solution to a system of inequalities is an ordered pair that satisfies *both* inequalities. Graphically, this means the ordered pair falls within the intersection (overlap) of the two shaded regions. The point (2, 5) lies within the intersection of the two shaded regions, so it is a solution to the system. None of the other points lie within the intersection, so (C) is correct.

4. C   Difficulty: Easy

Category: Problem Solving and Data Analysis / Rates, Ratios, Proportions, and Percentages

Getting to the Answer: Don't let the three-way ratio confuse you. You can answer this question just like any other ratio question. Before selecting your answer, make sure you answered the right question (how many *more* votes for the Independent candidate than for the Republican candidate).

Set up an equation using parts: 19 parts of the vote were cast for the Independent candidate, 18 parts for the Democrat, and 13 parts for the Republican. You don't know how big a part is, so call it x. Now, write and solve an equation:

$$19x + 18x + 13x = 510,000$$
$$50x = 510,000$$
$$x = 10,200$$

This means each part is equal to 10,200 votes. Now, you could multiply 19 by this number and 13 by this number, and then subtract. Or, you could recognize that the Independent received $19 - 13 = 6$ more parts of the vote than the Republican, or 6(10,200) = 61,200 more votes, which is (C).

5. B   Difficulty: Easy

Category: Problem Solving and Data Analysis / Rates, Ratios, Proportions, and Percentages

Getting to the Answer: Don't spend too much time reviewing the context of the question. Focus on the last couple of sentences, which tell you what you're looking for. You need to find the percent of states that use the Missouri Plan. There are 15 states that use the Missouri Plan and 50 states total, so use the formula Whole × percent = part. The whole is 50, the percent is unknown so call it x, and the part is 15, resulting in the equation $50x = 15$. Use division to find that x is $15 \div 50 = 0.3 = 30\%$, (B).

6. B   **Difficulty:** Easy

Category: Heart of Algebra / Linear Equations

Getting to the Answer: All you need to do is substitute 197 (number of seeds) for s and solve for r (rainfall) using inverse operations.

$$197 = 28.5r + 83$$
$$114 = 28.5r$$
$$4 = r$$

This means (B) is correct.

7. A   **Difficulty:** Medium

Category: Problem Solving and Data Analysis / Scatterplots

Getting to the Answer: The dendrologist uses an exponential function to model the data. When an exponential equation is written in the form of $f(x) = ab^x$, a is the starting amount and b is the rate of growth or decay. The dendrologist is studying the number of leaves shed, not the number of leaves left on the tree, so you can eliminate C and D. Remember, a is the starting amount, not the unit of time, so it can't represent the number of days, which means you can also eliminate B. Choice (A) is correct because 1.92 is b in the equation, which represents the growth rate, so it tells the dendrologist that the number of leaves shed almost doubles (192% is very close to 200%) each day.

8. D   **Difficulty:** Medium

Category: Heart of Algebra / Inequalities

Getting to the Answer: There is an open dot on the number line, which means the sign must be < or >,

so you can eliminate A and B. To decide between C and (D), you don't even need to solve the equation. Instead, look at the shading. The graph is shaded to the left, which means the graph shows $a < -4$. However, there is a negative sign in front of the a term, so the inequality will be reversed at some point in the solution, which means the original inequality sign must have been >. The correct answer is (D). You can check your answer by solving the inequality using the sign you chose. If you chose correctly, your answer should match the graph.

9. D   **Difficulty:** Medium

Category: Heart of Algebra / Linear Equations

Getting to the Answer: Take a quick peek at the answer choices. The equations are given in slope-intercept form, so start by finding the slope. This can be done by substituting two pairs of values from the table (try to pick easy ones, if possible) into the slope formula, $m = \dfrac{y_2 - y_1}{x_2 - x_1}$. Keep in mind that the projected number of units sold depends on the price, so the price is the independent variable (x) and the projected number is the dependent variable (y). Using the points (0.2, 150,000) and (0.4, 90,000), the slope is:

$$m = \frac{150,000 - 90,000}{0.2 - 0.4}$$
$$m = \frac{60,000}{-0.2}$$
$$m = -300,000$$

This means you can eliminate A and B because the slope is not correct. Don't let B fool you—the projected number of units sold goes down as the price goes up, so there is an inverse relationship, which means the slope must be negative. To choose between C and (D), you could find the y-intercept of the line, but this is a fairly time-intensive process. Instead, choose any pair of values from the table, such as (0.2, 150,000), and substitute into C and (D) only. Choice (D) is correct because 150,000 is indeed equal to $-300,000(0.2) + 210,000$.

10. A   Difficulty: Medium

Category: Heart of Algebra / Systems of Linear Equations

Getting to the Answer: Create a system of linear equations where e represents the number of packs with 8 boxes and t represents the number of packs with 20 boxes. Before selecting your final answer, make sure you answered the right question (the number of packs that have 20 boxes). The first equation should represent the total number of packs, $e + t = 61$. The second equation should represent the total number of boxes. Because e represents packs with 8 boxes and t represents packs with 20 boxes, the second equation should be $8e + 20t = 800$. Now, solve the system using substitution. Solve the first equation to find that $e = 61 - t$. Then, substitute the result into the second equation:

$$8e + 20t = 800$$
$$8(61 - t) + 20t = 800$$
$$488 - 8t + 20t = 800$$
$$488 + 12t = 800$$
$$12t = 312$$
$$t = 26$$

Because t represents the number of packs with 20 boxes, 26 packs have 20 boxes. This is what the question asks for, so you don't need to find the value of e. Choice (A) is correct.

11. C   Difficulty: Medium

Category: Additional Topics in Math / Imaginary Numbers

Getting to the Answer: To evaluate a high power of i, look for patterns and use the definition $\sqrt{-1} = i$ which, when written in a more useful form, is $i^2 = -1$. Write out enough powers of i for you to see the pattern:

$$i^1 = i$$
$$i^2 = -1 \, (\text{definition})$$
$$i^3 = i \times i^2 = i \times -1 = -i$$
$$i^4 = i^2 \times i^2 = -1 \times -1 = 1$$
$$i^5 = i^4 \times i = 1 \times i = i$$
$$i^6 = i^4 \times i^2 = 1 \times -1 = -1$$
$$i^7 = i^6 \times i = -1 \times i = -i$$
$$i^8 = i^4 \times i^4 = 1 \times 1 = 1$$

Notice that the pattern $(i, -1, -i, 1, i, -1, -i, 1)$ repeats on a cycle of 4. To evaluate i^{125}, divide 125 by 4. The result is 31, remainder 1, which means 31 full cycles and then back to i^1. This means i^{125} is equivalent to i^1, which is i. Because $i + i = 2i$, you are looking for the answer choice that is also equivalent to $2i$. Choices (C) and D look tempting (because of the 2), so start with them: (C) is correct because $45 \div 4 = 11$, remainder 1, which means i^{45} is equivalent to i and $2i^{45}$ is equal to $2i$.

12. A   Difficulty: Medium

Category: Passport to Advanced Math / Exponents

Getting to the Answer: Find the greatest common factor (GCF) that can be divided out of all of the terms in the expression. You need to find the greatest number and the variable to the highest power that each term has in common. To make finding the GCF easier, ignore the 2s in the denominators until you've decided on a GCF and then put the 2 back in. The greatest number that 9, 3, and 15 have in common is 3, so the GCF (with the 2 back in the denominator) is $\frac{3}{2}$. All terms in the expression have at least x^8, so you can also factor out x^8 from each term.

$$-\frac{9}{2}x^{10} - \frac{3}{2}x^9 + \frac{15}{2}x^8$$
$$= \frac{3}{2}x^8(-3x^2 - x + 5)$$

Unfortunately, this isn't one of the answer choices. However, in (A), $-\frac{3}{2}$ has been factored out, and all of the signs of the terms are reversed. This answer is equivalent to the one found above and is therefore correct.

13. A   Difficulty: Medium

Category: Passport to Advanced Math / Functions

Getting to the Answer: Pay careful attention to the axis labels as you read the answer choices. Time is graphed on the *x*-axis, and distance is graphed on the *y*-axis. Compare each answer choice to the graph, eliminating false statements as you go.

Choice (A): The truck is stopped when it is making a delivery. This means its distance is not changing, and the graph should be flat. Both flat sections of the graph span 30 minutes (20 to 50 and 70 to 100), so each delivery took 30 minutes. Choice (A) is correct. If you're confident in your answer, move on to the next question. If not, you can quickly check the other answer choices to be sure.

Choice B: The second delivery starts at (70, 18), which means it was about 18 miles away from the warehouse, not 70.

Choice C: When the truck arrived at the first delivery, it was about 8 miles from the warehouse, and when it was at the second delivery, it was about 18 miles from the warehouse. Then, it had to travel 18 miles back to the warehouse, so it traveled a total of 36 miles, not 18.

Choice D: The second delivery took place 18 miles from the warehouse, and the first delivery took place 8 miles from the warehouse, which means the second delivery was about 10 miles farther from the warehouse, not 18.

14. B   Difficulty: Medium

Category: Problem Solving and Data Analysis / Statistics and Probability

Getting to the Answer: Start by filling in any cells in the table that you can, using the information provided in the table itself (kind of like a sudoku puzzle).

Because there are 628 trees total and 402 are hybrids, you know that $628 - 402 = 226$ are not hybrids. Then, because 118 orange trees are not hybrids, you know that $226 - 118 = 108$ apple trees are not hybrids. Now, you've reached the point at which the table can't help you anymore. So, look at the question. It says that 45% of the apple trees are not hybrids. Use the formula Percent × whole = part to arrive at the equation $0.45w = 108$. Then, solve for *w* by dividing: $108 \div 0.45 = 240$, which tells you there are 240 apple trees in total. This means there are $240 - 108 = 132$ apple trees that are hybrids.

15. D   Difficulty: Medium

Category: Problem Solving and Data Analysis / Statistics and Probability

Getting to the Answer: Start by completing the rest of the table. Use the information you found in the previous question.

Because there are 402 hybrids in total, there are $402 - 132 = 270$ orange trees that are hybrids, which means there are $270 + 118 = 388$ orange trees in total. Now, find the probability that if the scientist selects one orange tree, it will be a hybrid. There are 388 orange trees total, and of those, 270 are hybrids, so the probability of picking a hybrid is $\frac{270}{388} = \frac{135}{194}$, which is (D).

16. C   Difficulty: Medium

Category: Passport to Advanced Math / Exponents

Getting to the Answer: Division and factoring are interchangeable, so think of factoring out the *x*. Then, instead of dividing by $\frac{1}{2}$, you can multiply by its reciprocal, 2. Using these two strategies will make solving a question like this considerably easier. First, divide (factor) out the *x* by subtracting 1 from each exponent:

$$\left(5x^4 - \frac{1}{4}x^3 + 3x\right) \div x = 5x^3 - \frac{1}{4}x^2 + 3$$

Now, multiply each term by 2 to get:

$$\left(5x^3 - \frac{1}{4}x^2 + 3\right) \div \frac{1}{2} = 2\left(5x^3 - \frac{1}{4}x^2 + 3\right)$$

$$= 10x^3 - \frac{1}{2}x^2 + 6$$

This matches (C).

17. C   Difficulty: Medium

Category: Heart of Algebra / Linear Equations

Getting to the Answer: Be careful—the 0 in the table is an *x*-value, which means it shows the *y*-intercept, not the *x*-intercept. You are looking for the point at which *y* = 0. You could use two of the points in the table and the slope formula to find the equation of the line, then substitute 0 for *y* and solve for *x*. However, this would use up valuable time. Instead, look for a pattern in the table. If you continue the pattern, the next ordered pair would be (3, −1), which would mean the line has dropped below the *x*-axis. This means the graph of the line crosses the *x*-axis somewhere between the *x*-values of 2 and 3. The only answer choice that is between 2 and 3 is (C).

18. C   Difficulty: Medium

Category: Problem Solving and Data Analysis / Rates, Ratios, Proportions, and Percentages

Getting to the Answer: There are a few ways to answer this question. You could think it through logically and use a weighted average for the two climb rates, or you could use the DIRT equation to set up two equations representing the climb up and the climb down. Using the second method, recall that Distance = rate × time. The tourist climbed up the mountain at a rate of 264 meters per hour for *x* hours, so the distance is *d* = 264*x* meters. She climbed down twice as fast (or 2(264)), and it took her 7 hours in all, so this part of the climb took 7 − *x* hours, making the distance *d* = 2(264)(7 − *x*) meters. Because the distance up the mountain is equal to the distance down the mountain (taking the same route), you can set the two equations equal to find the amount of time she hiked at each rate. Save yourself some

time by dividing both sides of the equation by 264 rather than distributing:

$$264x = 2(264)(7 - x)$$
$$x = 2(7 - x)$$
$$x = 14 - 2x$$
$$3x = 14$$
$$x = 4.6667$$

Be careful—this is not the answer! The question asks how tall Mount Fuji is, so don't forget to add the vertical distance she drove, 2,390 meters, to get 2,390 + 1,232 = 3,622 meters, which is (C).

19. A   Difficulty: Medium

Category: Passport to Advanced Math / Quadratics

Getting to the Answer: Even though one of the equations in this system isn't linear, you can still solve the system using substitution. You already know that *y* is equal to 3*x*, so substitute 3*x* for *y* in the second equation. Don't forget that when you square 3*x*, you must square both the coefficient and the variable.

$$-3x^2 + 2y^2 = 180$$
$$-3x^2 + 2(3x)^2 = 180$$
$$-3x^2 + 2(9x^2) = 180$$
$$-3x^2 + 18x^2 = 180$$
$$15x^2 = 180$$
$$x^2 = 12$$

The question asks for the value of x^2, not *x*, so there is no need to take the square root of 12 to find the value of *x*. The answer is (A).

20. C   Difficulty: Medium

Category: Passport to Advanced Math / Exponents

Getting to the Answer: Adding polynomials is typically safer than subtracting them, because you may forget to distribute the negative sign when subtracting more than one term. To find *M* − *N*, multiply each term of *N* by −1 and then add the two polynomials by combining like terms.

$$-1N = -5x^2 + 12$$
$$M + (-N) = 3x^2 + 9x - 4 - 5x^2 + 12$$
$$= -2x^2 + 9x + 8$$

Don't forget to multiply the resulting expression by 2 to get $2(-2x^2 + 9x + 8) = -4x^2 + 18x + 16$, (C).

21. B   Difficulty: Medium

Category: Problem Solving and Data Analysis / Statistics and Probability

Getting to the Answer: The *median* of a data set is the middle value when the data points are arranged from least to greatest (or greatest to least). When there is an even number of data points, the median is the average of the two middle values.

The histogram represents the lengths of 28 bridges, so the median length is the average of the 14th and 15th longest bridges. Because the number of bridges that are less than 6 miles long is 12, and the number of bridges that are less than 9 miles long is 12 + 8 = 20, the median length of the 28 bridges must be between 6 and 9 miles (because 14 and 15 lie between 12 and 20). Of the choices given, only (B) matches this criterion.

22. C   Difficulty: Medium

Category: Problem Solving and Data Analysis / Scatterplots

Getting to the Answer: It's a good idea to get comfortable with the vocabulary used in statistics questions. *Correlation* simply means relationship. The word *weak* refers to the strength of the relationship, which has no effect on slope, but rather on how closely the data points follow the line of best fit.

Be careful not to confuse slope and strength. Simply because a data set shows a weak correlation does not mean the slope will be close to zero. The data can still be gathered around a steep line of best fit. So, you can eliminate A and B. Also, keep in mind that the terms *weak* and *positive* are not related but rather are two independent descriptors of the correlation. So, the fact that the rate of change is positive has nothing to do with the strength of the correlation. In a weak correlation, the data points will follow the line of best fit, but not as closely as in a strong correlation, which means (C) is correct.

23. C   Difficulty: Medium

Category: Problem Solving and Data Analysis / Rates, Ratios, Proportions, and Percentages

Getting to the Answer: Pay careful attention to the units. You need to convert all of the dimensions to inches and then find the scale factor. There are 12 inches in one foot, so the height of the woolly mammoth was $10 \times 12 = 120 + 6 = 126$ inches. The tusk length was 11.5 feet, or $11.5 \times 12 = 138$ inches. The student plans to draw the mammoth 14 inches tall, so find the scale factor of the two heights by writing them as a fraction: $\frac{14}{126} = \frac{1}{9}$. This means the scale factor is $\frac{1}{9}$. Multiply this by the length of the real mammoth's tusks to find the scaled length: $138 \times \frac{1}{9} = \frac{138}{9} = 15\frac{1}{3}$. This means the student should make the tusks 15.33 inches long, (C).

24. D   Difficulty: Medium

Category: Heart of Algebra / Linear Equations

Getting to the Answer: When a real-world scenario is modeled using a linear equation, b is a flat fee or starting amount, m is a unit rate, x represents the number of units, and y represents a total amount. Write the equation in words first, adding the variables as you go. The total cost, y, is equal to the cost per pound, m, multiplied by the number of pounds, x, and added to the cost of the pail, b. You can eliminate A and B because b is 1.50 (the cost of the pail) and m is 3.99 (the cost per pound). You can also eliminate C because Johanna picks 3 pounds, so x is 3. Choice (D) is correct because the total cost of picking 3 pounds is $3.99(3) + 1.50 = 13.47$. This means 13.47 most likely represents the total cost, y.

25. B   Difficulty: Hard

Category: Problem Solving and Data Analysis / Rates, Ratios, Proportions, and Percentages

Getting to the Answer: Start by determining what the question is asking. You need to find the net percent change in the power reliance on solar panels over the course of a day. To do this, you need to know how much the solar panels were relied on at the beginning of the day and how much at the end (neither of which is given).

Whenever you aren't given a concrete starting point, pick one yourself. The best number to use when dealing with percents is 100. First, find how much power was derived from the solar panels after the first increase: $100 \times 0.6 = 60$. So, the company increased power from the solar panels to $100 + 60 = 160$. Next, find the amount after the decrease: $160 \times 0.3 = 48$, so the solar panels then provided $160 - 48 = 112$ units of power. Finally, find the amount after the last increase: $112 \times 0.75 = 84$, so the plant ended the day at $112 + 84 = 196$, which is $196 - 100 = 96$ more than it started the day with. To find the percent change, use the formula $\text{Percent change} = \dfrac{\text{amount of change}}{\text{original amount}}$ to get $\dfrac{96}{100} = 0.96 = 96\%$, which is (B).

26. D   Difficulty: Hard

Category: Problem Solving and Data Analysis / Rates, Ratios, Proportions, and Percentages

Getting to the Answer: A question like this requires a simple proportion. However, you need to convert the units so they are the same. Because the conversion given at the end of the question is feet to meters, convert the first snake length to meters by multiplying it by 0.3. Remember, 2 feet, 6 inches is the same as 2.5 feet: 2.5 feet × 0.3 meters per foot = 0.75 meters. Now, set up a proportion and solve. Let g be the number of grams of feed needed for a snake that is 1 meter long. Write the proportion in words first to keep the pieces organized:

$$\frac{\text{length of 1st snake}}{\text{food for 1st snake}} = \frac{\text{length of 2nd snake}}{\text{food for 2nd snake}}$$

$$\frac{0.75}{12} = \frac{1}{g}$$

$$0.75g = 12$$

$$g = 16$$

A snake that is 1 meter long should receive 16 grams of frog mash, (D).

27. D   Difficulty: Hard

Category: Additional Topics in Math / Trigonometry

Getting to the Answer: Take a peek at the answer choices—the angles of the trig functions are given in radians, rather than degrees (you know this because there is no degree symbol). This means you'll need to use the radian formula for finding arc length: $arcL = \theta \times r$, where θ is the central angle of the arc in radians and r is the radius of the circle. This will allow you to determine the measure of the central angle, half of which becomes one of the angles of a right triangle (*CDE*, for example). You know both the arc length (3.4) and the radius (2), so solve for the central angle.

$$arcL = \theta \times r$$
$$3.4 = \theta \times 2$$
$$1.7 = \theta$$

This means that $\angle DCF$ has a measure of 1.7 radians, and consequently, $\angle DCE$ has a measure of half that, or 0.85 radians. Add this measure to the triangle, or draw a quick right triangle off to the side like the one below:

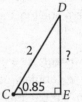

Now, if you can find the length of side *DE*, you can double it to find the length of chord *DF*. Side *DE* is opposite the angle measure that you found and you know the hypotenuse of the triangle; so, use the ratio $\sin x = \dfrac{\text{opposite}}{\text{hypotenuse}}$ to find the length of side *DE*:

$$\sin(0.85) = \frac{DE}{2}$$
$$2\sin(0.85) = DE$$

Multiply by 2 to find that $DF = 2 \times 2\sin(0.85) = 4\sin(0.85)$. Keep in mind that multiplying the angle (inside the parentheses) is not the same as multiplying the whole quantity by 2, so (D) is correct.

28. A   Difficulty: Hard

Category: Heart of Algebra / Systems of Linear Equations

Getting to the Answer: Don't let all the fractions intimidate you. There are two equations and two variables, so solve this system the same way you would solve any other system of equations. The first equation is already solved for y, so use substitution. To make the second equation easier to work with, multiply it by 4 to clear the fractions (even though you may have noticed the tempting 4 in the denominator of the desired expression).

$$4\left(\frac{3y}{4} + 11 = \frac{-x}{2}\right)$$
$$3y + 44 = -2x$$
$$3(12 - x) + 44 = -2x$$
$$36 - 3x + 44 = -2x$$
$$80 - 3x = -2x$$
$$80 = x$$

Next, substitute 80 for x into the first equation and solve for y.

$$y = 12 - 80$$
$$y = -68$$

Finally, substitute the values you found into the expression in the question, $\frac{x}{5} + \frac{y}{4}$.

$$\frac{80}{5} + \frac{(-68)}{4} = 16 + (-17) = -1$$

Choice (A) is correct.

29. B   Difficulty: Hard

Category: Problem Solving and Data Analysis / Scatterplots

Getting to the Answer: This question requires a conceptual understanding of modeling data and properties of quadratic equations. The graph of a quadratic equation is symmetric with respect to its axis of symmetry. The axis of symmetry occurs at the x-value of the vertex, which according to the graph is 20. You can also see from the graph that one of the x-intercepts is x = 8. This means that 8 is a solution to the quadratic equation. Unfortunately, 8 isn't one of the answer choices. However, because the graph of a quadratic equation is symmetric, the other solution (x-intercept) must be the same distance from the vertex as 8 is, which is 20 − 8 = 12 units. Therefore, the other solution to the equation must be x = 20 + 12 = 32.

30. D   Difficulty: Hard

Category: Passport to Advanced Math / Functions

Getting to the Answer: The key to answering this question is in having a conceptual understanding of function notation. Here, the input (x − 4) has already been substituted and simplified in the given function. Your job is to determine what the function would have looked like had x been the input instead. To keep things organized, let u = x − 4, the old input. This means x = u + 4. Substitute this into h(x − 4) and simplify:

$$h(x - 4) = 6x^2 + 2x + 10$$
$$h(u) = 6(u + 4)^2 + 2(u + 4) + 10$$
$$= 6(u^2 + 8u + 16) + 2u + 8 + 10$$
$$= 6u^2 + 48u + 96 + 2u + 8 + 10$$
$$= 6u^2 + 50u + 114$$

When working with function notation, you evaluate the function by substituting a given input value for the variable in the parentheses. Here, if the input value is x, then $h(x) = 6x^2 + 50x + 114$.

31. 42   Difficulty: Easy

Category: Problem Solving and Data Analysis / Statistics and Probability

Getting to the Answer: When a sample is a good representation of a population, you can apply the results of a study to the entire population. Start by finding the percent of the graduates who were surveyed that were not practicing law: 720 out of 3,000 is 720 ÷ 3,000 = 0.24, or 24%. The question asks about the number of graduates who *were* practicing law in 2012, so subtract from 100% to find that 76% of the graduates *were* practicing law in 2012. Apply this percentage to the whole population of graduates from 2000 who passed the bar: 55,200 × 0.76 = 41,952. Now, follow directions carefully—round to the nearest thousand (42,000) and enter your answer as the number of thousands, which is 42.

32. 4962 Difficulty: Easy

Category: Heart of Algebra / Linear Equations

Getting to the Answer: Create a linear equation to keep the information straight. The total number of miles driven by the car is equal to the miles per gallon times the number of gallons in the tank added to the existing number of miles on the odometer. The equation is $y = 48x + 4,386$. You are given the x-value, 12 gallons, so simply substitute it for x and solve for y.

$$y = 48(12) + 4,386$$
$$y = 576 + 4,386$$
$$y = 4,962$$

33. 28   Difficulty: Medium

Category: Passport to Advanced Math / Quadratics

Getting to the Answer: Graphically, a y-intercept is in the form $(0, y)$, so the y-intercept of the graph is the value of y when 0 is substituted for x in the equation. Don't forget to follow the correct order of operations as you simplify the expression.

$$y = 2(0 + 3)^2 + 10$$
$$= 2(3)^2 + 10$$
$$= 2(9) + 10$$
$$= 18 + 10$$
$$= 28$$

34. 60   Difficulty: Medium

Category: Additional Topics in Math / Geometry

Getting to the Answer: Whenever a question asks about the amount of space something covers (here,

the greenspace), you are looking for area. In this question, the area that you're looking for takes on the shape of a right triangle (actually, two of them), so use the formula $A = \frac{1}{2}bh$.

The key to answering this question is in labeling the diagram. The calculations are very straightforward once you have the correct dimensions of the triangles. You're given that the width of each parking lot is equal to the width of the City Hall building, so each parking lot is 540 ÷ 3 = 180 feet wide. This means the base of each triangle (at the top of the diagram) is 180 − 40 = 140 feet. The height of each triangle is the same as the length of the parking lot, which is 430 feet.

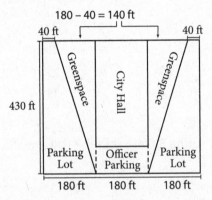

You now have all the numbers you need. The area of each triangle is $\frac{1}{2}(140)(430) = 30,100$, so both triangles together result in a greenspace that covers 60,200 square feet. Rounded to the nearest thousand, this is 60,000, which should be gridded in as 60.

35. 23   Difficulty: Medium

Category: Heart of Algebra / Inequalities

Getting to the Answer: When a question asks about a maximum (or minimum) amount, it usually means you need to create and solve an inequality. Write the inequality in words first. The cost of 3 cans of vegetables plus the cost of 1 bag of rice, all multiplied by the number of care packages Rasha makes, must be less than or equal to the amount of money he collected, $145. Because you are not asked to differentiate between cans and rice, they can be represented by the same variable. Just don't forget to multiply the cost of 1 can by 3 first ($0.89 × 3 = $2.67). Let p represent the number of care packages:

$$(2.67 + 3.49)p \leq 145$$
$$6.16p \leq 145$$
$$p \leq 23.54$$

Be careful, the question asks for *complete* care packages, so he can make only 23.

36. 1.7   Difficulty: Hard

Category: Problem Solving and Data Analysis / Rates, Ratios, Proportions, and Percentages

Getting to the Answer: Questions that involve distance, rate, and time can almost always be solved using the formula Distance = rate × time. Just make sure the rate and the time involve compatible units. For each of the three rail systems, you know how long the person traveled and their rate (after you adjust for the 30%). Use the formula to find the distance for each one. But be careful—the rates are given in miles per hour, which means you must use hours, not minutes, for the times.

New York City Subway:
Time = 6 minutes = 0.1 hours
Rate = 17.4 mph
Distance = 17.4 × 0.1 = 1.74 miles

Chicago L:
Time = 4.8 minutes = 0.08 hours
Rate = 1.3(17.4) = 22.62 mph
Distance = 22.62 × 0.075 = 1.8096 miles

DC Metro:
Time = 3.6 minutes = 0.06 hours
Rate = 1.3(22.62) = 29.406 mph
Distance = 29.406 × 0.05 = 1.76436 miles

Marc traveled the shortest distance between stops at about 1.7 miles (rounded to the nearest tenth).

37. 50   Difficulty: Medium

Category: Problem Solving and Data Analysis / Statistics and Probability

Getting to the Answer: The key to answering a question like this is in reading the labels on the graph carefully. You do not need to convert grams to micrograms or vice versa. They are simply the units for mercury content. Start by determining how many micrograms of mercury a person who weighs 82 kilograms can consume: 82 × 0.1 = 8.2 micrograms. Next, find *snapper* on the bar graph and determine how many micrograms it contains (per gram of weight): 0.165. Divide the number of micrograms the person can consume, 8.2, by the number in each gram of snapper to arrive at 8.2 ÷ 0.165 = 49.697, or about 50 grams.

38. 23   Difficulty: Hard

Category: Problem Solving and Data Analysis / Statistics and Probability

Getting to the Answer: There is a lot of information to sort through in a question like this. Make a plan and carry out the plan one step at a time. Don't try to keep all the calculations in your calculator; jot them down as you work through each step.

Multiply the average portion size (100 grams) by each mercury content shown in the bar graph. Don't forget to remove the swordfish, because it has the highest mercury content. Then, find the average—but be careful, you're finding an average over 7 days (the number of days in a week), not 5 (the number of portions the person consumes).

Haddock: 0.055 × 100 = 5.5
Tuna: 0.350 × 100 = 35
Snapper: 0.165 × 100 = 16.5
Marlin: 0.485 × 100 = 48.5
Orange Roughy: 0.570 × 10 = 57

The total is 162.5 micrograms, which means the average daily consumption over the whole week is 162.5 ÷ 7 = 23.214, or about 23 micrograms. (Note that unless this person weighs 230 kg, which is a little over 500 pounds, then they are consuming way too much mercury per day.)

ESSAY TEST RUBRIC

The Essay Demonstrates...

4—Advanced	• **(Reading)** A strong ability to comprehend the source text, including its central ideas and important details and how they interrelate; and effectively use evidence (quotations, paraphrases, or both) from the source text
	• **(Analysis)** A strong ability to evaluate the author's use of evidence, reasoning, and/or stylistic and persuasive elements, and/or other features of the student's own choosing; make good use of relevant, sufficient, and strategically chosen support for the claims or points made in the student's essay; and focus consistently on features of the source text that are most relevant to addressing the task
	• **(Writing)** A strong ability to provide a precise central claim; create an effective organization that includes an introduction and conclusion, as well as a clear progression of ideas; successfully employ a variety of sentence structures; use precise word choice; maintain a formal style and objective tone; and show command of the conventions of standard written English so that the essay is free of errors
3—Proficient	• **(Reading)** Satisfactory ability to comprehend the source text, including its central ideas and important details and how they interrelate; and use evidence (quotations, paraphrases, or both) from the source text
	• **(Analysis)** Satisfactory ability to evaluate the author's use of evidence, reasoning, and/or stylistic and persuasive elements, and/or other features of the student's own choosing; make use of relevant and sufficient support for the claims or points made in the student's essay; and focus primarily on features of the source text that are most relevant to addressing the task
	• **(Writing)** Satisfactory ability to provide a central claim; create an organization that includes an introduction and conclusion, as well as a clear progression of ideas; employ a variety of sentence structures; use precise word choice; maintain an appropriate formal style and objective tone; and show control of the conventions of standard written English so that the essay is free of significant errors

2—Partial	• **(Reading)** Limited ability to comprehend the source text, including its central ideas and important details and how they interrelate; and use evidence (quotations, paraphrases, or both) from the source text • **(Analysis)** Limited ability to evaluate the author's use of evidence, reasoning, and/or stylistic and persuasive elements, and/or other features of the student's own choosing; make use of support for the claims or points made in the student's essay; and focus on relevant features of the source text • **(Writing)** Limited ability to provide a central claim; create an effective organization for ideas; employ a variety of sentence structures; use precise word choice; maintain an appropriate style and tone; or show command of the conventions of standard written English, resulting in certain errors that detract from the quality of the writing
1—Inadequate	• **(Reading)** Little or no ability to comprehend the source text or use evidence from the source text • **(Analysis)** Little or no ability to evaluate the author's use of evidence, reasoning, and/or stylistic and persuasive elements; choose support for claims or points; or focus on relevant features of the source text • **(Writing)** Little or no ability to provide a central claim, organization, or progression of ideas; employ a variety of sentence structures; use precise word choice; maintain an appropriate style and tone; or show command of the conventions of standard written English, resulting in numerous errors that undermine the quality of the writing

ESSAY RESPONSE #1 (ADVANCED SCORE)

The State of the Union differs year to year in that each president speaks in a distinctive style while outlining specific policy proposals he or she would like to see enacted into law. However, all of the speeches probably have one thing in common: Any proposals the president makes are almost always connected to an emotional appeal based on American values such as freedom and opportunity. President Truman's 1948 State of the Union address was no exception. In the speech, he offers his ideas for social security, health care, education, and preservation of our natural resources. But he frames all of his ideas within one common narrative: The American ideals of democracy insist on the continued investment in the collective welfare and security of our citizens.

Truman's first goal is to convince Congress that investing in the nation's collective welfare is nothing less than ensuring that the essential human rights of U.S. citizens are met. He begins his speech in general terms by asking Congress to focus on the common aspirations they have for American citizens, such as freedom of speech and freedom of religion. This is an effective way to begin, because it allows him to establish common ground with his political opponents. After all, who doesn't believe in freedom? He then says what is probably the most important line of the speech: "Any denial of human rights is a denial of the basic beliefs of democracy and of our regard for the worth of each individual." He strengthens his position with the evidence that "some of our citizens are still denied equal opportunity for education, for jobs and economic advancement, and for the expression of their views at the polls," as well as equal protection under the law. This is a direct appeal to emotion, and it sets the tone for the rest of his speech because he continually equates the "right" of citizens to economic security and equality of opportunity with government investment in what he terms "human resources."

President Truman now makes the argument that to protect human freedoms, we must invest in human resources by improving the nation's social security, health, and education. He explains that further investment in social security programs, including unemployment compensation and old age benefits, would best ensure the economic security of Americans. President Truman argues that affordable health care is needed to protect people's economic security as well, reasoning that good doctors are of no use if you can't afford them, thereby making the implicit point that people who are sick suffer wage and job loss.

He then turns to education, using the powerful phrase "equality of opportunity" to argue that our democracy would be strengthened with better educated citizens. He also notes his concern for the educational inequalities that existed at that time between states, arguing, "If there are educational inadequacies in any state, the whole nation suffers." He mentions this in order to strengthen his argument for the federal government to help provide equitable reform throughout the nation.

President Truman uses similar language to discuss his goal of more thoughtful use and conservation of fields, forests, and mines, arguing that these "natural resources" are in need of the same investment and protection that we give to our "human resources." His rationale is based on a simple argument: Natural resources are essential to the nation's "growth and economic development." He argues for a good balance between conservation and use of our natural resources, and again turns to emotional appeals while doing so. He uses phrases such as "preservation of our national strength" and "an expanding future" to connect better use of natural resources with national pride and security.

Throughout his speech, President Truman continually ties his proposals to the essential ideals of our great nation. The speech makes it clear that he firmly believes our democracy is only as strong as the collective welfare of its citizens. He argues that the preservation of our democracy requires nothing less than continued investment in our human and natural resources, and that the values upon which our democracy is based actually demand such investment to ensure equality of freedom and opportunity. An appeal to emotion using such powerful words as "freedom," "opportunity," and "democracy" leaves the members of Congress, and the American public, with little room to argue against him.

ESSAY RESPONSE #2 (PROFICIENT SCORE)

U.S. presidents give a State of the Union address to Congress and the American people every year. They usually use the speech to introduce new ideas and proposals that they hope Congress will make into laws, so they have to persuade Congress to go along with their ideas. Presidents today do this, and many presidents in the past did this as well, including President Truman. In 1948, he gave a speech about the need to invest in human rights, human resources, and natural resources.

President Truman begins his speech talking about human rights. He speaks in general terms by asking Congress to think about the goals they have for American citizens, such as freedom of speech and freedom of religion, regardless of whether or not they support his policies. This is a good way to begin, because everyone believes in freedom and it was probably important for Truman to find common ground with his audience. He then says we should never deny human rights. This is important because he thought human rights included the right to freedom and opportunity. These are values that every American holds dear, so President Truman thought mentioning those values would help him convince his audience about the need to spend more money on things like social security and education. The best way to do that was to talk about how those things would help American democracy.

Then he talks about human resources. President Truman makes it clear that he believes that the rights of Americans should be protected with more investment in social security programs, including unemployment compensation and old age benefits. President Truman also reasons that affordable health care protects American rights as well. He then states that education is important for our democracy, and he uses phrases such as "equality of opportunity" to argue that our country would be better with better educated citizens.

Truman's final point is the need to protect and use natural resources wisely. He believes natural resources are just as important as human resources because natural resources are essential to the "growth and economic development" of the nation. He urges Congress to think about better use and conservation of natural resources like forests and water, and uses language like "preservation of our national strength" to tie this issue to America's strength and security.

Throughout his speech, President Truman talks about things that make our nation great, hoping to convince Congress to go along with his plans. He asserts that it is important to take care of American citizens and their rights to things like social security and education, and to take care of the environment. He also asserts that all these things, like human rights, human resources, and natural resources, are worth spending money for. By using words like "freedom" and "opportunity" to describe his plans and persuade Congress to make those plans laws, he makes it hard to argue against him, as all Americans want the best for their country.

SAT PRACTICE TEST 3 ANSWER SHEET

Remove (or photocopy) this answer sheet and use it to complete the test. See the answer key following the test when finished.

Start with number 1 for each section. If a section has fewer questions than answer spaces, leave the extra spaces blank.

SECTION 1

1. Ⓐ Ⓑ Ⓒ Ⓓ
2. Ⓐ Ⓑ Ⓒ Ⓓ
3. Ⓐ Ⓑ Ⓒ Ⓓ
4. Ⓐ Ⓑ Ⓒ Ⓓ
5. Ⓐ Ⓑ Ⓒ Ⓓ
6. Ⓐ Ⓑ Ⓒ Ⓓ
7. Ⓐ Ⓑ Ⓒ Ⓓ
8. Ⓐ Ⓑ Ⓒ Ⓓ
9. Ⓐ Ⓑ Ⓒ Ⓓ
10. Ⓐ Ⓑ Ⓒ Ⓓ
11. Ⓐ Ⓑ Ⓒ Ⓓ
12. Ⓐ Ⓑ Ⓒ Ⓓ
13. Ⓐ Ⓑ Ⓒ Ⓓ

14. Ⓐ Ⓑ Ⓒ Ⓓ
15. Ⓐ Ⓑ Ⓒ Ⓓ
16. Ⓐ Ⓑ Ⓒ Ⓓ
17. Ⓐ Ⓑ Ⓒ Ⓓ
18. Ⓐ Ⓑ Ⓒ Ⓓ
19. Ⓐ Ⓑ Ⓒ Ⓓ
20. Ⓐ Ⓑ Ⓒ Ⓓ
21. Ⓐ Ⓑ Ⓒ Ⓓ
22. Ⓐ Ⓑ Ⓒ Ⓓ
23. Ⓐ Ⓑ Ⓒ Ⓓ
24. Ⓐ Ⓑ Ⓒ Ⓓ
25. Ⓐ Ⓑ Ⓒ Ⓓ
26. Ⓐ Ⓑ Ⓒ Ⓓ

27. Ⓐ Ⓑ Ⓒ Ⓓ
28. Ⓐ Ⓑ Ⓒ Ⓓ
29. Ⓐ Ⓑ Ⓒ Ⓓ
30. Ⓐ Ⓑ Ⓒ Ⓓ
31. Ⓐ Ⓑ Ⓒ Ⓓ
32. Ⓐ Ⓑ Ⓒ Ⓓ
33. Ⓐ Ⓑ Ⓒ Ⓓ
34. Ⓐ Ⓑ Ⓒ Ⓓ
35. Ⓐ Ⓑ Ⓒ Ⓓ
36. Ⓐ Ⓑ Ⓒ Ⓓ
37. Ⓐ Ⓑ Ⓒ Ⓓ
38. Ⓐ Ⓑ Ⓒ Ⓓ
39. Ⓐ Ⓑ Ⓒ Ⓓ

40. Ⓐ Ⓑ Ⓒ Ⓓ
41. Ⓐ Ⓑ Ⓒ Ⓓ
42. Ⓐ Ⓑ Ⓒ Ⓓ
43. Ⓐ Ⓑ Ⓒ Ⓓ
44. Ⓐ Ⓑ Ⓒ Ⓓ
45. Ⓐ Ⓑ Ⓒ Ⓓ
46. Ⓐ Ⓑ Ⓒ Ⓓ
47. Ⓐ Ⓑ Ⓒ Ⓓ
48. Ⓐ Ⓑ Ⓒ Ⓓ
49. Ⓐ Ⓑ Ⓒ Ⓓ
50. Ⓐ Ⓑ Ⓒ Ⓓ
51. Ⓐ Ⓑ Ⓒ Ⓓ
52. Ⓐ Ⓑ Ⓒ Ⓓ

☐ # correct in Section 1

☐ # incorrect in Section 1

SECTION 2

1. Ⓐ Ⓑ Ⓒ Ⓓ
2. Ⓐ Ⓑ Ⓒ Ⓓ
3. Ⓐ Ⓑ Ⓒ Ⓓ
4. Ⓐ Ⓑ Ⓒ Ⓓ
5. Ⓐ Ⓑ Ⓒ Ⓓ
6. Ⓐ Ⓑ Ⓒ Ⓓ
7. Ⓐ Ⓑ Ⓒ Ⓓ
8. Ⓐ Ⓑ Ⓒ Ⓓ
9. Ⓐ Ⓑ Ⓒ Ⓓ
10. Ⓐ Ⓑ Ⓒ Ⓓ
11. Ⓐ Ⓑ Ⓒ Ⓓ

12. Ⓐ Ⓑ Ⓒ Ⓓ
13. Ⓐ Ⓑ Ⓒ Ⓓ
14. Ⓐ Ⓑ Ⓒ Ⓓ
15. Ⓐ Ⓑ Ⓒ Ⓓ
16. Ⓐ Ⓑ Ⓒ Ⓓ
17. Ⓐ Ⓑ Ⓒ Ⓓ
18. Ⓐ Ⓑ Ⓒ Ⓓ
19. Ⓐ Ⓑ Ⓒ Ⓓ
20. Ⓐ Ⓑ Ⓒ Ⓓ
21. Ⓐ Ⓑ Ⓒ Ⓓ
22. Ⓐ Ⓑ Ⓒ Ⓓ

23. Ⓐ Ⓑ Ⓒ Ⓓ
24. Ⓐ Ⓑ Ⓒ Ⓓ
25. Ⓐ Ⓑ Ⓒ Ⓓ
26. Ⓐ Ⓑ Ⓒ Ⓓ
27. Ⓐ Ⓑ Ⓒ Ⓓ
28. Ⓐ Ⓑ Ⓒ Ⓓ
29. Ⓐ Ⓑ Ⓒ Ⓓ
30. Ⓐ Ⓑ Ⓒ Ⓓ
31. Ⓐ Ⓑ Ⓒ Ⓓ
32. Ⓐ Ⓑ Ⓒ Ⓓ
33. Ⓐ Ⓑ Ⓒ Ⓓ

34. Ⓐ Ⓑ Ⓒ Ⓓ
35. Ⓐ Ⓑ Ⓒ Ⓓ
36. Ⓐ Ⓑ Ⓒ Ⓓ
37. Ⓐ Ⓑ Ⓒ Ⓓ
38. Ⓐ Ⓑ Ⓒ Ⓓ
39. Ⓐ Ⓑ Ⓒ Ⓓ
40. Ⓐ Ⓑ Ⓒ Ⓓ
41. Ⓐ Ⓑ Ⓒ Ⓓ
42. Ⓐ Ⓑ Ⓒ Ⓓ
43. Ⓐ Ⓑ Ⓒ Ⓓ
44. Ⓐ Ⓑ Ⓒ Ⓓ

☐ # correct in Section 2

☐ # incorrect in Section 2

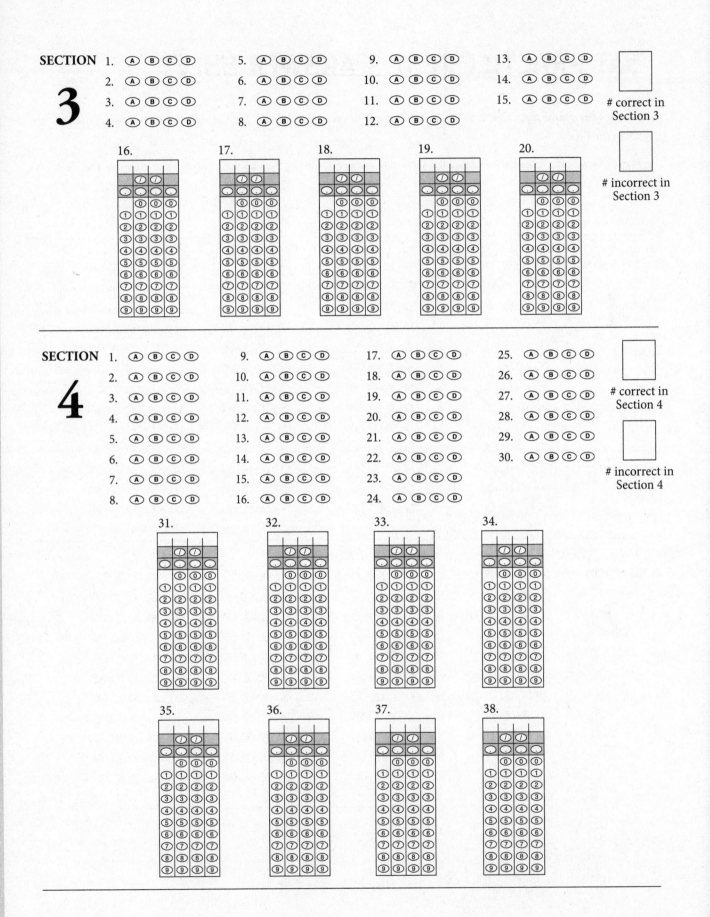

READING TEST

65 Minutes—52 Questions

This section corresponds to Section 1 of your answer sheet.

Directions: Read each passage or pair of passages, then answer the questions that follow. Choose your answers based on what the passage(s) and any accompanying graphics state or imply.

Questions 1-10 are based on the following passage.

The following passage is adapted from the short story "Village Opera," by early 20th-century Chinese writer Lu Hsun. The narrator recalls a childhood memory of being a guest, along with his mother, in his grandmother's home in Pingchao Village.

It was the custom in Luchen where we lived for married women who were not yet in charge of the household to go back to their parents' home
Line for the summer. Although my father's mother was
(5) then still quite strong, my mother had quite a few household duties. She could not spend many days at her own home during the summer. She could take a few days only after visiting the ancestral graves. At such times I always went with her to
(10) stay in her parents' house. It was in a place called Pingchao Village, not far from the sea, a very out-of-the-way little village on a river, with less than thirty households, peasants, and fishermen, and just one tiny grocery....
(15)   We spent most of our days digging up worms, putting them on little hooks made of copper wire, and lying on the river bank to catch shrimps. Shrimps are the silliest water creatures: they willingly use their own pincers to push the point of the hook
(20) into their mouths; so in a few hours we could catch a big bowlful. It became the custom to give these shrimps to me. Another thing we did was to take the buffaloes out together, but, maybe because they are animals of a higher species, oxen and buffaloes
(25) are hostile to strangers, and they treated me with contempt so that I never dared get too close to them. I could only follow at a distance and stand there....
What I looked forward to most was going to Chaochuang to see the opera. Chaochuang was
(30) a slightly larger village about two miles away. Since

Pingchiao was too small to afford to put on operas, every year it contributed some money for a performance at Chaochuang. At the time, I wasn't curious why they should have operas every year.
(35) Thinking about it now, I dare say it may have been for the late spring festival or for the village sacrifice.
That year when I was eleven or twelve, the long-awaited day arrived. But as ill luck would have it, there was no boat for hire that morning.
(40) Pingchiao Village had only one sailing boat, which left in the morning and came back in the evening. This was a large boat which it was out of the question to hire; and all the other boats were unsuitable because they were too small. Someone
(45) was sent round to the neighbouring villages to ask if they had boats, but no—they had all been hired already. My grandmother was very upset, blamed my cousins for not hiring one earlier, and began to complain. Mother tried to comfort her by saying
(50) the operas at Luchen were much better than in these little villages, and there were several every year, so there was no need to go today. But I was nearly in tears from disappointment, and mother did her best to impress on me that no matter what,
(55) I must not make a scene, because it would upset my grandmother; and I mustn't go with other people either, for then grandmother would be worried.
In a word, it had fallen through. After lunch, when all my friends had left and the opera had
(60) started, I imagined I could hear the sound of gongs and drums, and saw them, with my mind's eye, in front of the stage buying soya-bean milk.
I didn't catch shrimps that day, and didn't eat much either. Mother was very upset, but there was
(65) nothing she could do. By supper time grandmother

GO ON TO THE NEXT PAGE ▷

realized how I felt, and said I was quite right to be angry, they had been too negligent, and never before had guests been treated so badly. After the meal, youngsters who had come back from the
(70) opera gathered round and gaily described it all for us. I was the only one silent; they all sighed and said how sorry they were for me. Suddenly one of the brightest, called Shuang-hsi, had an inspiration, and said: "A big boat—hasn't Eighth Grand-uncle's
(75) boat come back?" A dozen other boys picked up the idea in a flash, and at once started agitating to take the boat and go with me. I cheered up. But grandmother was nervous, thinking we were all children and undependable. And mother said that
(80) since the grown-ups all had to work the next day, it wouldn't be fair to ask them to go with us and stay up all night. While our fate hung in the balance, Shuang-hsi went to the root of the question and declared loudly: "I give my word it'll be all right! It's
(85) a big boat, Brother Hsun never jumps around, and we can all swim!"

It was true. There wasn't one boy in the dozen who wasn't a fish in water, and two or three of them were first-rate swimmers.

(90)   Grandmother and mother were convinced and did not raise any more objections. They both smiled, and we immediately rushed out to the evening performance of the opera.

1. According to the passage, why does the narrator spend time in his mother's parents' home?

    A) He always goes with his mother when she visits there.

    B) His grandmother insists that he come with his mother.

    C) He lives with his grandmother most of the year.

    D) His grandmother needs extra help.

2. As used in line 54, "impress on me" most nearly means

    A) infer.

    B) emphasize.

    C) mark.

    D) understand.

3. The passage most strongly suggests that which of the following is true?

    A) The narrator's grandmother lets the narrator do whatever he wants.

    B) The narrator's mother does not enjoy visiting her mother's home.

    C) The narrator's mother is not head of her household.

    D) The narrator's grandmother thinks his mother is too strict with him.

4. Which choice provides the best evidence for the answer to the previous question?

    A) Lines 1-4 ("It was the . . . summer")

    B) Lines 9-10 ("At such times . . . parents' house")

    C) Lines 15-17 ("We spent . . . to catch shrimps")

    D) Lines 35-36 ("Thinking about it . . . the village sacrifice")

5. What theme does the passage communicate through the experiences of the narrator?

    A) Traditions are meant to be changed.

    B) Hope is hard to maintain.

    C) Hardship is a part of life.

    D) Problems can sometimes be solved.

 GO ON TO THE NEXT PAGE

6. Based on the passage, why do the narrator's mother and grandmother change their minds about letting him go to the opera?

   A) They decide they could trust the person who owns the boat.

   B) They want to please the narrator since he was so sad.

   C) They are assured that the boys would not be in danger.

   D) They realize that the boat is not that small.

7. Which choice provides the best evidence for the answer to the previous question?

   A) Lines 42-44 ("This was . . . too small")

   B) Lines 58-62 ("After lunch . . . soya-bean milk")

   C) Lines 79-82 ("And mother . . . all night")

   D) Lines 87-89 ("It was . . . swimmers")

8. The author's use of the phrase "with my mind's eye" (line 61) implies that the narrator

   A) sees visions.

   B) has poor eyesight.

   C) wants to go to sleep.

   D) has a good imagination.

9. As used in line 76, "agitating" most nearly means

   A) campaigning.

   B) shaking.

   C) disturbing.

   D) stirring.

10. Based on the tone of this passage, what emotion does the author want the reader to feel toward the narrator?

   A) Sympathy

   B) Criticism

   C) Indifference

   D) Hostility

Questions 11-20 are based on the following passage.

The following passage is adapted from a pivotal 1964 speech by South Africa's Nelson Mandela, called "An Ideal for Which I Am Prepared to Die." Mandela, later elected first president of democratic South Africa, gave this speech before his trial and imprisonment for activism against apartheid, a now-obsolete system of racial segregation in South Africa.

The lack of human dignity experienced by Africans is the direct result of the policy of white supremacy. . . . Menial tasks in South Africa are
Line invariably performed by Africans. When anything
(5) has to be carried or cleaned the white man will look around for an African to do it for him, whether the African is employed by him or not. Because of this sort of attitude, whites . . . do not look upon them as people with families of their own; they do not
(10) realise that they have emotions—that they fall in love like white people do; that they want to be with their wives and children like white people want to be with theirs; that they want to earn enough money to support their families properly, to feed
(15) and clothe them and send them to school. . . .

Pass laws[1], which to the Africans are among the most hated bits of legislation in South Africa, render any African liable to police surveillance at any time. I doubt whether there is a single African
(20) male in South Africa who has not at some stage had a brush with the police over his pass. Hundreds and thousands of Africans are thrown into jail each year under pass laws. Even worse than this is the fact that pass laws keep husband and wife apart and
(25) lead to the breakdown of family life.

Poverty and the breakdown of family life have secondary effects. Children wander about the streets of the townships because they have no schools to go to, or no money to enable them to go
(30) to school, or no parents at home to see that they go to school, because both parents (if there be two) have to work to keep the family alive. This leads to a breakdown in moral standards . . . and to growing

[1]Pass laws: Black South Africans were legally required to carry pass books, which were like internal passports with the purpose of restricting where Africans could go, thus maintaining racial segregation.

GO ON TO THE NEXT PAGE

violence which erupts not only politically, but
(35) everywhere. . . .

Africans want to perform work which they
are capable of doing, and not work which the
government declares them to be capable of.
Africans want to be allowed to live where they
(40) obtain work, and not be endorsed out of an area
because they were not born there. Africans want to
be allowed to own land in places where they work,
and not to be obliged to live in rented houses which
they can never call their own. Africans want to be
(45) part of the general population, and not confined
to living in their own ghettoes. African men want
to have their wives and children to live with them
where they work. . . . Africans want to be allowed
out after eleven o'clock at night and not to be
(50) confined to their rooms like little children. Africans
want to be allowed to travel in their own country
and to seek work where they want to and not where
the labour bureau tells them to. Africans want a
just share in the whole of South Africa; they want
(55) security and a stake in society.

Above all, we want equal political rights, because
without them our disabilities will be permanent. I
know this sounds revolutionary to the whites in this
country, because the majority of voters will be
(60) Africans. This makes the white man fear democracy.

But this fear cannot be allowed to stand in the
way of the only solution which will guarantee racial
harmony and freedom for all. It is not true that the
enfranchisement of all will result in racial domina-
(65) tion. Political division, based on colour, is entirely
artificial and, when it disappears, so will the domination of one colour group by another. The ANC[2] has
spent half a century fighting against racialism. When
it triumphs it will not change that policy.
(70) This then is what the ANC is fighting. Their
struggle is a truly national one. It is a struggle of
the African people, inspired by their own suffering
and their own experience. It is a struggle for the
right to live.
(75) During my lifetime I have dedicated myself to
this struggle of the African people. I have fought
against white domination, and I have fought
against black domination. I have cherished the
ideal of a democratic and free society in which all
(80) persons live together in harmony and with equal
opportunities. It is an ideal which I hope to live
for and to achieve. But if needs be, it is an ideal for
which I am prepared to die.

[2]ANC: African National Congress, the political organization that
spearheaded the movement for equal rights in South Africa.

11. The most likely intended purpose of this speech is to

A) explain the political goals of the ANC.

B) explain why Mandela is not guilty of the
crime of which he is accused.

C) argue that the laws passed under apartheid
are illegal.

D) explain to white South Africans why the
apartheid system must be abolished.

12. Which choice provides the best evidence for the
answer to the previous question?

A) Lines 1-3 ("The lack of . . . supremacy")

B) Lines 36-37 ("Africans want . . . of doing")

C) Lines 67-68 ("The ANC . . . racialism")

D) Lines 75-76 ("During . . . African people")

13. As used in line 40, the phrase "endorsed out of"
most nearly means

A) supported by.

B) restricted from.

C) authorized for.

D) approved to be in.

14. It can most reasonably be inferred that pass laws

A) led to the criminal behavior they were
designed to prevent.

B) were fundamentally European and incom-
patible with African life.

C) led to the passage of additional apartheid
laws.

D) were a necessary part of South Africa's
transition to democracy.

GO ON TO THE NEXT PAGE ⇨

15. Which choice provides the best evidence for the answer to the previous question?

    A) Lines 19-21 ("I doubt . . . his pass")

    B) Lines 21-23 ("Hundreds . . . pass laws")

    C) Lines 26-27 ("Poverty . . . effects")

    D) Lines 32-35 ("This leads to . . . but everywhere")

16. As used in line 66, "artificial" most nearly means

    A) simulated.

    B) not genuine.

    C) imitative.

    D) human-made.

17. According to Mandela's claims, what is true of democracy?

    A) It is fundamentally incompatible with white rule.

    B) It existed in South Africa before apartheid.

    C) It is a goal of white South Africans.

    D) It would lead to increased crime at all levels.

18. The statement in lines 67-69 ("The ANC . . . policy") is important to the overall argument in its suggestion that

    A) black South Africans will initiate steps to curb violence without pass laws.

    B) black South Africans will be happier once there are equal political rights.

    C) black South Africans will not retaliate once there are equal political rights.

    D) black South Africans will continue to endorse a separate but equal system.

19. It can most reasonably be inferred that Mandela would most likely support which of the following future policies?

    A) Reduction of domestic employment

    B) Job training for untrained workers

    C) Pass laws for all whites and blacks

    D) Investment in overseas business

20. The sixth paragraph of Mandela's speech can best be described as

    A) a promise that the changes he proposes will be good for all people.

    B) a contrast between his former beliefs and those he currently holds.

    C) an acknowledgment that he knows there is no perfect system.

    D) a thank-you for people's continued support in a difficult situation.

Questions 21-31 are based on the following passage and supplementary material.

The following passage discusses the surprisingly complex endeavor of keeping dictionaries up-to-date.

If you've ever played Scrabble, you know who the ultimate arbiter in that word game is: You challenge a word your opponent makes by reaching
Line for that infallible judge, the dictionary. After all,
(5) a dictionary is a definitive collection of words, spellings, and meanings, right?

Actually, that isn't quite so, because while we regard dictionaries as catalogs of correctness, the truth is that dictionaries do not tell the whole story.
(10) We can think of them as horses pulling tidy carts of our cluttered language, but in fact, as David Skinner wrote in the *New York Times* (May 17, 2013), "in following *Webster*'s you're following the followers."

That's because language is an ever-changing
(15) thing in which new words are invented all the time and old words are put to new use. Keeping up with this is daunting task, as the writers of the *Oxford English Dictionary,* or *OED,* found out over 100 years ago.

GO ON TO THE NEXT PAGE →

(20)   In 1879, members of the Philological Society of London began working with James Murray of Oxford University Press to produce a more complete dictionary than what was available at the time. In ten years, they estimated, they would (25) publish a four-volume, 6,400-page dictionary covering all English language vocabulary from the Early Middle English period (c. AD 1150) onward. However, five years along they were only as far as the word "ant"! The task of tracking new words and (30) new meanings of existing words while examining the previous seven centuries of the language's development proved monumental.

It turned out that their work required ten volumes, included over 400,000 words, and was not (35) fully published until 1924. Even then, the editors' first job after completion of the monstrous *OED* was to print an addendum, which came out a mere nine years later.

As Skinner says, "There is always much more to (40) know about a word than what a dictionary can tell you."

According to Global Language Monitor, a new word is created every 98 minutes; this results in an average of about 14 words per day. They (45) come from regular people; from writers; from specialized, often scientific fields; and from the Internet.

A short list of the words spawned by the Internet and its technologies includes "blog," "avatar," "spam," (50) and "webisode." Every year, Merriam-Webster's, publisher of America's premier dictionary, adds a jumble of words that have been coined by Web users and promulgated across the Internet's multitudinous channels: websites, chat rooms, forums, blogs, and, (55) of course, social media platforms.

Just like other professional and social realms, the Internet produces both new words and new definitions of old words. The word "troll," for example, dates back to 1616 as a name for "a (60) dwarf or giant in Scandinavian folklore inhabiting caves or hills." In the last decade, however, "troll" emerged as a term for someone who participates in Internet discussions, not to contribute meaningfully, but for the sole purpose of making

(65) harsh rebuttals and insults.

Dictionary makers are faced with tough decisions. Any dictionary that doesn't include Internet-produced words would be seen as being behind the times, although many feel that (70) dictionaries go too far in their role as recorders of what gets said rather than rule-makers of correct usage. One of the most controversial new entries happened in 2013, when several major dictionaries added a definition for "literally" that literally (75) means the literal opposite of its meaning! To some it seemed to erode the very purpose of a dictionary, but consensus prevailed, and Merriam-Webster's now lists "in effect; virtually" as one meaning of literally. In response to criticism it (80) received, Merriam-Webster's wrote, "the use is pure hyperbole intended to gain emphasis." Seemingly as a concession to those who call the definition incorrect, it added, "but it often appears in contexts where no additional emphasis is necessary."

(85)   For those who grumble about the imprecision that this entry enjoins, perhaps the best attitude to have is that expressed on the *Oxford English Dictionary*'s website: "An exhilarating aspect of a living language is that it continually changes."

Internet Words Added to Merriam-Webster's Dictionary

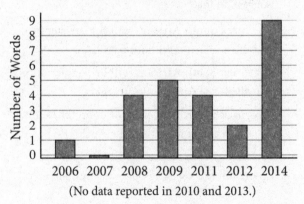

(No data reported in 2010 and 2013.)

Data from merriam-webster.com.

GO ON TO THE NEXT PAGE ⟶

21. The stance the author takes in the passage is best described as that of

    A) a columnist discussing a topic of interest.

    B) a pundit advocating support for a position.

    C) a reporter investigating a current event.

    D) a researcher cataloguing historical data.

22. According to the first two paragraphs, what claim does the author seek to refute?

    A) The assertion that Merriam-Webster's is the best authority to follow

    B) The assumption that Scrabble users rely on dictionaries for aid

    C) The notion that dictionaries are absolute and undeniable authorities

    D) The prediction that dictionaries will become cluttered over time

23. Which choice provides the best evidence for the answer to the previous question?

    A) Lines 1-2 ("If you've . . . game is")

    B) Lines 2-4 ("You challenge . . . dictionary")

    C) Lines 4-6 ("After all, . . . right")

    D) Lines 11-13 ("David Skinner . . . followers")

24. As used in line 32, "monumental" most nearly means

    A) important.

    B) impossible.

    C) tremendous.

    D) ungainly.

25. What idea does the author convey in lines 45-46 through the use of the succession of phrases "from regular people; from writers; from specialized, often scientific fields"?

    A) Definitions of words reflect usage for varied purposes among different people.

    B) Dictionaries must be accessible to users from all walks of life.

    C) People from several professional fields contributed to the development of the *OED*.

    D) Words come from many sources, including nonphilological ones.

26. What conclusion can most reasonably be inferred from lines 50-55 ("Every year . . . social media platforms")?

    A) Dictionaries are easily updated through online and other digital tools.

    B) Navigating the Web requires adopting new meanings for existing words.

    C) The Internet is the most prolific source of new words today.

    D) Words gain not only meaning but also legitimacy through usage.

27. Which choice provides the best evidence for the answer to the previous question?

    A) Lines 42-44 ("According to . . . per day")

    B) Lines 58-61 ("The word . . . or hills")

    C) Lines 61-65 ("In the last . . . insults")

    D) Lines 75-77 ("To some . . . a dictionary")

GO ON TO THE NEXT PAGE ▷

28. What statement is best supported by the data presented in the graphic?

    A) Before 2014, fewer than five words from the Internet were added.

    B) Fewer words from the Internet were added from 2006-2008 than during 2009.

    C) More words from the Internet were added in the years after 2010 than before 2010.

    D) So far, in the 21st century, twenty-six words from the Internet have been added.

29. As used in line 76, "erode" most nearly means

    A) diminish.

    B) dissolve.

    C) consume.

    D) wear.

30. As presented in the passage, the relationship between language and dictionaries is

    A) dictionaries reflect the flaws and inconsistencies of language.

    B) dictionaries attempt to address the idea that language changes over time.

    C) dictionaries establish definite meanings for new words.

    D) dictionaries support the opinion that the study of language is exhilarating.

31. Data in the graphic most directly support which conclusion from the passage?

    A) Dictionaries are imperfect records of the English language.

    B) Language changes in response to the needs of those who use it.

    C) Many new words originate from evolving technologies.

    D) Online usage constantly adapts the meaning of existing words.

Questions 32-42 are based on the following passages.

Passage 1 focuses on new techniques for tracking newborn loggerhead sea turtles, one species found in the Sargasso Sea. Passage 2 describes the unique wildlife habitat found in the Sargasso Sea.

Passage 1

A baby loggerhead sea turtle hatches in its nest buried deep in the sand. Soon, it emerges onto the beach with its siblings. The palm-sized creatures
Line venture across the sand and into the waves of
(5) the Atlantic Ocean. The tiny turtles must vanish quickly to avoid the many predators looming on the dunes or near the water. Seagulls, raccoons, and other animals are eager to make a meal out of the brand-new hatchlings.
(10) Until now, scientists have been unable to track where baby sea turtles go once they reach the water. Small satellite transmitters have allowed older loggerheads to be tracked and studied from afar, giving researchers a window into their migration
(15) patterns, their social behaviors, and other patterns that can be difficult to track in the ocean. But the travels of a newly hatched sea turtle have remained a mystery.

Scientists on the island of Boa Vista, off the coast
(20) of West Africa, have successfully tagged eleven hatchlings with nanoacoustic tags. This has allowed scientists to follow the baby turtles for their first eight hours in the ocean. The tags, which send a ping that the researchers can then plot, are glued
(25) to the shells of the baby loggerheads. The glue was specifically designed to dissolve completely within a few days. The tags are small enough to avoid interfering with the turtles' swimming.

The hatchlings surprised scientists with their
(30) speed. Once the turtles found the ocean currents that would transport them, they could travel at a speed of nearly 200 feet per minute. In the first eight hours of their journeys, some traveled more than nine miles. Tagged turtles released in various
(35) locations all eventually made their way to the Sargasso Sea in the Northern Atlantic Ocean. Here, they become part of the floating ecosystem, eating bite-sized prey and using the sargassum seaweed as rafts. They can sometimes spend up to a decade

GO ON TO THE NEXT PAGE

(40) here before returning to the shores where they hatched. The use of nanoacoustic tags should help protect this endangered species by giving scientists more information about these turtles and when they are most vulnerable.

Passage 2

(45)   A great number of species make their home in the vast waters of the Atlantic Ocean. Although the entire ocean makes up an ecosystem, many smaller habitats are found within, including an open-water habitat off the coast of the Northern Atlantic Ocean
(50) known as the Sargasso Sea. Sargassum is an algae that floats in masses that can continue for miles. The waters of the Gulf Stream push the water in a northward motion into this area. This constant motion and varying temperatures support the
(55) accumulation of the brown-colored seaweed.

     The Sargasso Sea is so immense that one method of information collection has not been enough for scientists to obtain an accurate picture of what takes place within this ecosystem. Researchers
(60) have needed to employ several methods of sampling. Methods such as dragging mesh nets over the surface of the water and videotaping beneath areas of sargassum have served scientists well. Information collected has shown that the Gulf
(65) Stream pushes brown algae from open water into the Sargasso Sea area, creating a diverse floating habitat in an area that would otherwise not support that wildlife.

     In the most recent study of the sargassum
(70) community off the shores of North Carolina, eighty-one fish species were documented as using the area as a microhabitat. This is an increase from previous studies. The types of fish found here are both commercially and environmentally important.
(75) Also found here are juvenile loggerhead sea turtles. The South Atlantic Fishery Management Council is working to regulate the harvesting of sargassum. The Council hopes to have the area classified as an Essential Fish Habitat, which would afford it
(80) certain protections.

     Further research needs to be done before scientists understand how best to protect the Sargasso Sea as well as understand how it goes about supporting so many important types of
(85) wildlife.

32. The central idea of Passage 1 is that

A) the island of Boa Vista, off the coast of Africa, has become a key research center for monitoring baby loggerhead sea turtles.

B) the number of baby loggerhead sea turtles decreases every year, which concerns scientists around the world.

C) scientists are using new technology to track the movements of newborn loggerhead sea turtles, and the results have surprised them.

D) scientists are interested in how long loggerhead sea turtles remain in the Sargasso Sea before returning to where they hatched.

33. Passage 1 most strongly suggests that which of the following is true of the scientists' usage of nanoacoustic tags?

A) The size of the tags is appropriate for baby turtles and will thus offer the most accurate readings.

B) The low cost of the tags is greatly preferable to the expensive satellite technology previously used.

C) The tags protect baby loggerhead turtles from the predators they are likely to meet in the first eight hours of their journey.

D) Scientists prefer gluing the tags because they believe it is more humane than clipping older satellite tags to flippers.

GO ON TO THE NEXT PAGE ⟶

34. Which choice provides the best evidence for the answer to the previous question?

    A) Lines 21-23 ("This has . . . ocean")

    B) Lines 23-25 ("The tags, which . . . loggerheads")

    C) Lines 27-28 ("The tags are . . . swimming")

    D) Lines 34-36 ("Tagged turtles . . . Ocean")

35. As used in line 44 of Passage 1, "vulnerable" most nearly means

    A) defenseless.

    B) inexperienced.

    C) naive.

    D) open.

36. Passage 2 most strongly suggests that which of the following is true of the importance of the Sargasso Sea research?

    A) The research is important in order to ensure that the Gulf Stream does not push the algae too far north.

    B) Data about the Sargasso ecosystem is valuable to conservationists and the fishing industry alike.

    C) The research is important for convincing politicians that fish species are disappearing from the ecosystem.

    D) Through these studies, scientists are able to eliminate predators from the North Carolina microhabitat.

37. Which choice provides the best evidence for the answer to the previous question?

    A) Lines 52-53 ("The waters of . . . area")

    B) Lines 53-55 ("This constant . . . seaweed")

    C) Lines 69-72 ("In the most . . . microhabitat")

    D) Lines 73-74 ("The types of fish . . . important")

38. As used in line 78 of Passage 2, "classified" most nearly means

    A) arranged.

    B) cataloged.

    C) categorized.

    D) pigeonholed.

39. It can most reasonably be inferred from the phrase "needs to be done" (line 81) that the author of Passage 2 thinks

    A) new methods for researching the ecosystem are required before funding continues.

    B) the Sargasso Sea is becoming a problem for shipping lanes and requires removal.

    C) the scientific community has ignored this complex and delicate ecosystem.

    D) the Sargasso ecosystem is worthy of our attention and requires intense study.

40. The author uses the words "great," "vast," and "immense" in Passage 2 in order to emphasize that

    A) the work researchers conduct is highly respected by a growing scientific community.

    B) the microhabitats are large despite their name and require extensive periods for study.

    C) the amount of funding required for Sargasso Sea research is commensurate with the large area that must be covered.

    D) the level of complexity for researchers is heightened by the large area that must be covered.

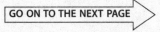

GO ON TO THE NEXT PAGE

41. Which statement best describes the difference between the purpose of Passage 1 and the purpose of Passage 2?

    A) The purpose of Passage 2 is to convince politicians to lend aid, while Passage 1 speaks to a general audience.

    B) Passage 1 aims to convince readers that these studies are futile, while Passage 2 has a more optimistic viewpoint of the research.

    C) Passage 2 discusses current research trends for an entire ecosystem, while Passage 1 focuses on a single species.

    D) The purpose of Passage 2 is to show that scientists cannot agree on a single research method, while they are able to do so in Passage 1.

42. Both passages support which generalization?

    A) The most dangerous period of time for young loggerhead turtles is the first eight hours of life.

    B) The technology used to research the ecosystem and its inhabitants continues to evolve.

    C) Recent studies show that the number of fish and turtle species in the Sargasso Sea is increasing.

    D) The ability of scientists to collect data on the Sargasso Sea properly depends on vital government grants.

Questions 43-52 are based on the following passage and supplementary material.

The following passage explains what causes colorblindness and why men are affected more often than women.

About eight percent of men of European descent are colorblind, but only about half a percent of women are affected by the same condition. Most of
Line these people are "red-green" colorblind, meaning
(5) they cannot see colors related to green or red. Not only are they unable to tell red and green apart, but yellows and oranges do not appear different, nor do blues and purples. Colorblindness is not "blindness" but is instead an inability to distinguish
(10) certain wavelengths of light. A red-green colorblind man looking at a red object can see the object and can see that it is not white; however, he is unable to tell whether the object is red or green, as they both appear similar to him.

(15) People with normal color vision see color because they have an array of three types of photosensitive cells, called cones, on the back of their retinas. Each type of cone has a different pigment that is sensitive to a certain part of the
(20) visible light spectrum. The visible light spectrum runs from smaller wavelengths at the blue end, through medium wavelengths in the green to yellow range, to long wavelengths at the red end.

The cones are often referred to as blue, green,
(25) and red cones, based on the wavelength of light they absorb most. The blue cones absorb the blue wavelengths of light most, although they also absorb a small amount of the green wavelengths. The green cones have their maximum absorption
(30) in the green wavelengths, but also absorb partially into the blue and up into the yellow wavelengths. The range that the red cones absorb significantly overlaps the range of the green cones; the red cone maximum absorption is in the yellow wave-
(35) lengths, but red cones also absorb a bit down into the green, through the yellow, and up into the red wavelengths.

Even though the green and red cones absorb much of the same part of the visible spectrum, a
(40) person who lacks the sensitive pigment in either red or green cones will have difficulty perceiving either color, because the brain compares the signals from both to determine exactly which region of light is being absorbed. With only one set of cones
(45) sending signals, the brain will perceive light from the green, yellow, and red wavelengths to be about the same.

A person will lack the pigment for either green or red cones if he or she lacks the gene necessary
(50) to make that pigment. Because genes are inherited

GO ON TO THE NEXT PAGE

from our parents, half from each parent, we would expect men and women to have an equal chance of being colorblind. The actual ratio is about sixteen colorblind men for each colorblind woman. The
(55) reason for this inequality becomes clear once we know that the genes for making the cone pigments are on the X chromosome.

Women have two X chromosomes, one from each parent. Men only have one X chromosome, which
(60) they get from their mother. A woman can receive a colorblind gene on an X chromosome from one parent, but if the other X chromosome has a normal cone pigment gene, she will still make normal pigments and have normal color vision.
(65) The woman would need to receive the colorblind gene from each parent to be colorblind. Since a man only has the one X chromosome, receiving the colorblind gene from his mother will always cause colorblindness in a man.
(70) Women who have only one copy of the colorblind gene are referred to as carriers because they carry the gene but are not affected by it. By tracking the family members with colorblindness, we can create a chart, called a pedigree, to determine which
(75) women in the family are carriers. A colorblind daughter must have had a colorblind father and either a colorblind or carrier mother, as she must have received a copy of the colorblind gene from each parent. A colorblind son also must have had
(80) either a colorblind or carrier mother, but whether or not the father was colorblind will not affect the son.

Pedigree Chart of Color Blindness
Within One Family

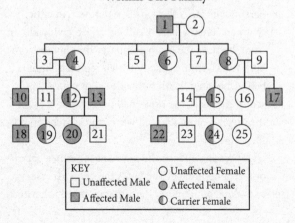

KEY
□ Unaffected Male   ○ Unaffected Female
■ Affected Male   ● Affected Female
    ◐ Carrier Female

43. The passage is primarily concerned with

A) how to determine whether a person is colorblind.

B) research being conducted about colorblindness.

C) how people who are colorblind perceive color.

D) the genetic and physiological causes of colorblindness.

44. Which choice provides the best evidence for the answer to the previous question?

A) Lines 1-3 ("About eight . . . condition")

B) Lines 15-18 ("People with . . . retinas")

C) Lines 24-26 ("The cones . . . absorb most")

D) Lines 48-50 ("A person . . . pigment")

45. In the sixth paragraph, the author mentions details about X chromosomes primarily to

A) give examples of other traits inherited from mothers.

B) explain why more men than women are colorblind.

C) illustrate how genes affect vision and colorblindness.

D) contrast colorblindness with other genetic disorders.

GO ON TO THE NEXT PAGE

46. Based on the information in the passage, which choice best describes what causes red and green to be the two colors that a colorblind person often cannot perceive?

    A) A colorblind person is missing both red and green cones on the back of the retinas.

    B) Because blue wavelengths are brighter, they overpower both red and green wavelengths.

    C) Because red and green absorption ranges overlap greatly, the colorblind person's brain has trouble interpreting the difference between those two colors.

    D) Red and green are on opposite sides of the color wheel, so their absorption ranges are at the farthest, opposite ends of the visible light spectrum.

47. Which choice would best support the author's line of reasoning in the first paragraph?

    A) Details about other types of colorblindness

    B) A more detailed explanation of the light spectrum

    C) A list of other genetic disorders that affect men

    D) Information about how colorblindness is diagnosed

48. As used in line 19, "sensitive" most nearly means

    A) delicate.

    B) responsive.

    C) sympathetic.

    D) vulnerable.

49. Based on the information in the passage, it can most reasonably be inferred that which of the following statements is true?

    A) Colorblindness can be corrected with treatments designed to encourage the growth of the missing genes that make pigments.

    B) A person with normal color vision can become colorblind as he or she ages and the photosensitive cells degenerate.

    C) A person who is colorblind will experience the visual world in a way that is different from a person with normal color vision.

    D) Colorblindness cannot be diagnosed without invasive and expensive genetic testing of both a person and his or her parents.

50. Which choice provides the best evidence for the answer to the previous question?

    A) Lines 10-14 ("A red-green . . . him")

    B) Lines 26-27 ("The blue cones . . . wavelengths")

    C) Lines 42-44 ("the brain . . . absorbed")

    D) Lines 72-75 ("By tracking . . . carriers")

GO ON TO THE NEXT PAGE

51. As used in line 72, "affected" most nearly means

    A) changed.

    B) concerned.

    C) exaggerated.

    D) involved.

52. Based on the information in the passage and the graphic, which of the following statements is true?

    A) A male with a colorblind mother and a father who is not colorblind has a 100% chance of being a carrier for the colorblind gene, but not colorblind himself.

    B) A male with a colorblind father and a mother who is a carrier has a 100% chance of being colorblind.

    C) A female with a colorblind father and a mother who is not a carrier has a 100% chance of being a carrier for the colorblind gene.

    D) A female with a mother who is a carrier but not colorblind and a colorblind father has a 100% chance of being colorblind.

WRITING AND LANGUAGE TEST

35 Minutes—44 Questions

This section corresponds to Section 2 of your answer sheet.

Directions: Each passage in this section is followed by several questions. Some questions will reference an underlined portion in the passage; others will ask you to consider a part of a passage or the passage as a whole. For each question, choose the answer that reflects the best use of grammar, punctuation, and style. If a passage or question is accompanied by a graphic, take the graphic into account in choosing your response(s). Some questions will have "NO CHANGE" as a possible response. Choose that answer if you think the best choice is to leave the sentence as written.

Questions 1-11 are based on the following passage and supplementary material.

Antarctic Treaty System in Need of Reform

The Antarctic Treaty System (ATS) was established in 1959 to provide governance over an entire continent and the surrounding Southern Ocean. Twelve member **1** countries, including the United States currently manage the affairs of Antarctica. In the next fifty years, however, it is likely that existing conflicts will **2** accelerate over the sovereignty and resources of Antarctica, challenging the ATS. Some countries feel the ATS should be reformed, while other countries argue that Antarctica should be designated as the shared heritage of humankind and be placed under the watch of the United Nations.

1. A) NO CHANGE
    B) countries including the United States, currently manage
    C) countries: including the United States currently manage
    D) countries including the United States currently manage

2. A) NO CHANGE
    B) anticipate
    C) decelerate
    D) vacillate

GO ON TO THE NEXT PAGE ⟶

[3] Altogether, opponents of the ATS believe that politics should trump science in Antarctica. A main objective of the ATS was to establish international research on a continent considered a "perfect laboratory." But new technological advances have countries **[4]** interested in Antarctic minerals, although mineral extraction is currently banned to protect the environment. **[5]** New players in Antarctic affairs such as China are oil-poor states. They view Antarctica's mineral resources as one solution to their increasing oil demands.

3. A) NO CHANGE
    B) Mainly,
    C) Surprisingly,
    D) Selfishly,

4. A) NO CHANGE
    B) thinking about
    C) curious about
    D) uninterested in

5. Which choice most effectively combines the underlined sentences?

    A) New players in Antarctic affairs such as China are oil-poor states, and so they view Antarctica's mineral resources as one solution to their increasing oil demands.

    B) New players in Antarctic affairs such as China are oil-poor states, even though they view Antarctica's mineral resources as one solution to their increasing oil demands.

    C) New players in Antarctic affairs such as China are oil-poor states, viewing Antarctica's mineral resources as the solution to their increasing oil demands.

    D) New players in Antarctic affairs such as China are oil-poor states, despite their view that Antarctica's mineral resources are one solution to their increasing oil demands.

[6] In the case of China, its future demand for energy from resources such as oil and coal is forecasted to surpass that of all other countries.

　　[7] Because of its many reserves such as coal, uranium, oil, and natural gas, Antarctica is indeed a rich continent. Yet, for environmental reasons, and because icebergs and weather have made mineral extraction expensive, there has never been commercial mining.

6. Which choice best supports the author's claim that China is an "oil-poor state" with accurate data based on the graphic?

   A) NO CHANGE

   B) In 2010, China's oil consumption exceeded production by approximately 10 million barrels per day.

   C) By 2015, China's oil consumption is forecasted to exceed production by approximately 7 million barrels per day.

   D) By 2015, China's oil production is forecasted to exceed consumption by approximately 7 million barrels per day.

7. A) NO CHANGE

   B) With reserves such as coal, uranium, oil, and natural gas,

   C) Because it has various reserves which include coal, uranium, oil, and natural gas,

   D) Due to its reserves like coal, uranium, and oil, and natural gas,

GO ON TO THE NEXT PAGE

But non-member countries believe that easier methods of extracting oil will bring the ATS's mineral ban into re-view. **8** <u>Right now, the ATS's superpowers choose to ig-nore the prediction that Antarctica may hold 200 billion barrels of oil.</u> When the protocol banning extraction is re-examined in 2048, **9** <u>it</u> will be waiting to capitalize on mineral claims in Antarctic locations.

There is also the economic issue of the Southern Ocean, because management of the commercial exploi-tation of marine resources is part of the ATS. **10** Fishing

8. A) NO CHANGE
    B) At the current moment, the superpowers of the ATS fail to realize the prediction that Antarctica may hold 200 billion barrels of oil.
    C) Currently, the ATS's superpowers are not addressing the prediction that Antarctica may hold 200 billion barrels of oil.
    D) For now, the ATS's superpowers don't seem to mind the prediction that Antarctica may hold 200 billion barrels of oil.

9. A) NO CHANGE
    B) an energy-hungry world
    C) they
    D) this banning protocol

10. At this point, the writer wants to add specific information that connects the ideas of the first sentence with the rest of the paragraph. Which choice most effectively accomplishes this goal?

    A) Antarctica has a wide variety of fish.
    B) This is one of several areas of responsibility assigned to the ATS.
    C) Other areas of the world have been heavily overfished.
    D) Non-member nations want to utilize the fishing ground.

 GO ON TO THE NEXT PAGE

is a primary industry for many countries; **11** therefore, Chinese Russian and other officials argue that forming marine preserves in Antarctica's periphery will seal off future fishing possibilities as fish stocks in the world are being depleted. Such a challenge has people wondering if national economic incentives are overwhelming the ATS's competing science and conservation values for the Southern Ocean.

These examples illustrate that after two decades, Antarctica's current governance structure isn't addressing new global priorities such as fuel and food security. As has probably been said by others before, detractors already feel that the continent could be better governed by the United Nations instead of the ATS. Without concessions or reform, many doubt the system can accommodate a wider community and survive in its current form.

11. A) NO CHANGE
    B) therefore Chinese Russian and other officials
    C) therefore Chinese Russian, and other officials
    D) therefore, Chinese, Russian, and other officials

China's Oil Production and Consumption, 1993-2015

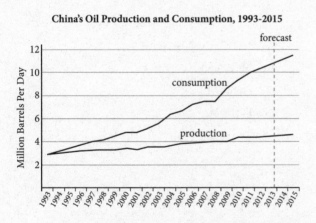

Adapted from U.S. Energy Information Administration, International Energy Statistics and Short-Term Energy Outlook, January 2014.

GO ON TO THE NEXT PAGE >

Questions 12-22 are based on the following passage.

Finding Pluto

Clyde Tombaugh sat down at an apparatus called a blink comparator, where he had spent hundreds of hours looking at photographic images of stars that appeared as [12] tiny little white specks on the black photographic plates. It was Thursday, February 13, 1930, and Tombaugh had been working at Lowell Observatory for about [13] thirteen months, he was looking for a planet that Percival Lowell had predicted would be at the far boundary of the solar system. [14] However, finding this elusive planet was not an easy task.

Tombaugh picked up the next set of photographic plates; weeks earlier, he had taken the photographs by pointing a telescope at a particular spot in the night sky, days apart but at the same time. If Lowell was right, one of the white specks would be in two different positions on the two plates. Tombaugh [15] loaded the images side by side in the blink comparator and looked through the eyepiece to compare the enlarged images.

12. A) NO CHANGE
    B) very tiny, little white specks
    C) tiny miniscule white specks
    D) tiny white specks

13. A) NO CHANGE
    B) thirteen months; he was looking
    C) thirteen months he was looking
    D) thirteen months, however, he was looking

14. Which choice most effectively concludes the paragraph?
    A) NO CHANGE
    B) The blink comparator is one of the most valuable tools astronomers have.
    C) Astronomy is among the oldest of the natural sciences.
    D) The Lowell Observatory is located in Flagstaff, Arizona.

15. A) NO CHANGE
    B) burdened
    C) changed
    D) led

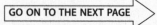

Like Lowell, Tombaugh believed there was an additional planet in our solar system, farther away than Neptune. Neptune's orbit did not exactly match the one predicted by calculations, and the presence of another planet could have caused that difference. [16]

Tombaugh moved a mirror in the viewer. It allowed him to look at a small area in the image on the left. When he moved the mirror again, he saw the image on the right in exactly the same place; the image did not change as he flipped back and forth, so he moved the images slightly and began looking at the next area, slowly working his way around the plates.

Tombaugh knew he could [17] check between a planet in our solar system and the stars; the planet, being closer, would change location in the sky relative to the stars. [18] Although, the farther the planet is from Earth, the more slowly that change happens, making it difficult to observe.

[1] Tombaugh continued to work his way, inch by inch, over the images, flipping back and forth with [19] the mirror; he saw no difference between the two images at each location, indicating he had nothing but far-away stars in the images. [2] Once more, he moved the images and flipped the mirror back and forth while looking through the eyepiece. [3] This time, as he blinked from one image to another, a speck seemed to move. [4] He knew immediately that it was significant; checking more images convinced him that he had found

16. At this point, the writer wants to add specific information that supports the central idea of the paragraph. Which choice most effectively accomplishes this goal?

A) Tombaugh wanted to find a new planet very badly.

B) This is because the gravitational pull of planets can affect the orbit of nearby planets.

C) Neptune is the eighth planet from the sun and has an elliptical orbit.

D) Lowell and Tombaugh disagreed about whether the presence of another planet could affect Neptune's orbit.

17. A) NO CHANGE

B) compliment

C) further

D) distinguish

18. A) NO CHANGE

B) Despite,

C) However,

D) Moreover,

19. A) NO CHANGE

B) the mirror, he saw no difference

C) the mirror he saw no difference

D) the mirror so he saw no difference

GO ON TO THE NEXT PAGE

a planet, which was eventually named Pluto. [5] Pluto was named for the Roman god of the underworld, because it was cold and far from the sun. [20]

Since that time, scientists [21] has determined that Pluto is smaller than it initially appeared and is actually a dwarf planet. [22] Pluto is, however, still a part of our solar system, located by calculations, careful observations, and a lot of patience.

20. Which sentence in the paragraph is least important to the main topic of the paragraph?

A) Sentence 2

B) Sentence 3

C) Sentence 4

D) Sentence 5

21. A) NO CHANGE

B) was determined

C) were determining

D) have determined

22. A) NO CHANGE

B) Pluto is however,

C) Pluto is; however,

D) Pluto is however

GO ON TO THE NEXT PAGE

Questions 23-33 are based on the following passage.

Public Relations: Build Your Brand While Building for Others

[23] Public relations is all about communicating— in print, in press interviews, in web content, and on social media. Public relations specialists are the people [24] behind, corporations, politicians, entertainers, and athletes. Practically anyone with a public image needs someone on his or her staff to maintain that image. With media expanding into every area of our lives, it is no surprise that U.S. government economists expect this field to experience [25] above-average growth through the year 2020!

As a public relations specialist for the Broome Corporation, a global pharmaceutical company, Janice Lin is responsible for drawing positive attention to the company and therefore enhancing its reputation. "A big part of my job is maintaining relationships with people in the media— [26] journalists, television personalities, online bloggers. I work with them to make sure the excellent work of the Broome Corporation is presented to the public accurately and often."

23. A) NO CHANGE
    B) Public relations is all about communicating. In print, in press interviews, in web content, and on social media.
    C) Public relations is all about communicating; in print, in press interviews, in web content, and on social media.
    D) Public relations is all about communicating; in print, in press interviews, in web content. And on social media.

24. A) NO CHANGE
    B) behind: corporations, politicians, entertainers, and athletes.
    C) behind—corporations, politicians, entertainers, athletes.
    D) behind corporations, politicians, entertainers, and athletes.

25. A) NO CHANGE
    B) above-average growth through the year 2020....
    C) above-average growth through the year 2020.
    D) above-average growth through the year 2020?

26. A) NO CHANGE
    B) journalists, a television personality, online bloggers.
    C) journalists, television personalities, an online blogger.
    D) a journalist, television personalities, online bloggers.

GO ON TO THE NEXT PAGE

Public relations specialists like Lin are often tasked with creating materials for use in print and on the Web. The materials must match [27] its company's brand and message. "I [28] provide press releases on a regular basis, but I also write scripts for web-based videos that can be found on our corporate website. I conduct interviews and review speeches, as well." In a media-savvy world, corporations and public figures are expected to communicate with the public across multiple platforms.

Most people in the public relations field have earned a bachelor's degree in communications, marketing, journalism, or other fields with [29] immovable skills. An entry-level position in public relations can pay $30,000 per year. Public relations specialists who rise in the field can earn increasingly higher salaries. [30] Many employees in upper-level management positions boast about their generous salaries. The Bureau of Labor Statistics expects the public relations field to grow 12 percent before 2022, which means an additional 27,400 jobs will be opening in the field.

27. A) NO CHANGE
    B) it's
    C) their
    D) they're

28. A) NO CHANGE
    B) form
    C) craft
    D) invent

29. A) NO CHANGE
    B) ordinary
    C) immobile
    D) transferable

30. Which choice best supports the claim made in the previous sentence?
    A) NO CHANGE
    B) Upper-level management positions pay significantly more at approximately $100,000 per year.
    C) PR workers who have been in the field for 30 or more years often rise to upper-level management positions.
    D) However, some PR specialists never rise in their field and rarely make more than $40,000 per year.

GO ON TO THE NEXT PAGE

[31] Lin has some advice for people who are considering a career in public relations: she suggests looking for local specialists in your area on a social media platform. [32] Reach out to them, request a meeting. [33] That will give you the opportunity of talking with them about their daily tasks and to observe how they talk to you about their company. You can learn a lot by listening. Also, consider joining a publication at your school. You'll learn to write effectively while also learning how to ask and answer difficult questions. That's the kind of thing I do every day.

31. Which sentence best establishes the central idea of the paragraph?

A) NO CHANGE

B) Lin expects social media to be the best method for connecting with specialists in the future.

C) Lin began her career as a public relations specialist before it was a popular career choice.

D) Lin believes that the Bureau of Labor Statistics offers support for students who want to pursue public relations careers.

32. A) NO CHANGE

B) Reach out to them, and request a meeting.

C) Reach out to them; and request a meeting.

D) Reach out to them; and, request a meeting.

33. A) NO CHANGE

B) That will give you the opportunity to talk to them about their daily tasks and to observe how they talk to you about their company.

C) That will give you the opportunity to talk to them about their daily tasks, and observing how they talk to you about their company.

D) That will give you the opportunity to talk to them about their daily tasks, and of observing how they are talking to you about their company.

GO ON TO THE NEXT PAGE ⟩

Questions 34-44 are based on the following passage and supplementary material.

Film, Culture, and Globalization

Globalization, or the integration of cultures across nations, is a prominent yet controversial topic. The controversy arises over concern about what is often called "cultural imperialism," or the notion of one culture's overpowering influence on another's cultural identity. [34] Some defend globalization for its benefits. Greater creativity and appreciation of heritage. Others argue that globalization damages cultures, especially in developing nations. For better or worse, advancing technology enables new levels of cross-cultural interconnectedness. The modern world is culturally intertwined, and there is no force more [35] inactive for globalization in the 21st century than the film industry.

[36] Filmmakers throughout the world are allowed to showcase their movies in the United States only if American film producers approve the project ahead of time. With multi-billion-dollar extranational revenues, Hollywood has inspired a global culture of moviemakers and moviegoers. Now, many nations enjoy booming domestic film markets that compare with or surpass the United States in production and popularity.

34. A) NO CHANGE
    B) Some defend globalization for its benefits greater creativity and appreciation of heritage.
    C) Some defend globalization for its benefits; greater creativity and appreciation of heritage.
    D) Some defend globalization for its benefits, including greater creativity and appreciation of heritage.

35. A) NO CHANGE
    B) ineffectual
    C) fragile
    D) potent

36. Which topic sentence most effectively establishes the central idea of the paragraph?
    A) NO CHANGE
    B) The past century has seen the rise of film and its predominance over much of popular culture, in and beyond the United States.
    C) This past century has seen Hollywood filmmakers striving to maintain their presence in the global cultural environment.
    D) Global filmmakers are anxious to share their products with the United States so that they may obtain the notoriety of American film producers.

As more countries produce and distribute films worldwide, the global sense of shared understanding and cultural appreciation [37] grow.

[38] Sharing cultural artifacts is central to globalization, and cultural artifacts are physical renderings of cultural identity. Foods, music, languages, books, art, and trade goods are all cultural artifacts. But films are cultural artifacts with more impact than others because of their vivid ability to document and portray a population's ideals, values, and commonalities. There is [39] naive appeal in viewers witnessing the heartfelt stories of people worlds away. Through film, the cross-cultural sharing of ideas, stories, ethics, humor, and much more can happen quickly.

The extent to which the world watches foreign, cross-cultural films is staggering. [40] Even as more countries increase film production the trend of cross-cultural film popularity is expected to remain; the difference will be the greater variety of cultures represented in those

37. A) NO CHANGE
    B) grows
    C) have grown
    D) were growing

38. A) NO CHANGE
    B) Cultural artifacts are physical renderings of cultural identity and are central to globalization.
    C) The sharing of cultural artifacts, which are physical renderings of cultural identity, is central to globalization.
    D) The sharing of cultural artifacts is central to globalization and they are physical renderings of cultural identity.

39. A) NO CHANGE
    B) senseless
    C) obtuse
    D) acute

40. A) NO CHANGE
    B) Even as more countries increase film production; the trend of cross-cultural film popularity is expected to remain
    C) Even as more countries increase film production; the trend of cross-cultural film popularity is expected to remain,
    D) Even as more countries increase film production, the trend of cross-cultural film popularity is expected to remain;

GO ON TO THE NEXT PAGE

films. **41** <u>Only the production of video games exceeds the film-making industry in the world market.</u>

Certainly, many individuals prefer films that reflect their own cultural identities, but trends indicate rising popular interest, even in Hollywood, in multicultural and cross-cultural movies. Despite valid concerns over cultural imperialism, the international film industry in many ways **42** <u>enables</u> positive culture sharing. **43** <u>Films are increasingly used to teach, treasuring, and to preserve cultures and peoples,</u> strengthening those groups' identities and raising worldwide awareness and appreciation of their stories.

41. Which choice provides the most relevant detail to the paragraph?

A) NO CHANGE

B) Cross-cultural experiences extend beyond the foreign film industry to cuisine in popular international restaurants.

C) Outside the few nations whose powerhouse filmmaking industries dominate their own markets, nearly every moviegoer's experience is markedly cross-cultural.

D) The cross-cultural concept of sharing ideas and stories through humor is the most popular type of filmmaking both in the United States and in the current international market.

42. A) NO CHANGE

B) enabled

C) will enable

D) was enabling

43. A) NO CHANGE

B) Films are increasingly used to teach, treasure, and preserve cultures and peoples,

C) Films are increasingly used to teach, treasure, and preserving cultures and peoples,

D) Films are increasingly used for teaching, to treasure, and preserve cultures and peoples,

 GO ON TO THE NEXT PAGE

Statistics indicate that the global population will continue to frequent films from a variety of origins. According to information from the UNESCO Institute for Statistics, while film production fluctuates in many nations, only ▮44▮ India demonstrated a consistent increase in the number of films produced from 2005 to 2011. Filmmakers have the opportunity both to protect cultures and to creatively pioneer the route to true, sustained intercultural appreciation. Understanding the industry's undeniable impact on cultural identities and globalization is crucial in the world's progression toward collective prosperity, protection, and peace.

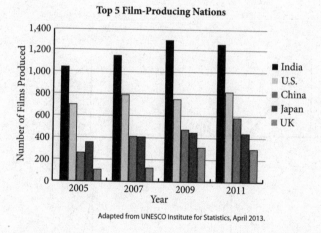

Top 5 Film-Producing Nations

Adapted from UNESCO Institute for Statistics, April 2013.

44. Which choice completes the sentence with accurate data based on the graphic?

A) NO CHANGE

B) China

C) the United States

D) the United Kingdom

MATH TEST

25 Minutes—20 Questions

NO-CALCULATOR SECTION

This section corresponds to Section 3 of your answer sheet.

Directions: For this section, solve each question and select the best answer choice. The available space on each page may be used for scratch work.

Notes:

1. Calculator use is NOT permitted.
2. All numbers used are real numbers, and all variables used represent real numbers, unless otherwise indicated.
3. Figures are drawn to scale and lie in a plane unless otherwise indicated.
4. Unless stated otherwise, the domain of any function f is assumed to be the set of all real numbers x, for which $f(x)$ is a real number.

Information:

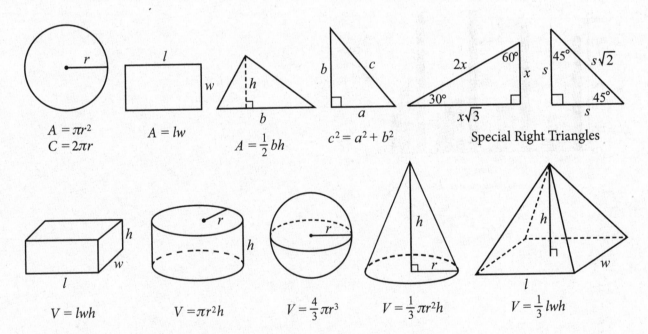

$A = \pi r^2$
$C = 2\pi r$

$A = lw$

$A = \frac{1}{2}bh$

$c^2 = a^2 + b^2$

Special Right Triangles

$V = lwh$

$V = \pi r^2 h$

$V = \frac{4}{3}\pi r^3$

$V = \frac{1}{3}\pi r^2 h$

$V = \frac{1}{3}lwh$

The sum of the degree measures of the angles in a triangle is 180.

The number of degrees of arc in a circle is 360.

The number of radians of arc in a circle is 2π.

GO ON TO THE NEXT PAGE

1. Tread depth is a measurement between the top of the rubber on a tire and the bottom of its deepest groove. The average tread depth on a new standard tire is $\frac{10}{32}$ inches. In most states, a tire is considered legally worn out, and therefore unsafe, when the tread depth reaches $\frac{2}{32}$ inches. Which inequality represents the range of safe tread depths, d, for a standard car tire?

   A) $\frac{2}{32} > d \le \frac{10}{32}$

   B) $\frac{2}{32} < d \ge \frac{10}{32}$

   C) $\frac{2}{32} < d \le \frac{10}{32}$

   D) $\frac{2}{32} > d \ge \frac{10}{32}$

2. If $x^2 - 8x = 48$ and $x < 0$, what is the value of $x + 10$?

   A) -2

   B) 4

   C) 6

   D) 8

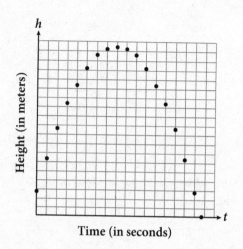

Time (in seconds)

3. A physics class is using simulation software to study water bottle rockets before attempting to build one for the National Physics Competition. Their first simulation is of a rocket without a parachute launched from the roof of the gymnasium. The scatterplot shows the approximate path of the rocket. The software program generates the equation $h = -4.9t^2 + 39.2t + 14$ to model the data, where h is the height in meters of the rocket t seconds after it was launched. What does the number 14 most likely represent in this equation?

   A) The number of seconds the rocket was in the air

   B) The height of the gymnasium from which the rocket was launched

   C) The number of seconds that it took the rocket to reach its maximum height

   D) The maximum height of the rocket

GO ON TO THE NEXT PAGE

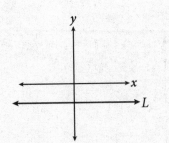

4. Line L shown in the graph could be the graph of which equation?

A) $x + y = -2$

B) $x + y = 0$

C) $x + y - 2 = x$

D) $x + y + 2 = x$

$$\begin{cases} 2x + 5y = 8 \\ x + 3y = 3 \end{cases}$$

5. If (x, y) is a solution to the system of equations above, what is the value of y^2?

A) 4

B) 9

C) 25

D) 81

6. An alloy is a metal made by mixing and melting two or more metals together. After the metals are mixed, the alloy must be cooled slowly to avoid crystallization. Suppose a metallurgist heats a mixture of metals to a temperature of 2,500°F and then removes the resulting alloy from the furnace. The alloy will then cool at a constant rate of 40°F every 15 minutes until it reaches room temperature. Which of the following functions represents the temperature T of the alloy h hours after it was removed from the furnace until it reaches room temperature?

A) $T(h) = -15h + 2,500$

B) $T(h) = -40h + 2,500$

C) $T(h) = -160h + 2,500$

D) $T(h) = -600h + 2,500$

7. If $\dfrac{3}{a - 1} = \dfrac{12}{w}$, such that $a \neq 1$ and $w \neq 0$, what is w in terms of a?

A) $4a - 4$

B) $4a - 12$

C) $12a - 4$

D) $\dfrac{1}{4}a + 1$

$$\frac{4 - (1 - 3n)}{36} = \frac{2(n - 3) + 7}{12}$$

8. In the equation above, what is the value of n?

A) 0

B) 2

C) 3

D) There is no value of n that satisfies the equation.

9. Which of the following functions has a domain of $x \geq 2$?

A) $f(x) = -x^2 + 2$

B) $g(x) = -\sqrt{x - 2}$

C) $h(x) = -\sqrt{x} + 2$

D) $k(x) = -|x - 2|$

10. If $\dfrac{1}{6}x - \dfrac{1}{2}y = 3$, what is the value of $x - 3y$?

A) 6

B) 12

C) 18

D) 36

GO ON TO THE NEXT PAGE
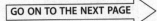

11. Suppose you know that $0° < m\angle\beta < 90°$ and $0 < m\angle\theta < 90°$, and that $\sin\beta = \cos\theta$. If $m\angle\beta = (7n - 12)°$ and $m\angle\theta = (3n - 8)°$, then what is the value of n ?

A) 1

B) 5

C) 8

D) 11

$$\begin{cases} ax + y = -5 \\ -\dfrac{1}{3}x - 2y = -1 \end{cases}$$

12. If the system of linear equations above has no solution, and a is a constant, what is the value of a ?

A) $-\dfrac{1}{3}$

B) $-\dfrac{1}{6}$

C) $\dfrac{1}{6}$

D) $\dfrac{1}{3}$

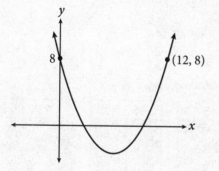

13. The range of the parabola shown in the graph is $y \geq -4$. If the equation $y = ax^2 + bx + c$ is used to represent the graph, what is the value of a ?

A) $\dfrac{1}{3}$

B) $\dfrac{2}{3}$

C) $\dfrac{3}{2}$

D) 3

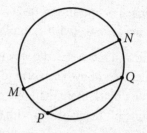

14. The circle shown has a radius of r centimeters. If chord PQ is parallel to diameter MN, and the length of chord PQ is $\dfrac{3}{4}$ of the length of the diameter, what is the distance in centimeters between $\overline{MN}$ and $\overline{PQ}$ in terms of r ?

A) $\dfrac{\sqrt{7}}{4}r$

B) $\dfrac{\sqrt{3}}{2}r$

C) $\dfrac{1}{4}\pi r$

D) $\dfrac{3}{4}\pi r$

15. Which of the following represents $16^{\frac{3}{2}}$ as an integer?

A) 4

B) 12

C) 48

D) 64

GO ON TO THE NEXT PAGE

Directions: For questions 16-20, enter your responses into the appropriate grid on your answer sheet, in accordance with the following:

1. You will receive credit only if the circles are filled in correctly, but you may write your answers in the boxes above each grid to help you fill in the circles accurately.

2. Don't mark more than one circle per column.

3. None of the questions with grid-in responses will have a negative solution.

4. Only grid in a single answer, even if there is more than one correct answer to a given question.

5. A **mixed number** must be gridded as a decimal or an improper fraction. For example, you would grid $7\frac{1}{2}$ as 7.5 or $\frac{15}{2}$.

   (Were you to grid it as $\boxed{7 \mid 1 \mid / \mid 2}$, this response would be read as $\frac{71}{2}$.)

6. A **decimal** that has more digits than there are places on the grid may be either rounded or truncated, but every column in the grid must be filled in order to receive credit.

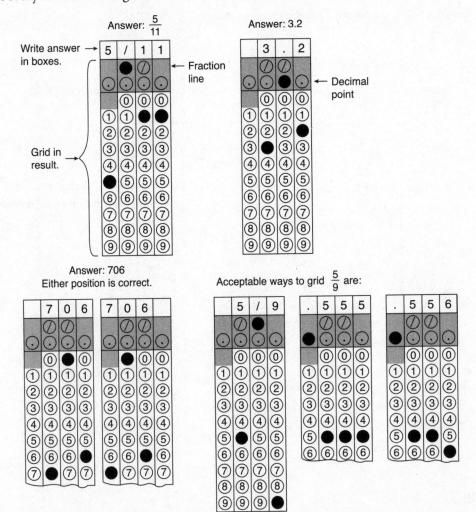

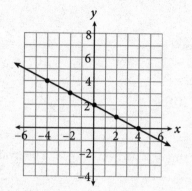

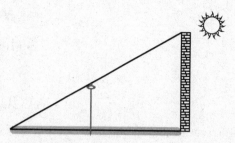

Note: Figure not drawn to scale.

16. If the equation that represents the graph shown above is written in standard form, $Ax + By = C$, and $A = 6$, what is the value of B?

17. If $\dfrac{1}{3} \leq 2 - \dfrac{d}{6} \leq \dfrac{5}{4}$, what is the minimum possible value of d?

$$g(x) = \begin{cases} x^2 - 1, & \text{if } x \leq 0 \\ \dfrac{x^2}{3} + 1, & \text{if } 0 < x \leq 3 \\ 5x + 3, & \text{if } x > 3 \end{cases}$$

18. For the piecewise-defined function $g(x)$ shown above, what is the value of $g(2)$?

19. A toy saber is stuck at a right angle into the ground 4 inches deep. It casts a shadow that is 4 feet long. The brick wall casts a shadow three times that long. If the wall is 7 feet 6 inches tall, how many inches long is the toy saber?

$$\frac{x}{x-1} - \frac{2}{x} = \frac{1}{x-1}$$

20. What is one possible solution to the rational equation given above?

MATH TEST

55 Minutes—38 Questions

CALCULATOR SECTION

This section corresponds to Section 4 of your answer sheet.

Directions: For this section, solve each question and select the best answer choice. The available space on each page may be used for scratch work.

Notes:

1. Calculator use is permitted.
2. All numbers used are real numbers, and all variables used represent real numbers, unless otherwise indicated.
3. Figures are drawn to scale and lie in a plane unless otherwise indicated.
4. Unless stated otherwise, the domain of any function f is assumed to be the set of all real numbers x, for which $f(x)$ is a real number.

Information:

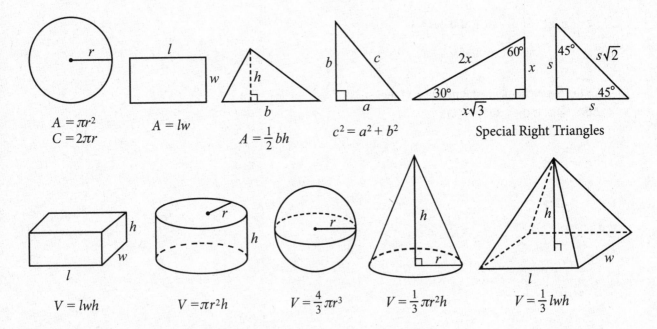

$$A = \pi r^2$$
$$C = 2\pi r$$

$$A = lw$$

$$A = \frac{1}{2} bh$$

$$c^2 = a^2 + b^2$$

Special Right Triangles

$$V = lwh$$

$$V = \pi r^2 h$$

$$V = \frac{4}{3} \pi r^3$$

$$V = \frac{1}{3} \pi r^2 h$$

$$V = \frac{1}{3} lwh$$

The sum of the degree measures of the angles in a triangle is 180.

The number of degrees of arc in a circle is 360.

The number of radians of arc in a circle is 2π.

GO ON TO THE NEXT PAGE

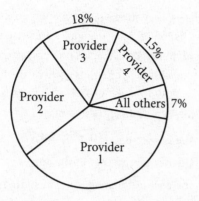

1. A company's market share is the percent of consumers who utilize the services or buy the products of that company. The pie chart above shows the different market shares of cable providers in a certain region. If the ratio of the market shares of Provider 1 to Provider 2 is 3:2, what is Provider 1's market share?

   A) 24%

   B) 30%

   C) 36%

   D) 42%

2. Which of the following number lines represents the solution to the inequality $3x + 29 > 5 - x$?

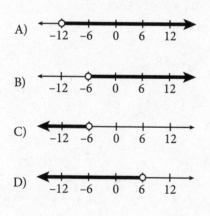

3. Water is vital to human health. An average person should consume approximately 2.5 ounces of water per hour. However, because of the salt in it, seawater actually dehydrates the human body and should not be consumed. This is why boats must carry a supply of fresh water when embarking on long trips. Suppose a sailboat is traveling at an average speed of 4 nautical miles per hour with 3 people on board and the trip is 232 nautical miles. What is the minimum number of ounces of water the boat should stock before leaving?

   A) 69.6

   B) 145

   C) 435

   D) 1,113.6

4. If $a = 0$ and $b < 0$, then which of the following could be the graph of $f(x) = (x - a)(x - b)$?

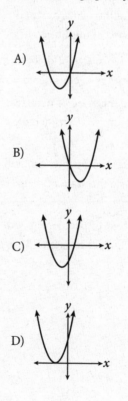

GO ON TO THE NEXT PAGE

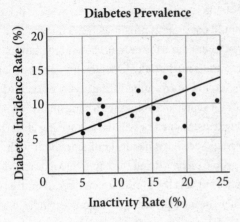

Diabetes Prevalence

Diabetes Incidence Rate (%) vs Inactivity Rate (%)

5. Increased physical activity has been linked to a lower incidence rate of diabetes. The scatterplot above shows the relationship between the percent of people in a certain country whose daily activity qualifies them as "inactive" and the incidence rate of diabetes in that country. The line of best fit for the data is also shown. Which of the following best represents the meaning of the y-intercept of the line of best fit in the context of this question?

A) The predicted incidence rate of diabetes when the entire country is considered active

B) The predicted incidence rate of diabetes when the entire country is considered inactive

C) The predicted percent of people who will be active when the incidence rate of diabetes is 0%

D) The predicted percent of people who will be inactive when the incidence rate of diabetes is 0%

6. At the grocery store, Gigi buys apples, a magazine, and a gallon of milk. The apples are priced per pound. In her state, there is no sales tax on food. If the total cost of her items is given by the function $C(p) = 1.89p + 1.07(3.99) + 4.49$, then the term $1.07(3.99)$ most likely represents

A) the cost of one gallon of milk.

B) the per-pound cost of the apples.

C) the cost of the magazine, including tax.

D) the cost of the magazine, not including tax.

7. When a homeowner hires a contractor to renovate a bathroom, the homeowner is charged for both labor and materials. By law, the contractor can charge sales tax on the materials, but not on the labor. If the contractor quotes the homeowner $3,000 for materials and $40 per hour for labor, and sales tax in the homeowner's state is 5.5%, which equation represents the total cost for the bathroom renovation if it takes the contractor h hours to complete the job?

A) $c = (40h + 3,000)(1.055)$

B) $c = 1.055(40 + 3,000)h$

C) $c = 40h(1.055) + 3,000$

D) $c = 40h + 1.055(3,000)$

8. A picture-framing shop sells ready-made frames and also does custom framing using different kinds and widths of wood or metal. The shop has a three-day sale. During the sale, for an 11-inch × 14-inch frame, a ready-made frame costs $12 and a custom frame costs $30. Over the course of the three days, the shop sells ninety-two 11 × 14 frames and collects $1,788. Solving which system of equations would yield the number of 11 × 14 ready-made frames r and the number of 11 × 14 custom frames c that the shop sold during the three-day sale?

A) $\begin{cases} r + c = 92 \\ 12r + 30c = \dfrac{1,788}{3} \end{cases}$

B) $\begin{cases} r + c = 1,788 \\ 12r + 30c = 92 \times 3 \end{cases}$

C) $\begin{cases} r + c = 1,788 \\ 12r + 30c = 92 \end{cases}$

D) $\begin{cases} r + c = 92 \\ 12r + 30c = 1,788 \end{cases}$

City	Cost per Square Foot
Detroit	$62.45
Atlanta	$74.19
New York City	$288.58
San Francisco	$420.99

9. In real estate, location is often the number one determinant of home prices. The table above shows the average price per square foot of houses in four cities. Assuming an average home size of 1,500 to 2,000 square feet, which inequality represents how much more in dollars a house in New York City would cost than in Detroit?

A) $x \geq 226.13$

B) $62.45 \leq x \leq 288.58$

C) $93,675 \leq x \leq 432,870$

D) $339,195 \leq x \leq 452,260$

10. If $5n - 3(n - 1) = \dfrac{1}{2}(4n + 16) - 5$, what is the value of n?

A) $n = 1$

B) $n = 3$

C) There is no value of n for which the equation is true.

D) There are infinitely many values of n for which the equation is true.

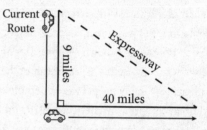

Note: Figure not drawn to scale.

11. The figure above shows the route that Max currently takes to work and back home every day. The city is planning to build an expressway that would cross through the city to help alleviate commuter traffic. Assuming an average gas consumption of 20 miles per gallon and a 5-day workweek, how many gallons of gas will Max save per week by taking the expressway to and from work each day instead of using his current route?

A) 2

B) 4

C) 8

D) 10.25

GO ON TO THE NEXT PAGE

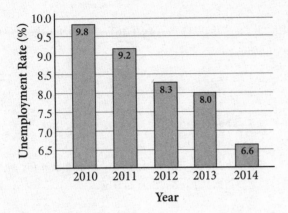

12. The bar graph shows the percent of the U.S. population that was unemployed as of January 1 on each of the years shown. A governmental agency wants to use the 5-year mean of the data to estimate how many people were unemployed in a certain geographic area between 2010 and 2014. If the total adult population of the area was 250,000, approximately how many adults were unemployed in that area during the indicated time period?

A) 16,950

B) 20,150

C) 20,950

D) 104,750

13. Which of the following expressions is equivalent to $(36x^4y^7)^{\frac{1}{2}}$?

A) $\dfrac{36x^4y^7}{2}$

B) $6xy^2\sqrt{y}$

C) $6x^2y^3\sqrt{y}$

D) $(36x^4y^7)^{-2}$

Questions 14 and 15 refer to the following information.

Use the data in the scatterplot and the line of best fit shown to answer the following questions.

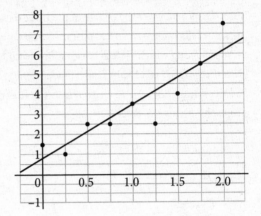

14. Which of the following values most accurately reflects the average rate of change of the data based on the line of best fit?

A) $\dfrac{3}{8}$

B) $\dfrac{3}{4}$

C) $\dfrac{4}{3}$

D) $\dfrac{8}{3}$

15. For how many of the data points is the difference between the actual y-value and the expected y-value greater than 2 ?

A) 3

B) 2

C) 1

D) 0

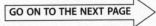

16. Which of the following are solutions to the quadratic equation $(x - 2)^2 = \dfrac{16}{25}$?

    A) $x = \pm\sqrt{\dfrac{4}{5}}$

    B) $x = -\dfrac{4}{5},\ x = \dfrac{4}{5}$

    C) $x = \dfrac{6}{5},\ x = \dfrac{14}{5}$

    D) $x = \dfrac{14}{5},\ x = -\dfrac{14}{5}$

17. If the slope of a line is $-\dfrac{5}{2}$ and a point on the line is $(2, -1)$, which of the following is the y-intercept of the line?

    A) -6

    B) $-\dfrac{1}{2}$

    C) 4

    D) 6

18. The Consumer Price Index (CPI) is a weighted average of the cost of certain categories of goods and services in the United States. It is one of the most widely used measures of inflation. According to the U.S. Census Bureau, the CPI was 130.7 in 1990 and was 218.1 in 2010. If the CPI continues to experience the same percent increase over the next 20 years, approximately what will the CPI be in 2030?

    A) 145.8

    B) 305.5

    C) 363.9

    D) 408.7

19. Given the function $f(x) = \dfrac{1}{4}x - 2$, what domain value corresponds to a range value of $-\dfrac{5}{3}$?

    A) $-\dfrac{29}{12}$

    B) $\dfrac{4}{3}$

    C) $\dfrac{7}{3}$

    D) $\dfrac{29}{12}$

$$T = 2\pi\sqrt{\dfrac{m}{k}}$$

20. When a spring is pressed tightly between two objects, it remains still. When one or both of those objects is disturbed, the spring starts to move. The equation above can be used to find the time period T in which a mass m, attached to a spring, makes a single oscillation (going all the way down and then back up). The variable k is a constant. Which of the following equations could be used to find the mass of the object?

    A) $m = \dfrac{2\pi k}{T^2}$

    B) $m = \dfrac{kT^2}{4\pi^2}$

    C) $m = \dfrac{T^2}{4\pi^2 k}$

    D) $m = \sqrt{\dfrac{T}{2\pi k}}$

GO ON TO THE NEXT PAGE

21. An educational polling company wants to determine whether parents of high school-age children believe using an electronic tablet in the classroom will improve student learning. To do this, the company conducted a survey by sending 50,000 text messages across the entire United States to randomly selected phones with text-messaging capabilities. For every text that the company sent, it received a response to the survey. Which of the following best explains why this random sample is unlikely to be a good representative sample of parents' opinions on the use of tablets in the classroom?

A) Most parents don't care about this issue, and their attitude is likely to skew the results.

B) Surveys conducted via text messaging are illegal and therefore are not considered reliable.

C) There is no way to verify whether the responders to the survey were parents of high school age-children.

D) The survey was biased because parents who own a cell phone probably also have a tablet and would want their children to learn how to use it.

22. A company that makes shoelaces has two machines, both of which run 24 hours a day. The first machine can produce 36,000 shoelaces per day. The second machine can produce 28,800 shoelaces per day. How many more shoelaces can the first machine make than the second machine in 8 minutes?

A)   5

B)   40

C)   160

D)   200

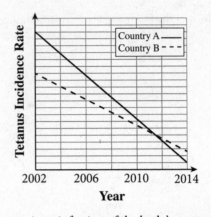

23. Tetanus is an infection of the body's nervous system. It is usually contracted by cutting oneself on a rusty metal object. In 2002, Country A started requiring students to have tetanus shots before entering public school. That same year, Country B started providing the vaccine free of charge to school-age children but has not required that they get it. The graph above shows the incidence rate of tetanus in these two countries starting in 2002. Which of the following statements is true?

A) Country A's vaccine requirement had a greater impact on the incidence rate than did Country B's free vaccines.

B) Country B's free vaccines had a greater impact on the incidence rate than did Country A's vaccine requirement.

C) Country A's vaccine requirement had about the same impact on the incidence rate as did Country B's free vaccines.

D) Because the countries started with different incidence rates, it is impossible to determine which country's actions had a greater impact.

GO ON TO THE NEXT PAGE

24. A college professor with several hundred students has office hours between classes to provide extra help when needed. His classes on Monday are from 9:00 AM to 10:45 AM and 2:30 PM to 3:45 PM. It takes him 5 minutes to walk from the classroom to his office, and he takes a lunch break from 12:00 PM to 1:00 PM. On a particular Monday, he plans to grade tests, which have all multiple-choice questions. If each test consists of 50 questions and it takes him 4 seconds to mark each question right or wrong, how many complete tests can he mark during his office hours if no students come for help? Assume that he does not take the time to add up the scores until after his afternoon class.

   A) 46

   B) 47

   C) 54

   D) 55

25. An optician charges $125 for an eye examination, frames, and clear glass lenses, but $197 for an eye examination, frames, and tinted glass lenses. If the tinted lenses cost three times as much as the clear lenses, how much do the clear glass lenses cost?

   A) $24

   B) $36

   C) $48

   D) $72

Registered to Vote?	1	2	3	4	5	Total
Yes	112	104	228	487	163	1,094
No	28	76	48	158	54	364
Total	140	180	276	645	217	1,458

26. An incumbent state senator (currently in office and running for an additional term) conducts a survey to see how favorably the people in her district view her. In the survey, responses of 1 or 2 represent an unfavorable view, a response of 3 is a neutral view, and responses of 4 or 5 are favorable. The results of the survey are recorded in the table. If one registered voter is chosen at random to attend a town hall meeting, what is the probability that the voter does not view the senator unfavorably?

   A) 40.6%

   B) 59.4%

   C) 78.1%

   D) 80.3%

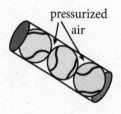

pressurized air

27. Higher-quality tennis balls are typically packaged in cylindrical cans, as shown above, which are pressurized with air to keep them fresh. If the can and the tennis balls have the same diameter, 2.6 inches, what is the volume in cubic inches of the air inside the can around the tennis balls? Assume that each tennis ball is tangent to the next and that the top and bottom tennis balls are tangent to the top and bottom of the can.

   A) 4.4π

   B) 8.1π

   C) 10.3π

   D) 29.3π

GO ON TO THE NEXT PAGE

28. If h is a rational number such that $-1 < h < 0$, which of the following could be the graph of the equation $y = hy + hx + x - 4$?

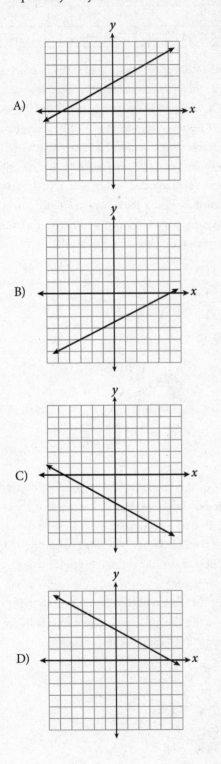

A)

B)

C)

D)

29. A scientist weighed a 1.0 cubic foot piece of granite and found that it weighed 168 pounds. The average density of Earth's inner core is approximately 12.8 g/cm³. How much denser, in g/cm³, is Earth's inner core than the piece of granite? Use any of the following conversions:

- 12 inches = 1 foot

- 16 ounces = 1 pound

- 1 inch = 2.54 cm

- 1 ounce = 28.35 grams

A) 2.7

B) 10.1

C) 15.55

D) 28.35

$$\dfrac{1}{\dfrac{1}{R_1} + \dfrac{1}{R_2}}$$

30. In electronic circuits, resistors are often paired to manage the flow of the electrical current. To find the total resistance of a pair of parallel resistors, electricians use the formula shown above, where R_1 is the resistance of the first resistor and R_2 is the resistance of the second resistor. Which of the following is another way to represent this formula?

A) $\dfrac{R_1 R_2}{R_1 + R_2}$

B) $\dfrac{R_1 + R_2}{R_1 R_2}$

C) $\dfrac{1}{R_2} - \dfrac{1}{R_1}$

D) $R_1 + R_2$

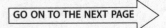

Directions: For questions 31-38, enter your responses into the appropriate grid on your answer sheet, in accordance with the following:

1. You will receive credit only if the circles are filled in correctly, but you may write your answers in the boxes above each grid to help you fill in the circles accurately.
2. Don't mark more than one circle per column.
3. None of the questions with grid-in responses will have a negative solution.
4. Only grid in a single answer, even if there is more than one correct answer to a given question.
5. A **mixed number** must be gridded as a decimal or an improper fraction. For example, you would grid $7\frac{1}{2}$ as 7.5 or $\frac{15}{2}$.

   (Were you to grid it as $\begin{array}{|c|c|c|c|}\hline 7 & 1 & / & 2 \\\hline\end{array}$, this response would be read as $\frac{71}{2}$.)
6. A **decimal** that has more digits than there are places on the grid may be either rounded or truncated, but every column in the grid must be filled in order to receive credit.

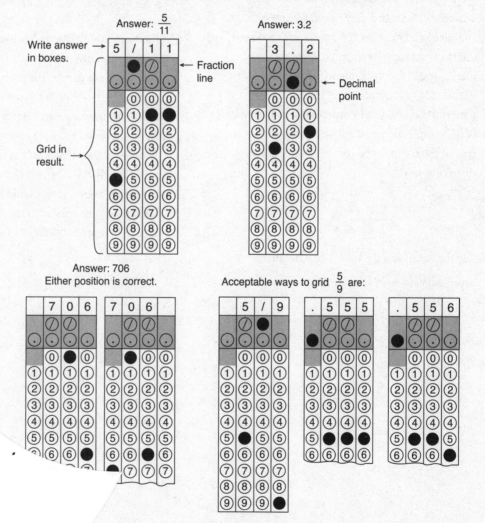

31. According to the U.S. Department of Agriculture, the linear equation $f = -3.7t + 872$ estimates the number of acres of farmland f in the United States t years after 2010, where f is given in millions of acres. Based on this equation, at the start of what year will the amount of farmland be below 800 million acres?

32. If $g(x) = x^2 + 2x + 9$, what is $g(5) - g(-1)$?

33. A North Carolina agricultural supply company is hoping to expand its services to three counties in rural Virginia. According to its research, there is a total of approximately 1,200 farms in these three counties. The company sends out surveys to a sample of 200 randomly selected farmers in the counties and finds that 120 are not satisfied with their current supply company. Based on other market research, the company is confident that it will be able to acquire 75% of the dissatisfied customers. Based on this information and the results of the sample survey, about how many customers should the company be able to acquire in these three counties?

$$\frac{4 + \sqrt{-16}}{2 + \sqrt{-4}}$$

34. Use the definition $\sqrt{-1} = i$ to write the expression above in simplest form.

35. Sometimes, companies will buy stock in businesses owned by one or more of their competitors in order to gain some control over the competing companies. Suppose Company X buys a 500-share block of stock in each of two of its competitors. The first competitor is a small regional company. The block of its stock cost $25,000 less than half as much as the block of the other competitor's stock, which is a large national company. Together, Company X pays $155,000 for the two blocks of stock. How many more thousands of dollars did Company X spend on acquiring the stock of the national competitor than the regional one? Enter your answer in thousands of dollars. (For example, enter $15,000 as 15.)

36. The Mackinac Bridge in Michigan is one of the longest suspension bridges in the Western Hemisphere, spanning approximately 1.63 miles from one end to the other. It has several pieces that are connected by anchorages (large blocks to which the suspension cables are attached). The longest piece is 3,800 feet long. In a scale drawing on a poster board, the length of the bridge is 28 inches. How many inches long should the longest piece be? Round your answer to the nearest tenth of an inch. (There are 5,280 feet in 1 mile.)

Questions 37 and 38 refer to the following information.

A restaurant sent out surveys to determine how long customers are willing to wait for a table on Friday night versus Saturday night. Participants randomly received either a Friday night or a Saturday night survey. Results are shown in the bar graph below.

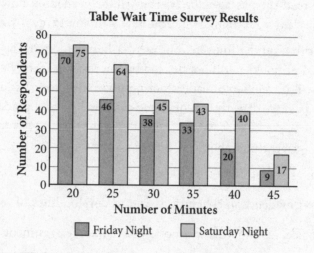

Table Wait Time Survey Results

37. If a customer is chosen at random from all of the survey respondents, what is the probability that the customer is willing to wait at least 30 minutes for a table?

38. On average, how many minutes longer are customers willing to wait for a table on Saturday night than on Friday night? Round your answer to the nearest whole minute.

ESSAY TEST

50 Minutes

You will be given a passage to read and asked to write an essay analyzing it. As you write, be sure to show that you have read the passage closely. You will be graded on how well you have understood the passage, how clear your analysis is, and how well you express your ideas.

Your essay must be written on the lines in your answer booklet. Anything you write outside the lined space in your answer booklet will not be read by the essay graders. Be sure to write or print in such a way that it will be legible to readers not familiar with your handwriting. Additionally, be sure to address the passage directly. An off-topic essay will not be graded.

As you read the passage, think about the author's use of

- evidence, such as statistics or other facts.

- logic to connect evidence to conclusions and to develop lines of reasoning.

- style, word choice, and appeals to emotion to make the argument more persuasive.

Adapted from President Lyndon Johnson's Voting Rights Address, delivered March 15, 1965.

1 I speak tonight for the dignity of man and the destiny of democracy.

2 I urge every member of both parties, Americans of all religions and of all races, from every section of this country, to join me in that cause.

3 At times history and fate meet at a single time in a single place to shape a turning point in man's unending search for freedom....

4 In our time we have come to live with moments of great crisis. Our lives have been marked with debate about great issues; issues of war and peace, issues of prosperity and depression. But rarely in any time does an issue lay bare the secret heart of America itself. Rarely are we met with a challenge, not to our growth or abundance, our welfare or our security, but rather to the values and the purposes and the meaning of our beloved Nation.

5 The issue of equal rights for African Americans is such an issue, and should we defeat every enemy, should we double our wealth and conquer the stars, and still be unequal to this issue, then we will have failed as a people and as a nation....

6 Many of the issues of civil rights are very complex and most difficult, but about this there can and should be no argument. Every American citizen must have an equal right to vote. There is no reason which can excuse the denial of that right. There is no duty which weighs more heavily on us than the duty we have to ensure that right.

7 Yet the harsh fact is that in many places in this country men and women are kept from voting simply because they are black.

8 Every device of which human ingenuity is capable has been used to deny this right. The African American citizen may go to register only to be told that the day is wrong, or the hour is late, or the official in charge is absent; and if he persists, and if he manages to present himself to the registrar, he may be disqualified because he did not spell out his middle name or because he abbreviated a word on the application.

GO ON TO THE NEXT PAGE ⟩

9   And if he manages to fill out an application he is given a test. The registrar is the sole judge of whether he passes this test. He may be asked to recite the entire Constitution, or explain the most complex provisions of state law. And even a college degree cannot be used to prove that he can read and write.

10 Experience has clearly shown that the existing process of law cannot overcome systematic and ingenious discrimination. No law that we now have on the books—and I have helped to put three of them there—can ensure the right to vote when local officials are determined to deny it.

11 In such a case our duty must be clear to all of us. The Constitution says that no person shall be kept from voting because of his race. We have all sworn an oath before God to support and to defend that Constitution. We must now act in obedience to that oath....

12 It is wrong—deadly wrong—to deny any of your fellow Americans the right to vote in this country....

13 We cannot, we must not, refuse to protect the right of every American to vote in every election that he may desire to participate in; and we ought not and we cannot and we must not wait another eight months before we get a bill. We have already waited a hundred years and more, and the time for waiting is gone....

14 Because it is not just African Americans, but really it is all of us, who must overcome the crippling legacy of bigotry and injustice—and we shall overcome.

15 As a man whose roots go deeply into Southern soil, I know how agonizing racial feelings are. I know how difficult it is to reshape the attitudes and the structure of our society.

16 But a century has passed, more than a hundred years, since the slave was freed, and he is not fully free tonight.

17 It was more than a hundred years ago that Abraham Lincoln, a great President of another party, signed the Emancipation Proclamation, but emancipation is a proclamation and not a fact.

Write an essay that analyzes the author's approach in persuading his readers that "emancipation is a proclamation and not a fact." Focus on specific features such as the ones listed in the box above the passage and explain how these features strengthen the author's argument. Your essay should discuss the most important rhetorical features of the passage.

Your essay should not focus on your own opinion of the author's conclusion, but rather on how the author persuades his readers.

ANSWER KEY
READING TEST

1. A	14. A	27. C	40. D
2. B	15. D	28. C	41. C
3. C	16. D	29. A	42. B
4. A	17. A	30. B	43. D
5. D	18. C	31. C	44. D
6. C	19. B	32. C	45. B
7. D	20. A	33. A	46. C
8. D	21. A	34. C	47. A
9. A	22. C	35. A	48. B
10. A	23. D	36. B	49. C
11. D	24. C	37. D	50. A
12. A	25. D	38. C	51. A
13. B	26. D	39. D	52. C

WRITING AND LANGUAGE TEST

1. D	12. D	23. A	34. D
2. A	13. B	24. D	35. D
3. B	14. A	25. C	36. B
4. A	15. A	26. A	37. B
5. A	16. B	27. C	38. C
6. C	17. D	28. C	39. D
7. B	18. C	29. D	40. D
8. C	19. A	30. B	41. C
9. B	20. D	31. A	42. A
10. D	21. D	32. B	43. B
11. D	22. A	33. B	44. B

MATH—NO CALCULATOR TEST

1. C	6. C	11. D	16. 12
2. C	7. A	12. C	17. 9/2 or 4.5
3. B	8. A	13. A	18. 7/3 or 2.33
4. D	9. B	14. A	19. 34
5. A	10. C	15. D	20. 2

MATH—CALCULATOR TEST

1. C	11. B	21. C	31. 2030
2. B	12. C	22. B	32. 36
3. C	13. C	23. A	33. 540
4. A	14. D	24. A	34. 2
5. A	15. D	25. B	35. 85
6. C	16. C	26. D	36. 12.4
7. D	17. C	27. A	37. .49
8. D	18. C	28. B	38. 1
9. D	19. B	29. B	
10. D	20. B	30. A	

ANSWERS AND EXPLANATIONS

READING TEST

"Village Opera"

Suggested Passage Map notes:

¶1: narrator goes with mother to visit grand-mother

¶2: catch shrimp, take buffalo out

¶3: liked going to opera

¶4: he and grandmother upset b/c can't go

¶5: imagines being at opera

¶6: makes plan with friends to get boat

¶7: plan not dangerous

¶8: mother & grandmother say ok

1. A   Difficulty: Easy

Category: Detail

Getting to the Answer: Predict an answer before you look at the answer choices. The first paragraph explicitly states that the narrator would always go with his mother to visit his grandmother, so (A) is the correct answer.

2. B   Difficulty: Medium

Category: Vocab-in-Context

Getting to the Answer: Use context clues to help you predict a word that could substitute for "impress on me." Choice (B) is the correct answer. Because the narrator's mother is commanding him to "not make a scene," "no matter what," predict she is trying to *emphasize* this command.

3. C   Difficulty: Medium

Category: Inference

Getting to the Answer: Look for clues in the passage that suggest which possibility is most likely true. The first paragraph explains the local custom

of married women who did not head the household visiting their parents. Since the narrator's mother visits her parents (though only for a short time, since she did have household duties), (C) is the logical choice. None of the others are suggested by the passage.

4. A   Difficulty: Hard

Category: Command of Evidence

Getting to the Answer: Eliminate answer choices that do not directly support your answer to the previous question or are about a different topic. The correct answer relates to why the narrator's mother goes to visit her mother in the summer. Choice (A) supports the logical assumption of the previous answer.

5. D   Difficulty: Medium

Category: Global

Getting to the Answer: The central theme of the passage is the insight about life that the author is trying to communicate to the reader. Eliminate any themes that are not revealed by the experiences of the narrator. Although you may agree personally with more than one of the themes presented, (D) is the correct answer choice. It is supported by details in the passage, specifically, those that relate to the fact that the narrator finally gets to go to the opera.

6. C   Difficulty: Medium

Category: Inference

Getting to the Answer: Eliminate answer choices that don't fit with your understanding of events in the passage. (C) is the correct answer. Although the narrator's mother and grandmother want him to go because he is disappointed, they ultimately approve because they are persuaded that the boys will not be in danger from going on the boat.

7. D   **Difficulty:** Medium

Category: Command of Evidence

Getting to the Answer: Reread each quote in the context of the passage. Watch out for answer choices that support an incorrect answer to the previous question. Choice (D) is the correct answer because the boys' ability to swim is the reason the adults were finally convinced to let the boys go on the boat.

8. D   **Difficulty:** Easy

Category: Rhetoric

Getting to the Answer: Think about the scene described in the passage and decide why the author chose to use the phrase "with my mind's eye." Choice (D) is the correct answer. The author chose this expression to show that the narrator was able to envision his friends enjoying the opera.

9. A   **Difficulty:** Medium

Category: Vocab-in-Context

Getting to the Answer: Predict a word that could substitute for "agitating" in context. The boys wanted the narrator to go to the opera. Predict they were *pushing*, or "campaigning," for that to happen. Choice (A) is the correct answer in this context.

10. A   **Difficulty:** Easy

Category: Rhetoric

Getting to the Answer: Eliminate answer choices that are clearly not representative of the author's attitude. With the numerous references to his mother, grandmother, and friends feeling sorry for the narrator, the passage's tone suggests that the author wishes the reader to feel sympathy toward the narrator. Therefore, (A) is the correct answer.

Nelson Mandela Speech

Suggested Passage Map notes:

¶1: how whites see/treat blacks in South Africa
¶2: black pass laws → jail, family separation: laws hated
¶3: poverty: ↓ moral standards, ↑ violence
¶4: Africans want security & fairness
¶5: most imp: want equal pol rights
¶6: ANC against racism
¶7: national struggle for blacks' right to live
¶8: M dedicated to democratic free society

11. D   **Difficulty:** Easy

Category: Rhetoric

Getting to the Answer: Consider the language Mandela uses in his speech. What emotions is he trying to stir in his audience? This should help you choose the correct answer. Mandela uses emotional language to make his audience understand the terrible consequences of the apartheid system for black South Africans. He sympathizes with whites' fears and tries to calm them by explaining that democracy is the only acceptable solution. He is clearly trying to help white South Africans understand why apartheid is morally wrong and must be repealed. Choice (D) conveys this idea.

12. A   **Difficulty:** Hard

Category: Command of Evidence

Getting to the Answer: Choose the quote that provides the most direct support for your answer to the previous question. Mandela opens his speech by asserting a key problem with the practice of white supremacy: the lack of dignity experienced by black Africans. Choice (A) provides the most direct support for the assertion that apartheid must be abolished.

13. B   Difficulty: Hard

Category: Vocab-in-Context

Getting to the Answer: Predict a phrase that could substitute for "endorsed out of" in context. Keep in mind that Mandela is describing a negative occurrence. Mandela is saying that Africans don't want to be "endorsed out of an area because they were not born there" (lines 40-41). In other words, Africans don't want to be "restricted from" an area through the use of a legal, signed document. Choice (B), "restricted from" is the correct answer.

14. A   Difficulty: Hard

Category: Inference

Getting to the Answer: Follow Mandela's logic closely throughout his discussion of pass laws. What are the consequences of this legislation? Mandela says that pass laws "render any African liable to police surveillance" (line 18) and "lead to the breakdown of family life" (line 25). In the next paragraph, Mandela suggests that this, in turn, leads to violence. Therefore, (A) is the correct answer; pass laws caused lawlessness.

15. D   Difficulty: Hard

Category: Command of Evidence

Getting to the Answer: Carefully reread the part of the passage that addresses pass laws. Identify the specific claims it makes. Choice (D) is the correct answer because it identifies the consequence of violence as a result of "breakdown in moral standards," which was previously linked to the "breakdown of family life" (line 25) from pass laws.

16. D   Difficulty: Medium

Category: Vocab-in-Context

Getting to the Answer: Examine the sentence in which the word appears. Which meaning of "artificial" fits with the idea that Mandela is trying to communicate? In this sentence, Mandela is arguing that "political division, based on colour" (line 65) is

entirely man-made and therefore will not "result in racial domination" (lines 64-65). Choice (D) is the correct answer.

17. A   Difficulty: Medium

Category: Rhetoric

Getting to the Answer: Search the passage for Mandela's discussion of the term "democracy." Remember that his claim about democracy may be implied rather than stated explicitly. Mandela identifies South Africa as undemocratic because of its racialized government. He seeks democracy but does not believe it exists presently under white rule. In fact, democracy is something the whites "fear" (line 60). Choice (A) is the correct answer, as it reflects this idea.

18. C   Difficulty: Hard

Category: Rhetoric

Getting to the Answer: Reread the quoted statement and think about how a white South African might react to this part of Mandela's speech. Mandela's and the ANC's goal is a nonracist democracy. He states that the ANC has spent many years fighting against racist practices and "will not change that policy" once given a chance to "triumph" (line 69). In doing so, Mandela is assuring white South Africans that black South Africans will not retaliate or enact unfair laws and practices, once equal political rights are established by law. Therefore, (C) is the correct answer.

19. B   Difficulty: Hard

Category: Inference

Getting to the Answer: Focus on the problems Mandela outlines throughout the speech. What future policy has the potential to impact one or more of these problems? Throughout his speech, Mandela talks about the lack of education and the lack of meaningful, rather than menial, employment for black South Africans. One can extrapolate that Mandela would be in favor of a future policy that makes sure that untrained workers would receive the training and education needed to attain meaningful employment. Choice (B) is the correct answer.

20. A   Difficulty: Easy

Category: Rhetoric

Getting to the Answer: Use your Passage Map to think about the paragraph's relationship to the other paragraphs in the passage. The previous paragraph acknowledges that some people fear a nonracialized political system. This paragraph answers that fear by promising that even when Africans constitute a majority of voters, they will not institute a new race-based system. Choice (A) is the correct answer.

Dictionary Passage

Suggested Passage Map notes:

¶1: dictionary is guide for Scrabble
¶2: dicts don't tell whole story
¶3: dicts can't keep up w/ changes
¶4: 1879 – after 5 yrs only at word "ant"
¶5: finished in 1924 then immediately needed more work
¶6: Skinner – dict can't tell you everything
¶7: details about creating new words
¶8: lots of new words come from Internet
¶9: Internet also gives old words new meanings
¶10: dict makers have to decide what words/ definitions to include
¶11: change is exhilarating

21. A   Difficulty: Medium

Category: Rhetoric

Getting to the Answer: Read the entire passage and consider the tone, purpose, and content presented by the author. The correct answer will reflect the intent of the passage and the tone in which its content is conveyed. The passage reports on the role of dictionaries in tracking language, the changing nature of language over time, and the difficulties for dictionary publishers in keeping up with evolving language. Although the passage contains historical and contemporary information and posits an opinion, it is presented in a somewhat casual, accessible tone without any concerted effort to sway the audience to adopt a specific position. The correct answer is (A).

22. C   Difficulty: Medium

Category: Rhetoric

Getting to the Answer: Consult your Passage Map notes for the first two paragraphs and look for the relationship between their ideas. Identify a claim that is made that seems to run counter to the position taken by the author. The author begins by questioning whether many Scrabble players rely on the dictionary because it is a "definitive" (line 5) source. The author then explains that many people assume that dictionaries are comprehensive when, in fact, they "do not tell the whole story" (line 9). The claim that the author tries to refute, then, is that dictionaries are absolute and undeniable authorities on language, making (C) correct.

23. D   Difficulty: Medium

Category: Command of Evidence

Getting to the Answer: The correct answer should provide direct support of the author refuting the claim identified in the previous question. The correct answer to the previous question explains that the author seeks to refute the claim that dictionaries are absolute and undeniable authorities on language. Choice (D) is correct because it provides evidence that the author doesn't think that dictionaries are the absolute authority on language.

24. C   Difficulty: Medium

Category: Vocab-in-Context

Getting to the Answer: Read the complete sentence in which the word appears and look for the specific meaning of the word in context. If needed, review surrounding sentences for additional context clues. The correct word will most naturally replace the existing word in the sentence while keeping flow and meaning. The contextual sentence refers to the task of tracking changes in language. Additional context clues in the paragraph suggest that authors of the dictionary expected to be done much sooner than they were, though the next paragraph explains that they did eventually complete a version of the project. In this way, the job turned out to be much bigger than anticipated; predict it was *huge*. Choice (C), "tremendous," is correct.

25. D   Difficulty: Medium

Category: Rhetoric

Getting to the Answer: Read the complete paragraph in which the phrases appear to understand the meaning that they convey in their specific sentence. Consider the content of preceding paragraphs, as well. The correct answer reflects an inference that can be made from the cited phrases. The paragraph in which the phrases appear begins by explaining that a new word is created every 98 minutes. This follows earlier paragraphs that discuss the development of the *Oxford English Dictionary* (*OED*), contrasting the sources of new words with philological authorities who first sought to provide a comprehensive dictionary for the English language. The inference is that new words not only come into use every day but also originate from many sources, including non-philological ones. Choice (D) is correct.

26. D   Difficulty: Medium

Category: Inference

Getting to the Answer: Read the complete sentence. Check each conclusion against the sentence to see if the specific rhetoric of the sentence supports that choice. The lines explain that Merriam-Webster's dictionary adds many words that come from common Internet usage. This suggests that words not only gain meaning but also accrue a certain legitimacy through their popular usage, making (D) correct.

27. C   Difficulty: Medium

Category: Command of Evidence

Getting to the Answer: Read each choice completely and check the meaning of the lines. The correct answer will provide direct support for the answer to the previous question. The answer to the previous question suggests that words gain meaning and legitimacy from usage. Lines 61-65 ("In the last . . . insults") explain how the meaning of *troll* changed over time through its use on the Internet. Choice (C) is correct.

28. C   Difficulty: Medium

Category: Synthesis

Getting to the Answer: Carefully study the graphic's data for each year. Check each answer choice against the data provided. The graphic shows that from 2011 to 2014, 15 words from the Internet were added. It also shows that from 2006 to 2009, 10 words from the Internet were added. This makes (C) correct.

29. A   Difficulty: Easy

Category: Vocab-in-Context

Getting to the Answer: Reread the sentence, pretending that the referenced word is a blank. Before reading the answer choices, predict which word might best fill that blank. Review the answer choices for the word that most nearly means the same as your prediction. The implication gained from the previous and subsequent sentences is that people do not like this meaning of "literally" and consider it contrary to the purpose of a dictionary. In this sense, predict "erode" means to *diminish* the underlying purpose of the dictionary. Choice (A) is correct.

30. B   Difficulty: Hard

Category: Connections

Getting to the Answer: Consider the overall claim that the author makes about how dictionaries function in our world. Which answer choice best reflects the relationship between dictionaries and our "living language" (lines 88-89)? The correct choice is (B). Based on the passage, one can conclude that dictionaries attempt to address the idea that language changes over time.

31. C   Difficulty: Medium

Category: Synthesis

Getting to the Answer: Study the data and read the title of the graphic carefully to identify the purpose of its data. Compare these data with the key conclusions drawn by the author of the passage. The correct answer will relate the purpose and nature of the data to a central argument in the passage. The title of the graphic indicates that its purpose is to show what new words from the Internet were added to the *Merriam-Webster Dictionary*. In the passage, the author explores the impact of changing Internet technologies on language usage. The correct answer is (C) because it ties together the purpose of the data in the chart with a central idea in the passage.

Paired Passages—Atlantic Ocean Wildlife

Suggested Passage Map notes:

Passage 1

¶1: baby sea turtles: hatch, get in water away from predators

¶2: where do babies go once they reach the water?

¶3: scientists tagged 11 babies off W. African coast

¶4: babies end up in Sargasso Sea: eat, use sargassum (seaweed) as rafts; info helps sci. protect turtles

Passage 2

¶1: Sargasso Sea has lots of seaweed

¶2: sci. use nets & video to get info

¶3: lots of fish, baby loggerheads; regulate sargassum harvest & preserve area

¶4: need more research to protect it

32. C   Difficulty: Medium

Category: Global

Getting to the Answer: Review your Passage Map to identify the author's central idea. Then choose the answer choice that best reflects this overarching idea. Beware of options that simply reflect facts presented in the passage. While other answer choices focus on details mentioned in the passage or on information not present, the idea presented in (C) is central to Passage 1.

33. A   Difficulty: Medium

Category: Inference

Getting to the Answer: Use your Passage Map to locate the paragraph that discusses scientists' use of nanoacoustic tags. Eliminate choices that might be true but that are not discussed in the passage, such as B. The third paragraph states that the tags are small enough not to interfere with the turtles' ability to swim, implying that larger tags might slow the turtles down and offer skewed data. Therefore, the correct answer is (A).

34. C   Difficulty: Medium

Category: Command of Evidence

Getting to the Answer: Begin by reviewing the line of reasoning you used to choose your answer to the previous question. Then choose the quote that supports that answer. The sentence noted in (C) indicates that the research tags are small enough not to hinder the ability of the turtles to swim. This directly supports the answer to the previous question, so (C) is correct.

35. A   Difficulty: Medium

Category: Vocab-in-Context

Getting to the Answer: Read the sentence for context clues, assess how the meaning of the sentence relates to the overall passage, and predict a word that could substitute for "vulnerable" in this context. Choice (A) is correct, as the sentence states the studies offer scientists data about the first hours of the turtles' lives, when they are unable to protect themselves from the predators mentioned earlier in the passage.

36. B   **Difficulty:** Easy

Category: Inference

Getting to the Answer: Use your Passage Map to find the paragraphs that discuss research. Eliminate answer choices that might be true but that are not discussed in the passage. The last two paragraphs suggest ways in which both the fishing industry and conservationists will find the research beneficial. Therefore, the correct answer is (B).

37. D   **Difficulty:** Medium

Category: Command of Evidence

Getting to the Answer: Avoid choices that provide evidence for incorrect answers to the previous question. Choice (D) indicates that the Sargasso research is commercially and environmentally important. This directly supports the correct answer to the previous question, the importance of Sargasso Sea research data to "conservationists and the fishing industry alike."

38. C   **Difficulty:** Easy

Category: Vocab-in-Context

Getting to the Answer: Read for context clues to understand the meaning of the sentence and predict a word that could appropriately substitute for "classified." The sentence discusses how the South Atlantic Fishery Management Council wants to have the sargassum community classified as an Essential Fish Habitat. If it received this classification, it would then receive additional protection. In this context, predict "classified" means identified; therefore, (C), "categorized," is correct. Choice B may be tempting, but "cataloged" means to "arrange multiple items according to a system" and is incorrect in this context.

39. D   **Difficulty:** Medium

Category: Inference

Getting to the Answer: Examine the sentence containing the selected phrase and decide how the sentence's tone reflects the author's point of view about the topic. Then choose the answer choice that correctly reflects this intention. The author is clearly in favor of more studies that could help protect the ecosystem, and because the author does not mention funding, shipping, or ways in which scientists have ignored the ecosystem, the correct answer choice is (D).

40. D   **Difficulty:** Hard

Category: Rhetoric

Getting to the Answer: Skim Passage 2 to locate the cited words and infer the author's intention for including them. Choice (D) is correct. The words are used to describe the large area of ocean in which a great number of species live. It's logical that this vast area would create a complex challenge for scientists studying the ecosystem, and in fact paragraph 2 explains that scientists need to use multiple methods to collect data from such a large area.

41. C   **Difficulty:** Medium

Category: Synthesis

Getting to the Answer: After reading both passages, predict each author's purpose and decide which answer choice explains the most accurate difference between the two. Choice (C) is correct. Both passages intend to inform a general audience about the various research methods used to study the Sargasso Sea and the importance of this research, but one passage focuses on a single species, while the other focuses on the entire ecosystem.

42. B   **Difficulty:** Medium

Category: Synthesis

Getting to the Answer: Use your Passage Map notes to identify the central idea in each passage and how scientists in each case approach their research. Then choose which answer choice best connects ideas from both passages. Avoid answer choices, such as A, that only address one of the passages. Choice (B) is correct, as both passages discuss the old and new research methods scientists have used to study the Sargasso Sea. This suggests that no matter what is being studied, a single species or an entire ecosystem, the research technology used is constantly evolving.

Colorblindness

Suggested Passage Map notes:

¶1: description of red/green colorblindness

¶2: depends on cones in eye

¶3: details about light spectrum

¶4: red & green absorption overlaps

¶5: lack of pigment comes from genes on X chromosome

¶6: women have 2 X chromos so can inherit one w/o colorblindness; men have 1 X chromo so always colorblindness

¶7: pedigree shows which women are carriers & who is colorblind

43. D   **Difficulty:** Medium

Category: Global

Getting to the Answer: Remember that you are determining the largest, most central, idea of the entire passage. Avoid answers that refer only to specific supporting details. This passage is mostly about what causes colorblindness. It discusses the physiological process of colorblindness in the human body, as well as the genetics involved in passing the trait through generations. Choice (D) is the correct answer.

44. D   **Difficulty:** Medium

Category: Command of Evidence

Getting to the Answer: All of the information presented in the passage supports the central idea, but the correct answer will provide direct support for the answer to the previous question. Avoid answers that provide evidence for incorrect answers to the previous question. The passage is mostly about what causes colorblindness. Choice (D) contains information about the physiological and genetic causes of colorblindness, so it is the correct answer.

45. B   **Difficulty:** Hard

Category: Rhetoric

Getting to the Answer: Consider how the information in paragraph 6 relates to the information in the rest of the passage. In paragraph 6, the author explains that more men than women are colorblind because of how the gene for colorblindness is passed from parents to their children. Because the gene is passed on the X chromosome and men have only one X chromosome, they need only inherit the gene from their mother rather than both parents (as women must) in order to be colorblind. Choice (B) is the correct answer.

46. C   **Difficulty:** Medium

Category: Inference

Getting to the Answer: Read the question stem carefully. Notice that it's asking you to infer a relationship between the colors red and green in the context of colorblindness. Choice (C) is correct. Overlapping absorption ranges mean that everyone's brain must compare red and green to tell which color is to be correctly interpreted. In the colorblind person, however, some of the information needed by the brain to tell the colors apart is missing due to the lack of either red or green pigment (lines 38-47).

47. A   Difficulty: Hard

Category: Rhetoric

Getting to the Answer: After reviewing the central idea of the first paragraph, evaluate each answer choice and consider what each would add to the passage. Choose the one that would best support the author's line of reasoning. In paragraph 1, the author states that most people who are colorblind are "red-green" colorblind. In identifying this specific type, the author suggests that there are other types as well. The author's central claim could be strengthened by including information about other types of colorblindness. Choice (A) is the correct answer.

48. B   Difficulty: Easy

Category: Vocab-in-Context

Getting to the Answer: Predict a word that is a synonym for "sensitive" in context. Eliminate answer choices that are synonyms of "sensitive" but do not make sense in context. In this context, predict "sensitive" most nearly means *responsive* because it is referring to how the eye's cones react to the light spectrum. Choice (B) is the correct answer.

49. C   Difficulty: Medium

Category: Inference

Getting to the Answer: Remember that the correct answer will not be stated directly in the text but will be supported by evidence presented in the passage. Eliminate answers that are not supported by evidence in the passage. The author compares the way in which a person who is colorblind experiences color with the way a person with normal color vision experiences color. It is reasonable to infer that a person who is colorblind experiences the visual world in a way that is different from the way a person who has normal color vision perceives it. Therefore, (C) is the correct answer.

50. A   Difficulty: Medium

Category: Command of Evidence

Getting to the Answer: Locate each answer choice in the passage and determine which one provides the strongest support for your answer to the previous question. In paragraph 1, the author explains how people who are colorblind perceive color, which has an impact on how they see the world. Lines 10-14 provide the strongest support for the answer to the previous question, so (A) is the correct answer.

51. A   Difficulty: Medium

Category: Vocab-in-Context

Getting to the Answer: Think about the fact that the topic being discussed in the sentence is human genes. Predict a word that would make sense in this context. The author is explaining that women who have only one colorblind gene are called carriers because they aren't "affected" by it. This means that the gene doesn't "change" their ability to see all colors. Choice (A) is the correct answer.

52. C   Difficulty: Hard

Category: Synthesis

Getting to the Answer: The correct answer will be supported by the evidence in both the passage and the graphic. Look for relationships between the variables in the graphic that are described in the passage. In paragraph 6, the author explains that females get one X chromosome from their father and one from their mother. If the father is colorblind, there is a 100% chance that the X chromosome he passes on to his daughter will have the colorblind gene, making her a carrier. The graphic shows this information as well. Therefore, (C) is the correct answer.

WRITING AND LANGUAGE TEST

Antarctic Treaty System in Need of Reform

1. D   Difficulty: Hard

Category: Punctuation

Getting to the Answer: Consider whether this sentence needs punctuation within it and, if so, what type. You should be able to come up with a specific reason a particular form of punctuation is needed. "Including the United States" is part of the subject of the sentence that begins with "Twelve member countries." Therefore, no punctuation is necessary to make this sentence grammatical. Choice (D) is the correct answer.

2. A   Difficulty: Medium

Category: Effective Language Use

Getting to the Answer: Ask yourself whether the sentence in its current form makes sense or whether another word is needed in place of "accelerate" to improve the meaning. The word "accelerate" indicates that the conflicts will increase in intensity, so the sentence in its current form makes sense, so (A) is the correct answer.

3. B   Difficulty: Medium

Category: Development

Getting to the Answer: Determine what specific relationship "opponents" have to their feelings about politics and science. What information should the introductory phrase in this sentence provide to help the reader understand exactly what the opponents feel? The rest of the paragraph implies that the opponents definitely believe "that politics should trump science." The sentence should emphasize that politics trumping science is the most important reason for their objection. The correct answer should also maintain the tone of the paragraph as a whole. Therefore, (B) is the correct answer.

4. A   Difficulty: Medium

Category: Effective Language Use

Getting to the Answer: Consider how strongly countries feel about Antarctic minerals. Which word among the answer choices best expresses their degree of interest? The countries appear to be extremely interested in accessing Antarctic minerals. Choice (A), "interested in," reflects that countries want to use Antarctica for its minerals and, therefore, is the correct answer. The other answer choices suggest a weak or nonexistent desire for obtaining resources from Antarctica.

5. A   Difficulty: Hard

Category: Effective Language Use

Getting to the Answer: Determine the relationship between the two sentences. Then decide which answer choice best reflects this relationship. The second sentence appears to have a cause-effect relationship with the first one; because China and similar states are oil-poor, they see Antarctica as a means to satisfying their oil demands. Choice (A) combines the two sentences in a way that makes this relationship clear and, therefore, is the correct answer.

6. C   Difficulty: Hard

Category: Quantitative

Getting to the Answer: Note that the graphic gives specific information about the amount of China's oil consumption and production per day over a period of approximately 22 years. Observe which data are labeled "forecast." Be sure that your choice is accurate and best supports the author's claim. Choice (C) accurately reflects the information in the graphic.

7. B   Difficulty: Medium

Category: Effective Language Use

Getting to the Answer: Read the answer choices carefully to determine how each would change the meaning or style of the sentence. Which change, if any, would result in the best sentence? All of the answer choices claim that Antarctica is "a rich continent" because of its mineral resources. Choice (B), however, expresses the same relationship most elegantly. In fewer words it articulates the same idea, so it is the correct answer.

8. C   Difficulty: Hard

Category: Effective Language Use

Getting to the Answer: Carefully reread the rest of the paragraph. Try to identify the answer choice that best matches the paragraph's tone and intent. The paragraph, like the passage as a whole, has an objective, factual tone. It is not critical of anyone in particular but is simply stating facts. Choice (C) is the most objective and succinct choice and is the correct answer.

9. B   Difficulty: Hard

Category: Usage

Getting to the Answer: Verify whether "it" matches the noun it stands for and choose a better replacement if needed. "It" seems to refer to "the protocol," but this does not make sense within the sentence; the protocol is not what will be "waiting for claims." A specific noun, rather than a pronoun, is needed. Replacing "it" with "an energy-hungry world" identifies the actual subject that "will be" waiting. Choice (B) is the correct answer.

10. D   Difficulty: Hard

Category: Development

Getting to the Answer: Before reading the answer choices, identify in your own words what purpose an appropriate sentence would serve in the paragraph. How should the first sentence be linked to the others? The first sentence states that there is an economic aspect to the discussion of the Southern Ocean. The rest of the sentences note that fishing is important to many countries. Therefore, the inserted sentence should provide a detail that links economics and fishing. Choice (D) accomplishes this.

11. D   Difficulty: Easy

Category: Punctuation

Getting to the Answer: Items in a list should be separated by appropriate punctuation. Review your knowledge of the rules governing lists to arrive at the correct answer choice. Choice (D) is the only one that uses correct punctuation.

Finding Pluto

12. D   Difficulty: Easy

Category: Effective Language Use

Getting to the Answer: Watch out for choices that are overly wordy and redundant, like B and C. The word "specks" suggests that these star images are small. It is better to be as direct and simple as possible. Additional words do not add more meaning to this content. (D) is the correct answer because it is the most concise and effective way of stating the information in the passage.

13. B   Difficulty: Easy

Category: Sentence Formation

Getting to the Answer: Think about the ways that two complete thoughts that are closely related can be separated. Be careful of inappropriate transition words. The semicolon is one option for dividing two independent clauses that are closely tied to one another. Choice (B) is the correct answer.

14. A   Difficulty: Medium

Category: Development

Getting to the Answer: Read the entire paragraph and then read each of the choices. Decide which one is a fitting conclusion for the rest of the information in the paragraph. Choice (A) is the correct answer because it most effectively concludes the paragraph by stating the overarching idea of the paragraph.

15. A   Difficulty: Easy

Category: Effective Language Use

Getting to the Answer: Pretend the word is a blank in the sentence. Predict what word could be substituted for the blank. Choose the word closest in meaning to your prediction. The passage later states that Tombaugh studied the images. You can guess that he had to load them into the machine first. Only (A) fits within the context of the sentence.

16. B   Difficulty: Medium

Category: Development

Getting to the Answer: Reread the paragraph to identify the central idea. Then review the answer choices to find the one that best provides support for that idea. Choice (B) explains how the gravitational pull of another planet could affect Neptune's orbit. This supports the central idea of the paragraph, that Tombaugh believed there was an additional planet in our solar system, farther away than Neptune. Choice (B) is correct.

17. D   Difficulty: Easy

Category: Effective Language Use

Getting to the Answer: Reread the sentence. Consider whether "check" appropriately fits in the context. The sentence describes how Tombaugh was able to tell the difference between planets and stars. Only (D) fits within the context of the sentence.

18. C   Difficulty: Easy

Category: Organization

Getting to the Answer: Look for the relationship between the previous sentence and this sentence. This will help you choose the appropriate transition word. Replace the word in the sentence to ensure that it makes sense. The sentence beginning with "Although" places a condition on the previous sentence. It describes a situation in which it would be difficult for Tombaugh to tell the difference between stars and planets. Only choice (C) is appropri-

ately and shows the correct relationship between the two sentences.

19. A   Difficulty: Medium

Category: Punctuation

Getting to the Answer: Ask yourself if the two clauses separated by the semicolon are independent or not. Be careful of inappropriate transition words. Choice (A) correctly places a semicolon between the two independent clauses.

20. D   Category: Development

Difficulty: Medium

Getting to the Answer: Review the choices and find the one that does not give information that is directly related to the paragraph's central idea. The central idea of the paragraph concerns Tombaugh working meticulously until he finds evidence of a planet. Choice (D) is the least essential sentence in the paragraph. The detail in this sentence is not directly tied to the paragraph's central idea, but rather is a detail about the planet itself.

21. D   Difficulty: Easy

Category: Usage

Getting to the Answer: Read the sentence and notice that the verb in question is not in agreement with the subject of the verb. The verb "has determined" is in a singular form, but the subject is "scientists," which is plural, so (D) is the correct answer.

22. A   Difficulty: Medium

Category: Punctuation

Getting to the Answer: Remember that words such as "however" show a relationship between two things or ideas and that to emphasize that relationship, they are typically set off with punctuation. Choice (A) is correct. Commas are needed to set off "however" from the rest of the sentence and to emphasize its meaning.

Public Relations: Build Your Brand While Building for Others

23. A   Difficulty: Hard

Category: Punctuation

Getting to the Answer: Determine whether the two parts of the sentence on either side of the dash can stand independently. The series "in print, in press interviews, in web content, and on social media" cannot stand on its own because it lacks a subject. Therefore, a dash, rather than a period or semicolon, should be used. Choice (A) is correct.

24. D   Difficulty: Medium

Category: Punctuation

Getting to the Answer: Consider whether the list of items is a series needing commas. Because there is a list in the sentence, commas should be used to separate the items. The preposition "behind" is not an item in the series and should not be followed by a comma or other punctuation. Choice (D) is correct.

25. C   Difficulty: Easy

Category: Punctuation

Getting to the Answer: Reread the paragraph and consider the author's purpose. Is it to inform? To entertain? To persuade? If you're not sure, read more of the passage. Then review the answer choices to find the one with punctuation that is appropriate for the author's purpose. This is an informational passage; the author does not use casual language or offer opinions. A period is most appropriate when the author's purpose is to inform. Choice (C) is correct.

26. A   Difficulty: Easy

Category: Usage

Getting to the Answer: Look back to find what noun this list must match. Is it in a singular or plural form? The noun "people" is plural. As the sentence is written, the nouns in the list are all plural, so no change is needed. Choice (A) is correct.

27. C   Difficulty: Medium

Category: Usage

Getting to the Answer: A pronoun must agree with its antecedent in number and gender. Find the antecedent of "its" and determine whether it is singular or plural. Make sure the pronoun you choose is spelled correctly. The antecedent, "materials," is plural. Choice (C) is correct.

28. C   Difficulty: Medium

Category: Effective Language Use

Getting to the Answer: Decide whether the word in the sentence is used correctly. Do any of the answer choices offer a clearer usage? "Provide" is a verb meaning "to make available for use"; the use of "craft" as a verb implies an artistic sense of creating something to support the company's brand message, just as Lin also "write[s] scripts." Choice (C) is correct.

29. D   Difficulty: Medium

Category: Effective Language Use

Getting to the Answer: Reread the sentence for context. Consider whether the word is used correctly in the sentence. If not, test the other choices in its place to identify a clearer meaning. The opening sentence of the paragraph refers to acquiring the skills necessary for a public relations position. The adjective "immovable" means incapable of being moved. "Transferable" is an adjective meaning "able to be passed," in this case, from one field to another. Choice (D) is the correct answer.

30. B   Difficulty: Medium

Category: Development

Getting to the Answer: Review the answer choices to find the one that provides concrete, factual evidence for the author's claim in sentence 3. The author is making a claim about the increase in salary for employees who are promoted to upper-management positions. The sentence that provides factual evidence for this claim is (B), which cites a specific numerical figure

($100,000 per year) to contrast with the $30,000 per year paid to entry-level employees.

31. A   Difficulty: Hard

Category: Development

Getting to the Answer: Reread the entire paragraph to establish the central idea. Make sure that the answer you choose is supported by all the sentences in the paragraph. All the sentences in this paragraph contain Lin's advice for success; therefore, (A) is correct.

32. B   Difficulty: Medium

Category: Sentence Formation

Getting to the Answer: Verify that there are two short but separate thoughts in the sentence. As the sentence is written, it is a run-on. Proper punctuation and the conjunction "and" eliminate the run-on. Choice (B) is correct.

33. B   Difficulty: Medium

Category: Sentence Formation

Getting to the Answer: Parallel ideas in a sentence must be expressed in the same grammatical form. Rephrase the actions in the sentence so they are parallel. In this sentence, the gerund "talking" is paired with the infinitive "to observe." These are different grammatical forms and, therefore, are not parallel. The correct choice pairs two infinitives: "to talk" and "to observe." Choice (B) is correct.

Film, Culture, and Globalization

34. D   Difficulty: Medium

Category: Sentence Formation

Getting to the Answer: Reread the underlined portion of the paragraph to see whether it contains incomplete thoughts that cannot stand alone. As written, the phrase "greater creativity and appreciation of heritage" is a fragment and must be combined with the sentence before it. Choice (D) is correct.

35. D   Difficulty: Easy

Category: Effective Language Use

Getting to the Answer: Decide how the word is used in the sentence. Make a prediction about what type of word would make the most sense in context. All the choices except (D) are negative representations of the film industry, but the passage is about the positive influences of the film industry. "Potent" means "robust and dynamic." Choice (D) is correct.

36. B   Difficulty: Medium

Category: Development

Getting to the Answer: Examine the sentences of the paragraph to determine the central idea. The paragraph is about the success of filmmakers who have expanded to global markets. The topic sentence must describe the spread of the worldwide appreciation of films and transition logically from the previous paragraph. Choice (B) is correct.

37. B   Difficulty: Medium

Category: Usage

Getting to the Answer: Identify the subject of the independent clause. Then predict the verb that is correctly used with the subject. "Global sense" is singular, so the singular verb "grows" is correct; do not be distracted by the prepositional phrase "of shared understanding and cultural appreciation." Choice (B) is correct.

38. C   Difficulty: Hard

Category: Sentence Formation

Getting to the Answer: Locate each independent idea in the statement. Determine whether the two independent ideas are equal in rank. As the sentence is written, the two ideas are presented as equal. However, the "physical renderings of cultural identity" is a description of cultural artifacts, making it subordinate to the main idea of the sentence. All choices except (C) incorrectly treat the two as equals. Choice (C) is correct.

39. D   Difficulty: Medium

Category: Effective Language Use

Getting to the Answer: Read the surrounding sentences to analyze the context in which the word is used. The previous sentence states that films have "more impact" than other cultural artifacts. This is a clue that you are looking for a word that means "powerful" or "important." Choice (D) is correct.

40. D   Difficulty: Medium

Category: Punctuation

Getting to the Answer: Reread the entire sentence carefully to find the error(s) in the underlined portion. Identify the different parts of the sentence. How can these be grammatically united? The subordinating conjunction "Even as" indicates that the first part of the sentence is a clause that cannot stand alone and should be separated from the main idea by a comma. The next two parts of the sentence each have a subject and verb, so there needs to be a semicolon before "the difference" to form two independent clauses. Choice (D) is correct.

41. C   Difficulty: Hard

Category: Development

Getting to the Answer: Identify the main idea of the paragraph in the topic sentence and the details presented to provide support. Both of the sentences in this paragraph refer to the increasing popularity of cross-cultural films, not to the subject matter of the films or other forms of entertainment. Choice (C) is correct.

42. A   Difficulty: Medium

Category: Usage

Getting to the Answer: Reread the paragraph. Which verb tense is used in the first and last sentences of the paragraph? The sentence is correct as written. All other choices create a shift in verb tense within the paragraph. Choice (A) is correct.

43. B   Difficulty: Medium

Category: Sentence Formation

Getting to the Answer: Notice that the underlined portion of the sentence contains a list of parallel ideas. Parallel ideas must be expressed in the same grammatical form. The list of how films are used is a series requiring the same form. Notice that in (B), the infinitive "to teach" matches "[to] treasure" and "[to] preserve." Choice (B) is correct.

44. B   Difficulty: Medium

Category: Quantitative

Getting to the Answer: Use the key in the graphic to identify the countries represented by each bar. Then identify the country that has shown a consistent increase in film production. According to the graphic, film production fluctuated in all countries except China. Choice (B) is correct.

MATH—NO CALCULATOR TEST

1. C   Difficulty: Easy

Category: Heart of Algebra / Inequalities

Getting to the Answer: When matching a real-world scenario to an inequality, try writing the inequality in words first, and then translate from English into math. On a new tire, the tread depth is $\frac{10}{32}$ inches. As the car is driven, the tread wears down, or is *less* over time, so the depth is always less than or equal to $\frac{10}{32}$. You can express this as $d \leq \frac{10}{32}$, which means you can eliminate B and D. For safety reasons, the tread depth must be *more* than $\frac{2}{32}$ inches. You can express this as $d > \frac{2}{32}$. Because the answer choices are written with the number first, turn the inequality around—but don't forget to keep the open end of the symbol pointed at d. The result is $\frac{2}{32} < d$. This means (C) is correct.

2. C   **Difficulty:** Easy

Category: Passport to Advanced Math / Quadratics

Getting to the Answer: There are a number of ways to solve quadratic equations. When the coefficient of x^2 is 1, the quickest way is usually to factor, if possible. You could also use the quadratic formula or completing the square.

To answer this question, first rewrite the equation in standard form, $x^2 - 8x - 48 = 0$, and then factor to arrive at $(x - 12)(x + 4) = 0$. Using the Zero-Product property to solve for x results in $x = 12$ and $x = -4$. It is given that $x < 0$, so x must equal -4. This means that $x + 10$ is equal to $-4 + 10 = 6$, which is (C).

3. B   **Difficulty:** Medium

Category: Passport to Advanced Math / Quadratics

Getting to the Answer: When a quadratic equation is written in standard form, $y = ax^2 + bx + c$, the value of c is the y-intercept of the equation's graph. This is because substituting 0 for x results in $y = a(0)^2 + b(0) + c = c$. In a real-world scenario, the y-intercept represents an initial amount. In this question, height is what is being measured, so the y-intercept represents the initial height of the bottle rocket. Because the rocket was fired from the roof of the gymnasium, the height of the gymnasium must be 14 meters, making (B) correct.

4. D   **Difficulty:** Medium

Category: Heart of Algebra / Linear Equations

Getting to the Answer: Horizontal and vertical lines have special forms. A horizontal line has a slope of 0 and an equation that always looks like $y = b$, where b is a constant. A vertical line has an undefined slope and always looks like $x = b$. Line L shown in the graph is horizontal, so you are looking for an equation that once simplified (or written in $y = mx + b$ form) looks like $y = b$. In other words, all the x terms must cancel out. In addition, because the line is below the x-axis, b must be a negative number. Check each answer choice to see if it takes on the desired form. Choice

$A \rightarrow y = -x - 2$, so eliminate it. Choice $B \rightarrow y = -x$, so eliminate it. Choice $C \rightarrow y = 2$, which is in the correct form, but 2 is positive and the graph would be above the x-axis, so eliminate it. This means (D) must be correct—subtracting x and 2 from both sides of the equation results in $y = -2$, which could be the equation of line L.

5. A   **Difficulty:** Medium

Category: Heart of Algebra / Systems of Linear Equations

Getting to the Answer: When solving a system of linear equations, always check to see if you can cancel out one of the variables by multiplying either of the equations by a fairly small number and then adding the equations. Before you choose an answer, check that you answered the right question (here, the value of y^2). Multiply the bottom equation by -2 and then combine the equations to eliminate the terms that have x's in them.

$$\begin{aligned} 2x + 5y = 8 &\rightarrow \cancel{2x} + 5y = 8 \\ -2[x + 3y = 3] &\rightarrow \underline{\cancel{-2x} - 6y = -6} \\ & \phantom{\rightarrow \cancel{-2x}} -y = 2 \\ & \phantom{\rightarrow \cancel{-2x}} y = -2 \end{aligned}$$

The question asks for the value of y^2, so you don't need to find the value of x. Simply square the value of y and you're done: $(-2)^2 = 4$, which is (A).

6. C   **Difficulty:** Medium

Category: Passport to Advanced Math / Functions

Getting to the Answer: In a real-world scenario, the slope of a line represents a rate of change (how fast the alloy cools) and the y-intercept represents a starting amount (the initial temperature of the alloy). Be careful—the rate is given in minutes while the question asks for a function in terms of hours. There are four 15-minute intervals in an hour, so the cooling rate per hour is $-40(4) = -160$ degrees. (The rate is negative because as the alloy cools, the temperature drops.) Look back at the answer choices—(C) is the only one that has a slope of -160, so (C) is correct.

7. A   Difficulty: Medium

Category: Passport to Advanced Math / Exponents

Getting to the Answer: Whenever an equation involves two fractional expressions set equal to each other, you can cross-multiply to solve. As you work through the algebra, don't skip steps. This will keep you from forgetting to distribute numbers and/or negative signs.

$$\frac{3}{a-1} = \frac{12}{w}$$
$$3(w) = 12(a-1)$$
$$3w = 12a - 12$$
$$\frac{\cancel{3}w}{\cancel{3}} = \frac{12a}{3} - \frac{12}{3}$$
$$w = 4a - 4$$

This matches the expression in (A).

8. A   Difficulty: Medium

Category: Heart of Algebra / Linear Equations

Getting to the Answer: Choose the best strategy to answer the question—cross-multiplying in this question (without a calculator) will create large numbers and possibly lead to errors. Instead, start by simplifying the numerators and then multiply both sides of the equation by the least common denominator, 36.

$$\frac{4 - (1 - 3n)}{36} = \frac{2(n - 3) + 7}{12}$$
$$\frac{4 - 1 + 3n}{36} = \frac{2n - 6 + 7}{12}$$
$$\frac{3 + 3n}{36} = \frac{2n + 1}{12}$$
$$\cancel{36} \times \left[\frac{3 + 3n}{\cancel{36}}\right] = \left[\frac{2n + 1}{\cancel{12}}\right] \times \cancel{36}^3$$
$$3 + 3n = 3(2n + 1)$$
$$3 + 3n = 6n + 3$$
$$0 = 3n$$
$$0 = n$$

Don't be fooled—this does not mean that there is no solution. The value of n just happens to be 0. If

the variable had been in the denominator of either of the expressions, you would need to check that the solution is valid, but it wasn't, so the correct answer is (A).

9. B   Difficulty: Medium

Category: Passport to Advanced Math / Functions

Getting to the Answer: The domain of a function is the set of x-values (inputs) for which the function is defined. Of all the parent functions, the only ones that have a *restricted* domain (a domain that is not all real numbers) are the square root function (because the square root of a negative number is imaginary) and the rational function (because you cannot divide by 0).

The domain in the question is restricted to numbers greater than or equal to 2, so you can immediately eliminate A and D—the domain of a quadratic function and an absolute function is all real numbers. To choose between (B) and C, you can draw a quick sketch or think about how transformations affect the domain of each function. The domain of the parent function $f(x) = \sqrt{x}$ is $x \geq 0$ (nonnegative numbers). In (B), the parent function is reflected vertically across the horizontal axis (which doesn't change the domain) and then shifted to the right 2 (making the domain $x \geq 2$), so (B) is correct. Note that in C, the function is reflected across the horizontal axis and then shifted *up* 2 units, which adds 2 to the *range* of the function, not the domain.

10. C   Difficulty: Medium

Category: Heart of Algebra / Linear Equations

Getting to the Answer: Only one equation is given, and it has two variables. This means that you don't have enough information to solve for either variable. Instead, look for the relationship between the variable terms in the equation and those in the expression that you are trying to find, $x - 3y$. The expression that you're looking for doesn't have fractions, so clear the fractions in the equation by multiplying both sides by 6. Don't forget to distribute the 6 to both terms on the left side of the equation.

$$\frac{1}{6}x - \frac{1}{2}y = 3$$

$$6\left(\frac{1}{6}x - \frac{1}{2}y\right) = 6(3)$$

$$x - 3y = 18$$

This yields the expression that you are looking for, $x - 3y$, so no further work is required—just read the value on the right-hand side of the equation. The answer is 18, which is (C).

11.   D   Difficulty: Medium

Category: Additional Topics in Math / Trigonometry

Getting to the Answer: Don't let the notation in this question intimidate you. You just need to understand the complementary angle property of sines and cosines. This property states that the sine of an acute angle is equal to the cosine of the angle's complement. Conversely, if the sine of an acute angle is equal to the cosine of another acute angle, then those angles must be complementary (i.e., the sum of the two angles is 90°).

It is given that $0° < m\angle\beta < 90°$ and $0° < m\angle\theta < 90°$ (i.e., they are acute angles) and that $\sin\beta = \cos\theta$, which means angles β and θ must be complementary. Thus, $m\angle\beta + m\angle\theta = 90°$. Substitute the expressions given for the measures of β and θ and solve for n:

$$m\angle\beta + m\angle\theta = 90$$
$$(7n - 12) + (3n - 8) = 90$$
$$10n - 20 = 90$$
$$10n = 110$$
$$n = 11$$

Choice (D) is correct.

12.   C   Difficulty: Hard

Category: Heart of Algebra / Systems of Linear Equations

Getting to the Answer: Graphically, a system of linear equations that has no solution indicates two parallel lines or, in other words, two lines that have the same slope. So, write each of the equations in slope-intercept form ($y = mx + b$) and set their slopes (m) equal to each other to solve for a. Before finding the slopes, multiply the bottom equation by -3 to make it easier to manipulate.

$$ax + y = -5 \rightarrow y = -ax - 5$$
$$-3\left(-\frac{1}{3}x - 2y = -1\right) \rightarrow x + 6y = 3$$
$$\rightarrow y = -\frac{1}{6}x + \frac{1}{2}$$

The slope of the first line is $-a$, and the slope of the second line is $-\frac{1}{6}$. Setting them equal and solving for a results in $-a = -\frac{1}{6}$ or $a = \frac{1}{6}$, which is (C).

13.   A   Difficulty: Hard

Category: Passport to Advanced Math / Quadratics

Getting to the Answer: To write the equation of a parabola, you need two things—the vertex and one other point. In this question, you already have a point, but you'll need to reason logically to find the vertex. The vertex of the parabola shown must lie on its axis of symmetry, which is halfway between the two points (0, 8) and (12, 8). This means the x-coordinate of the vertex is halfway between 0 and 12, which is 6. To find the y-coordinate of the vertex, look at the range: $y \geq -4$, which means that the minimum value of the graph, and hence the y-coordinate of the vertex, is -4. Now, use the vertex (6, -4) to set up a quadratic equation in vertex form: $y = a(x - h)^2 + k$. The result is $y = a(x - 6)^2 - 4$. Plug in either of the given points for x and y to find the value of a. Using (0, 8), the result is:

$$y = a(x - 6)^2 - 4$$
$$8 = a(0 - 6)^2 - 4$$
$$8 = 36a - 4$$
$$12 = 36a$$
$$a = \frac{12}{36} = \frac{1}{3}$$

This matches (A).

14. A   Difficulty: Hard

Category: Additional Topics in Math / Geometry

Getting to the Answer: Drawing in a radius or two is usually a good way to start a circle question, especially when there doesn't seem to be a lot of information given. This question asks about the distance between the chord and the diameter, so start by drawing that in. Then, see if drawing a radius will help. After you've drawn in anything that you think might help you answer the question, go back and label wherever possible. The radius has length r, so add that to the diagram. The chord is $\frac{3}{4}$ as long as the diameter, which means half the chord is $\frac{3}{4}$ as long as the radius, so add that to the diagram. You are looking for the distance between the chord and the diameter, so call that x.

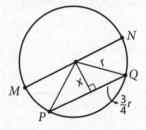

You now have a right triangle with enough labels to use the Pythagorean theorem.

$$a^2 + b^2 = c^2$$
$$x^2 + \left(\frac{3}{4}r\right)^2 = r^2$$
$$x^2 + \frac{9}{16}r^2 = r^2$$
$$x^2 = \frac{16}{16}r^2 - \frac{9}{16}r^2$$
$$x^2 = \frac{7}{16}r^2$$
$$x = \sqrt{\frac{7}{16}r^2} = \frac{\sqrt{7}}{4}r$$

Choice (A) is correct.

15. D   Difficulty: Hard

Category: Passport to Advanced Math / Exponents

Getting to the Answer: Use the rules of exponents to rewrite $\frac{3}{2}$ as a unit fraction raised to a power. Then write the expression in radical form and simplify.

$$16^{\frac{3}{2}} = \left(16^{\frac{1}{2}}\right)^3$$
$$= \left(\sqrt{16}\right)^3$$
$$= 4^3$$
$$= 4 \times 4 \times 4$$
$$= 64$$

Choice (D) is correct.

16. 12   Difficulty: Easy

Category: Heart of Algebra / Linear Equations

Getting to the Answer: The two things you can glean from the equation of a line are its slope and its y-intercept. In this question, you're given information about A and asked about B. Try writing the equation in slope-intercept form to see how A and B are related. Then look at the graph and see what you can add to this relationship. Start by writing the equation in slope-intercept form, $y = mx + b$.

$$Ax + By = C$$
$$By = -Ax + C$$
$$y = -\frac{A}{B}x + \frac{C}{B}$$

So, together A and B (specifically A over B) define the slope of the line. Look at the graph: Reading from left to right, the line falls 1 unit for every 2 units that it runs to the right, so the slope is $-\frac{1}{2}$. Don't forget—the question tells you that $A = 6$, so set the slope equal to $-\frac{6}{B}$ and solve for B:

$$-\frac{1}{2} = -\frac{6}{B}$$
$$B = 12$$

17. 9/2 or **4.5**   **Difficulty:** Medium

Category: Heart of Algebra / Inequalities

Getting to the Answer: You don't need to separate this compound inequality into pieces. Just remember, whatever you do to one piece, you must do to all three pieces, and don't forget to reverse the inequality symbols if you multiply or divide by a negative number. Here, the fractions make it look more complicated than it really is, so start by clearing the fractions by multiplying everything by 12.

$$\frac{1}{3} \le 2 - \frac{d}{6} \le \frac{5}{4}$$

$$12\left(\frac{1}{3}\right) \le 12\left(2 - \frac{d}{6}\right) \le 12\left(\frac{5}{4}\right)$$

$$4 \le 24 - 2d \le 15$$

$$-20 \le -2d \le -9$$

$$10 \ge d \ge \frac{9}{2}$$

The question asks for the minimum possible value of d, so turn the inequality around so that smaller numbers are written first: $\frac{9}{2} \le d \le 10$, making the minimum value $\frac{9}{2}$, or 4.5.

18. 7/3 or **2.33**   **Difficulty:** Medium

Category: Passport to Advanced Math / Functions

Getting to the Answer: The right-hand side of each piece of the function tells you what part of the domain (which x-values) goes with that particular function. In this function, only values of x that are less than zero go with the top function, values of x between 0 and 3 go with the middle function, and values of x that are greater than 3 go with the bottom function. Because 2 is between 0 and 3, plug it into the middle function and simplify:

$$g(2) = \frac{(2)^2}{3} + 1$$

$$= \frac{4}{3} + 1$$

$$= \frac{4}{3} + \frac{3}{3} = \frac{7}{3}$$

19. 34   Difficulty: Hard

Category: Additional Topics in Math / Geometry

Getting to the Answer: Add information from the question to the diagram. There are two right triangles—the smaller one formed by the saber, the path of the sun's rays, and the ground; and the larger one formed by the brick wall, the path of the sun's rays, and the ground. The two triangles share one angle (the small angle on the left side), and each has a 90-degree angle (where the saber and the brick wall each meet the ground), making the third pair of corresponding angles also congruent. This means the triangles are similar by AAA, and the sides of the triangles are proportional. You'll need to convert the height of the wall to inches because the question asks for the length of the saber in inches. (You could also convert the base lengths to inches, but it is not necessary because you can compare feet to feet in that ratio.)

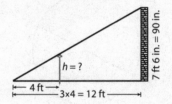

Now that you have a more detailed drawing, set up and solve a proportion:

$$\frac{\text{base of small triangle}}{\text{base of large triangle}} = \frac{\text{length of saber (in inches)}}{\text{height of wall (in inches)}}$$

$$\frac{4}{12} = \frac{h}{90}$$

$$4(90) = 12h$$

$$360 = 12h$$

$$30 = h$$

Don't forget to add the 4 inches that are stuck in the ground to find that the length of the saber is $30 + 4 = 34$ inches.

20. 2   Difficulty: Hard

Category: Passport to Advanced Math / Exponents

Getting to the Answer: Start by multiplying both sides of the equation (all three terms) by the common denominator, which is $x(x-1)$. Try to write neatly, especially when canceling terms, so you don't lose track of anything.

$$x \, \cancel{(x-1)} \left(\frac{x}{\cancel{x-1}} \right) - \cancel{x}(x-1) \left(\frac{2}{\cancel{x}} \right) =$$

$$x(x \cancel{-1}) \left(\frac{1}{\cancel{x-1}} \right)$$

$$x(x) - 2(x-1) = x(1)$$

$$x^2 - 2x + 2 = x$$

The resulting equation is quadratic, so set it equal to zero and either try to factor it or use the quadratic formula to solve it.

$$x^2 - 2x + 2 = x$$

$$x^2 - 3x + 2 = 0$$

$$(x-1)(x-2) = 0$$

$$x - 1 = 0 \text{ or } x - 2 = 0$$

$$x = 1 \text{ or } \qquad x = 2$$

Be careful here—whenever there is a variable in the denominator of the original equation, you must check to make sure that the solutions do not result in division by zero. The solution $x = 1$ *does* result in division by 0, so it is invalid. That means the only correct solution is $x = 2$.

MATH—CALCULATOR TEST

1. C   Difficulty: Easy

Category: Problem Solving and Data Analysis / Rates, Ratios, Proportions, and Percentages

Getting to the Answer: Break the question into steps. Before you can use the ratio, you need to find the percent of the market that utilizes Provider 1 and Provider 2. The ratio given in the question is 3:2, so write this as 3 parts (Provider 1) and 2 parts (Provider 2). You don't know how big a part is, so call it x. This means that $3x + 2x =$ the percent of consumers that utilize Provider 1 and Provider 2 for cable services, which is 100% minus all the other providers: $100 - (18 + 15 + 7) = 100 - 40 = 60$.

$$3x + 2x = 60$$

$$5x = 60$$

$$x = 12$$

Each part has a value of 12 and three parts use Provider 1, so Provider 1's market share is $3 \times 12 = 36\%$, which is (C).

2. B   Difficulty: Easy

Category: Heart of Algebra / Inequalities

Getting to the Answer: Solve the inequality using inverse operations. Then compare your answer with each of the number lines shown. Remember, on a number line, numbers to the right are greater than numbers to the left.

$$3x + 29 > 5 - x$$

$$4x + 29 > 5$$

$$4x > -24$$

$$x > -6$$

There should be an open dot at -6, with shading to the right, so (B) is correct. Don't be fooled by C. You only reverse the inequality symbol when you multiply or divide by a negative number, not when the answer is negative.

3. C   Difficulty: Easy

Category: Problem Solving and Data Analysis / Rates, Ratios, Proportions, and Percentages

Getting to the Answer: This is a question about rates, so pay careful attention to the units. First determine how long it will take the boat to complete the trip. Set up and solve a proportion:

$$\frac{4 \text{ nautical miles}}{1 \text{ hour}} = \frac{232 \text{ nautical miles}}{x \text{ hours}}$$

$$4x = 232$$

$$x = 58$$

The question asks for the total number of ounces of water needed. The recommended rate of consumption is given in ounces per hour, and you now know the number of hours that it will take the boat to complete the trip. Multiply the number of total hours by the number of ounces needed per hour: $58 \times 2.5 = 145$. Be careful—this isn't the answer. Remember, there are 3 people on board. This is the amount 1 person needs to consume during the trip, so multiply by 3 to get $145 \times 3 = 435$ ounces, (C).

4. A **Difficulty:** Medium

Category: Passport to Advanced Math / Quadratics

Getting to the Answer: If $a = 0$, then one factor must be $(a - 0)$, which means $x = 0$ is a root. This means the graph must cross through the origin, so you can eliminate C and D right away. Look at the remaining two choices, (A) and B. The question states that $b < 0$. This means b is negative, which means the other x-intercept must fall to the left of the y-axis, so (A) is correct.

Because this question is in the calculator section of the test, you could also use the Picking Numbers strategy. To do this, choose a value for b (that is less than 0), such as -2, and graph the equation $y = (x - 0)(x - (-2))$ to see what the graph looks like.

5. A **Difficulty:** Medium

Category: Problem Solving and Data Analysis / Scatterplots

Getting to the Answer: The y-intercept is the point at which $x = 0$. In this real-world scenario, the percent of people who are considered inactive is graphed on the x-axis, so the y-intercept occurs when 0% of the country is inactive. Now, look carefully at the way the answer choices are worded. Choice (A) is correct because it says the entire country is *active*, which is the same as saying 0% are inactive. Choice B says the entire country is *inactive*, which means 100% is inactive (not 0% inactive).

6. C **Difficulty:** Medium

Category: Heart of Algebra / Linear Equations

Getting to the Answer: In a real-world scenario, a one-time fee does not depend on the variable and is therefore a constant. A unit rate, however, is always multiplied by the independent variable.

The total cost consists of the gallon of milk (a constant), the per-pound cost of the apples (which depends on the number of pounds), and the cost of the magazine (which is the only taxed item). The constant in the equation is 4.49 and is, therefore, the cost of the gallon of milk; 1.89 is being multiplied by p (the number of pounds), so $1.89 must be the per-pound cost of the apples. That leaves the remaining term, 1.07(3.99), which must be the cost of the magazine ($3.99) plus a 7% sales tax. This matches (C).

7. D **Difficulty:** Medium

Category: Heart of Algebra / Linear Equations

Getting to the Answer: Organize information as you read the question; the total cost includes the labor cost, the cost of the materials, and the 5.5% tax on the *materials only*. If the contractor works h hours, the labor cost of the renovation is the per-hour rate ($40) multiplied by the number of hours (h) or $40h$. To this amount, add the $3,000 for materials, which are taxed at a rate of 5.5% and should therefore be multiplied by 1.055. The total cost is given by the equation $c = 40h + 1.055(3,000)$, which is (D).

8. D **Difficulty:** Medium

Category: Heart of Algebra / Systems of Linear Equations

Getting to the Answer: One equation should represent the total *number* of frames, while the other equation should represent the *revenue* from the frames. The number of custom frames c plus the number of ready-made frames r equals the total number of frames sold, 92. Therefore, one equation is $c + r = 92$. This means you can eliminate B and C. Now write the revenue equation: Revenue per custom frame ($30c$) plus revenue per ready-made frame ($12r$) equals the total amount collected (1,788). The revenue equation is $30c + 12r = 1,788$. Don't let A fool you. The question says nothing about the revenue *per day* of the sale, so there is no reason to divide by 3. Choice (D) is correct.

9. D   Difficulty: Medium

Category: Heart of Algebra / Inequalities

Getting to the Answer: The best way to answer this question is to pretend you are a homebuyer. How much more per square foot would your house cost in New York than Detroit? If the house was 1,500 square feet, how much more would this be? If the house was 2,000 square feet, how much more would this be?

Based on the data in the table, a house would cost $288.58 − $62.45 = $226.13 more per square foot in New York than in Detroit. If the house was 1,500 square feet, it would cost 1,500(226.13) = $339,195 more. If the house was 2,000 square feet, it would cost 2,000(226.13) = $452,260 more. So, the house would cost somewhere between $339,195 and $452,260 more, which can be expressed as the compound inequality $339{,}195 \leq x \leq 452{,}260$, (D).

10. D   Difficulty: Medium

Category: Heart of Algebra / Linear Equations

Getting to the Answer: Use the distributive property to simplify each of the terms that contain parentheses. You don't need to clear the fractions on the right-hand side, because you can easily take half of $4n$ and half of 16. Once you arrive at the simplified equation, make sure you understand what the result is telling you.

$$5n - 3(n - 1) = \frac{1}{2}(4n + 16) - 5$$
$$5n - 3n + 3 = 2n + 8 - 5$$
$$2n + 3 = 2n + 3$$
$$3 = 3$$

All of the variable terms cancel out, and the resulting numerical statement is true (3 always equals 3), so there are infinitely many solutions, or in other words, there are infinitely many values of n for which the equation is true, (D).

11. B   Difficulty: Medium

Category: Additional Topics / Geometry

Getting to the Answer: The roads form a right triangle with the expressway as the hypotenuse. The two legs are Max's current route. He travels on one road for 9 miles and the other for 40. You might recognize this as a Pythagorean triple: 9, 40, 41. Even if you don't, you can always use the Pythagorean theorem to solve for the length of the hypotenuse.

$$a^2 + b^2 = c^2$$
$$(9)^2 + (40)^2 = c^2$$
$$81 + 1{,}600 = c^2$$
$$1{,}681 = c^2$$
$$41 = c$$

Now that you know the length of the expressway, it's time to analyze what the question is actually asking.

The question asks how much gas he will save given that his car gets 20 miles per gallon. His current *round-trip* route is 2(9 + 40) = 2(49) = 98 miles, which will use 98 ÷ 20 = 4.9 gallons of gas per day, which is equal to 5(4.9) = 24.5 gallons per workweek. The *round-trip* expressway route is 2(41) = 82 miles, which will use 82 ÷ 20 = 4.1 gallons of gas per day, which is equal to 5(4.1) = 20.5 gallons per workweek. Thus, he will save 24.5 − 20.5 = 4 gallons of gas per week by taking the expressway, making (B) correct.

12. C   Difficulty: Medium

Category: Problem Solving and Data Analysis / Statistics and Probability

Getting to the Answer: The mean of a set of numbers is the same as the average, which is the sum of the terms divided by the number of terms. Use the graph to find the sum of the unemployment rates over all 5 years: 9.8 + 9.2 + 8.3 + 8 + 6.6 = 41.9. Now, divide by the number of years to calculate the mean: 41.9 ÷ 5 = 8.38. Read the axis labels carefully. The unemployment rate is given as a percent, so write 8.38 as 0.0838. According to the question stem there were 250,000 people in the geographic area, so approximately $250,000 \times 0.0838 = 20,950$ people, (C), were unemployed during the indicated time period.

13. C   Difficulty: Medium

Category: Passport to Advanced Math / Exponents

Getting to the Answer: To make the expression look more familiar, rewrite the fraction exponent as a radical. Then, find the largest perfect square for each factor and take its square root (which allows you to bring the square roots outside the radical).

$$
\begin{aligned}
&\left(36x^4y^7\right)^{\frac{1}{2}} \\
&= \sqrt{36x^4y^7} \\
&= \sqrt{\left(6^2\right)\left(x^2\right)^2\left(y^3\right)^2 y} \\
&= 6x^2y^3\sqrt{y}
\end{aligned}
$$

Choice (C) is correct.

14. D   Difficulty: Medium

Category: Problem Solving and Data Analysis / Scatterplots

Getting to the Answer: The average rate of change is the same as the slope of the line of best fit. Look for two points that lie on the line (or as close as possible to the line) and then find the slope using the slope formula, $m = \dfrac{y_2 - y_1}{x_2 - x_1}$. Pay careful attention to how the axes are labeled to make sure you write the points accurately. Using the points (1, 3.5) and (1.75, 5.5), the average rate of change is $\dfrac{5.5 - 3.5}{1.75 - 1} = \dfrac{2}{0.75} = 2.\overline{6}$ or $\dfrac{8}{3}$, which is (D).

15. D   Difficulty: Medium

Category: Problem Solving and Data Analysis / Scatterplots

Getting to the Answer: A line of best fit serves as an approximation of data from which you can estimate an output for a given input (or vice versa). Hence, the

actual value is the y-value of the data point and the *expected value* is the y-value along the line of best fit. The key is in reading the axis labels carefully. Notice that the distance between two consecutive grid lines on the vertical axis is 0.5 (*not* 1). Therefore, you are looking for points that are more than 4 grid-lines away from the line of best fit (because you want points for which the difference is greater than 2 and $0.5 \times 4 = 2$). There are no such points, so (D) is correct.

16. C   Difficulty: Medium

Category: Passport to Advanced Math / Quadratics

Getting to the Answer: Taking the square root is the inverse operation of squaring, and both sides of the equation are already perfect squares, so take their square roots. Then solve the resulting equations. Remember, there will be two equations to solve.

$$
\begin{aligned}
(x - 2)^2 &= \frac{16}{25} \\
\sqrt{(x - 2)^2} &= \sqrt{\frac{16}{25}} \\
x - 2 &= \pm\frac{\sqrt{16}}{\sqrt{25}} \\
x &= 2 \pm \frac{4}{5}
\end{aligned}
$$

Now, simplify each equation:

$$
x = 2 - \frac{4}{5} = \frac{10}{5} - \frac{4}{5} = \frac{6}{5}
$$

and

$$
x = 2 + \frac{4}{5} = \frac{10}{5} + \frac{4}{5} = \frac{14}{5}
$$

Choice (C) is correct.

17. C   Difficulty: Medium

Category: Heart of Algebra / Linear Equations

Getting to the Answer: When you know the slope and one point on a line, you can use $y = mx + b$ to write the equation. Substitute the slope for m and the coordinates of the point for x and y. The slope is given as $-\frac{5}{2}$, so substitute this for m. The point is given as $(2, -1)$, so $x = 2$ and $y = -1$. Now, find b:

$$y = mx + b$$
$$-1 = -\frac{5}{2}(2) + b$$
$$-1 = -5 + b$$
$$4 = b$$

The y-intercept of the line is 4, which is (C).

You could also very carefully graph the line using the given point and the slope. Start at $(2, -1)$ and move toward the y-axis by rising 5 and running to the left 2 (because the slope is negative). You should land at the point $(0, 4)$.

18. C   Difficulty: Medium

Category: Problem Solving and Data Analysis / Rates, Ratios, Proportions, and Percentages

Getting to the Answer: Find the percent increase using the formula, % Change $= \dfrac{\text{amount of change}}{\text{original amount}}$. Then apply the same percent increase to the 2010 CPI to find the expected value in 2030. The amount of increase is $218.1 - 130.7 = 87.4$, so the percent increase is $87.4 \div 130.7 = 0.6687$, or 66.87% over 20 years. If the total percent increase over the next 20 years is the same, the CPI will be about $218.1 \times 1.6687 = 363.9$, (C).

19. B   Difficulty: Medium

Category: Passport to Advanced Math / Functions

Getting to the Answer: The given range value is an output value, so substitute $-\frac{5}{3}$ for $f(x)$ and use inverse operations to solve for x, which gives you the corresponding domain value. Start by multiplying the equation by the greatest common multiple of 3 and 4, which is 12, in order to clear the fractions.

$$-\frac{5}{3} = \frac{1}{4}x - 2$$
$$(12)\left(-\frac{5}{3}\right) = 12\left(\frac{1}{4}x - 2\right)$$
$$-20 = 3x - 24$$
$$4 = 3x$$
$$\frac{4}{3} = x$$

Choice (B) is correct.

20. B   Difficulty: Medium

Category: Passport to Advanced Math / Exponents

Getting to the Answer: First, square both sides of the equation to get m out from under the radical. Then, divide both sides by $4\pi^2$. Finally, multiply both sides by k.

$$T = 2\pi\sqrt{\frac{m}{k}}$$
$$T^2 = (2\pi)^2\left(\frac{m}{k}\right)$$
$$T^2 = 4\pi^2\left(\frac{m}{k}\right)$$
$$\frac{T^2}{4\pi^2} = \frac{m}{k}$$
$$\frac{kT^2}{4\pi^2} = m$$

This matches (B).

21. C   Difficulty: Medium

Category: Problem Solving and Data Analysis / Statistics and Probability

Getting to the Answer: A good representative sample is not only random, but also a good representation of the population in question. Here, the population in question is parents of high school-age children. Not everyone with a cell phone is a parent of high school-age children. For example, single and married people who don't have children are likely to make up at least a portion of the random texts sent out by the polling company. This means that, despite being randomly selected, the sample is unlikely to be a good representative sample, making (C) correct. (Note that D also sounds reasonable, but the question asks for the best explanation that specifically addresses why the sample is unlikely to be a *good representative sample*.)

22. B   Difficulty: Medium

Category: Problem Solving and Data Analysis / Rates, Ratios, Proportions, and Percentages

Getting to the Answer: Let the units in this question, as in most rate questions, guide you to the answer. The rate at which each machine can produce shoelaces is given per day, but the question asks about the number of shoelaces each machine can produce in 8 minutes, so convert shoelaces per day to shoelaces per minute and multiply by 8. Then find the difference.

Machine 1:

$$\frac{36{,}000 \text{ laces}}{\text{day}} \times \frac{1 \text{ day}}{24 \text{ hr}} \times \frac{1 \text{ hr}}{60 \text{ min}} \times 8 \text{ min}$$
$$= 200 \text{ laces}$$

Machine 2:

$$\frac{28{,}800 \text{ laces}}{\text{day}} \times \frac{1 \text{ day}}{24 \text{ hr}} \times \frac{1 \text{ hr}}{60 \text{ min}} \times 8 \text{ min}$$
$$= 160 \text{ laces}$$

The first machine can produce $200 - 160 = 40$ more shoelaces in 8 minutes, (B).

23. A   Difficulty: Medium

Category: Heart of Algebra / Linear Equations

Getting to the Answer: Compare the differences in the two lines to the statements in the answer choices. Pay careful attention to which line represents each country. The lines both have different *y*-intercepts and different slopes. The dashed line (Country B) starts lower and has a more gradual

slope, while the solid line (Country A) starts higher and has a steeper slope. This means that, even though the incidence rate was initially higher, Country A's vaccine requirement had a greater impact on the incidence rate than Country B's free vaccines, (A). You can also think about it logically: The incidence rate in Country A started higher and ended lower than in Country B, which means there was a greater change.

24. A   Difficulty: Hard

Category: Problem Solving and Data Analysis / Rates, Ratios, Proportions, and Percentages

Getting to the Answer: Start by finding the time between classes. There are 3 hours and 45 minutes between classes. Now, subtract 10 minutes (5 minutes each way) for walking to and from the classroom, which leaves 3 hours and 35 minutes. Next, subtract the hour the professor takes for lunch, leaving 2 hours and 35 minutes, to grade papers. Now comes the tricky part. The question gives you the rate at which he can grade papers per second, so you need to convert the hours and minutes to seconds. There are 60 minutes in 1 hour, so 2 hours and 35 minutes is 155 minutes. There are 60 seconds in 1 minute, so the number of seconds the professor has to grade papers is 9,300. Now divide this by 4 to see how many questions he can grade: 2,325. The question asks how many complete tests he can grade, and there are 50 questions per test, so divide by 50 to get 46.5, which means he can completely grade 46 tests (he doesn't have time to finish the 47th test). Choice (A) is correct.

25. B   Difficulty: Hard

Category: Problem Solving and Data Analysis / Rates, Ratios, Proportions, and Percentages

Getting to the Answer: The trick to answering a question like this is figuring out what accounts for the difference in the prices. In each case, the examination and the frames are the same; the difference in the cost must be due to the difference in the cost of the lenses. Because tinted lenses cost three times as much as clear lenses, the *difference* in cost must be twice the cost of the clear lenses.

Difference in cost $=$ cost of tinted $-$ cost of clear
$= 3(\text{cost of clear}) - \text{cost of clear}$
$= 2(\text{cost of clear})$

The difference in cost is $197 - 125 = 72$. Because this is twice the cost of the clear lenses, the clear lenses must cost $72 \div 2 = 36$, (B).

26. D Difficulty: Hard

Category: Problem Solving and Data Analysis / Statistics and Probability

Getting to the Answer: Whenever a question involves a two-way table, read carefully to see which rows and/or columns you need to focus on. The question asks for the probability that the registered voter chosen will not view the senator *unfavorably*. This means the voter's view is either *neutral* or *favorable*, so look at columns 3, 4, and 5. Add the numbers together to get $228 + 487 + 163 = 878$. The probability that you're looking for is the quotient of this number divided by the total number of registered voters: $878 \div 1{,}094 = 0.8025$, or approximately 80.3%, (D).

27. A Difficulty: Hard

Category: Additional Topics / Geometry

Getting to the Answer: Make a plan before you start plugging values into the formulas: The volume of the air is equal to the volume of the can minus the volume of the three tennis balls. For both formulas, you will need the radius. The diameters of the cylinder and the balls are the same, 2.6, but you need the radius, so divide by 2 to get $2.6 \div 2 = 1.3$. For the cylinder, you also need the height. Because there are 3 tennis balls and the top and bottom balls are tangent to the top and bottom of the can, the height is simply the diameter multiplied by 3, which is $2.6 \times 3 = 7.8$. Now you're ready to use the formulas. A quick peek at the answer choices will tell you that you don't need to simplify completely.

First, find the volume of the whole can:

$$V = \pi r^2 h$$
$$V = \pi(1.3)^2(7.8)$$
$$V = \pi(1.69)(7.8)$$
$$V = 13.182\pi$$

Next, find the volume of three tennis balls:

$$V = 3\left(\frac{4}{3}\pi r^3\right)$$
$$V = \cancel{3}\left(\frac{4}{\cancel{3}}\pi(1.3)^3\right)$$
$$V = 4\pi(2.197)$$
$$V = 8.788\pi$$

Finally, subtract to get $13.182\pi - 8.788\pi = 4.394\pi$, or about 4.4π cubic inches of air, which is (A).

28. B Difficulty: Hard

Category: Heart of Algebra / Linear Equations

Getting to the Answer: None of the variables in the equation has an exponent greater than 1, so the equation is linear. Most of what we know about lines revolves around slope and y-intercepts, so start by rearranging the equation to look like $y = mx + b$.

$$y = hy + hx + x - 4$$
$$y - hy = hx + x - 4$$
$$y(1 - h) = x(h + 1) - 4$$
$$y = \frac{(h + 1)}{(1 - h)}x - \frac{4}{1 - h}$$

Once rewritten, you have a linear equation with a slope of $\frac{h + 1}{1 - h}$ and a y-intercept of $-\frac{4}{1-h}$. It is given in the question that $-1 < h < 0$ (or a negative fraction greater than -1), so the quantity $h + 1$ is positive and the quantity $1 - h$ is also positive, resulting in a positive slope and a negative y-intercept. Only (B) satisfies these conditions.

29. B   Difficulty: Hard

Category: Problem Solving and Data Analysis / Rates, Ratios, Proportions, and Percentages

Getting to the Answer: Let the units in this question guide you to the correct answer. Set up unit conversions so that the units you don't want will cancel out. Your goal is to find the density of the piece of granite so you can compare it to the density of Earth's inner core. You don't need a definition of *density*—you can see from the units that you need to convert to g/cm³, which tells you to divide the weight of the granite by the volume. You're not given a conversion from feet to centimeters or pounds to grams, so you'll need to convert 168 pounds per cubic foot to ounces per cubic inch, and then to grams per cubic centimeter. Try not to round too much as you work—rather, wait until the very end if possible.

$$\frac{168 \text{ lb}}{1 \text{ ft}^3} \times \frac{1 \text{ ft}}{12 \text{ in.}} \times \frac{1 \text{ ft}}{12 \text{ in.}} \times \frac{1 \text{ ft}}{12 \text{ in.}} = \frac{168 \text{ lb}}{1,728 \text{ in.}^3}$$

$$\frac{168 \text{ lb}}{1,728 \text{ in.}^3} \times \frac{16 \text{ oz}}{1 \text{ lb}} = \frac{2,688 \text{ oz}}{1,728 \text{ in.}^3}$$

$$\frac{2,688 \text{ oz}}{1,728 \text{ in.}^3} \times \frac{1 \text{ in.} \times 1 \text{ in.} \times 1 \text{ in.}}{2.54 \text{ cm} \times 2.54 \text{ cm} \times 2.54 \text{ cm}}$$

$$= \frac{2,688 \text{ oz}}{28,316.85 \text{ cm}^3}$$

$$\frac{2,688 \text{ oz}}{28,316.85 \text{ cm}^3} \times \frac{28.35 g}{1 \text{ oz}} = \frac{76,204.8 g}{28,316.85 \text{ cm}^3} \approx 2.7 \text{ g/cm}^3$$

But wait—that's not the final answer. Subtract this amount from 12.8 to find that Earth's inner core is $12.8 - 2.7 = 10.1$ g/cm³ denser than the piece of granite. Choice (B) is correct.

30. A   Difficulty: Hard

Category: Passport to Advanced Math / Exponents

Getting to the Answer: Simplifying a complex rational expression requires planning and patience. Here, you need to write the denominator of the big expression as a single fraction, and then you can simply "flip it" to adjust for the "1 over."

Start by writing $\frac{1}{R_1} + \frac{1}{R_2}$ as a single term. To do this, find the common denominator and write each piece of the sum in terms of that denominator. The common denominator is $R_1 R_2$.

$$\frac{1}{R_1} + \frac{1}{R_2} = \frac{R_2}{R_2}\left(\frac{1}{R_1}\right) + \frac{R_1}{R_1}\left(\frac{1}{R_2}\right)$$

$$= \frac{R_2}{R_1 R_2} + \frac{R_1}{R_1 R_2}$$

$$= \frac{R_1 + R_2}{R_1 R_2}$$

But remember, this fraction is the denominator under 1, so you need to write the reciprocal (flip it); the correct expression is $\frac{R_1 R_2}{R_1 + R_2}$, which matches (A).

31. 2030 Difficulty: Easy

Category: Heart of Algebra / Inequalities

Getting to the Answer: You want the cropland to be below, or less than 800, so set up and solve an inequality:

$$f < 800$$
$$-3.7t + 872 < 800$$
$$-3.7t < -72$$
$$t > 19.46$$

Here's the tricky part—should you round? To decide, plug 19 and 20, one at a time, into the original equation and simplify:

When $t = 19$, $f = -3.7(19) + 872 = 801.7$, which is not below 800.

This means $t = 20$, but be careful—that is not the answer! The question states that t represents the number of years after 2010, so the correct answer is $2010 + 20 = 2030$.

32. 36   Difficulty: Easy

Category: Passport to Advanced Math / Functions

Getting to the Answer: When evaluating a function, substitute the value inside the parentheses for x in the equation. Evaluate the function at $x = 5$ and at $x = -1$. Then subtract the second output from the first. Note that this is not the same as first subtracting $5 - (-1)$ and then evaluating the function at $x = 6$.

$$g(5) = (5)^2 + 2(5) + 9 = 25 + 10 + 9 = 44$$
$$g(-1) = (-1)^2 + 2(-1) + 9 = 1 - 2 + 9 = 8$$

$$g(5) - g(-1) = 44 - 8 = 36$$

33. 540   Difficulty: Medium

Category: Problem Solving and Data Analysis / Rates, Ratios, Proportions, and Percentages

Getting to the Answer: Work through this question one step at a time. Start by using the sample survey to find the percentage of farmers who are not satisfied with their current supply company. According to the sample survey, $\frac{120}{200} = 0.6$ (or 60%) of the farmers are not satisfied with their current supply company. Multiply the total number of farms in the population (the three counties) to find that $1,200 \times 0.6 = 720$ farmers are not satisfied. The company is confident that it can acquire 75% of these customers, or $720 \times 0.75 = 540$ customers.

34. 2   Difficulty: Medium

Category: Additional Topics / Imaginary Numbers

Getting to the Answer: Because $\sqrt{-1} = i$, rewrite each number under the radical as a product of -1 and itself. Then take the square root of each. If possible, cancel any factors that are common to the numerator and the denominator.

$$\frac{4 + \sqrt{-16}}{2 + \sqrt{-4}} = \frac{4 + \sqrt{16 \times (-1)}}{2 + \sqrt{4 \times (-1)}}$$
$$= \frac{4 + 4i}{2 + 2i}$$
$$= \frac{2(2 + 2i)}{2 + 2i}$$
$$= 2$$

35. 85   Difficulty: Medium

Category: Heart of Algebra / Systems of Linear Equations

Getting to the Answer: Write a system of equations with r = the cost of the block of the regional competitor's stock in thousands of dollars (so you don't have to deal with all the zeros) and n = the cost of the block of the national competitor's stock in thousands of dollars. Before entering your final answer, check that you answered the right question (how much more the national competitor's stock cost). The block of the regional competitor's stock cost 25 thousand dollars less than half as much as the block of the national competitor's stock, so $r = \frac{1}{2}n - 25$. Together, both stock acquisitions cost 155 thousand dollars, so $r + n = 155$.

The system of equations is:

$$\begin{cases} r + n = 155 \\ r = \dfrac{n}{2} - 25 \end{cases}$$

The bottom equation is already solved for r, so substitute $r = \frac{n}{2} - 25$ into the top equation for r and solve for n. To make the numbers easier to work with, multiply each term by 2 to clear the fractions:

$$\frac{n}{2} - 25 + n = 155$$
$$n - 50 + 2n = 310$$
$$3n = 360$$
$$n = 120$$

The national competitor's stock cost 120 thousand dollars, so the regional competitor's stock cost $(120 \div 2) - 25 = 60 - 25 = 35$ thousand dollars. This means the national competitor's stock cost $120 - 35 = 85$ thousand dollars more than the regional competitor's stock.

36. 12.4   Difficulty: Hard

Category: Problem Solving and Data Analysis / Rates, Ratios, Proportions, and Percentages

Getting to the Answer: Pay careful attention to the units. You don't need to convert all of the dimensions to inches, even though the answer asks for inches. The ratio will be the same. But you do need to convert the length of the bridge, given in miles, to feet, because the length of the longest piece of the bridge is given in feet: 1.63 miles × 5,280 feet = 8,606.4 feet. Now, set up a proportion and solve for the unknown. Use words first to help you keep the dimensions in the right places:

$$\frac{\text{actual longest piece}}{\text{actual total length}} = \frac{\text{drawing longest piece}}{\text{drawing total length}}$$

$$\frac{3,800}{8,606.4} = \frac{x}{28}$$

$$106,400 = 8,606.4x$$

$$12.36 \approx x$$

The length of the longest piece in the drawing should be 12.4 inches long.

37. .49   Difficulty: Medium

Category: Problem Solving and Data Analysis / Statistics and Probability

Getting to the Answer: Identify the parts of the bar graph that you will need to answer this question. You need to find a probability, which is always given by the number of favorable outcomes (willing to wait at least 30 minutes) divided by the total number of outcomes (all the responses to the survey). First, total the number of customers willing to wait 30 minutes or more. Be careful—the question doesn't specify Friday or Saturday, so use both days:

$$38 + 45 + 33 + 43 + 20 + 40 + 9 + 17 = 245$$

Now, find the total number of people who responded to the survey. You don't need to start over—just add the previous sum to the number of people willing to wait *less than* 30 minutes:

$$245 + 70 + 75 + 46 + 64 = 500$$

This means the probability that someone will be willing to wait more than 30 minutes is $\frac{245}{500} = \frac{49}{100}$, This fraction won't fit in the answer grid, so enter your answer as a decimal, .49.

38. 1   Difficulty: Hard

Category: Problem Solving and Data Analysis / Statistics and Probability

Getting to the Answer: The question asks *on average* how much *longer* customers are willing to wait. So, you will need to find a weighted average for each day. Start with Friday. Multiply each wait time by the height of the bar (the number of people willing to wait for that amount of time on that night):

$$20 \times 70 = 1,400$$
$$25 \times 46 = 1,150$$
$$30 \times 38 = 1,140$$
$$35 \times 33 = 1,155$$
$$40 \times 20 = 800$$
$$45 \times 9 = 405$$

Next, add the results to get 6,050, and then divide by the total number of people who took the Friday survey: (70 + 46 + 38 + 33 + 20 + 9 = 216) to get 6,050 ÷ 216 = 28.0 minutes. This is the average amount of time people are willing to wait for a table on Friday night. Now, do the same thing for Saturday.

$$20 \times 75 = 1,500$$
$$25 \times 64 = 1,600$$
$$30 \times 45 = 1,350$$
$$35 \times 43 = 1,505$$
$$40 \times 40 = 1,600$$
$$45 \times 17 = 765$$

Add the results, 8,320, and divide by the number of people: (75 + 64 + 45 + 43 + 40 + 17 = 284) to get 8,320 ÷ 284 = 29.3 minutes. So, people are willing to wait 29.3 − 28.0 = 1.3 minutes longer on Saturday than Friday. Don't forget to follow directions—1.3 rounded to the nearest whole minute is 1 minute.

ESSAY TEST RUBRIC

The Essay Demonstrates ...

4—Advanced	• **(Reading)** A strong ability to comprehend the source text, including its central ideas and important details and how they interrelate; and effectively use evidence (quotations, paraphrases, or both) from the source text. • **(Analysis)** A strong ability to evaluate the author's use of evidence, reasoning, and/or stylistic and persuasive elements, and/or other features of the student's own choosing; make good use of relevant, sufficient, and strategically chosen support for the claims or points made in the student's essay; and focus consistently on features of the source text that are most relevant to addressing the task. • **(Writing)** A strong ability to provide a precise central claim; create an effective organization that includes an introduction and conclusion, as well as a clear progression of ideas; successfully employ a variety of sentence structures; use precise word choice; maintain a formal style and objective tone; and show command of the conventions of standard written English so that the essay is free of errors.
3—Proficient	• **(Reading)** Satisfactory ability to comprehend the source text, including its central ideas and important details and how they interrelate; and use evidence (quotations, paraphrases, or both) from the source text. • **(Analysis)** Satisfactory ability to evaluate the author's use of evidence, reasoning, and/or stylistic and persuasive elements, and/or other features of the student's own choosing; make use of relevant and sufficient support for the claims or points made in the student's essay; and focus primarily on features of the source text that are most relevant to addressing the task. • **(Writing)** Satisfactory ability to provide a central claim; create an organization that includes an introduction and conclusion, as well as a clear progression of ideas; employ a variety of sentence structures; use precise word choice; maintain an appropriate formal style and objective tone; and show control of the conventions of standard written English so that the essay is free of significant errors.
2—Partial	• **(Reading)** Limited ability to comprehend the source text, including its central ideas and important details and how they interrelate; and use evidence (quotations, paraphrases, or both) from the source text. • **(Analysis)** Limited ability to evaluate the author's use of evidence, reasoning, and/or stylistic and persuasive elements, and/or other features of the student's own choosing; make use of support for the claims or points made in the student's essay; and focus on relevant features of the source text. • **(Writing)** Limited ability to provide a central claim; create an effective organization for ideas; employ a variety of sentence structures; use precise word choice; maintain an appropriate style and tone; or show command of the conventions of standard written English, resulting in certain errors that detract from the quality of the writing.

1—Inadequate	• **(Reading)** Little or no ability to comprehend the source text or use evidence from the source text.
	• **(Analysis)** Little or no ability to evaluate the author's use of evidence, reasoning, and/ or stylistic and persuasive elements; choose support for claims or points; or focus on relevant features of the source text.
	• **(Writing)** Little or no ability to provide a central claim, organization, or progression of ideas; employ a variety of sentence structures; use precise word choice; maintain an appropriate style and tone; or show command of the conventions of standard written English, resulting in numerous errors that undermine the quality of the writing.

ESSAY RESPONSE #1 (ADVANCED SCORE)

President Johnson is speaking to Americans during a time of great struggle involving national identity. The question posed is whether "American" is a designation to include all people equally, or a privilege reserved for white Americans only. Using evidence, emotional appeals, precisely chosen words, and a tone of reason, Johnson argues for the immediate expansion of voting rights to all citizens. The well-crafted construction of this speech enhances the persuasiveness of the argument.

In his speech, Johnson uses language and emotional appeals to address all Americans, making them feel unified in the common goal that the nation should deliver on the promise of its founding. He uses the pronouns "us" and "we" repeatedly. This is a deliberate choice designed to make his audience feel included in a grand project that will make the country a fair and just place. Johnson is addressing his fellow Americans directly, so if they reject this challenge, they are not simply ignoring the problem of injustice. Instead, they would be personally refusing to solve it.

In addition, Johnson uses personalized language to present the evidence for his case, which leads the audience, whatever their ethnic background, to sympathize with the victims of racial discrimination. He describes the specific details of how people are denied the right to vote by using a fictional African American citizen who must endure these insults. "He" must fill out paperwork (if he is lucky enough to be allowed to do so), and then must pass a ludicrous and unreasonable test, such as reciting the entire Constitution. Johnson could have simply listed what had to be changed by saying, for instance, "literacy tests are unfair." Instead, by personalizing the experience of injustice, Johnson makes his audience understand the way that injustice builds over time to produce humiliation and defeat.

The structure of Johnson's speech is powerful. It begins with a bold proclamation designed to capture the audience's attention; its subject is nothing less than "the dignity of man and the destiny of democracy." How could the audience not want to listen? He then proceeds to lay out the problem. Voting rights are denied to African Americans. This is a threat to democracy itself, Johnson argues. He goes on to argue point by point how "emancipation is a proclamation and not a fact." He enumerates each way black voters are denied their rights, backing up his argument with specific details. In this way, he builds an argument that drastic measures must be taken immediately to ensure all people can vote.

Johnson's speech is also powerful because his reasonable tone makes his a credible voice. He does not speak down to anyone in his audience, even those who might be inclined to disagree with him. Instead, he uses reason to make his argument seem obvious and sensible. He identifies the challenges that face the nation. He is not naive about the difficulties of race relations. He even reassures those who struggle with the debates of civil rights that he understands how challenging they are. He gains substantial credibility by noting that he himself is from the South and knows personally "how agonizing racial feelings are." As someone who shares their background but still feels the law must be changed, Johnson comes across not as a patronizing radical, but as a reasonable person not unlike them, who might be able to persuade them to change their minds.

Through the language, structure, and tone of his speech, Johnson stresses inclusivity: not only the extension of voting rights to all people, but the responsibility of all of "us" to ensure that it happens. Without a voting system free of racism, he argues, nothing else in our democracy matters.

ESSAY RESPONSE #2 (PROFICIENT SCORE)

President Johnson's speech was made during a time when the nation debated whether all citizens should be able to vote. Johnson believed that they should. He also believed that African Americans were being illegally denied their voting rights and that laws should be passed to make sure everyone could vote. Johnson's speech persuades the audience that this is true through his use of evidence, reasoning, and style.

Johnson's use of evidence makes it clear that the injustice taking place is obvious. He uses real examples and explains why the situation cannot be allowed to continue. He has answers for those who might ask, "But why is the situation so bad?" He can point to specific ways in which it is bad. In short, he has clearly thought through his ideas and can persuade people who disagree with him.

Johnson's reasoning is related to the Constitution. The United States is a democracy, and it is legally and morally right that citizens can vote. But even though the Emancipation Proclamation was signed a hundred years before, many African Americans still could not vote, for the reasons Johnson lists. The system legally allows people to prevent others from voting, but it is their right. This is why Johnson argues that things must change.

Johnson's language is about justice and a sense of belonging to a nation. He uses words like "us" and "we" a lot. This suggests that people in the audience are supposed to feel responsibility for the current situation. They cannot ignore it. In fact, he says, even if the United States accomplishes great things, if they do not get voting rights right, "we will have failed as a people and as a nation."

In conclusion, any intelligent person listening to Johnson's speech would be persuaded by his reasoning, evidence, and language that even though slaves were freed many years before, the system was still racist and needed to change. They would surely have supported Johnson's idea that laws should be written in order to make the system fair.

SAT PRACTICE TEST 4 ANSWER SHEET

Remove (or photocopy) this answer sheet and use it to complete the test. See the answer key following the test when finished.

Start with number 1 for each section. If a section has fewer questions than answer spaces, leave the extra spaces blank.

SECTION 1

1. Ⓐ Ⓑ Ⓒ Ⓓ	14. Ⓐ Ⓑ Ⓒ Ⓓ	27. Ⓐ Ⓑ Ⓒ Ⓓ	40. Ⓐ Ⓑ Ⓒ Ⓓ
2. Ⓐ Ⓑ Ⓒ Ⓓ	15. Ⓐ Ⓑ Ⓒ Ⓓ	28. Ⓐ Ⓑ Ⓒ Ⓓ	41. Ⓐ Ⓑ Ⓒ Ⓓ
3. Ⓐ Ⓑ Ⓒ Ⓓ	16. Ⓐ Ⓑ Ⓒ Ⓓ	29. Ⓐ Ⓑ Ⓒ Ⓓ	42. Ⓐ Ⓑ Ⓒ Ⓓ
4. Ⓐ Ⓑ Ⓒ Ⓓ	17. Ⓐ Ⓑ Ⓒ Ⓓ	30. Ⓐ Ⓑ Ⓒ Ⓓ	43. Ⓐ Ⓑ Ⓒ Ⓓ
5. Ⓐ Ⓑ Ⓒ Ⓓ	18. Ⓐ Ⓑ Ⓒ Ⓓ	31. Ⓐ Ⓑ Ⓒ Ⓓ	44. Ⓐ Ⓑ Ⓒ Ⓓ
6. Ⓐ Ⓑ Ⓒ Ⓓ	19. Ⓐ Ⓑ Ⓒ Ⓓ	32. Ⓐ Ⓑ Ⓒ Ⓓ	45. Ⓐ Ⓑ Ⓒ Ⓓ
7. Ⓐ Ⓑ Ⓒ Ⓓ	20. Ⓐ Ⓑ Ⓒ Ⓓ	33. Ⓐ Ⓑ Ⓒ Ⓓ	46. Ⓐ Ⓑ Ⓒ Ⓓ
8. Ⓐ Ⓑ Ⓒ Ⓓ	21. Ⓐ Ⓑ Ⓒ Ⓓ	34. Ⓐ Ⓑ Ⓒ Ⓓ	47. Ⓐ Ⓑ Ⓒ Ⓓ
9. Ⓐ Ⓑ Ⓒ Ⓓ	22. Ⓐ Ⓑ Ⓒ Ⓓ	35. Ⓐ Ⓑ Ⓒ Ⓓ	48. Ⓐ Ⓑ Ⓒ Ⓓ
10. Ⓐ Ⓑ Ⓒ Ⓓ	23. Ⓐ Ⓑ Ⓒ Ⓓ	36. Ⓐ Ⓑ Ⓒ Ⓓ	49. Ⓐ Ⓑ Ⓒ Ⓓ
11. Ⓐ Ⓑ Ⓒ Ⓓ	24. Ⓐ Ⓑ Ⓒ Ⓓ	37. Ⓐ Ⓑ Ⓒ Ⓓ	50. Ⓐ Ⓑ Ⓒ Ⓓ
12. Ⓐ Ⓑ Ⓒ Ⓓ	25. Ⓐ Ⓑ Ⓒ Ⓓ	38. Ⓐ Ⓑ Ⓒ Ⓓ	51. Ⓐ Ⓑ Ⓒ Ⓓ
13. Ⓐ Ⓑ Ⓒ Ⓓ	26. Ⓐ Ⓑ Ⓒ Ⓓ	39. Ⓐ Ⓑ Ⓒ Ⓓ	52. Ⓐ Ⓑ Ⓒ Ⓓ

☐ # correct in Section 1

☐ # incorrect in Section 1

SECTION 2

1. Ⓐ Ⓑ Ⓒ Ⓓ	12. Ⓐ Ⓑ Ⓒ Ⓓ	23. Ⓐ Ⓑ Ⓒ Ⓓ	34. Ⓐ Ⓑ Ⓒ Ⓓ
2. Ⓐ Ⓑ Ⓒ Ⓓ	13. Ⓐ Ⓑ Ⓒ Ⓓ	24. Ⓐ Ⓑ Ⓒ Ⓓ	35. Ⓐ Ⓑ Ⓒ Ⓓ
3. Ⓐ Ⓑ Ⓒ Ⓓ	14. Ⓐ Ⓑ Ⓒ Ⓓ	25. Ⓐ Ⓑ Ⓒ Ⓓ	36. Ⓐ Ⓑ Ⓒ Ⓓ
4. Ⓐ Ⓑ Ⓒ Ⓓ	15. Ⓐ Ⓑ Ⓒ Ⓓ	26. Ⓐ Ⓑ Ⓒ Ⓓ	37. Ⓐ Ⓑ Ⓒ Ⓓ
5. Ⓐ Ⓑ Ⓒ Ⓓ	16. Ⓐ Ⓑ Ⓒ Ⓓ	27. Ⓐ Ⓑ Ⓒ Ⓓ	38. Ⓐ Ⓑ Ⓒ Ⓓ
6. Ⓐ Ⓑ Ⓒ Ⓓ	17. Ⓐ Ⓑ Ⓒ Ⓓ	28. Ⓐ Ⓑ Ⓒ Ⓓ	39. Ⓐ Ⓑ Ⓒ Ⓓ
7. Ⓐ Ⓑ Ⓒ Ⓓ	18. Ⓐ Ⓑ Ⓒ Ⓓ	29. Ⓐ Ⓑ Ⓒ Ⓓ	40. Ⓐ Ⓑ Ⓒ Ⓓ
8. Ⓐ Ⓑ Ⓒ Ⓓ	19. Ⓐ Ⓑ Ⓒ Ⓓ	30. Ⓐ Ⓑ Ⓒ Ⓓ	41. Ⓐ Ⓑ Ⓒ Ⓓ
9. Ⓐ Ⓑ Ⓒ Ⓓ	20. Ⓐ Ⓑ Ⓒ Ⓓ	31. Ⓐ Ⓑ Ⓒ Ⓓ	42. Ⓐ Ⓑ Ⓒ Ⓓ
10. Ⓐ Ⓑ Ⓒ Ⓓ	21. Ⓐ Ⓑ Ⓒ Ⓓ	32. Ⓐ Ⓑ Ⓒ Ⓓ	43. Ⓐ Ⓑ Ⓒ Ⓓ
11. Ⓐ Ⓑ Ⓒ Ⓓ	22. Ⓐ Ⓑ Ⓒ Ⓓ	33. Ⓐ Ⓑ Ⓒ Ⓓ	44. Ⓐ Ⓑ Ⓒ Ⓓ

☐ # correct in Section 2

☐ # incorrect in Section 2

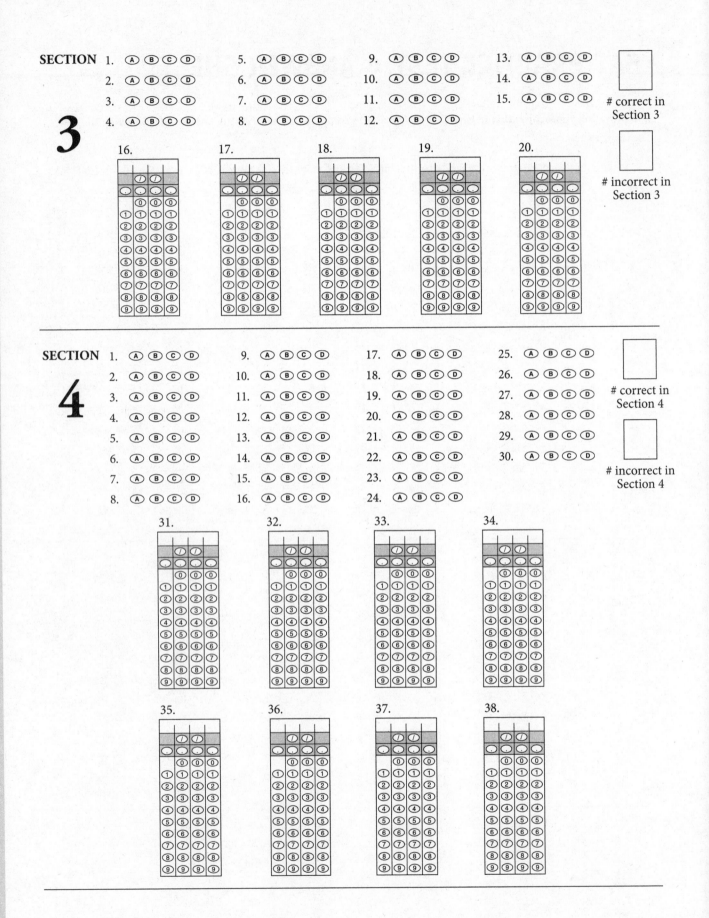

READING TEST

65 Minutes—52 Questions

This section corresponds to Section 1 of your answer sheet.

Directions: Read each passage or pair of passages, then answer the questions that follow. Choose your answers based on what the passage(s) and any accompanying graphics state or imply.

Questions 1-10 are based on the following passage.

The following passage is adapted from Willa Cather's 1918 novel *My Ántonia*. In this excerpt, the boy narrator, Jim Burden, has traveled from Virginia to his grandparents' Nebraska farm to spend the rest of his childhood there. On his first Nebraska morning, he goes outdoors to observe the landscape.

As I looked about me I felt that the grass was the country, as the water is the sea. The red of the grass made all the great prairie the colour of winestains,
Line or of certain seaweeds when they are first washed
(5) up. And there was so much motion in it; the whole country seemed, somehow, to be running.

I had almost forgotten that I had a grandmother, when she came out, her sunbonnet on her head, a grain-sack in her hand, and asked me if I did not
(10) want to go to the garden with her to dig potatoes for dinner. . . .

I can remember exactly how the country looked to me as I walked beside my grandmother along the faint wagon-tracks on that early September morning.
(15) Perhaps the glide of long railway travel was still with me, for more than anything else I felt motion in the landscape; in the fresh, easy-blowing morning wind, and in the earth itself, as if the shaggy grass were a sort of loose hide, and underneath it herds of wild
(20) buffalo were galloping, galloping. . . .

Alone, I should never have found the garden— except, perhaps, for the big yellow pumpkins that lay about unprotected by their withering vines— and I felt very little interest in it when I got there.
(25) I wanted to walk straight on through the red grass and over the edge of the world, which could not be very far away. The light air about me told me that

the world ended here: only the ground and sun and sky were left, and if one went a little farther there
(30) would be only sun and sky, and one would float off into them, like the tawny hawks which sailed over our heads making slow shadows on the grass. While grandmother took the pitchfork we found standing in one of the rows and dug potatoes, while I picked
(35) them up out of the soft brown earth and put them into the bag, I kept looking up at the hawks that were doing what I might so easily do.

When grandmother was ready to go, I said I would like to stay up there in the garden awhile.
(40) She peered down at me from under her sunbonnet. "Aren't you afraid of snakes?"

"A little," I admitted, "but I'd like to stay, anyhow." . . .

Grandmother swung the bag of potatoes over
(45) her shoulder and went down the path, leaning forward a little. The road followed the windings of the draw; when she came to the first bend, she waved at me and disappeared. I was left alone with this new feeling of lightness and content.
(50) I sat down in the middle of the garden, where snakes could scarcely approach unseen, and leaned my back against a warm yellow pumpkin. There were some ground-cherry bushes growing along the furrows, full of fruit. I turned back the papery triangular
(55) sheaths that protected the berries and ate a few. All about me giant grasshoppers, twice as big as any I had ever seen, were doing acrobatic feats among the dried vines. The gophers scurried up and down the ploughed ground. There in the sheltered draw-
(60) bottom the wind did not blow very hard, but I could hear it singing its humming tune up on the level, and I could see the tall grasses wave. The earth was warm under me, and warm as I crumbled it through my

GO ON TO THE NEXT PAGE ▷

fingers. Queer little red bugs came out and moved
(65) in slow squadrons around me. Their backs were
polished vermilion, with black spots. I kept as still as
I could. Nothing happened. I did not expect anything to happen. I was something that lay under the
sun and felt it, like the pumpkins, and I did not want
(70) to be anything more. I was entirely happy. Perhaps
we feel like that when we die and become a part of
something entire, whether it is sun and air, or good-
ness and knowledge. At any rate, that is happiness;
to be dissolved into something complete and great.
(75) When it comes to one, it comes as naturally as sleep.

1. According to the passage, why is Jim's grandmother initially concerned about leaving him in
   the garden?

   A) Jim doesn't know the way back home.

   B) She is worried he will encounter snakes.

   C) A bad storm is brewing on the horizon.

   D) She hoped Jim would help her cook dinner.

2. As used in line 51, "scarcely" most nearly means

   A) not easily.

   B) rapidly.

   C) with fear.

   D) narrowly.

3. Based on information in the passage, it can reasonably be inferred that

   A) the prairie reminds Jim of the landscape
      back in his native Virginia.

   B) the snakes and coyotes make the prairie a
      dangerous place.

   C) growing crops on the prairie is extremely
      difficult for farmers.

   D) it is very easy to get lost because there are
      few landmarks.

4. Which choice provides the best evidence for the
   answer to the previous question?

   A) Lines 1-2 ("As I looked . . . sea")

   B) Lines 21-24 ("Alone . . . there")

   C) Lines 46-48 ("The road . . . disappeared")

   D) Lines 50-52 ("I sat . . . pumpkin")

5. The central claim of the passage is that

   A) confronting fears allows a person to move
      forward in life.

   B) nature, though beautiful, can present many
      hidden dangers.

   C) family relationships can help a person
      adjust to new places.

   D) a natural setting can have a transforming
      effect on a person.

6. Based on information in the passage, it can reasonably be inferred that Jim's personality could best be
   described as

   A) aggressive.

   B) introspective.

   C) regretful.

   D) ambivalent.

7. Which choice provides the best evidence for the
   answer to the previous question?

   A) Lines 7-11 ("I had . . . for dinner")

   B) Lines 12-14 ("I can . . . morning")

   C) Lines 38-52 ("When grandmother . . .
      pumpkin")

   D) Lines 70-73 ("Perhaps we . . . knowledge")

GO ON TO THE NEXT PAGE

8. As used in line 74, "dissolved" most nearly means

    A) assimilated.

    B) destroyed.

    C) disintegrated.

    D) terminated.

9. The repetition of "galloping" in line 20 ("herds of . . . galloping, galloping") mainly serves to emphasize how

    A) fast the wind moved against the grass.

    B) much the Nebraska landscape seems like a dream.

    C) the recurrent motion of the landscape.

    D) wild buffalo and wild horses on the prairie are similar.

10. Through the perspective of a first-person narrator, the author is able to

    A) focus attention on the main character rather than on his grandmother.

    B) limit what we learn about the main character.

    C) describe in detail the thoughts and experiences of the main character.

    D) distance herself from her main character.

Questions 11-20 are based on the following passage.

The following passage is adapted from an open letter to the United Nations, written by Danish physicist and Nobel Prize winner Niels Bohr. Bohr completed important work on atomic structure long before World War II. After fleeing Denmark to escape the Nazis, he eventually went to work with the British as an adviser to U.S. scientists developing the first atomic bomb. The atomic bomb was then used to bring an end to World War II.

        I address myself to the organization, founded
    for the purpose to further co-operation between
    nations. . . .
Line   The fear of being left behind was a strong
(5) incentive in various countries to explore, in secrecy,
the possibilities of using such energy sources for
military purposes. The joint American-British
project remained unknown to me until, after my
escape from occupied Denmark in the autumn of
(10) 1943, I came to England at the invitation of the
British government. At that time I was taken into
confidence about the great enterprise which had
already then reached an advanced stage.

        Everyone associated with the atomic energy
(15) project was, of course, conscious of the serious
problems which would confront humanity once the
enterprise was accomplished. . . .

        It certainly surpasses the imagination of anyone
to survey the consequences of the project in years
(20) to come, where in the long run the enormous
energy sources which will be available may be
expected to revolutionize industry and transport.
The fact of immediate preponderance is, however,
that a weapon of an unparalleled power is being
(25) created which will completely change all future
conditions of warfare.

        This situation raises a number of problems
which call for most urgent attention. Unless,
indeed, some agreement about the control of the
(30) use of the new active materials can be obtained
in due time, any temporary advantage, however
great, may be outweighed by a perpetual menace to
human security.

        When the war ended and the great menaces
(35) of oppression to so many peoples had disappeared, an immense relief was felt all over the
world. Nevertheless, the political situation was
fraught with ominous forebodings. Divergences in
outlook between the victorious nations inevitably
(40) aggravated controversial matters arising in connection with peace settlements. Contrary to the
hopes for future fruitful co-operation, expressed
from all sides and embodied in the Charter of the
United Nations, the lack of mutual confidence soon
(45) became evident.

        The creation of new barriers, restricting the free
flow of information between countries, further
increased distrust and anxiety. . . .

        The very fact that knowledge is in itself the
(50) basis for civilization points directly to openness as
the way to overcome the present crisis. Whatever

GO ON TO THE NEXT PAGE

judicial and administrative international authorities may eventually have to be created in order to
stabilize world affairs, it must be realized that full
(55) mutual openness, only, can effectively promote
confidence and guarantee common security.

Any widening of the borders of our knowledge
imposes an increased responsibility on individuals
and nations through the possibilities it gives for
(60) shaping the conditions of human life. The forceful
admonition in this respect which we have received
in our time cannot be left unheeded and should
hardly fail in resulting in common understanding
of the seriousness of the challenge with which our
(65) whole civilization is faced. It is just on this background that quite unique opportunities exist to-day
for furthering co-operation between nations on the
progress of human culture in all its aspects.

11. The main purpose of this letter is to

   A) discuss the implications of the military use
      of atomic energy.

   B) explore the industrial potential of atomic
      energy development.

   C) compare the shared atomic energy goals of
      members of the United Nations.

   D) clarify the role of the United Nations in
      overseeing atomic energy use.

12. Which choice provides the best evidence for the
    answer to the previous question?

   A) Lines 7-11 ("The joint . . . government")

   B) Lines 11-13 ("At that time . . . stage")

   C) Lines 14-17 ("Everyone . . . accomplished")

   D) Lines 18-22 ("It certainly . . . transport")

13. As used in line 23, "preponderance" most nearly
    means

   A) eminence.

   B) importance.

   C) majority.

   D) prestige.

14. The passage most clearly suggests that Bohr's work
    before World War II

   A) began as a nonmilitary pursuit.

   B) led to the outbreak of the war.

   C) resulted from industrialization.

   D) undermined efforts to reach peace.

15. Which choice provides the best evidence for the
    answer to the previous question?

   A) Lines 4-7 ("The fear . . . purposes")

   B) Lines 7-11 ("The joint . . . government")

   C) Lines 23-26 ("The fact of . . . warfare")

   D) Lines 27-28 ("This situation . . . attention")

16. As used in line 38, "divergences" most nearly
    means

   A) differences.

   B) misinterpretations.

   C) perspectives.

   D) rebellions.

17. In lines 41-42, the author mentions "contrary to
    the hopes for fruitful co-operation" primarily to
    show that what happened after World War II?

   A) Countries decided to form the United
      Nations.

   B) Knowledge became the driving force behind
      civilization.

   C) Trust among nations declined because of
      political disagreements.

   D) New judicial and administrative authorities
      were established.

GO ON TO THE NEXT PAGE ⇨

18. The reference to knowledge in lines 49-51 ("The very fact . . . present crisis") mainly serves to

    A) explain the important uses of atomic energy.

    B) highlight the role of learning in societal progress.

    C) posit the benefits of regulating scientific investigation.

    D) justify the need for transparency among nations.

19. Based on information in the passage, it can reasonably be inferred that the author would most likely support international

    A) laws restricting the testing of nuclear bombs.

    B) monitoring of countries' nuclear technologies.

    C) regulation of nuclear power plants and materials.

    D) sanctions on nations with nuclear weapons.

20. The sentence in lines 60-65 ("The forceful admonition . . . is faced") mainly serves to

    A) emphasize the significance of the author's purpose.

    B) explain the author's credentials regarding the subject.

    C) offer evidence for a contrary point of view.

    D) summarize the author's arguments and evidence.

Questions 21-31 are based on the following passage and supplementary material.

The following passage is adapted from an article about the evolution of computers.

If you had to count every person who lived in the United States, and there were neither calculators nor computers of any kind to help you, how
Line would you do it?
(5)   That's the puzzle that nineteen-year-old engineer Herman Hollerith was faced with in the 1880s when he was employed by the U.S. Census Bureau. His solution was to invent a machine that stored information by putting patterns of holes in stiff
(10) pasteboard—an idea that Hollerith struck upon by observing the Jacquard loom, an automatic weaving machine that was controlled by specially coded punch cards. The machine, called the Hollerith tabulating machine and sorting box, was used to
(15) record the 1890 population census and shortened what had been a seven-year job to just three months.

Because Hollerith's machine used mechanical counters operated by electromagnets and circuits,
(20) it is considered the very first computer. Go anywhere today—a grocery store, an office, a school—and you see one of its many descendants, such as the calculator, personal computer, iPad, and smartphone. Though Hollerith retired to work
(25) at a cattle farm in Maryland, in 1924 the company he founded was renamed International Business Machines (IBM), which is still one of the largest technology corporations in the world.

Data Storage

As a data storage medium, Hollerith's invention
(30) was revolutionary, but one problem with it was the physical size and quantities of cards, each punch card holding only 960 bits of information. Many types of companies needed to hold more data in a smaller space. A big leap was made in the 1950s
(35) with the invention of magnetic tape, which consisted of long strips of plastic with a magnetized coating that could store as much data as 10,000 punch cards. A single reel was about the size of a dinner plate, and could be read from and written

GO ON TO THE NEXT PAGE ▷

(40) to rapidly. In 1963, Philips introduced magnetized tape in a small cassette, which became a popular choice for businesses to store data using computers.

Nevertheless, tapes were still cumbersome, and they would degrade over time. Then came the hard
(45) drive. IBM made one of the first, in 1956, called 305 RAMAC. It was bigger than a refrigerator and contained fifty discs, each two feet in diameter. The 305 RAMAC could store 4.4 megabytes of data. By comparison, at about the size of a wallet, three
(50) floppy discs, a popular medium from the 1980s and 1990s, held the same amount of information.

Hard drives have been constantly improving ever since, getting smaller, faster, and more energy-efficient. With the invention of the flash drive
(55) and the micro-SD card, our information storage platforms are almost too small to handle with our bare hands.

Over the years, the price of data storage space has decreased exponentially. In 1984, a 5-megabyte
(60) drive cost $1,400, or $280 per megabyte. Within five years, this was cut in half, and since then, the popularity of personal computers for home and business has driven the price even lower. In 2010, the cost per megabyte was less than ten cents.

Microprocessors

(65)   The microprocessor, or Central Processing Unit (CPU), is the brain inside every computer, tablet, and smartphone. It's a silicon semiconductor chip that contains the basic logic and arithmetic functions that the device needs in order to run.
(70) The CPU receives and decodes instructions from keyboards, touch screens, and Wi-Fi adapters and sends signals out in a timed sequence to devices such as monitors, printers, and networks.

The first microprocessor was devised in 1971
(75) and called the Intel 4004. Measuring just 1/8" by 1/16", it was as powerful as the electronic computer of 25 years prior, which weighed 30 tons and used 18,000 vacuum tubes. It was said about that computer that the lights of Philadelphia dimmed when
(80) it was turned on.

And yet, as fast as the Intel 4004 was, today's CPUs are thousands of times faster. One way that chips get faster is by the addition of more, and

smaller, transistors. Though the Intel 4004 proces-
(85) sor held 2,300 transistors, a typical Intel processor today, with a 32-nanometer processing die, holds 560,000,000 transistors. (One nanometer equals one-billionth of a meter.)

Manufacturers of microprocessors also speed up
(90) chips by making circuits smaller; when the circuits are more compact, the microprocessors become faster because electrons have less distance to travel. As chips get smaller, more of them can be etched onto the same diameter silicon wafer by improved fabrication
(95) equipment. Consequently, computers that used to require warehouses now fit in the palm of our hands.

Microchip Transistor Sizes, 2000-2020

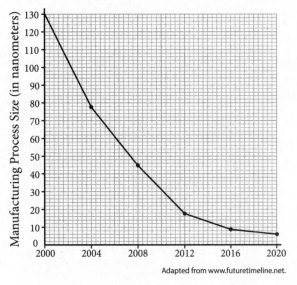

Adapted from www.futuretimeline.net.

21. Which choice best describes the narrator's view of technology?

A) A computer industry spokesperson explaining why innovation is good for the economy.

B) A consumer advocate explaining why the price of computers continues to fall.

C) A columnist outlining the evolution of computer speed and storage over time.

D) An efficiency expert discussing how the Census Bureau can improve its performance.

GO ON TO THE NEXT PAGE

22. An unstated assumption made by the author about Hollerith's invention is that

    A) the invention of the Jacquard loom was inspired by the success of Hollerith's machine.

    B) subsequent technological innovations were based on Hollerith's original design.

    C) the success of the 1890 census propelled IBM to the forefront of the computer industry.

    D) Hollerith's mechanical counters continued to be used years after their original debut.

23. Which choice provides the best evidence for the answer to the previous question?

    A) Lines 13-17 ("The machine . . . three months")

    B) Lines 18-20 ("Because Hollerith's . . . computer")

    C) Lines 20-24 ("Go anywhere . . . smart-phone")

    D) Lines 24-28 ("Though Hollerith . . . world")

24. As used in line 43, "cumbersome" most nearly means

    A) awkward.

    B) bulky.

    C) heavy.

    D) ponderous.

25. The main purpose of the opening sentence of the passage is to help readers

    A) understand the enormity of Hollerith's initial task.

    B) relive the bygone era in which Hollerith lived.

    C) appreciate the job of the U.S. Census Bureau.

    D) acknowledge how important computers are.

26. The passage most strongly suggests that

    A) the 1980s saw the most significant innovations in the history of personal computing.

    B) the price of data storage space has risen due to consumer demand for personal computers.

    C) continued innovation in data storage devices has resulted in increased value for consumers.

    D) computer industry profits have fallen as a result of decreased costs related to data storage.

27. Which choice provides the best evidence for the answer to the previous question?

    A) Lines 54-57 ("With the . . . hands")

    B) Lines 59-60 ("In 1984 . . . megabyte")

    C) Lines 60-63 ("Within five . . . lower")

    D) Lines 63-64 ("In 2010 . . . ten cents")

28. Data in the graph provide most direct support for which idea in the passage?

    A) The greatest decrease in microchip transistor sizes occurred between 2000 and 2008.

    B) The decline in microchip transistor sizes will most likely level out after the year 2020.

    C) Microchip transistor sizes are expected to increase to approximately 10 nanometers by the year 2020.

    D) The difference in microchip transistor sizes from 2004 and 2012 is 40 nanometers.

29. As used in line 44, "degrade" most nearly means

    A) corrupt.

    B) decay.

    C) humiliate.

    D) lower.

 GO ON TO THE NEXT PAGE

30. The description of how a computer in the 1940s dimmed the lights of Philadelphia (lines 78-80) mainly serves to demonstrate the relationship between

    A) the size of the Intel 4004 and of its predecessor.

    B) the speed of contemporary CPUs and of the Intel 4004.

    C) the manufacturing process in the 1970s and that of today.

    D) the number of transistors in the Intel 4004 and in CPUs today.

31. It can most reasonably be inferred from the passage and graphic that

    A) Herman Hollerith's ideas influenced contemporary computers and other devices.

    B) The price of data storage space has fallen in the face of continual consumer demand.

    C) Increased consumer demand corresponds to a decrease in transistor sizes in the 2000s.

    D) Smaller transistors have exponentially increased the processing speed of today's CPUs.

Questions 32-42 are based on the following passages.

The following passages discuss solar farming.

Passage 1

The largest solar farm in the world, known as Topaz, opened in late 2014. The plant, which cost $2.5 billion dollars to build, generates a whopping
Line 550 megawatts of power. To put this number into
(5) perspective, this amount of power will be used to supply 160,000 homes. This switch from fossil fuels to solar power will save the environment exposure to approximately 377,000 tons of carbon dioxide emissions per year, which is the equivalent of
(10) retiring 73,000 cars.

The benefits of constructing such a large-scale solar farm are not only environmental. There

are also significant economic benefits. Over 400 construction jobs were added to the area during
(15) the construction phase. $192 million in income was pumped into the local economy as a result. Economic benefits haven't stopped since the plant opened. Local energy suppliers are now able to enjoy $52 million in economic output.

(20) Located in San Luis Obispo County in California, the area where Topaz was built is part of California's Carrizo Plain. The plain is an area of native grassland northwest of Los Angeles. The land on which the plant sits was used as farmland
(25) in the past. Because of this, no new land disturbance was required in order to complete this large project. The land was no longer suitable for farming due to irrigation practices that stripped the soil of its nutrients. The 4,700 private acres provided
(30) the perfect setting for a solar plant, meeting the developer's standards for low-impact development, which was a priority considering the site's proximity to the Carrizo Plain National Monument, a protected area home to native species and plants.

(35) The plant's setup includes 460 panels mounted on steel support posts. The sunlight taken in by these panels is fed to power conversion stations. Each panel has its own conversion station. Made up of two inverters and a transformer each, the
(40) conversion stations are needed to make the power usable. The power is then sent to a substation that transforms it from 35.5 kilovolts to the standard 230 kilovolts. The Pacific Gas and Electric Company (PG&E) built a new switching station next to
(45) the solar farm. It is here that the power is looped into the grid that supplies neighboring areas.

Topaz will only remain the world's largest solar farm for a short period of time. The plant's owner, First Solar, is currently developing an even larger
(50) plant, also in California.

Passage 2

With more and more large-scale solar farms being developed in the sunny southwestern United States, researchers and conservationists alike are beginning to notice surprising environmental
(55) effects. While solar energy is known for its positive environmental impacts, officials at the National Fish and Wildlife Forensics Laboratory have come to

GO ON TO THE NEXT PAGE

recognize one of its significant downsides: Some species of birds that live in close proximity to large solar (60) plants are dying off, including endangered birds.

A recent federal investigation recovered 233 birds that had been killed as a direct result of solar plants. Researchers believe that some of the affected birds have mistaken the large, reflective (65) areas of the solar panels for bodies of water. This is a phenomenon referred to by scientists as "lake effect." The birds are drawn to what they assume to be water. They home in on the area and slam into the panels with great force. It is thought that the (70) insects that birds eat fall victim to "lake effect" as well, leading the birds into the panels.

Researchers estimate that between 1,000 and 28,000 birds are killed as a result of harvesting solar energy. The number of birds affected by wind (75) farming is much greater, ranging from 140,000 to 328,000. Coal-fired electricity has the largest negative effect on birds, killing nearly 8 million a year. These numbers make solar farming seem like the best option. However, conservationists (80) are quick to point out that the areas where solar is expected to boom between 2015 and 2020 are home to some of the rarest birds in the United States. This could put specific bird species at risk of extinction.

(85) There exists a state mandate in California that 20 percent of all electricity sold must be renewable by the year 2017. This has been one driving force behind the rapid development of huge solar farms. The industry, which is expecting to boom as a (90) result of this shift to renewable energy, is facing newly filed lawsuits by conservationist groups, citing the negative impact on wildlife. These lawsuits could prolong the approval process for the planned solar developments across the Southwest.

32. The central claim of Passage 1 is that solar farms

    A) are an accepted form of generating energy because of their benefits.

    B) were first thought impractical ways to generate energy.

    C) help to improve the environment.

    D) need large amounts of land to be developed.

33. In Passage 2, which choice best describes the narrator's view of solar farms?

    A) Using solar farms is the most viable way to create energy.

    B) More birds are endangered by wind farms than solar farming.

    C) Solar farms may not be as friendly to the environment as many people believe.

    D) Scientists need to find ways to discourage "lake effect" caused by solar farms.

34. It can most reasonably be inferred from Passage 1 that

    A) solar farms will most likely only be built in the state of California.

    B) the developer of Topaz is respectful of the environment.

    C) not many studies have been done on the impact of solar farms on the environment.

    D) the consumption of energy continues to grow greater each year.

35. Which choice provides the best evidence for the answer to the previous question?

    A) Lines 6-10 ("This switch . . . cars")

    B) Lines 13-15 ("Over 400 . . . phase")

    C) Lines 29-34 ("The 4,700 . . . and plants")

    D) Lines 47-48 ("Topaz will . . . of time")

GO ON TO THE NEXT PAGE

36. Passage 2 most strongly suggests that

    A) wind farms do less harm to the environment than solar farms.

    B) there are ways to create energy that do not harm wildlife.

    C) the life of solar farms will be short-lived because of their cost.

    D) birds can be easily confused by human-made structures.

37. Which choice provides the best evidence for the answer to the previous question?

    A) Lines 63-65 ("Researchers . . . of water")

    B) Lines 74-76 ("The number . . . 328,000")

    C) Lines 85-87 ("There exists . . . 2017")

    D) Lines 92-94 ("These lawsuits . . . Southwest")

38. Which of the following best describes the passages' central ideas?

    A) Passage 1 aims to convince readers that solar farming will be the primary form of developing energy in the future, while Passage 2 aims to show the limited benefits of solar farms.

    B) The purpose of Passage 1 is to show the many benefits of solar farming, while Passage 2 concentrates on the negative side effects of solar farming.

    C) Passage 1 discusses current research into the benefits of solar farms, while Passage 2 relates why solar farms are not practical in all locations.

    D) The purpose of Passage 1 is to show that producing energy is vital to the economy, while Passage 2 explains the ways in which solar farms can be developed.

39. As used in line 16 of Passage 1, "pumped" most nearly means

    A) drained.

    B) encouraged.

    C) extracted.

    D) funneled.

40. As used in line 58 of Passage 2, "recognize" most nearly means

    A) appreciate.

    B) credit.

    C) distinguish.

    D) realize.

41. In Passage 2, the word "surprising" (line 54) most directly suggests that

    A) solar farms require a lengthy development period.

    B) most people would be shocked by the size of solar farms.

    C) solar energy panels look strange to most people.

    D) most people think that solar energy is very beneficial.

42. On which of the following points would the authors of both passages most likely agree?

    A) Solar farms have effects that disturb some conservationists.

    B) Solar farms are an accepted way to generate electricity.

    C) All of the ways to create energy have negative side effects.

    D) Finding sites for solar farms is difficult to accomplish.

GO ON TO THE NEXT PAGE

Questions 43-52 are based on the following passage and supplementary material.

The following passage is adapted from an article about carbon dioxide in the atmosphere.

The concentration of carbon dioxide in our atmosphere has been steadily increasing since about 1750. Carbon dioxide lets in sun energy and
Line then traps it as heat energy, so the more carbon
(5) dioxide in the atmosphere, the higher the average global temperature. Scientists are concerned that even slight increases in global temperatures will significantly affect plant and animal life on Earth.

In the past, photosynthesis has been able to keep
(10) the level of carbon dioxide in the air at a lower level. Plants and algae convert water and carbon dioxide into oxygen and glucose, using the sun's energy. Carbon from carbon dioxide becomes trapped or "fixed" as the plant uses glucose to build
(15) cellulose and starches, which make up most of the plant's structure.

Human industry is the main cause of increased carbon dioxide in the atmosphere. Cutting down forests to make room for expanding cities or farm-
(20) land reduces the amount of carbon dioxide being removed. The wood is also often burned, releasing more carbon dioxide into the air. Burning fossil fuels for energy releases even more carbon dioxide that had previously been locked up in the coal, oil,
(25) or gas underground.

We can reduce the amount of carbon dioxide by reducing how much we release, either by burning fewer fossil fuels or by removing carbon dioxide as the fuel is being burned. We can burn fewer
(30) fossil fuels by switching to other forms of power that don't release carbon dioxide, such as solar or wind power, but these methods are more expensive. We can "scrub" the carbon dioxide from the air at the power plant where the fuel is burned, but
(35) that is also expensive. It also does not work for the carbon dioxide produced by cars, trucks, and airplanes. Reducing our output of carbon diox-

ide, though a commendable idea, may not reduce the levels enough to have a meaningful impact.
(40) We might need to go one step farther and try to remove carbon dioxide from the air.

Many research and development companies are now developing systems that will act like artificial "trees" and remove carbon dioxide from the atmos-
(45) phere. Several built their approach on a method used in submarines and space vehicles. They combine the carbon dioxide with a strong base called sodium hydroxide to produce sodium bicarbonate, also known as baking soda. Bubbling air through
(50) a solution of sodium hydroxide works well enough for the small amount of air in a space vehicle or submarine, but this would be a slow way to process a large amount of air.

One researcher found a way to make a plastic
(55) with hydroxide components that would remove carbon dioxide from air as it passes over the surface of the plastic. Filters made out of long strands of this plastic can then remove carbon dioxide as wind pushes the air through the strands. The filters,
(60) therefore, act much like leaves in a tree.

This plastic is inexpensive, but making it into filters, building towers that contain many "leaves" of the filters, and processing the plastic to remove the carbon dioxide so the plastic can be reused
(65) is currently very expensive. To pay for the cost, gasoline would end up increasing in price. If manufacturers could get the cost of this method down to $100 per metric ton of carbon dioxide removed, for example, the price of gas would still
(70) have to increase by about 88 cents to cover the cost. Researchers are optimistic that they could actually get the cost down to $25 per metric ton. If they achieve this goal, we someday may see artificial trees in our cities, assisting the real trees in clean-
(75) ing the air.

GO ON TO THE NEXT PAGE ▷

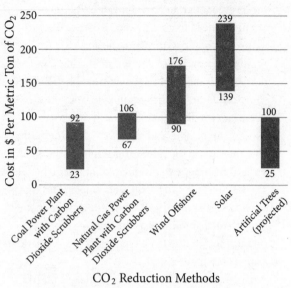

CO₂ Reduction Costs by Method

CO₂ Reduction Methods

Adapted from the Global CSS Institute.

43. The central claim of the passage is that

   A) methods to help remove carbon dioxide from the air are being developed.

   B) problems are caused by cutting down forests to make cities larger.

   C) increased levels of carbon dioxide in the atmosphere are a danger to humans.

   D) increased global temperatures will affect humans, plants, and animals.

44. Which choice provides the best evidence for the answer to the previous question?

   A) Lines 1-3 ("The concentration . . . 1750")

   B) Lines 11-13 ("Plants and . . . energy")

   C) Lines 17-18 ("Human industry . . . atmosphere")

   D) Lines 42-45 ("Many research . . . atmosphere")

45. In paragraph 2, the author helps structure the passage's claim by providing

   A) a detailed description of how real trees are different from artificial trees.

   B) examples of current methods of removing carbon dioxide from the air.

   C) an explanation of how carbon dioxide is naturally removed from the air.

   D) details about how the level of carbon dioxide in the air has been steadily increasing.

46. According to the passage, how do the filters described in paragraph 6 act like leaves in a tree?

   A) They contain long strands like veins in a leaf.

   B) They remove carbon dioxide from the air.

   C) They release oxygen into the atmosphere.

   D) They branch out from the plastic-like leaves.

47. Which of the following examples of evidence would most strengthen the author's line of reasoning?

   A) Details about the type of consequences plant and animal life could face if global temperatures increase in paragraph 1

   B) How many acres of forest are cut down each year to make room for bigger cities and more farmland in paragraph 3

   C) Descriptions of how solar and wind energy are harvested and converted to electricity in paragraph 4

   D) An analysis of how much people would be willing to pay for gas to offset the cost of plastic used to remove carbon dioxide from the air in paragraph 7

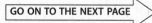

48. As used in line 11, "convert" most nearly means

    A) control.
    B) transform.
    C) substitute.
    D) adjust.

49. The passage most strongly suggests that

    A) solar and wind energy would become less expensive if more people used these forms of energy.
    B) technology that removes carbon dioxide from the air would not be necessary if more people rode bikes.
    C) global temperatures could reach levels dangerous to plant and animal life in the next 50 years.
    D) people will resist technology that removes carbon dioxide from the air if it is too expensive.

50. Which choice provides the best evidence for the answer to the previous question?

    A) Lines 3-6 ("Carbon dioxide . . . temperature")
    B) Lines 26-29 ("We can . . . burned")
    C) Lines 61-65 ("This plastic . . . very expensive")
    D) Lines 71-75 ("Researchers . . . the air")

51. As used in line 38, "commendable" most nearly means

    A) convincing.
    B) hopeful.
    C) admirable.
    D) effective.

52. Data in the graph provide most direct support for which idea in the passage?

    A) Solar and wind energy are the most expensive methods of reducing carbon dioxide emissions.
    B) Artificial trees remove more carbon dioxide from the air than scrubbers at power plants.
    C) Natural gas power plants with scrubbers provide the least expensive method of reducing carbon dioxide emissions.
    D) Coal power plants with scrubbers cost more to operate than natural gas power plants with scrubbers.

IF YOU FINISH BEFORE TIME IS CALLED, YOU MAY CHECK YOUR WORK ON THIS SECTION ONLY. DO NOT TURN TO ANY OTHER SECTION IN THE TEST. **STOP**

WRITING AND LANGUAGE TEST

35 Minutes—44 Questions

This section corresponds to Section 2 of your answer sheet.

Directions: Each passage in this section is followed by several questions. Some questions will reference an underlined portion in the passage; others will ask you to consider a part of a passage or the passage as a whole. For each question, choose the answer that reflects the best use of grammar, punctuation, and style. If a passage or question is accompanied by a graphic, take the graphic into account in choosing your response(s). Some questions will have "NO CHANGE" as a possible response. Choose that answer if you think the best choice is to leave the sentence as written.

Questions 1-11 are based on the following passage.

Vitamin C—Essential Nutrient or Wonder Drug?

Vitamin C has been considered a wonder drug by many people, including a two-time Nobel Prize winner. Unfortunately, although it is **1** so very essential for many growth and repair activities in the body, vitamin C does not live up to most other claims.

Linus Pauling was one of the earliest, and most famous, of the vitamin C supporters. He was a brilliant chemist and **2** deferential humanitarian who won both the Nobel Prize in Chemistry and the Nobel Peace Prize for his work. His later work on vitamin C still serves for many as proof that vitamin C is a wonder drug; **3** as a result, his work never supported his theories.

1. A) NO CHANGE
   B) very essential
   C) important and essential
   D) essential

2. A) NO CHANGE
   B) dedicated
   C) good
   D) loyal

3. A) NO CHANGE
   B) because
   C) however,
   D) so

GO ON TO THE NEXT PAGE →

[4] [1] In 1932, vitamin C was identified as the nutrient that prevents scurvy. [2] The symptoms of scurvy are caused mainly by the body's inability to repair and replace damaged cells. [3] The word "scurvy" has been in use since the 1500s and is believed to have Dutch and French origins. [4] These symptoms appear after months without sufficient vitamin C, usually because of a poor diet. [5] Getting enough vitamin C is therefore essential to good health. [6] Pauling and others [5] implied that increasing vitamin C intake beyond the amount found in a balanced diet could do more than just maintain good health.

For example, Pauling was certain that high doses of vitamin C could cure cancer. His research with cancer patients did not reveal any conclusive support [6] for his theory, very high doses of vitamin C slowed the growth of certain tumors but did not shrink them. The high levels of vitamin C were also dangerous and actually interfered with other cancer treatments.

Pauling and others were also convinced that high doses of vitamin C could prevent and cure colds. Research has shown that people with a high vitamin C intake recover from colds slightly faster than people with a normal intake. [7] However, for the average person, who gets a few a year, this means reducing sick days a little bit. Also, increasing levels of vitamin C in the body once a person has already come down with a cold unfortunately makes no difference.

4. Which choice provides the least relevant detail?

A) Sentence 1
B) Sentence 2
C) Sentence 3
D) Sentence 5

5. A) NO CHANGE
B) reasoned
C) judged
D) philosophized

6. A) NO CHANGE
B) for this theory, so very high doses
C) for his theory very high doses
D) for his theory; very high doses

7. Which choice most effectively supports the claim that vitamin C has only a slight effect on people's ability to recover from colds?

A) However, for most people, who get colds around 3 times a year, the reduced time frame is not that significant.
B) However, for an average person, who gets colds every year, this amounts to only about two or three days a year.
C) However, for most people, who get a lot of colds each year, this doesn't add up to be much time.
D) However, for the average person, who gets about 3 colds a year, this means reducing sick days from about 6 to about 4.

GO ON TO THE NEXT PAGE ▷

The recommended daily intake of vitamin C for adult males is 90 mg, and for women it is 75 mg. Amounts up to twice that much can be absorbed well by the digestive system, but anything beyond those amounts cannot. People who take high doses are able to absorb only about 50 percent of the vitamin. **8** The unabsorbed vitamin will have caused digestive problems, such as nausea, **9** diarrhea; and abdominal cramps. The slightly shorter cold duration obtained at high doses is not worth the possible side effects.

Vitamin C is important for **10** good health. People should make sure they get the recommended amount by eating a balanced diet. However, a person who takes higher doses through supplements will see almost no additional benefit, and may, in fact, feel worse from the side effects. **11** Vitamin C may not be a "wonder" drug, but it is an essential nutrient for all of us.

8. A) NO CHANGE
   B) The unabsorbed vitamin can cause digestive problems,
   C) The unabsorbed vitamin has caused digestive problems,
   D) The unabsorbed vitamin could have caused digestive problems,

9. A) NO CHANGE
   B) diarrhea—and abdominal cramps.
   C) diarrhea, and abdominal cramps.
   D) diarrhea, and, abdominal cramps.

10. Which choice most effectively combines the sentences at the underlined portion?
    A) good health, making sure
    B) good health, but people should make sure
    C) good health, and people should make sure
    D) good health; however making sure

11. The author wants a conclusion that summarizes the main point of the passage. Which choice accomplishes that goal?
    A) NO CHANGE
    B) Vitamin C is found in fruits and vegetables, such as oranges, peppers, tomatoes, and broccoli.
    C) Vitamin C supplements have always been accompanied by false claims, so choose one carefully.
    D) Vitamin C supplements are sold in a pharmacy or health food store near you.

Questions 12-22 are based on the following passage.

The Familiar Myth

Jermaine typed "Joseph Campbell" into his Internet browser. His teacher had said that Campbell's research held the key to understanding the universal motifs of literature from around the world. He clicked on a web page dedicated to the man's life and work. The first thing Jermaine noted was that American mythologist and author Joseph Campbell wrote in his **12** seminal work, *The Hero with a Thousand Faces,* "Myth is the secret opening through which the inexhaustible energies of the cosmos pour into human cultural manifestation." Online, Jermaine learned that **13** Campbell showcases what he calls the "monomyth" in this work. "Monomyth" is a term Campbell borrowed from fellow author James Joyce,

12. A) NO CHANGE
    B) initial
    C) primary
    D) fictitious

13. A) NO CHANGE
    B) Campbell is showcasing what he calls the "monomyth"
    C) Campbell showcased what he calls the "monomyth"
    D) Campbell showcased what he called the "monomyth"

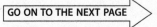
GO ON TO THE NEXT PAGE

referring to a story pattern that has served as the basis for many pieces of literature from around the world. The monomyth is often referred to as the "hero's journey."

Next, Jermaine clicked to view a graphic representation of the story structure. A plot diagram detailed the typical events of **14** a heros' journey. The start of the journey is referred to as "the call to adventure." It is followed by several challenges and encounters with people who appear to help him. The hero experiences revelations along the way, and these revelations are the catalyst for transformation. Most heroes undergo this transformation in order to reach **15** the end of there journey.

16 Jermaine sought out famous stories and myths to help him better understand the monomyth concept. Jermaine clicked a link titled "Cultural Representations." He learned that throughout time, many cultures have expressed their worldview through myths. While some of these stories are representative of humanity as a whole, the monomyth prominently featured one hero working for the good of all humans, experiencing **17** hardships, challenges, and will triumph. Two very recognizable instances of this structure from modern

14. A) NO CHANGE
    B) a hero's journey.
    C) a heroes journey.
    D) a heroes' journey.

15. A) NO CHANGE
    B) the journey they are ending.
    C) the end of their journey.
    D) the end of they're journey.

16. Which choice most effectively sets up the information that follows?

    A) NO CHANGE
    B) Jermaine wanted to write about the very first monomyth, so he chose to focus his research on that.
    C) Jermaine decided that religious figures were the best way to explore the monomyth concept.
    D) Jermaine didn't quite understand the progression of the hero's journey.

17. A) NO CHANGE
    B) hardships, challenges, and is triumphant.
    C) hardships, challenges, and triumph.
    D) hardships, challenges, and triumphs.

GO ON TO THE NEXT PAGE

times are the stories of superheroes found in comic **18** books. Such as Superman and Batman.

Jermaine then read monomyths found in other cultures. He learned about the Kayapo Indians and their myth about a boy who stole fire from a jaguar. The boy brought this fire to his people, enabling them to cook their food. To a large extent, this hero brought more to his people than just the **19** use of fire—in this story, fire symbolized civilization. Similarly, in Greek mythology, Prometheus also stole fire to bring to his people. In the mythology of the Daribi people, native to Papua New Guinea, Souw, a wanderer, brought his people livestock and crops. These stories are similar **20** not only in its structure but also in its symbolism. **21**

The monomyth, Jermaine learned, is a structure that people across all cultures are familiar and comfortable with to the point that they can picture themselves as the heroes in their own stories. It is because of this that the monomyth will continue to be a **22** timely story structure moving forward.

18. A) NO CHANGE
    B) books. And Superman and Batman.
    C) books, such as Superman and Batman.
    D) books, as well as Superman and Batman.

19. A) NO CHANGE
    B) use of fire, in this story,
    C) use of fire. In this story,
    D) use of fire: in this story,

20. A) NO CHANGE
    B) not only in their structure but also in their symbolism.
    C) not only in structure but also in its symbolism.
    D) not only in each structure but also symbolism.

21. Which detail, if added here, would best complete the paragraph?
    A) A description of a villain in a modern fairy tale
    B) The name of the website where Jermaine found this information
    C) The importance of animal figures in myths
    D) The location of the Kayapo Indians' homeland

22. A) NO CHANGE
    B) prevalent
    C) distinguished
    D) requisite

GO ON TO THE NEXT PAGE ⟶

Questions 23-33 are based on the following passage and supplementary material.

America's Love for Streetcars

The history of the electric trolley car can be traced to 1887, the era when electric motor technology was perfected. The street railway industry immediately hailed the new mode of public transport as a solution to horsecars, which were horse-drawn vehicles that ran on rails. Extremely popular, trolley lines had a large impact on cities such as San Francisco.

A streetcar, or trolley, is an electric vehicle that runs on rails; **23** they connect to form a system, typically providing public access to urban centers. Besides transportation, other benefits of the new technology abounded—for example, by World War I, streetcars had become America's fifth largest industry, employing over 100,000 workers nationwide.

24 People loved the trolleys. During the summer, special open trolleys called "breezers" allowed riders to enjoy cool air on hot days, but the main attraction was that electric cars **25** were faster, more speedy, and arrived sooner than the previous horsecars. The demand resulted in the creation of larger and more powerful trolleys, such as double-deckers.

The public's desire to travel between cities prompted a change in the late 1800s to intercity trolleys, also known as "interurbans." These electric trolleys were economical and thus were less expensive to ride than steam railroads. **26** Trolley routes within cities nonetheless continued to be common, however.

23. A) NO CHANGE
    B) these rails
    C) it
    D) which

24. Which choice most effectively sets up the information that follows?
    A) NO CHANGE
    B) Most people today have never seen a trolley in person.
    C) Trolleys remain popular outside America.
    D) The popularity of trolleys did not last in the United States.

25. A) NO CHANGE
    B) were faster and speedier
    C) were faster
    D) were faster, speedier, and arrived sooner

26. Which choice provides the most relevant detail?
    A) NO CHANGE
    B) Decades later, long-distance buses would become the transportation of choice.
    C) Although some still viewed railroads romantically, their time was coming to an end.
    D) Farmers saved money by using interurbans to get products to markets in large cities.

[1] As more automobiles became available, the competition caused trolley companies to cut back. [2] Henry Ford, however, changed the world with the 1908 introduction of the Model T, a car the average worker could afford. [3] Ultimately, this major factor led to the demise of such lines. [4] The World War II years ignited renewed interest in, and use of, some interurban lines, because gasoline and tire **27** <u>rationalizing</u> limited the use of automobiles. [5] This **28** <u>resumption</u> was short-lived, though, because once new cars hit the post-war market, people again chose mobility over scheduled public transportation. **29**

A modern resurgence in electric trolleys began in 2009, when federal funding became available for streetcar projects in key cities such as Atlanta. **30** <u>Critics argue that modern streetcars aren't any faster than local buses. Critics argue that this is the reason modern streetcars will never be cost-effective.</u> They also point out that a lot of streetcar projects start as economic development projects rather than as transit projects.

27. A) NO CHANGE
    B) rationing
    C) reasoning
    D) rating

28. A) NO CHANGE
    B) reparation
    C) renaissance
    D) renovation

29. To make this paragraph most logical, sentence 2 should be placed
    A) where it is now.
    B) before sentence 1.
    C) after sentence 3.
    D) after sentence 4.

30. Which choice most effectively combines the sentences at the underlined portion?
    A) Critics argue that modern streetcars aren't any faster than local buses and therefore will never be cost-effective.
    B) Critics argue that modern streetcars aren't any faster than local buses and that they will never be cost-effective.
    C) Critics argue that modern streetcars aren't any faster than local buses and critics argue they will never be cost-effective.
    D) Critics argue that modern streetcars aren't any faster than local buses, so critics say they will never be cost-effective.

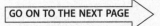
GO ON TO THE NEXT PAGE

Today, most commuters still get to work by car; **31** in fact, very few Americans in any metropolitan area use public transportation. Some communities are **32** embracing a revival, with light rail systems as the second generation of streetcars. Portland, Oregon, for example, boasts a successful light rail system serving the broad metropolitan area with an annual ridership of 39.12 million residents interested in car-free living.

From trolleys to light rail, the evolution of public transportation shows that if it is **33** reliable convenient comfortable, and fast, it's on the right track.

31. Which choice offers an accurate interpretation of the data in the chart?

A) NO CHANGE

B) however, public transportation is crucial to some cities.

C) it is only in rural areas that public transportation is still a valuable service.

D) nonetheless, public transportation use is on the rise in all metro areas.

32. A) NO CHANGE

B) accepting

C) tolerating

D) understanding

33. A) NO CHANGE

B) reliable—convenient, comfortable, and fast,

C) reliable; convenient, comfortable and fast

D) reliable, convenient, comfortable, and fast,

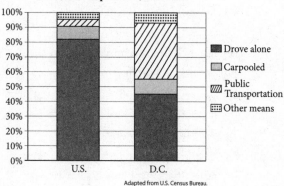

Means of Transportation, 2006-2010

Adapted from U.S. Census Bureau.

Questions 34-44 are based on the following passage and supplementary material.

Educating Early

Early childhood education (ECE) is the field **34** formed by those who teach young children, typically between ages three and five. Preschool teachers, teaching assistants, and childcare workers are today's most common ECE job titles. **35** Careers in ECE involve reward and challenge, as well as a healthy measure of fun.

For those interested in working with children up to about age eight, it is perhaps as important to develop nurturing skills as it is to undergo the proper training. Early childhood **36** educators must be patient, gentle, creative, and physically, energetic in order to address the many needs of young children. **37** Varying levels of educational training are also required for some entry-level childcare positions. A high school diploma is sufficient. For most teaching jobs, though, an associate's or bachelor's degree in an ECE-related discipline is expected. Some of these jobs also require staff to obtain credentials as Child Development Associates (CDA) or Child Care Professionals (CCP). Due to these variations in qualifications, it is important that anyone pursuing ECE find out specific expectations for the job of their choice.

The daily demands of ECE are multifaceted. Educators conscientiously interact with both children and parents and must plan in advance for the day's activities. They teach at the unique level of the children under

34. A) NO CHANGE
    B) consisting of
    C) epitomized by
    D) exclusive of

35. A) NO CHANGE
    B) Careers in ECE involve reward and challenge. As well as a healthy measure of fun.
    C) Careers in ECE involve reward and challenge; as well as a healthy measure of fun.
    D) Careers in ECE involve reward and challenge, as well as: a healthy measure of fun.

36. A) NO CHANGE
    B) educators must be patient, gentle, creative, and physically energetic
    C) educators must be: patient gentle creative and physically energetic
    D) educators must be, patient, gentle, creative, and physically energetic

37. A) NO CHANGE
    B) Varying levels of educational training are also required, for some entry-level childcare positions, a high school diploma is sufficient.
    C) Varying levels of educational training are also required. For some entry-level childcare positions, a high school diploma is sufficient.
    D) Varying levels of educational training are also required: for some entry-level childcare positions a high school diploma is sufficient.

GO ON TO THE NEXT PAGE

their care, continually working to prepare them for many coming years of formal education. Introducing concepts such as storytelling, reading, basic sciences, arts, and math, as well as healthy physical, social, and emotional activities, **38** these teachers instruct children in listening, learning, and enjoying school. The vital lessons taught to the preschool-aged child **39** equips young learners to succeed in kindergarten and beyond.

40 The field presents a challenging career path. The U.S. Department of Labor expects ECE jobs to grow moderately over the coming decade. As research continues to confirm early education's positive impact on children's lives, the U.S. government is spending more money to improve and expand opportunities. Parents and guardians of any socioeconomic status are urged to consider preschool because of **41** their influence on the future of both the individual child and the nation as a whole. These developments indicate **42** a ceaseless job market for early childhood educators. **43** Early childhood educators often choose to pursue graduate studies in fields such as education and psychology.

38. A) NO CHANGE
    B) these teachers instruct children listening, learning, and enjoying school.
    C) these teachers instruct children to listen, how to learn, and how to enjoy school.
    D) these teachers instruct children to listen, to learn, and enjoy of school.

39. A) NO CHANGE
    B) has equipped
    C) equipping
    D) equip

40. Which choice most effectively sets up the information that follows?
    A) NO CHANGE
    B) Job security in ECE is promising.
    C) The field is booming internationally.
    D) Unfortunately, pay for ECE positions is low.

41. A) NO CHANGE
    B) it's
    C) its
    D) they're

42. A) NO CHANGE
    B) an erratic
    C) an eternal
    D) an enduring

43. Which choice provides the most relevant detail?
    A) NO CHANGE
    B) Recent years have seen an increase in federal funding to preschool programs offered to low-income families.
    C) In Sweden, preschool is compulsory and is fully funded by the government.
    D) The benefits of preschool are apparent in longitudinal studies focusing on child development.

GO ON TO THE NEXT PAGE ⟶

Those pursuing ECE should anticipate a lower average yearly income than that of some other jobs. For those who love young children, activity, and an interactive, eventful, and playful workplace, however, this career offers what many would find to be a rewarding and stimulating life. The Bureau of Labor Statistics bears this out, **44** as schools and day care centers continue to be the most common places of employment for workers in ECE. The influence of such educators is irreplaceable. Inviting children each day to craft and imagine, these teachers form the minds that will someday imagine and craft the future of this world.

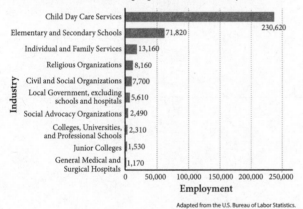

Industries with the Highest Employment Level for Preschool Teachers, Except Special Education, May 2013

Adapted from the U.S. Bureau of Labor Statistics.

44. Which choice offers an accurate interpretation of the data in the chart?

A) NO CHANGE

B) as civic and social organizations have seen a rapid decline in the number of ECE-trained employees.

C) as most students pursuing careers in ECE can anticipate finding work in the fast-paced medical field.

D) as the majority of ECE graduates find employment in rewarding local government positions.

MATH TEST

25 Minutes—20 Questions

NO-CALCULATOR SECTION

This section corresponds to Section 3 of your answer sheet.

Directions: For this section, solve each question and select the best answer choice. The available space on each page may be used for scratch work.

Notes:

1. Calculator use is NOT permitted.
2. All numbers used are real numbers, and all variables used represent real numbers, unless otherwise indicated.
3. Figures are drawn to scale and lie in a plane unless otherwise indicated.
4. Unless stated otherwise, the domain of any function f is assumed to be the set of all real numbers x, for which $f(x)$ is a real number.

Information:

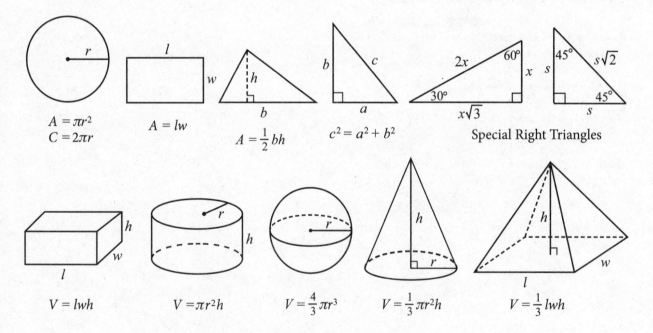

$A = \pi r^2$
$C = 2\pi r$

$A = lw$

$A = \frac{1}{2}bh$

$c^2 = a^2 + b^2$

Special Right Triangles

$V = lwh$

$V = \pi r^2 h$

$V = \frac{4}{3}\pi r^3$

$V = \frac{1}{3}\pi r^2 h$

$V = \frac{1}{3}lwh$

The sum of the degree measures of the angles in a triangle is 180.

The number of degrees of arc in a circle is 360.

The number of radians of arc in a circle is 2π.

GO ON TO THE NEXT PAGE

$$a = \frac{b - 3}{c}$$

1. In a certain board game, where playing involves a specific number of cards and a specific number of players, three cards are removed from the deck and kept in an envelope, while the rest of the cards are distributed equally among the players. The scenario can be represented by the equation given above. What does the variable c represent in this scenario?

    A) The number of players

    B) The number of cards left over

    C) The number of cards in the deck

    D) The number of cards dealt to each player

2. A hospital hosts an annual charity drive in which volunteers sell first aid kits to raise money for the pediatric ward. The hospital ordered too many kits last year, so it already has some to start this year's drive with. The project manager estimates, based on last year's sales, that the hospital needs to order an additional 50 boxes of kits. The function $k(b) = 12b + 32$, where b is the number of boxes ordered, represents the number of kits the hospital will have after the order arrives. When the project manager places the order, she is told that the company has changed the number of kits per box to 8. How many more boxes will she need to order to end up with the same number of kits that she had originally planned for?

    A) 25

    B) 32

    C) 75

    D) 200

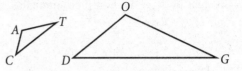

Note: Figure not drawn to scale.

3. If $\triangle CAT$ shown above is similar to $\triangle DOG$, and the ratio of the length of $\overline{TC}$ to $\overline{GD}$ is 2:7, which of the following ratios must also be equal to 2:7?

    A) $\overline{CA} : \overline{DG}$

    B) $m\angle C : m\angle D$

    C) area of $\triangle CAT$: area of $\triangle DOG$

    D) perimeter of $\triangle CAT$: perimeter of $\triangle DOG$

4. Which of the following expressions is equivalent to $\sqrt{16x^9 y^6}$?

    A) $4x^2 y^3$

    B) $4x^3 y^2$

    C) $4xy\sqrt{xy}$

    D) $4x^4 y^3 \sqrt{x}$

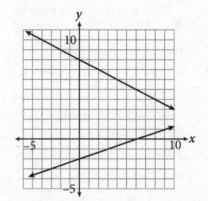

5. What is the solution to the system of equations shown in the graph?

    A) (11, 1.5)

    B) (12, 2)

    C) (13, 2.5)

    D) (14, 2.75)

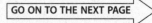GO ON TO THE NEXT PAGE

6. The value of $7x^2 + 3$ is how much more than the value of $7x^2 - 9$?

   A) 6

   B) 12

   C) $7x^2 - 6$

   D) $7x^2 + 12$

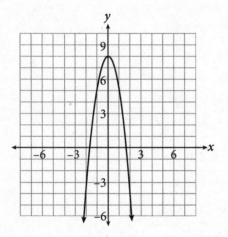

7. Vadim graphs the equation $y = -3x^2 + 8$, which is shown in the figure above. He realizes, however, that he miscalculated and should have graphed $y = -\dfrac{1}{3}x^2 + 8$. How will this affect his graph?

   A) It will change the y-intercept.

   B) It will make the parabola open in the opposite direction.

   C) It will make the parabola cross the x-axis closer to the origin.

   D) It will make the parabola cross the x-axis farther from the origin.

8. Which value of x makes the equation $\dfrac{9}{4}\left(x - \dfrac{7}{3}\right) = 5$ true?

   A) $-\dfrac{1}{9}$

   B) $\dfrac{41}{9}$

   C) $\dfrac{163}{12}$

   D) $\dfrac{67}{3}$

9. An egg farmer packs his eggs in standard 12-hole cartons and then packs the cartons in large shipping boxes. The number of boxes needed, b, to transport c cartons of eggs can be found using the function $b(c) = \dfrac{c}{40}$. If the carton-packing machine can pack a maximum of 4,000 cartons per day, and it does not pack partial boxes, what is the range of the function in this context?

   A) All integers from 0 to 100

   B) All integers from 0 to 4,000

   C) All integers greater than or equal to 40

   D) All integers greater than or equal to 100

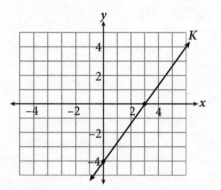

10. Where will the graph of $y = \dfrac{4}{3}x + 8$ intersect line K shown above?

   A) $(-3, 4)$

   B) $(9, 20)$

   C) The graphs will never intersect.

   D) It is not possible to determine where the graphs will intersect because the y-intercept of the given line does not fit on the coordinate plane.

GO ON TO THE NEXT PAGE

11. Some herbicides are more effective at killing weeds than others, relative to the amount of the herbicide needed to produce results. Which graph could represent the effectiveness of a more-effective herbicide, m, and a less-effective herbicide, l?

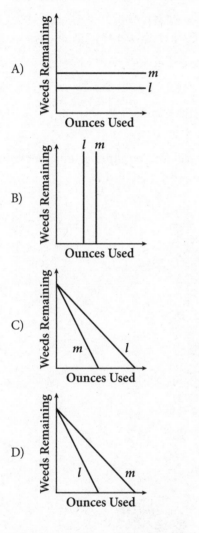

12. Which of the following values satisfies the inequalities $t - \dfrac{3}{4} > \dfrac{3}{2}$ and $\dfrac{t}{4} - \dfrac{1}{3} < \dfrac{5}{12}$?

    A) 1.75

    B) 2.25

    C) 2.75

    D) 3.25

13. If $p(x)$ is a polynomial function that has a simple zero at $x = 4$ and a double zero at $x = -\dfrac{1}{3}$, which of the following could be the factored form of $p(x)$?

    A) $p(x) = (x - 4)(x + 3)^2$

    B) $p(x) = (x - 4)(3x + 1)^2$

    C) $p(x) = 2(x - 4)(x + 3)$

    D) $p(x) = 2(x - 4)(3x + 1)$

14. Triangle ABC (not shown) is a right triangle, with $AB < AC < BC$. If the length of side AB is 6 and the length of side BC is 10, what is the area, in square units, of triangle ABC?

    A) 24

    B) 30

    C) 48

    D) 60

15. Water from rivers and streams is often unsafe to drink because of sediments and contaminants. One primitive way that water has been filtered in the past (and is still occasionally employed by avid campers and survivalists) is to use a charcoal filter, through which the water is allowed to trickle. Suppose three campers each make a charcoal filter. The first two campers make their filters using water bottles, each of which can filter enough water for all three campers in 8 hours. The third filter is made from a two-liter soda bottle and can filter the same amount of water in 4 hours. How long will it take the three filters working together to filter enough water for all three campers?

    A) $\dfrac{1}{2}$ hour

    B) 1 hour

    C) $1\dfrac{1}{2}$ hours

    D) 2 hours

GO ON TO THE NEXT PAGE

Directions: For questions 16-20, enter your responses into the appropriate grid on your answer sheet, in accordance with the following:

1. You will receive credit only if the circles are filled in correctly, but you may write your answers in the boxes above each grid to help you fill in the circles accurately.
2. Don't mark more than one circle per column.
3. None of the questions with grid-in responses will have a negative solution.
4. Only grid in a single answer, even if there is more than one correct answer to a given question.
5. A **mixed number** must be gridded as a decimal or an improper fraction. For example, you would grid $7\frac{1}{2}$ as 7.5 or $\frac{15}{2}$.

    (Were you to grid it as $\boxed{7\ 1\ /\ 2}$, this response would be read as $\frac{71}{2}$.)

6. A **decimal** that has more digits than there are places on the grid may be either rounded or truncated, but every column in the grid must be filled in order to receive credit.

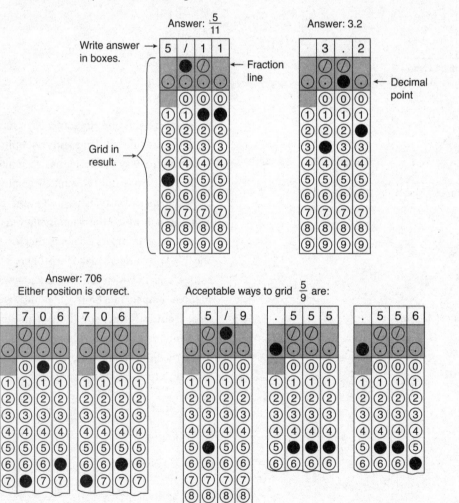

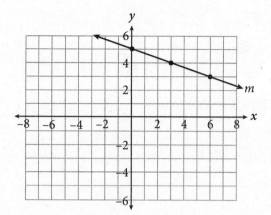

16. If line m shown above is reflected over the x-axis, what is the slope of the new line?

$$0 \leq \frac{1-k}{2} < \frac{7}{8}$$

17. If k lies within the solution set of the inequality shown above, what is the maximum possible value of k?

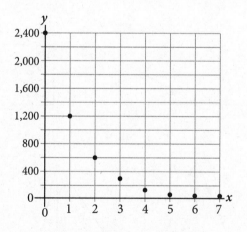

18. If an exponential function of the form $h(x) = a(b)^x$ is used to model the data shown in the graph above, what is the value of b?

19. What is the value of the complex number $\frac{1}{4}i^{42} + i^{60}$?

20. In medicine, when a drug is administered in pill form, it takes time for the concentration in the bloodstream to build up, particularly for pain medications. Suppose for a certain pain medication, the function $C(t) = \frac{1.5t}{t^2 + 4}$ is used to model the concentration, where t is the time in hours after the patient takes the pill. For this particular medication, the concentration reaches a maximum level of 0.375 about two hours after it is administered and then begins to decrease. If the patient isn't allowed to eat or drink until the concentration drops back down to 0.3, how many hours after taking the pill must the patient wait before eating or drinking?

MATH TEST

55 Minutes—38 Questions

CALCULATOR SECTION

This section corresponds to Section 4 of your answer sheet.

Directions: For this section, solve each question and select the best answer choice. The available space on each page may be used for scratch work.

Notes:

1. Calculator use is permitted.
2. All numbers used are real numbers, and all variables used represent real numbers, unless otherwise indicated.
3. Figures are drawn to scale and lie in a plane unless otherwise indicated.
4. Unless stated otherwise, the domain of any function f is assumed to be the set of all real numbers x, for which $f(x)$ is a real number.

Information:

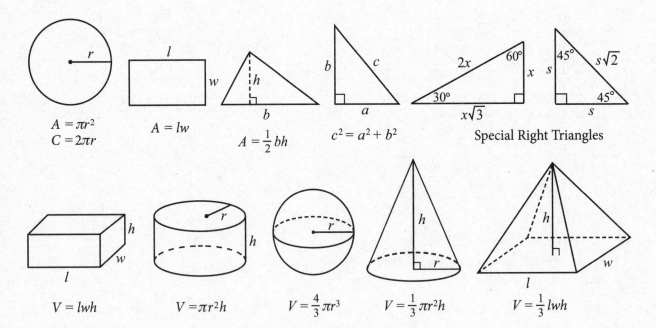

$A = \pi r^2$
$C = 2\pi r$

$A = lw$

$A = \frac{1}{2}bh$

$c^2 = a^2 + b^2$

Special Right Triangles

$V = lwh$

$V = \pi r^2 h$

$V = \frac{4}{3}\pi r^3$

$V = \frac{1}{3}\pi r^2 h$

$V = \frac{1}{3}lwh$

The sum of the degree measures of the angles in a triangle is 180.

The number of degrees of arc in a circle is 360.

The number of radians of arc in a circle is 2π.

GO ON TO THE NEXT PAGE

Rating Score	1	2	3	4	5
Frequency	0	4	6	8	2

1. In a market where approximately 44% of all book purchases are made online, customer reviews are extremely important from a sales and marketing perspective. Early reviews are most important, as they help or hinder a book's momentum in the marketplace. The frequency table shown above gives the first 20 customer ratings for a certain book sold online. What is the mean rating for this book?

   A) 3

   B) 3.4

   C) 3.7

   D) 4

2. Hardwood trees take much longer to grow than softwood trees. Once harvested, however, hardwood is much stronger and more durable. Because of its higher density, a piece of hardwood that is the same size as a piece of softwood weighs considerably more. A lumberyard ships both kinds of wood to home improvement stores. The cost C, in dollars, to ship a pallet of wood weighing p pounds can be found using the equation $C = 6.5p + 16$. What is the cost difference to ship a pallet of hardwood weighing 170 pounds versus a pallet of softwood weighing 80 pounds?

   A) $90

   B) $325

   C) $585

   D) $715

3. The First Transcontinental Railroad, which was 1,907 miles long, was completed in 1869 to connect the West Coast of the United States to the existing rail system that ran from the Missouri River to the East Coast. During the early years after building the railroad, dangerous conditions and mechanical problems could delay the train significantly. For a person traveling from one end of the First Transcontinental Railroad to the other, which inequality represents all possible values of t, where t is the time it took to complete the journey, if, while in motion, the train traveled at an average speed of m miles per hour?

   A) $t \geq \dfrac{m}{1,907}$

   B) $t \geq \dfrac{1,907}{m}$

   C) $t \geq 1,907m$

   D) $t \geq 1,907 + m$

$$\frac{3x + 7}{x - 2} = 16$$

4. Which value of x satisfies the equation given above?

   A) $\dfrac{9}{19}$

   B) $\dfrac{9}{13}$

   C) 2

   D) 3

GO ON TO THE NEXT PAGE

	Bargain	High-End
Price (per sq. ft)	$1.89	$5.49
Rating	2.8	8.2
Life Expectancy	5 years	

5. The table above shows the price per square foot, the average customer rating (out of 10), and the life expectancy (before needing replacement) of the bargain version and the high-end version of carpet at a flooring warehouse. If the ratio of the life expectancies is roughly the same as the ratios of the prices and the ratings, about how many years can the high-end carpet be expected to last?

A) 10

B) 12

C) 15

D) 18

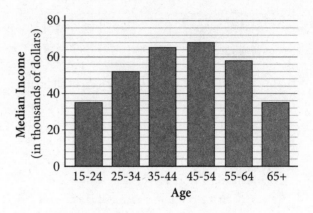

6. The bar graph shows median household incomes in a certain geographic region according to the age of the highest earner in the household. When presenting the data, the researcher who compiled the data decides to exclude the first age bracket (15-24), because it includes minors, which will likely skew the results because most minors do not have full-time jobs. The researcher also decides to exclude the last age bracket (65+) because it includes retirees, which is again likely to skew the results for the same reason. Which of the following statements most likely describes how this will affect the data overall?

A) It will significantly change the median, but not the mean.

B) It will significantly change the mean, but not the median.

C) There will be no significant change to either the mean or the median.

D) There is not enough information to determine what effect, if any, it will have on either the median or the mean.

7. If the graph of $y = mx + b$ passes through quadrants I, III, and IV on a coordinate plane, which of the following must be true about m and b?

A) $m < 0, b < 0$

B) $m < 0, b > 0$

C) $m > 0, b < 0$

D) $m > 0, b > 0$

GO ON TO THE NEXT PAGE

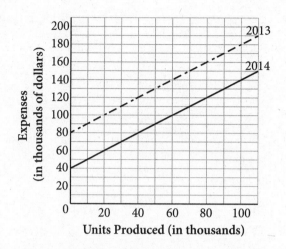

Units Produced (in thousands)

8. Manufacturing companies typically have a number of fixed costs (such as rent, machinery, insurance, etc.), which do not depend on output, and variable costs (such as wages, utilities, materials, etc.), which vary with output, usually at a constant rate. The graph shows a company's costs for manufacturing a particular product over the course of two years. Which of the following could explain the difference between the 2013 and 2014 costs?

A) The company reduced its fixed costs by 50%.

B) The company reduced its variable costs by 50%.

C) The company reduced the number of units produced by 50%.

D) The company reduced its fixed costs, variable costs, and the number of units produced by 50%.

$$\begin{cases} y = \dfrac{1}{4}x - 3 \\ y = -\dfrac{5}{2}x + 8 \end{cases}$$

9. Which of the following is the y-coordinate of the solution to the system of equations given above?

A) -8

B) -2

C) 2

D) 4

10. Premature babies are typically born underweight and are cared for in a neonatal intensive care unit (NICU). At a certain NICU, the mean weight of all the male babies is 4 pounds, and the mean weight of all the female babies is 3.6 pounds. Which of the following must be true about the mean weight w of the combined group of male and female babies at this NICU?

A) $w = 3.8$

B) $w > 3.8$

C) $w < 3.8$

D) $3.6 < w < 4$

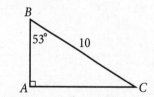

11. Given that $\sin 53° \approx 0.8$, what is the approximate length of side AB in the figure above?

A) 6

B) 7.2

C) 8

D) 8.5

GO ON TO THE NEXT PAGE ⟩

12. When most people buy a house, they take out a mortgage to cover at least part of the cost of the home and then pay the loan back over time. The most common kind of mortgage is a 30-year loan. A couple buys a home and takes out a 30-year loan in the amount of $220,000 (called the principal). They decide they want to pay it off early to save money on interest. They set a goal of reducing the principal amount of the loan to $170,000 in four years. Suppose during the first two years of their four-year timeline, the couple pays down the loan by 10%. By approximately what percent do they need to pay down the rest of the loan to reach their overall goal?

A) 10%

B) 14%

C) 18%

D) 20%

x	1	2	3	4	5	6
$f(x)$	3.5	0	−2.5	−4	−4.5	−4

13. The table above shows several points through which the graph of a quadratic function $f(x)$ passes. One of the x-intercepts for the graph is given in the table. What is the other x-intercept for the graph?

A) (−2, 0)

B) (5, 0)

C) (8, 0)

D) (10, 0)

Questions 14 and 15 refer to the following information.

A college cafeteria received a petition from students to offer healthier meat, vegetarian, and vegan dishes. In response to the petition, the cafeteria conducted an analysis of its existing menu to determine the current state of those options. The results are summarized in the table below. The analyst used a sliding scale based on the nutrient levels compared against calorie, sugar, and sodium counts to determine the health score, a score of 1 being the least healthy and 5 being the healthiest.

Health Score	Meat Dishes	Vegetarian Dishes	Vegan Dishes
1	3	1	1
2	4	3	1
3	8	5	4
4	5	4	2
5	0	1	0

14. What fraction of the vegetarian and vegan dishes received a health score greater than 2 ?

A) $\dfrac{7}{22}$

B) $\dfrac{8}{21}$

C) $\dfrac{8}{11}$

D) $\dfrac{11}{21}$

15. If a student chooses a dish at random for lunch one day, what is the probability that it will be a meat dish with a health score of at least 4 ?

A) $\dfrac{5}{42}$

B) $\dfrac{6}{21}$

C) $\dfrac{1}{4}$

D) $\dfrac{13}{42}$

GO ON TO THE NEXT PAGE

$$r = \sqrt[4]{\frac{8kl}{\pi R}}$$

16. Ideally, blood should flow smoothly through the arteries in our bodies. When there are problems, or as a natural part of aging, there is an increased amount of resistance to blood flow. *Viscosity* is a term used to describe the thickness or stickiness of the blood and is directly related to this resistance, as are the radius and the length of the artery through which the blood flows. The formula given above relates the radius (r) of an artery to the viscosity (k), resistance (R), and length (l) of that artery. Which of the following represents the viscosity in terms of the other variables?

A) $k = \dfrac{r^4 \pi R}{8l}$

B) $k = \sqrt[4]{\dfrac{8l}{\pi R r}}$

C) $k = \dfrac{1}{2} r \pi R l$

D) $k = \left(\dfrac{8l}{\pi R r}\right)^4$

17. Two muffins and a carton of milk cost \$3.35. If five muffins and a carton of milk cost \$5.60, what is the cost of two cartons of milk?

A) \$0.75

B) \$1.50

C) \$1.85

D) \$3.70

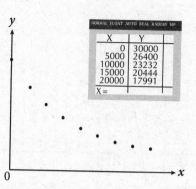

18. The calculator screenshot above shows the x- and y-values for the first few data points shown in the scatterplot, which can be modeled using an exponential function. Which of the following scenarios could be represented by this function?

A) The resale value of a car is cut in half for every 3,600 miles driven.

B) The resale value of a car decreases by \$5,000 for every 3,600 miles driven.

C) The resale value of a car decreases by \$3,600 for every 5,000 miles driven.

D) The resale value of a car decreases by approximately 12% for every 5,000 miles driven.

GO ON TO THE NEXT PAGE

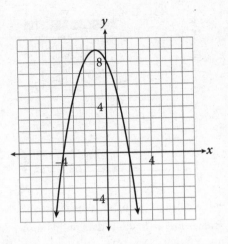

19. The graph of the function $f(x) = -x^2 - 2x + 8$ is shown in the figure above. For what values of x does $f(x) = 5$?

A) -4 and 2

B) -3 and 1

C) -1 and 9

D) 5 and 8

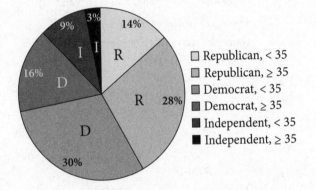

20. The pie chart above shows the distribution of registered voters in a certain district in Illinois by party and by age. If there are 8,640 voters in the district, what is the ratio of Republicans to Independents?

A) 3:1

B) 7:2

C) 22:3

D) 23:6

21. A DVD rental kiosk dispenses movies for $1 for a 24-hour rental. After the initial rental period has expired, customers are charged a $0.50 late fee for every 24 hours that the movie is returned late. If a customer rents four movies at one time, which of the following graphs represents the total possible charges in late fees, assuming he returns all the movies together?

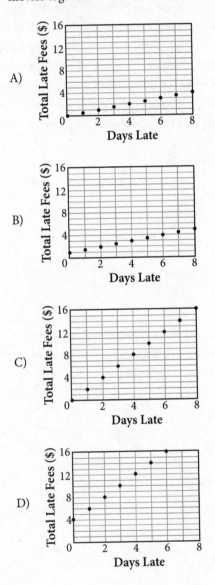

GO ON TO THE NEXT PAGE

22. There are many ways to defrost a turkey. One way is to let it thaw slowly in the refrigerator, at a thaw rate of about 4 pounds per day. Another way is to submerge the turkey in cold water, which thaws it at a rate of 1 pound per 30 minutes. Approximately how many more ounces of turkey can the cold-water method thaw in 2 hours than the refrigerator method? (1 pound = 16 ounces)

    A) 16

    B) 27

    C) 32

    D) 59

23. A freight train operator knows that on a 200-mile trip, if the freight cars are not fully loaded, she can save 1 hour of travel time by increasing her normal speed by 10 miles per hour. What is her normal speed in miles per hour?

    A) 40

    B) 45

    C) 55

    D) 60

24. A cable company offers movie rental packages. If you join the Movie Fan club, you get 10 movies for $20 and each movie after that costs $2.50. If you join the Movie Super Fan club, you get unlimited movies for a year for $75. How many movies would a person need to rent for each package to cost the same amount over a one-year period?

    A) 22

    B) 30

    C) 32

    D) 57

25. Many wholesale businesses charge customers less per item when they buy those items in bulk. Suppose a baseball cap distributor charges $6 per cap for the first 25 caps the customer purchases, $5 per cap for the next 75 purchased, and $4 per cap for all additional caps over 100. Which of the following piecewise functions represents this scenario, where C represents the total cost and n represents the number of caps purchased?

    A) $C(n) = \begin{cases} 6n, & \text{if } n \leq 25 \\ 5n, & \text{if } 25 < n \leq 100 \\ 4n, & \text{if } n > 100 \end{cases}$

    B) $C(n) = \begin{cases} 6n, & \text{if } n < 25 \\ 5n, & \text{if } 25 \leq n < 100 \\ 4n, & \text{if } n \geq 100 \end{cases}$

    C) $C(n) = \begin{cases} 6n, & \text{if } n \leq 25 \\ 150 + 5(n - 25), & \text{if } 25 < n \leq 100 \\ 500 + 4(n - 100), & \text{if } n > 100 \end{cases}$

    D) $C(n) = \begin{cases} 6n, & \text{if } n \leq 25 \\ 150 + 5(n - 25), & \text{if } 25 < n \leq 100 \\ 525 + 4(n - 100), & \text{if } n > 100 \end{cases}$

26. The decline of a certain animal species' population, currently estimated to be 22,000, can be modeled using the quadratic function $p(x) = -0.5x^2 + 22,000$, where x is the number of years after 2015. Based on only this information, and assuming no intervention to change the path of the population, which of the following statements must be true?

    A) This species will be extinct by the end of the year 2225.

    B) The animal population for this species is decreasing at a constant rate.

    C) In approximately 100 years, the animal population for this species will be about half what it was in 2015.

    D) The animal population will increase or decrease from the initial 2015 level, depending on the year after 2015.

GO ON TO THE NEXT PAGE

27. In geology, the water table is the level below which the ground is saturated with water. Wells must be dug below this point to bring water up into the well. Except in cases of severe flooding, the water level in a well does not rise above the water table. Suppose a cylindrical well is 6 feet wide and 60 feet deep in an area where the water table is 40 feet below ground level. Assuming no unusual circumstances, what is the volume in cubic feet of the water in the well at any given time?

A) 180π

B) 360π

C) 540π

D) 720π

28. Ramon graphed a line that has a slope of -2. The line he graphed passes through the point (3, 5). If Ramon doubles the slope of his line and then shifts it down 1 unit, through which point will the line pass?

A) $(3, -2)$

B) $(3, 9)$

C) $(6, 4)$

D) $(10, 2)$

California Earthquakes, 2003-2010

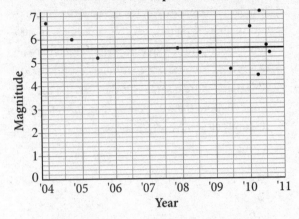

29. Earthquakes occur when energy is released from deep inside the earth, causing friction between the tectonic plates of the earth's crust. The magnitude, or intensity, of the earthquake is measured on the Richter scale. The scatterplot above shows the earthquakes experienced by California between December 2003 and December 2010. The line of best fit, which has a slope of 0, is a fairly good indicator in California. Approximately what percent of the earthquakes in California during this time period differed by 1 point or more on the Richter scale from the magnitude predicted by the line of best fit?

A) 22%

B) 27%

C) 33%

D) 36%

30. If the equation $\dfrac{2}{9}x^2 + \dfrac{8}{3}x - 7 = 3$ has solutions x_1 and x_2, what is the product of x_1 and x_2?

A) -45

B) -15

C) -5

D) 3

GO ON TO THE NEXT PAGE

Directions: For questions 31-38, enter your responses into the appropriate grid on your answer sheet, in accordance with the following:

1. You will receive credit only if the circles are filled in correctly, but you may write your answers in the boxes above each grid to help you fill in the circles accurately.

2. Don't mark more than one circle per column.

3. None of the questions with grid-in responses will have a negative solution.

4. Only grid in a single answer, even if there is more than one correct answer to a given question.

5. A **mixed number** must be gridded as a decimal or an improper fraction. For example, you would grid $7\frac{1}{2}$ as 7.5 or $\frac{15}{2}$.

   (Were you to grid it as ⬚, this response would be read as $\frac{71}{2}$.)

6. A **decimal** that has more digits than there are places on the grid may be either rounded or truncated, but every column in the grid must be filled in order to receive credit.

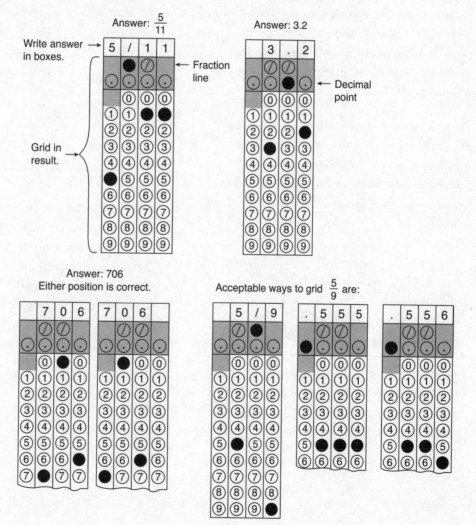

31. If $-10 < 14 - 2p < 6$, what is the greatest possible integer value of $7 - p$?

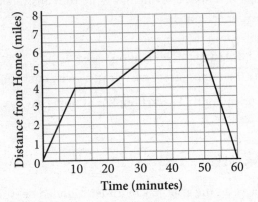

32. The graph above shows Umberto's distance from home over a one-hour period, during which time he first went to the bank, then went to the post office, and then returned home. How many minutes did Umberto spend at the bank and at the post office combined?

33. Selena is taking a 90-minute test that consists of 50 multiple-choice questions and 30 true-false questions. If she completes 48 questions in 50 minutes, how many seconds per question does she have on average to answer each of the remaining questions?

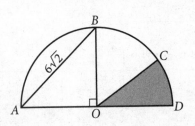

34. If $\overline{AD}$ is a diameter of the semicircle shown above, and the arc length of CD is π, what is the area of the shaded region? Use 3.14 to approximate π and round your answer to the nearest tenth.

35. A bag valve mask is used to resuscitate patients who have stopped breathing. It consists primarily of a bag attached to a mask. The mask is fitted to the patient's nose and mouth. Squeezing the bag pushes air through the mask and into the patient's lungs. For sanitary reasons, most of these masks are disposable. Suppose a hospital's mask supplier sells them in boxes of 48 or 144, and the supplier has 35 boxes in stock. If the supplier has 2,832 total masks in stock, how many masks would the hospital receive if it ordered all of the boxes of 144 that the supplier has in stock?

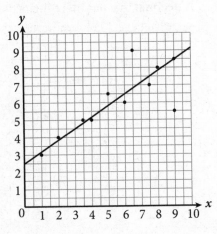

36. Patricia collected data for a school project, plotted the information on a scatterplot (shown above), and drew the line of best fit. In reviewing her notes, she realized that one of her data points was wrong, so she eliminated that point and redrew the line of best fit. If the new y-intercept of her line is 2 and the slope is steeper than before, what was the y-value of the point she eliminated?

GO ON TO THE NEXT PAGE ⟹

Questions 37 and 38 refer to the following information.

A company sponsors a health program for its employees by partnering with a local gym. If employees pay for a year-long membership at this gym, then for every day the employee uses his or her swipe card to enter the gym (and work out), the company reimburses the employee 0.2% of the cost of the $220 membership. Additionally, any employee who goes to the gym more than 60% of the days in the year gets one bonus paid day off of work. The company uses a 365-day year.

37. If 246 employees participate in the program and they each go to the gym an average of 84 days per year, how much money in membership reimbursements will the company pay out? Round your answer to the nearest whole dollar.

38. Giving employees additional paid time off also costs the company money because it is paying the salary of an employee who is not actually doing any work on that day. The pie graph below shows gym usage for the 246 employees who participated in the health program.

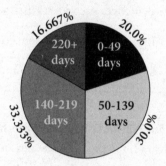

If the average salary of workers who participated was $14.90 per hour and one day off equals 8 hours, how much did the health program day-off benefit cost the company? Round your answer to the nearest whole dollar.

ESSAY TEST

50 Minutes

You will be given a passage to read and asked to write an essay analyzing it. As you write, be sure to show that you have read the passage closely. You will be graded on how well you have understood the passage, how clear your analysis is, and how well you express your ideas.

Your essay must be written on the lines in your answer booklet. Anything you write outside the lined space in your answer booklet will not be read by the essay graders. Be sure to write or print in such a way that it will be legible to readers not familiar with your handwriting. Additionally, be sure to address the passage directly. An off-topic essay will not be graded.

> As you read the passage, think about the author's use of
>
> - evidence, such as statistics or other facts.
>
> - logic to connect evidence to conclusions and to develop lines of reasoning.
>
> - style, word choice, and appeals to emotion to make the argument more persuasive.

**Adapted from Winston Churchill's speech "The Defence of Freedom and Speech (The Lights Are Going Out),"
broadcast by radio to the United States and London, October 16, 1938.**

1   I avail myself with relief of the opportunity of speaking to the people of the United States. I do not know how long such liberties will be allowed. The stations of uncensored expression are closing down; the lights are going out; but there is still time for those to whom freedom and parliamentary government mean something, to consult together. Let me, then, speak in truth and earnestness while time remains. . . .

2   The American people have, it seems to me, formed a true judgment upon the disaster which has befallen Europe. They realise, perhaps more clearly than the French and British publics have yet done, the far-reaching consequences of the abandonment and ruin of the Czechoslovak Republic. . . .

3   Has any benefit or progress ever been achieved by the human race by submission to organised and calculated violence? As we look back over the long story of the nations we must see that, on the contrary, their glory has been founded upon the spirit of resistance to tyranny and injustice, especially when these evils seemed to be backed by heavier force. Since the dawn of the Christian era a certain way of life has slowly been shaping itself among the Western peoples, and certain standards of conduct and government have come to be esteemed. After many miseries and prolonged confusion, there arose into the broad light of day the conception of the right of the individual; his right to be consulted in the government of his country; his right to invoke the law even against the State itself. . . .

4   We are confronted with another theme. It is not a new theme; it leaps out upon us from the Dark Ages—racial persecution, religious intolerance, deprivation of free speech, the conception of the citizen as a mere soulless fraction of the State. To this has been added the cult of war. Children are to be taught in their earliest schooling the delights and profits of conquest and aggression. A whole mighty community has been drawn painfully, by severe privations, into a warlike frame. They are held in this condition, which they relish no more than we do, by a party organisation, several millions strong, who derive all kinds of profits, good and bad, from the upkeep of the regime. Like the Communists, the Nazis tolerate no opinion but their own. Like the Communists, they

GO ON TO THE NEXT PAGE ➡

feed on hatred. Like the Communists, they must seek, from time to time, and always at shorter intervals, a new target, a new prize, a new victim. The Dictator, in all his pride, is held in the grip of his Party machine. . . .

5 The culminating question to which I have been leading is whether the world as we have known it—the great and hopeful world of before the war, the world of increasing hope and enjoyment for the common man, the world of honoured tradition and expanding science—should meet this menace by submission or by resistance. Let us see, then, whether the means of resistance remain to us today. We have sustained an immense disaster; the renown of France is dimmed. In spite of her brave, efficient army, her influence is profoundly diminished. No one has a right to say that Britain, for all her blundering, has broken her word—indeed, when it was too late, she was better than her word. Nevertheless, Europe lies at this moment abashed and distracted before the triumphant assertions of dictatorial power. In the Spanish Peninsula, a purely Spanish quarrel has been carried by the intervention, or shall I say the "non-intervention" (to quote the current Jargon) of Dictators into the region of a world cause.

6 Is this a call to war? Does anyone pretend that preparation for resistance to aggression is unleashing war? I declare it to be the sole guarantee of peace. We need the swift gathering of forces to confront not only military but moral aggression; the resolute and sober acceptance of their duty by the English-speaking peoples and by all the nations, great and small, who wish to walk with them. Their faithful and zealous comradeship would almost between night and morning clear the path of progress and banish from all our lives the fear which already darkens the sunlight to hundreds of millions of men.

> Write an essay that analyzes the author's approach in persuading his readers that the United States and Britain must mobilize their forces in preparation to resist the military aggression of Nazi Germany. Focus on specific features such as the ones listed in the box above the passage and explain how these features strengthen the author's argument. Your essay should discuss the most important rhetorical features of the passage.
>
> Your essay should not focus on your own opinion of the author's conclusion, but rather on how the author persuades his readers.

ANSWER KEY
READING TEST

1. B	14. A	27. C	40. D
2. A	15. B	28. A	41. D
3. D	16. A	29. B	42. B
4. B	17. C	30. A	43. A
5. D	18. D	31. D	44. D
6. B	19. B	32. A	45. C
7. D	20. A	33. C	46. B
8. A	21. C	34. B	47. A
9. C	22. B	35. C	48. B
10. C	23. C	36. D	49. D
11. A	24. B	37. A	50. D
12. C	25. A	38. B	51. C
13. B	26. C	39. D	52. A

WRITING AND LANGUAGE TEST

1. D	12. A	23. B	34. B
2. B	13. D	24. A	35. A
3. C	14. B	25. C	36. B
4. C	15. C	26. D	37. C
5. B	16. A	27. B	38. A
6. D	17. D	28. C	39. D
7. D	18. C	29. B	40. B
8. B	19. D	30. A	41. C
9. C	20. B	31. B	42. D
10. C	21. D	32. A	43. B
11. A	22. B	33. D	44. A

MATH—NO CALCULATOR TEST

1. A	6. B	11. C	16. 1/3 or .333
2. A	7. D	12. C	17. 1
3. D	8. B	13. B	18. 1/2 or .5
4. D	9. A	14. A	19. 3/4 or .75
5. B	10. C	15. D	20. 4

MATH—CALCULATOR TEST

1. B	11. A	21. C	31. 2
2. C	12. B	22. D	32. 25
3. B	13. C	23. A	33. 75
4. D	14. C	24. C	34. 9.4
5. C	15. A	25. D	35. 1728
6. D	16. A	26. A	36. 5.5
7. C	17. D	27. A	37. 9092
8. A	18. D	28. A	38. 4887
9. B	19. B	29. B	
10. D	20. B	30. A	

ANSWERS AND EXPLANATIONS

READING TEST

My Ántonia

Suggested Passage Map notes:

¶1: describing view

¶2: Jim lost in thought

¶3: Jim "feels" the land

¶4: vast land, wants to explore

¶5-7: Jim stays behind to enjoy, feels content

¶8: Jim describes view - plants, animals, insects; ponders being like this after death

1. B   Difficulty: Easy

Category: Detail

Getting to the Answer: Eliminate answer choices that are not reflected in the passage. When Jim asks if he can stay in the garden, his grandmother immediately asks if he's afraid of snakes, but relents and lets him stay. Thus, (B) is correct.

2. A   Difficulty: Easy

Category: Vocab-in-Context

Getting to the Answer: Read the sentence for context clues and determine which answer choice best matches the idea presented in the sentence. Jim explains that he sits in the middle of the garden, implying he can see a long way in all directions and that it will be difficult for anything to sneak up on him. This makes (A) the correct answer.

3. D   Difficulty: Hard

Category: Inference

Getting to the Answer: Reread the section of the passage concerning Jim's interaction with the land. Avoid answer choices that might be true but are not dealt with in the passage. Jim mentions that he never would have found the garden on his own and fre-

quently discusses the vastness and sameness of the prairie all around him. Choice (D) is the correct answer.

4. B   Difficulty: Medium

Category: Command of Evidence

Getting to the Answer: Reread each quote from the passage in its entirety. Then choose the one that supports the correct answer in the previous question. Choice (B) is correct, as it states that Jim would never have found the garden on his own in the vast prairie, which only had the pumpkins for a landmark.

5. D   Difficulty: Medium

Category: Global

Getting to the Answer: Review the passage to determine what major themes the author uses throughout the entire excerpt. Avoid answer choices that deal with only a small part of the excerpt. Most of the answer choices are suggested in small sections of the excerpt. Only (D) explains the main claim running throughout that a natural setting can have a transforming effect on a person.

6. B   Difficulty: Medium

Category: Inference

Getting to the Answer: Read the passage and consider the kinds of thoughts Jim has throughout. Then determine which answer choice best reflects his personality. Jim spends a lot of time reflecting on the landscape and how it affects his ideas about life. These are very introspective thoughts, making (B) the correct answer.

7. D   Difficulty: Medium

Category: Command of Evidence

Getting to the Answer: Locate each answer choice in the passage and decide which one provides evidence for the answer to the previous question.

Avoid answers that might hint at Jim's personality but do not give the strongest evidence. Choice (D) is the correct answer. In this quote, Jim reflects on the landscape, life, and the relationship between the two. This provides strong evidence of his introspective personality.

8. A   Difficulty: Medium

Category: Vocab-in-Context

Getting to the Answer: Read the surrounding sentences for context clues about how the author intended to use the word. Then determine which answer choice best serves the author's intention. Jim discusses his idea that death might feel the same as becoming a part of something bigger than ourselves. Choice (A) is correct because "assimilate" also means "to become a part of something bigger."

9. C   Difficulty: Hard

Category: Rhetoric

Getting to the Answer: Review the entire paragraph in which the repetition of "galloping" takes place. Then decide which answer choice best describes the author's reason for repeating this word. In paragraph 3, Jim explains "more than anything else I felt motion in the landscape" (lines 16-17). By repeating "galloping," the author is able to emphasize the landscape's motion. Therefore, (C) is the correct answer.

10. C   Difficulty: Easy

Category: Rhetoric

Getting to the Answer: Recall that a first-person narrator tells the story from his or her own perspective and uses pronouns such as "I," "me," and so on. Keep this in mind as you determine the author's reason for choosing this point of view. Choice (C) is the correct answer. A first-person narrator allows the author to describe the main character's thoughts and experiences with such precision that the reader often feels as though he or she is right there with the main character. Based on the amount of descriptive

detail Cather uses in the passage, one can assume that this was her reason for choosing the first-person point of view.

Bohr Letter

Suggested Passage Map notes:

¶1-2: Bohr escaped Denmark to England, went to work with Brits to develop A bomb
¶3-4: Bohr cautions - serious work, major impact on warfare
¶5: technology must be controlled
¶6-7: despite end to war, tensions high
¶8: must be mutually open in communication
¶9: great responsibility to cooperate and promote progress

11. A   Difficulty: Hard

Category: Rhetoric

Getting to the Answer: Reread the passage introduction, as it provides context for Bohr and his letter. This question requires you to think about this context as well as the rhetoric of Bohr's letter to draw conclusions about his intent. The passage introduction explains that Bohr began work on atomic energy before World War II, and before he advised other scientists on the development of the atomic bomb. The first few paragraphs of his letter discuss the development of atomic energy for military uses and resulting problems. This suggests that Bohr writes the letter to discuss the implications of the military use of atomic energy. Choice (A) is the correct answer.

12. C   Difficulty: Medium

Category: Command of Evidence

Getting to the Answer: Recall the purpose expressed in your answer to the preceding item. The correct answer will most clearly relate to that purpose and tie together your thinking. Be wary of answer choices that provide context but do not clearly support this correct answer. The answer to the previous question indicates that Bohr intends to discuss the implications of military uses of atomic weaponry. Although several answer choices provide context, only the rhetoric in (C) refers to the "serious problems" that arise as a result of the "enterprise," by which Bohr means the potential use of atomic energy for military purposes.

13. B   Difficulty: Medium

Category: Vocab-in-Context

Getting to the Answer: Substitute each answer choice for the word "preponderance." The correct answer will replace the word without changing the meaning of its sentence. The sentence states that the fact of immediate preponderance is a weapon of great power. The preceding sentences discuss the nonmilitary potential of that power. The implication is that the military application is a matter of greater importance that must be considered. Choice (B) is correct.

14. A   Difficulty: Medium

Category: Inference

Getting to the Answer: As you prepare to answer this question, think about the information provided in both the introduction and the first few paragraphs of Bohr's letter. The introduction states that before World War II, Bohr performed work on atomic structure, which does not necessarily have anything to do with military use of atomic energy. Paragraph 2 then states that Bohr knew nothing about the American-British project—in other words, the atomic bomb project—until he escaped from Denmark and joined their efforts. Based on these two clues, one can infer that Bohr's work probably began as a nonmilitary pursuit. Choice (A) is the correct answer.

15. B   Difficulty: Medium

Category: Command of Evidence

Getting to the Answer: Remember that the correct answer will support why the answer to the previous question is correct. The answer to the previous ques-

tion suggests that Bohr's work prior to World War II began as a nonmilitary pursuit. Choice (B) is correct because it provides evidence of Bohr's lack of knowledge about the atomic bomb project until he was invited to England by the British government.

16. A   Difficulty: Easy

Category: Vocab-in-Context

Getting to the Answer: Think of a definition for the word "divergences" as it is used in the sentence. Then, think about the meaning of each answer choice. The correct choice will most nearly match your own definition. In the sentence, the word "divergences" occurs in relation to the word "outlook" and implies discord and differences of opinion or perspective. Therefore, the correct answer is (A).

17. C   Difficulty: Easy

Category: Rhetoric

Getting to the Answer: Avoid answer choices that relate to other material in the passage but fail to relate specifically to the referenced lines. The sentence in which the quoted phrase appears states: "Contrary to the hopes for fruitful co-operation . . . the lack of mutual confidence soon became evident" (lines 41-45). The surrounding paragraphs refer to an ominous political situation and controversial matters during peace settlements. Choice (C) is correct because the author claims that confidence, or trust, broke down among nations because of this political discord.

18. D   Difficulty: Medium

Category: Rhetoric

Getting to the Answer: Predict what point the author is trying to make about knowledge in this section. Then select the answer choice that most nearly reflects your prediction. The referenced text suggests that because knowledge is the basis of civilization, openness—or transparency—is essential to resolving current problems. The correct answer is (D).

19. B   Difficulty: Medium

Category: Inference

Getting to the Answer: Paraphrase the author's concluding argument in your own words. Then, consider each answer choice. The correct choice will most nearly align with the argument that you paraphrased. In the concluding paragraphs, Bohr calls for greater openness and mutual cooperation among nations, particularly in the realm of atomic development. Only (B), the monitoring of countries' nuclear technologies, reflects this openness and mutual cooperation.

20. A   Difficulty: Hard

Category: Rhetoric

Getting to the Answer: Paraphrase the meaning of the quoted sentence. The correct answer will reflect how this sentence relates to the rest of the passage. The sentence primarily emphasizes the author's purpose for writing the letter: to explain the negative consequences of military use of atomic energy. Therefore, (A) is the correct answer.

Evolution of Computers Passage

Suggested Passage Map notes:

¶1: intro problem to solve

¶2: H.H. invented machine to use for 1890 census

¶3: machine considered first computer

¶4: machine very large, holds little data; magnetic tape and cassettes invented, smaller and held more data

¶5: tapes big and would not last, intro hard drive and floppy discs - smaller and holds more data

¶6: tech getting smaller and better

¶7: cost going down with popularity

¶8: info on microprocessors

¶9: MP intro in 1971, used less power

¶10: chips smaller and have more transistors

¶11: MP faster due to smaller circuits

21. C   Difficulty: Easy

Category: Rhetoric

Getting to the Answer: Read the entire passage carefully as you consider its content, purpose, and tone. The correct answer will reflect the passage's intent and how the author presents the information. The passage discusses how data storage and processing speeds of computers have improved over time, yet doesn't present a clear opinion about why or how this occurred in an attempt to persuade the reader. The correct answer is (C).

22. B   Difficulty: Easy

Category: Rhetoric

Getting to the Answer: Read the first three paragraphs carefully. Then examine each answer choice and decide which one reflects a claim that the author makes. The author notes that many contemporary technologies can be traced back to the original ideas in Hollerith's first computer. The correct answer is (B).

23. C   Difficulty: Medium

Category: Command of Evidence

Getting to the Answer: Read each answer choice carefully. The correct answer will support the claim identified in the previous question. The author is drawing a clear connection between Hollerith's machine and contemporary technologies when he refers to today's iPads and smartphones as "descendants" of Hollerith's machine. The correct answer is (C).

24. B   Difficulty: Easy

Category: Vocab-in-Context

Getting to the Answer: Read the previous paragraph to better understand how the word "cumbersome" is used in the context of the passage. In the previous paragraph, the author refers to computer magnetic tape as the "size of a dinner plate" and subsequent tapes as the size of a "small cassette." Given that the author suggests the desire to create increasingly smaller, more efficient storage units, the correct answer is (B).

25. A   Difficulty: Easy

Category: Rhetoric

Getting to the Answer: Consider why the author might have decided to start the passage with a question posed directly to readers. Though the rhetorical question at the beginning might help some readers to relive a bygone era, appreciate the U.S. Census, and acknowledge the importance of computers, the rhetorical question mainly helps readers understand the enormity of Hollerith's initial task of counting people for the U.S. Census Bureau in the 1880s. This, in turn, helps reinforce the importance of Hollerith's contribution.

26. C   Difficulty: Medium

Category: Inference

Getting to the Answer: Decide which answer choice deals with an important idea that the author suggests in the passage. The author notes that the cost per megabyte of data storage has fallen in the last few decades and that the computer industry is able to produce more powerful storage devices for less cost. Therefore, one can infer that consumers now get more data storage capability for significantly less cost. Choice (C) is the correct answer.

27. C   Difficulty: Medium

Category: Command of Evidence

Getting to the Answer: Remember that the correct answer will directly support the conclusion you reached in the previous question. The answer to the previous question suggests that consumers are getting more value for the money they spend on computers. Lines 60-63 ("Within five . . . lower") describe the relationship between lower costs and the subsequent rise in consumer demand, which suggests that consumers believe they are getting a good deal. The correct answer is (C). Choice D is incorrect because this sentence only discusses the cost of data storage devices in 2010.

28. A   Difficulty: Medium

Category: Synthesis

Getting to the Answer: Study the relationship between the size of microchip transistors in the y-axis and the passage of time in the x-axis. Be careful of answer choices that are not fully supported by the data in the graphic. The data in the graphic explicitly show that between 2000 and 2008, the size of microchip transistors experienced a larger absolute decrease than in other time periods shown. Therefore, (A) is the correct answer.

29. B   Difficulty: Easy

Category: Vocab-in-Context

Getting to the Answer: Reread the entire paragraph to better understand the overall context in which the word "degrade" is used. Decide which meaning fits this context. Choice (B), "decay," is the correct answer, as it indicates one of the problems encountered with early magnetized tapes. The other answer choices may be synonyms of "degrade," but not in this context.

30. A   Difficulty: Medium

Category: Connections

Getting to the Answer: Carefully reread the beginning of the section titled "Microprocessors," in which the reference to the computer of the 1940s occurs. Choice (A) is the correct answer. The author deliberately chose to include this fact to emphasize the size of the predecessor in the reader's mind. Contrasting the Intel 4004 with a predecessor helps the reader better understand the relationship between the two.

31. D   Difficulty: Hard

Category: Synthesis

Getting to the Answer: Remember that the correct answer will combine information in the passage with data presented in the graphic. Choice (D) is the correct answer. It connects the purpose of the graphic—to show how transistors have significantly decreased in size—with the conclusion in the passage that transistors have greatly increased in speed.

Paired Passages—Solar Farming

Suggested Passage Map notes:

Passage 1
¶1: Topaz largest solar farm
¶2: benefits of large solar farm
¶3: Topaz located in Cali, built with "low impact" development
¶4: describe layout and structure of Topaz
¶5: larger solar plant to come

Passage 2
¶1: downsides to solar farms - bad for birds
¶2: birds mistake solar panels for water
¶3: rates of birds killed due to energy production source
¶4: negative effects on wildlife could slow down renewable energy production

32. A   **Difficulty:** Medium

Category: Global

Getting to the Answer: When answering a central claim question, ask yourself what the passage is mostly about rather than concentrating on details. Choice (A) describes what the passage is mostly about, the benefits of solar energy production. The other choices are based on misinformation or are details that support the central claim.

33. C   **Difficulty:** Medium

Category: Rhetoric

Getting to the Answer: Watch out for choices that may be mentioned in passing or seem logical but do not reflect the author's overall perspective in Passage 2. While some of the choices are mentioned in the passage, the author's overall viewpoint, that solar farms may have some significant drawbacks, is best summed up by (C).

34. B   **Difficulty:** Medium

Category: Inference

Getting to the Answer: Look for information in the passage about each of the answer choices. Determine which one has the best support. Choice (B) is suggested by the passage in lines 29-31; the author states that developing the land with the least harm to the environment is important to the developer.

35. C   **Difficulty:** Hard

Category: Command of Evidence

Getting to the Answer: Avoid answer choices that do not provide direct evidence to support your answer to the previous question. Choice (C) directly supports the inference that the developer of Topaz is respectful of the environment because it states that the developer had a goal of low-impact development.

36. D   **Difficulty:** Medium

Category: Inference

Getting to the Answer: Use the clues in each answer choice to decide which inference is correct. Paragraph 3 of Passage 2 discusses the various methods of energy and the impact each has had on local bird populations; (D) is correct.

37. A   **Difficulty:** Medium

Category: Command of Evidence

Getting to the Answer: Make sure to choose the quote that best supports the inference you made in the previous question. The correct answer will have information that supports that inference directly. The idea that birds can easily be confused by human-made structures is best supported by (A), which tells how birds have mistaken solar panels for bodies of water.

38. B   **Difficulty:** Medium

Category: Synthesis

Getting to the Answer: Decide which answer choice explains the difference between the two purposes in the most accurate way. Choice (B) is correct. Passage 1 stresses the benefits of solar farms, while Passage 2 takes an opposite approach, showing the negative effects of these farms on birds.

39. D   **Difficulty:** Easy

Category: Vocab-in-Context

Getting to the Answer: Reread the sentence and substitute each word for the target word. The correct answer will fit the context of the sentence. The context of the sentence suggests that only (D) fits. This income was "funneled" into or "moved into," the economy.

40. D   **Difficulty:** Easy

Category: Vocab-in-Context

Getting to the Answer: Reread the sentence. Pretend the target word is a blank and place each choice in the sentence. Decide which word would work best in context. In the context provided, "realize" makes the most sense as a synonym for "recognize." Therefore, (D) is the correct answer.

41. D   **Difficulty:** Easy

Category: Inference

Getting to the Answer: Reread the sentence and figure out what idea the word "surprising" helps the author convey. Choice (D) is correct because it helps convey the idea that, contrary to most people's way of thinking, solar energy can have negative effects on the environment.

42. B   **Difficulty:** Medium

Category: Synthesis

Getting to the Answer: Avoid choices that are suggested by only one of the passages or are not mentioned at all. Choice (B) is the correct answer.

Though the passages convey different points of view on solar farms, both support the generalization that solar farms are an accepted way to generate electricity.

Carbon Dioxide Passage

Suggested Passage Map notes:

¶1: CO_2 concentration increasing, will affect plants and animals

¶2: photosynthesis is nature's way to control CO_2

¶3: humans causing increase from cutting down forests, burning fossils fuels, etc.

¶4: reduce CO_2 output needed but expensive

¶5: research methods to help with CO_2 problem

¶6: plastic that can filter CO_2

¶7: production cost is high, could affect price of gas

43. A   **Difficulty:** Easy

Category: Global

Getting to the Answer: Eliminate answer choices that contain details found in the passage but do not describe the central claim. The passage's central claim is about methods being developed to help remove carbon dioxide from the air. Choice (A) is the correct answer.

44. D   **Difficulty:** Medium

Category: Command of Evidence

Getting to the Answer: Consider your answer to the previous question. The correct answer to this question will provide the strongest support for the central claim of the passage. The central claim of this passage is primarily concerned with methods being developed to reduce levels of carbon dioxide in the atmosphere. Choice (D) provides the strongest support for this idea because it explains these methods.

45. C   Difficulty: Medium

Category: Connections

Getting to the Answer: Think about the relationship between paragraph 2 and the rest of the passage. Paragraph 2 helps structure the passage by explaining how carbon dioxide is removed from the air naturally through photosynthesis and mentions this in the context of the past. Choice (C) is the correct answer.

46. B   Difficulty: Medium

Category: Detail

Getting to the Answer: Think about why the author compares the filters to leaves. In what ways are the real and artificial leaves similar? In paragraph 6, the author suggests that the filters are like leaves because they can remove carbon dioxide from the air. Choice (B) is the correct answer.

47. A   Difficulty: Hard

Category: Rhetoric

Getting to the Answer: Think about the passage's central idea. Decide which answer choice would be the most meaningful addition to the passage in light of the central idea. The passage is mostly about the development of new methods to remove carbon dioxide from the air. Details about how increased global temperatures, caused by carbon dioxide, would help to explain why removing carbon dioxide from the air is so important. Choice (A) is the correct answer.

48. B   Difficulty: Easy

Category: Vocab-in-Context

Getting to the Answer: Read the sentence and replace "convert" with each of the answer choices. The correct answer will make sense in context and will not change the overall meaning of the sentence. In this context, "convert" most nearly means "change"; therefore, (B) is the correct answer.

49. D   Difficulty: Hard

Category: Inference

Getting to the Answer: For Inference questions, the correct answer will not be stated directly in the passage but will be supported by the details presented. It can be inferred from the passage that people will resist technology that removes carbon dioxide from the air if it is too expensive. Choice (D) is correct.

50. D   Difficulty: Hard

Category: Command of Evidence

Getting to the Answer: Locate each answer choice in the passage and decide which choice provides the strongest support for the answer to the previous question. In paragraph 7, the author discusses how the price of gasoline must increase to cover the cost of building artificial trees that remove carbon dioxide from the air. The author adds that if the cost comes down enough, these towers could be built and used. This supports the conclusion from the previous question that people will resist technology if it is too expensive. Choice (D) is the correct answer.

51. C   Difficulty: Medium

Category: Vocab-in-Context

Getting to the Answer: Before looking at the answer choices, try thinking of synonyms for "commendable" that would make sense in context. Then select the answer choice that closely matches the meaning of the synonym you came up with. In this context, "commendable" most nearly means "admirable." Choice (C) is the correct answer.

52. A   Difficulty: Easy

Category: Synthesis

Getting to the Answer: Study the data provided in the graphic. The correct answer will be a claim from the passage that is supported by the graphic. The passage states: "We can burn fewer fossil fuels by switching to other forms of power that don't release carbon dioxide, such as solar or wind power, but these methods are more expensive" (lines 29-33). The graphic supports this statement with data that show that solar and wind energy are the most expensive methods of reducing carbon dioxide in the air. Therefore, (A) is the correct answer.

WRITING AND LANGUAGE TEST

Vitamin C—Essential Nutrient or Wonder Drug?

1. D   Difficulty: Medium

Category: Effective Language Use

Getting to the Answer: Be wary of choices that are overly wordy and redundant. Look for the option that communicates what is meant in the most concise way. Choice (D) is the correct answer because it is the most concise and effective way of stating the information.

2. B   Difficulty: Medium

Category: Effective Language Use

Getting to the Answer: Pretend the word is a blank in the sentence. Predict which word could be substituted for the blank. Choose the word closest in meaning to your prediction. The sentence goes on to state that Pauling won the Nobel Peace Prize in addition to the Nobel Prize in Chemistry. You can assume that someone who wins a peace prize would be "dedicated" as a humanitarian. The other choices have similar meanings but are less precise in their connotations. Choice (B) is the correct answer.

3. C   Difficulty: Easy

Category: Organization

Getting to the Answer: Look for the relationship between the first part of the sentence and the second part. This will help you choose the appropriate transition word. Choice (C) shows the relationship between the two parts of the sentence and how the ideas contrast with one another. The transition word "however" suggests this contrast of ideas.

4. C   Difficulty: Easy

Category: Development

Getting to the Answer: Look for the sentence that does not support the central idea about the relationship between vitamin C and good health. Choice (C) does not reflect the central idea of the paragraph, which is about the relationship between vitamin C and good health. Instead, (C) focuses on the origins of the word "scurvy," making it the least relevant sentence and, therefore, the correct answer.

5. B   Difficulty: Medium

Category: Effective Language Use

Getting to the Answer: Read the sentence with each of the answer choices to see which one makes the most sense within the context of the sentence. In paragraph 2, the author calls Pauling "one of the earliest, and most famous, of the vitamin C supporters." This makes it clear that Pauling and others thought that increased amounts of vitamin C would be helpful. As a chemist, Pauling based his beliefs on reasoning so the word that makes the most sense in this context is "reasoned." Choice (B) is correct.

6. D   Difficulty: Easy

Category: Sentence Formation

Getting to the Answer: Two complete thoughts should be two separate sentences or clauses. Be careful of inappropriate transition words or incorrect punctuation. Think about how clauses that are closely related to each other can be connected but separate. The semicolon is one option for dividing two complete thoughts that are closely tied to one another. Choice (D) is correct.

7. D   Difficulty: Hard

Category: Development

Getting to the Answer: To find the sentence that offers the strongest support, look for the sentence that provides the most detailed evidence. Choice (D) has the most precise details about how much sick time is reduced when a lot of vitamin C is taken. It gives specific data that provide stronger support for the claim. (D) is the correct answer.

8. B   Difficulty: Easy

Category: Usage

Getting to the Answer: Read the entire paragraph to establish the verb tense. Identify the key verbs in the paragraph and their tenses. The verbs "is," "can," and "absorb" are present tense, making (B) the correct choice.

9. C   Difficulty: Medium

Category: Punctuation

Getting to the Answer: Study the words in the series. Decide which punctuation is required. Only one option includes the correct punctuation. Choice (C) is correct.

10. C   Difficulty: Medium

Category: Effective Language Use

Getting to the Answer: Watch out for choices that may have incorrect transition words and that may change the intended meaning of the sentence. Choice (C) joins the sentences concisely and correctly by using a transition word that makes sense in the context of the sentences. A comma plus the word "and" combines the two complete ideas.

11. A   Difficulty: Easy

Category: Organization

Getting to the Answer: Read the entire paragraph and then read each of the choices. Decide which one is a fitting conclusion for the rest of the information in the paragraph and the passage. Be careful of details that do not relate to the entire paragraph. Choice (A) best concludes the paragraph by stating the overall idea of the paragraph and of the entire passage.

The Familiar Myth

12. A   Difficulty: Hard

Category: Effective Language Use

Getting to the Answer: Read the entire paragraph for context clues and to assess the author's intention in the sentence. Then determine which adjective offers the most appropriate meaning. The author states that Campbell's work holds the "key" to understanding the topic at hand, implying that Campbell's book is influential and important. The correct answer is (A), as "seminal" means "highly influential."

13. D   Difficulty: Medium

Category: Usage

Getting to the Answer: Review the entire paragraph to understand what verb tense the author is using to convey the information. Then determine whether and how the sentence needs to change to become grammatically correct. The paragraph is about Jermaine's research on what Campbell said in the past, which creates a precedent for using the past tense. Only (D) adjusts the sentence so it consistently uses the past tense, making it the correct choice.

14. B   Difficulty: Easy

Category: Punctuation

Getting to the Answer: Review the sentence to assess the subject's ownership in the sentence. Then determine which form of the possessive noun correctly reflects this ownership. The sentence refers to a singular hero going on a journey. Choice (B) is the only choice that shows a singular hero in possession of his or her journey. Therefore, (B) is the correct answer.

15. C   Difficulty: Easy

Category: Usage

Getting to the Answer: Their, they're, and there are often confused with one another. Review each answer choice and choose the one that is logical and grammatically correct. Choice B is both wordy and confusing, and the adverb "there" in choice A refers to a location. Only (C) refers to the journey belonging to the heroes, making it the correct answer.

16. A   Difficulty: Medium

Category: Organization

Getting to the Answer: After reading the paragraph, evaluate each answer choice to determine which best summarizes the overall message of the paragraph. The paragraph discusses Jermaine's exploration of different cultures and how they tell stories using monomyth legends. The only choice that accurately summarizes this idea is (A), thus making it the correct answer.

17. D   Difficulty: Medium

Category: Sentence Formation

Getting to the Answer: In a parallel sentence, a series of items or actions that begin with a specific pattern must retain that pattern throughout. Review the sentence to ensure the items in the series follow a grammatically correct and parallel pattern. The sentence is not parallel as written because there is a break in the verb-noun pattern. Choice (D) corrects this problem.

18. C   Difficulty: Easy

Category: Sentence Formation

Getting to the Answer: Decide whether the underlined portion creates a grammatically correct and logical flow of ideas. If not, select the answer choice that does so. As is, the second "sentence" is a fragment, as it does not have both a verb and a subject. Choice (C) correctly combines the sentences.

19. D   Difficulty: Hard

Category: Punctuation

Getting to the Answer: Assess the relationship between the two portions of the sentences separated by the underlined punctuation. Then determine which answer choice creates a grammatically correct sentence with a logical relationship between each portion. Because the portion of the sentence that falls after the dash offers further explanation of the preceding portion (explaining what else the fire represents), a colon is the best choice. A comma would be grammatically incorrect; while a period is tempting, it indicates a stronger break than necessary between the two clauses. Choice (D) is the correct answer.

20. B   Difficulty: Easy

Category: Usage

Getting to the Answer: Reread the sentence to determine the correct relationship between the pronouns and the antecedent. Select the answer choice that creates a grammatically correct sentence. The two appearances of the pronoun "its" are singular and do not match the antecedent, "stories," which is plural. Choice (B) is correct because it creates a sentence that uses the proper pronoun "their" in each location to match the antecedent.

21. D   Difficulty: Hard

Category: Development

Getting to the Answer: Assess the paragraph's purpose and determine which additional fact noted in the answer choices would best complete the paragraph. The purpose of the paragraph is to explain how myths from different cultures share common ideals and symbols. Including the location of the Kayapo Indians' homeland would provide support that fits well within the existing paragraph, as the author has already included locations for other examples. Thus, (D) is correct.

22. B   Difficulty: Medium

Category: Effective Language Use

Getting to the Answer: Read the paragraph for context clues and determine which word's definition most appropriately matches the context. The author makes the point in the paragraph that the monomyth is widely accepted and understood. Answer choice (B) is correct, as it offers the definition that best conveys this idea.

America's Love for Streetcars

23. B   Difficulty: Medium

Category: Usage

Getting to the Answer: A pronoun such as "they" should always have a clear relationship to its antecedent. If it doesn't, then a revision is needed. The pronoun "they" is unclear; as used, it could refer to the rails or the trolleys themselves. Choice D introduces an error because a dependent clause cannot begin after a semicolon. Only (B) clarifies what the sentence means and is therefore the correct answer.

24. A   Difficulty: Easy

Category: Organization

Getting to the Answer: Identify in your own words what this paragraph is primarily about. Which choice matches your idea? The paragraph includes positive

information about trolleys in America. Choice (A) is correct.

25. C   Difficulty: Medium

Category: Effective Language Use

Getting to the Answer: Consider what each item in this series is communicating. Look at what items can be eliminated to make the sentence flow better while still making grammatical sense. All three of the ideas in this series say essentially the same thing. The entire list can be made more concise by shortening it to "were faster." Choice (C) is correct.

26. D   Difficulty: Hard

Category: Development

Getting to the Answer: The correct answer should provide information that adds support or additional detail to the prior sentences. The rest of the paragraph discusses the change to intercity trolleys and their financial advantage over steam railroads. Choice (D) provides an additional detail that shows how intercity trolleys were used by those needing to save money and is the correct answer.

27. B   Difficulty: Easy

Category: Usage

Getting to the Answer: Substitute each answer choice to see if one would make a good replacement for "rationalizing." Note the differences in meaning between these similar-looking words. "Rationalizing" means "justifying." In the context of the sentence, this does not make sense. However, (B), "rationing," means "distributing a limited amount among a group." This is what was done with gasoline during World War II. Choice (B) is correct.

28. C   Difficulty: Hard

Category: Effective Language Use

Getting to the Answer: Consider the subtle differences among the answer choices. Which best applies to a situation in which interest is renewed in an idea? As written, the sentence containing "resumption," which suggests starting where one left off after a brief pause or interruption. This is not quite an accurate description of what happened to the interest in interurban lines. In the previous sentence, "renewed interest in" clearly points to the idea of becoming popular again. Only (C), "renaissance," accurately conveys a "rebirth" of interest in the trolley lines. Choice (C) is correct.

29. B   **Difficulty:** Medium

Category: Organization

Getting to the Answer: Pay close attention to the events described in this paragraph and the words that signal a relationship among them. Then decide on a logical order for the sentences. To help ideas flow logically, it makes more sense to place the current sentence 2, in which the Model-T is introduced, before the current sentence 1, in which the increased availability of automobiles affects trolley operations. The word "however" in sentence 2 also suggests that the invention of the automobile should come as a surprise after whatever information has just been presented. Therefore, sentence 2 should follow the previous paragraph, in which trolleys seem to be popular and successful. Choice (B) is, therefore, the correct answer.

30. A   **Difficulty:** Medium

Category: Effective Language Use

Getting to the Answer: Remember that when connected ideas are combined into one sentence, the new sentence often eliminates some of the repeated words. The original sentences begin with the same words: "Critics argue. . . . " To create sentence variety, these sentences can be combined to express both ideas. Choices C and D still repeat the word "critics," which is unnecessary. Choice B is grammatically correct but changes the sentence's intended meaning by removing the cause-and-effect relationship between the speed and cost efficiency of modern streetcars. Only (A) combines the sentences in a concise and grammatically correct way. It uses "modern streetcars," the subject of the phrase beginning with

"that," as the subject for the verbs "aren't" and "will be." Choice (A) is the correct answer.

31. B   **Difficulty:** Medium

Category: Quantitative

Getting to the Answer: Study the graphic carefully and consider how its information connects to the content of the passage. The graphic shows that the use of cars is dominant in the United States as a whole but that a substantial percentage of residents in Washington, DC, uses public transportation. As written, the sentence ignores the popularity of public transportation in Washington, DC, so A is incorrect. Choice D is not supported, as there is no way to tell from the graphic how these numbers are changing. Choice C states the situation backward: it is in urban areas that public transportation is most useful. Choice (B) is correct because its information is supported directly by the graphic.

32. A   **Difficulty:** Medium

Category: Effective Language Use

Getting to the Answer: When presented with answer choices that are similar in meaning, reread the paragraph for context. Then choose the word with the connotation that best fits the context. A "revival" is an exciting event that provokes strong emotion. Only (A) accurately expresses the enthusiasm these communities feel about this revival and is the correct choice.

33. D   **Difficulty:** Easy

Category: Punctuation

Getting to the Answer: Determine whether all of the underlined terms are included as part of a list, and if so, punctuate them according to the rules for items in a series. All four items do seem to be part of a list; they are all attributes of public transportation. Therefore, a comma should be placed between each item in the list, and, in addition, a comma should be placed after "fast," because it ends a dependent clause. Choice (D) is correct.

Educating Early

34. B   **Difficulty:** Medium

Category: Effective Language Use

Getting to the Answer: Decide whether the words in the underlined portion of the sentence maintain the overall meaning and context of the paragraph. Determine which choice offers a clearer meaning. "Consisting of" means "made up of," which connects to the ideas in the next sentence listing the occupations that make up the field of early childhood education. Choice (B) is correct.

35. A   **Difficulty:** Easy

Category: Punctuation

Getting to the Answer: Carefully review the sentence as written to decide whether there is an error. Determine whether the two parts of the sentence can stand independently. The phrase "as well as a healthy measure of fun" cannot stand on its own because it lacks a verb, so the sentence is correct as written. Choice (A) is correct.

36. B   **Difficulty:** Easy

Category: Punctuation

Getting to the Answer: Determine whether the list of items is a series needing commas. Commas should separate only the items in the series. Because there is a list of attributes in the sentence, commas should be used to separate the items. However, a comma is not needed to separate "physically" from "energetic," as "physically" is an adverb that modifies "energetic." Choice (B) is correct.

37. C   **Difficulty:** Medium

Category: Punctuation

Getting to the Answer: Establish whether both of the underlined sentences are punctuated correctly to convey the author's meaning. If not, how can you change the punctuation to correct the problem? The period after "positions" is inappropriately placed, creating the sentence "A high school diploma is sufficient." This sentence does not make sense given that the previous sentence said that varying levels of training are required. Placing the period after "required" creates two sentences that make sense together. Choice (C) is correct.

38. A   **Difficulty:** Medium

Category: Sentence Formation

Getting to the Answer: Make sure the verbs in a series maintain the same grammatical structure. Parallel ideas must be expressed in the same grammatical form. Here, the infinitive "listening" is paired with the infinitives "learning" and "enjoying school." This maintains the same grammatical form throughout the series. Choice (A) is correct.

39. D   **Difficulty:** Medium

Category: Usage

Getting to the Answer: Look back to find what subject the verb must match. Then review the rest of the paragraph to determine the correct verb tense. "Lessons" is plural and the paragraph uses the present tense, so (D) is correct.

40. B   **Difficulty:** Hard

Category: Development

Getting to the Answer: Analyze the sentences of the paragraph to establish the overarching idea. Most of the sentences in the paragraph pertain to the growth of the field and opportunities for employment; therefore, (B) is correct.

41. C   **Difficulty:** Easy

Category: Usage

Getting to the Answer: Check that the pronoun agrees with its antecedent in number and gender. Remember that an apostrophe can indicate possession or a contraction. The antecedent, "preschool," is singular and the context requires the use of a possessive. The possessive form of "it" does not take an apostrophe. Choice (C) is correct.

42. D   Difficulty: Medium

Category: Effective Language Use

Getting to the Answer: Consider whether the word fits with the context clues in the rest of the paragraph. Test the other choices in its place to identify a more precise meaning. The paragraph focuses on positive growth and outcomes in the field of early childhood education. The adjective "enduring" accurately conveys a steady, lasting growth in the jobs in this field. Choice (D) is the most precise of the answer choices and is, therefore, correct.

43. B   Difficulty: Hard

Category: Development

Getting to the Answer: Identify the central idea of the paragraph before choosing the correct answer. The sentences in this paragraph all refer to the prospects for the job market in ECE. The paragraph offers evidence that more ECE programs are being funded to illustrate steady growth in the field. The correct answer will need to provide similar evidence. Choice (B) is correct.

44. A   Difficulty: Easy

Category: Quantitative

Getting to the Answer: Keep the central claim of the passage in mind as you review the graphic. The graphic shows that the vast majority of ECE jobs are in schools and day care centers. Choice (A) is correct.

MATH—NO CALCULATOR TEST

1. A   Difficulty: Easy

Category: Heart of Algebra / Linear Equations

Getting to the Answer: In the scenario, there are a specified number of cards in the deck, from which 3 are removed, or subtracted. This means b must represent the initial number of cards in the deck, from which the remaining cards ($b - 3$) are distributed, or divided, equally among the players. This means c

must represent the number of players among whom the cards are divided, making (A) correct. Although it is not asked for in the question, the result of performing all the operations (a) represents the number of cards each player receives.

2. A   Difficulty: Medium

Category: Passport to Advanced Math / Functions

Getting to the Answer: The function represents the number of kits the hospital will have, so $k(b)$ is the total number of kits. The question tells you that b is the number of boxes ordered, which you also know to be 50. Because b is multiplied by 12, this must be the number of kits per box. Finally, 32 is simply added to the equation, which must mean it represents the kits left over from last year's charity drive. Now, look at the question. It states that the company has changed the number of kits per box to 8. Evaluate the original function at $b = 50$ to see how many kits the hospital would have had: $k(50) = 12(50) + 32 = 632$.

Now, substitute this for $k(b)$ in the new function, replacing the 12 with the 8, and solve for b:

$$632 = 8b + 32$$
$$600 = 8b$$
$$75 = b$$

Be careful—this is not the answer. She needs to order $75 - 50 = 25$ more boxes than she would have had to order at 12 kits per box. Choice (A) is correct.

3. D   Difficulty: Medium

Category: Additional Topics in Math / Geometry

Getting to the Answer: Corresponding sides of similar triangles are proportional, and corresponding angles are congruent. You can eliminate B immediately because corresponding angles of similar triangles are congruent, so they are always in a 1:1 ratio. You can also eliminate A because side CA does not correspond to side DG (CA corresponds to DO), so you cannot say that they will be in the same ratio. Because the side lengths are proportional, when you add all the side lengths (the perimeter), this number will be in the same proportion, so (D) is correct. You can check this by assigning numbers that are in the ratio 2:7 and finding the perimeter of each triangle:

$TC = 2$ and $GD = 7$

$CA = 4$ and $DO = 14$

$AT = 6$ and $OG = 21$

Perimeter of triangle $CAT = 2 + 4 + 6 = 12$

Perimeter of triangle $DOG = 7 + 14 + 21 = 42$

The ratio is 12:42 which reduces to 2:7.

4. D   Difficulty: Medium

Category: Passport to Advanced Math / Exponents

Getting to the Answer: Whenever simplifying a square root, look for the largest perfect square of each factor. Bring the square root of the perfect squares outside the radical.

$$\sqrt{16x^9y^6}$$
$$= \sqrt{(4)^2 \cdot \left(x^4\right)^2 \cdot x \cdot \left(y^3\right)^2}$$
$$= 4x^4y^3\sqrt{x}$$

This matches (D).

5. B   Difficulty: Medium

Category: Heart of Algebra / Systems of Linear Equations

Getting to the Answer: Don't try to extend the graphs in a question like this. The answers are very close together, and it would be easy to make a mistake. Instead, think algebraically—the solution to a system of equations is the ordered pair that satisfies both equations. Thus, you need to find the equation of each line and solve the system using substitution.

Start with the top line. Its y-intercept is 8, and it falls 1 unit for every 2 units it runs, so its slope is $-\dfrac{1}{2}$, making the equation $y = -\dfrac{1}{2}x + 8$. The bottom line has a y-intercept of –2, and it rises 1 unit for every

3 units is runs, so its slope is $\dfrac{1}{3}$, making its equation $y = \dfrac{1}{3}x - 2$.

Set the two equations equal to one another. Multiply everything by the common denominator, 6, to clear the fractions. Then, solve for x:

$$\frac{1}{3}x - 2 = -\frac{1}{2}x + 8$$
$$2x - 12 = -3x + 48$$
$$5x = 60$$
$$x = 12$$

You do not need to substitute 12 for x and solve for y because there is only one answer with an x-coordinate of 12, which means (B) must be correct.

6. B   Difficulty: Medium

Category: Passport to Advanced Math / Exponents

Getting to the Answer: When you find the language confusing, try to put it in concrete terms. If you wanted to know how much more 8 was than 5, what would you do? You would subtract $8 - 5 = 3$ more. So you need to subtract these two algebraic expressions. Don't forget to distribute the negative when simplifying the difference:

$$\left(7x^2 + 3\right) - \left(7x^2 - 9\right) = \cancel{7x^2} + 3 - \cancel{7x^2} + 9 = 12$$

Choice (B) is correct.

7. D   Difficulty: Medium

Category: Passport to Advanced Math / Quadratics

Getting to the Answer: Changing the coefficient of x^2 from -3 to $-\dfrac{1}{3}$ will make the graph narrower or wider (in this case, wider), which means the only things that will change are the x-intercepts. This means you can eliminate A and B. To choose between C and (D), recall that fraction coefficients (between 0 and 1) result in wider graphs, so the x-intercepts will spread out and therefore be farther from the origin.

8. B **Difficulty:** Medium

Category: Heart of Algebra / Linear Equations

Getting to the Answer: This question has multiple fractions, so start by clearing the $\frac{9}{4}$ by multiplying both sides of the equation by its reciprocal, $\frac{4}{9}$. You might have to repeat this process to eliminate any remaining fractions.

$$\frac{9}{4}\left(x - \frac{7}{3}\right) = 5$$

$$\frac{\cancel{4}}{\cancel{9}}\left[\frac{\cancel{9}}{\cancel{4}}\left(x - \frac{7}{3}\right)\right] = \frac{4}{9}(5)$$

$$x - \frac{7}{3} = \frac{20}{9}$$

There are still a couple of fractions in the equation, so multiply by the common denominator this time, which is 9.

$$9\left(x - \frac{7}{3}\right) = \cancel{9}\left(\frac{20}{\cancel{9}}\right)$$

$$9x - 21 = 20$$

$$9x = 41$$

$$x = \frac{41}{9}$$

Choice (B) is correct.

9. A **Difficulty:** Medium

Category: Passport to Advanced Math / Functions

Getting to the Answer: Think about the scenario—if c represents the maximum number of crates (which is 4,000), then the range can certainly never be greater than this, so eliminate C and D. Now you need to think about the meaning of *range*—range refers to y-values, not x-values, so substitute 4,000 for c (which represents x in this scenario) to find that the y-values must fall between 0 and 100. The range consists only of integers because the question states that the machine does not pack partial boxes, so (A) is correct.

10. C **Difficulty:** Medium

Category: Heart of Algebra / Linear Equations

Getting to the Answer: You can't graph the given equation on the grid (because the y-intercept is too high), so find the equation of line K shown in the graph and go from there. Line K intersects the y-axis at -4. From there, it rises 4 units and runs 3 units to the next point, making its equation $y = \frac{4}{3}x - 4$. Now, you could set this equation equal to the one in the question and solve for x, or you could recognize that the two lines have the same slope but different y-intercepts, which means they are parallel lines and will never intersect, (C).

11. C **Difficulty:** Medium

Category: Heart of Algebra / Linear Equations

Getting to the Answer: Sometimes, the best way to answer a conceptual question, particularly one that involves graphs without number labels, is to add your own numbers to the graph. Then you can try to make sense of the axis labels and the numbers you added. Add reasonable numbers to each graph that make sense for that graph. Choice (C) is correct because logically, a more-effective herbicide requires fewer ounces to eliminate all of the weeds. In the sample graph that follows, the more effective herbicide (which is m) only takes 3 ounces to achieve 0% weeds remaining, while the less effective one (which is l) takes 5 ounces to produce the same results.

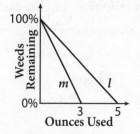

12. C **Difficulty:** Medium

Category: Heart of Algebra / Inequalities

Getting to the Answer: Although the answer choices are given in decimal form, don't convert the fractions in the inequalities to decimals—this will create very messy calculations. Solve each inequality for t by first clearing all the fractions.

First inequality:

$$4\left(t - \frac{3}{4}\right) > 4\left(\frac{3}{2}\right)$$
$$4t - 3 > 6$$
$$4t > 9$$
$$t > \frac{9}{4}$$

Second inequality:

$$12\left(\frac{t}{4} - \frac{1}{3}\right) < \cancel{12}\left(\frac{5}{\cancel{12}}\right)$$
$$3t - 4 < 5$$
$$3t < 9$$
$$t < 3$$

Now, because the answer choices are given in decimal form, convert $\frac{9}{4} = 2\frac{1}{4} = 2.25$. The correct answer is greater (but not equal) to 2.25 and less than 3. The only answer that falls within this range is 2.75, making (C) correct.

13. B   Difficulty: Medium

Category: Passport to Advanced Math / Exponents

Getting to the Answer: A *double zero* occurs in a polynomial when a factor is repeated, or in other words, squared. For example, the factor $(x - a)$ produces a simple zero at $x = a$, while $(x - b)^2$ produces a double zero at $x = b$. The polynomial has a simple zero at $x = 4$, which corresponds to a factor of $(x - 4)$, and all of the answers include this factor. The double zero at $x = -\frac{1}{3}$ results from a repeated (squared) factor, so you can eliminate C and D. To choose between A and (B), set each factor equal to 0 and then use inverse operations to solve for x (mentally if possible). The polynomial in A has zeroes at 4 and -3 (not $-\frac{1}{3}$), so you can eliminate A. Choice (B) is correct because it has a double zero when:

$$3x + 1 = 0$$
$$3x = -1$$
$$x = -\frac{1}{3}$$

14. A   Difficulty: Medium

Category: Additional Topics in Math / Geometry

Getting to the Answer: The formula for finding the area of a triangle is $A = \frac{1}{2}bh$. In the case of a right

triangle, the base and height are simply the legs of the triangle. To use the lengths given, you need to interpret the inequality. The longest side of a right triangle (which is side BC here) is always the hypotenuse, so you only know the length of one leg. Find the length of the other leg by using the Pythagorean Theorem (or by recognizing a 6-8-10 triangle):

$$a^2 + b^2 = c^2$$
$$a^2 + 6^2 = 10^2$$
$$a^2 + 36 = 100$$
$$a^2 = 64$$
$$a = 8$$

Now, substitute the lengths of the legs into the area formula and simplify:

$$A = \frac{1}{2} \times 6 \times 8 = \frac{1}{2} \times 48 = 24$$. Choice (A) is correct.

15. D   Difficulty: Hard

Category: Passport to Advanced Math / Exponents

Getting to the Answer: You're told that either of the two water-bottle-sized filters can filter the whole supply in 8 hours. This means one of these filters works at a rate of $\frac{1}{8}$ of the supply per hour. Likewise, the larger filter's rate is $\frac{1}{4}$ of the supply per hour. Add them all together, set them equal to $\frac{1}{t}$ (the rate for the entire task), and solve for t:

$$\frac{1}{8} + \frac{1}{8} + \frac{1}{4} = \frac{1}{t}$$
$$t\left(\frac{1}{8} + \frac{1}{8} + \frac{1}{4}\right) = \cancel{t}\left(\frac{1}{\cancel{t}}\right)$$
$$\frac{t}{8} + \frac{t}{8} + \frac{t}{4} = 1$$
$$\frac{2t}{8} + \frac{2t}{8} = 1$$
$$\frac{4t}{8} = 1$$
$$4t = 8$$
$$t = 2$$

Therefore, working together, it would take all three filters 2 hours, (D), to filter the entire water supply.

16. 1/3 or **.333**   **Difficulty:** Easy

Category: Heart of Algebra / Linear Equations

Getting to the Answer: Sketch the reflection on the grid in your test booklet:

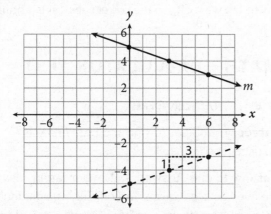

Use your sketch to count the vertical change and the horizontal change from one point to the next. Remember—slope is *rise over run*. The slope of the reflected line is $\frac{1}{3}$. Grid this in as 1/3 or .333.

17. 1   **Difficulty:** Medium

Category: Heart of Algebra / Inequalities

Getting to the Answer: Whenever expressions involve fractions, you can clear the fractions by multiplying each term in the expression by the least common denominator. Don't forget—when working with inequalities, if you multiply or divide by a negative number, you must flip the inequality symbol(s). The inequality in this question is a compound inequality, but you don't need to break it into parts. Just be sure that anything you do to one piece of the inequality, you do to all three pieces. Start by multiplying everything by 8 to clear the fractions.

$$0 \leq \frac{1-k}{2} < \frac{7}{8}$$

$$8(0) \leq {}^{4}\cancel{8}\left(\frac{1-k}{\cancel{2}}\right) < \cancel{8}\left(\frac{7}{\cancel{8}}\right)$$

$$0 \leq 4(1-k) < 7$$

$$0 \leq 4 - 4k < 7$$

$$-4 \leq -4k < 3$$

$$\frac{-4}{-4} \geq \frac{-4k}{-4} > \frac{3}{-4}$$

$$1 \geq k > -\frac{3}{4}$$

Turn the inequality around so the numbers are increasing from left to right: $-\frac{3}{4} < k \leq 1$. This tells you that k is less than or equal to 1, making 1 the maximum possible value of k.

18. 1/2 or **.5**   **Difficulty:** Medium

Category: Passport to Advanced Math / Functions

Getting to the Answer: Jot down the first few points and look for a pattern. The points are (0, 2,400), (1, 1,200), (2, 600), (3, 300), and so on. This means each y-value is half the previous value, so b, which is the decay rate, is $\frac{1}{2}$. Grid this in as 1/2 or .5.

19. 3/4 or **.75**   **Difficulty:** Hard

Category: Additional Topics in Math / Imaginary Numbers

Getting to the Answer: To evaluate a high power of i, look for patterns and use the definition $\sqrt{-1} = i$, which can be written in a more useful form as $i^2 = -1$. Write out enough powers of i that allow you to see the pattern:

$$i^1 = i$$
$$i^2 = -1\,(\text{definition})$$
$$i^3 = i \times i^2 = i \times -1 = -i$$
$$i^4 = i^2 \times i^2 = -1 \times -1 = 1$$
$$i^5 = i^4 \times i = 1 \times i = i$$
$$i^6 = i^4 \times i^2 = 1 \times -1 = -1$$
$$i^7 = i^6 \times i = -1 \times i = -i$$
$$i^8 = i^4 \times i^4 = 1 \times 1 = 1$$

Notice that the pattern $(i, -1, -i, 1, i, -1, -i, 1)$ repeats on a cycle of 4. To evaluate i^{42}, divide 42 by 4. The result is 10, remainder 2, which means 10 full cycles, and then back to i^2. This means i^{42} is equivalent to i^2, which is -1. Do the same for i^{60}: $60 \div 4 = 15$, remainder 0, which means stop on the 4th cycle to find that $i^{60} = 1$. Make these substitutions in the original equation:

$$\frac{1}{4}i^{42} + i^{60} = \frac{1}{4}(-1) + 1 = -\frac{1}{4} + 1 = \frac{3}{4}$$

Grid in the answer as 3/4 or .75.

20. 4   Difficulty: Hard

Category: Passport to Advanced Math / Functions

Getting to the Answer: Sometimes in a real-world scenario, you need to think logically to get a mental picture of what is happening. Think about the concentration of the medicine—it starts at 0, increases to a maximum of 0.375, and then decreases again as it begins to wear off. This means the concentration is 0.3 two times—once before it hits the max and once after. In this case, you're looking for the second occurrence. Set the function equal to 0.3 and solve for t. Don't stress out about the decimals—as soon as you have the equation in some kind of standard form, you can move the decimals to get rid of them.

$$0.3 = \frac{1.5t}{t^2 + 4}$$
$$0.3(t^2 + 4) = 1.5t$$
$$0.3t^2 + 1.2 = 1.5t$$

To make the equation easier to work with, move the decimal one place to the right in each term. The result is a fairly nice quadratic equation. Move everything to the left side, factor out a 3, and go from there.

$$3t^2 + 12 = 15t$$
$$3t^2 - 15t + 12 = 0$$
$$3(t^2 - 5t + 4) = 0$$
$$3(t - 1)(t - 4) = 0$$

$$t - 1 = 0 \quad \text{and} \quad t - 4 = 0$$
$$t = 1 \quad \text{and} \quad t = 4$$

Don't forget, you're looking for the second occurrence of a 0.3 concentration (after the medicine has started to wear off), so the correct answer is 4 hours.

MATH—CALCULATOR TEST

1. B   Difficulty: Easy

Category: Problem Solving and Data Analysis / Statistics and Probability

Getting to the Answer: The mean rating means the average score given. To find the average, multiply each score by the number of times it occurs (the frequency). Then, add the results and divide by the total number of scores, 20. The sum of the ratings is $(2 \times 4) + (3 \times 6) + (4 \times 8) + (5 \times 2) = 8 + 18 + 32 + 10 = 68$.

Divide by the number of ratings to find that the mean is $68 \div 20 = 3.4$, which is (B).

2. C   Difficulty: Easy

Category: Heart of Algebra / Linear Equations

Getting to the Answer: Find the difference in the costs of shipping each type of wood by substituting the two values given for p and then subtracting.

$$C = 6.5p + 16$$
$$C(\text{hardwood}) = 6.5(170) + 16 = 1,121$$
$$C(\text{softwood}) = 6.5(80) + 16 = 536$$
$$\$1,121 - \$536 = \$585$$

Choice (C) is correct.

3. B   Difficulty: Easy

Category: Heart of Algebra / Inequalities

Getting to the Answer: Use the DIRT formula, Distance = rate × time, and solve for time. Then, substitute the value given for distance, 1,907. Remember, m is the rate in this scenario. All of the inequality symbols are the same, so look for the inequality with the proper relationship among distance, rate, and time.

$$d = r \times t$$

$$\frac{d}{r} = t$$

$$t = \frac{1,907}{m}$$

Choice (B) is correct.

4. D   Difficulty: Easy

Category: Passport to Advanced Math / Exponents

Getting to the Answer: Don't let this rational equation intimidate you. Rather than finding a common denominator, move the 16 to the other side of the equation, write it over 1, and use cross-multiplication. Don't forget to check that your solution doesn't cause the denominator to be 0. If it does, then it's an invalid solution. After moving the 16, cross-multiply and then solve for x using inverse operations.

$$\frac{3x + 7}{x - 2} - 16 = 0$$

$$\frac{3x + 7}{x - 2} = \frac{16}{1}$$

$$3x + 7 = 16(x - 2)$$

$$3x + 7 = 16x - 32$$

$$3x + 39 = 16x$$

$$39 = 13x$$

$$3 = x$$

When substituted into the denominator of the original equation, 3 does not cause division by 0, so it is a valid solution, making (D) correct.

5. C   Difficulty: Easy

Category: Problem Solving and Data Analysis / Rates, Ratios, Proportions, and Percentages

Getting to the Answer: Write out the ratios of the prices and the ratings: 1.89 to 5.49 and 2.8 to 8.2.

Set up a proportion with the life expectancy and either ratio. Let e be the unknown life expectancy of the high-end carpet.

$$\frac{1.89}{5.49} = \frac{5}{e}$$

$$1.89e = 27.45$$

$$e = 14.52$$

You can check your answer using the other ratio:

$$\frac{2.8}{8.2} = \frac{5}{e}$$

$$2.8e = 41$$

$$e = 14.64$$

The high-end carpeting can be expected to last about 15 years, (C).

6. D   Difficulty: Medium

Category: Problem Solving and Data Analysis / Statistics and Probability

Getting to the Answer: Read the axis labels carefully. Neither axis indicates how many people are in each age bracket, so you have no idea what will happen after the two brackets are removed. Therefore, there is not enough information to determine what effect, if any, it will have on either the median or the mean, which is (D).

7. C   Difficulty: Medium

Category: Heart of Algebra / Linear Equations

Getting to the Answer: Draw a quick sketch of the line described and compare it to the answer choices. Don't forget, the quadrants start with I in the upper right corner and move counterclockwise. A sample sketch follows:

Notice that the line is increasing, so the slope is positive ($m > 0$). This means you can eliminate A and B. The line crosses the y-axis below the origin, so b is negative ($b < 0$), which means (C) is correct.

8. A   Difficulty: Medium

Category: Heart of Algebra / Linear Equations

Getting to the Answer: Compare the two lines. The second line (2014) has a lower y-intercept than the first (2013), which means the company reduced its fixed costs. You don't need to worry about the 50% because all the answer choices involve this same amount. You can eliminate B and C because they don't mention fixed costs. To determine whether the variable costs changed, look at the slopes. The lines are parallel, so the slope did not change, which means the variable costs did not change. Therefore, the company only reduced its fixed costs, and (A) is correct.

9. B   Difficulty: Medium

Category: Heart of Algebra / Systems of Linear Equations

Getting to the Answer: This system is set up perfectly to solve using substitution because both equations are already solved for y. Set both x expressions equal to one another and solve. Multiply the whole equation by 4 first, to get rid of the fractions.

$$4 \times \left[\frac{1}{4}x - 3 = -\frac{5}{2}x + 8 \right]$$
$$1x - 12 = -10x + 32$$
$$11x = 44$$
$$x = 4$$

The question asks for the y-coordinate of the solution, so substitute 4 for x in either equation and solve for y.

$$y = \frac{1}{4}(4) - 3$$
$$y = 1 - 3$$
$$y = -2$$

Choice (B) is correct.

As an alternate method, because the equations are already in slope-intercept form, you could graph both equations in your calculator and find the point of intersection, which is (4, −2).

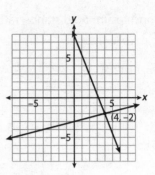

10. D   Difficulty: Medium

Category: Problem Solving and Data Analysis / Statistics and Probability

Getting to the Answer: Because the mean weights are different and you do not know how many male or how many female babies there are in the NICU, you need to reason logically to arrive at the correct answer. The mean weight of the female babies is lower than that of the male babies, so the combined mean cannot be greater than or equal to that of the male babies. Similarly, the mean weight of the male babies is greater than that of the female babies, so the combined mean cannot be less than or equal to the mean weight of the female babies. In other words, the combined mean weight must fall somewhere between the two means, making (D) correct.

11. A   Difficulty: Medium

Category: Additional Topics in Math / Trigonometry

Getting to the Answer: Use the given sine value (but think of it as $\frac{8}{10}$) and SOH CAH TOA. The sine of an angle is the ratio of the opposite side to the hypotenuse. You know from the figure that the hypotenuse is 10, so the length of the opposite side (AC) must be 8. Don't stop there—the question asks for the length of side AB, which is not the opposite side, so either use the Pythagorean theorem to find the other side length, or you might recognize that the triangle is a 6-8-10 triangle. Choice (A) is correct.

12. B   Difficulty: Medium

Category: Problem Solving and Data Analysis / Rates, Ratios, Proportions, and Percentages

Getting to the Answer: A question like this requires planning. Start by figuring out how much of the loan the couple has already paid down and how much they still have left to meet their goal. If they have reduced the principal amount by 10%, they have paid the loan down to $100 - 10 = 90\%$ of its original value. Use the formula % × whole = part to get $220,000 × 0.9 = $198,000 remaining on the principal. So, after two years, the value of the loan is $198,000, which means the couple still have $198,000 − $170,000 = $28,000 of the principal loan amount left to pay off to reach their goal. Now, determine what percent of the remaining whole this constitutes using the same formula again. The percent is unknown this time, so call it p:

$$p \times 198,000 = 28,000$$
$$p = 28,000 \div 198,000 = 0.1414 = 14.14\%$$

Therefore, the couple needs to pay down approximately 14%, (B), of the current principal amount to reach their goal.

13. C   Difficulty: Medium

Category: Passport to Advanced Math / Quadratics

Getting to the Answer: The graph of a parabola is symmetric with respect to its axis of symmetry (the imaginary vertical line that passes through the x-coordinate of the vertex). This means that each x-intercept must be the same distance from the vertex. Take a careful look at the values in the table. The y-values start at 3.5, decrease to a minimum value of -4.5, and then turn around. The points on each side of the minimum have the same y-values (-4), which means you've found the vertex, $(5, -4.5)$. The x-intercept given in the table is $(2, 0)$, which is 3 horizontal units to the left of 5. Therefore, the other x-intercept must be 3 horizontal units to the right of 5, which is $(8, 0)$. This means (C) is correct.

14. C   Difficulty: Easy

Category: Problem Solving and Data Analysis / Statistics and Probability

Getting to the Answer: The question asks about vegetarian and vegan dishes, so you are only concerned with those two columns. Find the total number of vegetarian and vegan dishes: $1 + 3 + 5 + 4 + 1 + 1 + 1 + 4 + 2 + 0 = 22$. You need to determine the fraction of these dishes that received a health score greater than 2 (which means 3 or higher), so look at those 3 rows of the last 2 columns and add those amounts: $5 + 4 + 1 + 4 + 2 + 0 = 16$. Now, write a fraction that represents 16 out of 22 and reduce to get $\dfrac{16}{22} = \dfrac{8}{11}$, which is (C).

15. A   Difficulty: Medium

Category: Problem Solving and Data Analysis / Statistics and Probability

Getting to the Answer: Reword the question: Find the probability that the student randomly chooses a dish that is both meat *and* has a health score of at least 4. This tells you that you are only interested in the combinations meat/4 and meat/5. The probability of randomly selecting one of these two combinations is (number of meat/4 + number of meat/5) divided by (number of all dishes). Now read the table and do the math. To save a bit of time, recall that you already found the total number of vegetarian and vegan dishes (22) in the previous question, so all you need to do is add the meat dishes:

$$p = \frac{5 + 0}{3 + 4 + 8 + 5 + 22} = \frac{5}{42}$$

Choice (A) is correct.

16. A   Difficulty: Medium

Category: Passport to Advanced Math / Exponents

Getting to the Answer: Don't worry too much about the scientific information. All you really need to know is that k is the viscosity, which means you're solving the equation for k.

The inverse of taking a fourth root is raising to the fourth power, so start by raising both sides of the equation to the fourth power to remove the radical, and then go from there.

$$(r)^4 = \sqrt[4]{\dfrac{8kl}{\pi R}}$$

$$r^4 = \dfrac{8kl}{\pi R}$$

$$r^4 \pi R = 8kl$$

$$\dfrac{r^4 \pi R}{8l} = k$$

This matches (A).

17. D   Difficulty: Medium

Category: Heart of Algebra / Systems of Linear Equations

Getting to the Answer: Write a system of equations with m = the number of muffins and c = the number of cartons of milk. Before you choose your answer, make sure you answered the right question (the cost of two cartons of milk). Translate from English into math to write the two equations: The first statement is translated as $2m + c = \$3.35$ and the second as $5m + c = \$5.60$. The system is

$$\begin{cases} 2m + c = 3.35 \\ 5m + c = 5.60 \end{cases}$$

You could solve the system using substitution, but elimination is quicker in this question, because subtracting the second equation from the first eliminates c, and you can solve for m:

$$\begin{array}{r} 2m + c = 3.35 \\ - (5m + c = 5.60) \\ \hline -3m = -2.25 \\ m = 0.75 \end{array}$$

Substitute this value for m in the first equation, and solve for c:

$$2(0.75) + c = 3.35$$
$$1.5 + c = 3.35$$
$$c = 1.85$$

So two cartons of milk would cost $2 \times \$1.85 = \$3.70$, (D).

18. D   Difficulty: Medium

Category: Problem Solving and Data Analysis / Scatterplots

Getting to the Answer: You are told that the function is exponential, which means the y-values are *not* changing by a constant amount (which is supported by the values in the calculator screenshot). You can immediately eliminate B and C because these describe linear functions (the value decreases by a constant amount each time). To choose between A and (D), think logically about how the graph would be labeled (if it had labels). The value of a car *depends* on how many miles it has been driven, so *value* would be plotted along the y-axis, and *miles driven* would be plotted along the x-axis. Now, apply this to the values in the calculator screenshot. The miles driven (x) increase by 5,000 each time, and for every 5,000-mile increase, the value of the car drops. This means (D) is correct. To check this answer, you can multiply each y-value in the table by $100 - 12 = 88\%$, or 0.88, to see if the values are in fact decreasing by 12% each time (which they are).

19. B   Difficulty: Medium

Category: Passport to Advanced Math / Quadratics

Getting to the Answer: Although you could set the second equation equal to 0 and solve for x, the solution can be found simply by looking at the graph. The statement $f(x) = 5$ means to find the x-values on the graph when y is 5. To do this, draw a horizontal line across the graph at $y = 5$ and read the x-coordinates of the points where the line intersects the parabola.

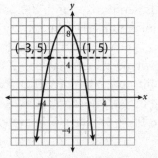

The function $y = -x^2 - 2x + 8$ has x-values of -3 and 1 when $y = 5$, so (B) is correct.

20. B   Difficulty: Medium

Category: Problem Solving and Data Analysis / Rates, Ratios, Proportions, and Percentages

Getting to the Answer: Because the figures in the pie chart are given as percentages, the ratio will be the same no matter how many voters there are in the district. All you need to do is compare Republicans to Independents. The question does not specify an age range, so add both together for each. The district consists of $14 + 28 = 42$ parts Republican and $9 + 3 = 12$ parts Independent, so the ratio is 42:12, which reduces to 7:2, (B).

21. C   Difficulty: Medium

Category: Heart of Algebra / Linear Equations

Getting to the Answer: Think about the question conceptually before you examine the graphs. The question asks about late fees *only*, not total charges. If the movies are returned on time, or 0 days late, the late fees will be $0, so the graph must start at the origin. Eliminate B and D. Next, the question asks about *total* late fees for all four movies. The late fee is $0.50 per movie per day, so the late fee for all four movies is $4 \times \$0.5 = \$2$ per day. This means (C) must be correct because the points increase at a rate of $2 per day. (Note that A shows the possible late fees for returning one movie late.)

22. D   Difficulty: Medium

Category: Problem Solving and Data Analysis / Rates, Ratios, Proportions, and Percentages

Getting to the Answer: Let the units in this question guide you to the solution. The thawing rates of the different methods are given in pounds, but one is given in pounds per day and the other in pounds per 30 minutes. Start by converting pounds to ounces. There are 16 ounces in 1 pound, so 4 pounds is 64 ounces and 1 pound is 16 ounces. Now, use the factor-label method to incorporate the time conversions.

Refrigerator Method:

$$\frac{64 \text{ oz}}{1 \text{ day}} \times \frac{1 \text{ day}}{24 \text{ hrs}} \times 2 \text{ hrs} = 5.33 \text{ oz}$$

Cold Water Method:

$$\frac{16 \text{ oz}}{30 \text{ min}} \times \frac{60 \text{ min}}{1 \text{ hr}} \times 2 \text{ hrs} = 64 \text{ oz}$$

In 2 hours, the cold water method can thaw approximately $64 - 5.33 = 58.67$ or about 59 more ounces, (D).

23. A   Difficulty: Medium

Category: Problem Solving and Data Analysis / Rates, Ratios, Proportions, and Percentages

Getting to the Answer: There are two rates and two times involved, so organize the information in a table.

	Distance	Rate	Time
Normal Trip	200	r	t
Faster Trip	200	$r + 10$	$t - 1$

Use the equation Distance = rate × time to set up a system of equations. The result is $200 = rt$ and $200 = (r + 10)(t - 1)$. Solve the system by solving the first equation for r and substituting the result into the second equation: $200 = rt \rightarrow r = \dfrac{200}{t}$.

Tip: Go ahead and FOIL the factors in the second equation before substituting the value of r.

$$200 = (r + 10)(t - 1)$$
$$200 = rt + 10t - r - 10$$
$$200 = \left(\frac{200}{t}\right)t + 10t - \frac{200}{t} - 10$$
$$200 = 200 + 10t - \frac{200}{t} - 10$$
$$0 = 10t - \frac{200}{t} - 10$$

Factor out a 10, find a common denominator, and you'll have a fairly nice quadratic equation to solve.

$$0 = 10\left(t - \frac{20}{t} - 1\right)$$
$$0 = \frac{t^2 - 20 - t}{t}$$
$$0 = t^2 - t - 20$$
$$0 = (t - 5)(t + 4)$$

The two solutions are $t = 5$ and $t = -4$. Time can't be negative, so $t = 5$. Substitute this back into the first equation (because the question asks about her original speed) and solve for r. Her normal speed is $\frac{200}{5} = 40$ miles per hour, (A).

You could also start with the answer choices and work backward. Start with (A): If her normal speed is 40 mph, then her time would be $200 \div 40 = 5$ hours. If she increases her speed 10 mph, then her time would be $200 \div 50 = 4$ hours. This represents a savings of 1 hour, which makes 40 mph the correct answer. This is a faster approach, but keep in mind that had this been a grid-in question, an algebraic solution would be necessary.

24. C   Difficulty: Medium

Category: Heart of Algebra / Linear Equations

Getting to the Answer: When a question asks for a number that results in the *same* amount of something, it usually means writing an equation with one expression set equal to the other. Let m represent the number of movie rentals. The Movie Super Fan package costs $75 for unlimited rentals, so write 75 on one side of the equal sign. The other package costs $2.50 per rental (not including the first 10 rentals), or $2.5(m - 10)$, plus a flat $20 fee for those first 10 rentals, so write $2.5(m - 10) + 20$ on the other side of the equal sign. Simplify the right-hand side of the equation and then solve for m.

$$75 = 2.5(m - 10) + 20$$
$$75 = 2.5m - 25 + 20$$
$$80 = 2.5m$$
$$32 = m$$

Renting 32 movies would result in equal package costs, so (C) is correct. Note that you could also work backward from the answer choices (even though it may use up valuable time). Try 32 in the scenario: The first 10 movies are free, so you must pay for 22 at a cost of $2.50 each, making the total cost of the Movie Fan package $20 + 22($2.50) = $75.

25. D   Difficulty: Hard

Category: Passport to Advanced Math / Functions

Getting to the Answer: Let n be the number of caps ordered. The supplier charges $6 per cap for up to and including 25 caps, so the first inequality should be the cost of the cap multiplied by the number ordered, or $6n$, given that $n \le 25$. You can eliminate B because it does not include 25 in the "if" statement. The distributor then charges $5 per cap for the next 75 caps, which means n is greater than 25, but less than or equal to $25 + 75 = 100$. The cost of the total order would be the cost of the first 25 caps ($6 \times 25 = 150$) added to the amount of the next set of caps, which is $5 times the number ordered minus the first 25 ordered (because they are at the $6 price point), or $150 + 5(n - 25)$, so you can now eliminate A. For the final price point, the inequality is simply any order of caps greater than 100, or $n > 100$. The cost equation is the cost of the first 25 caps (150) plus the cost of the next 75 caps ($75 \times 5 = 375$) plus the cost of the final set of caps, $4 multiplied by the number ordered, minus the first 100 ordered (because they are at either the $5 or $6 price points). The result is $525 + 4(n - 100)$, making (D) correct.

26. A   Difficulty: Hard

Category: Problem Solving and Data Analysis / Scatterplots

Getting to the Answer: One of the keys to doing well on Test Day is knowing when (and how) to use your calculator and when it would be quicker to solve something conceptually or by hand. You might try graphing the equation in your calculator, but finding a good viewing window may be very time-consuming. Instead, think about what you know about quadratic functions and how to evaluate them.

Skim through the answer choices to see which ones are easiest to eliminate. The question states that the function is quadratic; therefore, the population cannot be decreasing at a *constant* rate (or the function would be linear), so eliminate B. A quick examination of the equation tells you that the parabola opens downward ($-0.5x^2$) and its vertex has been shifted up 22,000 units to (0, 22,000). Because $x = 0$ represents 2015, for all years after 2015 (to the right of 0), the graph will always be decreasing, which means you can eliminate D. The other two choices involve actual numbers, so go back to A. The year 2225 is 210 years after 2015, so the statement translates as "at $x = 210$, $p(x) = 0$ (or less, depending on the month of the year)," which means $p(210) = 0$. Substitute 210 for x in the equation and see what happens (this is where your calculator is needed): $p(210) = -0.5(210)^2 + 22,000 = -50$. The population can't be negative, but this tells you that by the end of the year 2225, there will be no more of this species, meaning it will be extinct, so (A) is correct.

27. A   Difficulty: Hard

Category: Additional Topics in Math / Geometry

Getting to the Answer: Use the formula for finding the volume of a cylinder, $V = \pi r^2 h$. The well is 6 feet wide; this is its diameter, so $r = 3$. The height of the well is 60 feet, but the water table is 40 feet below ground level, which means only $60 - 40 = 20$ feet of the well is below the water table and thus has water in it, so $h = 20$.

$$V = \pi (3)^2 (20)$$
$$V = \pi (9)(20)$$
$$V = 180\pi$$

This matches (A).

28. A   Difficulty: Hard

Category: Heart of Algebra / Linear Equations

Getting to the Answer: You do not have enough information to answer this question using rules of transformations. Instead, you'll need to write the

equation of the original line, then follow the criteria given to change the equation and find the point. You already know the slope of the original line ($m = -2$), but you need the y-intercept. You also know a point through which the line passes. Plug the x- and y-values of this point into slope-intercept form of a line, and solve for b.

$$5 = -2(3) + b$$
$$5 = -6 + b$$
$$11 = b$$

The equation of the original line is $y = -2x + 11$. If Ramon doubles the slope, it goes from -2 to -4. If he shifts the line down one unit, the y-intercept becomes $11 - 1 = 10$, so the equation of the new line is $y = -4x + 10$. Graph the line in your graphing calculator and see that it passes through the point $(3, -2)$, which is (A). You could also plug the x- and y-values of the points in the answer choices into the new equation to see which one results in a true statement, but this could take more time depending on which choice is correct.

29. B   Difficulty: Hard

Category: Problem Solving and Data Analysis / Scatterplots

Getting to the Answer: Examine the graph, including the axis labels and numbering. On the vertical axis, there are 5 parts to each 1 unit, which means each grid-line represents 0.2 points on the Richter scale. So you are looking for points that are 5 or more grid-lines away from the line of best fit. There are 3 points that meet this criterion (one before 2004 and two between 2010 and 2011). Now, count the total number of data points: There are 11, and $3 \div 11 = 0.2727$, or about 27 percent, (B).

Note that you could also do the math to find that the magnitude predicted by the line of best fit is 5.6, so you're looking for points with a y-value of 4.6 or lower and 6.6 or greater.

30. A   Difficulty: Hard

Category: Passport to Advanced Math / Quadratics

Getting to the Answer: This is a quadratic equation, so you need one side to equal 0 and then, best-case scenario, you'll be able to factor. If not, you can rely on the quadratic formula. First, subtract 3 from both sides of the equation. Then multiply everything by 9 to clear the fractions.

$$\frac{2}{9}x^2 + \frac{8}{3}x - 7 = 3$$

$$\frac{2}{9}x^2 + \frac{8}{3}x - 10 = 0$$

$$9\left(\frac{2}{9}x^2 + \frac{8}{3}x - 10\right) = 9(0)$$

$$2x^2 + 24x - 90 = 0$$

Each number in the equation is divisible by 2, so factor out a 2 and go from there.

$$2x^2 + 24x - 90 = 0$$

$$2\left(x^2 + 12x - 45\right) = 0$$

$$2(x + 15)(x - 3) = 0$$

The solutions are −15 and 3, but be careful! The question asks for the product of the solutions, so the correct answer is (−15)(3) = −45 and (A) is correct.

31. 2   Difficulty: Easy

Category: Heart of Algebra / Inequalities

Getting to the Answer: When a question asks for the value of an expression, rather than the value of the variable alone, try to determine how the desired expression is related to what is given in the question. Notice that $7 - p$ is half of $14 - 2p$. This means you can cut all parts of the inequality in half to arrive at the correct answer.

$$\frac{-10}{2} < \frac{14 - 2p}{2} < \frac{6}{2}$$

$$-5 < 7 - p < 3$$

There is no need to solve for p because the question asks about $7 - p$. The inequality (<) doesn't include 3, so the greatest possible integer value of $7 - p$ is 2.

32. 25   Difficulty: Easy

Category: Passport to Advanced Math / Functions

Getting to the Answer: Pay careful attention to the axis labels as you read the answer choices. Time is graphed on the x-axis and distance is graphed on the y-axis. Try to visualize what is happening as Umberto runs his errands. Umberto was inside the bank and inside the post office when time was passing, but his distance was not changing (because he was stopped). This means you're looking for the portions of the graph where the line is horizontal (because distance is graphed on the vertical axis and you want no vertical change). This occurs from (10, 4) to (20, 4) and from (35, 6) to (50, 6). This means he spent 10 minutes in the bank and 15 minutes in the post office, for a total of 25 minutes in both.

33. 75   Difficulty: Medium

Category: Problem Solving and Data Analysis / Rates, Ratios, Proportions, and Percentages

Getting to the Answer: The test consists of a total of 50 + 30 = 80 questions. Selena has already answered 48 of the 80 questions. This means she has 80 − 48 = 32 questions left. She has used up 50 of the 90 minutes, leaving 40 minutes to complete the test. To find the amount of time per question she has left, divide the remaining time by the number of questions remaining: 40 minutes ÷ 32 questions = 1.25 minutes per question. Don't forget to change your answer to seconds. There are 60 seconds in 1 minute, so multiply 1.25 × 60 to find that she has 75 seconds per question.

34. 9.4   Difficulty: Hard

Category: Additional Topics in Math / Geometry

Getting to the Answer: Finding the area of a sector of a circle (the shaded region) requires knowing the degree measure of the corresponding interior angle. Given that information, your first step is to find the area of the entire circle. Then you'll find the proportional amount represented by the sector. To find the area of a circle, the only thing you need is the radius.

The radius is not shown in the figure, so you will have to think about special right triangles. In the figure, triangle ABO is formed by 2 radii and a 90° angle. This means the triangle must be a 45-45-90 triangle, and therefore its side lengths are in the ratio $1:1:\sqrt{2}$. The hypotenuse is given as $6\sqrt{2}$ so the side lengths of the triangle, and therefore the radius of the circle, must be 6, and the area of the entire circle is $A = \pi r^2 = \pi(6)^2 = 36\pi$. Now you need to find the portion of the circle represented by the shaded region by finding the measure of the angle inside the sector and dividing by 360. You'll need to use the given arc length, π, and the formula for finding arc length (arc length = θr, where θ is the interior angle and r is the length of the radius):

$$\pi = \theta(6)$$
$$\frac{\pi}{6} = \theta$$

If you know your unit circle, you know this corresponds to 30°. If you don't recall this fact, then you can convert radians to degrees by multiplying the radian measure by $\dfrac{180}{\pi}$ to get:

$$\frac{\cancel{\pi}}{6} \times \frac{180}{\cancel{\pi}} = \frac{180}{6} = 30$$

This means the shaded region makes up $\dfrac{30}{360} = \dfrac{1}{12}$ of the total area of the circle, so divide the total area by 12 to get $36\pi \div 12 = 3\pi$. The question tells you to approximate π using 3.14 and to round to the nearest tenth, so the final answer is 9.4.

35. 1728 Difficulty: Hard

Category: Heart of Algebra / Systems of Linear Equations

Getting to the Answer: Create a system of linear equations where x represents the number of boxes with 48 masks and y represents the number of boxes with 144 masks. The first equation should represent the total number of *boxes*, $x + y = 35$. The second equation should represent the total number of *masks*. Because x represents boxes with 48 masks and y represents boxes with 144 masks, the second

equation is $48x + 144y = 2{,}832$. Now solve the system using substitution. Solve the first equation for either variable; then substitute the result into the second equation:

$$x + y = 35$$
$$x = 35 - y$$
$$48(35 - y) + 144y = 2{,}832$$
$$1{,}680 - 48y + 144y = 2{,}832$$
$$96y = 1{,}152$$
$$y = 12$$

So 12 boxes have 144 masks. Because the question asks about boxes of 144, you don't need to find the value of x—but you're not done yet. The question asks how many *masks* the hospital would receive if it buys all of the boxes of 144 the supplier has, not the number of boxes. The hospital would receive $12 \times 144 = 1{,}728$ masks.

36. 5.5 Difficulty: Hard

Category: Problem Solving and Data Analysis / Scatterplots

Getting to the Answer: The y-intercept of the line in the graph is 2.5. Once Patricia removes the point, it is 2, which means the line is adjusted downward. The slope of the line, however, is steeper, which means the change in y-values will be greater compared to the change in x-values. Sketch this new line on the graph. After drawing the new line, you can see that the line still fits the data, except for point (9, 5.5), which has now become an outlier. This must have been the point Patricia eliminated, so grid in 5.5.

37. 9092 Difficulty: Medium

Category: Problem Solving and Data Analysis / Rates, Ratios, Proportions, and Percentages

Getting to the Answer: Break the solution into short steps.

Step one: Determine how many days total the company needs to make reimbursements for by multiplying the number of employees by the average number of days they each go to the gym: $246 \times 84 = 20{,}664$.

Step two: Determine the amount of money the company must reimburse per day by multiplying the daily reimbursement rate, 0.2% by the cost of the membership: $\$220 \times 0.002 = \$0.44$.

Step three: Find the total amount the company must pay in reimbursements by multiplying the total number of days for which it must make reimbursements by the amount it must pay per day: $20{,}664 \times \$0.44 = \$9{,}092.16 = \$9{,}092$.

38. 4887 **Difficulty:** Hard

Category: Problem Solving and Data Analysis / Rates, Ratios, Proportions, and Percentages

Getting to the Answer: Again, break the solution into short steps.

Step one: Determine how many days an employee needed to visit the gym to earn the bonus day off by multiplying the number of days in the year, 365, by 60%. The result is 219, but the question says more than 60% of the days, so an employee must have gone at least 220 days to qualify for the bonus day off.

Step two: Determine how many employees qualified for this benefit by looking to see what percent (according to the pie graph) went to the gym the required number of days. Then, multiply this number by the number of employees who participated in the health program: $246 \times 0.16667 = 41$ employees.

Step three: Find the total number of hours for which the company must pay for the days off: $41 \times 8 = 328$ hours.

Step four: Calculate the total cost of this benefit by multiplying by the average hourly rate: $328 \times \$14.90 = \$4{,}887.2$, which rounded to the nearest whole dollar is $\$4{,}887$.

ESSAY TEST RUBRIC

The Essay Demonstrates . . .

4—Advanced	• **(Reading)** A strong ability to comprehend the source text, including its central ideas and important details and how they interrelate; and to effectively use evidence (quotations, paraphrases, or both) from the source text
	• **(Analysis)** A strong ability to evaluate the author's use of evidence, reasoning, and/or stylistic and persuasive elements, and/or other features of the student's own choosing; make good use of relevant, sufficient, and strategically chosen support for the claims or points made in the student's essay; and focus consistently on features of the source text that are most relevant to addressing the task
	• **(Writing)** A strong ability to provide a precise central claim; create an effective organization that includes an introduction and conclusion, as well as a clear progression of ideas; successfully employ a variety of sentence structures; use precise word choice; maintain a formal style and objective tone; and show command of the conventions of standard written English so that the essay is free of errors
3—Proficient	• **(Reading)** Satisfactory ability to comprehend the source text, including its central ideas and important details and how they interrelate; and use evidence (quotations, paraphrases, or both) from the source text
	• **(Analysis)** Satisfactory ability to evaluate the author's use of evidence, reasoning, and/or stylistic and persuasive elements, and/or other features of the student's own choosing; make use of relevant and sufficient support for the claims or points made in the student's essay; and focus primarily on features of the source text that are most relevant to addressing the task
	• **(Writing)** Satisfactory ability to provide a central claim; create an organization that includes an introduction and conclusion, as well as a clear progression of ideas; employ a variety of sentence structures; use precise word choice; maintain an appropriate formal style and objective tone; and show control of the conventions of standard written English so that the essay is free of significant errors
2—Partial	• **(Reading)** Limited ability to comprehend the source text, including its central ideas and important details and how they interrelate; and use evidence (quotations, paraphrases, or both) from the source text
	• **(Analysis)** Limited ability to evaluate the author's use of evidence, reasoning, and/or stylistic and persuasive elements, and/or other features of the student's own choosing; make use of support for the claims or points made in the student's essay; and focus on relevant features of the source text
	• **(Writing)** Limited ability to provide a central claim; create an effective organization for ideas; employ a variety of sentence structures; use precise word choice; maintain an appropriate style and tone; or show command of the conventions of standard written English, resulting in certain errors that detract from the quality of the writing

1—Inadequate	• **(Reading)** Little or no ability to comprehend the source text or use evidence from the source text
	• **(Analysis)** Little or no ability to evaluate the author's use of evidence, reasoning, and/or stylistic and persuasive elements; choose support for claims or points; or focus on relevant features of the source text
	• **(Writing)** Little or no ability to provide a central claim, organization, or progression of ideas; employ a variety of sentence structures; use precise word choice; maintain an appropriate style and tone; or show command of the conventions of standard written English, resulting in numerous errors that undermine the quality of the writing

ESSAY RESPONSE #1 (ADVANCED SCORE)

In this speech, Churchill raises the specter of war in order to build the argument that the United States and Britain must prepare for war. Churchill takes an oblique approach to his argument by not coming right out and explaining his purpose. Instead, he begins by tackling the underlying motivators that he believes justify his goal. "The lights are going out," he warns, intimating that a great darkness has begun to sweep over Europe and the world. In the next lines, he establishes a kinship with his audience by invoking principles that the people of Britain and the United States have come to value: "liberties," "uncensored expression," "freedom," and "parliamentary government." He emphasizes the impending nature of the disaster with phrases such as "while time remains," suggesting that darkness will soon rule, and that the freedoms cherished by his listeners will soon be gone if they do not act.

Churchill's speech rests on a powerful appeal to emotion. First implicitly and then explicitly, he calls his audience to defend what they cherish and to resist what they fear. "The lights are going out" is metaphorical persuasion. Churchill invokes this rhetorical device to inspire fear and elicit the response that he wants, which he explains in greater detail later in the speech.

Churchill goes on to offer details supporting the theory that liberty and freedom are in danger—not only in Europe but also in the United States—in order to build a case for his culminating point. In the second paragraph, he cites the fall of the Czechoslovak Republic as evidence that darkness—even evil—is on the march. He continues to establish common ground with his audience by suggesting a certain like-mindedness with the American people: They already know what he knows. They understand what many British people do not—that appeasement will have "far-reaching consequences." The implication is that those consequences will prove disastrous and are tied to the encroaching dark of the first paragraph.

Churchill begins the third paragraph with a rhetorical question designed to elicit a specific response. To the question, "Has any benefit or progress ever been achieved by the human race by submission to organised and calculated violence?" the only answer can be "No." Churchill goes on to assert that this submission threatens the liberties that the United States and Britain have come to treasure. Churchill lists three such rights to drive home the importance of such liberty: "the right of the individual; his right to be consulted in the government of his country; his right to invoke the law even against the State."

Then, in the next paragraph, he creates a contrast with those rights by listing the forces that seek to sweep out the lights of freedom: "racial persecution, religious intolerance, deprivation of free speech, the conception of the citizen as a mere soulless fraction of the State," and "the cult of war." Again, Churchill is using powerful appeals to emotion: these are all things to be feared. He describes the state of repression in which the people of Germany and Czechoslovakia have been seized, and draws a comparison to the Communists, a political organization already feared by many within the United States. This is the fate that awaits Britain and the United States, if they do not take action to stop it.

Churchill brings his argument full circle with his final two paragraphs. "The culminating question," he says, is whether a world of hope, enjoyment, tradition, and science can survive by responding to the "menace" described in the preceding paragraph "by submission or by resistance." Here, Churchill draws a clear distinction between the light of the United States, Britain, and friendly nations and the dark that threatens them all. More significantly, he draws a distinction between continuing policies that let the darkness go unchecked and taking action to stop it.

Churchill addresses his audience's fear of waging war by asking the question that is undoubtedly in their minds: "Is this a call to war?" Churchill dispels this impending criticism and fear by reasoning that preparing to resist—to defend against—a great threat does not itself amount to starting a war. He asks only that the nations and their people be ready, that they not be caught like the people of Czechoslovakia. This preparation to resist, he argues, "is the sole guarantee of peace." The only way to avoid war, he seems to say, is to be ready for war.

Churchill makes clear his call that the United States and Britain must amass their military forces, that they have an obligation to do so to guard against not only the military threat of Nazi Germany but also the "moral aggression" that endangers the ideological underpinnings of their common society. This is the response that he sought to elicit with his opening invocation of fear. If the Nazis continue unchecked, the American and British way of life could be destroyed. In his final sentence, Churchill brings his speech back to the emotional appeal of its beginnings, echoing his previous warning that "the lights are going out." The United States and Britain must prepare for war because it is the threat of war that already looms over them—a "fear which already darkens the sunlight to hundreds of millions." To keep the lights on, they must be prepared to fight.

ESSAY RESPONSE #2 (PROFICIENT SCORE)

Churchill makes his speech on October 16, 1938, before World War II has officially begun. However, Churchill makes clear that horrible events are on the move. Churchill does not explain his main purpose right off the bat. He starts instead by making an emotional appeal to his audience—the people of the United States as well as the people of Britain who are also listening. He gets their attention by hitting on their fears. "The lights are going out," he says. By this, he suggests that a darkness is sweeping over Europe and threatens to sweep over the world. It is not just Europe, but also the United States, that is in danger. This darkness, he suggests, will wipe out values held by both Americans and British: "liberties," "uncensored expression," "freedom," and "parliamentary government." He says that he must tell the people of the United States a truth, "while time remains." The underlying implication is that Nazi Germany is a dark force—perhaps an evil force—bent on extinguishing the light of the United States and Britain. This wording builds toward Churchill's ultimate argument that the American and British people must protect what they love and defend against what they fear.

In the next paragraphs, Churchill gives supporting details that make the connection between the dark of Nazi Germany and the light of American and British liberties and freedoms. He reaches out to the American people as already knowing what he is telling them, as already understanding the dire consequences of inaction, of abandoning the Czechoslovakian people. In this way, he reels in their acceptance of the idea that current policies are doomed to fail. He argues against what he considers "submission to organized and calculated violence." This submission threatens the liberties that the United States and Britain value. Churchill lists three such liberties to drive home their importance. Then, he explains what the darkness trying to sweep out the lights of liberty is: "racial persecution, religious intolerance, deprivation of free speech, the conception of the citizen as a mere soulless fraction of the State," and "the cult of war." These are all things that his audience should fear. When he describes the horrible conditions in which the people of Germany and conquered lands must live, he is showing that this is what could happen to the rest of the world if the threat from Germany is not stopped. Churchill even compares the dark forces of Hitler and the Nazis with Communists, a political movement already feared by many in the United States.

In the final two paragraphs, Churchill makes clear his purpose. He draws a clear distinction between two paths that people hope will preserve the hope and joy and culture of the world: submission or resistance. Churchill has already made clear that submission, or letting the dark tides go unchecked, will not work. Submission can only have negative consequences. Instead, he explains that resistance offers the only hope of peace. "Is this a call to war?" Churchill asks, because he knows that many Americans and British do not want to fight another world war. He explains that preparing to resist a threat does not mean starting a war. He is asking people to get ready for war, not to start a war. He wants to make sure that Britain and the United States are not caught by surprise like Czechoslovakia.

Churchill calls on the United States and Britain to gather their military forces. They cannot simply expect the dark forces of the Nazis to go away, but must be ready to stop the "military and moral aggression" that endangers their societies. The Nazis cannot be left unchecked, he argues. In his final sentence, Churchill recalls the idea of the lights going out. The threat of war is already pulling darkness over the world. Hundreds of millions have already been denied the sunlight. In order to bring the light back, to keep the lights on, the United States and Britain must be prepared to fight.

SAT PRACTICE TEST 5 ANSWER SHEET

Remove (or photocopy) this answer sheet and use it to complete the test. See the answer key following the test when finished.

Start with number 1 for each section. If a section has fewer questions than answer spaces, leave the extra spaces blank.

SECTION 1

1. Ⓐ Ⓑ Ⓒ Ⓓ
2. Ⓐ Ⓑ Ⓒ Ⓓ
3. Ⓐ Ⓑ Ⓒ Ⓓ
4. Ⓐ Ⓑ Ⓒ Ⓓ
5. Ⓐ Ⓑ Ⓒ Ⓓ
6. Ⓐ Ⓑ Ⓒ Ⓓ
7. Ⓐ Ⓑ Ⓒ Ⓓ
8. Ⓐ Ⓑ Ⓒ Ⓓ
9. Ⓐ Ⓑ Ⓒ Ⓓ
10. Ⓐ Ⓑ Ⓒ Ⓓ
11. Ⓐ Ⓑ Ⓒ Ⓓ
12. Ⓐ Ⓑ Ⓒ Ⓓ
13. Ⓐ Ⓑ Ⓒ Ⓓ

14. Ⓐ Ⓑ Ⓒ Ⓓ
15. Ⓐ Ⓑ Ⓒ Ⓓ
16. Ⓐ Ⓑ Ⓒ Ⓓ
17. Ⓐ Ⓑ Ⓒ Ⓓ
18. Ⓐ Ⓑ Ⓒ Ⓓ
19. Ⓐ Ⓑ Ⓒ Ⓓ
20. Ⓐ Ⓑ Ⓒ Ⓓ
21. Ⓐ Ⓑ Ⓒ Ⓓ
22. Ⓐ Ⓑ Ⓒ Ⓓ
23. Ⓐ Ⓑ Ⓒ Ⓓ
24. Ⓐ Ⓑ Ⓒ Ⓓ
25. Ⓐ Ⓑ Ⓒ Ⓓ
26. Ⓐ Ⓑ Ⓒ Ⓓ

27. Ⓐ Ⓑ Ⓒ Ⓓ
28. Ⓐ Ⓑ Ⓒ Ⓓ
29. Ⓐ Ⓑ Ⓒ Ⓓ
30. Ⓐ Ⓑ Ⓒ Ⓓ
31. Ⓐ Ⓑ Ⓒ Ⓓ
32. Ⓐ Ⓑ Ⓒ Ⓓ
33. Ⓐ Ⓑ Ⓒ Ⓓ
34. Ⓐ Ⓑ Ⓒ Ⓓ
35. Ⓐ Ⓑ Ⓒ Ⓓ
36. Ⓐ Ⓑ Ⓒ Ⓓ
37. Ⓐ Ⓑ Ⓒ Ⓓ
38. Ⓐ Ⓑ Ⓒ Ⓓ
39. Ⓐ Ⓑ Ⓒ Ⓓ

40. Ⓐ Ⓑ Ⓒ Ⓓ
41. Ⓐ Ⓑ Ⓒ Ⓓ
42. Ⓐ Ⓑ Ⓒ Ⓓ
43. Ⓐ Ⓑ Ⓒ Ⓓ
44. Ⓐ Ⓑ Ⓒ Ⓓ
45. Ⓐ Ⓑ Ⓒ Ⓓ
46. Ⓐ Ⓑ Ⓒ Ⓓ
47. Ⓐ Ⓑ Ⓒ Ⓓ
48. Ⓐ Ⓑ Ⓒ Ⓓ
49. Ⓐ Ⓑ Ⓒ Ⓓ
50. Ⓐ Ⓑ Ⓒ Ⓓ
51. Ⓐ Ⓑ Ⓒ Ⓓ
52. Ⓐ Ⓑ Ⓒ Ⓓ

correct in Section 1

incorrect in Section 1

SECTION 2

1. Ⓐ Ⓑ Ⓒ Ⓓ
2. Ⓐ Ⓑ Ⓒ Ⓓ
3. Ⓐ Ⓑ Ⓒ Ⓓ
4. Ⓐ Ⓑ Ⓒ Ⓓ
5. Ⓐ Ⓑ Ⓒ Ⓓ
6. Ⓐ Ⓑ Ⓒ Ⓓ
7. Ⓐ Ⓑ Ⓒ Ⓓ
8. Ⓐ Ⓑ Ⓒ Ⓓ
9. Ⓐ Ⓑ Ⓒ Ⓓ
10. Ⓐ Ⓑ Ⓒ Ⓓ
11. Ⓐ Ⓑ Ⓒ Ⓓ

12. Ⓐ Ⓑ Ⓒ Ⓓ
13. Ⓐ Ⓑ Ⓒ Ⓓ
14. Ⓐ Ⓑ Ⓒ Ⓓ
15. Ⓐ Ⓑ Ⓒ Ⓓ
16. Ⓐ Ⓑ Ⓒ Ⓓ
17. Ⓐ Ⓑ Ⓒ Ⓓ
18. Ⓐ Ⓑ Ⓒ Ⓓ
19. Ⓐ Ⓑ Ⓒ Ⓓ
20. Ⓐ Ⓑ Ⓒ Ⓓ
21. Ⓐ Ⓑ Ⓒ Ⓓ
22. Ⓐ Ⓑ Ⓒ Ⓓ

23. Ⓐ Ⓑ Ⓒ Ⓓ
24. Ⓐ Ⓑ Ⓒ Ⓓ
25. Ⓐ Ⓑ Ⓒ Ⓓ
26. Ⓐ Ⓑ Ⓒ Ⓓ
27. Ⓐ Ⓑ Ⓒ Ⓓ
28. Ⓐ Ⓑ Ⓒ Ⓓ
29. Ⓐ Ⓑ Ⓒ Ⓓ
30. Ⓐ Ⓑ Ⓒ Ⓓ
31. Ⓐ Ⓑ Ⓒ Ⓓ
32. Ⓐ Ⓑ Ⓒ Ⓓ
33. Ⓐ Ⓑ Ⓒ Ⓓ

34. Ⓐ Ⓑ Ⓒ Ⓓ
35. Ⓐ Ⓑ Ⓒ Ⓓ
36. Ⓐ Ⓑ Ⓒ Ⓓ
37. Ⓐ Ⓑ Ⓒ Ⓓ
38. Ⓐ Ⓑ Ⓒ Ⓓ
39. Ⓐ Ⓑ Ⓒ Ⓓ
40. Ⓐ Ⓑ Ⓒ Ⓓ
41. Ⓐ Ⓑ Ⓒ Ⓓ
42. Ⓐ Ⓑ Ⓒ Ⓓ
43. Ⓐ Ⓑ Ⓒ Ⓓ
44. Ⓐ Ⓑ Ⓒ Ⓓ

correct in Section 2

incorrect in Section 2

SECTION

3

1. (A) (B) (C) (D)
2. (A) (B) (C) (D)
3. (A) (B) (C) (D)
4. (A) (B) (C) (D)

5. (A) (B) (C) (D)
6. (A) (B) (C) (D)
7. (A) (B) (C) (D)
8. (A) (B) (C) (D)

9. (A) (B) (C) (D)
10. (A) (B) (C) (D)
11. (A) (B) (C) (D)
12. (A) (B) (C) (D)

13. (A) (B) (C) (D)
14. (A) (B) (C) (D)
15. (A) (B) (C) (D)

correct in
Section 3

incorrect in
Section 3

16.
17.
18.
19.
20.

SECTION

4

1. (A) (B) (C) (D)
2. (A) (B) (C) (D)
3. (A) (B) (C) (D)
4. (A) (B) (C) (D)
5. (A) (B) (C) (D)
6. (A) (B) (C) (D)
7. (A) (B) (C) (D)
8. (A) (B) (C) (D)

9. (A) (B) (C) (D)
10. (A) (B) (C) (D)
11. (A) (B) (C) (D)
12. (A) (B) (C) (D)
13. (A) (B) (C) (D)
14. (A) (B) (C) (D)
15. (A) (B) (C) (D)
16. (A) (B) (C) (D)

17. (A) (B) (C) (D)
18. (A) (B) (C) (D)
19. (A) (B) (C) (D)
20. (A) (B) (C) (D)
21. (A) (B) (C) (D)
22. (A) (B) (C) (D)
23. (A) (B) (C) (D)
24. (A) (B) (C) (D)

25. (A) (B) (C) (D)
26. (A) (B) (C) (D)
27. (A) (B) (C) (D)
28. (A) (B) (C) (D)
29. (A) (B) (C) (D)
30. (A) (B) (C) (D)

correct in
Section 4

incorrect in
Section 4

31.
32.
33.
34.

35.
36.
37.
38.

READING TEST

65 Minutes—52 Questions

This section corresponds to Section 1 of your answer sheet.

Directions: Read each passage or pair of passages, then answer the questions that follow. Choose your answers based on what the passage(s) and any accompanying graphics state or imply.

Questions 1-10 are based on the following passage.

The following passage is adapted from Leo Tolstoy's 1873 novel, *Anna Karenina* (translated from the original Russian by Constance Garnett). Prior to this excerpt, one of the major characters, Levin, has realized that he is in love with his longtime friend Kitty Shtcherbatsky.

At four o'clock, conscious of his throbbing heart, Levin stepped out of a hired sledge at the Zoological Gardens, and turned along the path
Line to the frozen mounds and the skating ground,
(5) knowing that he would certainly find her there, as he had seen the Shtcherbatskys' carriage at the entrance.

It was a bright, frosty day. Rows of carriages, sledges, drivers, and policemen were standing in the
(10) approach. Crowds of well-dressed people, with hats bright in the sun, swarmed about the entrance and along the well-swept little paths between the little houses adorned with carving in the Russian style. The old curly birches of the gardens, all their twigs
(15) laden with snow, looked as though freshly decked in sacred vestments.

He walked along the path towards the skating-ground, and kept saying to himself—"You mustn't be excited, you must be calm. What's the matter
(20) with you? What do you want? Be quiet, stupid," he conjured his heart. And the more he tried to compose himself, the more breathless he found himself. An acquaintance met him and called him by his name, but Levin did not even recognize
(25) him. He went towards the mounds, whence came the clank of the chains of sledges as they slipped down or were dragged up, the rumble of the sliding

sledges, and the sounds of merry voices. He walked on a few steps, and the skating-ground lay open
(30) before his eyes, and at once, amidst all the skaters, he knew her.

He knew she was there by the rapture and the terror that seized on his heart. She was standing talking to a lady at the opposite end of the ground.
(35) There was apparently nothing striking either in her dress or her attitude. But for Levin she was as easy to find in that crowd as a rose among nettles. Everything was made bright by her. She was the smile that shed light on all round her. "Is it possible
(40) I can go over there on the ice, go up to her?" he thought. The place where she stood seemed to him a holy shrine, unapproachable, and there was one moment when he was almost retreating, so overwhelmed was he with terror. He had to make
(45) an effort to master himself, and to remind himself that people of all sorts were moving about her, and that he too might come there to skate. He walked down, for a long while avoiding looking at her as at the sun, but seeing her, as one does the sun,
(50) without looking.

On that day of the week and at that time of day people of one set, all acquainted with one another, used to meet on the ice. There were crack skaters there, showing off their skill, and learners clinging
(55) to chairs with timid, awkward movements, boys, and elderly people skating with hygienic motives. They seemed to Levin an elect band of blissful beings because they were here, near her. All the skaters, it seemed, with perfect self-possession, skated
(60) towards her, skated by her, even spoke to her, and were happy, quite apart from her, enjoying the capital ice and the fine weather.

GO ON TO THE NEXT PAGE ▷

Nikolay Shtcherbatsky, Kitty's cousin, in a short jacket and tight trousers, was sitting on a garden seat (65) with his skates on. Seeing Levin, he shouted to him:
"Ah, the first skater in Russia! Been here long? First-rate ice—do put your skates on."

1. According to the passage, how did Levin first know that Kitty was at the Zoological Gardens?

    A) Kitty's carriage was parked near the entrance.

    B) Nikolay said he had been skating with Kitty earlier.

    C) He saw her talking with another woman near the pond.

    D) Kitty invited him to meet her there at a certain time.

2. As used in line 11, "swarmed" most nearly means

    A) invaded.

    B) gathered.

    C) flew.

    D) obstructed.

3. The passage most strongly suggests that which of the following is true of Levin?

    A) He worries about his appearance.

    B) He wants Kitty to be more enthusiastic.

    C) He is a very passionate person.

    D) He is wary of his surroundings.

4. Which choice provides the best evidence for the answer to the previous question?

    A) Lines 8-13 ("It was a bright, frosty day . . . in the Russian style")

    B) Lines 23-28 ("An acquaintance met him . . . merry voices")

    C) Lines 41-47 ("The place where . . . there to skate")

    D) Lines 51-56 ("On that day . . . hygienic motives")

5. What theme does the passage communicate through the experiences of Levin?

    A) Love is a powerful emotion.

    B) People long to have company.

    C) Life should be filled with joy.

    D) People are meant to work hard.

6. The passage most strongly suggests that which of the following is true of how Levin appears to others?

    A) People think that Levin looks agitated because of the way he is acting.

    B) People think that Levin is sick because he seems to be feverish.

    C) People think that Levin seems normal because he is doing nothing unusual.

    D) People think that Levin is in trouble because he is not protecting himself emotionally.

7. Which choice provides the best evidence for the answer to the previous question?

    A) Lines 1-6 ("At four o'clock . . . at the entrance")

    B) Lines 10-13 ("Crowds . . . the Russian style")

    C) Lines 25-31 ("He went . . . he knew her")

    D) Lines 63-67 ("Nikolay Shtcherbatsky . . . your skates on")

8. As used in line 21, "conjured" most nearly means

    A) begged.

    B) created.

    C) summoned.

    D) tricked.

9. The author's use of the word "throbbing" in line 1 implies that Levin

    A) has cut himself badly.

    B) has a sudden pain in his chest.

    C) is about to collapse.

    D) is in an agitated state.

GO ON TO THE NEXT PAGE

10. Based on the tone of this passage, what emotion does the author wish the reader to feel about Levin?

    A) Empathy

    B) Cynicism

    C) Hostility

    D) Disgust

Questions 11-20 are based on the following passage.

This passage is adapted from a speech delivered by President Franklin Roosevelt on January 6, 1941, to the United States Congress. In the passage, Roosevelt reveals his intention to preserve and spread American ideals around the world.

The Nation takes great satisfaction and
much strength from the things which have
been done to make its people conscious of their
Line individual stake in the preservation of democratic
(5) life in America. Those things have toughened the
fibre of our people, have renewed their faith and
strengthened their devotion to the institutions we
make ready to protect.
        Certainly this is no time for any of us to stop
(10) thinking about the social and economic problems
which are the root cause of the social revolution
which is today a supreme factor in the world.
        For there is nothing mysterious about the
foundations of a healthy and strong democracy.
(15) The basic things expected by our people of their
political and economic systems are simple. They are:

• Equality of opportunity for youth and for others.

• Jobs for those who can work.

• Security for those who need it.

(20) • The ending of special privilege for the few.

• The preservation of civil liberties for all.

• The enjoyment of the fruits of scientific progress
in a wider and constantly rising standard of living.
        These are the simple, basic things that
(25) must never be lost sight of in the turmoil and
unbelievable complexity of our modern world. The

inner and abiding strength of our economic and
political systems is dependent upon the degree to
which they fulfill these expectations.
(30)   Many subjects connected with our social
economy call for immediate improvement.
        As examples:

• We should bring more citizens under the coverage
of old-age pensions and unemployment insurance.

(35) • We should widen the opportunities for adequate
medical care.

• We should plan a better system by which persons
deserving or needing gainful employment may
obtain it.

(40)   I have called for personal sacrifice. I am assured of the willingness of almost all Americans to
respond to that call.
        A part of the sacrifice means the payment of
more money in taxes. In my Budget Message I
(45) shall recommend that a greater portion of this
great defense program be paid for from taxation
than we are paying today. No person should try,
or be allowed, to get rich out of this program; and
the principle of tax payments in accordance with
(50) ability to pay should be constantly before our eyes
to guide our legislation.
        If the Congress maintains these principles, the
voters, putting patriotism ahead of pocketbooks,
will give you their applause.
(55)   In the future days, which we seek to make
secure, we look forward to a world founded upon
four essential human freedoms.
        The first is freedom of speech and expression—
everywhere in the world.
(60)   The second is freedom of every person to worship
God in his own way—everywhere in the world.
        The third is freedom from want—which,
translated into world terms, means economic
understandings which will secure to every nation
(65) a healthy peacetime life for its inhabitants—
everywhere in the world.
        The fourth is freedom from fear—which,
translated into world terms, means a world-wide
reduction of armaments to such a point and in
(70) such a thorough fashion that no nation will be in

GO ON TO THE NEXT PAGE ▷

a position to commit an act of physical aggression against any neighbor—anywhere in the world.

That is no vision of a distant millennium. It is a definite basis for a kind of world attainable in
(75) our own time and generation. That kind of world is the very antithesis of the so-called new order of tyranny which the dictators seek to create with the crash of a bomb.

To that new order we oppose the greater
(80) conception—the moral order. A good society is able to face schemes of world domination and foreign revolutions alike without fear.

Since the beginning of our American history, we have been engaged in change—in a perpetual
(85) peaceful revolution—a revolution which goes on steadily, quietly adjusting itself to changing conditions—without the concentration camp or the quick-lime in the ditch. The world order which we seek is the cooperation of free countries, working
(90) together in a friendly, civilized society.

This nation has placed its destiny in the hands and heads and hearts of its millions of free men and women; and its faith in freedom under the guidance of God. Freedom means the supremacy
(95) of human rights everywhere. Our support goes to those who struggle to gain those rights or keep them. Our strength is our unity of purpose. To that high concept there can be no end save victory.

11. The primary purpose of President Roosevelt's speech is to

   A) highlight the individuality inherent in patriotism.

   B) define the basic needs of the country.

   C) request money to support worthy causes.

   D) promote support for essential human rights.

12. Which choice provides the best evidence for the answer to the previous question?

   A) Lines 15-16 ("The basic things . . . are simple")

   B) Lines 30-31 ("Many subjects . . . improvement")

   C) Lines 52-54 ("If the Congress . . . applause")

   D) Lines 55-57 ("In the future days . . . freedoms")

13. As used in line 40, "sacrifice" most nearly means

   A) religious offerings to a deity.

   B) service in the military.

   C) losses of limbs in battle.

   D) surrender of interests to a greater good.

14. The passage most strongly suggests a relationship between which of the following?

   A) Protection of human rights abroad and military service

   B) Spread of freedom abroad and defense of democracy at home

   C) Defeat of tyrants abroad and establishment of democratic government at home

   D) Investment in global democracies abroad and strengthening of patriotism at home

15. Which choice provides the best evidence for the answer to the previous question?

   A) Lines 24-29 ("These are . . . expectations")

   B) Lines 52-54 ("If the Congress . . . applause")

   C) Lines 73-78 ("That is no . . . of a bomb")

   D) Lines 94-97 ("Freedom means . . . unity of purpose")

16. In line 53, "pocketbooks" most nearly refers to

   A) local, state, and national taxes.

   B) war debt accumulated by the nation.

   C) citizens' individual monetary interests.

   D) Americans' personal investment in the defense industry.

GO ON TO THE NEXT PAGE ⟶

17. In lines 73-75 ("That is no . . . generation"),
President Roosevelt is most likely responding to
what counterclaim to his own argument?

A) The spread of global democracy is idealistic
and unrealistic.

B) The defeat of tyrannical dictators in Europe
is implausible.

C) The commitment of the American people to
the war effort is limited.

D) The resources of the United States are
insufficient to wage war abroad.

18. Which choice offers evidence that the spread of
global democracy is achievable?

A) Lines 47-48 ("No person . . . this program")

B) Lines 56-57 ("we look forward . . . human
freedoms")

C) Lines 83-84 ("Since the beginning . . . in
change")

D) Line 97 ("Our strength . . . purpose")

19. In lines 62-66 ("The third is . . . world"), President
Roosevelt sets a precedent by which he would most
likely support which of the following policies?

A) Military defense of political borders

B) Investment in overseas business ventures

C) Aid to nations struggling due to conflict
and other causes

D) Reduction of domestic services to spur job
growth

20. The function of the phrase "the so-called new
order of tyranny" in lines 76-77 is to

A) connect the global conflict for human
rights to citizens on a personal level.

B) demonstrate the power of the global
opposition to the United States.

C) present an alternative vision of the world
without democracy.

D) provide examples of the political and social
revolutions underway.

**Questions 21-31 are based on the following passage
and supplementary material.**

The United States Constitution has been amended 27
times since its ratification. Rights such as freedom of
speech, religion, and press, for example, are granted
by the First Amendment. This passage focuses on the
Nineteenth Amendment, which gave women the right
to vote.

The American political landscape is constantly
shifting on a myriad of issues, but the voting process
itself has changed over the years as well. Electronic
Line ballot casting, for example, provides the
(5) public with instantaneous results, and statisticians
are more accurate than ever at forecasting our next
president. Voting has always been viewed as an
intrinsic American right and was one of the major
reasons for the nation's secession from Britain's
(10) monarchical rule. Unfortunately, although all men
were constitutionally deemed "equal," true equality of
the sexes was not extended to the voting booth until
1920.

The American women's suffrage movement
(15) began in 1848, when Elizabeth Cady Stanton
and Lucretia Mott organized the Seneca Falls
Convention. The meeting, initially an attempt
to have an open dialogue about women's rights,
drew a crowd of nearly three hundred women and
(20) included several dozen men. Topics ranged from
a woman's role in society to law, but the issue of
voting remained a contentious one. A freed slave
named Frederick Douglass spoke eloquently about
the importance of women in politics and swayed
(25) the opinion of those in attendance. At the end of
the convention, one hundred people signed the Seneca Falls Declaration, which demanded "immediate
admission to all the rights and privileges which
belong to [women] as citizens of the United States."
(30) Stanton and Mott's first victory came thirty years
later when a constitutional amendment allowing
women to vote was proposed to Congress in 1878.
Unfortunately, election practices were already a
controversial issue, as unfair laws that diminished
(35) the African American vote had been passed during

GO ON TO THE NEXT PAGE

Reconstruction. Questionable literacy tests and a "vote tax" levied against the poor kept minority turnout to a minimum. And while several states allowed women to vote, federal consensus was hardly (40) as equitable. The rest of the world, however, was taking note—and women were ready to act.

In 1893, New Zealand allowed women the right to vote, although women could not run for office in New Zealand. Other countries began reviewing (45) and ratifying their own laws as well. The United Kingdom took small steps by allowing married women to vote in local elections in 1894. By 1902, all women in Australia could vote in elections, both local and parliamentary.

(50) The suffrage movement in America slowly built momentum throughout the early twentieth century and exploded during World War I. President Woodrow Wilson called the fight abroad a war for democracy, which many suffragettes viewed as (55) hypocritical. Democracy, after all, was hardly worth fighting for when half of a nation's population was disqualified based on gender. Public acts of civil disobedience, rallies, and marches galvanized pro-women advocates while undermining defenders (60) of the status quo. Posters read "Kaiser Wilson" and called into question the authenticity of a free country with unjust laws. The cry for equality was impossible to ignore and, in 1919, with the support of President Wilson, Congress passed (65) the Nineteenth Amendment to the Constitution. It was ratified one year later by three-quarters of the states, effectively changing the Constitution. Only one signatory from the original Seneca Falls Declaration lived long enough to cast her first ballot (70) in a federal election.

America's election laws were far from equal for all, as tactics to dissuade or prohibit African Americans from effectively voting were still routinely employed. However, the suffrage (75) movement laid the groundwork for future generations. Laws, like people's minds, could change over time. The civil rights movement in the mid-to late-twentieth century brought an end to segregation and so-called Jim Crow laws that stifled (80) African American advancement. The Voting Rights Act of 1965 signaled the end of discriminatory

voting laws; what emerged was a free nation guided by elections in which neither skin color nor gender mattered, but only the will of all citizens.

Women's Suffrage in the United States

1848 ➤	Seneca Falls Convention.
1878 ➤	19th Amendment submitted; not ratified.
1911 ➤	Several states now grant women suffrage.
1914 ➤	Start of World War I.
1917 ➤	Picketing at the White House.
1918 ➤	Amendment passes in the House but fails in the Senate.
1919 ➤	Both the House and Senate pass the amendment.
1920 ➤	19th Amendment ratified.

21. The stance the author takes in the passage is best described as that of

A) an advocate of women's suffrage proposing a constitutional amendment.

B) a legislator reviewing the arguments for and against women's suffrage.

C) a scholar evaluating the evolution and impact of the women's suffrage movement.

D) a historian summarizing the motivations of women's suffrage leaders.

22. Lines 71-72 ("America's election laws . . . equal for all") most clearly support which claim?

A) The founders of the Constitution did not provide for free and fair elections.

B) The United States still had work to do to secure equal voting rights for some people.

C) Most women in the United States did not want suffrage and equal rights.

D) The women's suffrage movement perpetuated discriminatory voting laws.

GO ON TO THE NEXT PAGE ➤

23. Which choice provides the best evidence for the answer to the previous question?

    A) Lines 14-15 ("The American . . . in 1848")

    B) Lines 42-43 ("In 1893 . . . to vote")

    C) Lines 64-65 ("Congress . . . the Constitution")

    D) Lines 80-81 ("The Voting Rights Act . . . voting laws")

24. As used in line 58, "galvanized" most nearly means

    A) displaced.

    B) divided.

    C) excited.

    D) organized.

25. The function of lines 76-77 ("Laws, like . . . could change") is to

    A) connect the success of legislative reform with shifts in public sentiment.

    B) dissuade reformers from focusing on grassroots activity rather than political campaigns.

    C) evaluate the effectiveness of judicial rulings based on popular response to public polls.

    D) reject the need for legal actions and court proceedings to attain social change.

26. The passage most strongly suggests that

    A) the American government adapts to the changing needs and ideas of society.

    B) the best-organized reform movements are most likely to achieve their goals.

    C) the nation is more vulnerable to change during the confusion of wartime.

    D) the civil rights movement would not have happened without women suffragists.

27. Which choice provides the best evidence for the answer to the previous question?

    A) Lines 3-7 ("Electronic ballot casting . . . our next president")

    B) Lines 7-10 ("Voting has . . . monarchical rule")

    C) Lines 17-20 ("The meeting . . . dozen men")

    D) Lines 77-80 ("The civil rights . . . advancement")

28. The graphic most clearly illustrates which idea?

    A) The Nineteenth Amendment happened as a result of World War I.

    B) The states slowed reform of national voting rights laws.

    C) Women's suffrage resulted from a slow evolution of events.

    D) Acts of civil disobedience won support for suffrage in Congress.

29. In line 61, the word "authenticity" most nearly means

    A) reliability.

    B) realism.

    C) legitimacy.

    D) truth.

30. The passage suggests that President Wilson contributed to the success of the women's suffrage movement by

    A) circulating government propaganda in support of women's suffrage.

    B) framing the fight in World War I as a fight for democracy and freedom.

    C) engaging in a foreign war to distract the nation from political debate.

    D) working with legislators to write the Nineteenth Amendment.

GO ON TO THE NEXT PAGE

31. The graphic helps support which statement referred to in the passage?

    A) Early women suffragists did not live to vote in national elections.

    B) The Nineteenth Amendment passed within a few years of its introduction.

    C) A majority of state representatives opposed women's suffrage in 1918.

    D) Many state governments approved suffrage before the federal government did.

Questions 32-42 are based on the following passages and supplementary material.

Passage 1 is about how scientists use radioisotopes to date artifacts and remains. Passage 2 discusses the varying problems with radioactive contaminants.

Passage 1

Archaeologists often rely on measuring the amounts of different atoms present in an item from a site to determine its age. The identity of an atom
Line depends on how many protons it has in its nucleus;
(5) for example, all carbon atoms have 6 protons. Each atom of an element, however, can have a different number of neutrons, so there can be several versions, or isotopes, of each element. Scientists name the isotopes by the total number of protons
(10) plus neutrons. For example, a carbon atom with 6 neutrons is carbon-12 while a carbon atom with 7 neutrons is carbon-13.

Some combinations of protons and neutrons are not stable and will change over time. For example,
(15) carbon-14, which has 6 protons and 8 neutrons, will slowly change into nitrogen-14, with 7 protons and 7 neutrons. Scientists can directly measure the amount of carbon-12 and carbon-14 in a sample or they can use radiation measurements to calcu-
(20) late these amounts. Each atom of carbon-14 that changes to nitrogen-14 emits radiation. Scientists can measure the rate of emission and use that to calculate the total amount of carbon-14 present in a sample.
(25) Carbon-14 atoms are formed in the atmosphere at the same rate at which they decay. Therefore,

the ratio of carbon-12 to carbon-14 atoms in the atmosphere is constant. Living plants and animals have the same ratio of carbon-12 to carbon-14 in
(30) their tissues because they are constantly taking in carbon in the form of food or carbon dioxide. After the plant or animal dies, however, it stops taking in carbon and so the amount of carbon-14 atoms in its tissues starts to decrease at a predictable rate.

(35) By measuring the ratio of carbon-12 to carbon-14 in a bone, for example, a scientist can determine how long the animal the bone came from has been dead. To determine an object's age this way is called "carbon-14 dating." Carbon-14 dating can be
(40) performed on any material made by a living organism, such as wood or paper from trees or bones and skin from animals. Materials with ages up to about 50,000 years old can be dated. By finding the age of several objects found at different depths at an
(45) archeological dig, the archeologists can then make a timeline for the layers of the site. Objects in the same layer will be about the same age. By using carbon dating for a few objects in a layer, archeologists know the age of other objects in that layer, even if
(50) the layer itself cannot be carbon dated.

Passage 2

Radioactive materials contain unstable atoms that decay, releasing energy in the form of radiation. The radiation can be harmful to living tissue because it can penetrate into cells and damage their
(55) DNA. If an explosion or a leak at a nuclear power plant releases large amounts of radioactive materials, the surrounding area could be hazardous until the amount of radioactive material drops back to normal levels. The amount of danger from the
(60) radiation and the amount of time until the areas are safe again depends on how fast the materials emit radiation.

Scientists use the "half-life" of a material to indicate how quickly it decays. The half-life of a
(65) material is the amount of time it takes for half of a sample of that material to decay. A material with a short half-life decays more quickly than a material with a long half-life. For example, io-dine-131 and cesium-137 can both be released as
(70) a result of an accident at a nuclear power plant.

GO ON TO THE NEXT PAGE ⟩

Iodine-131 decays rapidly, with a half-life of 8 days. Cesium-137, however, decays more slowly, with a half-life of 30 years.

(75) If an accident releases iodine-131, therefore, it is a short-term concern. The amount of radiation emitted will be high but will drop rapidly. After two months, less than one percent of the original iodine-131 will remain. An accidental release of cesium-137, however, is a long-term concern. The

(80) amount of radiation emitted at first will be low but will drop slowly. It will take about 200 years for the amount of cesium-137 remaining to drop below one percent. The total amount of radiation emitted in both cases will be the same, for the same amount

(85) of initial material. The difference lies in whether the radiation is all released rapidly at high levels in a short time, or is released slowly at low levels, over a long time span.

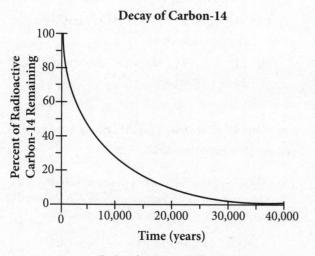

Decay of Carbon-14

This data is from the *Journal of Research of the National Bureau of Standards*, Vol. 64, No. 4, April 1951, pp. 328–333.

32. Based on the information in Passage 1, which of the following could be dated using carbon-14 dating?

A) An iron pot found in a cave

B) A rock at the bottom of a quarry

C) An arrowhead made from bone

D) The remains of a house made from stone

33. Which choice provides the best evidence for the answer to the previous question?

A) Lines 10-12 ("For example . . . carbon-13")

B) Lines 28-31 ("Living plants . . . dioxide")

C) Lines 31-34 ("After the plant . . . rate")

D) Lines 39-42 ("Carbon-14 dating . . . animals")

34. As used in line 26, "decay" most nearly means

A) yield.

B) deteriorate.

C) discharge.

D) circulated.

35. Which statement best describes the relationship between carbon-12 and carbon-14 in living tissue?

A) There is more carbon-14 than carbon-12.

B) There is more carbon-12 than carbon-14.

C) The ratio of carbon-12 to carbon-14 is constant.

D) The ratio of carbon-12 to carbon-14 fluctuates greatly.

36. Which choice provides the best evidence for the answer to the previous question?

A) Lines 13-14 ("Some combinations . . . time")

B) Lines 25-26 ("Carbon-14 atoms . . . decay")

C) Lines 28-31 ("Living plants . . . carbon dioxide")

D) Lines 31-34 ("After the plant . . . rate")

GO ON TO THE NEXT PAGE

37. In Passage 2, the author refers to an accident that results in the release of iodine-131 as a "short-term concern" (line 75) because the initial amount of radiation released is

    A) low but will drop slowly.

    B) high but will drop quickly.

    C) low and will drop quickly.

    D) high and will drop slowly.

38. According to Passage 2, living tissue exposed to radioactive material can

    A) be destroyed by high levels of heat caused by the radiation.

    B) become radioactive itself and damage surrounding tissue.

    C) suffer injury when the cells' components are damaged.

    D) be killed by extra protons released by the radioactive material.

39. As used in line 77, "original" most nearly means

    A) earliest.

    B) unique.

    C) unusual.

    D) critical.

40. According to Passage 2, scientists use the half-life of radioactive material to determine the

    A) amount of danger posed by radiation immediately following a nuclear accident.

    B) likelihood of a nuclear accident involving the release of radioactive material at any given location.

    C) amount of radiation contained in a sample of iodine-131 or cesium-137 used in nuclear reactions.

    D) length of time that must pass until an area is safe after the release of radioactive material.

41. Which generalization about the study of physics is supported by both passages?

    A) The study of atomic and nuclear physics can have many applications in a variety of fields.

    B) The study of physics has helped revolutionize how archaeologists study artifacts.

    C) Scientists use physics to keep people and wildlife safe following a nuclear accident.

    D) Scientists use different concepts to date ancient items and assess danger from nuclear accidents.

42. Based on the graph and the information in the passages, which statement is accurate?

    A) Carbon-14 has a half-life of about 5,400 years.

    B) The half-life of carbon-14 is similar to that of cesium-137.

    C) The half-life of iodine-131 is greater than that of cesium-137.

    D) All radioactive materials have a half-life of 30 to 5,400 years.

Questions 43-52 are based on the following passage and supplementary material.

The following passage is adapted from an essay about the field of biomimicry, which focuses on the design of materials and systems that are based on biological structures.

In 1948, Swiss chemist George de Mestral was impressed with the clinging power of burrs snagged in his dog's fur and on his pant legs after
Line he returned from a hike. While examining the
(5) burrs under a microscope, he observed many hundreds of small fibers that grabbed like hooks. He experimented with replicas of the burrs and eventually invented Velcro®, a synthetic clinging fabric that was first marketed as "the zipperless
(10) zipper." In the 1960s, NASA used de Mestral's invention on space suits, and now, of course, we see it everywhere.

GO ON TO THE NEXT PAGE

You might say that de Mestral was the father of biomimicry, an increasingly essential field that
(15) studies nature, looking for efficiencies in materials and systems, and asks the question "How can our homes, our electronics, and our cities work better?" As one biomimetics company puts it: "Nature is the largest laboratory that ever existed and ever will."

(20) Architecture is one field that is constantly exploring new ways to incorporate biomimicry. Architects have studied everything from beehives to beaver dams to learn how to best use materials, geometry, and physics in buildings. Termite
(25) mounds, for example, very efficiently regulate temperature, humidity, and airflow, so architects in Zimbabwe are working to apply what they've learned from termite mounds to human-made structures.

Says Michael Pawlyn, author of *Biomimicry in*
(30) *Architecture*, "If you look beyond the nice shapes in nature and understand the principles behind them, you can find some adaptations that can lead to new, innovative solutions that are radically more resource-efficient. It's the direction we need to take
(35) in the coming decades."

Designers in various professional fields are drawing on biomimicry; for example, in optics, scientists have examined the surface of insect eyes in hopes of reducing glare on handheld device
(40) screens. Engineers in the field of robotics worked to replicate the property found in a gecko's feet that allows adhesion to smooth surfaces.

Sometimes what scientists learn from nature isn't more advanced, but simpler. The abalone
(45) shrimp, for example, makes its shell out of calcium carbonate, the same material as soft chalk. It's not a rare or complex substance, but the unique arrangement of the material in the abalone's shell makes it extremely tough. The walls of the shell
(50) contain microscopic pieces of calcium carbonate stacked like bricks, which are bound together using proteins just as concrete mortar is used. The result is a shell three thousand times harder than chalk and as tough as Kevlar® (the material used in
(55) bullet-proof vests).

Often it is necessary to look at the nanoscale structures of a living material's exceptional properties in order to re-create it synthetically. Andrew Parker, an evolutionary biologist, looked at the skin of the
(60) thorny devil (a type of lizard) under a scanning electron microscope, in search of the features that let the animal channel water from its back to its mouth.

Examples like this from the animal world abound. Scientists have learned that colorful birds
(65) don't always have pigment in their wings but are sometimes completely brown; it's the layers of keratin in their wings that produce color. Different colors, which have varying wavelengths, reflect differently through keratin. The discovery of this
(70) phenomenon can be put to use in creating paints and cosmetics that won't fade or chip. At the same time, paint for outdoor surfaces can be made tougher by copying the structures found in antler bone. Hearing aids are being designed to capture
(75) sound as well as the ears of the *Ormia* fly do. And why can't we have a self-healing material like our own skin? Researchers at the Beckman Institute at the University of Illinois are creating just that; they call it an "autonomic materials system." A raptor's
(80) feathers, a whale's fluke, a mosquito's proboscis—all have functional features we can learn from.

The driving force behind these innovations, aside from improved performance, is often improved energy efficiency. In a world where
(85) nonrenewable energy resources are dwindling and carbon emissions threaten the planet's health, efficiency has never been more important. Pawlyn agrees: "For me, biomimicry is one of the best sources of innovation to get to a world of zero
(90) waste because those are the rules under which biological life has had to exist."

Biomimicry is a radical field and one whose practitioners need to be radically optimistic, as Pawlyn is when he says, "We could use natural
(95) products such as cellulose, or even harvest carbon from the atmosphere to create bio-rock."

GO ON TO THE NEXT PAGE ▷

Tiny florets in a sunflower's center are arranged in an interlocking spiral, which inspired engineers in the design of this solar power plant. Mirrors positioned at the same angle as the florets bounce light toward the power plant's central tower.

Adapted from David Ferris, "Innovate: Solar Designs from Nature." © 2014 by Sierra Club.

43. The central focus of the passage is

A) the field of biomimicry, which is the study of materials and systems found in nature and replicated in ways that benefit people.

B) the work of George de Mestral, the Swiss chemist who invented Velcro® after observing burrs under a microscope.

C) the ways in which architects use termite mounds as models for human-made structures in Zimbabwe.

D) how scientists are seeking ways to improve energy efficiency as nonrenewable energy sources decline.

44. Which choice provides the best evidence for the answer to the previous question?

A) Lines 1-6 ("In 1948 . . . hooks")

B) Lines 13-19 ("You might say . . . ever will'")

C) Lines 24-28 ("Termite mounds . . . structures")

D) Lines 82-87 ("The driving . . . more important")

45. The author includes a quote in paragraph 4 in order to

A) explain why architects are looking to biomimicry for solutions in architecture.

B) provide an argument for more scientists to study biomimicry.

C) give an explanation as to why someone might choose a career in architecture.

D) provide a counterargument to the author's central claim.

46. Based on the information in paragraph 6, how does the shell of an abalone shrimp compare with soft chalk?

A) The essential building blocks are arranged in a similar manner, but the material that makes up the shell of an abalone shrimp is harder.

B) Both are made from the same essential building blocks, but the shell of the abalone shrimp is much harder because of the manner in which the materials are arranged.

C) The essential building blocks of both are the same, but the abalone shrimp shell is harder because the soft chalk lacks a protein binding the materials together.

D) They are made from different essential building blocks, but they have a similar hardness because the materials are arranged in a similar manner.

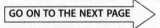

47. In paragraph 9, what is the function of the quote from Pawlyn about efficiency?

    A) To convince readers that Pawlyn is an expert in his field

    B) To prove that great strides are being made in creating products that do not generate waste

    C) To demonstrate the limits of what biomimicry can achieve

    D) To support the statement that energy efficiency "has never been more important"

48. In line 31, "principles" most nearly means

    A) sources.

    B) attitudes.

    C) standards.

    D) concepts.

49. Of the following, the most reasonable inference from the passage is that

    A) more scientists will utilize solutions developed through biomimicry in the future.

    B) the field of biomimicry will eventually decline as more nonrenewable resources are discovered.

    C) scientists will leave the fields they are currently working in and begin research in biomimicry.

    D) doctors will create a self-healing skin called an "autonomic materials system" using methods based in biomimicry.

50. Which choice provides the best evidence for the answer to the previous question?

    A) Lines 36-40 ("Designers . . . screens")

    B) Lines 56-58 ("Often it is . . . synthetically")

    C) Lines 63-67 ("Examples like . . . color")

    D) Lines 92-96 ("Biomimicry . . . bio-rock")

51. As used in line 92, "radical" most nearly means

    A) pervasive.

    B) drastic.

    C) essential.

    D) revolutionary.

52. The graphic and caption that accompany this passage help illustrate how biomimicry can be used to

    A) make a solar plant more attractive.

    B) increase waste generated by energy sources.

    C) improve the efficiency of existing technologies.

    D) replicate a pattern common in nature.

IF YOU FINISH BEFORE TIME IS CALLED, YOU MAY CHECK YOUR WORK ON THIS SECTION ONLY. DO NOT TURN TO ANY OTHER SECTION IN THE TEST. **STOP**

WRITING AND LANGUAGE TEST

35 Minutes—44 Questions

This section corresponds to Section 2 of your answer sheet.

Directions: Each passage in this section is followed by several questions. Some questions will reference an underlined portion in the passage; others will ask you to consider a part of a passage or the passage as a whole. For each question, choose the answer that reflects the best use of grammar, punctuation, and style. If a passage or question is accompanied by a graphic, take the graphic into account in choosing your response(s). Some questions will have "NO CHANGE" as a possible response. Choose that answer if you think the best choice is to leave the sentence as written.

Questions 1-11 are based on the following passage.

The Age of the Librarian

When Kristen Harris **1** is in college, she worked in her university's library and was constantly told, "You really should be studying to be a librarian; this is **2** your home" however Harris was pursuing a bachelor's degree in elementary education at the time. Little did she realize that becoming a school librarian was indeed **3** elective. During the 21st century, the age of information, what could be more necessary than an individual trained to gather, process, and disseminate information? So, after teaching children in the classroom, Harris went back to school to earn her Master of Library Science degree.

1. A) NO CHANGE
    B) has been
    C) was
    D) had been

2. A) NO CHANGE
    B) your home," however Harris
    C) your home."; However Harris
    D) your home." However, Harris

3. A) NO CHANGE
    B) imminent
    C) threatening
    D) optional

Today, Harris is preparing a story time for a group of young students. As it has done with everything else, the technology revolution has elevated the school library to "Library 2.0." Harris's tablet-integrated story time begins when she projects images for *The Very Cranky Bear* onto a projector screen. As a child, Harris got excited whenever a puppet appeared during story time, but now she uses an interactive app (application software) to enhance her own story time and **4** integrate this next generation of children.

As she introduces the children to the problem of cheering up a cranky **5** bear, Harris sees Miguel scouring the library shelves for another book by a popular author. **6** Miguel had said asking Harris for a book two weeks earlier "If you have any funny stories, I like those." "It will always be satisfying," reflects Harris, "to find books for students and have them return to say, 'I really liked that one. Are there any more by that author?'"

7 Harris maintains active profiles on multiple social media networks to connect with her students more effectively. Harris would call herself a media mentor as much as a librarian because she regularly visits her favorite websites for reviews of apps and other digital tools to suggest to students and parents. Librarians have always been an important resource for families in a community, but this importance has grown exponentially because of the advent of technology. Librarians are offering guidance about new media to address the changing information needs in our communities. Furthermore,

4. A) NO CHANGE
   B) enervate
   C) energize
   D) elucidate

5. A) NO CHANGE
   B) bear; Harris sees Miguel
   C) bear: Harris sees Miguel
   D) bear Harris sees Miguel

6. A) NO CHANGE
   B) Miguel had said, "If you have any funny stories, I like those," asking Harris for a book two weeks earlier.
   C) Asking Harris for a book two weeks earlier, Miguel had said, "If you have any funny stories, I like those."
   D) Miguel asked Harris for a book two weeks earlier had said, "If you have any funny stories, I like those."

7. Which sentence would most effectively establish the main idea of the paragraph?
   A) NO CHANGE
   B) In addition to finding books for students, Harris is expected to meet their digital needs.
   C) Librarians still perform many traditional tasks such as putting great literature in the hands of their students.
   D) In the future, many school libraries are unlikely to have books on the shelves because students prefer electronic media.

GO ON TO THE NEXT PAGE ▷

libraries are becoming increasingly technology driven, for example, [8] enabling access to collections of other libraries, offering remote access to databases, or they house video production studios. [9] Harris sponsors a weekly "Fun Read" book discussion club that is well attended by many of the students at her school. So, in Harris's opinion, librarians must be masters of the digital world.

Harris finishes her story time and heads across the library. A young student stops her and asks, "Ms. Harris, what's new in the library?" [10] She chuckles and thinks about the many collections, services, and programs their school library offers. "Have you seen the Trendy 10

8. A) NO CHANGE
   B) by enabling access to collections of other libraries, offering remote access to databases, or by housing video production studios.
   C) they enable access to collections of other libraries, offering remote access to databases, or they house video production studios.
   D) enabling access to collections of other libraries, offering remote access to databases, or housing video production studios.

9. Which sentence provides evidence that best supports the main idea of the paragraph?
   A) NO CHANGE
   B) Librarians continue to help students and teachers locate the perfect book in the library's collection.
   C) Teachers frequently ask Harris to recommend educational apps to support early literacy for their students.
   D) Many parents are concerned with online safety and digital citizenship due to the proliferation of social media.

10. A) NO CHANGE
    B) He chuckles
    C) Harris chuckles
    D) They chuckle

list? You read the books on the list and blog **11** your

ideas about them. I'll set you up with a password and

username so you can blog," says Harris. In this library

full of information, she's the gatekeeper.

Questions 12-22 are based on the following passage.

Unforeseen Consequences: The Dark Side of the Industrial Revolution

There is no doubt that the Industrial Revolu-

tion guided America through the nascent stages of

independence **12** and into being a robust economic

powerhouse. Inventions like the cotton gin revolu-

tionized the textile industry, and the steam engine

ushered in the advent of expeditious cross-country

distribution.

The Industrial Revolution marked a shift from

an agrarian to an industry-centered society. People

eschewed farming in favor of **13** more lucrative enter-

prises in urban areas which put a strain on existing lo-

cal resources. Necessary goods such as **14** food crops,

vegetables, and meat products also had to be shipped

in order to meet the dietary needs of a consolidated

population. And because there were fewer people

farming, food had to travel farther and in higher

quantities to meet demand. Issues like carbon dioxide

emissions, therefore, arose not only as byproducts

of industrial production but also from the delivery

of these products. Moreover, booming metropolises

11. A) NO CHANGE
    B) they're
    C) you're
    D) their

12. A) NO CHANGE
    B) and into the role of a robust economic powerhouse.
    C) and turned into a robust economic powerhouse.
    D) and then became a robust economic powerhouse.

13. A) NO CHANGE
    B) more lucrative enterprises in urban areas, which put a strain on
    C) more lucrative enterprises in urban areas; which put a strain on
    D) more lucrative enterprises in urban areas. Which put a strain on

14. A) NO CHANGE
    B) food
    C) food crops
    D) vegetables and meat products

GO ON TO THE NEXT PAGE

needed additional lumber, metal, and coal shipped from rural areas to sustain population and industrial growth.

15 [1] The negative effects of such expansion on humans were immediately apparent; improper water sanitization led to cholera outbreaks in big cities. [2] Miners suffered from black lung after spending hours harvesting coal in dark caverns. [3] Combusted fossil fuels **16** released unprecedented amounts of human-made carbon dioxide into the air, resulting in respiratory ailments. [4] The fact remains that smog, now an internationally recognized buzzword, simply did not exist before the factories that produced it.

The critical impact on the environment must also **17** be taken into account. Proper regulations were either not in place or not enforced. Industrial waste was often disposed of in the nearest river or buried in landfills, where it **18** polluted groundwater essential for wildlife to thrive. Deforestation across the United States served the dual purpose of providing inhabitable land and wood, but it also caused animals to migrate or die out completely.

15. To effectively transition from paragraph 2, which sentence should begin paragraph 3?

A) Sentence 1

B) Sentence 2

C) Sentence 3

D) Sentence 4

16. Which graphic would best support the underlined claim?

A) A line graph plotting an increase in atmospheric carbon dioxide over time

B) A pie chart comparing the present percentages of carbon dioxide and other atmospheric gases

C) A timeline tracking carbon dioxide emissions testing dates

D) A bar graph showing levels of atmospheric carbon dioxide in different locations

17. Which choice most effectively combines the sentences at the underlined portion?

A) be taken into account, and proper regulations

B) be taken into account since without proper regulations

C) be taken into account because proper regulations

D) be taken into account; however, proper regulations

18. A) NO CHANGE

B) disturbed

C) drained

D) enhanced

GO ON TO THE NEXT PAGE ⇒

Although the Industrial Revolution heralded an age of consumer ease and excess, it also invited a cyclical process of destruction and reduced resources. **19** Greenhouse gases were released into the atmosphere. Numerous health problems caused by **20** depressing working conditions prevented rural emigrants from thriving. And the environment that had cradled humankind since its inception was slowly being **21** degraded. All in the name of progress. **22**

19. Which choice should be added to the end of the underlined sentence to better support the claim in the preceding sentence?

A) NO CHANGE

B) while carbon dioxide-consuming trees were cut down to make way for new living spaces.

C) and caused an increase in global temperatures as well as a rise in coastal sea levels.

D) faster than they could be absorbed by the atmosphere's shrinking ozone layer.

20. A) NO CHANGE

B) urban

C) substandard

D) developing

21. A) NO CHANGE

B) degraded; all

C) degraded! All

D) degraded—all

22. Which choice most effectively states the central idea of the essay?

A) The Industrial Revolution created a new consumer society that replaced the existing farming society.

B) Politicians and historians today disagree about the true consequences of the Industrial Revolution.

C) Although some analysts suggest that industrialization had many problems, its immense benefits outweigh these concerns.

D) Unfortunately, progress came at the expense of environmental and ecological preservation and may well have ruined the future that once looked so bright.

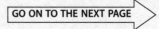 GO ON TO THE NEXT PAGE

Questions 23-33 are based on the following passage.

Remembering Freud

Psychology has grown momentously over the past century, largely due to the influence of Sigmund Freud, a pioneer of the field. This Austrian-born neurologist founded the practice of psychoanalysis and **23** began scientific study of the unconscious mind. **24** Since his career which ended in the mid-twentieth century, Freud has remained a common cultural and scientific reference point. **25** Even the abiding popularity of terms such as "id," "ego," and talking about a "Freudian slip" serves to indicate how this psychologist lingers powerfully in Western memory.

As neuroscience has progressed, many early practices and theories, including some of Freud's, have been dismissed as outdated, unscientific, or even harmful. Much of Freud's theory, clinical practice, and even lifestyle are now discredited. But when considered in his historical context, alongside the astounding progress catalyzed by his work, Freud's contribution was significant indeed.

26 Because he is now widely referred to as the Father of Psychoanalysis, Freud was among the first to develop the now-commonplace psychological method of inviting patients to speak freely. For Freud, this was both study and treatment. It helped doctors to understand patients, but more importantly it helped patients to understand themselves. Freud employed the classic (now

23. A) NO CHANGE
    B) continued
    C) spearheaded
    D) led to

24. A) NO CHANGE
    B) Since his career, which ended in the mid-twentieth century, Freud has remained
    C) Since his career ending in the mid-twentieth century; Freud has remained
    D) Since his career (ending in the mid-twentieth century) Freud has remained

25. A) NO CHANGE
    B) Even the abiding popularity of terms such as the "id," "ego," and a "Freudian slip"
    C) Even the abiding popularity of terms such as talking about an "id," "ego," and "Freudian slip"
    D) Even the abiding popularity of terms such as "id," "ego," and "Freudian slip"

26. A) NO CHANGE
    B) Widely remembered as the Father of Psychoanalysis, Freud was among the first to develop the now-commonplace psychological method of inviting patients to speak freely.
    C) Freud was among the first to develop the now-commonplace psychological method of inviting patients to speak freely, which is why he is now widely remembered as the Father of Psychoanalysis.
    D) Although he is widely remembered as the Father of Psychoanalysis, Freud was among the first to develop the now-commonplace psychological method of inviting patients to speak freely.

largely outdated) psychiatric style in which the patient lies face-up on a clinical bed, allegedly enabling access to deep **27** parts of the mind. These are better known as the unconscious or subconscious, and they fascinated Freud.

    28 He believed that uncovering repressed memories, was necessary for recovery. For Freud, understanding the activity of the innermost mind was essential. **29** In dealing with the conditions of patients, like neurosis or other psychological trauma, he suspected that there was a great deal going on beneath the "surface" of the psyche. He thought it was possible to reunite external, or conscious, thought with the internal, or unconscious. **30** At the same time that Freud practiced, many people were interested in spiritualism. Moreover, the method of inviting patients to speak and process their thoughts aloud remains central to today's psychological practice.

27. A) NO CHANGE
    B) recesses
    C) places
    D) components

28. A) NO CHANGE
    B) He believed that uncovering repressed memories, being necessary for recovery.
    C) He believed that uncovering repressed memories was necessary for recovery.
    D) He believed that uncovering, repressed memories was necessary for recovery.

29. A) NO CHANGE
    B) In dealing with patients' conditions, like neurosis or other psychological trauma, he suspected that
    C) In dealing with patients like neurosis or other psychological trauma conditions he suspected that
    D) He suspected that, in dealing with patients' conditions like neurosis or other psychological trauma,

30. Which sentence provides the best support for the ideas presented in this section?
    A) NO CHANGE
    B) Freud lived and worked mostly in London although he had originally trained in Austria.
    C) While some of Freud's more unusual practices have been criticized or abandoned, his interest in the unconscious altered the trajectory of the field.
    D) Psychologists today employ many theories, not just those developed by Freud.

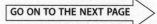 GO ON TO THE NEXT PAGE

Freud altered the course of twentieth-century medicine by initiating what would become a grand, global conversation about the [31] <u>still vastly mysterious human mind before Freud, medicine</u> had barely scratched the surface in understanding mental health. Patients were met with very few answers, let alone recovery protocols. [32] <u>Through trial and error—scientific method in action—Freud's finding of a method that seemed to work.</u> Since then, decades of ever-sharpening science have used his work as a launching pad. Therefore, as long as occasions arise to celebrate the progress of [33] <u>the field, Sigmund Freud will be remembered for groundbreaking work that</u> enabled countless advances.

31. A) NO CHANGE
   B) still vastly mysterious human mind. Before Freud, medicine
   C) still vastly mysterious human mind, before Freud, medicine
   D) still vastly mysterious human mind before Freud. Medicine

32. A) NO CHANGE
   B) Through trial and error—scientific method in action—Freud's finding a method that seems to work.
   C) Through trial and error—scientific method in action—Freud finds a method that seemed to work.
   D) Through trial and error—scientific method in action—Freud found a method that seemed to work.

33. A) NO CHANGE
   B) the field; Sigmund Freud will be remembered for groundbreaking work that
   C) the field Sigmund Freud will be remembered for groundbreaking work that
   D) the field Sigmund Freud will be remembered for groundbreaking work, and that

GO ON TO THE NEXT PAGE

Questions 34-44 are based on the following passage and supplementary material.

Success in Montreal

The Montreal Protocol on Substances That Deplete the Ozone Layer is an international treaty that was created to ensure that steps would be taken to reverse damage to Earth's ozone layer and **34** preventing future damage. **35** It was signed in 1987. This document created restrictions on chemicals that were known to be dangerous to the protective barrier that the ozone layer offers Earth. Without the ozone layer, the sun's dangerous UV rays would alter our climate so drastically, life on land and in water would cease to exist.

A hole in Earth's ozone layer was discovered over Antarctica **36** as long as two years prior to the signing of the treaty. The discovery brought the human impact on the environment to the forefront of **37** international conversation, the massive hole was evidence that a global response was necessary and that large-scale action was needed. The Montreal Protocol became effective January 1, 1989, and nearly 100 gases deemed dangerous to the ozone layer have been phased out. As a result, **38** the average size of the ozone hole decreased significantly during the 1990s.

34. A) NO CHANGE
    B) to prevent
    C) prevented
    D) was preventing

35. Which choice most effectively combines the sentences in the underlined portion?
    A) Signed in 1987, this document
    B) Because it was signed in 1987, this document
    C) It was signed in 1987, and this document
    D) It was signed in 1987 so this document

36. A) NO CHANGE
    B) long ago, two years prior.
    C) two years prior.
    D) years prior.

37. A) NO CHANGE
    B) international conversation, yet the massive hole
    C) international conversation. The massive hole
    D) international conversation, so the massive hole

38. Which choice completes the sentence with accurate data based on the graphic?
    A) NO CHANGE
    B) the average size of the ozone hole leveled off beginning in the 1990s.
    C) the average size of the ozone hole decreased beginning in the 2000s.
    D) the average size of the ozone hole increased beginning in the 1980s.

GO ON TO THE NEXT PAGE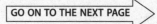

Now that a substantial amount of time has passed since the treaty was put into place, the effects can begin to be [39] looked at. As a part of the treaty, the Montreal Protocol's Scientific Assessment Panel was created to gauge [40] their effect on the hole in the ozone layer. The Panel has since reported the results every four years. The Panel predicts that the ozone layer will return to its former state of health by 2075. [41]

[1] While the treaty is already an obvious success, work continues to ensure that human strides in technology and industry do not reverse the healing process. [2] The Montreal Protocol's Multilateral Fund was established to help developing countries transition away from the consumption and production of harmful chemicals. [3] So far, over $3 billion has been invested by the Fund. [4] The developing countries are referred to as "Article 5 countries." [42]

39. A) NO CHANGE
    B) controlled
    C) measured
    D) governed

40. A) NO CHANGE
    B) its
    C) it's
    D) there

41. Which choice could be added to paragraph 3 to most effectively convey its central idea?

    A) It is the Panel's current estimation that the ozone layer is beginning to heal, but the rate of progress is slow.

    B) The Panel meets once a year to assess the increase or decrease of each gas that has been identified as dangerous.

    C) Of much concern to the Panel was the effect of ultraviolet radiation on the ozone layer.

    D) The Panel has recently updated procedures for the nomination and selection of its membership.

42. Which sentence in paragraph 4 provides the least amount of support for the central idea of the paragraph?

    A) Sentence 1
    B) Sentence 2
    C) Sentence 3
    D) Sentence 4

GO ON TO THE NEXT PAGE

[1] The Montreal Protocol is a living document. [2] A current amendment proposition has been put forth by the United States, Mexico, and Canada jointly. [3] It aims to cut down on harmful gases that were put into use as an alternative to the gases specified in the original Montreal Protocol treaty. [4] It has been amended four times since its inception. [5] Combating the erosion of our ozone layer will take time and flexibility, but the research is clear: If humans stay conscious of what we emit into the atmosphere, we can not only stall the damage we have done in the past, but we can change it.

43. A) NO CHANGE
    B) switch
    C) invert
    D) reverse

44. For the sake of cohesion of this paragraph, sentence 4 should be placed
    A) where it is now.
    B) before sentence 1.
    C) after sentence 1.
    D) after sentence 2.

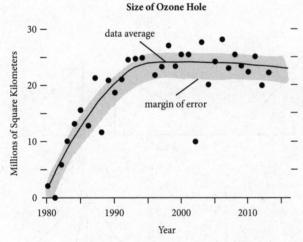

Adapted from Ozone Hole Watch, NASA Goddard Space Flight Center.

IF YOU FINISH BEFORE TIME IS CALLED, YOU MAY CHECK YOUR WORK ON THIS SECTION ONLY. DO NOT TURN TO ANY OTHER SECTION IN THE TEST.   **STOP**

MATH TEST

25 Minutes—20 Questions

NO-CALCULATOR SECTION

This section corresponds to Section 3 of your answer sheet.

Directions: For this section, solve each question and select the best answer choice. The available space on each page may be used for scratch work.

Notes:

1. Calculator use is NOT permitted.
2. All numbers used are real numbers, and all variables used represent real numbers, unless otherwise indicated.
3. Figures are drawn to scale and lie in a plane unless otherwise indicated.
4. Unless stated otherwise, the domain of any function f is assumed to be the set of all real numbers x, for which $f(x)$ is a real number.

Information:

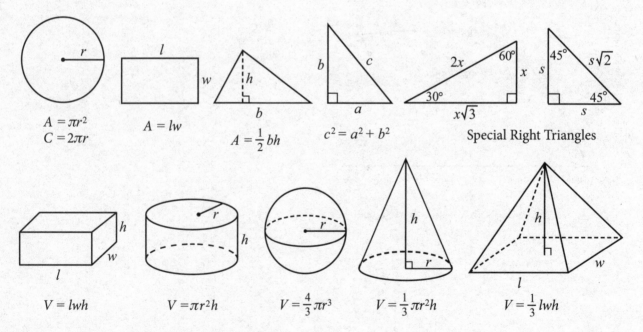

$A = \pi r^2$
$C = 2\pi r$

$A = lw$

$A = \frac{1}{2} bh$

$c^2 = a^2 + b^2$

Special Right Triangles

$V = lwh$

$V = \pi r^2 h$

$V = \frac{4}{3}\pi r^3$

$V = \frac{1}{3}\pi r^2 h$

$V = \frac{1}{3}lwh$

The sum of the degree measures of the angles in a triangle is 180.

The number of degrees of arc in a circle is 360.

The number of radians of arc in a circle is 2π.

GO ON TO THE NEXT PAGE

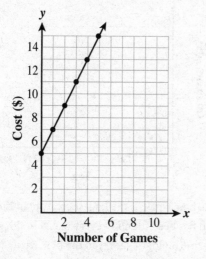

Number of Games

1. The graph above shows the amount that a new, high-tech video arcade charges its customers. What could the *y*-intercept of this graph represent?

   A) The cost of playing 5 games

   B) The cost per game, which is $5

   C) The entrance fee to enter the arcade

   D) The number of games that are played

$$\frac{3x}{x + 5} \div \frac{6}{4x + 20}$$

2. Which of the following is equivalent to the expression above, given that $x \neq -5$?

   A) $2x$

   B) $\dfrac{x}{2}$

   C) $\dfrac{9x}{2}$

   D) $2x + 4$

$$(x + 3)^2 + (y + 1)^2 = 25$$

3. The graph of the equation above is a circle. What is the area, in square units, of the circle?

   A) 4π

   B) 5π

   C) 16π

   D) 25π

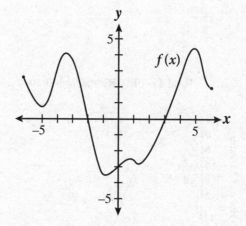

4. The figure above shows the graph of $f(x)$. For which value(s) of x does $f(x)$ equal 0 ?

   A) 3 only

   B) −3 only

   C) −2 and 3

   D) −3, −2, and 3

GO ON TO THE NEXT PAGE

$$\frac{4(d + 3) - 9}{8} = \frac{10 - (2 - d)}{6}$$

5. In the equation above, what is the value of d ?

A) $\dfrac{23}{16}$

B) $\dfrac{23}{8}$

C) $\dfrac{25}{8}$

D) $\dfrac{25}{4}$

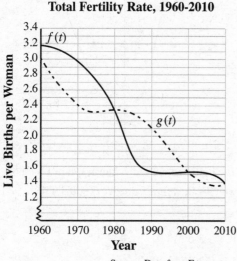

Total Fertility Rate, 1960-2010

Source: Data from Eurostat.

6. One indicator of a declining economy is a continued decline in birth rates. In 2010, birth rates in Europe were at an all-time low, with the average number of children that a woman has in her lifetime at well below two. In the figure above, $f(t)$ represents birth rates for Portugal between 1960 and 2010, and $g(t)$ represents birth rates in Slovakia for the same time period. For which value(s) of t is $f(t) > g(t)$?

A) $1960 < t < 1980$ only

B) $1980 < t < 2000$ only

C) $1960 < t < 1980$ and $1990 < t < 2000$

D) $1960 < t < 1980$ and $2000 < t < 2010$

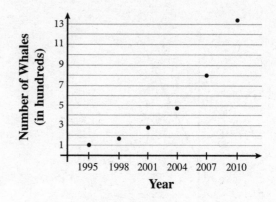

7. The blue whale is the largest creature in the world and has been found in every ocean in the world. A marine biologist surveyed the blue whale population in Monterey Bay, off the coast of California, every three years between 1995 and 2010. The figure above shows her results. If w is the number of blue whales present in Monterey Bay and t is the number of years since the study began in 1995, which of the following equations best represents the blue whale population of Monterey Bay?

A) $w = 100 + 2t$

B) $w = 100 + \dfrac{t^2}{4}$

C) $w = 100 \times 2^t$

D) $w = 100 \times 2^{\frac{t}{4}}$

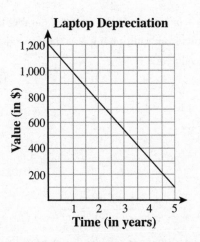

Laptop Depreciation

8. The figure above shows the straight-line depreciation of a laptop computer over the first five years of its use. According to the figure, what is the average rate of change in dollars per year of the value of the computer over the five-year period?

A) $-1,100$

B) -220

C) -100

D) 100

9. What is the coefficient of x^2 when $6x^2 - \dfrac{2}{5}x + 1$ is multiplied by $10x + \dfrac{1}{3}$?

A) -4

B) -2

C) 2

D) 4

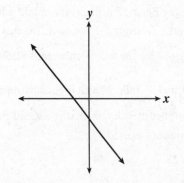

10. The graph above could represent which of the following equations?

A) $-6x - 4y = 5$

B) $-6x - 4y = -5$

C) $-6x + 4y = 5$

D) $-6x + 4y = -5$

$$\begin{cases} \dfrac{3}{4}x - \dfrac{1}{2}y = 12 \\ kx - 2y = 22 \end{cases}$$

11. If the system of linear equations above has no solution, and k is a constant, what is the value of k?

A) $-\dfrac{4}{3}$

B) $-\dfrac{3}{4}$

C) 3

D) 4

GO ON TO THE NEXT PAGE

12. In Delray Beach, Florida, you can take a luxury golf cart ride around downtown. The driver charges $4 for the first $\frac{1}{4}$ mile, plus $1.50 for each additional $\frac{1}{2}$ mile. Which inequality represents the number of miles, m, that you could ride and pay no more than $10 ?

A) $3.25 + 1.5m \leq 10$

B) $3.25 + 3m \leq 10$

C) $4 + 1.5m \leq 10$

D) $4 + 3m \leq 10$

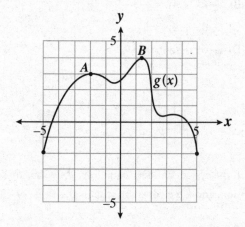

13. The graph of $g(x)$ is shown in the figure above. If $h(x) = -g(x) + 1$, which of the following statements is true?

A) The range of $h(x)$ is $-3 \leq y \leq 3$.

B) The minimum value of $h(x)$ is -4.

C) The coordinates of point A on the function $h(x)$ are $(2, 4)$.

D) The graph of $h(x)$ is increasing between $x = -5$ and $x = -2$.

14. If $a + bi$ represents the complex number that results from multiplying $3 + 2i$ times $5 - i$, what is the value of a ?

A) 2

B) 13

C) 15

D) 17

$$\frac{1}{x} + \frac{4}{x} = \frac{1}{72}$$

15. In order to create safe drinking water, cities and towns use water treatment facilities to remove contaminants from surface water and groundwater. Suppose a town has a treatment plant but decides to build a second, more efficient facility. The new treatment plant can filter the water in the reservoir four times as quickly as the older facility. Working together, the two facilities can filter all the water in the reservoir in 72 hours. The equation above represents the scenario. Which of the following describes what the term $\frac{1}{x}$ represents?

A) The portion of the water the older treatment plant can filter in 1 hour

B) The time it takes the older treatment plant to filter the water in the reservoir

C) The time it takes the older treatment plant to filter $\frac{1}{72}$ of the water in the reservoir

D) The portion of the water the new treatment plant can filter in 4 hours

GO ON TO THE NEXT PAGE

Directions: For questions 16-20, enter your responses into the appropriate grid on your answer sheet, in accordance with the following:

1. You will receive credit only if the circles are filled in correctly, but you may write your answers in the boxes above each grid to help you fill in the circles accurately.

2. Don't mark more than one circle per column.

3. None of the questions with grid-in responses will have a negative solution.

4. Only grid in a single answer, even if there is more than one correct answer to a given question.

5. A **mixed number** must be gridded as a decimal or an improper fraction. For example, you would grid $7\frac{1}{2}$ as 7.5 or $\frac{15}{2}$.

   (Were you to grid it as [7 1 / 2], this response would be read as $\frac{71}{2}$.)

6. A **decimal** that has more digits than there are places on the grid may be either rounded or truncated, but every column in the grid must be filled in order to receive credit.

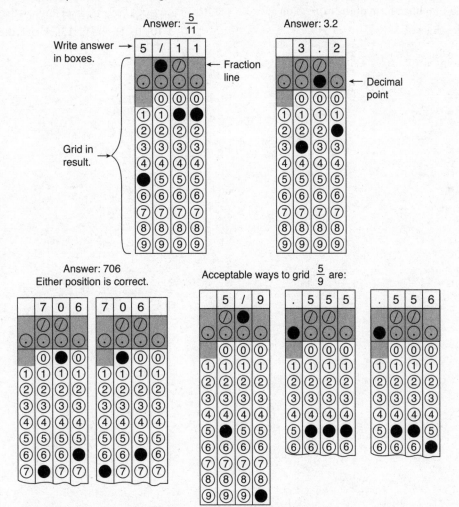

Answer: $\frac{5}{11}$

Write answer in boxes. ← → Fraction line

Grid in result.

Answer: 3.2 ← Decimal point

Answer: 706
Either position is correct.

Acceptable ways to grid $\frac{5}{9}$ are:

16. If $\dfrac{1}{4}x = 5 - \dfrac{1}{2}y$, what is the value of $x + 2y$?

$$\begin{cases} x + 3y \le 18 \\ 2x - 3y \le 9 \end{cases}$$

17. If (a, b) is a point in the solution region for the system of inequalities shown above and $a = 6$, what is the minimum possible value for b?

$$\dfrac{\sqrt{x} \cdot x^{\frac{5}{6}} \cdot x}{\sqrt[3]{x}}$$

18. If x^n is the simplified form of the expression above, what is the value of n?

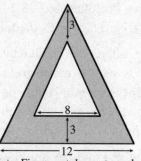

Note: Figure not drawn to scale.

19. In the figure above, the area of the shaded region is 52 square units. What is the height of the larger triangle?

20. If $y = ax^2 + bx + c$ passes through the points $(-3, 10)$, $(0, 1)$, and $(2, 15)$, what is the value of $a + b + c$?

MATH TEST

55 Minutes—38 Questions

CALCULATOR SECTION

This section corresponds to Section 4 of your answer sheet.

Directions: For this section, solve each question and select the best answer choice. The available space on each page may be used for scratch work.

Notes:

1. Calculator use is permitted.
2. All numbers used are real numbers, and all variables used represent real numbers, unless otherwise indicated.
3. Figures are drawn to scale and lie in a plane unless otherwise indicated.
4. Unless stated otherwise, the domain of any function f is assumed to be the set of all real numbers x, for which $f(x)$ is a real number.

Information:

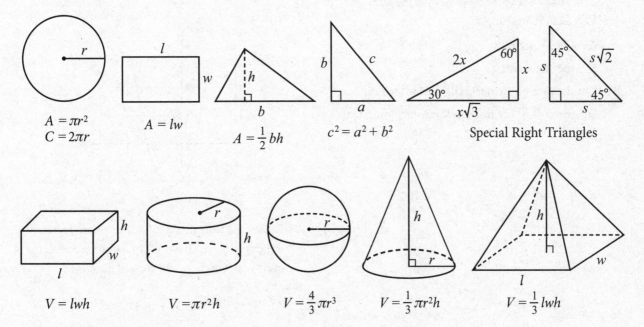

$A = \pi r^2$
$C = 2\pi r$

$A = lw$

$A = \frac{1}{2}bh$

$c^2 = a^2 + b^2$

Special Right Triangles

$V = lwh$

$V = \pi r^2 h$

$V = \frac{4}{3}\pi r^3$

$V = \frac{1}{3}\pi r^2 h$

$V = \frac{1}{3}lwh$

The sum of the degree measures of the angles in a triangle is 180.

The number of degrees of arc in a circle is 360.

The number of radians of arc in a circle is 2π.

GO ON TO THE NEXT PAGE

1. Oceans, seas, and bays represent about 96.5% of Earth's water, including the water found in our atmosphere. If the volume of the water contained in oceans, seas, and bays is about 321,000,000 cubic miles, which of the following best represents the approximate volume, in cubic miles, of all the world's water?

   A) 308,160,000

   B) 309,765,000

   C) 332,642,000

   D) 334,375,000

2. An electrician charges a one-time site visit fee to evaluate a potential job. If the electrician accepts the job, he charges an hourly rate plus the cost of any materials needed to complete the job. The electrician also charges for tax, but only on the cost of the materials. If the total cost of completing a job that takes h hours is given by the function $C(h) = 45h + 1.06(82.5) + 75$, then the term $1.06(82.5)$ represents

   A) the hourly rate.

   B) the site visit fee.

   C) the cost of the materials, including tax.

   D) the cost of the materials, not including tax.

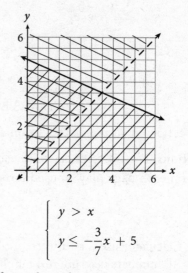

$$\begin{cases} y > x \\ y \le -\dfrac{3}{7}x + 5 \end{cases}$$

3. The figure above shows the solution set for the system of inequalities. Which of the following is not a solution to the system?

   A) $(0, 3)$

   B) $(1, 2)$

   C) $(2, 4)$

   D) $(3, 3)$

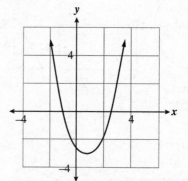

4. Each of the following quadratic equations represents the graph shown above. Which equation reveals the exact values of the x-intercepts of the graph?

   A) $y = \dfrac{1}{2}(2x - 5)(x + 1)$

   B) $y = x^2 - \dfrac{3}{2}x - \dfrac{5}{2}$

   C) $y + \dfrac{49}{16} = \left(x - \dfrac{3}{4}\right)^2$

   D) $y = \left(x - \dfrac{3}{4}\right)^2 - \dfrac{49}{16}$

GO ON TO THE NEXT PAGE

National Government Concerns

Average Annual Gas Prices

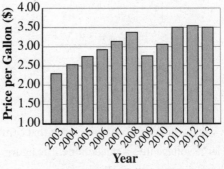

Data from U.S. Energy Information Administration.

5. Margo surveyed all the students in the government classes at her school to see what they thought should be the most important concern of a national government. The results of the survey are shown in the figure above. If the ratio of students who answered "Foreign Policy" to those who answered "Environment" was 5:3, what percentage of the students answered "Environment"?

   A) 16%

   B) 21%

   C) 24%

   D) 35%

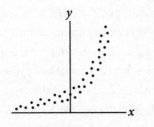

6. Which of the following best describes the type of association shown in the scatterplot above?

   A) Linear, positive

   B) Linear, negative

   C) Exponential, positive

   D) Exponential, negative

7. The figure above shows the average annual gas prices in the United States from 2003 to 2013. Based on the information shown, which of the following conclusions is valid?

   A) A gallon of gas cost more in 2008 than in 2013.

   B) The price more than doubled between 2003 and 2013.

   C) The drop in price from 2008 to 2009 was more than $1.00 per gallon.

   D) The overall change in price was greater between 2003 and 2008 than it was between 2008 and 2013.

$$\begin{cases} -2x + 5y = 1 \\ 7x - 10y = -11 \end{cases}$$

8. If (x, y) is a solution to the system of equations above, what is the sum of x and y ?

   A) $-\dfrac{137}{30}$

   B) -4

   C) $-\dfrac{10}{3}$

   D) -3

GO ON TO THE NEXT PAGE

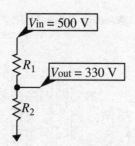

9. A voltage divider is a simple circuit that converts a large voltage into a smaller one. The figure above shows a voltage divider that consists of two resistors that together have a total resistance of 294 ohms. To produce the desired voltage of 330 volts, R_2 must be 6 ohms less than twice R_1. Solving which of the following systems of equations gives the individual resistances for R_1 and R_2?

A) $\begin{cases} R_2 = 2R_1 - 6 \\ R_1 + R_2 = 294 \end{cases}$

B) $\begin{cases} R_1 = 2R_2 + 6 \\ R_1 + R_2 = 294 \end{cases}$

C) $\begin{cases} R_2 = 2R_1 - 6 \\ R_1 + R_2 = \dfrac{294}{330} \end{cases}$

D) $\begin{cases} R_1 = 2R_2 + 6 \\ R_1 + R_2 = 330(294) \end{cases}$

10. If $\dfrac{2}{5}(5x) + 2(x - 1) = 4(x + 1) - 2$, what is the value of x?

A) $x = -2$

B) $x = 2$

C) There is no value of x for which the equation is true.

D) There are infinitely many values of x for which the equation is true.

11. Crude oil is being transferred from a full rectangular storage container with dimensions 4 meters by 9 meters by 10 meters into a cylindrical transportation container that has a diameter of 6 meters. What is the minimum possible length for a transportation container that will hold all of the oil?

A) 40π

B) $\dfrac{40}{\pi}$

C) 60π

D) $\dfrac{120}{\pi}$

12. The percent increase from 5 to 12 is equal to the percent increase from 12 to what number?

A) 16.8

B) 19.0

C) 26.6

D) 28.8

$$b = \frac{L}{4\pi d^2}$$

13. The brightness of a celestial body, like a star, decreases as you move away from it. In contrast, the luminosity of a celestial body is a constant number that represents its intrinsic brightness. The inverse square law, shown above, is used to find the brightness, b, of a celestial body when you know its luminosity, L, and the distance, d, in meters to the body. Which equation shows the distance to a celestial body, given its brightness and luminosity?

A) $d = \dfrac{1}{2}\sqrt{\dfrac{L}{\pi b}}$

B) $d = \sqrt{\dfrac{L}{2\pi b}}$

C) $d = \dfrac{\sqrt{L}}{2\pi b}$

D) $d = \dfrac{L}{2\sqrt{\pi b}}$

GO ON TO THE NEXT PAGE

Questions 14 and 15 refer to the following information.

Each month, the Bureau of Labor Statistics conducts a survey called the Current Population Survey (CPS) to measure unemployment in the United States. Across the country, about 60,000 households are included in the survey sample. These households are grouped by geographic region. A summary of the January 2014 survey results for male respondents in one geographic region is shown in the table below.

Age Group	Employed	Unemployed	Not in the Labor Force	Total
16 to 19	8	5	10	23
20 to 24	26	7	23	56
25 to 34	142	11	28	157
35 to 44	144	8	32	164
45 to 54	66	6	26	98
Over 54	65	7	36	152
Total	451	44	155	650

14. According to the data in the table, for which age group did the smallest percentage of men report that they were unemployed in January 2014?

A) 20 to 24 years

B) 35 to 44 years

C) 45 to 54 years

D) Over 54 years

15. If one unemployed man from this sample is chosen at random for a follow-up survey, what is the probability that he will be between the ages of 45 and 54?

A) 6.0%

B) 13.6%

C) 15.1%

D) 44.9%

16. Which of the following are solutions to the quadratic equation $(x - 1)^2 = \dfrac{4}{9}$?

    A) $x = -\dfrac{5}{3}, x = \dfrac{5}{3}$

    B) $x = \dfrac{1}{3}, x = \dfrac{5}{3}$

    C) $x = \dfrac{5}{9}, x = \dfrac{13}{9}$

    D) $x = 1 \pm \sqrt{\dfrac{2}{3}}$

17. Damien is throwing darts. He has a total of 6 darts to throw. He gets 5 points for each dart that lands in a blue ring and 10 points for each dart that lands in a red ring. If x of his darts land in a blue ring and the rest land in a red ring, which expression represents his total score?

    A) $10x$

    B) $10x + 5$

    C) $5x + 30$

    D) $60 - 5x$

18. Red tide is a form of harmful algae that releases toxins as it breaks down in the environment. A marine biologist is testing a new spray, composed of clay and water, hoping to kill the red tide that almost completely covers a beach in southern Florida. He applies the spray to a representative sample of 200 square feet of the beach. By the end of the week, 184 square feet of the beach is free of the red tide. Based on these results, and assuming the same general conditions, how many square feet of the 10,000-square-foot beach would still be covered by red tide if the spray had been used on the entire area?

    A)   800

    B)   920

    C) 8,000

    D) 9,200

$$\begin{cases} y = \dfrac{1}{2}x - 2 \\ y = -x^2 + 1 \end{cases}$$

19. If (a, b) is a solution to the system of equations above, which of the following could be the value of b?

    A) -3

    B) -2

    C)   1

    D)   2

20. Given the function $g(x) = \dfrac{2}{3}x + 7$, what domain value corresponds to a range value of 3?

    A) -6

    B) -2

    C)   6

    D)   9

21. A landscaper buys a new commercial-grade lawn mower that costs $2,800. Based on past experience, he expects it to last about 8 years, and then he can sell it for scrap metal with a salvage value of about $240. Assuming the value of the lawn mower depreciates at a constant rate, which equation could be used to find its approximate value after x years, given that $x < 8$?

    A) $y = -8x + 2,560$

    B) $y = -240x + 2,800$

    C) $y = -320x + 2,800$

    D) $y = 240x - 2,560$

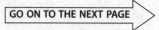

GO ON TO THE NEXT PAGE

22. A microbiologist is studying the effects of a new antibiotic on a culture of 20,000 bacteria. When the antibiotic is added to the culture, the number of bacteria is reduced by half every hour. What kind of function best models the number of bacteria remaining in the culture after the antibiotic is added?

    A) A linear function

    B) A quadratic function

    C) A polynomial function

    D) An exponential function

23. An airline company purchased two new airplanes. One can travel at speeds of up to 600 miles per hour and the other at speeds of up to 720 miles per hour. How many more miles can the faster airplane travel in 12 seconds than the slower airplane?

    A) $\dfrac{1}{30}$

    B) $\dfrac{2}{5}$

    C) 2

    D) 30

State	Minimum Wage per Hour
Idaho	$7.25
Montana	$7.90
Oregon	$9.10
Washington	$9.32

24. The table above shows the 2014 minimum wages for several states that share a border. Assuming an average workweek of between 35 and 40 hours, which inequality represents how much more a worker who earns minimum wage can earn per week in Oregon than in Idaho?

    A) $x \geq 1.85$

    B) $7.25 \leq x \leq 9.10$

    C) $64.75 \leq x \leq 74$

    D) $253.75 \leq x \leq 364$

25. In the United States, the maintenance and construction of airports, transit systems, and major roads is largely funded through a federal excise tax on gasoline. Based on the 2011 statistics given below, how much did the average household pay per year in federal gasoline taxes?

    • The federal gasoline tax rate was 18.4 cents per gallon.

    • The average motor vehicle was driven approximately 11,340 miles per year.

    • The national average fuel economy for noncommercial vehicles was 21.4 miles per gallon.

    • The average American household owned 1.75 vehicles.

    A) $55.73

    B) $68.91

    C) $97.52

    D) $170.63

GO ON TO THE NEXT PAGE

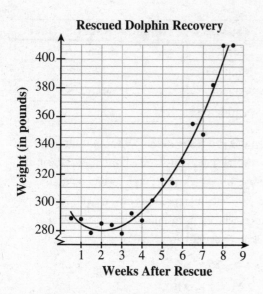

Rescued Dolphin Recovery

26. Following the catastrophic oil spill in the Gulf of Mexico in April of 2010, more than 900 bottlenose dolphins were found dead or stranded in the oil spill area. The figure above shows the weight of a rescued dolphin during its recovery. Based on the quadratic model fit to the data shown, which of the following is the closest to the average rate of change in the dolphin's weight between week 2 and week 8 of its recovery?

A) 4 pounds per week

B) 16 pounds per week

C) 20 pounds per week

D) 40 pounds per week

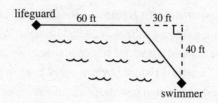

27. As shown in the figure above, a lifeguard sees a struggling swimmer who is 40 feet from the beach. The lifeguard runs 60 feet along the edge of the water at a speed of 12 feet per second. He pauses for 1 second to locate the swimmer again, and then dives into the water and swims along a diagonal path to the swimmer at a speed of 5 feet per second. How many seconds go by between the time the lifeguard sees the struggling swimmer and the time he reaches the swimmer?

A) 16

B) 22

C) 50

D) 56

28. What was the initial amount of gasoline in a fuel trailer, in gallons, if there are now x gallons, y gallons were pumped into a storage tank, and then 50 gallons were added to the trailer?

A) $x + y + 50$

B) $x + y - 50$

C) $y - x + 50$

D) $x - y - 50$

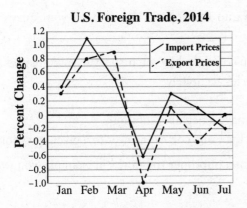

U.S. Foreign Trade, 2014

29. The figure above shows the net change, as a percentage, for U.S. import and export prices from January to July 2014 as reported by the Bureau of Labor Statistics. For example, U.S. import prices declined 0.2 percent in July while export prices remained unchanged for that month. Based on this information, which of the following statements is true for the time period shown in the figure?

A) On average, export prices increased more than import prices.

B) Import prices showed an increase more often than export prices.

C) Import prices showed the greatest change between two consecutive months.

D) From January to July, import prices showed a greater overall decrease than export prices.

$$\frac{3.86}{x} + \frac{180.2}{10x} + \frac{42.2}{5x}$$

30. The Ironman Triathlon originated in Hawaii in 1978. The format of the Ironman has not changed since then: It consists of a 3.86-km swim, a 180.2-km bicycle ride, and a 42.2-km run, all raced in that order and without a break. Suppose an athlete bikes 10 times as fast as he swims and runs 5 times as fast as he swims. The variable x in the expression above represents the rate at which the athlete swims, and the whole expression represents the number of hours that it takes him to complete the race. If it takes him 16.2 hours to complete the race, how many kilometers did he swim in 1 hour?

A) 0.85

B) 1.01

C) 1.17

D) 1.87

Directions: For questions 31-38, enter your responses into the appropriate grid on your answer sheet, in accordance with the following:

1. You will receive credit only if the circles are filled in correctly, but you may write your answers in the boxes above each grid to help you fill in the circles accurately.

2. Don't mark more than one circle per column.

3. None of the questions with grid-in responses will have a negative solution.

4. Only grid in a single answer, even if there is more than one correct answer to a given question.

5. A **mixed number** must be gridded as a decimal or an improper fraction. For example, you would grid $7\frac{1}{2}$ as 7.5 or $\frac{15}{2}$.

(Were you to grid it as $\boxed{7\ 1\ /\ 2}$, this response would be read as $\frac{71}{2}$.)

6. A **decimal** that has more digits than there are places on the grid may be either rounded or truncated, but every column in the grid must be filled in order to receive credit.

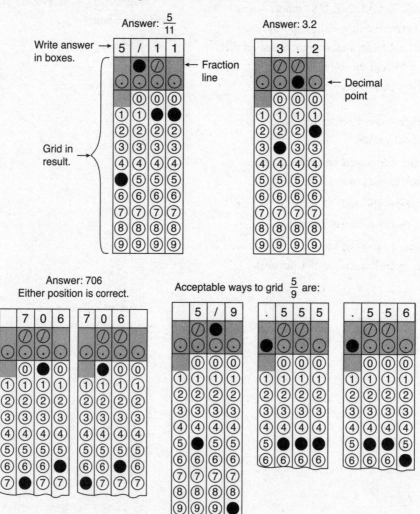

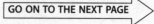

31. What value of x satisfies the equation $\frac{2}{3}(5x + 7) = 8x$?

32. Some doctors base the dosage of a drug to be given to a patient on the patient's body surface area (BSA). The most commonly used formula for calculating BSA is $BSA = \sqrt{\frac{wh}{3,600}}$, where w is the patient's weight (in kg), h is the patient's height (in cm), and BSA is measured in square meters. How tall (in cm) is a patient who weighs 150 kg and has a BSA of $2\sqrt{2}$ m^2?

33. A college math professor informs her students that rather than curving final grades, she will replace each student's lowest test score with the next to lowest test score, and then re-average the test grades. If Leeza has test scores of 86, 92, 81, 64, and 83, by how many points does her final test average change based on the professor's policy?

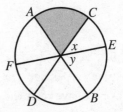

34. In the figure above, $\overline{AB}$, $\overline{CD}$, and $\overline{EF}$ are diameters of the circle. If $y = 2x - 12$, and the shaded area is $\frac{1}{5}$ of the circle, what is the value of x?

35. If the slope of a line is $-\frac{7}{4}$ and a point on the line is $(4, 7)$, what is the y-intercept of the line?

36. Rory left home and drove straight to the airport at an average speed of 45 miles per hour. He returned home along the same route, but traffic slowed him down and he only averaged 30 miles per hour on the return trip. If his total travel time was 2 hours and 30 minutes, how far is it, in miles, from Rory's house to the airport?

Questions 37 and 38 refer to the following information.

Chemical Makeup of One Mole of Chloroform

Element	Number of Moles	Mass per Mole (grams)
Carbon	1	12.011
Hydrogen	1	1.008
Chlorine	3	35.453

A chemical solvent is a substance that dissolves another to form a solution. For example, water is a solvent for sugar. Unfortunately, many chemical solvents are hazardous to the environment. One eco-friendly chemical solvent is chloroform, also known as trichloromethane ($CHCl_3$). The table above shows the chemical makeup of one mole of chloroform.

37. Carbon makes up what percent of the mass of one mole of chloroform? Round your answer to the nearest whole percent and ignore the percent sign when entering your answer.

38. If a chemist starts with 1,000 grams of chloroform and uses 522.5 grams, how many moles of chlorine are left?

IF YOU FINISH BEFORE TIME IS CALLED, YOU MAY CHECK YOUR WORK ON THIS SECTION ONLY. DO NOT TURN TO ANY OTHER SECTION IN THE TEST.   **STOP**

ESSAY TEST

50 Minutes

You will be given a passage to read and asked to write an essay analyzing it. As you write, be sure to show that you have read the passage closely. You will be graded on how well you have understood the passage, how clear your analysis is, and how well you express your ideas.

Your essay must be written on the lines in your answer booklet. Anything you write outside the lined space in your answer booklet will not be read by the essay graders. Be sure to write or print in such a way that it will be legible to readers not familiar with your handwriting. Additionally, be sure to address the passage directly. An off-topic essay will not be graded.

As you read the passage, think about the author's use of

- evidence, such as statistics or other facts.

- logic to connect evidence to conclusions and to develop lines of reasoning.

- style, word choice, and appeals to emotion to make the argument more persuasive.

Adapted from Elisabeth Woodbridge Morris's essay "The Tyranny of Things." In this portion, Morris paints a portrait of American consumerism in 1917 and offers a distinct perspective on the joy of freedom from "things, things, things."

1   Two fifteen-year-old girls stood eyeing one another on first acquaintance. Finally one little girl said, "Which do you like best, people or things?" The other little girl said, "Things." They were friends at once.

2   I suppose we all go through a phase when we like things best; and not only like them, but want to possess them under our hand. The passion for accumulation is upon us. We make "collections," we fill our rooms, our walls, our tables, our desks, with things, things, things.

3   Many people never pass out of this phase. They never see a flower without wanting to pick it and put it in a vase, they never enjoy a book without wanting to own it, nor a picture without wanting to hang it on their walls. They keep photographs of all their friends and Kodak albums of all the places they visit, they save all their theater programmes and dinner cards, they bring home all their alpenstocks.* Their houses are filled with an undigested mass of things, like the terminal moraine where a glacier dumps at length everything it has picked up during its progress through the lands.

4   But to some of us a day comes when we begin to grow weary of things. We realize that we do not possess them; they possess us. Our books are a burden to us, our pictures have destroyed every restful wall-space, our china is a care, our photographs drive us mad, our programmes and alpenstocks fill us with loathing. We feel stifled with the sense of things, and our problem becomes, not how much we can accumulate, but how much we can do without. We send our books to the village library, and our pictures to the college settlement. Such things as we cannot give away, and have not the courage to destroy, we stack in the garret, where they lie huddled in dim and dusty heaps, removed from our sight, to be sure, yet still faintly importunate.

GO ON TO THE NEXT PAGE

5   Then, as we breathe more freely in the clear space that we have made for ourselves, we grow aware that we must not relax our vigilance, or we shall be once more overwhelmed....

6   It extends to all our doings. For every event there is a "souvenir." We cannot go to luncheon and meet our friends but we must receive a token to carry away. Even our children cannot have a birthday party, and play games, and eat good things, and be happy. The host must receive gifts from every little guest, and provide in return some little remembrance for each to take home. Truly, on all sides we are beset, and we go lumbering along through life like a ship encrusted with barnacles, which can never cut the waves clean and sure and swift until she has been scraped bare again. And there seems little hope for us this side our last port.

7   And to think that there was a time when folk had not even that hope! When a man's possessions were burned with him, so that he might, forsooth, have them all about him in the next world! Suffocating thought! To think one could not even then be clear of things, and make at least a fresh start! That must, indeed, have been in the childhood of the race.

8   Once upon a time, when I was very tired, I chanced to go away to a little house by the sea.... There was nothing in the house to demand care, to claim attention, to cumber my consciousness with its insistent, unchanging companionship. There was nothing but a shelter, and outside, the fields and marshes, the shore and the sea. These did not have to be taken down and put up and arranged and dusted and cared for. They were not things at all, they were powers, presences....

9   If we could but free ourselves once for all, how simple life might become! One of my friends, who, with six young children and only one servant, keeps a spotless house and a soul serene, told me once how she did it. "My dear, once a month I give away every single thing in the house that we do not imperatively need. It sounds wasteful, but I don't believe it really is...."

> Write an essay that analyzes the author's approach in persuading her readers that possessions are oppressive. Focus on specific features such as the ones listed in the box above the passage and explain how these features strengthen the author's argument. Your essay should discuss the most important rhetorical features of the passage.
>
> Your essay should not focus on your own opinion of the author's conclusion, but rather on how the author persuades her readers.

ANSWER KEY
READING TEST

1. A	14. B	27. D	40. D
2. B	15. D	28. C	41. A
3. C	16. C	29. C	42. A
4. C	17. A	30. B	43. A
5. A	18. D	31. D	44. B
6. C	19. C	32. C	45. A
7. D	20. C	33. D	46. B
8. A	21. C	34. B	47. D
9. D	22. B	35. C	48. D
10. A	23. D	36. C	49. A
11. D	24. C	37. B	50. C
12. D	25. A	38. C	51. D
13. D	26. A	39. A	52. C

WRITING AND LANGUAGE TEST

1. C	12. B	23. C	34. B
2. D	13. B	24. B	35. A
3. B	14. B	25. D	36. C
4. C	15. A	26. B	37. C
5. A	16. A	27. B	38. B
6. C	17. C	28. C	39. C
7. B	18. A	29. B	40. B
8. D	19. B	30. C	41. A
9. C	20. C	31. B	42. D
10. C	21. D	32. D	43. D
11. A	22. D	33. A	44. C

MATH—NO CALCULATOR TEST

1. C	6. D	11. C	16. 20
2. A	7. D	12. B	17. 1
3. D	8. B	13. A	18. 2
4. C	9. B	14. D	19. 14
5. B	10. A	15. A	20. 6

MATH—CALCULATOR TEST

1. C	11. B	21. C	31. 1
2. C	12. D	22. D	32. 192
3. D	13. A	23. B	33. 3.4
4. A	14. D	24. C	34. 40
5. B	15. B	25. D	35. 14
6. C	16. B	26. C	36. 45
7. D	17. D	27. A	37. 10
8. B	18. A	28. B	38. 12
9. A	19. A	29. B	
10. C	20. A	30. D	

ANSWERS AND EXPLANATIONS

READING TEST

Anna Karenina

Suggested Passage Map notes:

¶1: Levin goes to skating rink to find Kitty

¶2: description of day, people

¶3: walks to skating area; nervous, sees K skating

¶4: knows her right away, still nervous

¶5: lots of happy people skating

¶6: cousin greets him

1. A.   Difficulty: Easy

Category: Detail

Getting to the Answer: Make sure to read the passage closely so events are clearly understood. The first paragraph explicitly states how Levin knew that Kitty was there: he saw her family's carriage. Choice (A) matches the information stated in the passage.

2. B   Difficulty: Medium

Category: Vocab-in-Context

Getting to the Answer: Use context clues to help you distinguish the shades of meaning each word has. Two of the answer choices have a somewhat negative connotation. The author is not describing the scene in a negative way. In this passage, the word "swarmed" means "gathered." Therefore, (B) is the correct answer. The other words' connotations do not fit with the context of the sentence.

3. C   Difficulty: Hard

Category: Inference

Getting to the Answer: Look for clues in the text that suggest what Levin is like. Emotionally charged phrases, such as "the rapture and the terror that seized on his heart," help reveal Levin's personality. Choice (C) reflects the depiction of Levin as a passionate person.

4. C   Difficulty: Hard

Category: Command of Evidence

Getting to the Answer: Eliminate answer choices that don't include a description of Levin. Because the excerpt focuses on Levin's feelings toward Kitty, evidence of the kind of person he is will probably reflect this. Choice (C) provides the best evidence.

5. A   Difficulty: Medium

Category: Global

Getting to the Answer: The central theme of a passage is the insight about life that the author is trying to get across to the reader. Eliminate any themes that are not revealed by the experiences of Levin. Though you may personally agree with more than one of the themes presented, (A) is the only answer choice that is supported by details in the passage. Levin's feelings and actions support this theme.

6. C   Difficulty: Medium

Category: Inference

Getting to the Answer: Examine the passage to see what other characters do in response to Levin. The other skaters go about their business. Most take little notice of Levin. Therefore, (C) is the correct answer.

7. D   Difficulty: Medium

Category: Command of Evidence

Getting to the Answer: Reread each quote in the context of the passage. This will help you decide the correct answer. Of all the answer choices, Nikolay's way of greeting Levin is the strongest evidence that people think Levin seems normal. Choice (D) is the correct answer.

8. A   **Difficulty:** Medium

Category: Vocab-in-Context

Getting to the Answer: The context of the passage can help reveal the meaning of the word. Insert each choice in the sentence to see which one makes the most sense. Levin speaks directly to his heart, asking it to behave. Choice (A), "begged," comes closest to meaning the same thing as "conjured" in this context.

9. D   **Difficulty:** Medium

Category: Rhetoric

Getting to the Answer: Think about the entire scene described in the passage and decide why the author chose to describe Levin's heart as "throbbing." Choice (D) is the correct answer. The author chose this word to capture Levin's agitated state.

10. A   **Difficulty:** Hard

Category: Rhetoric

Getting to the Answer: Eliminate answer choices that are clearly not representative of the author's feelings or attitude about Levin. The author presents Levin's situation as one that is painful. The passage's tone suggests that Levin is worthy of the reader's empathy. Choice (A) fits this tone.

Franklin Delano Roosevelt Speech

Suggested Passage Map notes:

    ¶1: US devoted to democracy
    ¶2: must think about soc. & eco problems which → soc. revol.
    ¶3: list of basics of dem.
    ¶4: must maintain basics
    ¶5: list of what should be improved
    ¶6: Americans will personally sacrifice for them
    ¶7: explain tax changes
    ¶8: people will be ok with them
    ¶9: four essential human freedoms
    ¶10: freedom speech and expression
    ¶11: freedom of religion

    ¶12: freedom from want
    ¶13: freedom from fear
    ¶14: are attainable now; against new order of tyranny
    ¶15: moral order
    ¶16: change can made done peacefully
    ¶17: US supports human rights everywhere and will win

11. D   **Difficulty:** Hard

Category: Rhetoric

Getting to the Answer: The introduction to the passage states that President Roosevelt intends to preserve and spread democracy. Choice (D) makes clear that the president wants to promote human rights, which can be achieved by spreading "American ideals around the world."

12. D   **Difficulty:** Hard

Category: Command of Evidence

Getting to the Answer: Be careful of choices that do not provide direct evidence to support the president's purpose. The correct answer will relate specifically to the stated purpose, or intent, of the passage. President Roosevelt makes clear that his intention is to provide support for global efforts to end tyranny and spread democracy and to garner the support of the American people for these goals. In the previous question, his stated purpose is "to make its people conscious of their individual stake in the preservation of democratic life in America." Only (D) provides direct evidence for the previous question.

13. D   **Difficulty:** Easy

Category: Vocab-in-Context

Getting to the Answer: All answer choices are alternate meanings of the word "sacrifice." The correct answer will relate directly to the context of the passage. Despite the fact that Roosevelt gave the speech on the eve of America's involvement in World War II, neither B nor C is the meaning he's after. Choice (D), "surrender of interests to a greater good," is the correct answer.

14. B   Difficulty: Hard

Category: Connections

Getting to the Answer: Keep in mind that you're looking for a relationship that is suggested, not stated. To reach the correct answer, you must infer, or make a logical guess, based on information in the passage. The correct answer will provide support for the stated purpose of the passage while demonstrating a logical relationship. Choice (B) provides support for the stated goal of winning support among U.S. citizens for the spread of democracy abroad. It does so by suggesting that the security of U.S. democracy depends on the advancement of human rights and freedoms globally.

15. D   Difficulty: Medium

Category: Command of Evidence

Getting to the Answer: Avoid answers that provide evidence for incorrect answers to the previous question. The correct answer will use language reflective of the correct answer above to demonstrate a relationship. Principles and ideas such as democracy, freedom, and protection of human rights are used interchangeably throughout Roosevelt's speech. The lines in (D) draw the connection between freedom at home and freedom everywhere.

16. C   Difficulty: Easy

Category: Vocab-in-Context

Getting to the Answer: Substitute each answer choice for the word in question and decide which one fits the context provided in the passage. In the context of the passage, (C) works best. It draws a distinction between individual citizens' monetary interests, or their pocketbooks, and the cause of patriotism, or the greater good.

17. A   Difficulty: Medium

Category: Rhetoric

Getting to the Answer: Keep in mind that the correct answer will relate directly to the meaning of the elements in the identified lines. President Roosevelt is arguing against those who would oppose the overarching goal of his speech, namely to garner support for the spread of democracy overseas. Choice (A) fits best; Roosevelt asserts that his goals are realistic and attainable, not just idealistic visions, as his opponents might claim.

18. D   Difficulty: Medium

Category: Rhetoric

Getting to the Answer: Be wary of answers like A and B that seem to offer specific advice or state specific goals relevant to the purpose of the passage without suggesting how those goals might be achieved. The correct answer will offer a tool, a condition, or another asset for achieving the passage's claim—in this case, the spread of democracy. The previous question identifies that President Roosevelt considers the spread of global democracy achievable. This question asks you to identify how the president envisions achieving that purpose. Choice (D) matches the intent. In this line, President Roosevelt identifies "our unity of purpose" as an asset that will help achieve his goal.

19. C   Difficulty: Hard

Category: Inference

Getting to the Answer: Be careful of answers that cite other policies that the president might support that are not related to the lines quoted. The correct answer will relate directly to the specific lines in question. In this speech, Roosevelt identifies four freedoms that he views the United States as obligated to defend. The freedom from want signifies a commitment to helping struggling populations at home and abroad. Choice (C) fits. The president urges economic understandings among nations to help those in need.

20. C   Difficulty: Medium

Category: Rhetoric

Getting to the Answer: Be careful of answers like

A that offer other viable uses of rhetoric within the larger passage. The correct answer will relate specifically to the text cited in the question. Roosevelt suggests that the preservation of American freedoms cannot exist without the preservation of human rights on a global scale. To cement this connection, he contrasts democratic movements with tyrannical movements occurring in the world. Choice (C) is the correct answer. President Roosevelt references "the so-called new order of tyranny" in order to show what might happen should the United States and the American people not support other nations in their fight against such tyranny.

Women's Suffrage

Suggested Passage Map notes:

¶1: Changes in Am. voting process

¶2: women's voting history; Seneca Falls declaration

¶3: 1878 – amendment proposed, federal gov't not ready

¶4: women voting in New Zealand, Australia, United Kingdom

¶5: WWI → female activism; 19th Amendment passed in 1919, ratified 1920

¶6: elections still not equal b/c Af. Americans often disenfranchised; 1965 Voting Rights Act → voting equality for all

21. C   Difficulty: Medium

Category: Rhetoric

Getting to the Answer: Keep in mind that the "stance" of an author refers to his or her perspective or attitude toward the topic. The passage is written by a scholar or a historian who is looking back on the events that led to the adoption of the Nineteenth Amendment. It is not written by a primary source, such as a legislator or an advocate in the midst of the movement's events. For this reason, (C) is the correct answer. The author of the passage is clearly a scholar

evaluating not just the motivation of women's suffrage leaders but the key events and impact of the movement as a whole.

22. B   Difficulty: Hard

Category: Rhetoric

Getting to the Answer: Avoid answers like A that refer to related issues not relevant to the passage's purpose and answers like D that go too far. The correct answer will identify a claim that is supported by the quotation. In the quote, the author notes that election laws following passage of the Nineteenth Amendment did not secure equal voting rights for all. From this statement, it becomes clear that other groups of people still needed support for their voting rights. Answer (B) is correct.

23. D   Difficulty: Medium

Category: Command of Evidence

Getting to the Answer: Reread the line quoted in the previous question and notice that it occurs in the passage after ratification of the Nineteenth Amendment. Therefore, the evidence you're looking for will refer to an event that came later. The author suggests that the Nineteenth Amendment did not win equal voting rights for all citizens but that it did serve as an important step on the way to free and fair elections. Choice (D) demonstrates that a later event expanded voting rights further, to citizens regardless not only of gender but also of race.

24. C   Difficulty: Easy

Category: Vocab-in-Context

Getting to the Answer: Consider the events that are being described in the paragraph in which the word appears. This will help you choose the best answer. It's clear in this paragraph that the women's suffrage movement was gaining momentum at this time. Events and tactics excited those who supported the movement and attracted more supporters. Therefore, (C) reflects the correct meaning of "galvanized."

25. A **Difficulty:** Hard

Category: Rhetoric

Getting to the Answer: Carefully review the paragraph in which the line appears before choosing the best answer. Choice (A) demonstrates the connection between successfully changing one element (people's minds) in order to change the other (laws).

26. A **Difficulty:** Hard

Category: Inference

Getting to the Answer: Be wary of answers like D that go too far in asserting unsubstantiated causal relationships. The correct answer will reference an idea or a relationship that is supported by the content of the passage. Choice (A) expresses the idea implicit in the passage that the American government responds, sometimes slowly, to the changing needs and sentiments of the American people.

27. D **Difficulty:** Hard

Category: Command of Evidence

Getting to the Answer: Watch for answers like A and C that cite specific changes or examples but do not provide direct support. The correct answer to the previous question states the idea implicit in the passage that the government responds and adapts to changes in U.S. society. This suggests a gradual change. Choice (D) demonstrates the idea that both society and the government have changed over time as the civil rights movement of the late twentieth century overcame social and legal inequalities inherited from earlier in the nation's history.

28. C **Difficulty:** Medium

Category: Synthesis

Getting to the Answer: Be careful of answers that aren't backed by sufficient evidence in the graphic. The graphic shows proof that women's suffrage unfolded through a series of events over a long period of time. Choice (C) is the correct answer.

29. C **Difficulty:** Medium

Category: Vocab-in-Context

Getting to the Answer: Read the sentence in which the word appears. The correct answer should be interchangeable with the word. The passage states that "Posters . . . called into question the authenticity of a free country with unjust laws." Choice (C) is the correct answer, as "legitimacy" refers to something that is in accordance with established principles.

30. B **Difficulty:** Medium

Category: Inference

Getting to the Answer: Be cautious about answers that present accurate facts but that do not directly relate to the content of the question. Choice (B) is the correct answer. Wilson's framing of the conflict abroad as a fight for democracy and freedom helped women suffragists draw attention to the fact that the U.S. government was fighting for justice abroad while denying justice at home.

31. D **Difficulty:** Medium

Category: Synthesis

Getting to the Answer: A question like this is asking you to compare information provided in the graphic with information provided in the passage text. Consider each answer choice as you make your comparison. Choice (D) is the correct answer. Both the graphic and the passage indicate that women's suffrage gained early victories in several states quite a few years before becoming law at the federal level through passage of the Nineteenth Amendment.

Paired Passages—Radioisotopes

Suggested Passage Map notes:

Passage 1

¶1: (central idea): use atoms to date things; isotopes def. & exs.

¶2: isotopes unstable; measure C-14

¶3: C-14 decay = predictable

¶4: C-14 dating; materials; timeline based on layers

Passage 2

¶1: def. radioactive; why dangerous; danger = radiation rate

¶2: half-life def. = decay rate; exs.

¶3: long half-life = long problem

32. C   Difficulty: Hard

Category: Inference

Getting to the Answer: Use your Passage Map to locate the paragraph that explains carbon-14 dating. This paragraph will contain the description of what materials can be dated using this method. In paragraph 4, the author states that carbon-14 dating can be used on materials made by a living organism. An arrowhead made from a bone is constructed of such material, choice (C).

33. D   Difficulty: Hard

Category: Command of Evidence

Getting to the Answer: Locate each of the answer choices in the passage. The correct answer should provide direct support for the answer to the previous question: the bone arrowhead can be dated using carbon-14 dating. In paragraph 4, the author describes the process for carbon-14 dating. Choice (D) is correct because this sentence provides a direct description of the materials that can be dated using carbon-14 dating.

34. B   Difficulty: Medium

Category: Vocab-in-Context

Getting to the Answer: Pretend that the word "decay" is a blank. Reread around the cited word to predict a word that could substitute for "decay" in context. The previous paragraph discusses how scientists measure the rate of emission to calculate the amount of carbon-14 in a sample. "Emission" means release; therefore, the amount of carbon-14 is be-

coming smaller if the atoms are releasing it. In this sentence, therefore, predict "decay" means to *decrease*, which matches "deteriorate," choice (B).

35. C   Difficulty: Easy

Category: Connections

Getting to the Answer: Look at your notes for paragraph 3. Summarize the ratio of carbon-12 to carbon-14 in living tissue in your own words. Look for the answer choice that most closely matches your prediction. In paragraph 3, the author explains that the ratio of carbon-12 to carbon-14 for living things is the same as the ratio in the atmosphere: constant. Choice (C) is correct.

36. C   Difficulty: Medium

Category: Command of Evidence

Getting to the Answer: Review what part of the passage you used to predict an answer for the previous question: the ratio is constant for living things. Of the answer choices, only lines 28-31 explain the ratio of carbon-12 to carbon-14 in living things. Choice (C) is correct.

37. B   Difficulty: Medium

Category: Detail

Getting to the Answer: Read around the cited lines. The author directly states why a release of iodine-131 is not cause for long-term concern. In paragraph 3, the author explains that the initial release of radiation from an accident involving iodine-131 will be high, but the level of radiation will drop quickly (lines 75–76). Choice (B) is correct.

38. C   Difficulty: Medium

Category: Detail

Getting to the Answer: Use your Passage Map to find the information about why exposure to radiation is dangerous.

Getting to the Answer: In paragraph 1, lines 53-55, the author explains that radiation is harmful to living tissue because it can cause damage to the cells'

DNA, which matches choice (C).

39. A   Difficulty: Easy

Category: Vocab-in-Context

Getting to the Answer: Pretend that the word "original" is a blank. Reread around the cited word to predict a word that could substitute for "original" in context. The previous paragraph explains how scientists use "half-life" to determine how quickly material decays. If the material is decaying, then predict "original" refers to the *first* material. Choice (A) matches your prediction.

40. D   Difficulty: Medium

Category: Detail

Getting to the Answer: Review your notes for Passage 2. Try to put into your own words how scientists use half-life calculations of radioactive materials. Look for the answer that most closely matches your idea. In paragraph 1, the author explains that the level of danger posed by radiation released during a nuclear accident depends on how quickly radiation is released (lines 59-62). In paragraph 2, the author discusses how the half-life of radioactive material is used to determine how long a material will emit radiation. Paragraph 3 then explains how different half-lives translate into short-term or long-term radiation concerns. Choice (D) is correct because it most clearly paraphrases the information in the passage about how scientists use half-life calculations.

41. A   Difficulty: Hard

Category: Synthesis

Getting to the Answer: The central idea will be supported by all of the evidence presented in both passages. Review the central idea you identified for each passage in your Passage Maps. Passage 1 discusses the application of atomic and nuclear physics in archaeology while Passage 2 details how scientists apply atomic and nuclear physics to studies of radioactivity in nuclear power plant accidents. Choice (A) is correct.

42. A   Difficulty: Hard

Category: Synthesis

Getting to the Answer: Analyze the graph to see that it describes the decay of carbon-14 over time. Think about how this data relates to the texts. The graph portrays the decay of carbon-14 as described in Passage 1. The definition of "half-life" is given in Passage 2. The half-life of a material is the amount of time it takes for half of that material to decay. The graph shows that about 50 percent of carbon-14 remains after 5,400 years. Choice (A) is correct.

Biomimicry Passage

Suggested Passage Map notes:

¶1: George de Mestral – invented velcro

¶2: biomimicry – study nature to improve people's homes, cities, etc.

¶3: used in architecture

¶4: Michael Pawlyn - adapt principles behind natural shapes → innovative solutions

¶5: used in optics and robotics

¶6: some natural stuff not advanced but simple: abalone shell

¶7: nanoscale features; Andrew Parker – skin of thorny devil

¶8: can learn from animal features

¶9: improve energy efficiency

¶10: radical, optimistic field

43. A   Difficulty: Medium

Category: Global

Getting to the Answer: Look for the answer choice that describes an idea supported throughout the passage rather than a specific detail. The passage cites several examples of biomimicry, the study of how materials and systems found in nature can be replicated to benefit humans. Therefore, (A) is the best summary of the central idea of the passage.

44. B **Difficulty:** Medium

Category: Command of Evidence

Getting to the Answer: Think back to why you chose your answer to the previous question. This will help you pick the correct quote as evidence. Choice (B) is the correct answer because it provides evidence for the central idea that the author presents about the field of biomimicry.

45. A **Difficulty:** Hard

Category: Rhetoric

Getting to the Answer: Think about the primary purpose of the quote. Eliminate any answer choices that don't support this purpose. The quote, which is from a book on architecture, explains why architects turn to biomimicry for solutions in their work. Choice (A) is the correct answer.

46. B **Difficulty:** Medium

Category: Connections

Getting to the Answer: Reread the paragraph that the question is asking about. Look for specific details about the abalone shrimp shell and soft chalk. The passage clearly states that the abalone shrimp shell is harder than soft chalk because of the way the basic material composing each is arranged, so (B) is the correct answer.

47. D **Difficulty:** Medium

Category: Rhetoric

Getting to the Answer: In order to understand why an author includes a quote from another person, examine the surrounding sentences. This often makes clear the author's reason for including the quotation. The author includes the quote from Pawlyn to support and strengthen his or her own view that energy efficiency "has never been more important." Therefore, (D) is the correct answer.

48. D **Difficulty:** Easy

Category: Vocab-in-Context

Getting to the Answer: Replace the word in ques-

tion with each of the answer choices. This will help you eliminate the ones that don't make sense in the context. Choice (D), "concepts," is the only answer choice that makes sense in this context because it reflects the foundational reasons behind the structures.

49. A **Difficulty:** Medium

Category: Inference

Getting to the Answer: Keep in mind that you're being asked to make an inference, a logical guess based on information in the passage. Therefore, the correct answer is not stated in the passage. The variety of examples of biomimicry mentioned in the passage make it reasonable to infer that more scientists will utilize solutions developed through biomimicry in the future. Choice (A) is the correct answer.

50. C **Difficulty:** Medium

Category: Command of Evidence

Getting to the Answer: Reread each quotation in the context of the passage. Consider which one is the best evidence to support the inference made in the previous question. The examples cited in (C) provide strong evidence for the inference that more scientists will probably make use of biomimicry in years to come.

51. D **Difficulty:** Medium

Category: Vocab-in-Context

Getting to the Answer: Eliminate answer choices that are synonyms for the word in question but do not work in the context of the sentence. Because biomimicry is such an innovative approach, it makes sense that the meaning of "radical" in this context is closest to (D), "revolutionary."

52. C **Difficulty:** Hard

Category: Synthesis

Getting to the Answer: Remember that a graphic might not refer to something explicitly stated in the passage. Instead, it often provides a visual example of how an important concept discussed in the passage works. The graphic and its caption help illustrate an example of biomimicry not mentioned in the passage: that of a solar power plant designed to mimic the arrangement of petals in a sunflower. This directs more energy toward the power plant's central tower and improves the efficiency of the power plant. Choice (C) is the correct answer.

WRITING AND LANGUAGE TEST

The Age of the Librarian

1. C   **Difficulty:** Easy

Category: Usage

Getting to the Answer: Examine the verb tense in the rest of the sentence. This will help you find the correct answer. As written, the sentence switches verb tense mid-sentence. Other verbs in the sentence, "worked" and "was," indicate that the events happened in the past. Choice (C) is the correct choice because it correctly uses the past tense of the target verb.

2. D   **Difficulty:** Medium

Category: Punctuation

Getting to the Answer: Pay attention to the quotation marks. Reading through the sentence and the answer choices shows that two issues might need correcting. The sentence inside the quotation marks is a complete sentence. The correct answer needs to punctuate that sentence before closing the quote. Additionally, "however" is being used as a connector or transition word and needs to be followed by a comma after beginning the new sentence. Choice (D) appropriately uses a period prior to the end quotes and correctly inserts a comma after the transition word "However."

3. B   **Difficulty:** Medium

Category: Effective Language Use

Getting to the Answer: Watch out for choices that distort the tone of the passage. The passage suggests that people expected or anticipated that Harris would become a librarian. Evidence for this idea is found in the statement that she was "constantly told" that she "should be studying to be a librarian." Harris was certainly aware that people anticipated this course of study for her, but the presence of the phrase "Little did she realize" tells you that she didn't expect to become one. The correct choice is (B), "imminent," meaning that becoming a librarian was about to occur despite her own expectations.

4. C   **Difficulty:** Hard

Category: Effective Language Use

Getting to the Answer: Read the sentence carefully for context clues. Also, think about the tone of what is being described. This will help you choose the best answer. Given the phrasing of the sentence, the answer must be close in meaning to "excited," which is used earlier in the sentence. Therefore, (C) is the correct answer.

5. A   **Difficulty:** Medium

Category: Punctuation

Getting to the Answer: Determine whether a clause is dependent or independent to decide between a comma and a semicolon. Choice (A) is the correct answer. The sentence is correctly punctuated as written because it uses a comma at the end of the introductory dependent clause.

6. C   **Difficulty:** Medium

Category: Sentence Formation

Getting to the Answer: Read the sentence carefully. The sentence sounds clunky and awkward. Look for an answer choice that makes the sentence clear and easy to understand. Notice that the word "asking" is part of a participial phrase that modifies "Miguel." A participial phrase should be placed as close as possible to the noun it modifies. When a participial phrase begins a sentence, it should be set off with a comma. Choice (C) is correct. The placement of commas and modifiers makes the content easy to understand, and the sentence is free of grammatical or punctuation errors.

7. B   Difficulty: Medium

Category: Development

Getting to the Answer: Read the entire paragraph carefully and predict the main idea. Then look for a close match with your prediction. The paragraph discusses how the role of librarian has changed due to an increased use of technology. Choice (B) is the correct answer, as it explicitly addresses the changing role of the librarian.

8. D   Difficulty: Medium

Category: Sentence Formation

Getting to the Answer: Read the sentence and note the series of examples. A series should have parallel structure. The sentence is not correct as written. The items in the series switch forms from participial phrases beginning with "enabling" and "offering" to "they house." All of the items need to fit the same pattern or form. Choice (D) is correct because it appropriately begins each item in the series with a participle.

9. C   Difficulty: Hard

Category: Development

Getting to the Answer: Don't be fooled by answer choices that are true statements but do not directly support the main idea of the paragraph. The paragraph concerns how the role of the librarian has changed due to an increased use of technology. The correct answer needs to support the idea that librarians work with technology in new ways. Choice (C) works best. It offers a specific example of how teachers look to the librarian to be a "media mentor" and illustrates this new role for school librarians.

10. C   Difficulty: Easy

Category: Usage

Getting to the Answer: Read the sentence prior to the pronoun and determine whom the pronoun is referencing. Pronouns should not be ambiguous, and they must match the verb in number. The sentence is ambiguous as written. "She" would presumably refer back to the "young student," but it seems unlikely that the student would be laughing and thinking about the collections in the library after asking the librarian a question. Choice (C) is the best choice. It clearly indicates the subject of the sentence (Harris) and avoids ambiguity.

11. A   Difficulty: Medium

Category: Usage

Getting to the Answer: Figure out whom the pronoun refers to and make sure it matches the antecedent in number. Watch out for confusing contractions and possessives. The pronoun in the sentence needs to indicate who will have the ideas. Harris is talking to a single student, so the sentence will need a singular possessive pronoun. Choice (A) is correct. As it is, the sentence correctly uses a singular possessive pronoun.

Unforeseen Consequences: The Dark Side of the Industrial Revolution

12. B   Difficulty: Medium

Category: Sentence Formation

Getting to the Answer: Be careful of answers that sound correct when they stand alone but do not conform to the structure of the sentence as a whole. The existing text is incorrect, as it does not maintain parallel structure. Choice (B) is the correct answer, as it maintains the parallel structure of preposition ("into") + noun ("the role").

13. B   Difficulty: Easy

Category: Punctuation

Getting to the Answer: Eliminate answers that confuse the usage of commas and semicolons. Choice (B) is correct. Without the comma, the following clause modifies "urban areas" when it should modify the entire preceding clause.

14. B   Difficulty: Medium

Category: Effective Language Use

Getting to the Answer: Avoid choices that are redundant and imprecise. The correct answer will use the clearest, most concise terminology to communicate the idea. Choice (B) is correct. It is the most concise—and clearest—word choice because all of the items listed in the original sentence are simply types of food. The other choices use more words than necessary to convey meaning.

15. A   Difficulty: Medium

Category: Organization

Getting to the Answer: The first sentence should function as a transition between ideas in the previous paragraph and ideas in the current paragraph. Choice (A) makes sense. This choice connects ideas from the previous paragraph with the content of paragraph 3. The sentences that follow provide details to support that introductory idea.

16. A   Difficulty: Hard

Category: Quantitative

Getting to the Answer: Eliminate answers like B that fail to support the cited sentence directly. The underlined sentence references "unprecedented amounts of human-made carbon dioxide into the air." This suggests an increase in the amount of carbon dioxide in the atmosphere over time. Therefore, (A) is the correct answer.

17. C   Difficulty: Medium

Category: Effective Language Use

Getting to the Answer: Choose the answer that

presents the correct relationship between ideas. Choice (C) is correct. It shows the causal relationship without adding verbiage.

18. A   Difficulty: Easy

Category: Effective Language Use

Getting to the Answer: Plug in the answer choices and select the one that reflects a specific meaning relevant to the sentence. The paragraph focuses on the negative effects of industrialization and waste production. Therefore, (A) is the correct answer.

19. B   Difficulty: Hard

Category: Development

Getting to the Answer: Be careful of choices that relate to the underlined portion of the text without showing clearly how the underlined portion supports the full implications of the preceding sentence. The paragraph explains that industrialization resulted in the destruction of resources. The correct answer, (B), serves as clear evidence of the "process of destruction and reduced resources."

20. C   Difficulty: Medium

Category: Effective Language Use

Getting to the Answer: Be careful of answers that make sense but do not fully support the meaning of the content. The correct answer will not only flow logically but will also reflect the precise purpose and meaning of the larger sentence and paragraph. Choice (C) is the correct answer. "Substandard" communicates clearly that the working conditions were the cause of the health problems.

21. D   Difficulty: Medium

Category: Sentence Formation

Getting to the Answer: Eliminate choices that result in sentence fragments or fragmented clauses. The correct answer will maintain appropriate syntax without misusing punctuation. Choice (D) is correct.

It sets off the dependent clause without using incorrect punctuation to signal a hard break before an independent clause or second complete sentence.

22. D   **Difficulty:** Hard

Category: Development

Getting to the Answer: Avoid answers that draw on similar ideas but combine those ideas in a way that communicates a proposition not supported by the essay as a whole. The correct answer will make sense within the larger context of the essay. The central idea of the entire essay is that industrialization and progress came at a cost that made the promise of a bright future difficult to fulfill. Choice (D) is the correct answer.

Remembering Freud

23. C   **Difficulty:** Hard

Category: Effective Language Use

Getting to the Answer: Consider the fact that there may be a choice that helps make the meaning of the sentence very precise. Choice (C) most accurately indicates that Freud led a whole movement.

24. B   **Difficulty:** Medium

Category: Punctuation

Getting to the Answer: Plug in each answer choice and select the one that seems most correct. Choice (B) makes it clear to the reader that this is extra information modifying the word "career."

25. D   **Difficulty:** Medium

Category: Sentence Formation

Getting to the Answer: Remember that in a list, all things listed should be presented with the same grammatical structure. "Id," "ego," and "Freudian slip" are all nouns. Choice (D) is the correct answer because it uses a parallel structure for all three nouns.

26. B   **Difficulty:** Hard

Category: Development

Getting to the Answer: Notice that the underlined sentence is the first sentence in the paragraph. Think about which choice would make the best topic sentence, given the content of the rest of the paragraph. Choice (B) correctly makes the free-speaking technique the focus of the paragraph's topic sentence, while suggesting that the technique was radical enough to earn Freud his title.

27. B   **Difficulty:** Medium

Category: Effective Language Use

Getting to the Answer: Eliminate any choices that don't seem as precise as others. Choice (B) is correct. The word "recesses" is more precise; it connotes smaller parts of the brain and a sense of being hidden.

28. C   **Difficulty:** Easy

Category: Punctuation

Getting to the Answer: Think about how the sentence sounds when read aloud. This often helps you get a good sense of whether or not a comma is needed. Choice (C) would fit here. The sentence eliminates the unneeded comma.

29. B   **Difficulty:** Hard

Category: Sentence Formation

Getting to the Answer: Remember that a modifier should be adjacent to the noun it is modifying and set off by punctuation. Choice (B) is correct. The modifier "like neurosis or other psychological trauma" should come directly after "conditions."

30. C   **Difficulty:** Hard

Category: Development

Getting to the Answer: Consider how this sentence relates to the one before it and the one that follows it. Does it offer strong support of the connecting ideas? This section discussed the development and lasting influence of Freud's ideas. The best supporting sentence will provide details connecting these concepts. Choice (C) is correct. It emphasizes that Freud developed new ideas that have had a lasting influence on psychological practices.

31. B   Difficulty: Medium

Category: Sentence Formation

Getting to the Answer: Notice that you are dealing with a run-on sentence. Identify the point in the run-on where it appears two sentences have been fused together. Choice (B) is correct. This choice splits the run-on sentence into two separate, grammatically correct sentences.

32. D   Difficulty: Easy

Category: Sentence Formation

Getting to the Answer: Eliminate answer choices that are not complete sentences or do not maintain the correct verb tense. Choice (D) correctly changes the phrase "Freud's finding of a method" to "Freud found a method," making the sentence complete. It also corrects the verb tense.

33. A   Difficulty: Hard

Category: Sentence Formation

Getting to the Answer: Recall that when a dependent clause precedes an independent clause, it should be set off with a comma. Choice (A) is the best choice. Although lengthy, the dependent clause in the sentence ("as long as occasions arise . . .") is correctly combined with its independent clause ("Sigmund Freud will be remembered . . .") by use of a comma.

Success in Montreal

34. B   Difficulty: Easy

Category: Sentence Formation

Getting to the Answer: Always check whether two

or more verbs that serve the same function have a parallel structure. Choice (B) is correct. "To prevent" is in the infinitive form like the earlier verb in the sentence, "to reverse."

35. A   Difficulty: Hard

Category: Effective Language Use

Getting to the Answer: Look for the choice that most concisely and correctly joins the two sentences. Choice (A) is the best fit. This option joins the sentences concisely and correctly.

36. C   Difficulty: Medium

Category: Effective Language Use

Getting to the Answer: Remember that the best answer is the most concise and effective way of stating the information while ensuring that the information is complete. Choice (C) works best here. It uses the fewest necessary words to convey the complete information.

37. C   Difficulty: Medium

Category: Sentence Formation

Getting to the Answer: Eliminate any choices that use transition words inappropriately. Two complete thoughts should be separated into two different sentences. Therefore, (C) is the best choice.

38. B   Difficulty: Hard

Category: Quantitative

Getting to the Answer: Examine the graphic for details that suggest which answer is correct. Choice (B) accurately reflects the information in the graphic. Beginning in the 1990s, the size of the ozone hole began to level off.

39. C   Difficulty: Medium

Category: Effective Language Use

Getting to the Answer: Check each word to see how it fits with the context of the sentence. While all of the words have similar meanings, only one fits the context of the paragraph. Choice (C), "measured," has a connotation that corresponds to "gauge" in the following sentence.

40. B   Difficulty: Easy

Category: Usage

Getting to the Answer: Remember that the possessive form must agree with its antecedent. The correct answer will reflect the gender and number of its antecedent; in this case, the word "treaty." Therefore, (B) is correct.

41. A   Difficulty: Hard

Category: Development

Getting to the Answer: To find the central idea of a paragraph, identify important details and then summarize them in a sentence or two. Then find the choice that is the closest to your summary. Choice (A) most clearly states the paragraph's central idea, that the ozone layer is beginning to return to normal.

42. D   Difficulty: Medium

Category: Development

Getting to the Answer: To find the correct answer, first determine the central idea of the paragraph. Choice (D) is the least essential sentence in the paragraph, so it is the correct answer.

43. D   Difficulty: Medium

Category: Effective Language Use

Getting to the Answer: Context clues indicate which word is appropriate in the sentence. Check to see which word fits best in the sentence. The word "reverse," (D), fits with the context of the sentence and connotes a more precise action than does "change."

44. C   Difficulty: Hard

Category: Organization

Getting to the Answer: Examine the entire paragraph. Decide whether the sentence provides more information about a topic mentioned in one of the other sentences. This sentence provides more information related to sentence 1, "The Montreal Protocol is a living document"; it describes how the document is "living." Choice (C) is the correct answer.

MATH—NO CALCULATOR TEST

1. C   Difficulty: Easy

Category: Heart of Algebra / Linear Equations

Getting to the Answer: To determine what the y-intercept could mean in the context of a word problem, examine the labels on the graph and note what each axis represents. According to the labels, the y-axis represents cost, and the x-axis represents the number of games played. The y-intercept, $(0, 5)$, has an x-value of 0, which means 0 games were played, yet there is still a cost of $5. The cost must represent a flat fee that is charged before any games are played, such as an entrance fee to enter the arcade, (C).

2. A   Difficulty: Easy

Category: Passport to Advanced Math / Exponents

Getting to the Answer: To divide one rational expression by another, multiply the first expression by the reciprocal (the flip) of the second expression. Rewrite the division as multiplication, factor any factorable expressions, and then simplify if possible.

$$\frac{3x}{x+5} \div \frac{6}{4x+20} = \frac{3x}{x+5} \cdot \frac{4x+20}{6}$$
$$= \frac{3x}{x+5} \cdot \frac{4(x+5)}{6}$$
$$= \frac{12x}{6}$$
$$= 2x$$

Note that the question also states that $x \neq -5$. This doesn't affect your answer—it is simply stated because the denominators of rational expressions cannot equal 0. Choice (A) is correct.

3. D   Difficulty: Easy

Category: Additional Topics in Math / Geometry

Getting to the Answer: When the equation of a circle is written in the form $(x - h)^2 + (y - k)^2 = r^2$, the point (h, k) represents the center of the circle on a coordinate plane, and r represents the length of the radius. To find the area of a circle, use the formula, $A = \pi r^2$. In the equation given in the question, r^2 is the constant on the right-hand side (25)—you don't even need to solve for r because the area formula involves r^2, not r. So, the area is $\pi(25)$ or 25π, (D).

4. C   Difficulty: Easy

Category: Passport to Advanced Math / Functions

Getting to the Answer: When using function notation, $f(x)$ is simply another way of saying y, so this question is asking you to find the values of x for which $y = 0$, or in other words, where the graph crosses the x-axis. The graph crosses the x-axis at the points $(-2, 0)$ and $(3, 0)$, so the values of x for which $f(x) = 0$ are -2 and 3, (C).

5. B   Difficulty: Medium

Category: Heart of Algebra / Linear Equations

Getting to the Answer: Choose the best strategy to answer the question. You could start by cross-multiplying to get rid of the denominators, but simplifying the numerators first will make the calculations easier.

$$\frac{4(d + 3) - 9}{8} = \frac{10 - (2 - d)}{6}$$
$$\frac{4d + 12 - 9}{8} = \frac{10 - 2 + d}{6}$$
$$\frac{4d + 3}{8} = \frac{8 + d}{6}$$
$$6(4d + 3) = 8(8 + d)$$
$$24d + 18 = 64 + 8d$$
$$16d = 46$$
$$d = \frac{46}{16} = \frac{23}{8}$$

Choice (B) is correct.

6. D   Difficulty: Medium

Category: Passport to Advanced Math / Functions

Getting to the Answer: This is a crossover question, so quickly skim the first couple of sentences. Then look for the relevant information in the last couple of sentences. It may also help to circle the portions of the graph that meet the given requirement.

Because *greater* means *higher* on a graph, the statement $f(t) > g(t)$ translates to "Where is $f(t)$ above $g(t)$?" The solid curve represents f and the dashed curve represents g, so $f > g$ between the years 1960 and 1980 and again between the years 2000 and 2010. Look for these time intervals in the answer choices: $1960 < t < 1980$ and $2000 < t < 2010$. This matches (D).

7. D   Difficulty: Medium

Category: Passport to Advanced Math / Scatterplots

Getting to the Answer: Use the shape of the data to predict the type of equation that might be used as a model. Then, use specific values from the graph to choose the correct equation. According to the graph, the population of the whales grew slowly at first and then more quickly. This means that an exponential model is probably the best fit, so you can eliminate A (linear) and B (quadratic). The remaining equations are both exponential, so choose a data point and see which equation is the closest fit. Be careful—the vertical axis represents *hundreds* of whales, and the question states that t represents the number of years since the study began, so $t = 0$ for 1995, $t = 3$ for 1998, and so on. If you use the data for 1995, which is the point $(0, 100)$, the results are the same for both equations, so choose a different point. Using the data for 2007, $t = 2007 - 1995 = 12$, and the number of whales was 800. Substitute these values into C and D to see which one is true. Choice C is not true because $800 \neq 100 \times 2^{12}$. Choice (D) is correct because:

$$800 = 100 \times 2^{\frac{12}{4}} = 100 \times 2^3 = 100 \times 8$$

8. B   **Difficulty:** Medium

Category: Heart of Algebra / Linear Equations

Getting to the Answer: To find the average rate of change over the 5-year period, find the slope between the starting point (0, 1,200) and the ending point (5, 100).

$$m = \frac{y_2 - y_1}{x_2 - x_1} = \frac{100 - 1{,}200}{5 - 0} = \frac{-1{,}100}{5} = -220$$

Choice (B) is correct. (The average rate of change is negative because the laptop decreases in value over time.)

Note: Because the question involves *straight-line* depreciation, you could have used any two points on the graph to find the slope. As a general rule, however, you should use the endpoints of the given time interval.

9. B   **Difficulty:** Medium

Category: Passport to Advanced Math / Exponents

Getting to the Answer: When multiplying polynomials, carefully multiply each term in the first factor by each term in the second factor. This question doesn't ask for the entire product, so check to make sure you answered the right question (the coefficient of x^2).

$$\left(6x^2 - \frac{2}{5}x + 1\right)\left(10x + \frac{1}{3}\right)$$

$$= 6x^2\left(10x + \frac{1}{3}\right) - \frac{2}{5}x\left(10x + \frac{1}{3}\right) + 1\left(10x + \frac{1}{3}\right)$$

$$= 60x^3 + \underline{2x^2 - 4x^2} - \frac{2}{15}x + 10x + \frac{1}{3}$$

The coefficient of x^2 is $2 + (-4) = -2$, which is (B).

10. A   **Difficulty:** Medium

Category: Heart of Algebra / Linear Equations

Getting to the Answer: The line is decreasing, so the slope (m) is negative. The line crosses the y-axis below 0, so the y-intercept (b) is also negative. Put each answer choice in slope-intercept form, one at a time, and examine the signs of m and b. Begin with (A):

$$-6x - 4y = 5$$
$$-4y = 6x + 5$$
$$y = \frac{6x}{-4} + \frac{5}{-4}$$
$$y = -\frac{3}{2}x - \frac{5}{4}$$

You don't need to check any of the other equations. Choice (A) has a negative slope and a negative y-intercept, so it is the correct equation.

11. C   **Difficulty:** Hard

Category: Heart of Algebra / Systems of Linear Equations

Getting to the Answer: Graphically, a system of linear equations that has no solution indicates two parallel lines or, in other words, two lines that have the same slope. So, write each of the equations in slope-intercept form ($y = mx + b$) and set their slopes (m) equal to each other to solve for k. Before finding the slopes, multiply the top equation by 4 to make it easier to manipulate.

$$4\left(\frac{3}{4}x - \frac{1}{2}y = 12\right) \rightarrow 3x - 2y = 48 \rightarrow y = \frac{3}{2}x - 24$$

$$kx - 2y = 22 \rightarrow -2y = -kx + 22 \rightarrow y = \frac{k}{2}x - 11$$

The slope of the first line is $\frac{3}{2}$, and the slope of the second line is $\frac{k}{2}$. Set them equal and solve for k.

$$\frac{3}{2} = \frac{k}{2}$$
$$2(3) = 2(k)$$
$$6 = 2k$$
$$3 = k$$

Choice (C) is correct.

12. B   **Difficulty:** Hard

Category: Heart of Algebra / Inequalities

Getting to the Answer: Before you write the inequality, you need to find the per-mile rate for the remaining miles. The driver charges $4.00 for the first $\frac{1}{4}$ mile, which is a flat fee, so write 4. The additional charge is $1.50 per $\frac{1}{2}$ mile, or 1.50 times 2 = $3.00 per mile. The number of miles after the first $\frac{1}{4}$ mile is $m - \frac{1}{4}$, so the cost of the trip, not including the first $\frac{1}{4}$ mile, is $3\left(m - \frac{1}{4}\right)$. This means the cost of the whole trip is $4 + 3\left(m - \frac{1}{4}\right)$. The clue "no more than $10" means that much or less, so use the symbol ≤. The inequality is $4 + 3\left(m - \frac{1}{4}\right) \leq 10$, which simplifies to $3.25 + 3m \leq 10$. This matches (B).

13. A   Difficulty: Hard

Category: Passport to Advanced Math / Functions

Getting to the Answer: Based on the equation, the graph of $h(x) = -g(x) + 1$ is a vertical reflection of $g(x)$, over the x-axis, that is then shifted up 1 unit. The graph looks like the dashed line in the following graph:

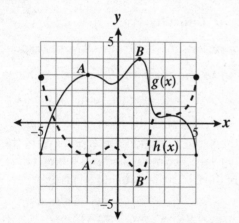

Now, compare the dashed line to each of the answer choices: The range of $h(x)$ is the set of y-values from lowest to highest (based on the dashed line). The lowest point occurs at point B' and has a y-value of -3; the highest value occurs at both ends of the

graph and is 3, so the range is $-3 \leq y \leq 3$. This means (A) is correct and you can move on to the next question. Don't waste valuable time checking the other answer choices unless you are not sure about the range. (Choice B: The minimum value of $h(x)$ is -3, not -4. Choice C: The coordinates of point A on $h(x)$ are $(-2, -2)$, not $(2, 4)$. Choice D: the graph of $h(x)$ is decreasing, not increasing, between $x = -5$ and $x = -2$.)

14. D   Difficulty: Medium

Category: Additional Topics in Math / Imaginary Numbers

Getting to the Answer: Multiply the two complex numbers just as you would two binomials (using FOIL). Then, combine like terms and use the definition $i^2 = -1$ to simplify the result.

$$
\begin{aligned}
(3 + 2i)(5 - i) &= 3(5 - i) + 2i(5 - i) \\
&= 15 - 3i + 10i - 2i^2 \\
&= 15 + 7i - 2(-1) \\
&= 15 + 7i + 2 \\
&= 17 + 7i
\end{aligned}
$$

The question asks for a in $a + bi$, so the correct answer is 17, (D).

15. A   Difficulty: Hard

Category: Passport to Advanced Math / Exponents

Getting to the Answer: Think of the rate given in the question in terms of the constant term you see on the right-hand side of the equation. Working together, the two treatment plants can filter the water in 72 hours. This is equivalent to saying that they can filter $\frac{1}{72}$ of the water in 1 hour. If $\frac{1}{72}$ is the portion of the water the two treatment plants can filter *together*, then each term on the left side of the equation represents the portion that each plant can filter *individually* in 1 hour. Because the new facility is 4 times as fast as the older facility, $\frac{4}{x}$ represents the portion of the water the new plant can filter in

1 hour, and $\dfrac{1}{x}$ represents the portion of the water the older plant can filter in 1 hour. This matches (A).

16. 20   **Difficulty:** Medium

Category: Heart of Algebra / Linear Equations

Getting to the Answer: Only one equation is given, and it has two variables. This means that you don't have enough information to solve for either variable. Instead, look for the relationship between the variable terms in the equation and those in the expression that you are trying to find, $x + 2y$. First, move the y-term to the left side of the equation to make it look more like the expression you are trying to find. The expression doesn't have fractions, so clear the fractions in the equation by multiplying both sides by 4. This yields the expression that you are looking for, $x + 2y$, so no further work is required—just read the value on the right-hand side of the equation. The answer is 20.

$$\frac{1}{4}x = 5 - \frac{1}{2}y$$
$$\frac{1}{4}x + y\frac{1}{2} = 5$$
$$4\left(\frac{1}{4}x + \frac{1}{2}y\right) = 4(5)$$
$$x + 2y = 20$$

17. 1   **Difficulty:** Medium

Category: Heart of Algebra / Inequalities

Getting to the Answer: This question is extremely difficult to answer unless you draw a sketch. It doesn't have to be perfect—you just need to get an idea of where the solution region is. Don't forget to flip the inequality symbol when you graph the second equation.

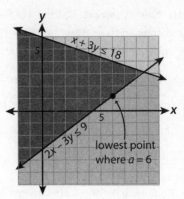

If (a, b) is a solution to the system, then a is the x-coordinate of any point in the darkest shaded region and b is the corresponding y-coordinate. When $a = 6$, the minimum possible value for b lies on the lower boundary line, $2x - 3y \le 9$. It looks like the y-coordinate is 1, but to be sure, substitute $x = 6$ into the equation and solve for y. You can use $=$ in the equation, instead of the inequality symbol, because you are finding a point on the boundary line.

$$2x - 3y = 9$$
$$2(6) - 3y = 9$$
$$12 - 3y = 9$$
$$-3y = -3$$
$$y = 1$$

18. 2   **Difficulty:** Hard

Category: Passport to Advanced Math / Exponents

Getting to the Answer: Write each factor in the expression in exponential form: $\sqrt{x} = x^{\frac{1}{2}}$ and $\sqrt[3]{x} = x^{\frac{1}{3}}$. Then use the rules of exponents to simplify the expression. Add the exponents of the factors that are being multiplied and subtract the exponent of the factor that is being divided:

$$\frac{\sqrt{x} \cdot x^{\frac{5}{6}} \cdot x}{\sqrt[3]{x}} = \frac{x^{\frac{1}{2}} \cdot x^{\frac{5}{6}} \cdot x^{1}}{x^{\frac{1}{3}}}$$
$$= x^{\frac{1}{2} + \frac{5}{6} + \frac{1}{1} - \frac{1}{3}}$$
$$= x^{\frac{3}{6} + \frac{5}{6} + \frac{6}{6} - \frac{2}{6}}$$
$$= x^{\frac{12}{6}} = x^2$$

Because n is the power of x, the value of n is 2.

19. 14   Difficulty: Hard

Category: Additional Topics in Math / Geometry

Getting to the Answer: The shaded region is the area of the larger triangle minus the area of the smaller triangle. Set up and solve an equation using the information from the figure. You don't know the height of the smaller triangle, so call it h. You do know the area of the shaded region—it's 52 square units.

Larger triangle: base = 12; height = $h + 3 + 3$

Smaller triangle: base = 8; height = h

Shaded area = large area − small area

$$52 = \left[\left(\frac{1}{2}\right)(12)(h + 6)\right] - \left[\left(\frac{1}{2}\right)(8)(h)\right]$$
$$52 = 6(h + 6) - 4h$$
$$52 = 6h + 36 - 4h$$
$$52 = 2h + 36$$
$$16 = 2h$$
$$8 = h$$

The question asks for the height of the *larger* triangle, so the correct answer is 8 + 3 + 3 = 14.

20. 6   Difficulty: Hard

Category: Passport to Advanced Math / Quadratics

Getting to the Answer: The highest power of x in the equation is 2, so the function is quadratic. Writing quadratic equations can be tricky and time-consuming. If you know the roots, you can use factors to write the equation. If you don't know the roots, you need to create a system of equations to find the coefficients of the variable terms. You don't know the roots of this equation, so start with the point that has the easiest values to work with, (0, 1), and substitute them into the equation $y = ax^2 + bx + c$.

$$1 = a(0)^2 + b(0) + c$$
$$1 = c$$

Now your equation looks like $y = ax^2 + bx + 1$. Next, use the other two points to create a system of two equations in two variables.

$$(-3, 10) \rightarrow 10 = a(-3)^2 + b(-3) + 1 \rightarrow 9 = 9a - 3b$$
$$(2, 15) \rightarrow 15 = a(2)^2 + b(2) + 1 \rightarrow 14 = 4a + 2b$$

You now have a system of equations to solve. None of the variables has a coefficient of 1, so use elimination to solve the system. If you multiply the top equation by 2 and the bottom equation by 3, the b terms will eliminate each other.

$$2[9a - 3b = 9] \rightarrow 18a - 6b = 18$$
$$3[4a + 2b = 14] \rightarrow \underline{12a + 6b = 42}$$
$$30a = 60$$
$$a = 2$$

Now, find b by substituting $a = 2$ into either of the original equations. Using the top equation, you get:

$$9(2) - 3b = 9$$
$$18 - 3b = 9$$
$$-3b = -9$$
$$b = 3$$

The value of $a + b + c$ is 2 + 3 + 1 = 6.

MATH—CALCULATOR TEST

1. C   Difficulty: Easy

Category: Problem Solving and Data Analysis / Rates, Ratios, Proportions, and Percentages

Getting to the Answer: You can use the formula $\text{Percent} = \dfrac{\text{part}}{\text{whole}} \times 100\%$ whenever you know two out of the three quantities. The clue "all" tells you that the "whole" is what you don't know. The percent is 96.5, and the part is 321,000,000.

$$96.5 = \frac{321,000,000}{w} \times 100\%$$

$$96.5w = 32,100,000,000$$

$$w = \frac{32,100,000,000}{96.5}$$

$$w = 332,642,487$$

The answer choices are rounded to the nearest thousand, so the answer is 332,642,000, (C).

2. C   Difficulty: Easy

Category: Heart of Algebra / Linear Equations

Getting to the Answer: The total cost consists of the one-time site visit fee (a constant), an hourly cost (which depends on the number of hours), and the cost of the materials (which are taxed). The constant in the equation is 75 and is therefore the site visit fee; 45 is being multiplied by h (the number of hours), so $45 must be the hourly rate. That leaves the remaining term, 1.06(82.5), which must be the cost of the materials ($82.50) plus a 6% tax. This matches (C).

3. D   Difficulty: Easy

Category: Heart of Algebra / Inequalities

Getting to the Answer: The intersection (overlap) of the two shaded regions is the solution to the system of inequalities. Check each point to see whether it lies in the region with the darkest shading. Don't forget to check that you answered the right question—you are looking for the point that is *not* a solution to the system. Each of the first three points clearly lies in the overlap. The point (3, 3) looks like it lies on the dashed line, which means it is *not* included in the solution. To check this, plug (3, 3) into the easier inequality: $3 \not> 3$ (3 is equal to itself, not greater than itself), so (D) is correct.

4. A   Difficulty: Easy

Category: Passport to Advanced Math / Quadratics

Getting to the Answer: Quadratic equations can be written in several forms, each of which reveals something special about the graph. The factored

form of a quadratic equation reveals the solutions to the equation, which graphically represent the x-intercepts. Choice (A) is the only equation written in this form and therefore must be correct. You can set each factor equal to 0 and solve to find that the x-intercepts of the graph are $x = \frac{5}{2}$ and $x = -1$.

5. B   Difficulty: Easy

Category: Problem Solving and Data Analysis / Rates, Ratios, Proportions, and Percentages

Getting to the Answer: Break the question into steps. Before you can use the ratio, you need to find the percent of the students who answered either "Foreign Policy" or "Environment." The ratio given in the question is 5:3, so write this as 5 parts "Foreign Policy" and 3 parts "Environment." You don't know how big a *part* is, so call it x. This means that $5x + 3x$ equals the percent of the students who answered either "Foreign Policy" or "Environment," which is 100% minus all the other answers:

$$100 - (16 + 14 + 9 + 5) = 100 - 44 = 56$$

$$5x + 3x = 56$$

$$8x = 56$$

$$x = 7$$

Each part has a value of 7, and 3 parts answered "Environment," so the correct percentage is $3(7) = 21\%$, (B).

6. C   Difficulty: Easy

Category: Problem Solving and Data Analysis / Scatterplots

Getting to the Answer: A data set that has a linear association follows the path of a straight line; a data set that is exponential follows a path that is similar to linear data, but with a curve to it because the rate of increase (or decrease) changes over time. This data set has a curve to it, so "exponential" describes the association better than "linear." This means you can eliminate A and B. A positive association between two variables is one in which higher values of one variable correspond to higher values of the other variable, and vice versa. In other words, as the x-values of the data points go up, so do the y-values. This is indeed the case for this data set, so (C) is correct.

7. D   Difficulty: Easy

Category: Problem Solving and Data Analysis / Statistics and Probability

Getting to the Answer: Your only choice for this question is to compare each statement to the figure. Don't waste time trying to figure out the exact value for each bar—an estimate is good enough to determine whether each statement is true. Choice A is incorrect because the price in 2008 was slightly less (not more) than $3.50, while the price in 2013 was right around $3.50. Choice B is incorrect because the price in 2003 was more than $2.00, and the price in 2013 was not more than twice that ($4.00). Choice C is incorrect because the price in 2008 was about $3.25 and the price in 2009 was about $2.75—this is not a difference of more than $1.00. This means (D) must be correct. You don't have to check it—just move on. (Between 2003 and 2008, the change in price was about $3.40 − $2.30 = $1.10; between 2008 and 2013, the change in price was only about $3.50 − $3.40 = $0.10; the change in price was greater between 2003 and 2008.)

8. B   Difficulty: Medium

Category: Heart of Algebra / Systems of Linear Equations

Getting to the Answer: Because none of the variable terms has a coefficient of 1, solve the system of equations using elimination (combining the equations). Before you choose an answer, check that you answered the right question (the sum of x and y). Multiply the top equation by 2 to eliminate the terms that have y's in them.

$$2[-2x + 5y = 1] \rightarrow -4x + 10y = 2$$
$$7x - 10y = -11 \rightarrow \underline{7x - 10y = -11}$$
$$3x = -9$$
$$x = -3$$

Now, substitute the result into either of the original equations and simplify to find y:

$$-2x + 5y = 1$$
$$-2(-3) + 5y = 1$$
$$6 + 5y = 1$$
$$5y = -5$$
$$y = -1$$

The question asks for the *sum*, so add x and y to get $-3 + (-1) = -4$, which is (B).

9. A   Difficulty: Medium

Category: Heart of Algebra / Systems of Linear Equations

Getting to the Answer: Take a quick peek at the answers just to see what variables are being used, but don't study the equations. Instead, write your own system using the same variables as given in the answer choices. One of the equations in the system needs to represent the sum of the two resistors $(R_1 + R_2)$, which is equal to 294. This means you can eliminate C and D. The second equation needs to satisfy the condition that R_2 is 6 less than twice R_1, or $R_2 = 2R_1 - 6$. This means (A) is correct.

10. C   Difficulty: Medium

Category: Heart of Algebra / Linear Equations

Getting to the Answer: Use the distributive property to simplify each of the terms that contains parentheses. Then use inverse operations to solve for x.

$$\frac{2}{3}\left(3x\right) + 2(x - 1) = 4(x + 1) - 2$$
$$2x + 2x - 2 = 4x + 4 - 2$$
$$4x - 2 = 4x + 2$$
$$-2 \neq 2$$

All of the variable terms cancel out, and the resulting numerical statement is false (because negative 2 does not equal positive 2), so there is no solution to the equation. Put another way, there is no value of x for which the equation is true, (C).

11. B **Difficulty:** Medium

Category: Additional Topics in Math / Geometry

Getting to the Answer: Think about this question logically before you start writing things down—after it's transferred, the volume of the oil in the cylindrical container will be the same volume as the rectangular container, so you need to set the two volumes equal and solve for h. The volume of the rectangular container is $4 \times 9 \times 10$, or 360 cubic meters. The volume of a cylinder equals the area of its base times its height, or $\pi r^2 h$. Because the diameter is 6 meters, the radius, r, is half that, or 3 meters. Now we're ready to set up an equation and solve for h (which is the height of the cylinder or, in this case, the length of the transportation container):

Volume of oil $=$ Volume of rectangular container

$$\pi(3)^2 h = 360$$
$$9\pi h = 360$$
$$h = \frac{360}{9\pi} = \frac{40}{\pi}$$

Choice (B) is correct.

12. D **Difficulty:** Medium

Category: Problem Solving and Data Analysis / Rates, Ratios, Proportions, and Percentages

Getting to the Answer: Even though this question uses the word *percent*, you are never asked to find the actual percent itself. Set this question up as a proportion to get the answer more quickly. Remember, percent change equals amount of change divided by the original amount.

$$\frac{12 - 5}{5} = \frac{x - 12}{12}$$
$$\frac{7}{5} = \frac{x - 12}{12}$$
$$12(7) = 5(x - 12)$$
$$84 = 5x - 60$$
$$144 = 5x$$
$$28.8 = x$$

Choice (D) is correct.

13. A **Difficulty:** Medium

Category: Passport to Advanced Math / Exponents

Getting to the Answer: Focus on the question at the very end—it's just asking you to solve the equation for d. First, cross-multiply to get rid of the denominator. Then, divide both sides of the equation by $4\pi b$ to isolate d^2. Finally, take the square root of both sides to find d.

$$b\left(4\pi d^2\right) = L$$
$$\frac{b\left(4\pi\, d^2\right)}{4\pi b} = \frac{L}{4\pi b}$$
$$d^2 = \frac{L}{4\pi b}$$
$$\sqrt{d^2} = \sqrt{\frac{L}{4\pi b}}$$
$$d = \sqrt{\frac{L}{4\pi b}}$$

Unfortunately, this is not one of the answer choices, so you'll need to simplify further. You can take the square root of 4 (it's 2), but be careful—it's in the denominator of the fraction, so it comes out of the square root as $\frac{1}{2}$. The simplified equation is $d = \frac{1}{2}\sqrt{\frac{L}{\pi b}}$. This matches (A).

14. D **Difficulty:** Easy

Category: Problem Solving and Data Analysis / Statistics and Probability

Getting to the Answer: To calculate the percentage of men in each age group who reported being unemployed in January 2014, divide the number in *that* age group who were unemployed by the total number in *that* age group. There are six age groups but only four answer choices, so don't waste time on the age groups that aren't represented. Choice (D) is correct because $7 \div 152 \approx 0.046 = 4.6\%$, which is a lower percentage than that for any other age group (20 to 24 $= 12.5\%$; 35 to 44 $= 4.9\%$; 45 to 54 $= 6.1\%$).

15. B   Difficulty: Medium

Category: Problem Solving and Data Analysis / Statistics and Probability

Getting to the Answer: The follow-up survey targets only those respondents who said they were unemployed, so focus on that column in the table. There were 6 respondents out of 44 unemployed males who were between the ages of 45 and 54, so the probability is $\frac{6}{44} = 0.1\overline{36}$, or about 13.6%, (B).

16. B   Difficulty: Medium

Category: Passport to Advanced Math / Quadratics

Getting to the Answer: Taking the square root is the inverse operation of squaring, and both sides of the equation are already perfect squares, so take their square roots. Then solve the resulting equations. Remember, there will be two equations to solve.

$$(x - 1)^2 = \frac{4}{9}$$

$$\sqrt{(x - 1)^2} = \sqrt{\frac{4}{9}}$$

$$x - 1 = \pm\frac{\sqrt{4}}{\sqrt{9}}$$

$$x = 1 \pm \frac{2}{3}$$

Now, simplify each equation: $x = 1 + \frac{2}{3} = \frac{3}{3} + \frac{2}{3} = \frac{5}{3}$

and $x = 1 - \frac{2}{3} = \frac{3}{3} - \frac{2}{3} = \frac{1}{3}$. Choice (B) is correct.

17. D   Difficulty: Medium

Category: Heart of Algebra / Linear Equations

Getting to the Answer: Write the expression in words first: points per blue ring (5) times number of darts in blue ring (x), plus points per red ring (10) times number of darts in red ring ($6 - x$). Now, translate the words into numbers, variables, and operations: $5x + 10(6 - x)$. This is not one of the answer choices, so simplify the expression by distributing the 10 and then combining like terms: $5x + 10(6 - x) = 5x + 60 - 10x = 60 - 5x$. This matches (D).

18. A   Difficulty: Medium

Category: Problem Solving and Data Analysis / Statistics and Probability

Getting to the Answer: This is a science crossover question. Read the first two sentences quickly—they are simply describing the context of the question. The last two sentences pose the question, so read those more carefully. In the sample, 184 out of 200 square feet were free of red tide after applying the spray. This is $\frac{184}{200} = 0.92 = 92\%$ of the area. For the whole beach, $0.92(10,000) = 9,200$ square feet should be free of the red tide. Be careful—this is *not* the answer. The question asks how much of the beach would still be covered by red tide, so subtract to get $10,000 - 9,200 = 800$ square feet, (A).

19. A   Difficulty: Medium

Category: Passport to Advanced Math / Quadratics

Getting to the Answer: The solution to a system of equations is the point(s) where their graphs intersect. You can solve the system algebraically by setting the equations equal to each other, or you can solve it graphically using your calculator. Both equations are given in calculator-friendly format ($y = ...$), so graphing them is probably the more efficient approach. The graph looks like:

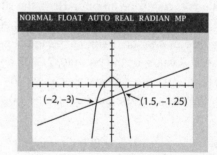

The solution point in the question is given as (a, b), so b represents the y-coordinate of the solution. The y-coordinates of the points of intersection are -3 and -1.25, so choice (A) is correct.

20. A   Difficulty: Medium

Category: Passport to Advanced Math / Functions

Getting to the Answer: The given range value is an output value, so substitute 3 for $g(x)$ and use inverse operations to solve for x, which is the corresponding domain value.

$$g(x) = \frac{2}{3}x + 7$$

$$3 = \frac{2}{3}x + 7$$

$$-4 = \frac{2}{3}x$$

$$-12 = 2x$$

$$-6 = x$$

Choice (A) is correct. Note that you could also graph the function and find the value of x (the domain value) for which the value of y (the range value) is 3. The point on the graph is $(-6, 3)$.

21. C   Difficulty: Medium

Category: Heart of Algebra / Linear Equations

Getting to the Answer: Write your own equation using the initial cost and the rate of change in the value of the lawn mower. Remember—when something changes at a constant rate, it can be represented by a linear equation. When a linear equation in the form $y = mx + b$ is used to model a real-world scenario, m represents the constant rate of change, and b represents the starting amount. Here, the starting amount is easy—it's the purchase price, $2,800. To find the rate of change, think of the initial cost as the value at 0 years, or the point $(0, 2,800)$, and the salvage amount as the value at 8 years, or the point $(8, 240)$. Substitute these points into the slope formula:

$$m = \frac{y_2 - y_1}{x_2 - x_1} = \frac{240 - 2,800}{8 - 0} = \frac{-2,560}{8} = -320$$

The correct equation is $y = -320x + 2,800$. This matches (C).

22. D   Difficulty: Medium

Category: Problem Solving and Data Analysis / Functions

Getting to the Answer: Determine whether the change in the number of bacteria is a common difference (linear function) or a common ratio (exponential function) or if the number of bacteria changes direction (quadratic or polynomial function). The question tells you that the number of bacteria is reduced by half every hour after the antibiotic is applied. The microbiologist started with 20,000, so after one hour, there are 10,000 left, or $20,000 \times \frac{1}{2}$. After 2 hours, there are 5,000 left, or $20,000 \times \frac{1}{2} \times \frac{1}{2}$, and so on. The change in the number of bacteria is a common ratio $\left(\frac{1}{2}\right)$, so the best model is an exponential function, (D), of the form $y = a\left(\frac{1}{2}\right)^x$. In this scenario, a is 20,000.

23. B   Difficulty: Medium

Category: Problem Solving and Data Analysis / Rates, Ratios, Proportions, and Percentages

Getting to the Answer: Let the units in this question guide you to the solution. The speeds of the airplanes are given in miles per hour, but the question asks about the number of miles each airplane can travel in 12 seconds, so convert miles per hour to miles per second and multiply by 12 seconds.

Slower airplane:

$$\frac{600 \text{ mi}}{\cancel{hr}} \times \frac{1 \cancel{hr}}{60 \cancel{min}} \times \frac{1 \cancel{min}}{60 \cancel{sec}} \times 12 \cancel{sec} = 2 \text{ mi}$$

Faster airplane:

$$\frac{720 \text{ mi}}{\cancel{hr}} \times \frac{1 \cancel{hr}}{60 \cancel{min}} \times \frac{1 \cancel{min}}{60 \cancel{sec}} \times 12 \cancel{sec} = 2.4 \text{ mi}$$

The faster plane can travel $2.4 - 2 = 0.4$ miles farther, which is the same as $\frac{2}{5}$ miles, (B).

24. C   Difficulty: Medium

Category: Heart of Algebra / Inequalities

Getting to the Answer: Based on the data in the

table, a worker would earn $9.10 − $7.25 = $1.85 more for one hour of work in Oregon than in Idaho. If he worked 35 hours per week, he would earn 35(1.85) = $64.75 more. If he worked 40 hours per week, he would earn 40(1.85) = $74 more. So, the worker would earn somewhere between $64.75 and $74 more per week, which can be expressed as the compound inequality 64.75 ≤ x ≤ 74. This matches (C).

25. D   Difficulty: Medium

Category: Problem Solving and Data Analysis / Rates, Ratios, Proportions, and Percentages

Getting to the Answer: This is another question where the units can help you find the answer. Use the number of vehicles owned to find the total number of miles driven to find the total number of gallons of gas used to find the total tax paid. Phew!

$$1.75 \text{ vehicles} \times \frac{11{,}340 \text{ miles}}{\text{vehicle}} = 19{,}845 \text{ miles}$$

$$19{,}845 \text{ miles} \times \frac{1 \text{ gallon of gas}}{21.4 \text{ miles}} = 927.336 \text{ gallons}$$

$$927.336 \text{ gallons} \times \frac{\$0.184}{\text{gallon}} = \$170.63$$

Choice (D) is correct.

26. C   Difficulty: Medium

Category: Problem Solving and Data Analysis / Scatterplots

Getting to the Answer: The average rate of change of a function over a given interval, from a to b, compares the change in the outputs, f(b) − f(a), to the change in the inputs, b − a. In other words, it is the slope of the line that connects the endpoints of the interval, so you can use the slope formula. Look at the quadratic model, not the data points, to find that the endpoints of the given interval, week 2 to week 8, are (2, 280) and (8, 400). The average rate of change is $\frac{400 - 280}{8 - 2} = \frac{120}{6} = 20$, so the dolphin's weight increased by about 20 pounds per week, (C).

27. A   Difficulty: Hard

Category: Additional Topics in Math / Geometry

Getting to the Answer: In this question, information is given in both the diagram and the text. You need to relate the text to the diagram, one piece of information at a time, to calculate how long the lifeguard ran along the beach and how long he swam. Before you find the swim time, you need to know how *far* he swam. Whenever you see a right triangle symbol in a diagram, you should think Pythagorean theorem or, in this question, special right triangles. All multiples of 3-4-5 triangles are right triangles, so the length of the lifeguard's swim is the hypotenuse of a 30-40-50 triangle, or 50 feet. Add this number to the diagram. Now calculate the times using the distances and the speeds given. Don't forget the 1 second that the lifeguard paused.

$$\text{Run time} = 60 \text{ ft} \times \frac{1 \sec}{12 \text{ ft}} = \frac{60}{12} = 5 \sec$$

Pause time = 1 second

$$\text{Swim time} = 50 \text{ ft} \times \frac{1 \sec}{5 \text{ ft}} = \frac{50}{5} = 10 \sec$$

Total time = 5 + 1 + 10 = 16 seconds, (A).

28. B   Difficulty: Hard

Category: Heart of Algebra / Linear Equations

Getting to the Answer: Call the initial amount A. After you've written your equation, solve for A.

Amount now (x) = Initial amount (A) minus y, plus 50

$$x = A - y + 50$$
$$x + y - 50 = A$$

The initial amount was x + y − 50 gallons, (B). Note that you could also use Picking Numbers to answer this question.

29. B   Difficulty: Hard

Category: Problem Solving and Data Analysis / Statistics and Probability

Getting to the Answer: When a question involves

reading data from a graph, it is sometimes better to skip an answer choice if it involves long calculations. Skim the answer choices for this question—A involves finding two averages, each of which is composed of 7 data values. Skip this choice for now. Start with (B). Be careful—you are not looking for places where the line segments are increasing. The y-axis already represents the change in prices, so you are simply counting the number of positive values for the imports (5) and for the exports (4). There are more for the imports, so (B) is correct and you don't need to check any of the other statements. Move on to the next question.

30. D   Difficulty: Hard

Category: Passport to Advanced Math / Exponents

Getting to the Answer: The key to answering this question is deciding what you're trying to find. The question tells you that x represents the athlete's swim rate, and you are looking for the number of kilometers he swam in one hour—these are the same thing. If you find x (in kilometers per hour), you will know how many kilometers he swam in one hour. Set the equation equal to the total time, 16.2, and solve for x. To do this, write the variable terms over a common denominator, $10x$, and combine them into a single term. Then cross-multiply and go from there.

$$16.2 = \frac{10}{10}\left(\frac{3.86}{x}\right) + \frac{180.2}{10x} + \frac{2}{2}\left(\frac{42.2}{5x}\right)$$

$$16.2 = \frac{38.6}{10x} + \frac{180.2}{10x} + \frac{84.4}{10x}$$

$$16.2 = \frac{303.2}{10x}$$

$$10x(16.2) = 303.2$$

$$162x = 303.2$$

$$x = \frac{303.2}{162} \approx 1.87$$

Choice (D) is correct.

31. 1   Difficulty: Easy

Category: Heart of Algebra / Linear Equations

Getting to the Answer: Choose the best strategy to answer the question. If you distribute the $\frac{2}{3}$, it creates messy calculations. Instead, clear the fraction by multiplying both sides of the equation by 3. Then use the distributive property and inverse operations to solve for x.

$$\frac{2}{3}(5x + 7) = 8x$$

$$3 \cdot \frac{2}{3}(5x + 7) = 3 \cdot 8x$$

$$2(5x + 7) = 24x$$

$$10x + 14 = 24x$$

$$14 = 14x$$

$$1 = x$$

32. 192   Difficulty: Medium

Category: Passport to Advanced Math / Exponents

Getting to the Answer: Before you start substituting values, quickly check that the units given match the units required to use the equation—they do, so proceed. The patient's weight (w) is 150 and the patient's BSA is $2\sqrt{2}$, so the equation becomes $2\sqrt{2} = \sqrt{\dfrac{150h}{3,600}}$. The only variable left in the equation is h, and you are trying to find the patient's height, so you're ready to solve the equation. To do this, square both sides of the equation and then continue using inverse operations. Be careful when you square the left side—you must square both the 2 and the root 2.

$$2\sqrt{2} = \sqrt{\frac{150h}{3,600}}$$

$$\left(2\sqrt{2}\right)^2 = \left(\sqrt{\frac{150h}{3,600}}\right)^2$$

$$2^2\left(\sqrt{2}\right)^2 = \frac{150h}{3,600}$$

$$4(2) = \frac{150h}{3,600}$$

$$28,800 = 150h$$

$$192 = h$$

33. 3.4   Difficulty: Medium

Category: Problem Solving and Data Analysis / Statistics and Probability

Getting to the Answer: The test average is the same as the mean of the data. The *mean* is the sum of all the values divided by the number of values. Break the question into short steps to keep your calculations organized. Before gridding in your answer, make sure you answered the right question (how much the final test average changes).

Step 1: Find the original test average:

$$\frac{86 + 92 + 81 + 64 + 83}{5} = \frac{406}{5} = 81.2$$

Step 2: Find the average of the tests after replacing the lowest score (64) with the next to lowest score (81):

$$\frac{86 + 92 + 81 + 81 + 83}{5} = \frac{423}{5} = 84.6$$

Step 3: Subtract the original average from the new average: $84.6 - 81.2 = 3.4$.

34. 40   Difficulty: Hard

Category: Additional Topics in Math / Geometry

Getting to the Answer: Because $\overline{AB}$, $\overline{CD}$, and $\overline{EF}$ are diameters, the sum of x, y, and the interior angle of the shaded region is 180 degrees. The question tells you that the shaded region is $\frac{1}{5}$ of the circle, so the interior angle must equal $\frac{1}{5}$ of the degrees in the whole circle, or $\frac{1}{5}$ of 360. Use what you know about y (that it is equal to $2x - 12$) and what you know about the shaded region (that it is $\frac{1}{5}$ of 360 degrees) to write and solve an equation.

$$x + y + \frac{1}{5}(360) = 180$$
$$x + (2x - 12) + 72 = 180$$
$$3x + 60 = 180$$
$$3x = 120$$
$$x = 40$$

35. 14   Difficulty: Hard

Category: Heart of Algebra / Linear Equations

Getting to the Answer: When you know the slope and one point on a line, you can use $y = mx + b$ to write the equation. The slope is given as $-\frac{7}{4}$, so substitute this for m. The point is given as $(4, 7)$, so $x = 4$ and $y = 7$. Now, find b:

$$y = mx + b$$
$$7 = -\frac{7}{\cancel{4}}\left(\cancel{4}\right) + b$$
$$7 = -7 + b$$
$$14 = b$$

The y-intercept of the line is 14.

You could also very carefully graph the line using the given point and the slope. Start at $(4, 7)$ and move toward the y-axis by rising 7 and running *to the left* 4 (because the slope is negative). You should land at the point $(0, 14)$.

36. 45   Difficulty: Hard

Category: Problem Solving and Data Analysis / Rates, Ratios, Proportions, and Percentages

Getting to the Answer: Make a chart that represents rate, time, and distance and fill in what you know.

	Rate	Time	Distance
To airport	45 mph	t	d
Back to home	30 mph	$2.5 - t$	d

Now use the formula $d = r \times t$ for both parts of the trip: $d = 45t$ and $d = 30(2.5 - t)$. Because both are equal to d, you can set them equal to each other and solve for t:

$$45t = 30(2.5 - t)$$
$$45t = 75 - 30t$$
$$75t = 75$$
$$t = 1$$

Now plug the value of t back in to solve for d:

$$d = 45t$$
$$d = 45(1)$$
$$d = 45$$

37. 10   Difficulty: Medium

Category: Problem Solving and Data Analysis / Rates, Ratios, Proportions, and Percentages

Getting to the Answer: You don't need to know chemistry to answer this question. All the information you need is in the table. Use the formula $\text{Percent} = \dfrac{\text{part}}{\text{whole}} \times 100\%$. To use the formula, find the part of the mass represented by the carbon; there is 1 mole of carbon, and it has a mass of 12.011 grams. Next, find the whole mass of the mole of chloroform: 1 mole carbon (12.011 g) + 1 mole hydrogen (1.008 g) + 3 moles chlorine (3 × 35.453 = 106.359 g) = 12.011 + 1.008 + 106.359 = 119.378. Now use the formula:

$$\text{Percent} = \frac{12.011}{119.378} \times 100\%$$
$$= 0.10053 \times 100\%$$
$$= 10.053\%$$

Before you grid in your answer, make sure you follow the directions—round to the nearest whole percent, which is 10.

38. 12   Difficulty: Hard

Category: Problem Solving and Data Analysis / Rates, Ratios, Proportions, and Percentages

Getting to the Answer: Think about the units given in the question and how you can use what you know to find what you need. Start with grams of chloro-

form; the chemist starts with 1,000 and uses 522.5, so there are 1,000 − 522.5 = 477.5 grams left. From the previous question, you know that 1 mole of chloroform has a mass of 119.378 grams, so there are 477.5 ÷ 119.378 = 3.999, or about 4 moles of chloroform left. Be careful—you're not finished yet. The question asks for the number of moles of *chlorine*, not chloroform. According to the table, each mole of chloroform contains 3 moles of chlorine, so there are 4 × 3 = 12 moles of chlorine left.

ESSAY TEST RUBRIC

The Essay Demonstrates...

4—Advanced	• **(Reading)** A strong ability to comprehend the source text, including its central ideas and important details and how they interrelate; and effectively use evidence (quotations, paraphrases, or both) from the source text.
	• **(Analysis)** A strong ability to evaluate the author's use of evidence, reasoning, and/or stylistic and persuasive elements, and/or other features of the student's own choosing; make good use of relevant, sufficient, and strategically chosen support for the claims or points made in the student's essay; and focus consistently on features of the source text that are most relevant to addressing the task.
	• **(Writing)** A strong ability to provide a precise central claim; create an effective organization that includes an introduction and conclusion, as well as a clear progression of ideas; successfully employ a variety of sentence structures; use precise word choice; maintain a formal style and objective tone; and show command of the conventions of standard written English so that the essay is free of errors.
3—Proficient	• **(Reading)** Satisfactory ability to comprehend the source text, including its central ideas and important details and how they interrelate; and use evidence (quotations, paraphrases, or both) from the source text.
	• **(Analysis)** Satisfactory ability to evaluate the author's use of evidence, reasoning, and/or stylistic and persuasive elements, and/or other features of the student's own choosing; make use of relevant and sufficient support for the claims or points made in the student's essay; and focus primarily on features of the source text that are most relevant to addressing the task.
	• **(Writing)** Satisfactory ability to provide a central claim; create an organization that includes an introduction and conclusion, as well as a clear progression of ideas; employ a variety of sentence structures; use precise word choice; maintain an appropriate formal style and objective tone; and show control of the conventions of standard written English so that the essay is free of significant errors.
2—Partial	• **(Reading)** Limited ability to comprehend the source text, including its central ideas and important details and how they interrelate; and use evidence (quotations, paraphrases, or both) from the source text.
	• **(Analysis)** Limited ability to evaluate the author's use of evidence, reasoning, and/or stylistic and persuasive elements, and/or other features of the student's own choosing; make use of support for the claims or points made in the student's essay; and focus on relevant features of the source text.
	• **(Writing)** Limited ability to provide a central claim; create an effective organization for ideas; employ a variety of sentence structures; use precise word choice; maintain an appropriate style and tone; or show control of the conventions of standard written English, resulting in certain errors that detract from the quality of the writing.

1—Inadequate	• **(Reading)** Little or no ability to comprehend the source text or use evidence from the source text. • **(Analysis)** Little or no ability to evaluate the author's use of evidence, reasoning, and/or stylistic and persuasive elements; choose support for claims or points; or focus on relevant features of the source text. • **(Writing)** Little or no ability to provide a central claim, organization, or progression of ideas; employ a variety of sentence structures; use precise word choice; maintain an appropriate style and tone; or show control of the conventions of standard written English, resulting in numerous errors that undermine the quality of the writing.

SAMPLE ESSAY RESPONSE #1 (ADVANCED SCORE)

As anyone knows who has had to help their family move house, find a textbook in a cluttered room, or even just clean a crowded apartment, possessions can have a huge amount of power over people. Far from being simply objects that we enjoy or that bring us pleasure, it can sometimes feel that our possessions oppress us. This is the point Morris eloquently makes in her essay "The Tyranny of Things." By using anecdotes, examples, reasoning, and powerful imagery, Morris argues that the very things we cherish are nearly crushing the life out of us.

The author begins by relating an anecdote about two teenagers becoming fast friends over their love of things. It is a touching moment, one to which readers can easily relate; even Morris herself says that we all probably go through this phase. This helps establish her credibility with readers, because her examples make sense to them. Gradually, however, Morris makes it clear that this touching moment has a sinister side—the love of things will only result in resentment.

Morris reasons that while it's natural to go through a phase of wanting objects, it is unhealthy to remain in this state. "Many people never pass out of this phase," she writes ominously. "They never see a flower without wanting to pick it … they bring home all their alpenstocks." It begins to sound obsessive, this need to control things. Morris goes on to develop her argument by suggesting that possessions are metaphorically suffocating us. She makes the idea of too many possessions sound repulsive by describing them as "an undigested mass of things." The things almost take on a kind of life force, according to Morris: "they possess us." They "have destroyed" our empty spaces and we feel "stifled."

Another way Morris supports her argument is by giving examples of the unnecessary "tokens" associated with social occasions. She describes how at events, luncheons, and parties, gifts are given and received. She then uses powerful negative imagery to describe the effects of these gifts, comparing the recipient to a "ship encrusted with barnacles" that needs to be "scraped bare again." This language suggests that the gifts are burdensome and even harmful.

By contrast, the imagery Morris uses to describe a simple life filled with fewer things is imagery of ease and relaxation. "We breathe more freely in the clear space that we have made for ourselves," she writes. It is not just that we have literally regained control from our possessions and are now acting rather than being acted upon; it is that we are physically more at ease.

In her conclusion, Morris longs for a day when we can live more simply, with fewer possessions. She describes a "house by the sea" that was simple and empty; it did not "demand care" or "claim attention" or otherwise act upon her. Her wish is that "we could but free ourselves" from the tyranny of things that she feels is draining us of our freedom. And at this point, it is likely the reader's wish, too.

SAMPLE ESSAY RESPONSE #2 (PROFICIENT SCORE)

Although as people we like to think of ourselves as owners of things, in fact it can sometimes feel like the things we own end up owning us. At least this is what Morris argues in her essay "The Tyranny of Things." Through her use of evidence, reasoning, and word choice, she makes a strong argument that we should own fewer things if we ever want to be truly happy.

Morris tells a story about two teenage girls who instantly know they will be friends because they both like things. They are not happy just to be. They have to own things. It's like their own experiences aren't enough for them. But Morris says that this is bad for people, because they will end up feeling like their possessions own them.

Morris's reasoning is that we can basically get control back over our own lives if we stop needing things so much. If we have too many things, "they possess us." So we have to get rid of things, and then we can feel better. At least these days we aren't buried with our things anymore, like they were in the olden days.

The word choices in the essay are interesting. She talks about the way things become a problem for us: "our books are a burden to us, our pictures have destroyed every restful wall-space, our china is a care." By using a lot of repetition, it shows how powerful things are.

Morris's essay encourages people to free themselves from their things. If they do so, they will be happier. Through her personal anecdotes, reasoning, and repetitive word choices, she makes her essay very powerful.

SAT PRACTICE TEST 6 ANSWER SHEET

Remove (or photocopy) this answer sheet and use it to complete the test. See the answer key following the test when finished.

Start with number 1 for each section. If a section has fewer questions than answer spaces, leave the extra spaces blank.

SECTION 1

1. Ⓐ Ⓑ Ⓒ Ⓓ
2. Ⓐ Ⓑ Ⓒ Ⓓ
3. Ⓐ Ⓑ Ⓒ Ⓓ
4. Ⓐ Ⓑ Ⓒ Ⓓ
5. Ⓐ Ⓑ Ⓒ Ⓓ
6. Ⓐ Ⓑ Ⓒ Ⓓ
7. Ⓐ Ⓑ Ⓒ Ⓓ
8. Ⓐ Ⓑ Ⓒ Ⓓ
9. Ⓐ Ⓑ Ⓒ Ⓓ
10. Ⓐ Ⓑ Ⓒ Ⓓ
11. Ⓐ Ⓑ Ⓒ Ⓓ
12. Ⓐ Ⓑ Ⓒ Ⓓ
13. Ⓐ Ⓑ Ⓒ Ⓓ

14. Ⓐ Ⓑ Ⓒ Ⓓ
15. Ⓐ Ⓑ Ⓒ Ⓓ
16. Ⓐ Ⓑ Ⓒ Ⓓ
17. Ⓐ Ⓑ Ⓒ Ⓓ
18. Ⓐ Ⓑ Ⓒ Ⓓ
19. Ⓐ Ⓑ Ⓒ Ⓓ
20. Ⓐ Ⓑ Ⓒ Ⓓ
21. Ⓐ Ⓑ Ⓒ Ⓓ
22. Ⓐ Ⓑ Ⓒ Ⓓ
23. Ⓐ Ⓑ Ⓒ Ⓓ
24. Ⓐ Ⓑ Ⓒ Ⓓ
25. Ⓐ Ⓑ Ⓒ Ⓓ
26. Ⓐ Ⓑ Ⓒ Ⓓ

27. Ⓐ Ⓑ Ⓒ Ⓓ
28. Ⓐ Ⓑ Ⓒ Ⓓ
29. Ⓐ Ⓑ Ⓒ Ⓓ
30. Ⓐ Ⓑ Ⓒ Ⓓ
31. Ⓐ Ⓑ Ⓒ Ⓓ
32. Ⓐ Ⓑ Ⓒ Ⓓ
33. Ⓐ Ⓑ Ⓒ Ⓓ
34. Ⓐ Ⓑ Ⓒ Ⓓ
35. Ⓐ Ⓑ Ⓒ Ⓓ
36. Ⓐ Ⓑ Ⓒ Ⓓ
37. Ⓐ Ⓑ Ⓒ Ⓓ
38. Ⓐ Ⓑ Ⓒ Ⓓ
39. Ⓐ Ⓑ Ⓒ Ⓓ

40. Ⓐ Ⓑ Ⓒ Ⓓ
41. Ⓐ Ⓑ Ⓒ Ⓓ
42. Ⓐ Ⓑ Ⓒ Ⓓ
43. Ⓐ Ⓑ Ⓒ Ⓓ
44. Ⓐ Ⓑ Ⓒ Ⓓ
45. Ⓐ Ⓑ Ⓒ Ⓓ
46. Ⓐ Ⓑ Ⓒ Ⓓ
47. Ⓐ Ⓑ Ⓒ Ⓓ
48. Ⓐ Ⓑ Ⓒ Ⓓ
49. Ⓐ Ⓑ Ⓒ Ⓓ
50. Ⓐ Ⓑ Ⓒ Ⓓ
51. Ⓐ Ⓑ Ⓒ Ⓓ
52. Ⓐ Ⓑ Ⓒ Ⓓ

☐ # correct in Section 1

☐ # incorrect in Section 1

SECTION 2

1. Ⓐ Ⓑ Ⓒ Ⓓ
2. Ⓐ Ⓑ Ⓒ Ⓓ
3. Ⓐ Ⓑ Ⓒ Ⓓ
4. Ⓐ Ⓑ Ⓒ Ⓓ
5. Ⓐ Ⓑ Ⓒ Ⓓ
6. Ⓐ Ⓑ Ⓒ Ⓓ
7. Ⓐ Ⓑ Ⓒ Ⓓ
8. Ⓐ Ⓑ Ⓒ Ⓓ
9. Ⓐ Ⓑ Ⓒ Ⓓ
10. Ⓐ Ⓑ Ⓒ Ⓓ
11. Ⓐ Ⓑ Ⓒ Ⓓ

12. Ⓐ Ⓑ Ⓒ Ⓓ
13. Ⓐ Ⓑ Ⓒ Ⓓ
14. Ⓐ Ⓑ Ⓒ Ⓓ
15. Ⓐ Ⓑ Ⓒ Ⓓ
16. Ⓐ Ⓑ Ⓒ Ⓓ
17. Ⓐ Ⓑ Ⓒ Ⓓ
18. Ⓐ Ⓑ Ⓒ Ⓓ
19. Ⓐ Ⓑ Ⓒ Ⓓ
20. Ⓐ Ⓑ Ⓒ Ⓓ
21. Ⓐ Ⓑ Ⓒ Ⓓ
22. Ⓐ Ⓑ Ⓒ Ⓓ

23. Ⓐ Ⓑ Ⓒ Ⓓ
24. Ⓐ Ⓑ Ⓒ Ⓓ
25. Ⓐ Ⓑ Ⓒ Ⓓ
26. Ⓐ Ⓑ Ⓒ Ⓓ
27. Ⓐ Ⓑ Ⓒ Ⓓ
28. Ⓐ Ⓑ Ⓒ Ⓓ
29. Ⓐ Ⓑ Ⓒ Ⓓ
30. Ⓐ Ⓑ Ⓒ Ⓓ
31. Ⓐ Ⓑ Ⓒ Ⓓ
32. Ⓐ Ⓑ Ⓒ Ⓓ
33. Ⓐ Ⓑ Ⓒ Ⓓ

34. Ⓐ Ⓑ Ⓒ Ⓓ
35. Ⓐ Ⓑ Ⓒ Ⓓ
36. Ⓐ Ⓑ Ⓒ Ⓓ
37. Ⓐ Ⓑ Ⓒ Ⓓ
38. Ⓐ Ⓑ Ⓒ Ⓓ
39. Ⓐ Ⓑ Ⓒ Ⓓ
40. Ⓐ Ⓑ Ⓒ Ⓓ
41. Ⓐ Ⓑ Ⓒ Ⓓ
42. Ⓐ Ⓑ Ⓒ Ⓓ
43. Ⓐ Ⓑ Ⓒ Ⓓ
44. Ⓐ Ⓑ Ⓒ Ⓓ

☐ # correct in Section 2

☐ # incorrect in Section 2

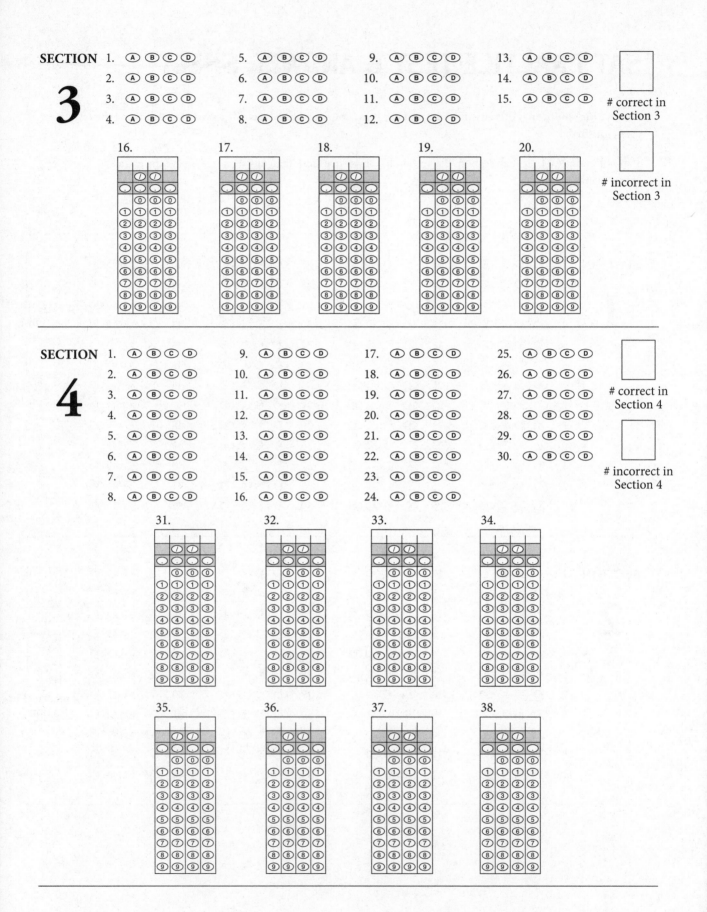

READING TEST

65 Minutes—52 Questions

This section corresponds to Section 1 of your answer sheet.

Directions: Read each passage or pair of passages, then answer the questions that follow. Choose your answers based on what the passage(s) and any accompanying graphics state or imply.

Questions 1-10 are based on the following passage.

The following passage is adapted from Henry David Thoreau's *Walden*, a mid-19th-century philosophical and personal reflection on the writer's experience living in nature and simplicity. This excerpt is from the chapter titled "Where I Lived, and What I Lived For."

It matters not what the clocks say or the attitudes and labors of men. Morning is when I am awake and there is a dawn in me. Moral reform is the
Line effort to throw off sleep. Why is it that men give so
(5) poor an account of their day if they have not been slumbering? They are not such poor calculators. If they had not been overcome with drowsiness, they would have performed something. The millions are awake enough for physical labor; but only one in a
(10) million is awake enough for effective intellectual exertion, only one in a hundred millions to a poetic or divine life. To be awake is to be alive. I have never yet met a man who was quite awake. How could I have looked him in the face?
(15)   We must learn to reawaken and keep ourselves awake, not by mechanical aids, but by an infinite expectation of the dawn, which does not forsake us in our soundest sleep. I know of no more encouraging fact than the unquestionable ability of man to
(20) elevate his life by a conscious endeavor. It is something to be able to paint a particular picture, or to carve a statue, and so to make a few objects beautiful; but it is far more glorious to carve and paint the very atmosphere and medium through which we
(25) look, which morally we can do. To affect the quality of the day, that is the highest of arts. Every man is tasked to make his life, even in its details, worthy of

the contemplation of his most elevated and critical hour. If we refused, or rather used up, such paltry
(30) information as we get, the oracles would distinctly inform us how this might be done.

I went to the woods because I wished to live deliberately, to front only the essential facts of life, and see if I could not learn what it had to teach,
(35) and not, when I came to die, discover that I had not lived. I did not wish to live what was not life, living is so dear; nor did I wish to practice resignation, unless it was quite necessary. I wanted to live deep and suck out all the marrow of life, to live so
(40) sturdily and Spartan-like as to put to rout all that was not life, to cut a broad swath and shave close, to drive life into a corner, and reduce it to its lowest terms, and, if it proved to be mean, why then to get the whole and genuine meanness of it, and publish
(45) its meanness to the world; or if it were sublime, to know it by experience, and be able to give a true account of it in my next excursion. For most men, it appears to me, are in a strange uncertainty about it, whether it is of the devil or of God, and have
(50) somewhat hastily concluded that it is the chief end of man here to "glorify God and enjoy him forever."

Still we live meanly, like ants; though the fable tells us that we were long ago changed into men; like pygmies we fight with cranes; it is error upon
(55) error, and clout upon clout, and our best virtue has for its occasion a superfluous and evitable wretchedness. Our life is frittered away by detail.

An honest man has hardly need to count more than his ten fingers, or in extreme cases he may
(60) add his ten toes, and lump the rest. Simplicity, simplicity, simplicity! I say, let your affairs be as two

GO ON TO THE NEXT PAGE

or three, and not a hundred or a thousand; instead of a million count half a dozen, and keep your accounts on your thumb-nail. In the midst of this
(65) chopping sea of civilized life, such are the clouds and storms and quicksands and thousand-and-one items to be allowed for, that a man has to live, if he would not founder and go to the bottom and not make his port at all, by dead reckoning, and he
(70) must be a great calculator indeed who succeeds. Simplify, simplify. Instead of three meals a day, if it be necessary eat but one; instead of a hundred dishes, five; and reduce other things in proportion.

1. The activities described in lines 20-25 ("It is something . . . morally we can do") explain how people can

   A) develop a satisfying and morally upright career.

   B) give an elevated and proper account of their day.

   C) learn to reawaken and live by conscious endeavor.

   D) awaken enough for effective intellectual exhaustion.

2. As used in lines 37-38, "resignation" most nearly means

   A) complacency.

   B) departure.

   C) quitting.

   D) revival.

3. The first paragraph of the passage most strongly suggests that which of the following is true of the author?

   A) He believes that to affect the quality of the day is the highest form of art.

   B) He feels that people perform poorly at work because they sleep too much.

   C) He is determined to spend as many waking hours as possible working.

   D) He believes that most people have yet to realize their fullest potential in life.

4. Which choice provides the best evidence for the answer to the previous question?

   A) Lines 4-6 ("Why is . . . slumbering")

   B) Lines 8-12 ("The millions . . . life")

   C) Line 12 ("To be . . . alive")

   D) Lines 12-13 ("I have . . . awake")

5. What central claim does the author make about our society as a whole?

   A) The few artists in our society do not receive the recognition they deserve.

   B) Our society willingly focuses too much on drudgery and insignificant details.

   C) Too many people hastily choose to dedicate their lives to religion.

   D) People should move to the woods to find their own conscious endeavor.

6. What can reasonably be inferred about the author's views on religion?

   A) He believes too few people critically examine their religious beliefs.

   B) He thinks that his studies in the woods will prove that God is sublime.

   C) He thinks that meanness and the sublime are the same in nature.

   D) He believes that oracles give us clues about how to live a sublime life.

7. Which choice provides the best evidence for the
    answer to the previous question?

    A) Lines 26-29 ("Every man . . . hour")

    B) Lines 32-36 ("I went . . . not lived")

    C) Lines 38-47 ("I wanted . . . excursion")

    D) Line 47-51 ("For most . . . forever")

8. As used in line 40, "Spartan-like" most nearly
    means

    A) indulgent.

    B) rigid.

    C) pioneering.

    D) austere.

9. The author uses such words as "meanly" and
    "wretchedness" in lines 52-57 in order to imply
    that

    A) people are cruel to one another.

    B) society will destroy itself in time.

    C) many people's lives are harsh and mundane.

    D) negative tendencies ruin our intelligence.

10. Which of the following describes an approach to
    life that is similar to the one Thoreau promotes in
    this passage?

    A) Taking courses and acquiring books on how
        to simplify your life

    B) Hiring people to help you do your chores so
        you can live more simply

    C) Cleaning out your closet so that you are left
        with only the most essential items of clothing

    D) Traveling to a cabin without cell phone
        service to get away from life's complications
        for a weekend

Questions 11-20 are based on the following passage.

This passage is adapted from "The Opening of the
Library" by W.E.B. DuBois, professor of Economics and
History at Atlanta University, published in the *Atlanta
Independent* on April 3, 1902.

"With simple and appropriate exercises the
beautiful new Carnegie Library was thrown open
to the public yesterday." So says the morning paper
Line of Atlanta, Georgia . . . .
(5)   The white marble building, the gift of Andrew
Carnegie, is indeed fair to look upon. The site was
given the city by a private library association, and
the City Council appropriates $5,000 annually
of the city moneys for its support. If you will climb
(10) the hill where the building sits, you may look down
upon the rambling city. Northward and southward
are 53,905 whites, eastward and westward are
35,912 blacks.
        And so in behalf of these 36,000 people my
(15) companions and I called upon the trustees of the
Library on this opening day, for we had heard that
black folk were to have no part in this "free public
library," and we thought it well to go ask why. It was
not pleasant going in, for people stared and won-
(20) dered what business we had there; but the trustees,
after some waiting, received us courteously and
gave us seats—some eight of us in all. To me, had
fallen the lot to begin the talking. I said, briefly:
        "Gentlemen, we are a committee come to ask
(25) that you do justice to the black people of Atlanta
by giving them the same free library privileges that
you propose giving the whites. Every argument
which can be adduced to show the need of libraries for whites applies with redoubled force to the
(30) blacks. More than any other part of our population,
they need instruction, inspiration and proper di-
version; they need to be lured from the temptations
of the streets and saved from evil influences, and
they need a growing acquaintance with what the
(35) best of the world's souls have thought and done and
said. It seems hardly necessary in the 20th century
to argue before men like you on the necessity and
propriety of placing the best means of human
uplifting into the hands of the poorest and lowest
(40) and blackest. . . .

GO ON TO THE NEXT PAGE

I then pointed out the illegality of using public money collected from all for the exclusive benefit of a part of the population, or of distributing public utilities in accordance with the amount of

(45) taxes paid by any class or individual, and finally I concluded by saying:

"The spirit of this great gift to the city was not the spirit of caste or exclusion, but rather the catholic spirit which recognizes no artificial differ-

(50) ences of rank or birth or race, but seeks to give all men equal opportunity to make the most of themselves. It is our sincere hope that this city will prove itself broad enough and just enough to administer this trust in the true spirit in which it was given."

(55) Then I sat down. There was a little pause, and the chairman, leaning forward, said: "I should like to ask you a question: Do you not think that allowing whites and blacks to use this library would be fatal to its usefulness?"

(60) There come at times words linked together which seem to chord in strange recurring resonance with words of other ages and one hears the voice of many centuries and wonders which century is speaking . . . .

(65) I said simply, "I will express no opinion on that point."

Then from among us darker ones another arose. He was an excellent and adroit speaker. He thanked the trustees for the privilege of being there, and

(70) reminded them that but a short time ago even this privilege would have been impossible. He said we did not ask to use this library, we did not ask equal privileges, we only wanted some privileges somewhere. And he assured the trustees that he had

(75) perfect faith in their justice.

The president of the Trustee Board then arose, gray-haired and courteous. He congratulated the last speaker and expressed pleasure at our call. He then gave us to understand four things:

(80) 1. Blacks would not be permitted to use the Carnegie Library in Atlanta.

2. That some library facilities would be provided for them in the future.

3. That to this end the City Council would be
(85) asked to appropriate a sum proportionate to the amount of taxes paid by blacks in the city.

4. That an effort would be made, and had been made, to induce Northern philanthropists
(90) to aid such a library, and he concluded by assuring us that in this way we might eventually have a better library than the whites.

Then he bade us adieu politely and we walked home wondering.

11. Which choice best explains why DuBois wrote this passage?

A) To encourage philanthropists such as Andrew Carnegie to fund new libraries

B) To present the trustees' explanation of why African Americans could not use the library

C) To contrast his position on public access to libraries with that of the trustees

D) To state his support for construction of a new library for just African Americans

12. Which choice provides the best evidence for the answer to the previous question?

A) Lines 14-18 ("And so . . . ask why")

B) Lines 41-45 ("I then . . . or individual")

C) Lines 68-71 ("He thanked . . . impossible")

D) Lines 88-92 ("That an effort . . . than the whites")

13. As used in line 23, "lot" most nearly means

A) a predictable result.

B) a random decision.

C) an unaccepted consequence.

D) an agreed-upon responsibility.

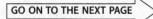
GO ON TO THE NEXT PAGE

14. It can reasonably be inferred from the passage that

   A) the trustees would consider the construction of segregated public library facilities.

   B) the trustees agreed with DuBois's arguments in favor of expanding access to public libraries.

   C) the trustees were open to the idea of integrating Atlanta's public library system.

   D) the trustees proposed concrete plans to provide public library facilities for African Americans.

15. Which choice provides the best evidence for the answer to the previous question?

   A) Lines 55-59 ("There was a little . . . to its usefulness")

   B) Lines 76-78 ("The president . . . at our call")

   C) Lines 80-81 ("Blacks . . . in Atlanta")

   D) Lines 82-83 ("That some . . . in the future")

16. As used in line 34, "growing acquaintance" most nearly means

   A) a friendly relationship.

   B) an increasing comprehension.

   C) an active involvement.

   D) a brief initiation.

17. Which claim does DuBois make to the trustees?

   A) Allowing all of Atlanta's residents to use the new library would render it useless.

   B) Blacks will benefit less from access to public libraries than white residents.

   C) Poor blacks have greater need for a public library than other residents.

   D) Atlanta should invest in public libraries and schools for all of its residents.

18. DuBois uses the example of a "catholic spirit" (line 49) to support the argument that

   A) the city's neighborhoods continue to be segregated by race and economic class.

   B) Atlanta has an obligation to provide equal opportunity for all its residents to better themselves.

   C) access to public libraries should be based on the amount of taxes one pays.

   D) Northern philanthropists should provide private money to help pay for a public library.

19. The author's reflections expressed in lines 60-64 most likely indicate that he

   A) wishes he lived in a different century.

   B) is frustrated that people's attitudes have not changed over time.

   C) is thinking about a time when another person said the exact same words to him.

   D) is planning a detailed response to the chairman's question.

20. The four-point list in the passage can be described as

   A) a summary of the author's supporting points.

   B) an acknowledgement of a counterargument.

   C) an introduction to a counterargument.

   D) a response to the author's main argument.

Questions 21-31 are based on the following passage and supplementary material.

The following passage is adapted from an essay about Denis Diderot, an 18th century French philosopher.

   Over a thirty-year period, Denis Diderot tirelessly undertook a bold endeavor; the philosopher and writer furthered technology education by
Line creating one of the most important books of the
(5) 18th century. He documented the Western world's collective knowledge through a massive set of

GO ON TO THE NEXT PAGE ⇨

volumes called the *Encyclopédie*. Today, Diderot's *Encyclopédie* remains one of the most accessible primary sources for the study of technology during (10) the Enlightenment, having received exposure in recent times through the Internet.

Since Diderot didn't know all there was to know, he sought contributors, more than 150, and organized their 72,000 articles into entries on politics, (15) economics, technology, and other topics. His goal was to create an intellectual work instructionally useful to all, but soon, his *Encyclopédie* became mired in controversy, and this precursor to the modern encyclopedia was seized after its inception, (20) its publication banned by the French government. The encyclopedia, however, had already sparked mass interest in the secrets of manufacturing and more, and so this "how-to" compendium was widely circulated underground after eventually be-(25)ing published in 1765 by a Swedish printer.

Undoubtedly, the *Encyclopédie* served then as a beacon of free thought, and questions about control of its content caused critics to boil over. For in building a compilation of human knowledge, Diderot (30) made a direct political statement. Essentially, the political statement was: You, the average person, can now know what only kings knew before.

In particular, Diderot created an "encyclopedic revolution" by integrating scientific discover-(35)ies with the liberal arts. He linked technology to culture when he divided the *Encyclopédie* into three categories: history, philosophy, and poetry. Diderot then assigned subjects to these three groupings such as industry, political theory, theology, (40) agriculture, and the arts and sciences.

The execution was deceptively simple enough because Diderot pursued everyday trade topics such as cloth dying, for example, accompanying his explanations with diagrams and illustrations. Thus, (45) Diderot elevated "unacademic" craft knowledge to a scholarly status, challenging viewpoints about erudition held by the aristocratic ruling class of the time. More important, Diderot suggested that everyone could have access to the rational, down-to-earth truth, (50) since he believed that knowledge about reality could be obtained by reason alone, rather than through authority or other means.

Not surprisingly, such rationalist philosophy was considered radical. The new idea of showing (55) in amazing detail how the production techniques used in tanning and metalwork were accomplished displeased those in power. Trade guilds held control of such knowledge, and so Diderot's *Encyclopédie* was viewed as a threat to the establishment. (60) Diderot's ideology of progress by way of better quality materials, technical research, and greater production speed was unprecedented in printed books.

Royal authorities did not want the masses (65) exposed to Diderot's liberal views such as this one: "The good of the people must be the great purpose of government. By the laws of nature and of reason, the governors are invested with power to that end. And the greatest good of the people is liberty."

(70) But the opposition was too late. Despite an official ban, the *Encyclopédie's* beautiful bookplates survived, recording production techniques dating to the Middle Ages. Ironically, with the advent of both the English Industrial Revolution and the (75) French Revolution, the trades shown in Diderot's work changed significantly after the encyclopedia's publication. Therefore, instead of becoming a technical dictionary, the *Encyclopédie* rather serves today as a history of technology, showing us what (80) trades were like before machines swept in to transform industry.

GO ON TO THE NEXT PAGE ⇨

1500-1800 Scientific Revolution

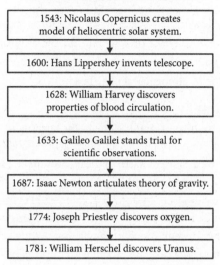

1543: Nicolaus Copernicus creates model of heliocentric solar system.

1600: Hans Lippershey invents telescope.

1628: William Harvey discovers properties of blood circulation.

1633: Galileo Galilei stands trial for scientific observations.

1687: Isaac Newton articulates theory of gravity.

1774: Joseph Priestley discovers oxygen.

1781: William Herschel discovers Uranus.

21. Which choice expresses a central idea of the passage?

A) Diderot crafted a revolutionary guide for the development of industrial technology.

B) Diderot provided students with a superb reference for the study of scientific principles.

C) Diderot's *Encyclopédie* continues to serve as a valuable technical resource.

D) Diderot's *Encyclopédie* helped promote the liberalization and expansion of knowledge.

22. The passage most clearly reflects the author's

A) devotion to the study of science.

B) disdain for intellectualism.

C) interest in early printing methods.

D) respect for individual innovation.

23. Which choice provides the best evidence for the answer to the previous question?

A) Lines 33-35 ("In particular . . . liberal arts")

B) Lines 54-57 ("The new idea . . . in power")

C) Lines 64-67 ("Royal . . . of government")

D) Lines 73-77 ("Ironically . . . publication")

24. According to the passage, Diderot's main goal in developing the *Encyclopédie* was to

A) express his views.

B) challenge political authority.

C) provide information and instruction.

D) create a historical record of technology.

25. As used in line 24, "underground" most nearly means

A) cautiously.

B) secretly.

C) perilously.

D) privately.

26. In lines 26-27, the function of the phrase "a beacon of free thought" is to suggest that Diderot's work

A) attracted more people to the pursuit of knowledge.

B) provided information for people most likely to use it.

C) encouraged revolutionary thinking.

D) spread scientific theory among intellectual circles.

27. The passage most strongly suggests that during this time period

A) access to information was limited to select demographics.

B) advances in printing resulted in comparable advances in other fields.

C) demands for political and social reform were severely punished.

D) intellectuals were widely respected and elevated to elite status.

GO ON TO THE NEXT PAGE ⟩

28. Which choice provides the best evidence for the answer to the previous question?

    A) Lines 12-15 ("Since Diderot . . . topics")

    B) Lines 41-44 ("The execution . . . illustrations")

    C) Lines 57-59 ("Trade guilds . . . establishment")

    D) Lines 70-73 ("Despite . . . Middle Ages")

29. As used in lines 46-47, "erudition" most nearly means

    A) hierarchy.

    B) sophistication.

    C) skill.

    D) learning.

30. Which choice best describes how the impact of the *Encyclopédie* changed over time?

    A) Advances in science and industry made the *Encyclopédie* obsolete.

    B) Advances in science and industry changed the *Encyclopédie* from a "how-to" source into a history of technology.

    C) Advances in science and industry turned the *Encyclopédie* into an affordable, mass-produced publication used by millions.

    D) Advances in science and industry led to an expansion of the number of *Encyclopédie* volumes in each set.

31. Based on the passage and the graphic, which of the following is most likely to be true?

    A) Diderot would not have included information about Galileo's scientific observations.

    B) Diderot would have included information on the production techniques used to create the first telescope.

    C) Diderot would not have included information about the discovery of Uranus.

    D) Diderot would have included information about Einstein's theory of relativity.

Questions 32-42 are based on the following passages.

The following passages discuss acidity. Passage 1 describes the effect of acid rain on the environment, while Passage 2 focuses on how the human body responds to abnormal acidity levels.

Passage 1

In the past century, due to the burning of fossil fuels in energy plants and cars, acid rain has become a cause of harm to the environment. How-
Line ever, rain would still be slightly acidic even if these
(5) activities were to stop. Acid rain would continue to fall, but it would not cause the problems we see now. The environment can handle slightly acidic rain; it just cannot keep up with the level of acid rain caused by burning fossil fuels.
(10) A pH of 7 is considered neutral, while pH below 7 is acidic and pH above 7 is alkaline, or basic. Pure rain water can have a pH as low as 5.5. Rain water is acidic because carbon dioxide gas in the air reacts with the water to make carbonic acid.
(15) Since it is a weak acid, even a large amount of it will not lower the pH of water much.

Soil, lakes, and streams can tolerate slightly acidic rain. The water and soil contain alkaline materials that will neutralize acids. These include
(20) some types of rocks, plant and animal waste, and ashes from forest fires. Altogether, these materials can easily handle the slightly acidic rain that occurs naturally. The alkaline waste and ashes will slowly be used up, but more will be made to replace it.
(25) Anthropomorphic causes of acid rain, such as the burning of fossil fuels, release nitrogen oxide and sulfur oxide gases. These gases react with water to make nitric acid and sulfuric acid. Since these are both strong acids, small amounts can lower
(30) the pH of rain water to 3 or less. Such a low pH requires much more alkaline material to neutralize it. Acid rain with a lower pH uses up alkaline materials faster, and more cannot be made quickly enough to replace what is used up. Soil and water
(35) become more acidic and remain that way, as they are unable to neutralize the strong acid.

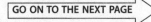
GO ON TO THE NEXT PAGE

Passage 2

In humans, keeping a constant balance between acidity and alkalinity in the blood is essential. If blood pH drops below 7.35 or rises above 7.45,
(40) all of the functions in the body are impaired and life-threatening conditions can soon develop. Many processes in the body produce acid wastes, which would lower the pH of blood below the safe level unless neutralized. Several systems are in place
(45) to keep pH constant within the necessary range. Certain conditions, however, can cause acids to be made faster than these systems can react.

Most of the pH control involves three related substances: carbon dioxide, carbonic acid, and
(50) bicarbonate ions. Carbonic acid is formed when carbon dioxide reacts with water. Bicarbonate ions are formed when the carbonic acid releases a hydrogen ion. Excess carbonic acid lowers the pH, while excess bicarbonate ions raise it.

(55) The kidneys store bicarbonate ions and will release or absorb them to help adjust the pH of the blood. Breathing faster removes more carbon dioxide from the blood, which reduces the amount of carbonic acid; in contrast, breathing more slowly has
(60) the opposite effect. In a healthy body, these systems automatically neutralize normal amounts of acid wastes and maintain blood pH within the very small range necessary for the body to function normally.

In some cases, these systems can be overwhelmed.
(65) This can happen to people with diabetes if their blood sugar drops too low for too long. People with type 1 diabetes do not make enough insulin, which allows the body's cells to absorb sugar from the blood to supply the body with energy. If a
(70) person's insulin level gets too low for too long, the body breaks down fats to use for energy. The waste produced from breaking down fats is acidic, so the blood pH drops. If the kidneys exhaust their supply of bicarbonate ions, and the lungs cannot remove
(75) carbon dioxide fast enough to raise pH, other functions in the body begin to fail as well. The person will need medical treatment to support these functions until the pH balancing system can catch up. The system will then keep the blood pH constant,
(80) as long as the production of acid wastes does not exceed the body's capacity to neutralize them.

32. Passage 1 most strongly suggests that

A) the environment will be damaged seriously if people do not reduce the burning of fossil fuels.

B) scientists must find a way to introduce more alkaline materials into the water supply to combat acid rain.

C) acid rain will not be a problem in the future as we move away from fossil fuels and toward alternative energy sources.

D) acidic rain water is more of a problem than acidic soil because soil contains more alkaline materials.

33. Which choice provides the best evidence for the answer to the previous question?

A) Lines 7-9 ("The environment . . . fuels")

B) Lines 13-14 ("Rain water . . . acid")

C) Lines 17-18 ("Soil, lakes . . . rain")

D) Lines 25-27 ("Anthropomorphic . . . gases")

34. According to the information in Passage 1, which pH level for rain water would cause the most damage to the environment?

A) 2.25

B) 4

C) 5

D) 9.1

35. As used in line 17, "tolerate" most nearly means

A) accept.

B) endure.

C) acknowledge.

D) distribute.

GO ON TO THE NEXT PAGE

36. Passage 2 most strongly suggests that

    A) a pH of 7.35 is ideal for blood in the human body.

    B) acid wastes in the blood multiply if not neutralized.

    C) the normal range of blood pH narrows as a person ages.

    D) small amounts of acid wastes in the blood are a normal condition.

37. Which choice provides the best evidence for the answer to the previous question?

    A) Lines 38-41 ("If blood pH . . . develop")

    B) Lines 46-47 ("Certain conditions . . . react")

    C) Lines 60-63 ("In a healthy . . . normally")

    D) Lines 66-69 ("People with . . . energy")

38. As used in line 73, "exhaust" most nearly means

    A) fatigue.

    B) consume.

    C) deplete.

    D) dissolve.

39. Which of the following plays a role in the environment most similar to the role played by excess bicarbonate ions in the blood?

    A) Acid rain

    B) Ashes from a forest fire

    C) Sulfur oxide gases

    D) Fossil fuels

40. Based on the information in Passage 2, which of the following can cause the body to break down fats to use for energy?

    A) An excess of carbonic acid

    B) Low blood pH

    C) A drop in blood sugar

    D) Not enough insulin

41. Which of the following best describes a shared purpose of the authors of both passages?

    A) To encourage readers to care for delicate systems such as the environment and human body

    B) To explain how the human body neutralizes acid wastes that it produces and deposits in the blood

    C) To describe systems that can neutralize small amounts of acids but become overwhelmed by large amounts

    D) To persuade readers to work toward reducing acid rain by cutting consumption of fossil fuels

42. Both passages support which of the following generalizations?

    A) The human body and environment are delicate systems that require balance to function properly.

    B) There are many similarities between the systems that make up the human body and the water cycle.

    C) Acid rain is an important issue that will continue to impact the environment until we reduce the use of fossil fuels.

    D) Medical treatment is necessary when the pH of a person's blood drops below 7.35 or rises above 7.45.

Questions 43-52 are based on the following passage and supplementary material.

The following passage discusses the benefits of using hydrogen as a renewable energy source.

Scientists worldwide have been working diligently to advance hydrogen as a renewable energy source. Hydrogen, the most abundant
Line element in the universe, is found primarily with
(5) oxygen in water. Because it can be safely used as fuel, it is a candidate for gasoline replacement in passenger vehicles.

GO ON TO THE NEXT PAGE

The potential benefits to moving away from petroleum-based fuel are plentiful. Since hydro-
(10) gen can be produced within the United States, discovering ways to safely and economically switch to hydrogen fuel would drastically reduce our dependency on other petroleum-producing nations. In addition to making us more independent, hydro-
(15) gen produces no pollution, including greenhouse gasses, when used as fuel. For this reason alone, forward-thinking scientists have made it a priority to invent new ways to use hydrogen.

Until now, there have been several challenges
(20) preventing hydrogen from becoming a mainstream form of clean energy. In the United States, engines that run on hydrogen are much more expensive than gasoline. Additionally, it is difficult to store enough hydrogen to get comparable mileage to a
(25) gasoline vehicle. However, these factors have not been the biggest drawback in producing hydrogen for use in fuel cells; the biggest drawback has been that fossil fuels were needed to generate large amounts of hydrogen. Relying on fossil
(30) fuels to produce this element nearly negates the environmental benefit behind the concept.

Recently, a new method has been discovered, allowing scientists to create large quantities of the element using lower amounts of energy derived
(35) from renewable sources. As in traditional methods, scientists employ electrolysis, a process during which electricity is used to break the bonds between the atoms found in water by passing a current through the water via a semiconductor. Once the water mol-
(40) ecules are broken into separate hydrogen and oxygen atoms, both are released as individual gasses and the hydrogen can be harvested.

When people think of solar power, huge panels usually come to mind, the type of panels that
(45) could not be used to power consumer vehicles in a way equivalent to gasoline. However, scientists have recently been successful at employing solar power as the catalyst in electrolysis, harvesting energy from the sun and using it to break apart
(50) water molecules. The same scientists who made this achievement then built a semiconductor out of affordable, oxide-based materials. When these two advances are coupled, they also reduce the

economic and environmental cost of generating
(55) and processing hydrogen.

Another bonus to this new method of production is that it is significantly more efficient than older production methods. The team of researchers attained the most efficient solar-to-fuel conversion to date, and
(60) they did it without using cost-prohibitive materials.

There are still several challenges to be overcome before hydrogen is a viable gasoline replacement. This new method of production, though, is a huge
(65) step in the right direction. There are many ongoing research initiatives that aim to make hydrogen extraction even more cost-effective, as well as easy to store. When these issues are solved, hydrogen will become a fuel that works for humanity and the
(70) earth at the same time.

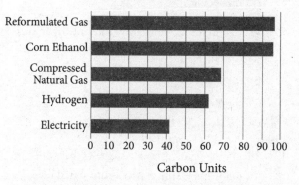

**Alternative Fuel Emissions
in California Passenger Cars**

Carbon Units

Adapted from U.S. Department of Energy Alternative Fuels Data Center.

43. With which of the following statements would the author most likely agree?

A) Scientists should consider the final cost to consumers when exploring alternatives to petroleum-based fuels.

B) The development of hydrogen fuel for automobiles will give a boost to the economy in the United States.

C) Safety concerns surrounding hydrogen used as fuel pose the biggest problem for scientists studying alternative energy.

D) Gasoline must be eliminated as a source of fuel for automobiles within the next decade.

GO ON TO THE NEXT PAGE ⟶

44. Which choice provides the best evidence for the answer to the previous question?

    A) Lines 5-7 ("Because it . . . vehicles")

    B) Lines 9-13 ("Since hydrogen . . . nations")

    C) Lines 21-23 ("In the United States . . . gasoline")

    D) Lines 52-70 ("When these . . . time")

45. According to the passage, which of the following is true of hydrogen?

    A) It exists mostly with oxygen in water molecules in its natural state.

    B) It is more efficient than solar power as an energy source.

    C) It can be used as fuel in most types of engines.

    D) It can be easily harvested from water molecules.

46. As used in line 2, "diligently" most nearly means

    A) impulsively.

    B) persistently.

    C) rapidly.

    D) perpetually.

47. The passage most strongly suggests that which of the following is true of petroleum-based fuel?

    A) Its cost is higher than most alternative fuels.

    B) Its use has a negative effect on the environment.

    C) It cannot be produced in the United States.

    D) It is more efficient than other types of fuel.

48. Which choice provides the best evidence for the answer to the previous question?

    A) Lines 1-3 ("Scientists . . . source")

    B) Lines 14-16 ("In addition . . . as fuel")

    C) Lines 56-58 ("Another bonus . . . methods")

    D) Lines 58-61 ("The team . . . materials")

49. In paragraph 2, why does the author explain that hydrogen energy will reduce our dependency on petroleum-producing nations?

    A) To illustrate why scientists in other countries are not working to develop hydrogen energy

    B) To highlight how hydrogen energy is superior to other forms of alternative energy

    C) To suggest how hydrogen energy can help protect the environment

    D) To clarify why the development of hydrogen as a fuel source is important

50. As used in line 34, "derived" most nearly means

    A) gained.

    B) received.

    C) obtained.

    D) copied.

GO ON TO THE NEXT PAGE

51. The passage most strongly suggests that which of the following is true about methods of extracting hydrogen from water?

    A) Much additional research is needed to perfect hydrogen extraction.

    B) Scientific breakthroughs will soon make hydrogen extraction unnecessary.

    C) Scientists are on course to develop a safe way to extract hydrogen within one year.

    D) It is unlikely that hydrogen extraction will ever be done in an environmentally friendly way.

52. Information from both the passage and the graphic support the conclusion that

    A) compressed natural gas is the most environmentally friendly form of automobile fuel.

    B) scientists are making great advances in the development of hydrogen as a fuel for automobiles.

    C) electricity produces less air pollution than hydrogen and compressed natural gas.

    D) switching from gasoline to hydrogen to fuel automobiles would significantly reduce air pollution.

WRITING AND LANGUAGE TEST

35 Minutes—44 Questions

This section corresponds to Section 2 of your answer sheet.

Directions: Each passage in this section is followed by several questions. Some questions will reference an underlined portion in the passage; others will ask you to consider a part of a passage or the passage as a whole. For each question, choose the answer that reflects the best use of grammar, punctuation, and style. If a passage or question is accompanied by a graphic, take the graphic into account in choosing your response(s). Some questions will have "NO CHANGE" as a possible response. Choose that answer if you think the best choice is to leave the sentence as written.

Questions 1-11 are based on the following passage and supplementary material.

Sorting Recyclables for Best Re-Use

From the time a plastic container is thrown into a recycling bin to the time the plastic **1** are actually recycled, it passes through several sorting cycles. In addition to being separated from the non-plastic items, the plastics themselves must be **2** detached, because not all plastics are alike, making some easier to recycle than others.

3 Special machines have been developed to assist in sorting plastics. During manual sorting, people

1. A) NO CHANGE
   B) is
   C) has been
   D) will be

2. A) NO CHANGE
   B) demolished,
   C) flanked,
   D) categorized,

3. Which choice most effectively sets up the information that follows?

   A) NO CHANGE
   B) Sorting by hand is less efficient than using machines to sort plastics.
   C) Classifying plastics can be done manually or by machines.
   D) Plastics are widely used today, so they need to be recycled.

[4] very thoroughly check the numbers on the bottom of each plastic item. The numbers indicate the type of plastic each is made from. Some sorting can be automated by using machines that can detect the composition of the plastic. The detectors in these machines use infrared light to characterize and sort the plastics, similar to how a human might use visible light to sort materials by their color. By either method, the plastics can eventually be arranged into bins or piles corresponding to the recycling code numbers running from one to seven.

In some cases, plastics are further sorted by the method by which they were manufactured. [5] However, [6] bottles, tubs and, trays are typically [7] made from either PET (polyethylene terephthalate) or HDPE (high density polyethylene), two of the least recovered plastics. Bottles are produced by a process called blow-molding, in which the plastic is heated until soft, then blown up, much like a balloon, while being pushed against a mold. Tubs and trays are usually made by a process called injection molding, in which the plastic is heated until it can be pushed through nozzles into a mold. Different additives are added to the plastics before [8] molding. It depends on the method. Since the additives for injection molding might not be suitable for blow-molding of the recycled plastic, PET and HDPE bottles are often separated out from the other PET and HDPE plastics.

4. A) NO CHANGE
   B) completely and thoroughly check
   C) thoroughly check
   D) make sure to thoroughly check

5. A) NO CHANGE
   B) For example,
   C) Consequently,
   D) Similarly,

6. A) NO CHANGE
   B) bottles, tubs, and trays
   C) bottles tubs, and trays,
   D) bottles, tubs, and, trays

7. Which choice completes the sentence with accurate data based on the graphic?

   A) NO CHANGE
   B) made from PET (polyethylene terephthalate) or HDPE (high density polyethylene), the two most recovered plastics after the leading type, LDPE.
   C) made from PP (polypropene) or PS (polystyrene), the two most recovered plastics after the leading type, PVC.
   D) made from PP (polypropene) or PS (polystyrene), the two most recovered plastics after the leading type, EPS.

8. Which choice most effectively combines the sentences at the underlined portion?

   A) molding, however, it depends
   B) molding, depending
   C) molding despite depending
   D) molding, it depends

GO ON TO THE NEXT PAGE

While the numbers 1 through 6 indicate a [9] specific plastic, number 7 indicates that the plastic is either one of many other plastics, or that it is a blend of plastics. These plastics are more difficult to recycle, as different amounts of the various types of number 7 plastics will be sent to recycling each day. They are typically used for products in which the plastic will be mixed with other materials.

Although there are many types of plastics to be found in a typical recycling bin, each one can play a part in a recycled [10] product, the many cycles of sorting guarantee that each piece can be correctly processed and sent off for re-use. [11]

9. A) NO CHANGE
   B) vague
   C) common
   D) pending

10. A) NO CHANGE
    B) product the many
    C) product. The many
    D) product, so the many

11. Which choice most effectively establishes a concluding sentence for the paragraph?

    A) Sorting ensures that plastics will not linger in the landfills, but continue to be of use.

    B) Sorting different types of plastics is done in many ways, either by hand or machine.

    C) Oftentimes, people are required to sort their own plastics by type.

    D) There are many different kinds of plastics, and each one is useful.

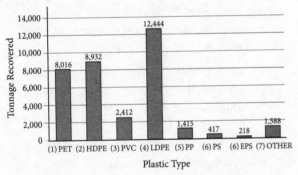

Breakdown of Recovered Plastic by Material Type (2004)

Original graph at http://www.recycle.co.nz/symbols.php.

Questions 12-22 are based on the following passage.

Interpreter at America's Immigrant Gateway

[12] Among the many diverse and fascinating possibilities for a career, David Kaufman chose language interpretation. Throughout his career as an interpreter at America's largest immigrant processing station, Kaufman has spent many ferry rides mentally preparing himself for the vivid realities of his job. Although some of his contemporaries might consider his work menial or inconsequential, he cherishes his opportunity to witness and contribute to the unfolding stories of countless immigrants. These immigrant stories, Kaufman knows, hold [13] great significance for his and American history. Most of the brave, sea-worn travelers who disembark at Ellis Island will soon depart as new Americans, [14] lugging all there courage, hope, and worldly possessions into New York City. Many [15] will remain in the city and some other people will disperse across the nation.

12. Which choice provides the most appropriate introduction to the passage?

   A) NO CHANGE

   B) Many people never consider language interpretation as a job, but David Kaufman knows all about it.

   C) All jobs come with difficulties, and David Kaufman believes language interpretation is no different.

   D) A pale horizon meets the early-morning sky as David Kaufman's commuter ferry crosses the New York Harbor, bound for Ellis Island.

13. A) NO CHANGE

   B) great significance for his—and America's—history.

   C) great significance for his: and America's history.

   D) great significance for his, and America's, history.

14. A) NO CHANGE

   B) lugging all they're courage,

   C) lugging all their courage,

   D) lugging all there are courage,

15. A) NO CHANGE

   B) will remain in the city, but other people will nonetheless disperse across the

   C) will remain in the city; many others will disperse across the

   D) will remain in the city, though yet others will disperse across the

GO ON TO THE NEXT PAGE ⟶

[1] The year is 1907: the busiest year Kaufman, or Ellis Island, has seen. [2] One and a quarter million immigrants have been admitted to the U.S. this year. [3] Only about 2 percent of Ellis Island's immigrants are denied, typically for perceived potential criminal or public health threats. [4] The rest will establish life in America, although not without difficulty and perseverance. [5] At the immigration station, Kaufman regularly sees the range of raw human emotion, from deep, exhausted grief to powerful hope. [6] He has witnessed it all. `16`

`17` Many Ellis Island interpreters were born to European immigrants. `18` His heritage, and surrounding community, enabled him to learn six languages. Fluency in six languages is typical for Ellis Island interpreters, although Kaufman knows some who speak as many as twelve or thirteen. Kaufman knows that in some ways, his ability to listen and translate effectively can impact the course of an immigrant's future. For this reason, he constantly hones his language skills, picking up various `19` shades and dialects in hopes to better help those he serves.

16. Sentence 1 should be placed

A) where it is now.

B) after sentence 2.

C) after sentence 3.

D) after sentence 4.

17. Which sentence most effectively establishes the central idea of the paragraph?

A) NO CHANGE

B) Like many Ellis Island interpreters, Kaufman was born to European immigrants.

C) Language ability was especially important among Ellis Island interpreters.

D) Some accused children of European immigrants of having an unfair advantage in getting jobs at Ellis Island.

18. A) NO CHANGE

B) His heritage, and surrounding community enabled him to learn six languages.

C) His heritage and surrounding community, enabled him to learn six languages.

D) His heritage and surrounding community enabled him to learn six languages.

19. A) NO CHANGE

B) meanings

C) tricks

D) nuances

Kaufman assists colleagues at every checkpoint. Ellis Island is equipped with a hospital, dining room, and boarding room, in addition to the more central processing facilities. **20** Kaufman is one of an army of Ellis Island employees spread around the enormous compound. This morning, he helps an Italian family discuss their child's health with nurses. Later, he translates for a Polish woman who expects to meet her brother soon. When Kaufman meets immigrants whose language he cannot speak, he finds another interpreter **21** to help speak to them instead of him doing it.

To some extent, Kaufman sees himself distinctly in the shoes of these immigrants. He intimately knows the reality that almost all Americans, somewhere in their ancestry, were not native to this nation. With every encounter, Kaufman hopes that these immigrants will soon find whatever they crossed oceans to seek. He hopes, as he still does for his own family, that life in America will someday render the **22** advantages of leaving home worthwhile.

20. Which sentence best supports the central idea of the paragraph?

A) NO CHANGE

B) From medical screening to records confirmation to inspection, Kaufman interprets as needs arise.

C) Sometimes, Kaufman feels the stress of being pulled in many different directions, but ultimately he finds his job worthwhile.

D) Kaufman and his colleagues work, eat, and practically live together, making them feel closer than typical coworkers.

21. A) NO CHANGE

B) to help speak instead of him.

C) helping him out with speaking.

D) to help.

22. A) NO CHANGE

B) journeys

C) difficulties

D) penalties

GO ON TO THE NEXT PAGE

Questions 23-33 are based on the following passage.

Software Sales: A Gratifying Career

Ever since she was a young girl, Stephanie Morales took on the role of family problem-solver. [23] <u>She remembers her brother never being able to find his favorite movie when he wanted to watch it: So, she alphabetized the family DVD collection.</u> [24] <u>"They're</u> about efficiency and what makes sense to a user," Morales says, "and putting systems in place so that using something becomes effortless."

Growing up, Morales became notorious amongst her friends as the one to plan parties and trips, and she was always voted team captain because everyone knew she could see the big picture and enact a plan. [25] <u>After college, she tried a career in interior design, but homes and offices didn't excite her.</u> "I didn't have a passion for furniture or architecture. I knew there must be a field out there that really tapped into my particular skill set," Morales says.

23. A) NO CHANGE
    B) She remembers her brother never being able to find his favorite movie, when he wanted to watch it so she alphabetized the family DVD collection.
    C) She remembers her brother never being able to find his favorite movie; when he wanted to watch it, so she alphabetized the family DVD collection.
    D) She remembers her brother never being able to find his favorite movie when he wanted to watch it, so she alphabetized the family DVD collection.

24. A) NO CHANGE
    B) It's
    C) Their
    D) Its

25. A) NO CHANGE
    B) After college, she tried a career in interior design,—but homes and offices; didn't excite her.
    C) After college, she tried a career in interior design but homes, and offices didn't excite her.
    D) After college she tried a career, in interior design; but homes and offices didn't excite her.

GO ON TO THE NEXT PAGE →

[1]To her surprise, that career turned out to be software consulting. [2] Morales returned from a backpacking trip around Europe to her parents' New Hampshire home, needing income. [3] New Hampshire also has many fine backpacking trails. [4] **26** <u>Although she had no direct experience in the field, Morales convinced</u> a family friend to hire her as a software consultant to work with new clients. **27** **28** <u>She had helped many of her friends with their computers. Knowing her interpersonal skills were strong.</u>

26. A) NO CHANGE
    B) Although she had no direct experience in the field, Morales convinces
    C) Although she has no direct experience in the field, Morales convinced
    D) Although she will have no direct experience in the field, Morales convinces

27. Which sentence does not support the paragraph's topic and purpose?

    A) Sentence 1
    B) Sentence 2
    C) Sentence 3
    D) Sentence 4

28. A) NO CHANGE
    B) She had helped many of her friends; with their computers and she knew her interpersonal skills were strong.
    C) She had helped many of her friends with their computers; knowing her interpersonal skills were strong.
    D) She had helped many of her friends with their computers, and she knew her interpersonal skills were strong.

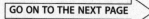 GO ON TO THE NEXT PAGE

29 Because she was willing to work in a factory, she was able to achieve success as a consultant. For example, Morales worked with a manufacturing company that was growing quickly but had trouble **30** maintaining employees. The company's human resources department could not keep up with regular payroll and billing, plus running advertisements and interviewing potential replacement employees. Morales used staff management software to gather data about employee satisfaction. Analysis showed that employees found the shift work too challenging for their schedules. The company changed the hours of the morning and evening shifts to meet employees' needs, which led to fewer workers leaving the company.

Nowadays, Morales works with what she calls "big data," such as information about consumer habits gathered through a supermarket membership card. These stores of information are a treasure trove to Morales, because they tell the story of how people interact with the world around them. She uses the data to make changes—just like alphabetizing a DVD collection. Her goal is to **31** vacillate into the health care field, where

29. Which choice most logically introduces the paragraph?

A) NO CHANGE

B) Morales's management of data led to the success of the company's advertising campaign.

C) Where the job really matched up with her strengths was in problem-solving and finding creative solutions.

D) Morales's advice to the human resources department resulted in higher wages for employees.

30. A) NO CHANGE

B) retaining

C) containing

D) detaining

31. A) NO CHANGE

B) convert

C) transition

D) fluctuate

she wants to bring the benefits of technology to people's physical and mental well-being. **32** For example, Morales is also interested in whether people pay for their medications with credit or debit cards.

Morales knows that people's health is extremely important, and every time someone fills a prescription online or has a follow-up visit with their doctor, that information helps medical experts better determine the efficacy of the medication. The technological revolution has the power **33** to quicken doctor's visits, improve the care we get, and even save lives.

Questions 34-44 are based on the following passage.

The Art of Collecting

At an art exhibition for artist Henri Matisse, enthusiasts can also view a black and white photograph of two siblings. These sisters, wearing Victorian-style dresses and top hats, are the renowned art collectors Claribel and Etta Cone. When Etta passed away in 1949, she **34** bequeathed some 3,000 objects to the Baltimore Museum of Art (BMA). Now, works from the Cone Collection, internationally renowned and consisting of masterpieces by early 20th century artists, travel on loan from BMA so that people can experience the Cone sisters' visionary passion for and dedication to modern art.

32. Which choice best supports the topic sentence of the paragraph?

A) NO CHANGE

B) For example, Morales spends countless hours walking through discount stores surveying the customers.

C) For example, Morales still gets great satisfaction from organizing her friends' and family's DVD collections.

D) For example, Morales can use "big data" to determine how many patients from a particular clinic use online automated refills.

33. A) NO CHANGE

B) to quicken doctor's visits improve the care we get, and even save lives.

C) to quicken doctor's visits, improve the care we get, and even, save lives.

D) to quicken doctor's visits; improve the care we get, and even save lives.

34. A) NO CHANGE

B) liquidated

C) delivered

D) allotted

GO ON TO THE NEXT PAGE

[35] <u>Henri Matisse was a well-known supporter of female artists and art patrons, and he revealed these unconventional attitudes in his work.</u> What made the Cone sisters innovative was their recognition of the value of art pieces by virtually unknown avant-garde artists of their time, such as Pablo Picasso. Critics failed to understand the Cones' [36] <u>tastes and such opinions</u> did not squelch the sisters' passion for collecting. According to Katy Rothkopf, senior curator at the BMA, Matisse's use of vibrant color, for example, was initially shocking. "At first the Cones . . . really found [the art] quite scary," states Rothkopf. However, the siblings befriended Matisse and other artists, gaining respect for the painters' unorthodox experimentation. As the Cones began buying and collecting art, [37] <u>there</u> selections improved.

"It took a lot of gall—guts—to paint it," Matisse once said about a controversial painting, "but much

35. Which choice best establishes the central idea of the paragraph?

A) NO CHANGE

B) Together the Cones, supported by the wealth from their family's textile business, gathered one of the finest collections of French art in the United States.

C) The Cones became great contributors to the Baltimore Museum of Art, and their renowned exhibition was praised by artists around the globe.

D) During this time period, only the wealthy could afford to purchase original artworks, and the Cones became famous for spending their entire fortune on art.

36. A) NO CHANGE

B) tastes, so such opinions

C) tastes therefore such opinions

D) tastes, but such opinions

37. A) NO CHANGE

B) they're

C) their

D) her

more to buy it." Claribel and Etta had that kind of gall. [38] Each had took risks by not purchasing traditional landscape paintings and instead amassing works that at the time were considered contemptuous and wild.

[1] A further legacy of the Cone Collection was its documentation of post-World War I Europe. [2] The art the Cones collected [39] suggested changes in Europe, such as the increasing use of machines in contemporary life and the emergence of modern thinking. [3] Traditional limitations in art were overcome by experimental forms and new media, allowing artists to explore their creativity. [4] Today, there are even more experimental forms of art than there were after World War I. [40]

[41] Additionally in visiting Paris, Budapest, Athens, Cairo, and Shanghai, the Cones represented the beginning of the new woman at the turn of the century. [42] Though their unconventional lifestyle, the far-seeing Cone sisters experienced freedom from narrower roles.

38. A) NO CHANGE
    B) They took risks
    C) They have taken risks
    D) Each will take risks

39. A) NO CHANGE
    B) depicted
    C) referenced
    D) divulged

40. Which sentence should be deleted to best maintain the theme of the paragraph?
    A) Sentence 1
    B) Sentence 2
    C) Sentence 3
    D) Sentence 4

41. A) NO CHANGE
    B) Additionally, in visiting: Paris,
    C) Additionally, in visiting Paris,
    D) Additionally in visiting Paris

42. A) NO CHANGE
    B) Therefore
    C) Thorough
    D) Through

GO ON TO THE NEXT PAGE

They avoided the gross inequalities between genders by becoming connoisseurs of radical art. 43

Public acceptance of the 44 Cone's avant-garde collection testifies to their accomplishments. While the estimated value of their artwork is one billion dollars, their larger contribution is inestimable. As bold patrons, the Cones advanced appreciation for modern art for generations to come.

43. What changes to the paragraph would best strengthen the author's claims?

A) The author should define the terms "new woman" and "narrower roles."

B) The author should list more nations and cities visited by the Cone sisters.

C) The precise centuries referenced by "turn of the century" should be included.

D) The author should add reactions from contemporary critics to the Cones' travels.

44. A) NO CHANGE
B) Cones'
C) Cones
D) Cones's

MATH TEST

25 Minutes—20 Questions

NO-CALCULATOR SECTION

This section corresponds to Section 3 of your answer sheet.

Directions: For this section, solve each question and select the best answer choice. The available space on each page may be used for scratch work.

Notes:

1. Calculator use is NOT permitted.
2. All numbers used are real numbers, and all variables used represent real numbers, unless otherwise indicated.
3. Figures are drawn to scale and lie in a plane unless otherwise indicated.
4. Unless stated otherwise, the domain of any function f is assumed to be the set of all real numbers x, for which $f(x)$ is a real number.

Information:

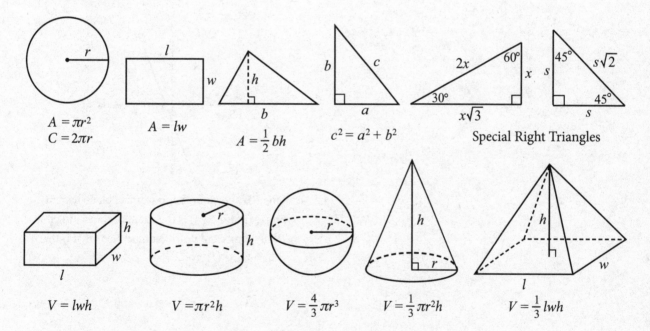

$A = \pi r^2$
$C = 2\pi r$

$A = lw$

$A = \frac{1}{2}bh$

$c^2 = a^2 + b^2$

Special Right Triangles

$V = lwh$

$V = \pi r^2 h$

$V = \frac{4}{3}\pi r^3$

$V = \frac{1}{3}\pi r^2 h$

$V = \frac{1}{3}lwh$

The sum of the degree measures of the angles in a triangle is 180.

The number of degrees of arc in a circle is 360.

The number of radians of arc in a circle is 2π.

GO ON TO THE NEXT PAGE ▷

1. A biologist develops the equation $y = 20.942x + 127$ to predict the regrowth of a certain species of plant x months after a natural disaster occurred. Which of the following describes what the number 20.942 represents in this equation?

    A) The estimated number of the plants after x months

    B) The estimated monthly increase in the number of the plants

    C) The estimated monthly decrease in the number of the plants

    D) The estimated number of the plants that survived the natural disaster

2. Which of the following expressions is equivalent to $25x^2 - \dfrac{4}{9}$?

    A) $\sqrt{5x - \dfrac{2}{3}}$

    B) $x\left(5x - \dfrac{2}{3}\right)$

    C) $\left(5x + \dfrac{2}{3}\right)\left(5x - \dfrac{2}{3}\right)$

    D) $\left(25x + \dfrac{2}{3}\right)\left(25x - \dfrac{2}{3}\right)$

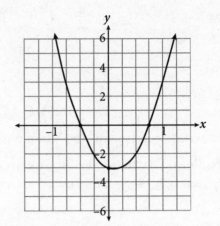

3. Which of the following could be the factored form of the equation graphed in the figure shown?

    A) $y = (2x + 1)(4x - 3)$

    B) $y = (x + 2)(x - 3)$

    C) $y = \left(x - \dfrac{1}{2}\right)\left(x + \dfrac{3}{4}\right)$

    D) $y = \dfrac{1}{2}(x + 1)(x - 3)$

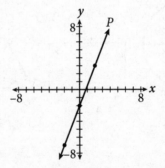

4. Line P is shown in the coordinate plane here. If line Q (not shown) is the result of translating line P left 4 units and down 3 units, then what is the slope of line Q?

    A) $-\dfrac{4}{3}$

    B) -1

    C) $\dfrac{4}{3}$

    D) $\dfrac{5}{2}$

$$a = \frac{v_f - v_i}{t}$$

5. Acceleration is the rate at which the velocity of an object changes with respect to time, or in other words, how much an object is speeding up or slowing down. The average acceleration of an object can be found using the formula shown above, where t is the time over which the acceleration is being measured, v_f is the final velocity, and v_i is the initial velocity. Which of the following represents t in terms of the other variables?

A) $t = \dfrac{a}{v_f - v_i}$

B) $t = \dfrac{v_f - v_i}{a}$

C) $t = a(v_f - v_i)$

D) $t = \dfrac{1}{a(v_f - v_i)}$

6. Which of the following equations could represent a parabola that has a minimum value of -5 and whose axis of symmetry is the line $x = 1$?

A) $y = (x - 5)^2 + 1$

B) $y = (x + 5)^2 + 1$

C) $y = (x - 1)^2 - 5$

D) $y = (x + 1)^2 - 5$

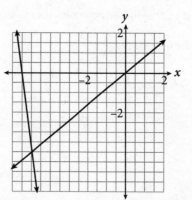

7. If (A, B) is the solution to the system of equations shown in the graph above, what is the value of $A + B$?

A) -18

B) -9

C) 1

D) 5.5

8. If $A = x^2 + 4x + 9$ and $B = x^3 + 6x - 2$, what is $3A + B$?

A) $4x^2 + 18x + 25$

B) $x^3 + x^2 + 10x + 7$

C) $x^3 + 3x^2 + 18x + 25$

D) $3x^3 + 3x^2 + 30x + 29$

9. How many real values of x satisfy the quadratic equation $9x^2 - 12x + 4 = 0$?

A) 0

B) 1

C) 2

D) 4

GO ON TO THE NEXT PAGE

10. Which of the following represents the solution set for the inequality $\frac{3}{5}\left(x + \frac{2}{7}\right) > -6$?

    A) $x > -\dfrac{72}{7}$

    B) $x > -\dfrac{216}{35}$

    C) $x > -\dfrac{136}{35}$

    D) $x > -\dfrac{18}{7}$

11. Acetaminophen is one of the most common drugs given to children and one of the most difficult to give correctly because it's sold in several different forms and different concentrations. For example, the old concentration given by dropper was 90 milligrams of acetaminophen per 1 milliliter of liquid, while the new concentration given by syringe is 160 milligrams per 5 milliliters. Several dosages are shown in the table below.

Infant Acetaminophen Dosages			
Age	0–3 mo	4–11 mo	12–23 mo
Dropper	0.5 ml	1.0 ml	1.5 ml
Syringe	1.25 ml	2.5 ml	3.75 ml

    Which linear function represents the relationship between the amount of liquid in the dropper, d, and the amount of liquid in the syringe, s?

    A) $s = 0.4d$

    B) $s = 1.25d$

    C) $s = 2d$

    D) $s = 2.5d$

12. Which of the following equations, when graphed on a coordinate plane, will not cross the y-axis?

    A) $0.5(4x + y) = y - 9$

    B) $2(x + 7) - x = 4(y + 3)$

    C) $0.25(8y + 4x) - 7 = -2(-y + 1)$

    D) $6x - 2(3y + x) = 10 - 3y$

$$\begin{cases} Hx + 2y = -8 \\ Kx - 5y = -13 \end{cases}$$

13. If the solution to the system of equations shown above is $(2, -1)$, what is the value of $\dfrac{K}{H}$?

    A) -3

    B) $-\dfrac{1}{3}$

    C) $\dfrac{1}{3}$

    D) 3

14. It is given that $\sin A = k$, where A is an angle measured in radians and $\pi < A < \dfrac{3\pi}{2}$. If $\sin B = k$, which of the following could be the value of B?

    A) $A - \pi$

    B) $\pi + A$

    C) $2\pi - A$

    D) $3\pi - A$

15. Which of the following is equivalent to the expression $\left(\dfrac{x^{\frac{1}{2}}}{x^{-2}}\right)^2$?

    A) x^2

    B) $\left(\dfrac{x^2}{x}\right)^{\frac{1}{2}}$

    C) $\left(\dfrac{(x^2)(x^{\frac{1}{3}})}{x^4}\right)^3$

    D) $\left(\dfrac{(x^3)(x^4)}{x^{-3}}\right)^{\frac{1}{2}}$

GO ON TO THE NEXT PAGE

Directions: For questions 16-20, enter your responses into the appropriate grid on your answer sheet, in accordance with the following:

1. You will receive credit only if the circles are filled in correctly, but you may write your answers in the boxes above each grid to help you fill in the circles accurately.

2. Don't mark more than one circle per column.

3. None of the questions with grid-in responses will have a negative solution.

4. Only grid in a single answer, even if there is more than one correct answer to a given question.

5. A **mixed number** must be gridded as a decimal or an improper fraction. For example, you would grid $7\frac{1}{2}$ as 7.5 or $\frac{15}{2}$.

    (Were you to grid it as $\boxed{\begin{array}{cccc} 7 & 1 & / & 2 \end{array}}$, this response would be read as $\frac{71}{2}$.)

6. A **decimal** that has more digits than there are places on the grid may be either rounded or truncated, but every column in the grid must be filled in order to receive credit.

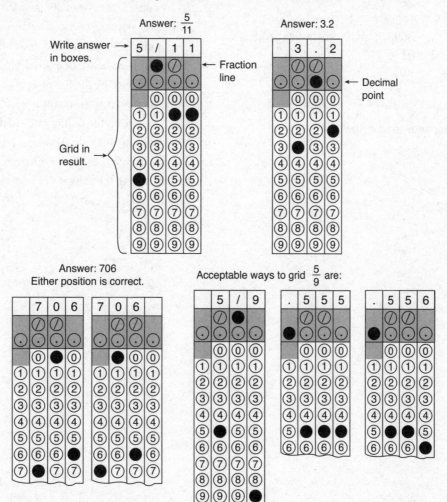

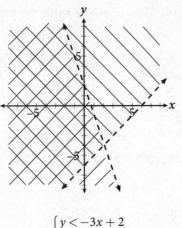

$$\begin{cases} y < -3x + 2 \\ y > x - 6 \end{cases}$$

16. The figure above shows the solution set for the given system of inequalities. Suppose (a, b) is a solution to the system. If $a = 0$, what is the greatest possible integer value of b?

17. Given the function $f(x) = \dfrac{2}{3}x - 5$, what input value corresponds to an output of 3?

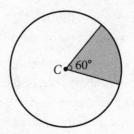

18. If the area of the shaded sector in circle C shown above is 6π square units, what is the diameter of the circle?

19. What is the diameter of the circle given by the equation $x^2 + y^2 + 10x - 4y = 20$?

20. In economics, the law of demand states that as the price of a commodity rises, the demand for that commodity goes down. A company determines that the monthly demand for a certain item that it sells can be modeled by the function $q(p) = -2p + 34$, where q represents the quantity sold in hundreds and p represents the selling price in dollars. It costs \$7 to produce this item. How much more per month in profits can the company expect to earn by selling the item at \$12 instead of \$10? (Profit = sales − costs)

MATH TEST

55 Minutes—38 Questions

CALCULATOR SECTION

This section corresponds to Section 4 of your answer sheet.

Directions: For this section, solve each question and select the best answer choice. The available space on each page may be used for scratch work.

Notes:

1. Calculator use is permitted.
2. All numbers used are real numbers, and all variables used represent real numbers, unless otherwise indicated.
3. Figures are drawn to scale and lie in a plane unless otherwise indicated.
4. Unless stated otherwise, the domain of any function f is assumed to be the set of all real numbers x, for which $f(x)$ is a real number.

Information:

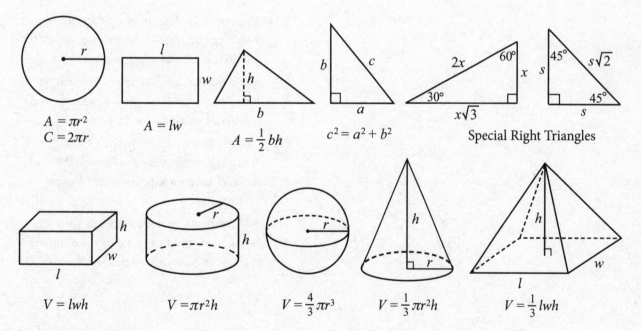

$A = \pi r^2$
$C = 2\pi r$

$A = lw$

$A = \frac{1}{2}bh$

$c^2 = a^2 + b^2$

Special Right Triangles

$V = lwh$

$V = \pi r^2 h$

$V = \frac{4}{3}\pi r^3$

$V = \frac{1}{3}\pi r^2 h$

$V = \frac{1}{3}lwh$

The sum of the degree measures of the angles in a triangle is 180.

The number of degrees of arc in a circle is 360.

The number of radians of arc in a circle is 2π.

GO ON TO THE NEXT PAGE ▷

1. The USDA recommends that adult females consume 75 milligrams of ascorbic acid, also known as vitamin C, each day. Because smoking inhibits vitamin absorption, smokers are encouraged to consume an additional 35 milligrams daily. If one grapefruit contains 40 mg of vitamin C and one serving of spinach contains 10 milligrams, which of the following inequalities represents the possible intake of grapefruit, g, and spinach, s, that a smoking female could consume to meet or surpass the USDA's recommended amount of vitamin C?

A) $40g + 10s \geq 75$

B) $40g + 10s \geq 110$

C) $40g + 10s > 110$

D) $\dfrac{40}{g} + \dfrac{10}{s} \geq 110$

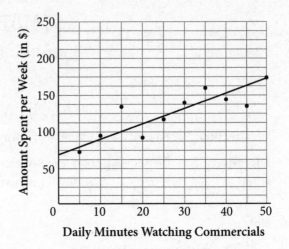

Daily Minutes Watching Commercials

2. The scatterplot above shows the relationship between the amount of time spent watching commercials each day and the amount of money spent each week on brand name grocery products for 10 consumers. The line of best fit for the data is also shown. Which of the following best represents the meaning of the slope of the line of best fit in the context of this question?

A) The predicted amount of time spent watching commercials when a person spends 0 dollars on brand name products

B) The predicted amount of money spent on brand name products when a person spends 0 minutes watching commercials

C) The predicted increase in time spent watching commercials for every dollar increase in money spent on brand name products

D) The predicted increase in money spent on brand name products for every one-minute increase in time spent watching commercials

3. There are very few states in the United States that require public schools to pay sales tax on their purchases. For this reason, many schools pay for student portraits and then the parents reimburse the school. Parents can choose between the basic package for $29.50 and the deluxe package for $44.50. If 182 parents ordered packages and the school's total bill was $6,509, which of the following systems of equations could be used to find the number of parents who ordered a basic package, b, and the number who ordered a deluxe package, d, assuming no parent ordered more than one package?

A) $\begin{cases} b+d=6,509 \\ 29.5b+44.5d=182 \end{cases}$

B) $\begin{cases} b+d=182 \\ 29.5b+44.5d=6,509 \end{cases}$

C) $\begin{cases} 2(b+d)=182 \\ 29.5b+44.5d=6,509 \end{cases}$

D) $\begin{cases} b+d=182 \\ 29.5b+44.5d=\dfrac{6,509}{2} \end{cases}$

5. If $4x+3=19$, what is the value of $4x-3$?

A) −19

B)   4

C)   13

D)   19

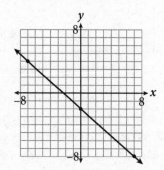

6. What is the slope of the line shown in the graph?

A) −2

B) $-\dfrac{7}{6}$

C) $-\dfrac{6}{7}$

D)   2

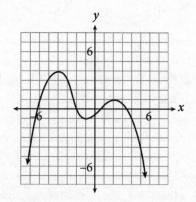

4. The graph of a polynomial function $p(x)$ is shown above. For what value(s) of x does $p(x)=-4$?

A) −1

B)   4

C) −7 and 5

D) −7, 4, and 5

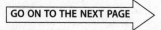 GO ON TO THE NEXT PAGE

Legislation Impact

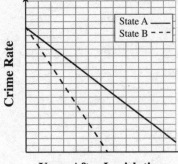

Years After Legislation

7. Most crimes in the United States are governed by state law rather than federal. Suppose two states passed laws that raised the penalty for committing armed robbery. The figure above represents the crime rate for armed robbery in both states after the laws were passed. Based on the graph, which of the following statements is true?

A) State A's law had a more positive impact on the crime rate for armed robbery.

B) State B's law had a more positive impact on the crime rate for armed robbery.

C) The laws in both states had the same impact on the crime rate for armed robbery.

D) Without axis labels, it is not possible to determine which state's law had a bigger impact.

8. On average, for every 2,500 cans of colored paint a home improvement chain mixes, exactly 40 are the wrong color (defective). At this rate, how many cans of paint were mixed during a period in which exactly 128 were defective?

A) 5,200

B) 7,500

C) 8,000

D) 10,200

9. According to the American Association of University Women, the mean age of men who have a college degree at their first marriage is 29.9 years. The mean age of women with a college degree at their first marriage is 28.4 years. Which of the following must be true about the combined mean age m of all people with college degrees at their first marriage?

A) $m = 29.15$

B) $m > 29.15$

C) $m < 29.15$

D) $28.4 < m < 29.9$

10. When scuba divers ascend from deep water, they must either rise slowly or take safety breaks to avoid nitrogen buildup in their lungs. The length of time a diver should take to ascend is directly proportional to how many feet she needs to ascend. If a scuba diver can safely ascend 165 feet in 5.5 minutes, then how many feet can she ascend in 90 seconds?

A) 45

B) 60

C) 75

D) 90

11. The chief financial officer of a shoe company calculates that the cost C of producing p pairs of a certain shoe is $C = 17p + 1,890$. The marketing department wants to sell the shoe for $35 per pair. The shoe company will make a profit only if the total revenue from selling p pairs is greater than the total cost of producing p pairs. Which of the following inequalities gives the number of pairs of shoes p that the company needs to sell in order to make a profit?

A) $p < 54$

B) $p > 54$

C) $p < 105$

D) $p > 105$

GO ON TO THE NEXT PAGE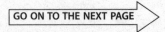

12. The human body has a very limited ability to store carbohydrates, which is why it is important for athletes to consume them during long training sessions or competitions. It is recommended that athletes consume approximately 3 calories per minute in situations like these. How many calories would an athlete biking a 74-mile race need to consume, assuming he bikes at an average speed of 9.25 miles per hour during the race?

A) 480

B) 1,440

C) 1,665

D) 2,053.5

x	3	−1	−5	−7
y	0	14	28	?

13. If the values in the table represent a linear relationship, what is the missing value?

A) 21

B) 30

C) 35

D) 42

Questions 14 and 15 refer to the following information.

The figure shows the age distribution of homebuyers and the percent of the market each age range makes up in a particular geographic region.

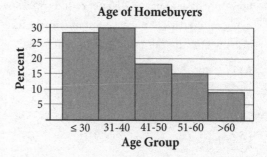

Age of Homebuyers

14. A new real estate agent is deciding which age group she should market toward in order to get the most clients. Which of the following measures of the data would be best for her to use when making this decision?

A) Mean

B) Mode

C) Range

D) Median

15. Based on the information in the figure, which of the following statements is true?

A) The shape of the data is skewed to the right, so the mean age of homebuyers is greater than the median.

B) The shape of the data is skewed to the left, so the median age of homebuyers is greater than the mean.

C) The shape of the data is fairly symmetric, so the mean age of homebuyers is approximately equal to the median.

D) The data has no clear shape, so it is impossible to make a reliable statement comparing the mean and the median.

GO ON TO THE NEXT PAGE

16. A railway company normally charges $35 round trip from the suburbs of a city into downtown. The company also offers a deal for commuters who use the train frequently to commute from their homes in the suburbs to their jobs in the city. Commuters can purchase a discount card for $900, after which they only have to pay $12.50 per round trip. How many round trips, t, must a commuter make in order for the discount card to be a better deal?

A) $t < 40$

B) $t > 40$

C) $t < 72$

D) $t > 72$

17. Most people save money before going on vacation. Suppose Etienne saved $800 to spend during vacation, 20 percent of which he uses to pay for gas. If he budgets 25 percent of the remaining money for food, allots $300 for the hotel, and spends the rest of the money on entertainment, what percentage of the original $800 did he spend on entertainment?

A) 14.5%

B) 17.5%

C) 22.5%

D) 28.5%

18. A microbiologist placed a bacteria sample containing approximately 2,000 microbes in a petri dish. For the first 7 days, the number of microbes in the dish tripled every 24 hours. If n represents the number of microbes after h hours, then which of the following equations is the best model for the data during the 7-day period?

A) $n = 2{,}000(3)^{\frac{h}{24}}$

B) $n = 2{,}000(3)^{24h}$

C) $n = \dfrac{h}{24} \times 2{,}000$

D) $n = 24h \times 2{,}000$

	For	Against	Undecided	Total
1L	32	16	10	58
2L	24	12	28	64
3L	17	25	13	55
Total	73	53	51	177

19. A survey is conducted regarding a proposed change in the attendance policy at a law school. The table above categorizes the results of the survey by year of the student (1L, 2L, or 3L) and whether they are for, against, or undecided about the new policy. What fraction of all 1Ls and 2Ls are against the new policy?

A) $\dfrac{14}{61}$

B) $\dfrac{24}{61}$

C) $\dfrac{28}{53}$

D) $\dfrac{28}{177}$

20. Which of the following expressions is equivalent to $(6 + 5i)^3$? (Note: $i = \sqrt{-1}$)

A) $11 + 60i$

B) $216 - 125i$

C) $-234 + 415i$

D) $-3{,}479 + 1{,}320i$

GO ON TO THE NEXT PAGE

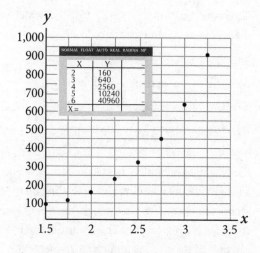

21. If an exponential function is used to model the data shown in the figure, and it is written in the form $f(x) = f(0)(1 + r)^x$, what would be the value of r?

A) 2

B) 3

C) 4

D) 5

22. The Great Pyramid of Giza, built in the 26th century BC just outside of Cairo, Egypt, had an original height of 480 feet, 8 inches, before some of the stones in which it was encased fell away. Inside the pyramid is a 53.75-foot passage, called the Dead End Shaft, which archeologists have yet to discover the purpose of. Suppose a museum is building a scale model of the pyramid for patrons to explore. Because of the museum's ceiling height, they can only make the pyramid 71 feet, 6 inches tall. About how many feet long should the museum's Dead End Shaft be?

A) 8

B) 12

C) 30

D) 96

$$\frac{-x^2 - 10x + 24}{2 - x}$$

23. Which of the following is equivalent to the expression above, given that $x \ne 2$?

A) $-x - 12$

B) $x - 12$

C) $12 - x$

D) $x + 12$

24. Ethanol is an alcohol commonly added to gasoline to reduce the use of fossil fuels. A commonly used ratio of ethanol to gasoline is 1:4. Another less common and more experimental additive is methanol, with a typical ratio of methanol to gasoline being 1:9. A fuel producer wants to see what happens to cost and fuel efficiency when a combination of ethanol and methanol are used. In order to keep the ratio of gasoline to total additive the same, what ratio of ethanol to methanol should the company use?

A) 1:1

B) 4:9

C) 9:4

D) 36:9

GO ON TO THE NEXT PAGE

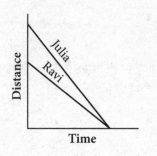

Distance

Julia

Ravi

Time

25. Julia and Ravi are meeting at a museum. The figure above represents the drives from their homes to the museum. Based on the figure, which of the following statements is true?

A) Julia drove to the museum at a faster speed than Ravi.

B) Julia and Ravi drove to the museum at about the same speed.

C) It took Ravi longer to arrive at the museum because his home is farther away.

D) It took Julia longer to arrive at the museum because her home is farther away.

26. If the graph of the function $g(x)$ passes through the point $(8, -3)$, then through which point does the graph of $-g(x - 4) - 6$ pass?

A) $(-12, -9)$

B) $(-12, -3)$

C) $(4, -3)$

D) $(12, -3)$

27. If $f(x) = x - 1$, $g(x) = x^3$, and $x \leq 0$, which of the following could not be in the range of $f(g(x))$?

A) -27

B) -3

C) -1

D) 1

28. Given the equation $y = -3(x - 5)^2 + 8$, which of the following statements is not true?

A) The y-intercept is $(0, 8)$.

B) The axis of symmetry is $x = 5$.

C) The vertex is $(5, 8)$.

D) The parabola opens downward.

29. Every weekend for 48 hours, a law firm backs up all client files by scanning and uploading them to a secure remote server. On average, the size of each client file is 2.5 gigabytes. The law firm's computer can upload the scans at a rate of 5.25 megabytes per second. What is the maximum number of client files the law firm can back up each weekend? (1 gigabyte = 1,000 megabytes)

A) 362

B) 363

C) 476

D) 477

30. Main Street and 2nd Street run parallel to each other. Both are one-way streets. Main Street runs north, and 2nd Street runs south. The city is planning to build a new road, also one-way, that runs toward the southeast and cuts through both streets at an angle. Traffic turning off of Main Street would have to make a 125° turn onto the new road. What angle would traffic turning off of 2nd Street have to make turning onto the new road?

A) 55°

B) 65°

C) 125°

D) 235°

GO ON TO THE NEXT PAGE ▷

Directions: For questions 31-38, enter your responses into the appropriate grid on your answer sheet, in accordance with the following:

1. You will receive credit only if the circles are filled in correctly, but you may write your answers in the boxes above each grid to help you fill in the circles accurately.

2. Don't mark more than one circle per column.

3. None of the questions with grid-in responses will have a negative solution.

4. Only grid in a single answer, even if there is more than one correct answer to a given question.

5. A **mixed number** must be gridded as a decimal or an improper fraction. For example, you would grid $7\frac{1}{2}$ as 7.5 or $\frac{15}{2}$.

    (Were you to grid it as [7 1 / 2], this response would be read as $\frac{71}{2}$.)

6. A **decimal** that has more digits than there are places on the grid may be either rounded or truncated, but every column in the grid must be filled in order to receive credit.

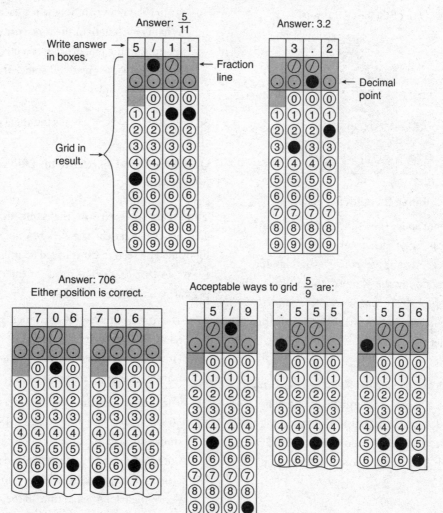

Answer: $\frac{5}{11}$

Write answer in boxes. ← Fraction line

Grid in result.

Answer: 3.2 ← Decimal point

Answer: 706
Either position is correct.

Acceptable ways to grid $\frac{5}{9}$ are:

GO ON TO THE NEXT PAGE

$$\frac{4h - (21 - 8h)}{3} = \frac{15 + 6(h - 1)}{2}$$

31. What is the value of h in the equation above?

32. A company is buying two warehouses near their production plants in two states, New York and Georgia. As is always the case in the real estate market, the geographic location plays a major role in the price of the property. Consequently, the warehouse in New York costs $30,000 less than four times the Georgia warehouse. Together, the two warehouses cost the company $445,000. How many more thousand dollars does the New York property cost than the Georgia property?

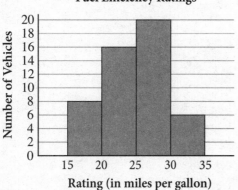

Fuel Efficiency Ratings

33. The histogram above shows the number of vehicles that a car rental agency currently has available to rent, categorized by fuel efficiency ratings. If a customer randomly selects one of the available cars, what is the probability that he will get a car that has a fuel efficiency rating of at least 25 miles per gallon? Enter your answer as a decimal number.

34. The volume of a rectangular shipping crate being loaded onto a barge for international shipment across the Panama Canal is 10,290 cubic feet. If the length to width to height ratio of the crate is 3:5:2 (in that order), what is the length of the crate in feet?

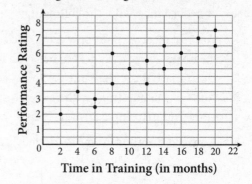

Regional Manager Job Performance

35. A company conducted a study comparing the overall job performance of its regional managers with the length of time each one spent in the company's management-training program. The scatterplot above shows the results of the study. What is the length of the time spent in training, in months, of the manager represented by the data point that is the greatest distance from the line of best fit (not shown)?

36. If $(2^{32})^{(2^{32})} = 2^{(2^x)}$, what is the value of x?

Questions 37 and 38 refer to the following information.

Three cars all arrive at the same destination at 4:00 PM. The first car traveled 144 miles mostly by highway. The second car traveled 85 miles mainly on rural two-lane roads. The third car traveled 25 miles primarily on busy city streets.

37. The first car traveled at an average speed of 64 mph. The second car started its drive at 2:18 PM. How many minutes had the first car already been traveling before the second car started its drive?

38. The third car encountered heavy traffic for the first 60% of its trip and only averaged 15 mph. Then traffic stopped due to an accident, and the car did not move for 20 minutes. After the accident was cleared, the car averaged 30 mph for the remainder of the trip. At what time in the afternoon did the third car start its trip? Use only digits for your answer. (For example, enter 1:25 PM as 125.)

ESSAY TEST

50 Minutes

You will be given a passage to read and asked to write an essay analyzing it. As you write, be sure to show that you have read the passage closely. You will be graded on how well you have understood the passage, how clear your analysis is, and how well you express your ideas.

Your essay must be written on the lines in your answer booklet. Anything you write outside the lined space in your answer booklet will not be read by the essay graders. Be sure to write or print in such a way that it will be legible to readers not familiar with your handwriting. Additionally, be sure to address the passage directly. An off-topic essay will not be graded.

As you read the passage, think about the author's use of

- evidence, such as statistics or other facts.

- logic to connect evidence to conclusions and to develop lines of reasoning.

- style, word choice, and appeals to emotion to make the argument more persuasive.

Adapted from William Faulkner's Nobel Prize Acceptance Speech, delivered in Stockholm on December 10, 1950.

1   I feel that this award was not made to me as a man, but to my work—a life's work in the agony and sweat of the human spirit, not for glory and least of all for profit, but to create out of the materials of the human spirit something which did not exist before. So this award is only mine in trust. It will not be difficult to find a dedication for the money part of it commensurate with the purpose and significance of its origin. But I would like to do the same with the acclaim too, by using this moment as a pinnacle from which I might be listened to by the young men and women already dedicated to the same anguish and travail, among whom is already that one who will some day stand where I am standing.

2   Our tragedy today is a general and universal physical fear so long sustained by now that we can even bear it. There are no longer problems of the spirit. There is only the question: When will I be blown up? Because of this, the young man or woman writing today has forgotten the problems of the human heart in conflict with itself which alone can make good writing because only that is worth writing about, worth the agony and the sweat.

3   He must learn them again. He must teach himself that the basest of all things is to be afraid: and, teaching himself that, forget it forever, leaving no room in his workshop for anything but the old verities and truths of the heart, the universal truths lacking which any story is ephemeral and doomed—love and honor and pity and pride and compassion and sacrifice. Until he does so, he labors under a curse. He writes not of love but of … defeats in which nobody loses anything of value, of victories without hope, and, worst of all, without pity or compassion. His griefs grieve on no universal bones, leaving no scars …

4   Until he learns these things, he will write as though he stood among and watched the end of man. I decline to accept the end of man. It is easy enough to say that man is immortal because he will endure: that when the last ding-dong of doom has clanged and faded from the last worthless rock hanging tideless in the last red and dying evening, that even then there will still be one more sound: that of his puny inexhaustible voice, still talking. I refuse to accept this. I believe that man will not merely endure: he will prevail. He is immortal, not because he

GO ON TO THE NEXT PAGE ⇨

alone among creatures has an inexhaustible voice, but because he has a soul, a spirit capable of compassion and sacrifice and endurance. The poet's, the writer's, duty is to write about these things. It is his privilege to help man endure by lifting his heart, by reminding him of the courage and honor and hope and pride and compassion and pity and sacrifice which have been the glory of his past. The poet's voice need not merely be the record of man, it can be one of the props, the pillars to help him endure and prevail.

Write an essay that analyzes the author's approach in persuading his readers that authors must write from the heart to ensure that mankind prevails. Focus on specific features such as the ones listed in the box above the passage and explain how these features strengthen the author's argument. Your essay should discuss the most important rhetorical features of the passage.

Your essay should not focus on your own opinion of the author's conclusion, but rather on how the author persuades his readers.

ANSWER KEY
READING TEST

1. C	14. A	27. A	40. D
2. A	15. D	28. C	41. C
3. D	16. B	29. D	42. A
4. B	17. C	30. B	43. A
5. B	18. B	31. C	44. C
6. A	19. B	32. A	45. A
7. D	20. D	33. A	46. B
8. D	21. D	34. A	47. B
9. C	22. D	35. B	48. B
10. C	23. A	36. D	49. D
11. C	24. C	37. C	50. C
12. A	25. B	38. C	51. A
13. D	26. A	39. B	52. D

WRITING AND LANGUAGE TEST

1. B	12. D	23. D	34. A
2. D	13. B	24. B	35. C
3. C	14. C	25. A	36. D
4. C	15. C	26. A	37. C
5. B	16. A	27. C	38. B
6. B	17. B	28. D	39. B
7. B	18. D	29. C	40. D
8. B	19. D	30. B	41. C
9. A	20. B	31. C	42. D
10. C	21. D	32. D	43. A
11. A	22. C	33. A	44. B

MATH—NO CALCULATOR TEST

1. B	6. C	11. D	16. 1
2. C	7. B	12. C	17. 12
3. A	8. C	13. D	18. 12
4. D	9. B	14. D	19. 14
5. B	10. A	15. D	20. 800

MATH—CALCULATOR TEST

1. B	11. D	21. B	31. 11.5 or **23/2** or **69/6**
2. D	12. B	22. A	32. 255
3. B	13. C	23. D	33. .52
4. C	14. B	24. C	34. 21
5. C	15. A	25. A	35. 8
6. C	16. B	26. D	36. 37
7. B	17. C	27. D	37. 33
8. C	18. A	28. A	38. 220
9. D	19. A	29. A	
10. A	20. C	30. A	

ANSWERS AND EXPLANATIONS

READING TEST

Walden

Suggested Passage Map notes:

¶1: sleep more do better

¶2: man is responsible for being present in life

¶3: HDT wanted to live fully, used nature to achieve it

¶4: let go of small things

¶5: keep life simple

1. C   Difficulty: Medium

Category: Detail

Getting to the Answer: Reread the entire paragraph to assess the intention of the sentence in question, and determine which answer choice best shows the author's reason for including this sentence. The author's previous statements in the paragraph directly relate to the idea that the conscious endeavors described are the very activities that will reawaken people; therefore, (C) is correct.

2. A   Difficulty: Hard

Category: Vocab-in-Context

Getting to the Answer: Read the complete sentence for context clues, and determine which answer choice's definition best serves the idea presented. The sentence suggests the author wants to live actively and "suck out all the marrow of life" (line 39) rather than live in a resigned, accepting manner; thus, (A) is correct because it best describes how the author does not wish to live.

3. D   Difficulty: Medium

Category: Inference

Getting to the Answer: Read the first paragraph expressly for the purpose of determining the author's

views. The author suggests that most people are only awake enough for physical labor, some for intellectual discussions, and very few for a higher calling. This implies that he feels most people are not working toward their fullest potential, so (D) is correct.

4. B   Difficulty: Hard

Category: Command of Evidence

Getting to the Answer: Choose the quote from the passage that best supports the correct answer of the previous question. Choice (B) is the correct answer not just because it shows the author's belief that most people are not truly awake, but also because it shows that the author thinks most people spend their lives pursuing goals beneath their human potential.

5. B   Difficulty: Easy

Category: Global

Getting to the Answer: Consider the entire passage to determine the author's central claim about society. Then choose the answer choice that correctly reflects this. Throughout the passage, the author frequently mentions that our society focuses on mundane labor and details and that we shun a life of conscious endeavors; therefore, (B) is the correct answer.

6. A   Difficulty: Medium

Category: Inference

Getting to the Answer: Because the author's views on religion are not explicitly stated, you must make inferences by examining details in the entire passage. Throughout the third paragraph, the author explains that he is going to the woods to determine the sublime or mean qualities of nature and God, and he states that far too many people hastily agree to preconceived ideas on these topics. Choice (A) is correct.

7. D   **Difficulty:** Easy

Category: Command of Evidence

Getting to the Answer: Choose the quote from the passage that best supports the correct answer in the previous question. Choice (D) is the correct answer, because it offers the most direct evidence that the author believes a person should critically examine his or her religious beliefs before dedicating a life to them.

8. D   **Difficulty:** Medium

Category: Vocab-in-Context

Getting to the Answer: Read the sentence for context clues, and determine which answer choice comes closest to reflecting the author's intent. The sentence and paragraph as a whole describe the author's indifference to the harshness of life for the sake of accomplishing a goal; therefore, (D), "austere," is correct.

9. C   **Difficulty:** Medium

Category: Rhetoric

Getting to the Answer: Carefully read the paragraph and ask yourself how these particular words help Thoreau convey his message. The author touches on many broad, negative aspects of human nature and existence in the paragraph, and the use of "meanly" and "wretchedness" strengthen the negative tone of the message. Choice (C) is correct.

10. C   **Difficulty:** Medium

Category: Inference

Getting to the Answer: Think about the author's intention in this passage when he discusses his views on how life should be lived. Identify the types of actions he promotes and review the answer choices to find the one that is most similar. The author urges readers to "simplify," and as an example he urges them to eat one meal a day instead of three and to reduce the number of dishes from 100 to 5. You can infer from this that Thoreau would advocate paring

down one's clothing to the bare essentials. Choice (C) is correct.

"The Opening of the Library"

Suggested Passage Map notes:

¶1: new library
¶2: library still segregated
¶3: African Am excluded from using library
¶4: WEB wants African Am to be allowed to use it: education will keep them off the streets
¶5-6: public money means it should be used by all
¶7: chairman says integration will kill library
¶8: segregation should be in the past
¶9-10: African Am in crowd spoke, thanked the trustees for listening
¶11-12: trustees gave response: said no

11. C   **Difficulty:** Medium

Category: Rhetoric

Getting to the Answer: Consider which answer choice describes an idea that is supported throughout the text. The passage begins with DuBois's arguments in favor of expanding access to public libraries and ends with the trustees' response to his arguments, highlighting the difference between the two positions. Therefore, (C) is correct.

12. A   **Difficulty:** Medium

Category: Command of Evidence

Getting to the Answer: The correct answer will support your response to the previous question. Choice (A) indicates that DuBois would present an argument "in behalf" (line 14) of others while asking the trustees to explain their side.

13. D   **Difficulty:** Medium

Category: Vocab-in-Context

Getting to the Answer: Make sure that your answer choice does not alter the meaning of the sentence in the passage. The paragraph in which the word appears indicates that speaking on behalf of so many others was not a responsibility DuBois took lightly, and the decision about who would speak had been previously decided. Choice (D) is correct.

14. A   Difficulty: Medium

Category: Inference

Getting to the Answer: Eliminate answer choices that are not suggested in the passage. Choice (A) is correct. The president of the Trustee Board did not make assurances, but he detailed a course of action that would potentially result in a new library for African Americans if the city council approved funding.

15. D   Difficulty: Hard

Category: Command of Evidence

Getting to the Answer: Review your answer to the previous question. Read each choice and figure out which one provides specific support for that answer. Choice (D) indicates the trustees' support for separate library facilities with approved funding. It best supports the idea that segregated library facilities would at least be considered.

16. B   Difficulty: Medium

Category: Vocab-in-Context

Getting to the Answer: Look for context clues in the sentence to help you determine the correct meaning. Choice (B) reflects the meaning of the phrase in the sentence; DuBois was arguing for the necessity of literacy and a strong comprehension of the books that a library offers.

17. C   Difficulty: Hard

Category: Rhetoric

Getting to the Answer: Pay close attention to the reasons DuBois presents that support his argument for expanding access to public libraries. Avoid choices that sound plausible but take the ideas too far.

Choice (C) is correct. DuBois specifically argues that the reason whites need public libraries "applies with redoubled force" (line 29) to poor African Americans.

18. B   Difficulty: Medium

Category: Rhetoric

Getting to the Answer: Look for the argument in the passage that this particular example supports. Choice (B) is correct. Note that DuBois's mention of the "catholic spirit" (line 49) is used to remind the trustees that we create differences between us, and what we have in common should inspire us to ensure that everyone has equal opportunity to improve themselves.

19. B   Difficulty: Medium

Category: Inference

Getting to the Answer: Read the cited lines, and then read them in the context of the paragraphs that come before and after. Think about how the chairman's words are affecting the author at this point in the passage. The chairman has just suggested that integrating the library "would be fatal to its usefulness" (lines 58-59), implying that African Americans and whites would be unable to use the library alongside each other without violence or chaos. Because DuBois's aim is to integrate the library, he is frustrated by the chairman's words, which echo the assumptions of past centuries. Choice (B) is correct.

20. D   Difficulty: Medium

Category: Rhetoric

Getting to the Answer: Keep in mind that the question is asking how this portion of the passage functions in relation to the passage as a whole. DuBois argued in favor of expanding access to public libraries for all citizens. The Trustee Board's president then responded to DuBois's persuasive argument. Therefore, (D) is correct.

Diderot Passage

Suggested Passage Map notes:

¶1: DD created volumes of documented tech advances during his time

¶2: DD found people to contribute, volumes were controversial

¶3: encyclopedie was progressive

¶4: science merged with liberal arts

¶5: made mundane crafts scholarly

¶6: angered people who protected trade secrets

¶7: upper society was angry

¶8: opposition too late, encyclo eventually became historical book

21. D   Difficulty: Medium

Category: Global

Getting to the Answer: Keep in mind that the correct answer will reflect the central purpose and opinion of the author as expressed in the passage. The passage explores the impact and influence of Diderot's *Encyclopédie*. The author states that the value of the work is not in its merit as a lasting technical reference or dictionary, but as a repository of historical knowledge and as an early attempt to extend the knowledge of the day to the masses. Choice (D) is correct.

22. D   Difficulty: Medium

Category: Rhetoric

Getting to the Answer: Choose the answer that reflects that author's overall point of view, or perspective, suggested by the passage. The passage examines the individual achievements of Diderot, specifically his efforts to extend the access to knowledge to a greater segment of European society. Choice (D) is correct, because it speaks to the author's obvious respect for Diderot as an innovator.

23. A   Difficulty: Medium

Category: Command of Evidence

Getting to the Answer: Reread each quote in the context of the passage. This will help you decide the correct answer. The correct answer to the previous question asserts that the author admires the individual accomplishments of innovators such as Diderot. Choice (A) is correct, because it calls attention to Diderot's contributions as revolutionizing encyclopedic thought.

24. C   Difficulty: Medium

Category: Detail

Getting to the Answer: Scan the passage for statements about Diderot's intentions and goals. Be sure not to confuse the results of his efforts with his goals. The passage states that Diderot's goal "was to create an intellectual work instructionally useful to all" (lines 16-17). While the work did create political controversy and also became part of the historical record, neither of these was his main goal. Choice (C) is correct.

25. B   Difficulty: Easy

Category: Vocab-in-Context

Getting to the Answer: Decide which answer choice could be substituted for the word without changing the meaning of the sentence. The paragraph states that Diderot's work was banned by the French government; therefore, the work's circulation, once published, was done secretly. Choice (B) is correct.

26. A   Difficulty: Medium

Category: Rhetoric

Getting to the Answer: The correct answer will reflect the meaning and intention behind the excerpted phrase as well as the surrounding text. The term "beacon" means a light that can be seen far away, usually with the purpose of guiding or attracting people to it. The phrase "free thought" in this context refers to the right of people to pursue knowledge. The surrounding text describes Diderot's work as having political purpose in expanding access to knowledge beyond the established elite to the masses. Therefore, (A) is correct.

27. A   **Difficulty:** Medium

Category: Inference

Getting to the Answer: Eliminate answer choices that don't represent the author's ideas. The passage refers repeatedly to the impact of Diderot's work in making information accessible to more people. The author states that political, economic, and intellectual elites opposed the publication of his encyclopedia because it lessened their control on trades and other valuable information. Choice (A) is correct.

28. C   **Difficulty:** Medium

Category: Command of Evidence

Getting to the Answer: Avoid answers that provide evidence for incorrect answers to the previous question. The correct answer to the previous question asserts that information was limited to a specific demographic, or segment of the population, at that time. Choice (C) is correct because it states clearly that the trade guilds, a select demographic, controlled certain knowledge and opposed the expansion of access to such knowledge.

29. D   **Difficulty:** Medium

Category: Vocab-in-Context

Getting to the Answer: Remember that you're looking for the answer that will make the most sense when substituted for the original word. The sentence discusses the way in which Diderot changed the perception and exploration of knowledge, making (D) correct. The word "erudition" refers to learning acquired by reading and study.

30. B   **Difficulty:** Medium

Category: Connections

Getting to the Answer: Remember that the correct answer must be based on information in the passage, not on speculation. Based on the last sentence of the passage and the information in paragraph 4, (B) is correct. It's the only answer choice directly supported by information in the passage.

31. C   **Difficulty:** Medium

Category: Synthesis

Getting to the Answer: Eliminate answer choices that cannot be inferred from the information in the passage and graphic. Choice (C) is the correct answer; Uranus was discovered after Diderot's *Encyclopédie* was published. Other answer choices are either impossible, as in the case of D, or cannot be inferred from the information provided.

Paired Passages—Acidity

Suggested Passage Map notes:

Passage 1
¶1: acid rain is a problem
¶2: explain pH scale
¶3: slightly acidic rain ok
¶4: man made problems make bad acid rain

Passage 2
¶1: human blood needs controlled pH
¶2: pH controlled in body
¶3: kidneys aid in maintaining pH
¶4: uncontrolled pH causes problems - ex: diabetes

32. A   **Difficulty:** Medium

Category: Inference

Getting to the Answer: Consider what the author of Passage 1 is saying in the first paragraph about the causes and consequences of acid rain. Avoid answers like C that go too far and are not directly supported by the evidence in the passage. The author clearly states that acid rain, largely caused by the burning of fossil fuels, is bad for the environment. It is reasonable to conclude that if the burning of fossil fuels is not reduced, the environment will be damaged. Therefore, (A) is correct.

33. A   **Difficulty:** Medium

Category: Command of Evidence

Getting to the Answer: Look back at your answer to the previous question. Think about the information you found in the passage that helped you choose this answer. The last sentence in the first paragraph provides the strongest evidence for the idea that burning fossil fuels will seriously damage the environment. Therefore, (A) is correct.

34. A   Difficulty: Easy

Category: Detail

Getting to the Answer: Find where Passage 1 discusses the pH of rain water. Determine whether lower or higher pH levels indicate that rain water is dangerously acidic. The passage states that the pH of pure rain water can be as low as 5.5, and a pH level of 3 can cause soil and water to become too acidic. A pH level of 2.25 is less than 3, meaning it is even more dangerously acidic; therefore, the correct answer is (A).

35. B   Difficulty: Easy

Category: Vocab-in-Context

Getting to the Answer: Remember that some answer choices might be synonyms for "tolerate" but do not reflect the meaning of the word in this context. In this context, "tolerate" most nearly means "endure." Choice (B) is the correct answer.

36. D   Difficulty: Hard

Category: Inference

Getting to the Answer: Reread the text, looking for evidence to support each of the answer choices. The first paragraph of Passage 2 states: "Many processes in the body produce acid wastes" (lines 41-42), from which you can infer that it's normal to have acid wastes in the blood. Choice (D), therefore, is the correct answer.

37. C   Difficulty: Medium

Category: Command of Evidence

Getting to the Answer: Look for evidence that supports the inference you made in the previous ques-

tion. In lines 60-63, the author explains how normal amounts of acid are neutralized in the blood. Choice (C) is correct.

38. C   Difficulty: Medium

Category: Vocab-in-Context

Getting to the Answer: Eliminate any answer choices that don't make sense in the context of the sentence. In this context, "exhaust" means "to use up" or "deplete." Therefore, (C) is the correct answer.

39. B   Difficulty: Hard

Category: Inference

Getting to the Answer: Read paragraph 2 of Passage 2 again, and determine the role of excess bicarbonate ions in the blood. Each answer choice is mentioned in Passage 1. Determine how each acts in the environment. Choice (B) is the correct answer. In Passage 2, the author explains that excess bicarbonate ions raise the pH of the blood, neutralizing acid wastes. In paragraph 3 of Passage 1, the author explains that alkaline materials in the environment, such as ashes from a forest fire, neutralize acid in the water supply.

40. D   Difficulty: Medium

Category: Connections

Getting to the Answer: You are looking for a cause-and-effect relationship to answer this question. Skim Passage 2, looking for an explanation of what causes the body to break down fats for energy. In paragraph 4 of Passage 2, the author explains that low insulin will cause the body to break down fats for energy. Therefore, (D) is the correct answer.

41. C   Difficulty: Medium

Category: Synthesis

Getting to the Answer: Consider the main topic and purpose of each passage. Decide what the passages have in common. Each passage describes a different system, the environment and the human body respectively, and how each system deals with acid. In each passage, the author describes how acid can be introduced into the system and neutralized in small amounts but also describes the ways in which large amounts of acid can damage or overwhelm each system, making (C) the correct answer.

42. A   Difficulty: Easy

Category: Synthesis

Getting to the Answer: The question is asking you about both passages. Eliminate answers that only address the information found in one of the passages. Although Passage 1 is about the environment and Passage 2 is about the human body, both passages are about delicate systems that need balance to remain healthy, so (A) is correct.

Hydrogen Passage

Suggested Passage Map notes:

¶1: hydrogen next renewable resource

¶2: looking for safe, low cost hydrogen fuel

¶3: challenges to hydrogen fuel production

¶4: new method for harvesting hydrogen

¶5: using solar power to harvest hydrogen, reduces cost of harvesting

¶6: more efficient way to harvest

¶7: more research to be done

43. A   Difficulty: Medium

Category: Inference

Getting to the Answer: Avoid answers like B, which are related to details presented but take the ideas too far. Think about the arguments presented by the author throughout the passage. In paragraph 3, the author lists drawbacks to hydrogen fuel as a replacement for gasoline. In this paragraph, the author notes that engines that run on hydrogen are more expensive than those that use gasoline. Choice (A) is the correct answer.

44. C   Difficulty: Medium

Category: Command of Evidence

Getting to the Answer: Read the previous question again. Look at each quote from the passage and decide which provides the strongest evidence. Choice (C) is the correct answer, as it provides the strongest evidence that the author is concerned with the cost to consumers of using hydrogen fuel.

45. A   Difficulty: Medium

Category: Detail

Getting to the Answer: Eliminate answer choices that contain details that are not stated directly in the text. In paragraph 1, the author states that hydrogen is found primarily with oxygen in water; therefore, (A) is correct.

46. B   Difficulty: Easy

Category: Vocab-in-Context

Getting to the Answer: Read the sentence again and replace "diligently" with each of the answer choices. Look for the answer that does not change the meaning of the sentence. When you consider the overall meaning of the sentence, (B) is the best choice. In this context, "persistently" means nearly the same thing as "diligently."

47. B   Difficulty: Medium

Category: Inference

Getting to the Answer: Pay attention to the parts of the passage that refer to petroleum-based fuels and the reasons scientists are seeking alternatives. Though the author does not explicitly state that petroleum-based fuels are bad for the environment, he or she does give the fact that hydrogen produces no pollution as a reason to look toward hydrogen and away from petroleum products. You can infer, then, that (B) is the correct answer.

48. B   Difficulty: Medium

Category: Command of Evidence

Getting to the Answer: Read the previous question again. Look at each quote from the passage and decide which most clearly supports the idea stated in the correct answer for that question. In paragraph 2, the author lists potential benefits for using hydrogen energy over petroleum-based energy sources. No pollution is one of the potential benefits, which leads to the conclusion that petroleum products are bad for the environment. Choice (B) is therefore the correct answer.

49. D   Difficulty: Medium

Category: Rhetoric

Getting to the Answer: Think about the purpose that paragraph 2 serves in creating the author's overall argument. In paragraph 2, the author asserts that decreasing dependence on other petroleum-producing countries is a potential benefit to the development of hydrogen as a fuel. The inclusion of this point helps clarify why hydrogen fuel is important. Choice (D) is correct.

50. C   Difficulty: Medium

Category: Vocab-in-Context

Getting to the Answer: Keep in mind that although all answer choices might be synonyms of "derived," only one fits the context of the sentence in which the word appears. In this context, "derived" most nearly means (C), "obtained."

51. A   Difficulty: Medium

Category: Inference

Getting to the Answer: Locate the parts of the passage that discuss advances in extracting hydrogen molecules from water. Then, find the answer choice that makes the most sense in the context of the passage. In lines 65-70, the author discusses research initiatives that focus on hydrogen extraction. You can infer from the fact that there are "many ongoing research initiatives" (lines 65-66) that much more research will be needed before hydrogen extraction is perfected. Choice (A) is correct.

52. D   Difficulty: Medium

Category: Synthesis

Getting to the Answer: Avoid answer choices that are supported only by the information in one of the sources. Look for the answer that is supported by both the passage and the graphic. The data presented in the graphic supports the author's argument that hydrogen fuel produces less greenhouse gas than gasoline. Choice (D) is correct.

WRITING AND LANGUAGE TEST

Sorting Recyclables for Best Re-Use

1. B   Difficulty: Easy

Category: Usage

Getting to the Answer: Read the sentence and check to see whether the verb agrees with the subject. The verb "are" is in a plural form, but the subject is singular. Choice (B) is correct because it is the singular form of the verb "to be."

2. D   Difficulty: Medium

Category: Effective Language Use

Getting to the Answer: Read the sentences surrounding the word to better understand the context in which the word appears. Then substitute each answer choice into the sentence to see which fits into the context best. The passage states that the plastics are sorted by types. Only (D) has the correct connotation and fits within the context of the sentence.

3. C   Difficulty: Hard

Category: Development

Getting to the Answer: Read the entire paragraph and write down the central idea. Then review the answer choices and look for a close match with your prediction. The paragraph discusses the two methods used to sort plastics. Choice (C) is closest to this summation.

4. C   Difficulty: Easy

Category: Effective Language Use

Getting to the Answer: Watch out for choices like A and B, which use extra words that do not add meaning to the sentence. It is better to be as direct and simple as possible. The word "thoroughly" indicates that the people doing the job are paying attention to every detail. Additional words such as "very" or "completely" do not add more meaning to this sentence. Choice (C) is the most concise and effective way of stating the information.

5. B   Difficulty: Medium

Category: Organization

Getting to the Answer: Look for the relationship between this sentence and the previous one. This will help you choose the appropriate transition word. Read the sentence using the word you chose to ensure that it makes sense. Choice (B) shows the relationship between the two sentences by giving an example of how the products are manufactured.

6. B   Difficulty: Medium

Category: Punctuation

Getting to the Answer: Study the words in a series to see where a comma might need to be placed or eliminated. Only one answer choice will include the correct punctuation. Choice (B) is correct.

7. B   Difficulty: Hard

Category: Quantitative

Getting to the Answer: The graphic gives specific information about how much of each type of plastic was recovered. Study the graphic in order to select the correct answer choice. Choice (B) accurately reflects the information in the graphic.

8. B   Difficulty: Medium

Category: Effective Language Use

Getting to the Answer: Watch out for choices that may include incorrect transition words. Choice (B) uses the present participle "depending" to join the sentences concisely and correctly.

9. A   Difficulty: Easy

Category: Effective Language Use

Getting to the Answer: Check each answer choice for its connotations, and be sure to pick one that fits with the context of the sentence. Substitute each answer choice for the word to see which works best. Notice that the sentence sets up a contrast between plastics numbered 1 through 6 and plastics with the number 7, which may consist of one of many other plastics or a blend of plastics. Choice (A) is correct because the word "specific" indicates that each of the numbers 1 through 6 is used for only one type of plastic.

10. C   Difficulty: Medium

Category: Sentence Formation

Getting to the Answer: Two complete thoughts should be two separate sentences. Be careful of inappropriate transition words. Choice (C) divides the two thoughts into two complete sentences by adding a period and capitalizing the first word of the second sentence.

11. A   Difficulty: Medium

Category: Development

Getting to the Answer: Read the entire paragraph and then read each of the choices. Decide which one sums up the paragraph best by stating the overall central idea. Choice (A) is the correct answer. It concludes the paragraph by stating the overall central idea of the paragraph and passage.

Interpreter at America's Immigrant Gateway

12. D   **Difficulty:** Hard

Category: Development

Getting to the Answer: Read the entire first paragraph. The correct answer should offer descriptive details and introduce David Kaufman as a character. The first paragraph discusses David Kaufman specifically and his relationship to his job. While A, B, and C are informative, they do not add beauty or descriptive interest to the paragraph. Only (D) sparks the reader's interest with descriptive language and relates directly to the following sentences.

13. B   **Difficulty:** Medium

Category: Punctuation

Getting to the Answer: Determine whether the information is all one thought or whether the sentence suggests that some part of it is an aside. The sentence is mainly discussing Kaufman, but it also introduces the idea of America's history almost as an afterthought. By setting this aside within dashes, the sentence will draw attention to its parenthetical relationship to the rest of the sentence. Choice (B) is correct.

14. C   **Difficulty:** Easy

Category: Usage

Getting to the Answer: Determine whether the underlined word is being used as a place or a possessive. Then consider which answer choice would be most appropriate here. In this sentence, "there" is describing "baggage" belonging to these new Americans. It should therefore be changed to the correct possessive form "their," making (C) correct.

15. C   **Difficulty:** Medium

Category: Effective Language Use

Getting to the Answer: Eliminate unnecessary words. Then reorder the nouns and verbs to achieve the most concise language possible. Choice (C) contains no unnecessary words. It concisely explains the actions taken by the two different groups of people and is the correct answer.

16. A   **Difficulty:** Medium

Category: Organization

Getting to the Answer: Consider the function of this sentence. At what point in the paragraph should this function be employed? The sentence is setting a scene, so it should be placed where it is now, at the beginning of the paragraph. To place it later would cause confusion in the following sentences, as the reader does not have all the information he or she needs. Choice (A), leaving it in its current position, is the correct answer.

17. B   **Difficulty:** Medium

Category: Development

Getting to the Answer: The correct answer should introduce an idea that is supported by the sentences that follow. Consider whether the current sentence should be revised to do this. The rest of the paragraph discusses the relationship between immigrant communities and language ability, as well as information about Kaufman's position. Therefore, the introductory sentence to this paragraph should tie together these thoughts. Choice (B) is the correct answer, as it ties Kaufman to his background in an immigrant community.

18. D   **Difficulty:** Easy

Category: Punctuation

Getting to the Answer: Determine whether the information enclosed in commas is separate or should be integrated into the rest of the sentence. The subject of the sentence is a compound noun: "his heritage and surrounding community." Therefore, the nouns making up this compound noun should not be separated by commas. Choice (D) punctuates this sentence correctly.

19. D   Difficulty: Hard

Category: Effective Language Use

Getting to the Answer: Consider the tone of this sentence as well as its meaning. Then review the answer choices to determine which one best matches both the tone and the meaning. The sentence suggests that Kaufman is trying to make his language abilities more refined and precise in order to help the immigrants. While C, "tricks," is tempting, it does not match the more formal tone of the passage. Choice (D), "nuances," conveys the fact that Kaufman is trying to understand the subtleties of language; this answer maintains the passage's formal tone.

20. B   Difficulty: Medium

Category: Development

Getting to the Answer: Reread the rest of the paragraph to determine which answer choice would most effectively add specific, relevant detail to this section of the passage. The paragraph notes that Kaufman helps "at every checkpoint," then mentions the variety of facilities Ellis Island possesses. Choice (B) adds detail about the variety of ways Kaufman helps at Ellis Island and is therefore the correct answer.

21. D   Difficulty: Medium

Category: Effective Language Use

Getting to the Answer: Consider whether the sentence's intended meaning can be conveyed in fewer words. All that is really needed in this sentence is "to help." The reader will still understand what is happening. The other options are wordy and awkward. Choice (D) is the correct answer.

22. C   Difficulty: Medium

Category: Effective Language Use

Getting to the Answer: Before looking at the answer choices, identify a word on your own that will convey the correct meaning for the context. The context of the sentence makes clear that the correct

word is something that is "rendered . . . worthwhile." In other words, it is a challenging situation that will be made worthwhile by living in America. While both (C) and D are negative words, (C), "difficulties," specifically connotes something hard or troubling, so it is the correct answer.

Software Sales: A Gratifying Career

23. D   Difficulty: Medium

Category: Punctuation

Getting to the Answer: Determine the relationship between the two different parts of the sentence. Then choose the punctuation that fits best. In this sentence, two independent clauses are joined by the coordinating conjunction "so." When two independent clauses are joined in this manner, a comma is needed before the conjunction. Only (D) combines the two independent clauses correctly.

24. B   Difficulty: Easy

Category: Usage

Getting to the Answer: Substitute the phrases for their contractions, such as "It is," for "It's" to determine the correct usage. "They're" and "Their" are inappropriate because when the subject is not clear (such as "It is raining"), it is grammatically correct to use "it" instead of "they." Choice (B) is correct.

25. A   Difficulty: Medium

Category: Punctuation

Getting to the Answer: Commas should be used sparingly to help the reader understand the passage. Only one comma is needed to successfully combine two independent clauses with a conjunction. Choice (A) is the correct answer.

26. A   Difficulty: Hard

Category: Usage

Getting to the Answer: Read the entire paragraph

to establish the verb tense. Identify the key verbs in the paragraph and their tenses. Both "turned" and "returned" are past tense, making (A) the correct choice.

27. C   Difficulty: Medium

Category: Development

Getting to the Answer: Determine the focus of the paragraph by identifying its topic and purpose. Then read the answer choices, looking for the choice that is least relevant. The paragraph has an informational purpose and is about the unusual route Morales took to a career in software sales. The opinion that "New Hampshire also has many fine backpacking trails" is extraneous to this topic and purpose. Choice (C) is correct.

28. D   Difficulty: Medium

Category: Sentence Formation

Getting to the Answer: Identify whether the underlined portion contains sentences or fragments, or a combination of both. Then determine the best way to join them. The underlined portion contains a sentence and a fragment. Only (D) correctly rewords the fragment to make it an independent clause and then uses a conjunction to join the two parts of the sentence.

29. C   Difficulty: Medium

Category: Development

Getting to the Answer: Read the entire paragraph and summarize the supporting details to help you determine the appropriate topic sentence. The supporting details of the paragraph all relate to Morales's ability to come up with a creative solution to a company's problem. Choice (C) is the correct topic sentence of the paragraph.

30. B   Difficulty: Medium

Category: Effective Language Use

Getting to the Answer: Notice the prefixes used in the answer choices and think about what they mean. Then choose the word that best fits into the context of the sentence. The prefix "re-" means "back," as in "return" or "replace." "Retaining" means to keep or hold back. This fits into the context of the sentence, so (B) is correct.

31. C   Difficulty: Medium

Category: Effective Language Use

Getting to the Answer: Read the sentence to determine which word provides the correct meaning in context. "Vacillate" means to be indecisive, "convert" means to change into a different form, and "fluctuate" means to change continually. Choice (C), "transition," means to move from one thing to another. Morales's goal is to move from one field to another, so (C) is the correct answer.

32. D   Difficulty: Medium

Category: Development

Getting to the Answer: Identify the topic sentence in the paragraph. Then review the answer choices to find the one that best supports it. The topic sentence of the paragraph is about "big data." Morales's use of "big data" to gather information regarding health care supports the topic sentence. The other choices do not involve capturing data from outside sources. Choice (D) is correct.

33. A   Difficulty: Medium

Category: Punctuation

Getting to the Answer: When a sentence contains a series of actions, make sure the elements are parallel and punctuated correctly. Then, determine whether you should eliminate or insert any commas. Choice (A) is correct, because there are three identifiable actions in the series: "quicken," "improve," and "save."

The Art of Collecting

34. A   Difficulty: Medium

Category: Effective Language Use

Getting to the Answer: Read for context clues and determine which answer offers the most appropriate word choice. The sentence states that Etta "passed away" before her art was given to the BMA. Because this was a gift after death, "bequeathed" is the most appropriate word choice in this sentence. Choice (A) is correct.

35. C   Difficulty: Hard

Category: Development

Getting to the Answer: After reading the paragraph, reread each sentence to determine which one summarizes the overall message of the paragraph. Aside from (C), all other sentences offer details and ideas that are not supported by the rest of the paragraph. Only (C) encapsulates the central idea that the Cones contributed their art to the BMA.

36. D   Difficulty: Medium

Category: Sentence Formation

Getting to the Answer: Reread the sentence to figure out what is meant. Then choose the coordinating conjunction that creates the most logical and grammatically correct sentence. Choice (D) is correct. Because the second independent clause discusses what the sisters did despite the statement in the first independent clause, the coordinating conjunction "but" is most appropriate here.

37. C   Difficulty: Easy

Category: Usage

Getting to the Answer: Read for context clues and determine which answer choice is most logical and grammatically correct. The possessive determiner "their" is grammatically correct and correctly explains the sisters' ownership of the selections, so (C) is the correct answer.

38. B   Difficulty: Medium

Category: Usage

Getting to the Answer: Read the surrounding sentences for context clues to determine which pronoun and verb combination creates the clearest and most effective sentence. The pronoun must be "they," as it refers to both Etta and Claribel. The rest of the paragraph is written in the past tense, making "took" the correct verb. Choice (B) is correct.

39. B   Difficulty: Medium

Category: Effective Language Use

Getting to the Answer: Read the sentence for context clues, and determine which answer offers the most appropriate word choice. The sentence describes what the art collected by the Cones showed, or "depicted." The other answer choices are less precise, making (B) the correct answer.

40. D   Difficulty: Hard

Category: Development

Getting to the Answer: Read the entire paragraph and determine the central idea. Then read the answer choices, looking for the choice that distracts from the paragraph's focus. The central idea of the paragraph is that the Cone collection documented the changes in post–World War I Europe. The statement "Today, there are more experimental forms of art than there were after World War I" may be accurate, but it does not relate to the central idea. Choice (D) is the correct answer.

41. C   Difficulty: Medium

Category: Punctuation

Getting to the Answer: Reread the sentence to determine which set of punctuation marks creates a grammatically correct sentence. Introductory words such as "additionally" are followed by a comma when they begin a sentence. The word "Paris" is the beginning of a list and also should be followed by a comma. No other punctuation is required in this portion of the sentence, so (C) is correct.

42. D **Difficulty:** Medium

Category: Usage

Getting to the Answer: Reread the sentence for context clues to determine which answer choice provides the correct meaning. The current underlined word, "though," means "despite," creating an illogical contrast between the two parts of the sentence. The definitions for B, "therefore" (for that reason), and C, "thorough" (completed with exacting detail), likewise do not create logical sentences. The definition of "through" best expresses the idea that the sisters experienced freedom "by means of" their lifestyle. Choice (D) is the correct answer.

43. A **Difficulty:** Hard

Category: Development

Getting to the Answer: Determine the central idea of the paragraph, and decide which additional facts noted in the answer choices would have the greatest benefit to the reader. Because the paragraph is about how the Cones challenged traditional views of women, and because the author uses several undefined but important terms, (A) is the correct answer.

44. B **Difficulty:** Medium

Category: Punctuation

Getting to the Answer: Review the sentence to assess which answer choice offers the correct use of plural punctuation to convey the proper sense of possession. The possessive plural of "Cones" refers to both sisters owning something, and requires an apostrophe after the "s" with no additional letters or punctuation. Choice (B) is correct.

MATH—NO CALCULATOR TEST

1. B **Difficulty:** Easy

Category: Heart of Algebra / Linear Equations

Getting to the Answer: Look at the structure of the equation. It is written in the form $y = mx + b$. The question is asking about 20.942, which is m in the equation, and therefore represents a rate of change. The variable x represents number of months. The value of m is positive, so it represents the estimated monthly increase in the number of the plants after the natural disaster occurred, (B).

2. C **Difficulty:** Easy

Category: Passport to Advanced Math / Quadratics

Getting to the Answer: The expression is a difference of two squares, so write each term as a quantity squared and then use the difference of squares rule $a^2 - b^2 = (a + b)(a - b)$.

$$25x^2 - \frac{4}{9}$$
$$= \left(5x\right)^2 - \left(\frac{2}{3}\right)^2$$
$$= \left(5x + \frac{2}{3}\right)\left(5x - \frac{2}{3}\right)$$

Choice (C) is correct.

3. A **Difficulty:** Medium

Category: Passport to Advanced Math / Quadratics

Getting to the Answer: Factored form of a quadratic equation reveals the roots, or x-intercepts, of the equation, so start by identifying the x-intercepts on the graph. An x-intercept is an x-value that corresponds to a y-value of 0. Read the axis labels carefully—each grid-line represents $\frac{1}{4}$, so the x-intercepts of the graph, and therefore the roots of the equation, are $x = -\frac{1}{2}$ and $x = \frac{3}{4}$. This means you are looking for factors that when solved result in these values of x. Choice (A) is correct because $2x + 1$ gives you $x = -\frac{1}{2}$ and $4x - 3$ gives you $x = \frac{3}{4}$.

4. D **Difficulty:** Easy

Category: Heart of Algebra / Linear Equations

Getting to the Answer: Don't jump right into translating the line. Think about how the translation would affect the slope—it wouldn't. Translating the line moves all the points by the same amount, so the slope doesn't change. Find the slope of line P by counting the rise and the run from one point to the next, and you'll have your answer. From the y-intercept $(0, -2)$, the line rises 5 units and runs 2 units to the point $(2, 3)$, so the slope is $\frac{5}{2}$, (D).

5. B   Difficulty: Easy

Category: Passport to Advanced Math / Exponents

Getting to the Answer: Solve the equation for t. Multiply both sides of the equation by t to get it out of the denominator, and then divide both sides by a.

$$a = \frac{v_f - v_i}{t}$$

$$t\left(a = \frac{v_f - v_i}{t}\right)t$$

$$ta = v_f - v_i$$

$$t = \frac{v_f - v_i}{a}$$

This matches (B).

6. C   Difficulty: Medium

Category: Passport to Advanced Math / Quadratics

Getting to the Answer: Imagine the graph of a parabola. The minimum value is the y-coordinate of its vertex, and the axis of symmetry also passes through the vertex. Use these properties to identify the vertex, and then use it to write the equation of the parabola in vertex form, $y = a(x - h)^2 + k$, where (h, k) is the vertex. If the minimum of the parabola is -5, then the vertex of the parabola looks like $(x, -5)$. The axis of symmetry, $x = 1$, tells you the x-coordinate—it's 1. That means (h, k) is $(1, -5)$, and the equation of the parabola looks like $y = a(x - 1)^2 - 5$. The value of a in each of the answer choices is 1, so (C) is correct.

7. B   Difficulty: Medium

Category: Heart of Algebra / Systems of Linear Equations

Getting to the Answer: The solution to a system of linear equations shown graphically is the point where the lines intersect. Read the axis labels carefully. Each grid-line represents $\frac{1}{2}$. The two lines intersect at $(-5, -4)$, so $A + B = -5 + (-4) = -9$, (B).

8. C   Difficulty: Easy

Category: Passport to Advanced Math / Exponents

Getting to the Answer: When adding or subtracting polynomial expressions, simply combine like terms (terms that have the same variable part). Pay careful attention to the exponents. To keep things organized, arrange the terms in descending order before you combine them. Substitute the given expressions for A and B into $3A + B$. Distribute the 3 to each term of A and then combine like terms. Be careful—the first term of B is x^3, not x^2, so these cannot be combined.

$$3\left(x^2 + 4x + 9\right) + \left(x^3 + 6x - 2\right)$$
$$= 3x^2 + 12x + 27 + x^3 + 6x - 2$$
$$= x^3 + 3x^2 + 12x + 6x + 27 - 2$$
$$= x^3 + 3x^2 + 18x + 25$$

This matches (C).

9. B   Difficulty: Medium

Category: Passport to Advanced Math / Quadratics

Getting to the Answer: A quadratic equation can have zero, one, or two real solutions. There are several ways to determine exactly how many. You could graph the equation and see how many times it crosses the x-axis; you could calculate the discriminant (the value under the square root in the quadratic formula); or you could try to factor the equation. Use whichever method gets you to the answer the quickest. Notice that the first and last terms in the equation are perfect squares—this is a hint that it could be a perfect square trinomial, which it is. The factored form of the equation is $(3x - 2)(3x - 2)$. Both factors are the same, so there is only one real value, $x = \dfrac{2}{3}$, that satisfies the equation, so (B) is correct.

10. A   Difficulty: Medium

Category: Heart of Algebra / Inequalities

Getting to the Answer: When an equation or an inequality involves fractions, there are a number of ways to approach it. You could distribute the fractions or you could clear the fractions by multiplying both sides by the lowest common denominator. In this question, clearing one fraction at a time will prevent having to work with messy fractions and large numbers. First, multiply everything by 5, and then divide by 3—this will clear the first fraction:

$$\cancel{5} \cdot \left[\frac{3}{\cancel{5}}\left(x + \frac{2}{7}\right)\right] > [-6] \cdot 5$$

$$3\left(x + \frac{2}{7}\right) > -30$$

$$\frac{\cancel{3}\left(x + \frac{2}{7}\right)}{\cancel{3}} > \frac{-30}{3}$$

$$x + \frac{2}{7} > -10$$

Now, multiply everything by 7 and go from there:

$$7 \cdot \left[x + \frac{2}{7}\right] > [-10] \cdot 7$$

$$7x + 2 > -70$$

$$7x > -72$$

$$x > -\frac{72}{7}$$

Choice (A) is correct.

11. D   Difficulty: Medium

Category: Heart of Algebra / Linear Equations

Getting to the Answer: Don't let all the contextual information confuse you. The question at the end tells you that you are looking for the linear relationship between the pairs of numbers in the last two rows of the table. This amounts to writing an equation in the form $y = mx + b$. Take a peek at the answers—none of the equations have a y-intercept, so all you need to do is write the equation $y = mx$, or here, $s = md$. To find m, use any two ordered pairs from the table and the slope formula. Be careful—d represents x in the equation, so the dropper amounts should be written first in the ordered pairs. Using (0.5, 1.25) and (1.0, 2.5), the slope is:

$$\begin{aligned} m &= \frac{y_2 - y_1}{x_2 - x_1} \\ &= \frac{2.5 - 1.25}{1.0 - 0.5} \\ &= \frac{1.25}{0.5} \\ &= 2.5 \end{aligned}$$

This means the equation is $s = 2.5d$, which matches (D).

12. C   Difficulty: Medium

Category: Heart of Algebra / Linear Equations

Getting to the Answer: Think conceptually before you start simplifying the equations. The only type of line that does not cross the y-axis is a vertical line (because it runs parallel to the axis). All vertical lines take the form $x = a$. In other words, a vertical line does not have a y term. Eliminate equations that will clearly have a y term once simplified. You don't need to worry about the x terms or the constants.

Choice A: Although it may appear that the y terms will cancel, you must first distribute 0.5. The result is $0.5y$ on the left side of the equation and y on the right, which do not cancel, so eliminate A.

Choice B: No y terms on the left, but $4y$ on the right, so eliminate B.

Choice (C): $0.25(8y) = 2y$ on the left and $-2(-y) = 2y$ on the right, which do indeed cancel, so (C) is correct.

You don't need to waste time checking D—just move on to the next question. (*Choice D:* $-6y$ on the left and $-3y$ on the right, which do not cancel.)

13. D   Difficulty: Medium

Category: Heart of Algebra / Systems of Linear Equations

Getting to the Answer: Typically, solving a system of equations means finding the values of x and y that satisfy both equations simultaneously. Because the solution to the system satisfies both equations, you can substitute 2 and -1, for x and y respectively, and then solve for H and K. Before selecting your answer, check that you found what the question was asking for (the value of $\frac{K}{H}$).

$$Hx + 2y = -8$$
$$H(2) + 2(-1) = -8$$
$$2H - 2 = -8$$
$$2H = -6$$
$$H = -3$$

$$Kx - 5y = -13$$
$$K(2) - 5(-1) = -13$$
$$2K + 5 = -13$$
$$2K = -18$$
$$K = -9$$

So, $\frac{K}{H} = \frac{-9}{-3} = 3$, (D).

14. D   Difficulty: Hard

Category: Additional Topics in Math / Trigonometry

Getting to the Answer: If an angle with measure A such that $\pi < A < \frac{3\pi}{2}$ is drawn on a unit circle, its terminal side will fall in Quadrant III, and $\sin A = k$ will be a negative value (because sine represents the y-value of the point that intersects the unit circle). If $\sin B = k$ also (and k is negative), then the terminal side of B must land in either of Quadrants III or IV (because sine is negative in those quadrants). Choose an easy radian measure (in Quadrant III) for angle A, such as $\frac{5\pi}{4}$. Try each answer choice to see which one results in an angle that lies in the third or

fourth quadrant:

Choice A: $\frac{5\pi}{4} - \pi = \frac{5\pi}{4} - \frac{4\pi}{4} = \frac{\pi}{4}$, which is in Quadrant I, so eliminate A.

Choice B: $\pi + \frac{5\pi}{4} = \frac{4\pi}{4} + \frac{5\pi}{4} = \frac{9}{4}$, which is in Quadrant I (because it is the same as $\frac{\pi}{4}$ rotated one full circle), so eliminate B.

Choice C: $2\pi - \frac{5\pi}{4} = \frac{8\pi}{4} - \frac{5\pi}{4} = \frac{3\pi}{4}$, which is in Quadrant II, so eliminate C.

Choice (D): $3\pi - \frac{5\pi}{4} = \frac{12\pi}{4} - \frac{5\pi}{4} = \frac{7\pi}{4}$, which is in Quadrant IV, so (D) is correct.

15. D   Difficulty: Hard

Category: Passport to Advanced Math / Exponents

Getting to the Answer: For this question, use the following rules of exponents: When you raise a power to a power, you multiply the exponents, and when you divide with exponents, you subtract them. Distribute the 2 outside the parentheses to the exponent in the numerator and in the denominator:

$$\left(\frac{x^{\frac{1}{2}}}{x^{-2}}\right)^2 = \frac{x^{\frac{1}{2}\times 2}}{x^{-2\times 2}} = \frac{x^1}{x^{-4}}$$

Now, subtract the exponents:

$$\frac{x}{x^{-4}} = x^{1-(-4)} = x^{1+4} = x^5$$

Unfortunately, x^5 is not one of the answer choices, so look for an answer choice that is also equivalent to x^5. You can eliminate A right away, and the exponents in B look too small, so start with C, which simplifies to $\frac{x^7}{x^{12}} = \frac{1}{x^5}$ and is therefore not correct. Choice (D) is correct because:

$$\left(\frac{\left(x^3\right)\left(x^4\right)}{x^{-3}}\right)^{\frac{1}{2}} = \left(\frac{x^7}{x^{-3}}\right)^{\frac{1}{2}}$$

$$= \left(x^{7-(-3)}\right)^{\frac{1}{2}}$$

$$= \left(x^{10}\right)^{\frac{1}{2}}$$

$$= x^5$$

16. 1   **Difficulty:** Medium

Category: Heart of Algebra / Inequalities

Getting to the Answer: If (a, b) is a solution to the system, then a is the x-coordinate of any point in the region where the shading overlaps and b is the corresponding y-coordinate. When $a = 0$ (or $x = 0$), the maximum possible value for b lies on the upper boundary line, $y < -3x + 2$. (You can tell which boundary line is the upper line by looking at the y-intercept.) The point on the boundary line is $(0, 2)$, but the boundary line is dashed (because the inequality is strictly less than), so you cannot include $(0, 2)$ in the solution set. This means 1 is the greatest possible integer value for b when $a = 0$.

17. 12   **Difficulty:** Medium

Category: Passport to Advanced Math / Functions

Getting to the Answer: For any function $f(x)$, the x is the input value, and the output is the result after plugging in the input and simplifying. The question tells you that the *output* is 3 (not the input), so set the equation equal to 3 and solve for x.

$$3 = \frac{2}{3}x - 5$$

$$8 = \frac{2}{3}x$$

$$3 \times 8 = \cancel{3} \times \frac{2}{\cancel{3}}x$$

$$24 = 2x$$

$$12 = x$$

18. 12   **Difficulty:** Medium

Category: Additional Topics in Math / Geometry

Getting to the Answer: Use the relationship $\dfrac{\text{area of sector}}{\text{area of circle}} = \dfrac{\text{central angle}}{360°}$. To help you remember this relationship, just think $\dfrac{\text{partial area}}{\text{whole area}} = \dfrac{\text{partial angle}}{\text{whole angle}}$. The unknown in this question is the diameter of the circle, which is twice the radius. You can find the radius of the circle by first finding the area of the whole circle, and then by using the area equation, $A = \pi r^2$. You have everything you need to find the area of the circle. Because this is a no-calculator question, you can bet that numbers will simplify nicely.

$$\frac{\text{area of sector}}{\text{area of circle}} = \frac{\text{central angle}}{360°}$$

$$\frac{6\pi}{A} = \frac{60}{360}$$

$$\frac{6\pi}{A} = \frac{1}{6}$$

$$A = 36\pi$$

Now, solve for r using $A = \pi r^2$:

$$36\pi = \pi r^2$$

$$36 = r^2$$

$$\pm 6 = r$$

The radius can't be negative, so it must be 6, which means the diameter of the circle is twice that, or 12.

19. 14   **Difficulty:** Hard

Category: Additional Topics in Math / Geometry

Getting to the Answer: When the equation of a circle is in the form $(x - h)^2 + (y - k)^2 = r^2$, the r represents the length of the radius. To get the equation into this form, complete the squares. You already have an x^2 and a y^2 in the given equation and the coefficients of x and y are even, so completing the square is fairly straightforward—there are just a lot of steps. Start by grouping the xs and ys together. Then, take the coefficient of the x term and divide it by 2, square it, and add it to the two terms with x variables. Do the same with the y term. Don't forget to add these amounts to the other side of the equation as well. This creates a perfect square of x terms and y terms, so take the square root of each.

$$x^2 + y^2 + 10x - 4y = 20$$
$$x^2 + 10x + y^2 - 4y = 20$$
$$\left(x^2 + 10x + 25\right) + \left(y^2 - 4y + 4\right) = 20 + 25 + 4$$
$$\left(x + 5\right)^2 + \left(y - 2\right)^2 = 49$$

The equation tells you that $r^2 = 49$, which means that the radius is 7 and the diameter is twice that, or 14.

20. 800 Difficulty: Hard

Domain: Passport to Advanced Math / Functions

Getting to the Answer: Think about the question logically and in terms of function notation. Find the quantity that the company can expect to sell at each price using the demand function. Don't forget that the quantity is given in hundreds. Then, find the total sales, the total costs, and the total profits using multiplication.

Price	$12	$10
Quantity	$q(12) = -2(12) + 34$ $= -24 + 34$ $= 10$	$q(10) = -2(10) + 34$ $= -20 + 34$ $= 14$
In hundreds	$10(100) = 1,000$	$14(100) = 1,400$
Sales	$1,000(12) = \$12,000$	$1,400(10) = \$14,000$
Costs	$1,000(7) = \$7,000$	$1,400(7) = \$9,800$
Profits	$5,000	$4,200

The company will earn $5,000 − $4,200 = $800 more per month.

MATH—CALCULATOR TEST

1. B   Difficulty: Easy

Category: Heart of Algebra / Inequalities

Getting to the Answer: When trying to match an inequality to a real-world scenario, you need to examine the numbers, the variables, and the inequal-ity symbol. The question asks how much is needed to *meet or surpass* the recommended amount, which is another way of saying *greater than or equal to*, so you can eliminate C. Adult females should consume 75 milligrams of vitamin C, and smokers should consume an additional 35 mg, so the total amount that a smoking female should consume is 75 + 35 = 110 milligrams. This means the right-hand side of the equation should be ≥ 110, and you can elimi-nate A. To choose between (B) and D, think in con-crete terms. *Multiplying* (not dividing) the number of milligrams in each grapefruit or serving of spinach yields the total amount of vitamin C in each, so (B) is correct.

2. D   Difficulty: Easy

Category: Problem Solving and Data Analysis / Scatterplots

Getting to the Answer: You don't need to know the slope of the line of best fit to answer the question, so don't waste valuable time trying to find it. Instead, use the labels on the axes to determine the meaning of the slope. On a graph, slope means the change in the y-values (rise) compared to the change in the x-values (run). In a real-world scenario, this is the same as the unit rate. In this context, the rise is the amount of money spent, and the run is the number of min-utes watching commercials. Thus, the unit rate, or slope, represents the predicted increase in money spent on brand name products for every one-minute increase in time spent watching commercials, (D).

3. B   Difficulty: Easy

Category: Heart of Algebra / Systems of Linear Equations

Getting to the Answer: Whenever a question gives you information about a total number of items and a total cost of those items, you should write one equation that represents the total number (here, the number of packages) and a second equation that represents the total cost (here, the cost of the portraits). The number of parents who ordered basic packages plus the number who ordered deluxe packages equals the total number of parents (182), so one equation is $b + d = 182$. This means you can eliminate A and C. Now write the cost equation: cost per basic package (29.5) times number ordered (b) plus cost per deluxe package (44.5) times number ordered (d) equals the total bill ($6,509). The cost equation is $29.5b + 44.5d = 6,509$. Together, these two equations form the system in (B). Don't let D fool you—there are two choices of packages, but this does not impact the total amount of the school's bill.

4. C   Difficulty: Easy

Category: Passport to Advanced Math / Functions

Getting to the Answer: Understanding the language of functions will make answering this question very simple. Another way of saying "For what values of x does $f(x) = -4$?" is "What is the x-value when $y = -4$?" Draw a horizontal line across the graph at $y = -4$ and find the x-coordinates of any points that hit your line.

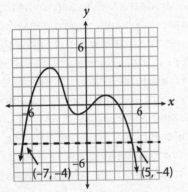

The line hits the graph at $x = -7$ and at $x = 5$, (C).

5. C   Difficulty: Easy

Category: Heart of Algebra / Linear Equations

Getting to the Answer: Don't let this fairly simple question fool you. Just because 3 and −3 are opposites, this does not mean the value on the right-hand side of the equals sign will be the opposite of 19. Solve for x, then substitute that value into the second equation for x and simplify.

$$4x + 3 = 19$$
$$4x = 16$$
$$x = 4$$

Thus, $4x - 3 = 4(4) - 3 = 16 - 3 = 13$, (C).

You might also recognize that $4x - 3$ is 6 less than $4x + 3$, so you can simply subtract 6 from 19 to arrive at 13. This is a great shortcut, but only works when the variable terms are identical.

6. C   Difficulty: Easy

Category: Heart of Algebra / Linear Equations

Getting to the Answer: To find the slope of a line from its graph, either count the rise and the run from one point to the next, or choose two points that lie on the line and substitute them into the slope formula, $m = \dfrac{y_2 - y_1}{x_2 - x_1}$. Use whichever method gets you to the answer the quickest. Pay careful attention to negative signs. Using the points $(0, -2)$ and $(7, -8)$, the slope is:

$$m = \frac{-8 - (-2)}{7 - 0}$$
$$= \frac{-6}{7}$$
$$= -\frac{6}{7}$$

Choice (C) is correct.

7. B   Difficulty: Easy

Category: Heart of Algebra / Linear Equations

Getting to the Answer: Compare the differences in the two lines to the statements in the answer choices. Pay careful attention to which line represents each state. Be careful—this is a real-world scenario, and the word "positive" does not refer to the slope of the lines. The key difference between the lines in the graph is their slopes. The dashed line (State B) has a steeper negative slope, while the solid line (State A) has a more gradual slope. This means that the crime rate for armed robbery in State B decreased at a faster rate than in State A. Because, in the real world, a positive impact means fewer crimes, State B's law had a more positive impact on the crime rate for armed robbery. This matches (B).

8. C   Difficulty: Easy

Category: Problem Solving and Data Analysis / Rates, Ratios, Proportions, and Percentages

Getting to the Answer: When ratios involve large numbers, simplify if possible to make the calculations easier. Let p equal the number of cans of paint mixed. Set up a proportion and solve for p. Try writing the proportion in words first.

$$\frac{4\cancel{0}\text{ defective}}{2,50\cancel{0}\text{ mixed}} = \frac{128\text{ defective}}{p\text{ mixed}}$$
$$\frac{4}{250} = \frac{128}{p}$$
$$4p = 32{,}000$$
$$p = 8{,}000$$

Choice (C) is correct.

9. D   Difficulty: Medium

Category: Problem Solving and Data Analysis / Statistics and Probability

Getting to the Answer: Because the mean ages are different and you do not know how many men or women have college degrees and get married, you need to reason logically to arrive at the correct answer. The mean age of the women is lower than that of the men, so the combined mean cannot be greater than or equal to that of the men. Similarly, the mean age of the men is greater than that of the women, so the combined mean cannot be less than or equal to the mean age of the women. In other words, the combined mean age must fall somewhere between the two means, making (D) correct.

10. A   Difficulty: Easy

Category: Problem Solving and Data Analysis / Rates, Ratios, Proportions, and Percentages

Getting to the Answer: To answer a question that says "directly proportional," set two ratios equal to

each other and solve for the missing amount. Don't forget—match the units in the numerators and in the denominators on both sides. Let f equal the number of feet that the diver can safely ascend in 90 seconds. Set up a proportion and solve for f. Because the first rate is given in terms of minutes, write 90 seconds as 1.5 minutes.

$$\frac{165\text{ feet}}{5.5\text{ minutes}} = \frac{f\text{ feet}}{1.5\text{ minutes}}$$
$$1.5(165) = 5.5(f)$$
$$247.5 = 5.5f$$
$$45 = f$$

Choice (A) is correct.

11. D   Difficulty: Medium

Category: Heart of Algebra / Inequalities

Getting to the Answer: You could graph the cost function ($y = 17p + 1{,}890$) and the revenue function ($y = 35x$) and try to determine where the revenue function is greater (higher on the graph). However, the numbers are quite large and this may prove to be very time-consuming. Instead, create and solve an inequality comparing revenue and cost. If the revenue from a single pair of shoes is $35, then the total revenue from p pairs is $35p$. If revenue must be greater than cost, then the inequality should be $35p > 17p + 1{,}890$. Now, solve for p using inverse operations:

$$35p > 17p + 1{,}890$$
$$18p > 1{,}890$$
$$p > 105$$

This matches (D).

12. B   Difficulty: Easy

Category: Problem Solving and Data Analysis / Rates, Ratios, Proportions, and Percentages

Getting to the Answer: This is a question about rates, so pay careful attention to the units. As you read the question, decide how and when you will need to convert units. First, determine how long it will take the athlete to complete the race. Set up a proportion.

$$\frac{9.25 \text{ miles}}{1 \text{ hour}} = \frac{74 \text{ miles}}{x \text{ hours}}$$

$$9.25x = 74$$

$$x = 8$$

The question asks for the total number of calories needed. The recommended rate of consumption is given in calories per minute, and you now know the number of hours that it will take the athlete to complete the race. You could convert the number of hours to minutes (8×60 minutes = 480 minutes) and then multiply this by 3 (the calorie per minute rate given) to find that the athlete should consume $480 \times 3 = 1,440$ calories, (B). Or, you could also convert the given rate (3 calories per minute) to a per-hour rate ($3 \times 60 = 180$ calories per hour) and then multiply this by the number of hours it will take the athlete to finish the race ($180 \times 8 = 1,440$ calories).

13. C   Difficulty: Medium

Category: Heart of Algebra / Linear Equations

Getting to the Answer: The rate of change (or slope) of a linear relationship is constant, so find the rate and apply it to the missing value. You could also look for a pattern in the table. Choose any two points (preferably ones with the nicest numbers) from the table, and substitute them into the slope formula. Using the points (3, 0) and (−1, 14), the slope is $\frac{14 - 0}{-1 - 3} = \frac{14}{-4} = \frac{7}{-2}$. This means that for every 2 units the x-value decreases, the y-value increases by 7, and the decrease from $x = -5$ to $x = -7$ happens to be −2. So, increase the y-value by 7 one time: $28 + 7 = 35$, (C).

14. B   Difficulty: Medium

Category: Problem Solving and Data Analysis / Statistics and Probability

Getting to the Answer: Think about what the question is asking. The real estate agent wants to figure out which measure of the data (mean, mode, range,

or median) is going to be most useful. The *mode* of a data set tells you the data point, or in this case the age range, that occurs most often. If the real estate agent markets to the age range that represents the mode, (B), she will be marketing to the largest group of clients possible.

15. A   Difficulty: Hard

Category: Problem Solving and Data Analysis / Statistics and Probability

Getting to the Answer: Some data sets have a *head*, where many data points are clustered in one area, and one or two *tails*, where the number of data points slowly decreases to 0. Examining the tail will help you describe the shape of the data set. A data set is *skewed* in the direction of its longest tail. The graph in this question has its tail on the right side, so the data is skewed to the right. When data is skewed to the right, the mean is greater than the median because the mean is more sensitive to the higher data values in the tail than is the median, so (A) is correct. If you're not sure about the mean/median part, read the rest of the answer choices—none of them describes the data as skewed to the right, so you can eliminate all of them.

16. B   Difficulty: Medium

Category: Heart of Algebra / Inequalities

Getting to the Answer: The question states that t represents the number of round trips. The cost of one round trip without the discount card is $35 per trip, or $35t$. If a commuter purchases the discount card, round trips would equal the cost of the card plus $12.50 per trip, or $900 + 12.5t$. Combine these into an inequality, remembering which way the inequality symbol should be oriented. You want the cost with the discount card to be less than (<) the cost without the card, so the inequality should be $900 + 12.5t < 35t$. Now, solve for t:

$$900 + 12.5t < 35t$$

$$900 < 22.5t$$

$$40 < t$$

Turn the inequality around to find that $t > 40$, which means a commuter must make more than 40 trips for the discount card to be a better deal, which is (B).

17. C **Difficulty:** Medium

Category: Problem Solving and Data Analysis / Rates, Ratios, Proportions, and Percentages

Getting to the Answer: Etienne starts with $800. He spends 20% of $800, or 0.2(800) = $160, on gas. He has $800 − $160 = $640 left over. He budgets 25% of $640, or 0.25(640) = $160, for food and allots $300 for the hotel. He spends all the remaining money on entertainment, which is $640 − $160 − $300 = $180. Divide this amount by the original amount to find the percent he spent on entertainment: $\frac{180}{800} = 0.225 = 22.5\%$, (C).

18. A **Difficulty:** Medium

Category: Passport to Advanced Math / Scatterplots

Getting to the Answer: When the dependent variable in a relationship increases by a scale factor, like doubling, tripling, etc., there is an exponential relationship between the variables which can be written in the form $y = a(b)^x$, where a is the initial amount, b is the scale factor, and x is time. The question states that the number of microbes tripled every 24 hours, so the relationship is exponential. This means you can eliminate C and D right away. Choices (A) and B are written in the form $y = a(b)^x$, with the initial amount equal to 2,000 and the scale factor equal to 3, so you can't eliminate either one at first glance. To choose between them, try an easy number for h (like 24) in each equation to see which one matches the information given in the question. In the first equation, $n = 2,000(3)^{\frac{24}{24}} = 2,000 \times (3)^1 = 6,000$, which is 2,000 tripled, so (A) is correct.

19. A **Difficulty:** Medium

Category: Problem Solving and Data Analysis / Statistics and Probability

Getting to the Answer: When working with two-way tables, always read the question carefully, identifying which pieces of information you need. Here, you need to focus on the "Against" column and the "1L" and "2L" rows. To stay organized, it may help to circle these pieces of information in the table. There are 58 1Ls and 64 2Ls in the survey sample, for a total of 58 + 64 = 122 1Ls and 2Ls. There are 16 1Ls and 12 2Ls against the policy, for a total of 16 + 12 = 28. This means that 28 out of the 122 1Ls and 2Ls are against the new policy. Written as a fraction, this is $\frac{28}{122}$, which reduces to $\frac{14}{61}$, (A).

20. C **Difficulty:** Medium

Category: Additional Topics in Math / Imaginary Numbers

Getting to the Answer: You will not be expected to raise a complex number like the one in this question to the third power by hand. That's a clue that you should be able to use your calculator. The definition of i has been programmed into all graphing calculators, so you can perform basic operations on complex numbers using the calculator (in the Calculator Section of the test). Enter the expression as follows: $(6 + 5i)^3$. On the TI83/84 calculators, you can find i on the button with the decimal point. After entering the expression and pressing Enter, the calculator should return $−234 + 415i$, which is (C).

You could, however, expand the number by hand, by writing it as $(6 + 5i)(6 + 5i)(6 + 5i)$ and carefully multiplying it all out.

21. B **Difficulty:** Hard

Category: Problem Solving and Data Analysis / Scatterplots

Getting to the Answer: When an exponential function is written in the form $f(x) = f(0)(1 + r)^x$, the quantity $(1 + r)$ represents the growth rate or the decay rate depending on whether the y-values are increasing or decreasing. The y-values are increasing in this graph, so r represents a growth rate. Because the data is modeled using an exponential function (not a linear function), the rate is not the same as the slope. Look at the y-values in the calculator screen-shot—they are quadrupling as the x-values increase by 1. In the equation, this means that $(1 + r) = 4$. Solve this equation to find that $r = 3$, (B).

22. A   Difficulty: Medium

Category: Problem Solving and Data Analysis / Rates, Ratios, Proportions, and Percentages

Getting to the Answer: Pay careful attention to the units. You need to convert all of the dimensions to inches and then set up and solve a proportion. There are 12 inches in one foot, so the real pyramid's height was $(480 \times 12) + 8 = 5,760 + 8 = 5,768$ inches; the length of the passage in the real pyramid was $53.75 \times 12 = 645$ inches; the museum's pyramid height will be 71 feet, 6 inches, or 858 inches; and the length of the museum's passage is unknown. Set up a proportion and solve for the unknown. Use words first to help you keep the measurements in the right places:

$$\frac{\text{real passage length}}{\text{real height}} = \frac{\text{museum passage length}}{\text{museum height}}$$

$$\frac{645}{5,768} = \frac{x}{858}$$

$$553,410 = 5,768x$$

$$95.94 = x$$

The museum should make the length of its passage about 96 inches, or $96 \div 12 = 8$ feet, (A).

23. D   Difficulty: Medium

Category: Passport to Advanced Math / Exponents

Getting to the Answer: You could use polynomial long division to answer this question, or you could try to factor the numerator and see if any terms cancel. It is very tricky to factor a quadratic equation with a negative coefficient on x^2, so start by factoring -1 out of both the numerator and the denominator. To factor the resulting quadratic in the numerator, you need to find two numbers whose product is -24 and whose sum is 10. The numbers are -2 and $+12$.

$$\frac{-x^2 - 10x + 24}{2 - x} = \frac{\cancel{-1}(x^2 + 10x - 24)}{\cancel{-1}(x - 2)}$$

$$= \frac{(\cancel{x - 2})(x + 12)}{\cancel{x - 2}}$$

$$= x + 12$$

This matches (D).

24. C   Difficulty: Hard

Category: Problem Solving and Data Analysis / Rates, Ratios, Proportions, and Percentages

Getting to the Answer: You're given two ratios: ethanol to gasoline and methanol to gasoline. Your job is to "merge" them so you can directly compare ethanol to methanol. Both of the given ratios contain gasoline, but the gasoline amounts (4 and 9) are not identical. To directly compare them, find a common multiple (36). Multiply each ratio by the factor that will make the number of parts of gasoline equal to 36 in each:

Ethanol to Gasoline: $(1:4) \times (9:9) = 9:36$

Methanol to Gasoline: $(1:9) \times (4:4) = 4:36$

Now that the number of parts of gasoline needed is the same in both ratios, you can merge the two ratios to compare ethanol to methanol directly: 9:36:4. So the proper ratio of ethanol to methanol is 9:4, which is (C).

25. A   Difficulty: Medium

Category: Heart of Algebra / Linear Equations

Getting to the Answer: Add reasonable numbers to the graph such as the ones shown in the following example:

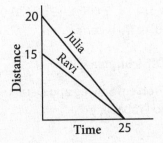

Use the numbers to help you evaluate each statement. It took Julia and Ravi each 25 minutes to drive to the museum, so you can eliminate C and D. Julia drove 20 miles in 25 minutes, while Ravi only drove 15 miles in 25 minutes; their rates are not the same, so B is not correct. This means (A) must be correct. Julia starts out farther away than Ravi, so Julia must have driven at a faster speed than Ravi to arrive at the museum in the same amount of time.

26. D   Difficulty: Hard

Category: Passport to Advanced Math / Functions

Getting to the Answer: Transformations that are grouped with the x in a function shift the graph horizontally and therefore affect the x-coordinates of points on the graph. Transformations that are not grouped with the x shift the graph vertically and therefore affect the y-coordinates of points on the graph. Remember, horizontal shifts are always backward of what they look like.

Perform each transformation on the coordinates of the point, one at a time, following the same order of operations that you use when simplifying arithmetic expressions. Start with $(x − 4)$. This shifts the graph right 4 units, so add 4 to the x-coordinate of the given point: $(8, −3) \rightarrow (8 + 4, −3) = (12, −3)$. Next, apply the negative in front of g, which is not grouped with the x, so it makes the y-coordinate the opposite of what it was: $(12, −3) \rightarrow (12, 3)$. Finally, the $−6$ is not grouped with x, so subtract 6 from the y-coordinate: $(12, 3) \rightarrow (12, 3 − 6) = (12, −3)$. Therefore, (D) is correct. You could also plot the point on a coordinate plane, perform the transformations (right 4, reflect vertically over the x-axis, and then down 6), and find the resulting point.

27. D   Difficulty: Medium

Category: Passport to Advanced Math / Functions

Getting to the Answer: Sometimes, a question requires thought rather than brute force. Here, you need to understand that when dealing with compositions, the range of the inner function be-

comes the domain of the outer function, which in turn produces the range of the composition. In the composition $f(g(x))$, the function $g(x) = x^3$ is the inner function. Because the question states that x is either zero or a negative number ($x \le 0$), every value of x, when substituted into this function, will result in zero or a negative number (because a negative number raised to an odd power is always negative). This means that the largest possible range value for $g(x)$ is 0, and consequently that the largest possible domain value for $f(x)$ is also 0. Substituting 0 for x in $f(x)$ results in $−1$, which is the largest possible range value for the composition. Because $1 > −1$, it is not in the range of $f(g(x))$, so (D) is correct.

28. A   Difficulty: Hard

Category: Passport to Advanced Math / Quadratics

Getting to the Answer: To answer this question, you need to recall nearly everything you've learned about quadratic graphs. The equation is given in vertex form ($y = a(x − h)^2 + k$), which reveals the vertex (h, k), the direction in which the parabola opens (upward when $a > 0$ and downward when $a < 0$), the axis of symmetry ($x = h$), and the minimum/maximum value of the function (k).

Start by comparing each answer choice to the equation, $y = −3(x − 5)^2 + 8$. The only choice that you cannot immediately compare is (A), because vertex form does not readily reveal the y-intercept, so start with B. Don't forget, you are looking for the statement that is not true. *Choice B:* The axis of symmetry is given by $x = h$, and h is 5, so this statement is true and therefore not correct. *Choice C:* The vertex is given by (h, k), so the vertex is indeed (5, 8) and this choice is not correct. *Choice D:* The value of a is $−3$, which indicates that the parabola opens downward, so this choice is also incorrect. That means (A) must be the correct answer. To confirm, you could substitute 0 for x in the equation to find the y-intercept.

$$y = -3(x - 5)^2 + 8$$
$$= -3(0 - 5)^2 + 8$$
$$= -3(-5)^2 + 8$$
$$= -3(25) + 8$$
$$= -75 + 8$$
$$= -67$$

The y-intercept is $(0, -67)$, not $(0, 8)$, so the statement is not true and therefore the correct answer.

29. A   Difficulty: Hard

Category: Problem Solving and Data Analysis / Rates, Ratios, Proportions, and Percentages

Getting to the Answer: Don't let all the technical words in this question overwhelm you. Solve it step-by-step, examining the units as you go. Notice that some of the numbers in the answer choices are just 1 apart, so think carefully before selecting your answer.

Step 1: Determine the number of megabytes the computer can upload in 1 weekend (48 hours):

$$\frac{5.25\,\text{megabytes}}{1\,\text{sec}} \times \frac{60\,\text{sec}}{1\,\text{min}} \times \frac{60\,\text{min}}{1\,\text{hr}} \times 48\,\text{hr}$$
$$= 907{,}200\,\text{megabytes}$$

Step 2: Convert this amount to gigabytes (because the information about the scans is given in gigabytes, not megabytes):

$$907{,}200\,\text{megabytes} \times \frac{1\,\text{gigabyte}}{1{,}000\,\text{megabytes}}$$
$$= 907.2\,\text{gigabytes}$$

Step 3: Each client file is about 2.5 gigabytes in size, so divide this number by 2.5 to determine how many client files the computer can upload to the remote server: $907.2 \div 2.5 = 362.88$ files. Remember, you should round this number down to 362, because the question asks for the maximum number the computer can upload, and it cannot complete the 363rd scan in the time allowed. Choice (A) is correct.

30. A   Difficulty: Medium

Category: Additional Topics in Math / Geometry

Getting to the Answer: This question does not provide a graphic, so sketch a quick diagram of the information presented. Be sure to show the direction of traffic for each street. The question describes two parallel streets, cut by a transversal. Start with that, and then add all the details.

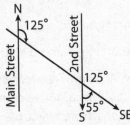

Traffic traveling north on Main Street must make a 125° turn onto the new road. This is the angle between where the traffic was originally headed and where it is headed after it makes the turn. Traffic on 2nd Street is traveling south, the opposite direction. As shown in the diagram, the angle that the southbound traffic would make is supplementary to the corresponding angle made by the northbound traffic. When two parallel lines are cut by a transversal, corresponding angles are congruent, which means that cars turning off of 2nd Street will make a $180 - 125 = 55°$ turn onto the new road. Choice (A) is correct.

31. 11.5 or **23/2** or **69/6   Difficulty:** Easy

Category: Heart of Algebra / Linear Equations

Getting to the Answer: Simplify each numerator. Then, cross-multiply. Finally, isolate the variable using inverse operations.

$$\frac{4h - (21 - 8h)}{3} = \frac{15 + 6(h - 1)}{2}$$

$$\frac{4h - 21 + 8h}{3} = \frac{15 + 6h - 6}{2}$$

$$\frac{12h - 21}{3} = \frac{6h + 9}{2}$$

$$2(12h - 21) = 3(6h + 9)$$

$$24h - 42 = 18h + 27$$

$$6h = 69$$

$$h = \frac{69}{6} = \frac{23}{2} = 11.5$$

32. 255   Difficulty: Medium

Category: Heart of Algebra / Systems of Linear Equations

Getting to the Answer: Translate English into math to write the two equations: The New York property costs 30 thousand dollars less than four times the cost of the Georgia property, so $N = 4G - 30$; together, the two properties cost 445 thousand dollars, so $N + G = 445$.

The system of equations is:

$$\begin{cases} N = 4G - 30 \\ N + G = 445 \end{cases}$$

The top equation is already solved for N, so substitute $4G - 30$ into the second equation for N and solve for G:

$$4G - 30 + G = 445$$

$$5G - 30 = 445$$

$$5G = 475$$

$$G = 95$$

The Georgia property costs 95 thousand dollars, so the New York property costs $4(95) - 30 = 350$ thousand dollars. This means the New York property costs $350 - 95 = 255$ thousand more dollars than the Georgia property.

33. .52   Difficulty: Medium

Category: Problem Solving and Data Analysis / Statistics and Probability

Getting to the Answer: The probability that an event will occur is the number of desired outcomes (number of available cars that have a rating of at least 25 mpg) divided by the number of total possible outcomes (total number of cars). "At least" means that much or greater, so find the number of cars represented by the two bars to the right of 25 in the histogram: $20 + 6 = 26$ cars. Now find the total number of available cars: $8 + 16 + 20 + 6 = 50$. Finally, divide to find the indicated probability: $\frac{26}{50} = 0.52$.

34. 21   Difficulty: Medium

Category: Additional Topics in Math / Geometry

Getting to the Answer: Use the formula for finding the volume of a rectangular solid, $V = lwh$, to write an equation. Because the dimensions are given as the ratio 3:5:2, let the length, width, and height be represented by $3x$, $5x$, and $2x$. Substitute the expressions into the formula and solve for x:

$$10,290 = (3x)(5x)(2x)$$

$$10,290 = 30x^3$$

$$343 = x^3$$

$$7 = x$$

The length was represented by $3x$, so multiply to find that the length is $3(7) = 21$ feet.

35. 8   Difficulty: Medium

Category: Problem Solving and Data Analysis / Scatterplots

Getting to the Answer: Draw the line of best fit so that approximately half the data points fall above the line and half fall below it:

Regional Manager Job Performance

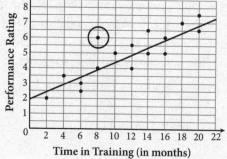

Look for the point that is farthest from the line you drew, which is (8, 6). Because time is plotted along the horizontal axis, this point represents a manager who spent 8 months in the training program.

36. 37   Difficulty: Hard

Category: Passport to Advanced Math / Exponents

Getting to the Answer: Although this question is in the calculator portion of the test, you get an overflow error if you try to use your calculator. This is because the numbers are simply too large. You'll need to rely on the rules of exponents to answer this question. When a power is raised to a power, multiply the exponents. You want to be able to add the exponents later, so the bases need to be the same, and you'll need to recognize that 32 is the same as 2 raised to the 5th power.

$$\left(2^{32}\right)^{\left(2^{32}\right)}$$
$$= 2^{\left(32 \times 2^{32}\right)}$$
$$= 2^{\left(2^5 \times 2^{32}\right)}$$

Now that the two bases in the exponent are the same, you can add their exponents.

$$= 2^{\left(2^{5+32}\right)}$$
$$= 2^{\left(2^{37}\right)}$$

Therefore, $x = 37$.

37. 33   Difficulty: Medium

Category: Problem Solving and Data Analysis / Rates, Ratios, Proportions, and Percentages

Getting to the Answer: Questions that involve distance, rate, and time can almost always be solved using the formula Distance = rate × time. Use the speed, or rate, of the first car (64 mph) and its distance from the destination (144 mi) to determine how long it traveled. You don't know the time, so call it t.

$$\text{Distance} = \text{rate} \times \text{time}$$
$$144 = 64t$$
$$2.25 = t$$

This means it took 2.25 hours for the first car to arrive. You need the number of minutes, so multiply 2.25 by 60 to get $60 \times 2.25 = 135$ minutes. Now determine how long it took the second car. It started its drive at 2:18 PM and arrived at 4:00 PM, so it took 1 hour and 42 minutes, or 102 minutes. This means that the first car had been traveling for $135 - 102 = 33$ minutes before the second car started its drive.

38. 220   Difficulty: Hard

Category: Problem Solving and Data Analysis / Rates, Ratios, Proportions, and Percentages

Getting to the Answer: To get started, you'll need to find the distance for each part of the third car's trip—the question only tells you the total distance (25 miles). Then, use the formula Distance = rate × time to find how long the car traveled at 15 mph and then how long it traveled at 30 mph.

First part of trip: (60% of the drive)

$$0.6 \times 25\,\text{mi} = 15\,\text{mi}$$
$$15 = 15t$$
$$1 = t$$

So the first part of the trip took 1 hour. Then the car did not move for 20 minutes due to the accident.

Last part of trip: (40% of the drive remained)

$$0.4 \times 25\,\text{mi} = 10\,\text{mi}$$
$$10 = 30t$$
$$\frac{10}{30} = t$$
$$t = \frac{1}{3}$$

So the last part of the trip took one-third of an hour, or 20 minutes. This means it took the third car a total of 1 hour and 40 minutes to arrive at the destination. Because the car arrived at 4:00 PM, it must have left at 2:20 PM. Enter the answer as 220.

ESSAY TEST RUBRIC

The Essay Demonstrates ...

4—Advanced	• **(Reading)** A strong ability to comprehend the source text, including its central ideas and important details and how they interrelate; and effectively use evidence (quotations, paraphrases, or both) from the source text. • **(Analysis)** A strong ability to evaluate the author's use of evidence, reasoning, and/or stylistic and persuasive elements, and/or other features of the student's own choosing; make good use of relevant, sufficient, and strategically chosen support for the claims or points made in the student's essay; and focus consistently on features of the source text that are most relevant to addressing the task. • **(Writing)** A strong ability to provide a precise central claim; create an effective organization that includes an introduction and conclusion, as well as a clear progression of ideas; successfully employ a variety of sentence structures; use precise word choice; maintain a formal style and objective tone; and show command of the conventions of standard written English so that the essay is free of errors.
3—Proficient	• **(Reading)** Satisfactory ability to comprehend the source text, including its central ideas and important details and how they interrelate; and use evidence (quotations, paraphrases, or both) from the source text. • **(Analysis)** Satisfactory ability to evaluate the author's use of evidence, reasoning, and/or stylistic and persuasive elements, and/or other features of the student's own choosing; make use of relevant and sufficient support for the claims or points made in the student's essay; and focus primarily on features of the source text that are most relevant to addressing the task. • **(Writing)** Satisfactory ability to provide a central claim; create an organization that includes an introduction and conclusion, as well as a clear progression of ideas; employ a variety of sentence structures; use precise word choice; maintain an appropriate formal style and objective tone; and show control of the conventions of standard written English so that the essay is free of significant errors.
2—Partial	• **(Reading)** Limited ability to comprehend the source text, including its central ideas and important details and how they interrelate; and use evidence (quotations, paraphrases, or both) from the source text. • **(Analysis)** Limited ability to evaluate the author's use of evidence, reasoning, and/or stylistic and persuasive elements, and/or other features of the student's own choosing; make use of support for the claims or points made in the student's essay; and focus on relevant features of the source text. • **(Writing)** Limited ability to provide a central claim; create an effective organization for ideas; employ a variety of sentence structures; use precise word choice; maintain an appropriate style and tone; or show control of the conventions of standard written English, resulting in certain errors that detract from the quality of the writing.

1—Inadequate	• **(Reading)** Little or no ability to comprehend the source text or use evidence from the source text.
	• **(Analysis)** Little or no ability to evaluate the author's use of evidence, reasoning, and/or stylistic and persuasive elements; choose support for claims or points; or focus on relevant features of the source text.
	• **(Writing)** Little or no ability to provide a central claim, organization, or progression of ideas; employ a variety of sentence structures; use precise word choice; maintain an appropriate style and tone; or show control of the conventions of standard written English, resulting in numerous errors that undermine the quality of the writing.

ESSAY RESPONSE #1 (ADVANCED SCORE)

When William Faulkner made his Nobel Prize Acceptance Speech in 1950, he was speaking at the height of the Cold War. The memory of the devastation of the atomic bombs dropped on Japan was still fresh in people's minds, and it's clear from Faulkner's speech that people were afraid more destruction was to come. Faulkner felt strongly that in order for mankind to prevail, writers must write from the heart, rather than writing from fear. In this speech, he uses several techniques to persuade his audience of his claim: he establishes his authority, uses vivid language and imagery, and appeals to his audience's sense of duty.

At the ceremony, Faulkner was speaking from a position of strength and expertise, having just been awarded the Nobel Prize for Literature. In a subtle way, he reminds his audience of this expertise throughout the speech, lending credibility to his claims. In the first paragraph, he redefines the award as an honor for his life's work in mining the human spirit to create great literature. He then reminds the audience of his position as an elder statesman by directing his speech to the "young men and women" who are also engaged in this great work, and goes on to tell them what they must "learn" and "teach themselves" about life and writing. By framing the speech as a lesson for younger writers based on his career-long exploration of the human spirit, Faulkner establishes his authority and commands respect for his ideas.

Faulkner also uses vivid language and imagery to create a vision of a higher purpose to which he would like his audience to aspire. In paragraphs 2 and 3, he paints a picture of the writer as an artist involved in a great struggle, which he characterizes with words like "agony" and "sweat." According to Faulkner, a writer will never succeed if he avoids universal truths, and until the writer realizes this, "he labors under a curse." To Faulkner, a writer who writes from a place of fear instead of compassion creates meaningless work that touches upon "no universal bones, leaving no scars." On the other hand, a writer who writes with pity and compassion lifts the reader's heart and reminds him of his "immortal" nature. This type of vivid language, which is clearly written from Faulkner's heart, helps to support his argument that writing from the heart is the way to create great literature that inspires mankind to prevail.

Finally, in speaking to his audience of younger writers, he calls upon their sense of duty. It's clear earlier in the speech that Faulkner is concerned that younger writers are being defeated by fear, and are failing to explore the rich material of the human heart. He asserts that rather than writing about defeat, they should elevate humans by reminding them of their great capacity for courage, compassion, sacrifice, and other noble qualities. These characteristics are unique to humans and are the "glory" of their past, which Faulkner exhorts them to carry into the future. In the final line, Faulkner calls upon writers to be more than just record-keepers—rather, they should actively inspire humankind to prevail.

In a time of great fear, William Faulkner used his Nobel Prize acceptance speech to express his belief that writers must write from the heart in order to ensure the success of mankind. To convince his audience that they should accept his claim, he first establishes his authority, then uses vivid language and imagery to illustrate the value of writing from the heart, and finally calls upon his audience's sense of duty to elevate the human race. Through skillful use of these features, he constructs a persuasive argument.

ESSAY RESPONSE #2 (PROFICIENT SCORE)

William Faulkner believed that authors must write from their hearts to make sure that humans prevail on Earth. In his Nobel Prize Acceptance Speech, Faulkner uses his expertise, vivid language, and calls to his audience's sense of responsibility to make his case.

In this speech, Faulkner speaks as both a writer and a teacher. He acknowledges that young writers are listening to him; and he has lessons to give to them. Since he just won the Nobel Prize his listeners believe him to be an expert and this makes them more willing to accept his message. He tells his young listeners that they have lost their way, and they must relearn the "problems of the human heart," which are what make good writing. Faulkner tells his listeners that being afraid is the lowest of human feelings, and they need to put their fears aside and instead explore the higher truths of the human heart. Faulkner knows that his young audience is looking up to him, and so he uses his position of authority to guide them to strive for something greater than their fear.

Faulkner also uses vivid language to enhance his argument. Twice he uses the phrase "agony and sweat" to describe the struggle of the writer who writes from the heart. This type of vivid language makes the writer's struggle seem like a goal worth fighting for. Faulkner describes writing that avoids the problems of the human heart as having no "bones" or "scars." By using words that evoke the human body, Faulkner implies that this type of writing has no weight or depth. Faulkner uses very vivid language to paint a picture of a world after a nuclear apacalypse, which is what his audience fears. In this picture, the evening is "red and dying," the rocks are "worthless" and man's voice is "puny" but still talking. Faulkner then tells his audience he refuses to accept this bleak image—that man will do more than just exist, he will prevail. By using vivid language to describe the defeatist view of mankind, Faulkner makes his audience feel revulsion at this image, and makes the alternative seem much more appealing.

Faulkner wanted writers to write about courage, hope, love, compassion, and pity because these things uplift the human spirit. Faulkner calls upon his listeners' sense of responsibility by telling them that they have a duty to write about these subjects. His implication is that if they don't, mankind will fall back into the bleakness he described previously. He also says that the writer has a responsibility to be a "pillar" holding up mankind. By making his audience feel that they have a responsibility to help mankind, Faulkner strengthens his position.

In this speech, Faulkner makes an effective argument that writers must write from the heart to save mankind and help it prevail. To strengthen his argument, he uses the features of expertise, vivid language, and calls to responsibility.

SAT PRACTICE TEST 7 ANSWER SHEET

Remove (or photocopy) this answer sheet and use it to complete the test. See the answer key following the test when finished.

Start with number 1 for each section. If a section has fewer questions than answer spaces, leave the extra spaces blank.

SECTION 1

1. Ⓐ Ⓑ Ⓒ Ⓓ	14. Ⓐ Ⓑ Ⓒ Ⓓ	27. Ⓐ Ⓑ Ⓒ Ⓓ	40. Ⓐ Ⓑ Ⓒ Ⓓ
2. Ⓐ Ⓑ Ⓒ Ⓓ	15. Ⓐ Ⓑ Ⓒ Ⓓ	28. Ⓐ Ⓑ Ⓒ Ⓓ	41. Ⓐ Ⓑ Ⓒ Ⓓ
3. Ⓐ Ⓑ Ⓒ Ⓓ	16. Ⓐ Ⓑ Ⓒ Ⓓ	29. Ⓐ Ⓑ Ⓒ Ⓓ	42. Ⓐ Ⓑ Ⓒ Ⓓ
4. Ⓐ Ⓑ Ⓒ Ⓓ	17. Ⓐ Ⓑ Ⓒ Ⓓ	30. Ⓐ Ⓑ Ⓒ Ⓓ	43. Ⓐ Ⓑ Ⓒ Ⓓ
5. Ⓐ Ⓑ Ⓒ Ⓓ	18. Ⓐ Ⓑ Ⓒ Ⓓ	31. Ⓐ Ⓑ Ⓒ Ⓓ	44. Ⓐ Ⓑ Ⓒ Ⓓ
6. Ⓐ Ⓑ Ⓒ Ⓓ	19. Ⓐ Ⓑ Ⓒ Ⓓ	32. Ⓐ Ⓑ Ⓒ Ⓓ	45. Ⓐ Ⓑ Ⓒ Ⓓ
7. Ⓐ Ⓑ Ⓒ Ⓓ	20. Ⓐ Ⓑ Ⓒ Ⓓ	33. Ⓐ Ⓑ Ⓒ Ⓓ	46. Ⓐ Ⓑ Ⓒ Ⓓ
8. Ⓐ Ⓑ Ⓒ Ⓓ	21. Ⓐ Ⓑ Ⓒ Ⓓ	34. Ⓐ Ⓑ Ⓒ Ⓓ	47. Ⓐ Ⓑ Ⓒ Ⓓ
9. Ⓐ Ⓑ Ⓒ Ⓓ	22. Ⓐ Ⓑ Ⓒ Ⓓ	35. Ⓐ Ⓑ Ⓒ Ⓓ	48. Ⓐ Ⓑ Ⓒ Ⓓ
10. Ⓐ Ⓑ Ⓒ Ⓓ	23. Ⓐ Ⓑ Ⓒ Ⓓ	36. Ⓐ Ⓑ Ⓒ Ⓓ	49. Ⓐ Ⓑ Ⓒ Ⓓ
11. Ⓐ Ⓑ Ⓒ Ⓓ	24. Ⓐ Ⓑ Ⓒ Ⓓ	37. Ⓐ Ⓑ Ⓒ Ⓓ	50. Ⓐ Ⓑ Ⓒ Ⓓ
12. Ⓐ Ⓑ Ⓒ Ⓓ	25. Ⓐ Ⓑ Ⓒ Ⓓ	38. Ⓐ Ⓑ Ⓒ Ⓓ	51. Ⓐ Ⓑ Ⓒ Ⓓ
13. Ⓐ Ⓑ Ⓒ Ⓓ	26. Ⓐ Ⓑ Ⓒ Ⓓ	39. Ⓐ Ⓑ Ⓒ Ⓓ	52. Ⓐ Ⓑ Ⓒ Ⓓ

☐ # correct in Section 1

☐ # incorrect in Section 1

SECTION 2

1. Ⓐ Ⓑ Ⓒ Ⓓ	12. Ⓐ Ⓑ Ⓒ Ⓓ	23. Ⓐ Ⓑ Ⓒ Ⓓ	34. Ⓐ Ⓑ Ⓒ Ⓓ
2. Ⓐ Ⓑ Ⓒ Ⓓ	13. Ⓐ Ⓑ Ⓒ Ⓓ	24. Ⓐ Ⓑ Ⓒ Ⓓ	35. Ⓐ Ⓑ Ⓒ Ⓓ
3. Ⓐ Ⓑ Ⓒ Ⓓ	14. Ⓐ Ⓑ Ⓒ Ⓓ	25. Ⓐ Ⓑ Ⓒ Ⓓ	36. Ⓐ Ⓑ Ⓒ Ⓓ
4. Ⓐ Ⓑ Ⓒ Ⓓ	15. Ⓐ Ⓑ Ⓒ Ⓓ	26. Ⓐ Ⓑ Ⓒ Ⓓ	37. Ⓐ Ⓑ Ⓒ Ⓓ
5. Ⓐ Ⓑ Ⓒ Ⓓ	16. Ⓐ Ⓑ Ⓒ Ⓓ	27. Ⓐ Ⓑ Ⓒ Ⓓ	38. Ⓐ Ⓑ Ⓒ Ⓓ
6. Ⓐ Ⓑ Ⓒ Ⓓ	17. Ⓐ Ⓑ Ⓒ Ⓓ	28. Ⓐ Ⓑ Ⓒ Ⓓ	39. Ⓐ Ⓑ Ⓒ Ⓓ
7. Ⓐ Ⓑ Ⓒ Ⓓ	18. Ⓐ Ⓑ Ⓒ Ⓓ	29. Ⓐ Ⓑ Ⓒ Ⓓ	40. Ⓐ Ⓑ Ⓒ Ⓓ
8. Ⓐ Ⓑ Ⓒ Ⓓ	19. Ⓐ Ⓑ Ⓒ Ⓓ	30. Ⓐ Ⓑ Ⓒ Ⓓ	41. Ⓐ Ⓑ Ⓒ Ⓓ
9. Ⓐ Ⓑ Ⓒ Ⓓ	20. Ⓐ Ⓑ Ⓒ Ⓓ	31. Ⓐ Ⓑ Ⓒ Ⓓ	42. Ⓐ Ⓑ Ⓒ Ⓓ
10. Ⓐ Ⓑ Ⓒ Ⓓ	21. Ⓐ Ⓑ Ⓒ Ⓓ	32. Ⓐ Ⓑ Ⓒ Ⓓ	43. Ⓐ Ⓑ Ⓒ Ⓓ
11. Ⓐ Ⓑ Ⓒ Ⓓ	22. Ⓐ Ⓑ Ⓒ Ⓓ	33. Ⓐ Ⓑ Ⓒ Ⓓ	44. Ⓐ Ⓑ Ⓒ Ⓓ

☐ # correct in Section 2

☐ # incorrect in Section 2

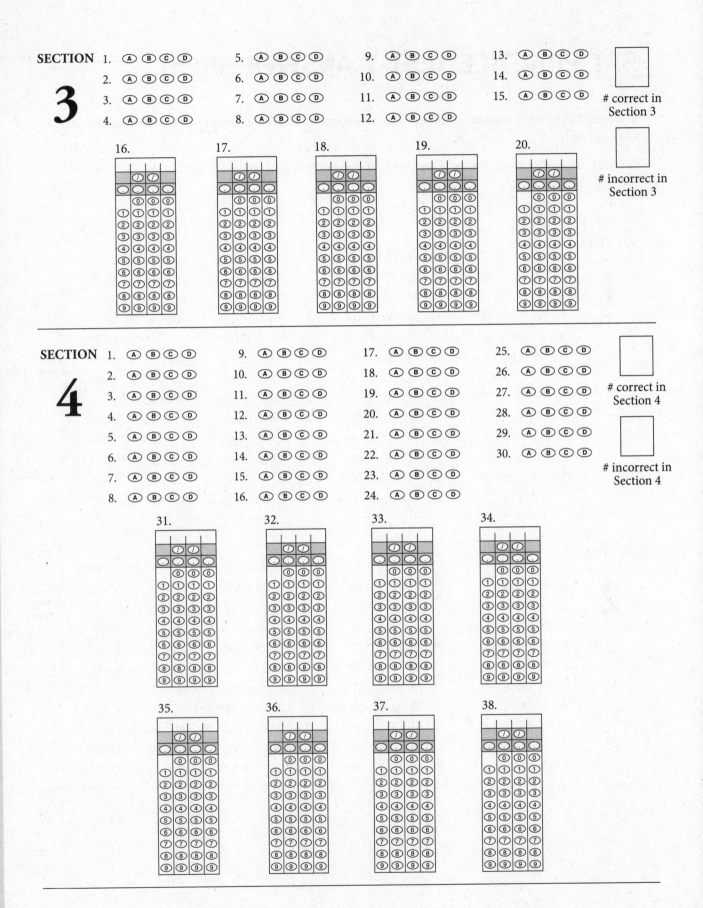

READING TEST

65 Minutes—52 Questions

This section corresponds to Section 1 of your answer sheet.

Directions: Read each passage or pair of passages, then answer the questions that follow. Choose your answers based on what the passage(s) and any accompanying graphics state or imply.

Questions 1-10 are based on the following passage.

The following passage is adapted from Charles Dickens's 1860 novel *Great Expectations*. In this scene, the narrator, a boy named Pip, eats breakfast with his older sister's acquaintance, Mr. Pumblechook. Pumblechook has agreed to take Pip to see Miss Havisham, a wealthy woman who has requested this visit, although Pip has never met her.

Mr. Pumblechook and I breakfasted at eight o'clock in the parlor behind the shop, while the shopman took his mug of tea and hunch of bread and butter
Line on a sack of peas in the front premises. I considered
(5) Mr. Pumblechook wretched company. Besides being possessed by my sister's idea that a mortifying and penitential character ought to be imparted to my diet,[1]—besides giving me as much crumb as possible in combination with as little butter, and putting
(10) such a quantity of warm water into my milk that it would have been more candid to have left the milk out altogether,—his conversation consisted of nothing but arithmetic. On my politely bidding him Good morning, he said, pompously, "Seven times nine,
(15) boy?" And how should I be able to answer, dodged in that way, in a strange place, on an empty stomach! I was hungry, but before I had swallowed a morsel, he began a running sum that lasted all through the breakfast. "Seven?" "And four?" "And eight?" . . . And
(20) so on. And after each figure was disposed of, it was as much as I could do to get a bite or a sup, before the next came; while he sat at his ease guessing nothing, and eating bacon and hot roll, in (if I may be allowed the expression) a gorging and gormandizing manner.

(25) For such reasons, I was very glad when ten o'clock came and we started for Miss Havisham's; though I was not at all at my ease regarding the manner in which I should acquit myself under that lady's roof. Within a quarter of an hour we came to Miss
(30) Havisham's house, which was of old brick, and dismal, and had a great many iron bars to it. Some of the windows had been walled up; of those that remained, all the lower were rustily barred. There was a courtyard in front, and that was barred; so we
(35) had to wait, after ringing the bell, until some one should come to open it. While we waited at the gate, I peeped in (even then Mr. Pumblechook said, "And fourteen?" but I pretended not to hear him), and saw that at the side of the house there was a large
(40) brewery. No brewing was going on in it, and none seemed to have gone on for a long long time.

A window was raised, and a clear voice demanded "What name?" To which my conductor replied, "Pumblechook." The voice returned, "Quite right,"
(45) and the window was shut again, and a young lady came across the courtyard, with keys in her hand.

"This," said Mr. Pumblechook, "is Pip."

"This is Pip, is it?" returned the young lady, who was very pretty and seemed very proud; "come in, Pip."

(50) Mr. Pumblechook was coming in also, when she stopped him with the gate.

"Oh!" she said. "Did you wish to see Miss Havisham?"

"If Miss Havisham wished to see me," returned
(55) Mr. Pumblechook, discomfited.

"Ah!" said the girl; "but you see she don't."

She said it so finally, and in such an

---

[1]Pip's sister indicated to Pumblechook that Pip should be grateful, even penitent (unreasonably so) for his help.

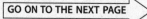
GO ON TO THE NEXT PAGE

undiscussible way, that Mr. Pumblechook,
though in a condition of ruffled dignity, could not
(60) protest. But he eyed me severely,—as if I had done
anything to him!—and departed with the words
reproachfully delivered: "Boy! Let your behavior
here be a credit unto them which brought you up
by hand!"[2] I was not free from apprehension that
(65) he would come back to propound through the gate,
"And sixteen?" But he didn't.

[2]Pumblechook is speaking of Pip's sister, who often boasts that
she raised him "by hand."

1. According to the first paragraph, Pip's breakfast
   with Mr. Pumblechook is

   A) eaten on the run.

   B) small and of poor quality.

   C) better than Pip usually receives.

   D) carefully cooked and served.

2. As used in line 5, "wretched" most nearly means

   A) shameful.

   B) deprived.

   C) distressing.

   D) heartbroken.

3. Based on the passage, it can be inferred that
   Mr. Pumblechook

   A) has looked forward to his morning with Pip.

   B) is as uncomfortable as Pip is during
      breakfast.

   C) has known Pip and his sister for a very
      long time.

   D) is indifferent to Pip's discomfort during
      breakfast.

4. Which choice provides the best support for the
   answer to the previous question?

   A) Lines 1-4 ("Mr. Pumblechook and I . . .
      premises")

   B) Lines 5-13 ("Besides . . . arithmetic")

   C) Lines 43-44 ("To which my . . .
      Pumblechook")

   D) Lines 57-60 ("She said . . . not protest")

5. What theme is communicated through the
   experiences of Pip, the narrator?

   A) The world can be a puzzling and sometimes
      cruel place.

   B) Young people are misunderstood by their
      elders.

   C) Mean-spirited people deserve to be treated
      harshly.

   D) The favors one receives in life should be
      reciprocated.

6. Which word best describes the young lady's
   demeanor when she approaches Pip and Mr.
   Pumblechook?

   A) Rude

   B) Timid

   C) Self-centered

   D) Authoritative

7. Which of the following is true when
   Mr. Pumblechook leaves Pip at Miss Havisham's
   house?

   A) Pip is excited to finally meet Miss
      Havisham.

   B) Pip is nervous about being away from his
      sister for so long.

   C) Pip is relieved to be away from Mr.
      Pumblechook.

   D) Pip is anxious about spending time with the
      young lady who greets them.

8. Which choice provides the best support for the
   answer to the previous question?

   A) Lines 1-4 ("Mr. Pumblechook . . . premises")

   B) Lines 42-43 ("A window . . . name")

   C) Lines 57-60 ("She said it . . . protest")

   D) Lines 64-66 ("I was not . . . he didn't")

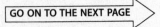
GO ON TO THE NEXT PAGE

9. As used in line 59, "condition" most nearly means

    A) illness.

    B) prerequisite.

    C) state.

    D) limitation.

10. The function of the parenthetical comment in lines 23-24 is to reveal that

    A) Pip is usually more polite in his references to others.

    B) Mr. Pumblechook appreciates gourmet food.

    C) Pip is very angered that his own breakfast is so meager.

    D) Mr. Pumblechook has no qualms about overeating in public.

Questions 11-20 are based on the following passage.

This passage is adapted from Martin Luther King, Jr.'s "Letter from Birmingham Jail."

...I think I should give the reason for my being in Birmingham, since you have been influenced by the argument of "outsiders coming in." I have
Line the honor of serving as president of the Southern
(5) Christian Leadership Conference, an organization operating in every Southern state with headquarters in Atlanta, Georgia. We have some eighty-five affiliate organizations all across the South, one being the Alabama Christian Movement for
(10) Human Rights. Whenever necessary and possible we share staff, educational, and financial resources with our affiliates. Several months ago our local affiliate here in Birmingham invited us to be on call to engage in a nonviolent direct action program if such
(15) were deemed necessary. We readily consented and when the hour came we lived up to our promises. So I am here, along with several members of my staff, because we were invited here. I am here because I have basic organizational ties here. Beyond this, I
(20) am in Birmingham because injustice is here. . . .

Moreover, I am cognizant of the interrelatedness of all communities and states. I cannot sit idly by in Atlanta and not be concerned about what happens in Birmingham. Injustice anywhere is a
(25) threat to justice everywhere. We are caught in an inescapable network of mutuality, tied in a single garment of destiny. Whatever affects one directly affects all indirectly. Never again can we afford to live with the narrow, provincial "outside agitator"
(30) idea. Anyone who lives inside the United States can never be considered an outsider anywhere in this country. . . .

You may well ask, "Why direct action? Why sit-ins, marches, etc.? Isn't negotiation a better path?" You
(35) are exactly right in your call for negotiation. Indeed, this is the purpose of direct action. Nonviolent direct action seeks to create such a crisis and establish such creative tension that a community that has constantly refused to negotiate is forced to confront the issue. It
(40) seeks so to dramatize the issue that it can no longer be ignored. I just referred to the creation of tension as a part of the work of the nonviolent resister. This may sound rather shocking. But I must confess that I am not afraid of the word tension. I have earnestly
(45) worked and preached against violent tension, but there is a type of constructive nonviolent tension that is necessary for growth. Just as Socrates felt that it was necessary to create a tension in the mind so that individuals could rise from the bondage of myths and
(50) half-truths to the unfettered realm of creative analysis and objective appraisal, we must see the need of having nonviolent gadflies to create the kind of tension in society that will help men rise from the dark depths of prejudice and racism to the majestic
(55) heights of understanding and brotherhood. So the purpose of the direct action is to create a situation so crisis-packed that it will inevitably open the door to negotiation. We, therefore, concur with you in your call for negotiation. Too long has our beloved
(60) Southland been bogged down in the tragic attempt to live in monologue rather than dialogue. . . .

GO ON TO THE NEXT PAGE

My friends, I must say to you that we have not made a single gain in civil rights without determined legal and nonviolent pressure.

(65) History is the long and tragic story of the fact that privileged groups seldom give up their privileges voluntarily. Individuals may see the moral light and voluntarily give up their unjust posture; but as Reinhold Niebuhr has reminded us, groups are

(70) more immoral than individuals.

We know through painful experience that freedom is never voluntarily given by the oppressor; it must be demanded by the oppressed. . . . For years now I have heard the word "Wait!" It rings in

(75) the ear of every African American with a piercing familiarity. This "wait" has almost always meant "never." It has been a tranquilizing thalidomide, relieving the emotional stress for a moment, only to give birth to an ill-formed infant of frustra-

(80) tion. We must come to see with the distinguished jurist of yesterday that "justice too long delayed is justice denied." We have waited for more than three hundred and forty years for our constitutional and God-given rights. The nations of Asia and Africa

(85) are moving with jet-like speed toward the goal of political independence, and we still creep at horse and buggy pace toward the gaining of a cup of coffee at a lunch counter. . . .

11. King's purpose for writing this letter is

A) to explain why he came to Birmingham to protest.

B) to launch a nonviolent protest movement in Birmingham.

C) to open an affiliate of the Southern Christian Leadership Conference in Birmingham.

D) to support fellow civil rights activists in Birmingham.

12. Which choice provides the best evidence for the answer to the previous question?

A) Lines 1-2 ("I think . . . in Birmingham")

B) Lines 3-7 ("I have . . . Atlanta, Georgia")

C) Lines 7-10 ("We have some . . . Rights")

D) Lines 24-25 ("Injustice anywhere . . . everywhere")

13. The passage most strongly suggests that which of the following statements is true?

A) King was warmly welcomed when he arrived in Birmingham.

B) King received criticism for his decision to come to Birmingham.

C) King did not want to cause a disruption by coming to Birmingham.

D) King was abandoned by his supporters when he arrived in Birmingham.

14. As used in lines 21-22, "interrelatedness of all communities and states" most nearly means that

A) King has personal connections to people in the town.

B) the Southern Christian Leadership Conference needs national support.

C) events in one part of the country affect everyone in the nation.

D) local civil rights groups operate independently of one another.

15. Based on paragraph 3, it can be reasonably inferred that King believed circumstances in Birmingham at the time

A) were unfair and wrong.

B) constituted an isolated event.

C) justified his arrest.

D) required federal intervention.

GO ON TO THE NEXT PAGE

16. Which choice provides the best evidence for the answer to the previous question?

    A) Lines 21-22 ("Moreover, . . . states")

    B) Lines 24-25 ("Injustice anywhere . . . everywhere")

    C) Lines 25-27 ("We are caught . . . destiny")

    D) Lines 28-30 ("Never again . . . idea")

17. As used in line 40, "dramatize" most nearly means

    A) cast events in an appealing light.

    B) draw attention to significant events.

    C) exaggerate events to seem more important.

    D) turn events into a popular performance.

18. Which choice most clearly paraphrases a claim made by King in paragraph 4?

    A) A failure to negotiate in the South has provoked secret action by civil rights activists.

    B) A focus on dialogue blinds reformers to the necessity for direct action to promote change.

    C) Direct action is necessary to motivate people to talk about prejudice and racism.

    D) Nonviolent protest encourages a sense of brotherhood and understanding among citizens.

19. Paragraph 4 best supports the claims made in paragraph 3 by

    A) arguing that nonviolent pressure is most likely to spur just action by individuals.

    B) clarifying that throughout history, privileged classes have been reluctant to let go of privilege.

    C) drawing a distinction between the morality of individuals and of groups.

    D) pointing out that few gains in civil rights have been made without nonviolent pressure.

20. King refers to "the gaining of a cup of coffee at a lunch counter" (lines 87-88) primarily to

    A) call attention to the sedative effect of delaying civil rights reform in the United States.

    B) emphasize that white Americans will not willingly end oppression against black Americans.

    C) describe the progress made toward the winning of equal rights in other countries.

    D) underscore the contrast between progress made in other countries and the United States.

Questions 21-31 are based on the following passages and supplementary material.

The idea of a World Bank became a reality in 1944, when delegates to the Bretton Woods Conference pledged to "outlaw practices which are agreed to be harmful to world prosperity." Passage 1 discusses the benefits of the World Bank, while Passage 2 focuses on the limited lifespan of the Bretton Woods system.

Passage 1

In 1944, 730 delegates from forty-four Allied nations met in Bretton Woods, New Hampshire, just as World War II was ending. They were attend-
Line ing an important conference. This mostly forgotten
(5) event shaped our modern world because delegates at the Bretton Woods Conference agreed on the establishment of an international banking system.

To ensure that all nations would prosper, the United States and other allied nations set rules
(10) for a postwar international economy. The Bretton Woods system created the International Monetary Fund (IMF). The IMF was founded as a kind of global central bank from which member countries could borrow money. The countries needed money
(15) to pay for their war costs. Today, the IMF facilitates international trade by ensuring the stability of the international monetary and financial system.

The Bretton Woods system also established the World Bank. Although the World Bank shares

GO ON TO THE NEXT PAGE

(20) similarities with the IMF, the two institutions remain distinct. While the IMF maintains an orderly system of payments and receipts between nations, the World Bank is mainly a development institution. The World Bank initially gave loans to European countries dev-
(25) astated by World War II, and today it lends money and technical assistance specifically to economic projects in developing countries. For example, the World Bank might provide a low-interest loan to a country attempting to improve education or
(30) health. The goal of the World Bank is to "bridge the economic divide between poor and rich countries." In short, the organizations differ in their purposes. The Bank promotes economic and social progress so people can live better lives, while the IMF represents
(35) the entire world in its goal to foster global monetary cooperation and financial stability.

These two specific accomplishments of the Bretton Woods Conference were major. However, the Bretton Woods system particularly benefited
(40) the United States. It effectively established the U.S. dollar as a global currency. A global currency is one that countries worldwide accept for all trade, or international transactions of buying and selling. Because only the U.S. could print dollars, the United
(45) States became the primary power behind both the IMF and the World Bank. Today, global currencies include the U.S. dollar, the euro (European Union countries), and the yen (Japan).

The years after Bretton Woods have been
(50) considered the golden age of the U.S. dollar. More importantly, the conference profoundly shaped foreign trade for decades to come.

Passage 2

The financial system established at the 1944 Bretton Woods Conference endured for many years. Even
(55) after the United States abrogated agreements made at the conference, the nation continued to experience a powerful position in international trade by having other countries tie their currencies to the U.S. dollar. The world, however, is changing.
(60) In reality, the Bretton Woods system lasted only three decades. Then, in 1971, President Richard Nixon introduced a new economic policy by ending the convertibility of the dollar to gold. It marked the end of the Bretton Woods international monetary

(65) framework, and the action resulted in worldwide financial crisis. Two cornerstones of Bretton Woods, however, endured: the International Monetary Fund (IMF) and the World Bank.

Since the collapse of the Bretton Woods system,
(70) IMF members have been trading using a flexible exchange system. Namely, countries allow their exchange rates to fluctuate in response to changing conditions. The exchange rate between two currencies, such as the Japanese yen and the U.S.
(75) dollar, for example, specifies how much one currency is worth in terms of the other. An exchange rate of 120 yen to dollars means that 120 yen are worth the same as one dollar.

Even so, the U.S. dollar has remained the most
(80) widely used money for international trade, and having one currency for all trade may be better than using a flexible exchange system.

This seems to be the thinking of a powerful group of countries. The Group of Twenty (G20), which has
(85) called for a new Bretton Woods, consists of governments and leaders from 20 of the world's largest economies including China, the United States, and the European Union. In 2009, for example, the G20 announced plans to create a new global currency
(90) to replace the U.S. dollar's role as the anchor currency. Many believe that China's yuan, quickly climbing the financial ranks, is well on its way to becoming a major world reserve currency.

In fact, an earlier 1988 article in *The Economist*
(95) stated, "30 years from now, Americans, Japanese, Europeans, and people in many other rich countries and some relatively poor ones will probably be paying for their shopping with the same currency."

The article predicted that the world supply of
(100) currency would be set by a new central bank of the IMF. This prediction seems to be coming to fruition since the G20 indicated that a "world currency is in waiting." For an international construct such as the original Bretton Woods to last some 26
(105) years is nothing less than amazing. But move over Bretton Woods; a new world order in finance could be on the fast track.

GO ON TO THE NEXT PAGE ⇨

Top 10 International Currencies						
(Percent Shares of Average Daily Currency Trading)						
	2007		2010		2013	
	Share	*Rank*	*Share*	*Rank*	*Share*	*Rank*
U.S. Dollar (USD)	85.6%	1	84.9%	1	87.0%	1
Euro (EUR)	37.0%	2	39.1%	2	33.4%	2
Japanese Yen (JPY)	17.2%	3	19.0%	3	23.0%	3
UK Pound (GBP)	14.9%	4	12.9%	4	11.8%	4
Australian Dollar (AUD)	6.6%	6	7.6%	5	8.6%	5
Swiss Franc (CHF)	6.8%	5	6.3%	6	5.2%	6
Canadian Dollar (CAD)	4.3%	7	5.3%	7	4.6%	7
Mexican Peso (MXN)	1.3%	12	1.3%	14	2.5%	8
Chinese Yuan (CNY)	0.5%	20	0.9%	17	2.2%	9
New Zealand Dollar	1.9%	11	1.6%	10	2.0%	10

Adapted from Mauldin Economics; Bank for International Settlements,
September 2013 Triennial Central Bank Survey.

21. Based on Passage 1, it can reasonably be inferred that

   A) world leaders recognized the need for markets to function independently.

   B) Bretton Woods increased U.S. economic influence around the world.

   C) the IMF and the World Bank work closely together to ensure prosperity.

   D) the conclusion of World War II had little influence on events at Bretton Woods.

22. Which choice provides the best evidence for the answer to the previous question?

   A) Lines 8-10 ("To ensure . . . economy")

   B) Lines 10-12 ("The Bretton . . . Fund")

   C) Lines 44-46 ("Because only . . . World Bank")

   D) Lines 50-52 ("More importantly . . . to come")

23. As used in line 35, "foster" most nearly means

   A) publicize.

   B) rear.

   C) stabilize.

   D) encourage.

GO ON TO THE NEXT PAGE

24. Which statement best explains the difference between the purposes of the IMF and the World Bank?

    A) The IMF provides money to pay for war costs, while the World Bank offers assistance to rebuild countries recovering from war across the globe.

    B) The IMF encourages stability in the global financial system, while the World Bank promotes economic development in relatively poor nations.

    C) The IMF supports the U.S. dollar in international markets, while the World Bank provides low-interest loans to many nations around the world.

    D) The IMF offers governments advice about participation in global markets, while the World Bank encourages monetary cooperation between nations.

25. Based on the second paragraph in Passage 2, it can be reasonably inferred that

    A) the United States did not support the goals of the IMF and the World Bank.

    B) Bretton Woods was originally intended to last for three decades.

    C) President Nixon acted to reinforce the decisions made at Bretton Woods.

    D) some U.S. policy decisions differed from international consensus over Bretton Woods.

26. Which choice provides the best evidence for the answer to the previous question?

    A) Lines 60-61 ("In reality . . . three decades")

    B) Lines 61-63 ("Then, in 1971 . . . to gold")

    C) Lines 66-68 ("Two cornerstones . . . World Bank")

    D) Lines 69-71 ("Since the collapse . . . exchange system")

27. As used in line 90, "anchor" most nearly means

    A) key.

    B) fastening.

    C) rigid.

    D) supporting.

28. It can reasonably be inferred from both Passage 2 and the graphic that

    A) international markets are increasingly comfortable using the yuan as trade currency.

    B) the United States favors using the yuan as one of the world's reserve currencies.

    C) the G20 wants to replace the yuan and other currencies with a new global currency.

    D) the IMF continues to support the yuan and other currencies in a flexible exchange system.

29. The last paragraph of Passage 2 can be described as

    A) a refutation of opponents' criticisms.

    B) an indication of the author's opinion.

    C) a summary of the author's main points.

    D) an introduction of a contradictory position.

30. Which statement most effectively compares the authors' purposes in both passages?

   A) Passage 1's purpose is to contrast the functions of the IMF and World Bank, while Passage 2's purpose is to outline the benefits of a flexible trade system to the United States.

   B) Passage 1's purpose is to describe the history of international trade in the 20th century, while Passage 2's purpose is to explain why the Bretton Woods system collapsed.

   C) Passage 1's purpose is to describe Bretton Woods' effect on the global economy, while Passage 2's purpose is to suggest that a new currency for global trade may soon be implemented.

   D) Passage 1's purpose is to promote the economic benefits of the IMF and World Bank, while Passage 2's purpose is to encourage the reestablishment of the Bretton Woods system.

31. Both passages support which generalization about the global economy?

   A) U.S. influence on global trade has continued under a flexible exchange system.

   B) The purposes of the International Monetary Fund and the World Bank are indirectly related.

   C) The Group of Twenty represents the financial interests of the world's largest economies.

   D) International institutions such as the IMF continue to influence economic trade and development.

Questions 32-42 are based on the following passage.

This passage is adapted from an article about treating paralysis.

According to a study conducted by the Christopher and Dana Reeve Foundation, more than six million people in the United States suffer from debilitating
Line paralysis. That's close to one person in every fifty
(5) who suffers from a loss of the ability to move or feel in areas of his or her body. Paralysis is often caused by illnesses, such as stroke or multiple sclerosis, or injuries to the spinal cord. Research scientists have made advances in the treatment of paralysis, which
(10) means retraining affected individuals to become as independent as possible. Patients learn how to use wheelchairs and prevent complications that are caused by restricted movement. This retraining is key in maintaining paralytics' quality of life; however, an actual
(15) cure for paralysis has remained elusive—until now.

In 2014, surgeons in Poland collaborated with the University College London's Institute of Neurology to treat a Polish man who was paralyzed from the chest down as a result of a spinal cord in-
(20) jury. The scientists chose this patient for their study because of the countless hours of physical therapy he had undergone with no signs of progress. Twenty-one months after their test subject's initial spinal cord injury, his condition was considered
(25) complete as defined by the American Spinal Injury Association (ASIA)'s Impairment Scale. This meant that he experienced no sensory or motor function in the segments of his spinal cord nearest to his injury.

(30) The doctors used a technique refined during forty years of spinal cord research on rats. They removed one of two of the patient's olfactory bulbs, which are structures found at the top of the human nose. From this structure, samples of olfactory ensheath-
(35) ing cells, responsible for a portion of the sense of smell, were harvested. These cells allow the olfactory system to renew its cells over the course of a human life. It is because of this constant regeneration that scientists chose these particular cells to implant into

GO ON TO THE NEXT PAGE

(40) the patient's spinal cord. After being harvested, the cells were reproduced in a culture. Then, the cells were injected into the patient's spinal cord in 100 mini-injections above and below the location of his injury. Four strips of nerve tissue were then placed

(45) across a small gap in the spinal cord.

After surgery, the patient underwent a tailor-made neurorehabilitation program. In the nineteen months following the operation, not only did the patient experience no adverse effects, but his condi-

(50) tion improved from ASIA's class A to class C. Class C is considered an incomplete spinal cord injury, meaning that motor function is preserved to a certain extent and there is some muscle activity. The patient experienced increased stability in the trunk

(55) of his body, as well as partial recovery of voluntary movements in his lower extremities. As a result, he was able to increase the muscle mass in his thighs and regain sensation in those areas. In late 2014, he took his first steps with the support of only a walker.

(60) These exciting improvements suggest that the nerve grafts doctors placed in the patient's spinal cord bridged the injured area and prompted the regeneration of fibers. This was the first-ever clinical study that showed beneficial effects of cells transplanted into the

(65) spinal cord. The same team of scientists plans to treat ten more patients using this "smell cell" transplant technique. If they have continued success, patients around the world can have both their mobility and their hope restored.

32. The passage is primarily concerned with

A) how various diseases and injuries can cause permanent paralysis.

B) ways in which doctors and therapists work to improve patients' quality of life.

C) one treatment being developed to return mobility to patients suffering paralysis.

D) methods of physical therapy that can help patients with spinal cord injuries.

33. The author includes a description of retraining paralytics in lines 8-13 primarily to

A) describe how people with paralysis cope with everyday tasks.

B) appeal to the reader's sympathies for people with paralysis.

C) show that most research scientists do not believe a cure can be found.

D) help readers appreciate the significance of research that may lead to a cure.

34. Based on the information in the passage, it can be inferred that the author

A) believes more research should be done before patients with paralysis are subjected to the treatment described in the passage.

B) feels that increased mobility will have a positive impact on patients suffering from all levels of paralysis.

C) thinks that more scientists should study paralysis and ways to improve the quality of life for patients with limited mobility.

D) was part of the research team that developed the new method of treating paralysis described in the passage.

35. Which choice provides the best support for the answer to the previous question?

A) Lines 6-8 ("Paralysis is . . . spinal cord")

B) Lines 16-20 ("In 2014 . . . injury")

C) Lines 53-56 ("The patient . . . extremities")

D) Lines 67-69 ("If they . . . restored")

36. As used in line 13, "restricted" most nearly means

A) confidential.

B) dependent.

C) increased.

D) limited.

GO ON TO THE NEXT PAGE

37. In lines 46-47, the author's use of the word "tailor-made" helps reinforce the idea that

    A) the injected cells were from the patient and were therefore well-suited to work in his own body.

    B) spinal cord cells were replaced during the transplant portion of the individualized treatment.

    C) olfactory bulbs were removed from rats and placed in the patient's spinal cord during surgery.

    D) the method used by doctors to locate the damaged area required expertise and precision.

38. It can reasonably be inferred from the passage that

    A) the patient's treatment would have been more successful if scientists had used cells from another area of his body instead of from his olfactory bulbs.

    B) cells from olfactory bulbs will be used to cure diseases that affect areas of the body other than the spinal cord.

    C) the patient who received the experimental treatment using cells from olfactory bulbs would not have regained mobility without this treatment.

    D) soon doctors will be able to treat spinal injuries without time-consuming and demanding physical therapy.

39. Which choice provides the best evidence for the answer to the previous question?

    A) Lines 8-11 ("Research scientists . . . possible")

    B) Lines 20-22 ("The scientists . . . progress")

    C) Lines 31-33 ("They removed . . . nose")

    D) Lines 60-63 ("These exciting . . . fibers")

40. As used in line 30, "refined" most nearly means

    A) advanced.

    B) improved.

    C) experienced.

    D) treated.

41. The success of the patient's treatment was due in large part to

    A) studies done on other patients.

    B) research conducted by other doctors in Poland.

    C) many experiments performed on rats.

    D) multiple attempts on various types of animals.

42. The procedure described in which cells from olfactory bulbs are injected into a damaged area of the spinal cord is most analogous to which of the following?

    A) Replacing a diseased organ in a patient with an organ from a donor who has the same tissue type

    B) Giving a patient with a high fever an injection of medication to bring the core body temperature down

    C) Placing a cast on a limb to hold the bone in place to encourage healing after suffering a break

    D) Grafting skin from a healthy area of the body and transplanting it to an area that has suffered severe burns

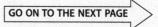

GO ON TO THE NEXT PAGE

Questions 43-52 are based on the following passage and supplementary material.

The following passage is adapted from an essay about mercury in fish.

Mercury is an unusual element; it is a metal but is liquid at room temperature. It is also a neuro-toxin and a teratogen, as it causes nerve damage
Line and birth defects. Mercury can be found just about
(5) everywhere; it is in soil, in air, in household items, and even in our food. Everyday objects, such as thermometers, light switches, and fluorescent light-bulbs, contain mercury in its elemental form. Bat-teries can also contain mercury, but they contain
(10) it in the form of the inorganic compound mercury chloride. Mercury can also exist as an organic compound, the most common of which is methyl-mercury. While we can take steps to avoid both elemental and inorganic mercury, it is much harder
(15) to avoid methylmercury.

Most of the mercury in the environment comes from the emissions of coal-burning power plants; coal contains small amounts of mercury, which are released into the air when coal burns. The concen-
(20) tration of mercury in the air from power plants is very low, so it is not immediately dangerous. However, the mercury is then washed out of the air by rain-storms and eventually ends up in lakes and oceans.

The mercury deposited in the water does not in-
(25) stantaneously get absorbed by fish, as elemental mer-cury does not easily diffuse through cell membranes. However, methylmercury diffuses into cells easily, and certain anaerobic bacteria in the water convert the elemental mercury to methylmercury as a by-
(30) product of their metabolic processes. Methylmer-cury released into the water by the bacteria diffuses into small single-celled organisms called plankton. Small shrimp and other small animals eat the plank-ton and absorb the methylmercury in the plankton
(35) during digestion. Small fish eat the shrimp and then larger fish eat the smaller fish; each time an animal preys on another animal, the predator absorbs the

methylmercury. Because each animal excretes the methylmercury much more slowly than it absorbs
(40) it, methylmercury builds up in the animal over time and is passed on to whatever animal eats it, resulting in a process called bioaccumulation.

As people became aware of the bioaccumulation of mercury in fish, many reacted by eliminating
(45) seafood from their diet. However, seafood contains certain omega-3 fatty acids that are important for good health. People who do not eat enough of these fatty acids, especially eicosapentaenoic acid (EPA) and docosahexaenoic acid (DHA), are more likely
(50) to have heart attacks than people who have enough EPA and DHA in their diet. Because fish and shell-fish, along with some algae, are the only sources of these fatty acids, eliminating them from our diet might have worse health effects than consuming
(55) small amounts of mercury.

Scientists have studied the effects of mercury by conducting tests on animals and by studying vari-ous human populations and recording the amount of mercury in their blood. By determining the lev-
(60) els of mercury consumption that cause any of the known symptoms of mercury poisoning, they were able to identify a safe level of mercury consump-tion. The current recommendation is for humans to take in less than 0.1 microgram of mercury for
(65) every kilogram of weight per day. This means that a 70-kilogram person (about 155 pounds) could safely consume 7 micrograms of mercury per day. Because haddock averages about 0.055 micrograms of mercury per gram, that person could safely eat
(70) 127 grams (about 4.5 ounces) of haddock per day. On the other hand, swordfish averages about 0.995 micrograms of mercury per gram of fish, so the 70-kilogram person could safely eat only about 7 grams (about one-quarter of an ounce) of swordfish
(75) per day.

Nutritionists recommend that, rather than eliminate fish from our diet, we try to eat more of the low-mercury fish and less of the high-mercury fish. Low-mercury species tend to be smaller
(80) omnivorous fish while high-mercury species tend

GO ON TO THE NEXT PAGE →

to be the largest carnivorous fish. Awareness of the particulars of this problem, accompanied by mindful eating habits, will keep us on the best course for healthy eating.

Species	Average Weight Range (grams)	Average Mercury Concentration (parts per billion)
Alaskan Pollock	227–1,000	31
Atlantic Haddock	900–1,800	55
Atlantic Herring	100–600	84
Chub Mackerel	100–750	88
Cod	800–4,000	111
Skipjack Tuna	2,000–10,000	144
Black-Striped Bass	6,820–15,900	152
Albacore Tuna	4,540–21,364	358
Marlin	180,000	485

43. The author of the passage would most likely agree with which of the following statements?

A) Mercury poisoning is only one of many concerns that should be considered when choosing which fish to add to one's diet.

B) More should be done by scientists and nutritionists to inform people about the dangers of mercury poisoning.

C) Fish is an essential part of a healthy diet and can be eaten safely if recommendations for mercury consumption are kept in mind.

D) The mercury present in the air is more dangerous to people than the mercury consumed by eating fish with high mercury levels.

44. Which choice provides the best evidence for the answer to the previous question?

A) Lines 16-17 ("Most of . . . plants")

B) Lines 30-32 ("Methylmercury released . . . plankton")

C) Lines 56-59 ("Scientists . . . their blood")

D) Lines 81-84 ("Awareness . . . eating")

45. In addition to the levels of mercury in a specific species of fish, people should also consider which of the following when determining a safe level of consumption?

A) Their own body weight

B) Where the fish was caught

C) The other meats they are eating

D) What they ate the day before

46. As used in lines 19-20, "concentration" most nearly means

A) focus.

B) application.

C) density.

D) awareness.

47. The passage most strongly suggests which of the following statements is accurate?

A) It is not possible to completely avoid environmental exposure to mercury.

B) Inorganic mercury is more dangerous to humans than organic mercury.

C) Most of the exposure to mercury experienced by humans comes from fish consumption.

D) Mercury is one of the most abundant elements found in nature.

GO ON TO THE NEXT PAGE

48. Which choice provides the best evidence for the answer to the previous question?

    A) Lines 1-2 ("Mercury is an unusual . . . temperature")

    B) Lines 4-6 ("Mercury . . . our food")

    C) Lines 19-21 ("The concentration . . . dangerous")

    D) Lines 27-30 ("However, methylmercury . . . processes")

49. The main purpose of paragraph 3 is to explain

    A) the reasons why mercury deposited in water is not harmful to fish.

    B) the relationships between predators and prey in aquatic animals.

    C) how the largest fish accumulate the greatest amounts of mercury.

    D) the difference between methylmercury and other types of mercury.

50. Which of the following pieces of evidence would most strengthen the author's line of reasoning?

    A) More examples in paragraph 1 of places mercury is found

    B) Details in paragraph 2 about the levels of mercury found in the air

    C) An explanation in paragraph 4 of how to treat mercury poisoning

    D) More examples in paragraph 5 of how many micrograms of mercury people of different weights could eat

51. As used in line 82, "particulars" most nearly means

    A) data.

    B) specifics.

    C) points.

    D) evidence.

52. Based on the information in the passage and the graphic, which of the following statements is true?

    A) The fish with the lowest average weight is the safest to eat.

    B) A person can safely eat more marlin than albacore tuna in one day.

    C) Eating large fish carries a lower risk of mercury poisoning than eating small fish.

    D) A person can safely eat more Alaskan pollock than black striped bass in one day.

WRITING AND LANGUAGE TEST

35 Minutes—44 Questions

This section corresponds to Section 2 of your answer sheet.

Directions: Each passage in this section is followed by several questions. Some questions will reference an underlined portion in the passage; others will ask you to consider a part of a passage or the passage as a whole. For each question, choose the answer that reflects the best use of grammar, punctuation, and style. If a passage or question is accompanied by a graphic, take the graphic into account in choosing your response(s). Some questions will have "NO CHANGE" as a possible response. Choose that answer if you think the best choice is to leave the sentence as written.

Questions 1-11 are based on the following passage and supplementary material.

The UN: Promoting World Peace

The United Nations (UN) is perhaps the most important political contribution of the 20th century. Some may argue that the work of the UN **1** ; an international peacekeeping organization—has proven futile, given persisting global conflict. But the UN's worldwide influence demands a closer look. This organization's global impact is undeniable. The UN is a strong political organization determined to create opportunities for its member nations to enjoy a peaceful and productive world. **2**

1. A) NO CHANGE
    B) —an international peacekeeping organization;
    C) —an international peacekeeping organization—
    D) ; an international peacekeeping organization,

2. Which choice would most clearly end the paragraph with a restatement of the author's claim?
    A) The UN is an organization dedicated to advancing social and political justice around the world.
    B) Those who argue otherwise are not well educated about geopolitical issues in the 20th century or today.
    C) The UN has had its share of corruption over the years, but it has a well-earned reputation of effectively settling international disputes.
    D) A better understanding of the UN suggests that the UN enables far greater peace in today's world than could have been possible otherwise.

GO ON TO THE NEXT PAGE ⟶

3 Decades ago, provoked by the events of World Wars I and II, world leaders began imagining a politically neutral force for international peace. The UN was born in 1945 with 51 participating nations. It was to be a collective political authority for global peace and security. Today, 193 nations are UN members. **4** In keeping with the original hope, the UN still strives toward peaceful international relations.

Understandably, no single organization can perfectly solve the world's countless, complex problems. But the UN has offered consistent relief for many of the past half-century's most difficult disasters and conflicts. It also provides a safe space for international conversation. Moreover, it advocates for issues such as justice, trade, hunger relief, human rights, health, and gender **5** equality, the UN also coordinates care for those displaced by disaster and conflict, **6** dictates environmental protection, and works toward conflict reconciliation.

3. A) NO CHANGE
    B) Recently,
    C) Consequently,
    D) In other words,

4. A) NO CHANGE
    B) In having kept with the original hope, the UN still strives toward peaceful international relations.
    C) In keeping with the original hope, the UN still strived toward peaceful international relations.
    D) In keeping with the original hope, the UN still strove toward peaceful international relations.

5. A) NO CHANGE
    B) equality. The UN
    C) equality: the UN
    D) equality, The UN

6. A) NO CHANGE
    B) prefers
    C) promotes
    D) celebrates

GO ON TO THE NEXT PAGE

[7] The UN's budget, goals, and personnel count have significantly expanded to meet more needs. **[8]** The year 2014 witnessed the UN peacekeeping force grow to over 100,000 strong. These uniformed, volunteer, civilian personnel represent 128 nations. The UN's budget has also grown over the years to support an international court system, as well as countless agencies, committees, and centers addressing sociopolitical topics. Today's UN does big things, and it functions with remarkable organization and efficiency. Critics highlight shortcomings to discount the UN's effectiveness. But considering the countless disasters to which the UN has responded over its six decades of existence, today's world might enjoy **[9]** far less peace, freedom, and safety without the UN.

7. Which choice provides the most logical introduction to the paragraph?

A) NO CHANGE

B) The UN has developed over the years, but critics charge it has met with limited success.

C) The responsibilities of the UN have expanded in recent years in response to challenging events.

D) The UN has maintained a quiet but effective voice on the world stage in spite of criticism.

8. Which choice best completes the sentence with accurate data based on the graphic?

A) NO CHANGE

B) The year 2010 led to an increase of approximately 100,000 in the UN peacekeeping force.

C) The year 2010 saw the UN peacekeeping force grow to approximately 100,000 strong.

D) The year 2010 saw the UN peacekeeping force decrease to just over 100,000 strong.

9. A) NO CHANGE

B) considerably less peace, less freedom, and less safety

C) much less peace, less freedom, and less safety

D) significantly less peace and freedom, and less safety

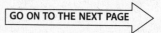 GO ON TO THE NEXT PAGE

[1] From promoting overarching sociopolitical change to offering food and care for displaced groups, the UN serves to protect human rights. [2] Equally **10** quotable are its initiatives to foster international collaboration, justice, and peace. [3] The UN provided aid to the Philippines after the disastrous 2013 typhoon. [4] Certainly, this work is not finished. [5] But no other organization compares with the work and influence of the UN. [6] This brave endeavor to insist on and strive for peace, whatever the obstacles, has indeed united hundreds of once-divided nations. [7] Today, with eleven Nobel Peace Prizes to its name, the UN is undoubtedly an irreplaceable and profoundly successful force for peace. **11**

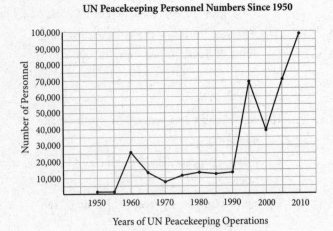

UN Peacekeeping Personnel Numbers Since 1950

Years of UN Peacekeeping Operations

10. A) NO CHANGE
    B) luminous
    C) noteworthy
    D) repeatable

11. Which sentence should be removed to improve the focus of the concluding paragraph?

    A) Sentence 1
    B) Sentence 3
    C) Sentence 5
    D) Sentence 6

GO ON TO THE NEXT PAGE

Questions 12-22 are based on the following passage.

DNA Analysis in a Day

Jane Saunders, a forensic DNA specialist, arrives at work and finds a request waiting for her: She needs to determine if the DNA of a fingernail with a few skin cells on it **12** match any records in the criminal database.

"Human DNA is a long, double-stranded **13** molecule; each strand consists of a complementary set of nucleotides," she explains. "DNA has four nucleotides: **14** adenine (A), thymine (T), guanine (G), and, cytosine (C). On each strand is a sequence of nucleotides that 'match,' or pair up with the nucleotides on the other, or complementary, strand. **15** On the other hand, when there is an adenine on one strand, there is a thymine on the complementary strand, and where there is guanine on one strand, there is cytosine on the complementary strand."

She begins by **16** moving the DNA from the rest of the sample, transferring it to a **17** reaction tube. She adds a solution of primers, DNA polymerase, and nucleotides. Her goal is to separate the two strands of the DNA molecules and then make complementary copies of each strand.

12. A) NO CHANGE
    B) matches
    C) has matched
    D) will be matching

13. A) NO CHANGE
    B) molecule, each strand consists
    C) molecule each strand consists
    D) molecule but each strand consists

14. A) NO CHANGE
    B) adenine (A), thymine (T), guanine (G), and cytosine (C).
    C) adenine (A), thymine (T) guanine (G) and cytosine (C).
    D) adenine (A) thymine (T), guanine (G) and cytosine (C).

15. A) NO CHANGE
    B) Specifically,
    C) However,
    D) Similarly,

16. A) NO CHANGE
    B) reviewing
    C) changing
    D) detaching

17. Which choice most effectively combines the sentences at the underlined portion?
    A) reaction tube since she adds
    B) reaction tube, however, she adds
    C) reaction tube, and adding
    D) reaction tube, she adds

[18] <u>The process of testing the DNA includes several steps and many changes in temperature.</u> After mixing the primers, DNA polymerase, and nucleotides with the evidence DNA, Saunders closes the reaction tube and puts it in a thermocycler. It is programmed to raise the temperature to 94°C to separate the double strands into single strands, and then lower the temperature to 59°C to attach the primers to the single strands. Finally, it raises the temperature to 72°C for the DNA polymerase to build the complementary strands. The thermocycler holds each temperature for one minute and repeats the cycle of three temperatures for at least 30 cycles. At the end of each cycle, the number of DNA segments containing the sequence marked by the primers doubles. If the original sample contains only 100 DNA strands, [19] <u>the absolute final sample</u> will have billions of segments.

18. Which sentence most effectively establishes the central idea?

A) NO CHANGE

B) The object of testing the DNA is to recreate many strands of the DNA in question.

C) Saunders uses a variety of machines in order to analyze the DNA.

D) Saunders would be unable to identify the DNA without the thermocycler.

19. A) NO CHANGE

B) absolutely the final sample

C) the final sample

D) the most final sample

[1] After a short lunch break, Saunders needs to separate and identify the copied DNA segments. [2] She had used primers that bind to 13 specific sites in human DNA called short tandem repeats, or STRs. [3] The 13 STRs are segments of four nucleotides that repeat, such as GATAGATAGATA. [4] "Now here's where the real magic happens!" Saunders says excitedly. [5] "Most DNA is identical for all humans. [6] But STRs vary greatly. [7] The chances of any two humans—other than identical twins—having the same set of 13 STRs is less than one in one trillion." **20**

Saunders knows that the detectives will be **21** prepared to hear her findings, so she sits down at her desk to compare her results with the criminal database in the hopes of finding a match. **22** Is it possible that too much time is spent identifying DNA in cases that are relatively easy to solve?

20. Where should sentence 1 be placed to make the paragraph feel cohesive?

A) Where it is now

B) After sentence 2

C) After sentence 3

D) After sentence 4

21. A) NO CHANGE

B) eager

C) impatient

D) conditioned

22. At this point, the writer wants to add a conclusion that best reflects Jane's feelings conveyed in the passage. Which choice accomplishes that?

A) NO CHANGE

B) It takes a good deal of work and expense to identify DNA in the world of modern forensics.

C) She takes pride in the fact that her scientific expertise plays such a key role in bringing criminals to justice.

D) She marvels at how far science has come in DNA analysis.

GO ON TO THE NEXT PAGE

Questions 23-33 are based on the following passage.

Will Your Start-Up Succeed?

According to research from Harvard Business School, the majority of small businesses ²³ fail in fact the success rate for a first-time company owner is a meager 18 percent. With odds so dismal, why would anyone become a business entrepreneur?

²⁴ Many people desire the freedom of being their own boss, but to be successful, an entrepreneur must also be productive, persistent, and creative. Veteran entrepreneurs achieve a higher 30 percent success rate, so the most predictive factor for success appears to be the number of innovations that a person has "pushed out." More specifically, the people who succeed at building a robust start-up are the ones who have previously tried. Finally, many entrepreneurs ²⁵ grab the idea for their business by solving practical problems, and it's more than luck; 320 new entrepreneurs out of 100,000 *do* succeed by starting a company at the right time in the right industry.

23. A) NO CHANGE
    B) fail, in fact,
    C) fail; in fact,
    D) fail: in fact

24. Which sentence most effectively establishes the central idea?

    A) NO CHANGE
    B) The Small Business Administration defines a small business as one with fewer than 500 employees and less than $7 million in sales annually.
    C) Many small businesses fail because company founders are not realistic about the amount of time it takes for a company to become profitable.
    D) Running a small business can take up a lot more time than punching a clock for someone else and might not be enjoyable for everyone.

25. A) NO CHANGE
    B) derive
    C) achieve
    D) grasp

GO ON TO THE NEXT PAGE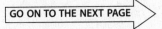

Mitch Gomez is evidence of this data. He 26 <u>did graduate</u> from college with a degree in accounting. "I quickly realized that I have too big of a personality to be content practicing accounting," he laughs. He first built a successful insurance claims 27 <u>service, and next</u> founded his own independent insurance agency. "I continually employ my accounting skills, but I've ascertained that I'm an even more effective salesperson."

Similarly, Barbara Vital, the woman behind Vital Studio, explains, "I love spending as much time with my family as possible." Vital saw an opportunity to 28 <u>launch</u> a monogramming business when her two young sons started school, so she founded a company that offers monogrammed backpacks and water bottles for kids, as well as 29 <u>totes, rain boots; and</u> baseball caps for college students. What is the secret to Vital's success? "I'm always learning how to incorporate social media and add functionality to my product website to keep customers happy," she says.

Finally, Chris Roth is an entrepreneur who can step out of his comfort zone. Always seeking a new 30 <u>challenge his company</u> designed and manufactured technology to keep the nozzles of water misting systems clean. Roth has also established a corporate travel agency and

26. A) NO CHANGE
    B) has graduated
    C) graduated
    D) would have graduated

27. A) NO CHANGE
    B) service. And next
    C) service and next
    D) service; and next

28. A) NO CHANGE
    B) present
    C) propel
    D) impact

29. A) NO CHANGE
    B) totes; rain boots; and
    C) totes, rain boots, and,
    D) totes, rain boots, and

30. A) NO CHANGE
    B) challenge: his company
    C) challenge; his company
    D) challenge, his company

GO ON TO THE NEXT PAGE ▷

a truck customization company, most recently claiming he has become an innovator who beat the odds by "striving to serve customers better than my competition." **31** Large companies often employ corporate travel agencies to arrange travel for their employees and clients.

Gomez, Vital, and Roth **32** agrees that although being an entrepreneur can be a formidable challenge, exceptionally skillful entrepreneurs have important strategies for success, including stretching **33** his personal boundaries and recovering from failures. "And nothing beats being your own boss," adds Gomez.

31. Which sentence would best support the central idea?

A) NO CHANGE

B) Savvy entrepreneurs know which risks are worth taking and which risks can tank their business before their doors open.

C) Now Roth's small business installs water misters on restaurant patios and even sets up misting stations at outdoor music festivals.

D) Many new small businesses fail because company founders fail to do market research and identify the needs of their community.

32. A) NO CHANGE

B) agree

C) should agree

D) had agreed

33. A) NO CHANGE

B) their

C) our

D) her

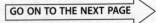 GO ON TO THE NEXT PAGE

Questions 34-44 are based on the following passage and supplementary material.

Edgard Varèse's Influence

Today's music, from rock to jazz, has many [34] influences. And perhaps none is as unique as the ideas from French composer Edgard Varèse. Called "the father of electronic music," he approached compositions from a different theoretical perspective than classical composers such as Bartók and Debussy. He called his [35] works "organized sound"; they did not [36] endear melodies but waged assaults of percussion, piano, and human voices. He thought of sounds as having intelligence and treated music spatially, as "sound objects floating in space."

His unique vision can be credited to his education in science. Born in 1883 in France, Varèse was raised by a great-uncle and grandfather in the Burgundy region. He was interested in classical music and composed his first opera as a teenager. While the family lived [37] in Italy he studied engineering in Turin, where he learned math and science and was inspired by the work of the artist Leonardo da Vinci.

In 1903, he returned to France to study music at the Paris Conservatory. There, he composed the radical percussion performance piece *Ionisation*, which featured cymbals, snares, bass drum, xylophone, and sirens wailing. Later compositions were scored for the theremin, a new electronic instrument controlled by [38] the player's hands waving over its antennae, which sense their posi-

34. A) NO CHANGE
    B) influences, and perhaps none is as
    C) influences, but perhaps none is as
    D) influences. Or perhaps none is as

35. A) NO CHANGE
    B) works "organized sound": They
    C) works "organized sound", they
    D) works—"organized sound"— they

36. A) NO CHANGE
    B) amplify
    C) deprive
    D) employ

37. A) NO CHANGE
    B) in Italy, he studied engineering in Turin, where he
    C) in Italy he studied engineering in Turin where he
    D) in Italy, he studied engineering in Turin; where he

38. A) NO CHANGE
    B) the players' hands
    C) the players hands
    D) the player's hands'

GO ON TO THE NEXT PAGE

tion. No composer had ever scored any music for the theremin before.

In his thirties, Varèse moved to New York City, where he played piano in a café and conducted other composers' works until his own compositions gained success. His piece *Amériques* was performed in Philadelphia in 1926. Varèse went on to travel to the western United States, where he recorded, lectured, and collaborated with other musicians. By the 1950s, he was using tape recordings in [39] contention with symphonic performance. His piece *Déserts* was aired on a radio program amid selections by Mozart and Tchaikovsky but was received by listeners with hostility. [40]

Varèse's ideas were more forward-thinking than could be realized. One of his most ambitious scores, called *Espace*, was a choral symphony with multilingual lyrics, which was to be sung simultaneously by choirs in Paris, Moscow, Peking, and New York. He wanted the timing to be orchestrated by radio, but radio technology did not support worldwide transmission. If only Varèse [41] had had the Internet!

39. A) NO CHANGE
    B) conjunction
    C) appropriation
    D) supplication

40. If added to the paragraph, which fact would best support the author's claims?
    A) The critical response to his 1926 performance in Philadelphia
    B) The selections by Mozart and Tchaikovsky that were played on the radio
    C) Which specific states he traveled to in the western United States
    D) The cities in which the radio program was aired

41. A) NO CHANGE
    B) would have had
    C) would have
    D) have had

Although many of [42] their written compositions were lost in a fire in 1918, many modern musicians and composers have been influenced by Varèse, including Frank Zappa, John Luther Adams, and John Cage, who wrote that Varèse is "more relevant to present musical necessity than even the Viennese masters." [43] Despite being less famous than Stravinsky or Shostakovich, his impact is undeniable. [44] Varèse's love of science and mathematics is shown in his later compositions, but less so in his early works.

Composer	Number of Surviving Works
Edgard Varèse	14
Benjamin Britten	84
Charles Ives	106
Igor Stravinsky	129
Arnold Schoenberg	290
Dmitri Shostakovich	320

42. A) NO CHANGE
    B) its
    C) our
    D) his

43. Which choice most accurately and effectively represents the information in the graph?
    A) NO CHANGE
    B) Despite having fewer surviving works than his contemporaries, his impact is undeniable.
    C) Even though he wrote pieces using a wider range of instruments than other composers, his impact is undeniable.
    D) Even though far fewer of his works are now performed compared with those of his contemporaries, his impact is undeniable.

44. Which sentence best summarizes the central idea?
    A) NO CHANGE
    B) In contrast with his newfound popularity, Varèse's early works have long been ignored due to increasing critical hostility.
    C) Varèse and his innovative compositions became an inspiration for artists seeking to challenge traditional musical beliefs.
    D) Though Varèse's contemporary critics failed to call him a "Viennese master," this distinction is changing.

IF YOU FINISH BEFORE TIME IS CALLED, YOU MAY CHECK YOUR WORK ON THIS SECTION ONLY. DO NOT TURN TO ANY OTHER SECTION IN THE TEST.   **STOP**

MATH TEST

25 Minutes—20 Questions

NO-CALCULATOR SECTION

This section corresponds to Section 3 of your answer sheet.

Directions: For this section, solve each question and select the best answer choice. The available space on each page may be used for scratch work.

Notes:

1. Calculator use is NOT permitted.
2. All numbers used are real numbers, and all variables used represent real numbers, unless otherwise indicated.
3. Figures are drawn to scale and lie in a plane unless otherwise indicated.
4. Unless stated otherwise, the domain of any function f is assumed to be the set of all real numbers x, for which $f(x)$ is a real number.

Information:

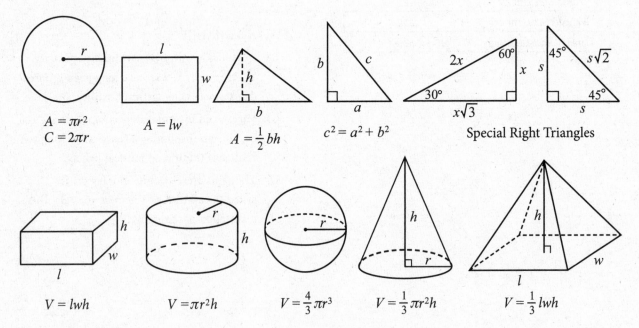

$A = \pi r^2$
$C = 2\pi r$

$A = lw$

$A = \frac{1}{2}bh$

$c^2 = a^2 + b^2$

Special Right Triangles

$V = lwh$

$V = \pi r^2 h$

$V = \frac{4}{3}\pi r^3$

$V = \frac{1}{3}\pi r^2 h$

$V = \frac{1}{3}lwh$

The sum of the degree measures of the angles in a triangle is 180.

The number of degrees of arc in a circle is 360.

The number of radians of arc in a circle is 2π.

GO ON TO THE NEXT PAGE

$$\frac{4(n-2)+5}{2} = \frac{13-(9+4n)}{4}$$

1. In the equation above, what is the value of n?

   A) $\frac{5}{6}$

   B) $\frac{5}{2}$

   C) There is no value of n that satisfies the equation.

   D) There are infinitely many values of n that satisfy the equation.

$$\frac{18x^3 + 9x^2 - 36x}{9x^2}$$

2. Which of the following is equivalent to the expression above?

   A) $2x - \dfrac{4}{x}$

   B) $18x^3 - 36x$

   C) $2x + 1 - \dfrac{4}{x}$

   D) $18x^3 - 36x + 1$

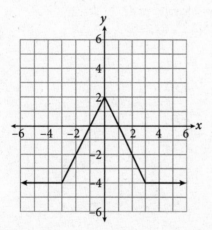

3. The figure above shows the graph of $f(x)$. For which value(s) of x does $f(x)$ equal 0?

   A) -3 and 3

   B) -1 and 1

   C) -1, 1, and 2

   D) 2 only

Start-Up Businesses

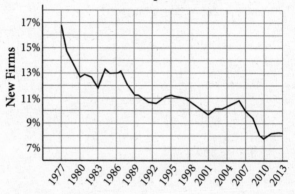

4. A start-up business is typically one that offers a "new" type of service or produces a "new" product. Start-ups are designed to search for a sustainable business model. The function shown in the graph represents new business start-up rates in the United States from 1977 to 2013 as reported by the U.S. Census Bureau. If t represents the year, then which of the following statements correctly describes the function?

   A) The function is increasing overall.

   B) The function is decreasing overall.

   C) The function is increasing for all t such that $1977 < t < 2013$.

   D) The function is decreasing for all t such that $1977 < t < 2013$.

5. Which of the following systems of inequalities has no solution?

   A) $\begin{cases} y \geq x \\ y \leq 2x \end{cases}$

   B) $\begin{cases} y \geq x \\ y \leq -x \end{cases}$

   C) $\begin{cases} y \geq x+1 \\ y \leq x-1 \end{cases}$

   D) $\begin{cases} y \geq -x+1 \\ y \leq x-1 \end{cases}$

GO ON TO THE NEXT PAGE

6. At what value(s) of x do the graphs of $y = -2x + 1$ and $y = 2x^2 + 5x + 4$ intersect?

   A) -8 and $\dfrac{1}{2}$

   B) -3 and $-\dfrac{1}{2}$

   C) -3 and 3

   D) $-\dfrac{1}{2}$ and 3

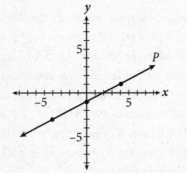

7. If line P shown in the graph is reflected over the x-axis and shifted up 3 units, what is the new y-intercept?

   A) $(0, -4)$

   B) $(0, -2)$

   C) $(0, 2)$

   D) $(0, 4)$

8. Which of the following are roots of the equation $3x^2 - 6x - 5 = 0$?

   A) $1 \pm 2\sqrt{6}$

   B) $\dfrac{1 \pm 2\sqrt{2}}{3}$

   C) $\dfrac{3 \pm 2\sqrt{2}}{3}$

   D) $\dfrac{3 \pm 2\sqrt{6}}{3}$

9. If $m = \dfrac{1}{n^{-\frac{1}{4}}}$, where both $m > 0$ and $n > 0$, which of the following gives n in terms of m?

   A) $n = m^4$

   B) $n = \dfrac{1}{m^4}$

   C) $n = \dfrac{1}{\sqrt[4]{m}}$

   D) $n = m^{\frac{1}{4}}$

$$\begin{cases} y = 3x - 1 \\ y = \dfrac{5x + 8}{2} \end{cases}$$

10. If (x, y) represents the solution to the system of equations shown above, what is the value of y?

    A) 10

    B) 19

    C) 29

    D) 31

11. If $0 < \dfrac{d}{2} + 1 \leq \dfrac{8}{5}$, which of the following is not a possible value of d?

    A) -2

    B) $-\dfrac{6}{5}$

    C) 0

    D) $\dfrac{6}{5}$

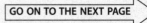

GO ON TO THE NEXT PAGE

12. The value of cos 40° is the same as which of the following?

    A) sin 50°

    B) sin(−40°)

    C) cos(−50°)

    D) cos 140°

13. A business's "break-even point" is the point at which revenue (sales) equals expenses. When a company breaks even, no profit is being made, but the company is not losing any money either. Suppose a manufacturer buys materials for producing a particular item at a cost of $4.85 per unit and has fixed monthly expenses of $11,625 related to this item. The manufacturer sells this particular item to several retailers for $9.50 per unit. How many units must the manufacturer sell per month to reach the break-even point for this item?

    A)   810

    B)   1,225

    C)   2,100

    D)   2,500

14. If $\frac{1}{2}y - \frac{3}{5}x = -16$, what is the value of $6x - 5y$?

    A)   32

    B)   80

    C)   96

    D)   160

15. If $f(g(2)) = -1$ and $f(x) = x + 1$, then which of the following could define $g(x)$?

    A) $g(x) = x - 6$

    B) $g(x) = x - 4$

    C) $g(x) = x - 2$

    D) $g(x) = x - 1$

GO ON TO THE NEXT PAGE

Directions: For questions 16-20, enter your responses into the appropriate grid on your answer sheet, in accordance with the following:

1. You will receive credit only if the circles are filled in correctly, but you may write your answers in the boxes above each grid to help you fill in the circles accurately.

2. Don't mark more than one circle per column.

3. None of the questions with grid-in responses will have a negative solution.

4. Only grid in a single answer, even if there is more than one correct answer to a given question.

5. A **mixed number** must be gridded as a decimal or an improper fraction. For example, you would grid $7\frac{1}{2}$ as 7.5 or $\frac{15}{2}$.

   (Were you to grid it as [7 1 / 2], this response would be read as $\frac{71}{2}$.)

6. A **decimal** that has more digits than there are places on the grid may be either rounded or truncated, but every column in the grid must be filled in order to receive credit.

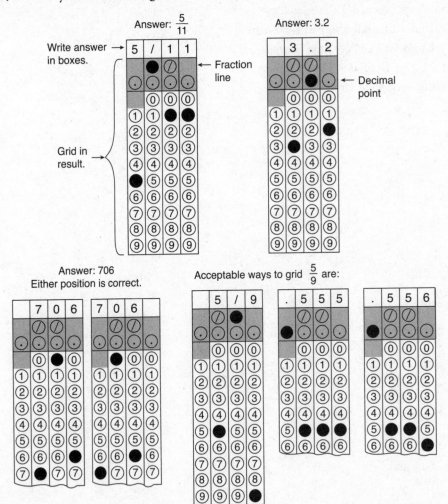

$$k(10x - 5) = 2(3 + x) - 7$$

16. If the equation above has infinitely many solutions and k is a constant, what is the value of k?

17. A right triangle has leg lengths of 18 and 24 and a hypotenuse of $15n$. What is the value of n?

$$\frac{\sqrt{x} \cdot x^{\frac{5}{4}} \cdot x^2}{\sqrt[4]{x^3}}$$

18. If the expression above is combined into a single power of x with a positive exponent, what is that exponent?

19. If the product of $\left(3 + \sqrt{-16}\right)\left(1 - \sqrt{-36}\right)$ is written as a complex number in the form $a + bi$, what is the value of a? (Note: $\sqrt{-1} = i$)

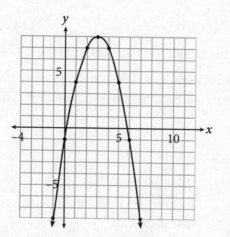

20. If the equation of the parabola shown in the graph is written in standard quadratic form, $y = ax^2 + bx + c$, and $a = -1$, then what is the value of b?

MATH TEST

55 Minutes—38 Questions

CALCULATOR SECTION

This section corresponds to Section 4 of your answer sheet.

Directions: For this section, solve each question and select the best answer choice. The available space on each page may be used for scratch work.

Notes:

1. Calculator use is permitted.
2. All numbers used are real numbers, and all variables used represent real numbers, unless otherwise indicated.
3. Figures are drawn to scale and lie in a plane unless otherwise indicated.
4. Unless stated otherwise, the domain of any function f is assumed to be the set of all real numbers x, for which $f(x)$ is a real number.

Information:

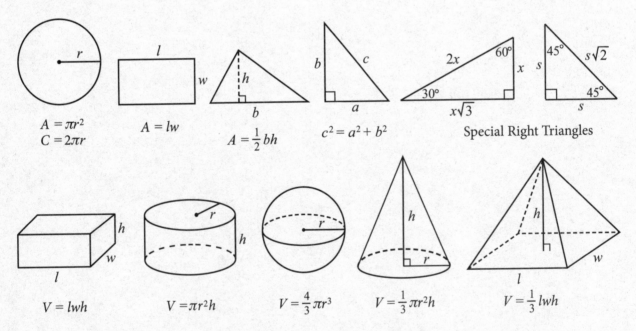

$A = \pi r^2$
$C = 2\pi r$

$A = lw$

$A = \frac{1}{2}bh$

$c^2 = a^2 + b^2$

Special Right Triangles

$V = lwh$

$V = \pi r^2 h$

$V = \frac{4}{3}\pi r^3$

$V = \frac{1}{3}\pi r^2 h$

$V = \frac{1}{3}lwh$

The sum of the degree measures of the angles in a triangle is 180.

The number of degrees of arc in a circle is 360.

The number of radians of arc in a circle is 2π.

GO ON TO THE NEXT PAGE

$$\begin{cases} 4x + y = -5 \\ -4x - 2y = -2 \end{cases}$$

1. What is the *y*-coordinate of the solution to the system of equations shown above?

A) −7

B) −3

C) 0

D) 7

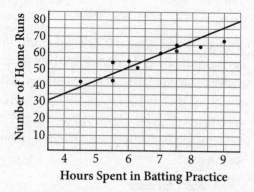

2. The scatterplot above shows data collected from 10 major league baseball players comparing the average weekly time each one spent in batting practice and the number of home runs he hit in a single season. The line of best fit for the data is also shown. What does the slope of the line represent in this context?

A) The estimated time spent in batting practice by a player who hits 0 home runs

B) The estimated number of single-season home runs hit by a player who spends 0 hours in batting practice

C) The estimated increase in time that a player spends in batting practice for each home run that he hits in a single season

D) The estimated increase in the number of single-season home runs hit by a player for each hour he spends in batting practice

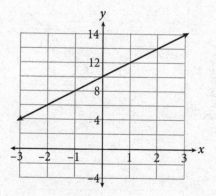

3. Where will the line shown in the graph above intersect the *x*-axis?

A) −5.5

B) −5

C) −4.5

D) −4

4. The function $f(x)$ is defined as $f(x) = -3g(x)$, where $g(x) = x + 2$. What is the value of $f(5)$?

A) −21

B) −1

C) 4

D) 7

5. Sara is grocery shopping. She needs laundry detergent, which is on sale for 30% off its regular price of $8.00. She also needs dog food, which she can buy at three cans for $4.00. Which of the following represents the total cost, before tax, if Sara buys *x* bottles of laundry detergent and 12 cans of dog food?

A) $C = 2.4x + 48$

B) $C = 5.6x + 16$

C) $C = 5.6x + 48$

D) $C = 8.4x + 16$

GO ON TO THE NEXT PAGE

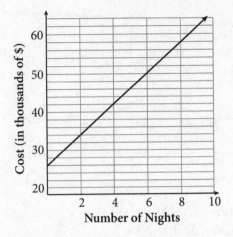

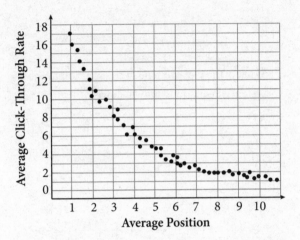

6. The graph above shows the average cost of back surgery followed by a hospital stay in the United States. The hospital charges for the surgery itself plus all the costs associated with recovery care for each night the patient remains in the hospital. Based on the graph, what is the average cost per night spent in the hospital?

A) $2,600

B) $4,000

C) $6,600

D) $8,000

7. The figure above represents a click-through rate curve, which shows the relationship between a search result position in a list of Internet search results and the number of people who clicked on advertisements on that result's page. Which of the following regression types would be the best model for this data?

A) A linear function

B) A quadratic function

C) A polynomial function

D) An exponential function

GO ON TO THE NEXT PAGE

8. Kudzu is a vine-like plant that grows indigenously in Asia. It was brought over to the United States in the early 20th century to help combat soil erosion. As can often happen when foreign species are introduced into a non-native habitat, kudzu growth exploded and it became invasive. In one area of Virginia, kudzu covered approximately 3,200 acres of a farmer's cropland, so he tried a new herbicide. After two weeks of use, 2,800 acres of the farmer's cropland were free of the kudzu. Based on these results, and assuming the same general conditions, how many of the 30,000 acres of kudzu-infested cropland in that region would still be covered if all the farmers in the entire region had used the herbicide?

A) 3,750

B) 4,000

C) 26,000

D) 26,250

x	-2	-1	0	1	2	3
$g(x)$	5	3	1	-1	-3	-5
$h(x)$	-3	-2	-1	0	1	2

9. Several values for the functions $g(x)$ and $h(x)$ are shown in the table. What is the value of $g(h(3))$?

A) -5

B) -3

C) -1

D)   2

10. Mae-Ling made 15 shots during a basketball game. Some were 3-pointers and others were worth 2 points each. If s shots were 3-pointers, which expression represents her total score?

A) $3s$

B) $s + 30$

C) $3s + 2$

D) $5s + 30$

11. Crude oil is sold by the barrel, which refers to both the physical container and a unit of measure, abbreviated as bbl. One barrel holds 42 gallons and, consequently, 1 bbl = 42 gallons. An oil company is filling an order for 2,500 barrels. The machine the company uses to fill the barrels pumps at a rate of 37.5 gallons per minute. If the oil company has 8 machines working simultaneously, how long will it take to fill all the barrels in the order?

A) 5 hours and 50 minutes

B) 12 hours and 45 minutes

C) 28 hours and 30 minutes

D) 46 hours and 40 minutes

GO ON TO THE NEXT PAGE

	Jan	Feb	Mar	April
Company A	54	146	238	330
Company B	15	30	60	120

12. Company A and Company B are selling two similar toys. The sales figures for each toy are recorded in the table above. The marketing department at Company A predicts that its monthly sales for this particular toy will continue to be higher than Company B's through the end of the year. Based on the data in the table, and assuming that each company sustains the pattern of growth the data suggests, which company will sell more of this toy in December of that year and how much more?

    A) Company A; 182

    B) Company A; 978

    C) Company B; 29,654

    D) Company B; 60,282

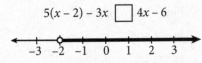

$$5(x - 2) - 3x \ \boxed{} \ 4x - 6$$

13. Which symbol correctly completes the inequality whose solution is shown above?

    A) <

    B) >

    C) ≤

    D) ≥

Questions 14 and 15 refer to the following information.

A student is drawing the human skeleton to scale for a school assignment. The assignment permits the student to omit all bones under a certain size because they would be too small to draw. The longest bone in the human body is the femur, or thighbone, with an average length of 19.9 inches. The tenth longest bone is the sternum, or breastbone, with an average length of 6.7 inches.

14. If the scale factor of the drawing is one-eighth, about how long in inches should the student draw the femur?

    A) 2

    B) 2.5

    C) 2.8

    D) 3

15. The student draws the femur, but then realizes she drew it too long, at 3.5 inches. She doesn't want to erase and start over, so she decides she will adjust the scale factor to match her current drawing instead. Based on the new scale factor, about how long in inches should she draw the sternum?

    A) 0.8

    B) 1

    C) 1.2

    D) 1.5

GO ON TO THE NEXT PAGE

16. If a line that passes through the ordered pairs $(4 - c, 2c)$ and $(-c, -8)$ has a slope of $\frac{1}{2}$, what is the value of c?

A) -5

B) -3

C) -2

D) 2

From	Distance to LHR
DCA	3,718
MIA	4,470

17. Two airplanes departed from different airports at 5:30 AM, both traveling nonstop to London Heathrow Airport (LHR). The distances the planes traveled are recorded in the table. The Washington, D.C. (DCA) flight flew through moderate cloud cover and as a result only averaged 338 mph. The flight from Miami (MIA) had good weather conditions for the first two-thirds of the trip and averaged 596 mph, but then encountered some turbulence and only averaged 447 mph for the last part of the trip. Which plane arrived first and how long was it at the London airport before the other plane arrived?

A) MIA; 2 hours, 40 minutes

B) MIA; 3 hours, 30 minutes

C) DCA; 1 hour, 20 minutes

D) DCA; 3 hours, 40 minutes

18. Which of the following quadratic equations has no solution?

A) $0 = -3(x + 1)(x - 8)$

B) $0 = 3(x + 1)(x - 8)$

C) $0 = -3(x + 1)^2 + 8$

D) $0 = 3(x + 1)^2 + 8$

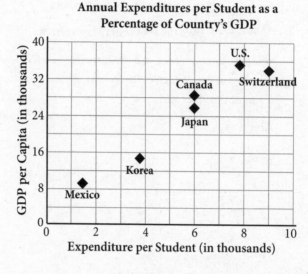

Annual Expenditures per Student as a Percentage of Country's GDP

Adapted from the Organization for Economic Cooperation and Development (OECD), 2003.

19. A student looked at the graph above and determined based on the data that spending more money per student causes the gross domestic product (GDP) to increase. Which of the following statements is true?

A) The student is correct; the data shows that increased spending on students causes an increase in the GDP.

B) The student is incorrect; the data shows that having a higher GDP causes an increase in the amount of money a country spends on students.

C) The student is incorrect; there is no correlation and, therefore, no causation between GDP and expenditures on students.

D) The student is incorrect; the two variables are correlated, but changes in one do not necessarily cause changes in the other.

GO ON TO THE NEXT PAGE

20. In chemistry, the combined gas law formula

$\dfrac{p_1V_1}{T_1} = \dfrac{p_2V_2}{T_2}$ gives the relationship between the volumes, temperatures, and pressures for two fixed amounts of gas. Which of the following gives p_2 in terms of the other variables?

A) $p_1 = p_2$

B) $\dfrac{p_1T}{V} = p_2$

C) $\dfrac{p_1V_1T_2}{T_1V_2} = p_2$

D) $\dfrac{p_1V_1V_2}{T_1T_2} = p_2$

21. An object's weight is dependent upon the gravitational force being exerted upon the object. This is why objects in space are weightless. If 1 pound on Earth is equal to 0.377 pounds on Mars and 2.364 pounds on Jupiter, how many more pounds does an object weighing 1.5 tons on Earth weigh on Jupiter than on Mars?

A) 1,131

B) 4,092

C) 5,961

D) 7,092

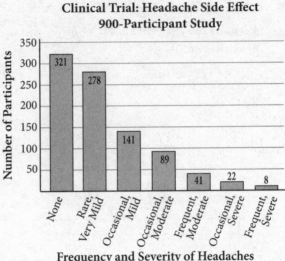

Clinical Trial: Headache Side Effect 900-Participant Study

Frequency and Severity of Headaches

22. When a drug company wants to introduce a new drug, it must subject the drug to rigorous testing. The final stage of this testing is human clinical trials, in which progressively larger groups of volunteers are given the drug and carefully monitored. One aspect of this monitoring is keeping track of the frequency and severity of side effects. The figure above shows the results for the side effect of headaches for a certain drug. According to the trial guidelines, all moderate and severe headaches are considered to be adverse reactions. Which of the following best describes the data?

A) The data is symmetric with over 50% of participants having adverse reactions.

B) The data is skewed to the right with over 50% of participants having adverse reactions.

C) The data is skewed to the right with over 75% of participants failing to have adverse reactions.

D) The data is skewed to the right with approximately 50% of participants having no reaction at all.

GO ON TO THE NEXT PAGE

23. In the legal field, "reciprocity" means that an attorney can take and pass a bar exam in one state, and be allowed to practice law in a different state that permits such reciprocity. Each state bar association decides with which other states it will allow reciprocity. For example, Pennsylvania allows reciprocity with the District of Columbia. It costs $25 less than 3 times as much to take the bar in Pennsylvania than in D.C. If both bar exams together cost $775, how much less expensive is it to take the bar exam in D.C. than in Pennsylvania?

A) $200

B) $275

C) $375

D) $575

24. A grain producer is filling a cylindrical silo 20 feet wide and 60 feet tall with wheat. Based on past experience, the producer has established a protocol for leaving the top 5% of the silo empty to allow for air circulation. Assuming the producer follows standard protocol, what is the maximum number of cubic feet of wheat that should be put in the silo?

A) $5,144\pi$

B) $5,700\pi$

C) $20,577\pi$

D) $22,800\pi$

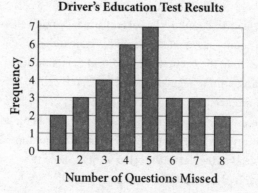

Driver's Education Test Results

25. Mr. Juno took his driver's education class to the Department of Motor Vehicles to take their driver's license test. The number of questions missed by each student in the class is recorded in the bar graph above. Which of the following statements is true?

A)   More than half of the students missed 5 or more questions.

B)   The mean number of questions missed was between 4 and 5.

C)   More students missed 3 questions than any other number of questions.

D)   Thirty-six students from Mr. Juno's class took the driver's license test that day.

26. If the graph of the equation $y = ax^2 + bx + c$ passes through the points $(0, 2)$, $(-6, -7)$, and $(8, -14)$, what is the value of $a + b + c$?

A) -19

B) -2

C) 1.75

D) 2.25

GO ON TO THE NEXT PAGE

27. A bakery sells three sizes of muffins—mini, regular, and jumbo. The baker plans daily muffin counts based on the size of his pans and how they fit in the oven, which results in the following ratios: mini to regular equals 5 to 2, and regular to jumbo equals 5 to 4. When the bakery caters events, it usually offers only the regular size, but it recently decided to offer a mix of mini and jumbo instead of regular. If the baker wants to keep the sizes in the same ratio as his daily counts, what ratio of mini to jumbo should he use?

A) 1:1

B) 4:2

C) 5:2

D) 25:8

$$\begin{cases} \dfrac{1}{3}x + \dfrac{1}{2}y = 5 \\ kx - 4y = 16 \end{cases}$$

28. If the system of linear equations shown above has no solution, and k is a constant, what is the value of k?

A) $-\dfrac{8}{3}$

B) -2

C) $\dfrac{1}{3}$

D) 3

29. What is the value of $3^{90} \times 27^{90} \div \left(\dfrac{1}{9}\right)^{30}$?

A) 9^{60}

B) 9^{120}

C) 9^{150}

D) 9^{210}

30. If a right cone is three times as wide at its base as it is tall, and the volume of the cone is 384π cubic inches, what is the diameter in inches of the base of the cone?

A) 8

B) 12

C) 16

D) 24

Directions: For questions 31-38, enter your responses into the appropriate grid on your answer sheet, in accordance with the following:

1. You will receive credit only if the circles are filled in correctly, but you may write your answers in the boxes above each grid to help you fill in the circles accurately.

2. Don't mark more than one circle per column.

3. None of the questions with grid-in responses will have a negative solution.

4. Only grid in a single answer, even if there is more than one correct answer to a given question.

5. A **mixed number** must be gridded as a decimal or an improper fraction. For example, you would grid $7\frac{1}{2}$ as 7.5 or $\frac{15}{2}$.

   (Were you to grid it as $\boxed{7\ 1\ /\ 2}$, this response would be read as $\frac{71}{2}$.)

6. A **decimal** that has more digits than there are places on the grid may be either rounded or truncated, but every column in the grid must be filled in order to receive credit.

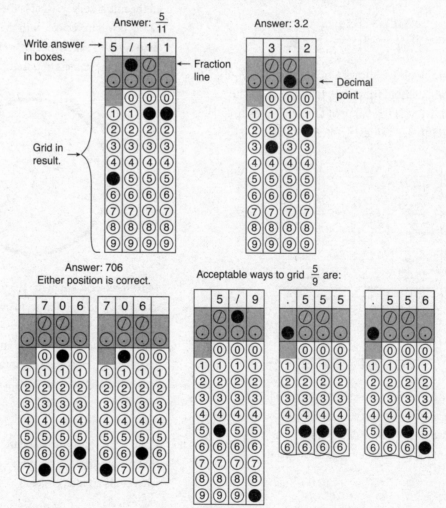

31. If $0.004 \le m \le 0.4$ and $1.6 \le n \le 16$, what is the maximum value of $\frac{m}{n}$?

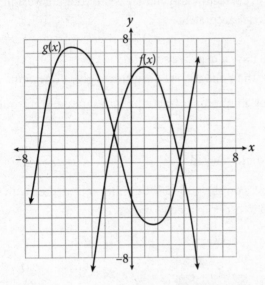

32. The graph above shows a quadratic function $f(x)$ and a cubic function $g(x)$. Based on the graph, what is the value of $(f - g)(3)$, assuming all integer values?

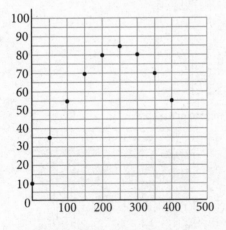

33. Nine data points were used to generate the scatterplot shown above. Assuming all whole number values for the data points, what is the maximum value in the range of the data?

Years at Company	Female	Male
$y < 1$	38	30
$1 \le y \le 3$	15	19
$y > 3$	54	48

34. A company conducts a survey among its employees and categorizes the results based on gender and longevity (the number of years the employee has been working for the company). The Director of Human Resources wants to conduct a small follow-up focus group meeting with a few employees to discuss the overall survey results. If the HR Director randomly chooses four employees that participated in the initial survey, what is the probability that all of them will have been with the company for longer than 3 years? Enter your answer as a decimal and round to the nearest hundredth.

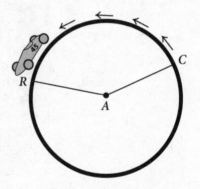

35. Most racetracks are in the shape of an ellipse (an elongated circle similar to an oval), but Langhorne Speedway in Pennsylvania was originally a circular track. If a racecar is traveling around this track, starting at point C and traveling 1,500 feet to point R, and the radius of the track is 840 feet, what is the measure to the nearest degree of minor angle CAR ?

36. If $Ax + By = C$ is the standard form of the line that passes through the points $(-4, 1)$ and $(3, -2)$, where A is an integer greater than 1, what is the value of B ?

GO ON TO THE NEXT PAGE ▷

Questions 37 and 38 refer to the following information.

The Great Depression began in 1929 and lasted until 1939. It was a period of extreme poverty, marked by low prices and high unemployment. The main catalytic event to the Great Depression was the Wall Street Crash (stock market crash). The Dow, which measures the health of the stock market, started Black Thursday (October 24, 1929) at approximately 306 points.

37. The stock market had been in steady decline since its record high the month before. If the market had declined by 19.5% between its record high and opening on Black Thursday, what was the approximate value of the Dow at its record high? Round your answer to the nearest whole point.

38. By the end of business on Black Thursday, the Dow had dropped by 2%. Over the course of Friday and the half-day Saturday session, there was no significant change. Unfortunately, the market lost 13% on Black Monday, followed by another 12% on Black Tuesday. What was the total percent decrease from opening on Black Thursday to closing on Black Tuesday? Round your answer to the nearest whole percent and ignore the percent sign when entering your answer.

IF YOU FINISH BEFORE TIME IS CALLED, YOU MAY CHECK YOUR WORK ON THIS SECTION ONLY. DO NOT TURN TO ANY OTHER SECTION IN THE TEST. **STOP**

ESSAY TEST

50 Minutes

You will be given a passage to read and asked to write an essay analyzing it. As you write, be sure to show that you have read the passage closely. You will be graded on how well you have understood the passage, how clear your analysis is, and how well you express your ideas.

Your essay must be written on the lines in your answer booklet. Anything you write outside the lined space in your answer booklet will not be read by the essay graders. Be sure to write or print in such a way that it will be legible to readers not familiar with your handwriting. Additionally, be sure to address the passage directly. An off-topic essay will not be graded.

As you read the passage, think about the author's use of

- evidence, such as statistics or other facts.

- logic to connect evidence to conclusions and to develop lines of reasoning.

- style, word choice, and appeals to emotion to make the argument more persuasive.

Adapted from Robert F. Kennedy's address to the National Union of South African Students' Day of Affirmation, 6 June 1966.

1   We stand here in the name of freedom.

2   At the heart of that Western freedom and democracy is the belief that the individual man, the child of God, is the touchstone of value, and all society, groups, the state, exist for his benefit. Therefore the enlargement of liberty for individual human beings must be the supreme goal and the abiding practice of any Western society.

3   The first element of this individual liberty is the freedom of speech.

4   The right to express and communicate ideas, to set oneself apart from the dumb beasts of field and forest; to recall governments to their duties and obligations; above all, the right to affirm one's membership and allegiance to the body politic—to society—to the men with whom we share our land, our heritage and our children's future.

5   Hand in hand with freedom of speech goes the power to be heard—to share the decisions of government which shape men's lives. Everything that makes life worthwhile—family, work, education, a place to rear one's children and a place to rest one's head—all this rests on decisions of government; all can be swept away by a government which does not heed the demands of its people. Therefore, the essential humanity of men can be protected and preserved only where government must answer—not just to those of a particular religion, or a particular race; but to all its people.

6   These are the sacred rights of Western society. These are the essential differences between us and Nazi Germany, as they were between Athens and Persia. . . .

GO ON TO THE NEXT PAGE

7   For two centuries, my own country has struggled to overcome the self-imposed handicap of prejudice and discrimination based on nationality, social class or race—discrimination profoundly repugnant to the theory and command of our Constitution. Even as my father grew up in Boston, signs told him that "No Irish need apply."

8   Two generations later President Kennedy became the first Catholic to head the nation; but how many men of ability had, before 1961, been denied the opportunity to contribute to the nation's progress because they were Catholic, or of Irish extraction.

9   In the last five years, the winds of change have blown as fiercely in the United States as anywhere in the world. But they will not—they cannot—abate.

10 For there are millions of African Americans untrained for the simplest jobs, and thousands every day denied their full equal rights under the law; and the violence of the disinherited, the insulated, the injured, looms over the streets of Harlem and Watts and South Chicago.

11 But an African American trains as an astronaut, one of mankind's first explorers into outer space; another is the chief barrister of the United States Government, and dozens sit on the benches of court; and another, Dr. Martin Luther King, is the second man of African descent to win the Nobel Peace Prize for his nonviolent efforts for social justice between the races.

12 We must recognize the full human equality of all our people before God, before the law, and in the councils of government. We must do this not because it is economically advantageous, although it is; not because the laws of God and man command it, although they do command it; not because people in other lands wish it so. We must do it for the single and fundamental reason that it is the right thing to do.

13 And this must be our commitment outside our borders as well as within.

14 It is your job, the task of the young people of this world, to strip the last remnants of that ancient, cruel belief from the civilization of man. Each nation has different obstacles and different goals, shadowed by the vagaries of history and experience. Yet as I talk to young people around the world I am impressed not by the diversity but by the closeness of their goals, their desires and concerns and hopes for the future. There is discrimination in New York, apartheid in South Africa and serfdom in the mountains of Peru. People stagnate in the streets of India; intellectuals go to jail in Russia; thousands are slaughtered in Indonesia; wealth is lavished on armaments everywhere. These are differing evils. But they are common works of man.

15 And therefore they call upon common qualities of conscience and of indignation, a shared determination to wipe away the unnecessary sufferings of our fellow human beings at home and particularly around the world.

Write an essay that analyzes the author's approach in persuading his readers that the expansion of liberty for all must be the guiding principle of any Western society. Focus on specific features such as the ones listed in the box above the passage and explain how these features strengthen the author's argument. Your essay should discuss the most important rhetorical features of the passage.

Your essay should not focus on your own opinion of the author's conclusion, but rather on how the author persuades his readers.

ANSWER KEY
READING TEST

1. B	14. C	27. A	40. B
2. C	15. A	28. A	41. C
3. D	16. B	29. B	42. D
4. B	17. B	30. C	43. C
5. A	18. C	31. D	44. D
6. D	19. D	32. C	45. A
7. C	20. D	33. D	46. C
8. D	21. B	34. B	47. A
9. C	22. C	35. D	48. B
10. A	23. D	36. D	49. C
11. A	24. B	37. A	50. D
12. A	25. D	38. C	51. B
13. B	26. B	39. B	52. D

WRITING AND LANGUAGE TEST

1. C	12. B	23. C	34. C
2. D	13. A	24. A	35. A
3. A	14. B	25. B	36. D
4. A	15. B	26. C	37. B
5. B	16. D	27. C	38. A
6. C	17. C	28. A	39. B
7. A	18. A	29. D	40. A
8. C	19. C	30. D	41. A
9. A	20. A	31. C	42. D
10. C	21. B	32. B	43. B
11. B	22. C	33. B	44. C

MATH—NO CALCULATOR TEST

1. A	6. B	11. A	16. 1/5 or .2
2. C	7. D	12. A	17. 2
3. B	8. D	13. D	18. 3
4. B	9. A	14. D	19. 27
5. C	10. C	15. B	20. 6

MATH—CALCULATOR TEST

1. D	11. A	21. C	31. 1/4 or .25
2. D	12. C	22. C	32. 6
3. B	13. A	23. C	33. 85
4. A	14. B	24. B	34. 0.06
5. B	15. C	25. B	35. 102
6. B	16. B	26. C	36. 7
7. D	17. A	27. D	37. 380
8. A	18. D	28. A	38. 25
9. B	19. D	29. D	
10. B	20. C	30. D	

ANSWERS AND EXPLANATIONS

READING TEST

Great Expectations

Suggested Passage Map notes:

¶1: Pip eating paltry breakfast, Mr. P making him do math while he eats, Pip does not like Mr. P
¶2: Pip visiting Miss H, Miss H's house in disrepair
¶3-9: lady let's in Pip, makes Mr. P go away
¶10: Pip happy to be rid of Mr. P for now

1. B   Difficulty: Easy

Category: Detail

Getting to the Answer: Examine the description of breakfast in the first paragraph before choosing the correct answer. In lines 8-9, Pip uses "crumb" and "little butter" to describe what he ate, and he also says that "a quantity of warm water" had been added to his milk. Therefore, it's clear that Pip's breakfast with Mr. Pumblechook is (B), "small and of poor quality."

2. C   Difficulty: Medium

Category: Vocab-in-Context

Getting to the Answer: Eliminate answer choices that might be synonyms of "wretched" but don't make sense in the context of the passage. When Pip describes Mr. Pumblechook's company to be "wretched," he means "distressing," or "causing misery." Choice (C) is the correct answer.

3. D   Difficulty: Medium

Category: Inference

Getting to the Answer: Review the passage for details that reveal Mr. Pumblechook's attitude. By his actions, you can infer that Mr. Pumblechook is indifferent to Pip's discomfort. Choice (D) is the correct answer.

4. B   Difficulty: Medium

Category: Command of Evidence

Getting to the Answer: Find each answer choice in the passage. Think about your answer for the previous question, and determine which lines provide the strongest support for that answer. In the first paragraph, Pip describes how Mr. Pumblechook offers him a meager breakfast and quizzes him on arithmetic during their meal rather than making conversation. Choice (B) is the correct answer.

5. A   Difficulty: Hard

Category: Global

Getting to the Answer: Study the answer choices. Eliminate any that go too far in their interpretation of characters and events in the passage. Though B seems to reflect what might be true of Pip and Mr. Pumblechook's relationship, and one might believe that C and D are true, the correct answer is (A). This theme most clearly reflects the message conveyed through Pip's experiences in this passage.

6. D   Difficulty: Medium

Category: Detail

Getting to the Answer: Review the section of the passage that describes the young lady's appearance and actions. Select the answer choice that describes her entire demeanor, not just part of it. In line 49, the young lady is described as seeming "very proud." When she tells Mr. Pumblechook that he may not enter, she speaks "finally" (line 57) and in an "undiscussible way" (line 58). This indicates that she is being authoritative. The correct answer is (D).

7. C   Difficulty: Medium

Category: Inference

Getting to the Answer: Think about details in the passage that relate to the characters' relationships.

What do they reveal about how Pip probably feels at the end of the passage? It is reasonable to infer that Pip is relieved when he is no longer in Mr. Pumblechook's company. Therefore, (C) is the correct answer.

8. D   Difficulty: Hard

Category: Command of Evidence

Getting to the Answer: Locate each answer in the passage and decide which one provides the best support for the answer to the previous question. At the end of the passage, Pip "was not free from apprehension" (line 64) that Mr. Pumblechook would return but then tells the reader that no return took place. Choice (D) best supports the idea that Pip is relieved to be away from Mr. Pumblechook.

9. C   Difficulty: Easy

Category: Vocab-in-Context

Getting to the Answer: Substitute each answer choice for "condition." The correct answer will not change the meaning of the sentence. Choice (C) is the correct answer. The narrator says that Mr. Pumblechook is "in a condition of ruffled dignity." In this context, "state" means the same as "condition."

10. A   Difficulty: Medium

Category: Rhetoric

Getting to the Answer: Think of what the parenthetical comment by Pip tells you about his personality. In a sense, Pip is apologizing for what he is about to say of Mr. Pumblechook. The parenthetical comment reveals that Pip is usually more polite in his references to others. Choice (A) is the correct answer.

"Letter from Birmingham Jail"

Suggested Passage Map notes:

¶1: MLK states why he is Birmingham, history of SCLC, in Birmingham due to injustice

¶2: MLK cannot let injustice continue, we are one people

¶3: MLK explains why peaceful protests are needed, benefits of tension to open negotiations

¶4: non-violent pressure only way to enact change

¶5: justice must be demanded by the oppressed

11. A   Difficulty: Medium

Category: Rhetoric

Getting to the Answer: Avoid answer choices that deal with related issues but do not address the main purpose of the letter. The passage as a whole addresses why King came to Birmingham, and then builds on his explanation for being in Birmingham to explore his cause. Choice (A) is correct.

12. A   Difficulty: Easy

Category: Command of Evidence

Getting to the Answer: Choose the answer that relates directly to the purpose you identified in the previous question. King begins the letter by stating "I think I should give the reason for my being in Birmingham," which clearly explains his purpose for writing the letter from the jail. Choice (A) is correct.

13. B   Difficulty: Medium

Category: Inference

Getting to the Answer: Determine whether the details in the passage and its title, which relate to how King was treated when he arrived in Birmingham, indicate a positive or negative reception. The title of the passage, "Letter from Birmingham Jail," indicates that King was incarcerated after his arrival in Birmingham. Furthermore, he is writing to an audience that considered him an "[outsider] coming in" (line 3). It is reasonable to infer from these details that King received criticism for his decision to come to Birmingham; therefore, (B) is correct.

14. C   Difficulty: Easy

Category: Vocab-in-Context

Getting to the Answer: Read the complete sentence and the surrounding paragraph to best understand the meaning of the phrase within its greater context. In the paragraph, King goes on to explain that events in Birmingham must necessarily concern him. He states that an injustice in one place threatens justice everywhere, and even writes, "Whatever affects one directly affects all indirectly" (lines 27-28). This suggests that events in Birmingham affect people throughout the nation. Choice (C) is correct, as it explains that the "interrelatedness of all communities and states" refers to the idea that events in one part of the country affect the entire nation.

15. A   Difficulty: Easy

Category: Inference

Getting to the Answer: Predict King's opinions before reviewing the answer choices. The correct answer can be inferred directly from King's views as expressed in the paragraph. In this paragraph, King refers specifically to injustice and how it affects people everywhere. From this, you can most clearly infer that King considered circumstances in Birmingham to be unfair and wrong. Choice (A) is correct.

16. B   Difficulty: Easy

Category: Command of Evidence

Getting to the Answer: Review the answer to the previous question. Read the answer choices to identify the one whose rhetoric provides clear support for the inference. Although the entire paragraph provides general support and context for the inference, only (B) suggests that circumstances in Birmingham were unjust, that is, unfair and wrong.

17. B   Difficulty: Medium

Category: Vocab-in-Context

Getting to the Answer: Before viewing the answer choices, think about the purpose of the word in the sentence, and form an alternate explanation of the word. Then identify the answer choice that best reflects that meaning and intent. King says that direct action in Birmingham aims to "dramatize the issue that it can no longer be ignored." This suggests that the issue, or events, in Birmingham are of great significance and demand attention that they have not received. Therefore, (B) is correct.

18. C   Difficulty: Hard

Category: Rhetoric

Getting to the Answer: Consider the overall thrust of King's argument in this paragraph. Choose the answer that encapsulates this idea. In paragraph 4, King responds to charges that activists should focus on negotiation, not direct action. He argues that direct action is needed to spur negotiations. King reasons that nonviolent protests create the tension between forces in society needed to bring people to the table to discuss the relevant issues of prejudice and racism. His claim in the paragraph is that direct action is needed to spur negotiation, making choice (C) correct.

19. D   Difficulty: Hard

Category: Rhetoric

Getting to the Answer: Identify an idea in paragraph 4 that provides clear support to the claim made in the previous paragraph. In paragraph 3, King claims that nonviolent direct action is needed to prompt negotiations on civil rights. In paragraph 4, he supports that argument by explaining that no gains have been made in civil rights without such nonviolent action, as choice (D) states.

20. D   Difficulty: Medium

Category: Rhetoric

Getting to the Answer: Read the complete paragraph to best understand the context and purpose of the cited line. The correct answer will identify what the phrase helps achieve in the paragraph. At the start of the paragraph, King argues that oppressors do not willingly give more freedom to the people whom they oppress. He goes on to explain the delay tactics that have kept African Americans from winning equal rights, and concludes that oppressed peoples in other nations are winning independence while African Americans still cannot get a cup of coffee at a lunch counter. The phrase helps King underscore the contrast between these two scenarios, so (D) is the correct answer.

Paired Passages—Bretton Woods

Suggested Passage Map notes:

Passage 1
¶1: background of Bretton Woods
¶2: created IMF to facilitate international trade
¶3: created World Bank to give loans to war affected countries, bridge rich and poor countries
¶4: BW made US dollar global currency
¶5: shaped foreign trade
¶6: BW made US powerful

Passage 2:
¶1: BW only lasted 3 decades, Nixon changed economic policy
¶2: BW collapsed, IMF began flexible exchange system for currency
¶3: US dollar still widely used
¶4: G20 wants to create global currency
¶5-6: predicts worldwide currency, new world order in finance coming

21. B   **Difficulty:** Medium

Category: Inference

Getting to the Answer: Remember that you are being asked to choose an inference suggested by Passage 1, not a statement of fact. The passage notes that the U.S. dollar became a global currency that nations around the world accept for trade, leaving the United States in a stronger position to influence international markets. Choice (B) is the correct answer.

22. C   **Difficulty:** Medium

Category: Command of Evidence

Getting to the Answer: The correct choice should support your answer to the previous question. Consider which choice best shows a clear relationship with your answer to the item above. Choice (C) explicitly states the United States became the "primary power" behind the institutions established at Bretton Woods.

23. D   **Difficulty:** Medium

Category: Vocab-in-Context

Getting to the Answer: Predict an answer based on the context of the passage. The correct answer should not alter the meaning of the sentence in the passage. Then choose the option that best fits your prediction. The passage states that the IMF gives loans to member countries to ensure their continued stability. Choice (D) is correct because it most closely reflects the IMF's goals of proactively promoting global economic growth and stability.

24. B   **Difficulty:** Medium

Category: Connections

Getting to the Answer: Locate information in the passage that accurately summarizes the purposes of both institutions. Then ask yourself how these purposes differ. Both institutions encourage economic growth. However, Passage 1 notes that the IMF maintains payments and receipts between nations. The World Bank, on the other hand, focuses on "economic and social progress" (line 33) in individual countries. Choice (B) is the correct answer.

25. D   **Difficulty:** Hard

Category: Inference

Getting to the Answer: Eliminate any answer choices that are not suggested in the passage. Choice (D) is correct. The paragraph states that President Nixon's decision broke with the Bretton Woods framework. It can be reasonably inferred that the decision differed from the consensus of other nations, given the fact that many nations had agreed to Bretton Woods.

26. B   Difficulty: Medium

Category: Command of Evidence

Getting to the Answer: The answer choice should support your answer to the previous question. The paragraph states that President Nixon's decision "marked the end" of the Bretton Woods framework, which best supports the inference that the United States did not have the support of other nations. The correct answer is (B).

27. A   Difficulty: Medium

Category: Vocab-in-Context

Getting to the Answer: Reread the sentence in which the word appears and decide which meaning makes the most sense in context. The sentence is referring to a new global currency that might take the place of the U.S. dollar as the major, or key, currency. Therefore, (A) is the correct definition of "anchor" in this context.

28. A   Difficulty: Hard

Category: Synthesis

Getting to the Answer: Study the yuan's percent share of use in daily trading relative to other currencies in the graphic over time. What does this suggest about global views of the yuan? Passage 2 explicitly states that the yuan is "becoming a major world reserve currency" (lines 92-93). This is supported by the data in the chart, which shows the yuan's percent share of use in daily trading climbing from 0.5% in 2007 to 2.2% in 2013. Choice (A) is correct.

29. B   Difficulty: Medium

Category: Rhetoric

Getting to the Answer: Determine what purpose

the final paragraph of Passage 2 serves in relation to the rest of the passage. Passage 2 is mostly about the changes to the world's financial system since the 1944 Bretton Woods Conference. The last paragraph of Passage 2 discusses a prediction about that system with which the author appears to agree. This is an opinion rather than a fact; therefore, (B) is correct.

30. C   Difficulty: Medium

Category: Synthesis

Getting to the Answer: Identify the overall purpose of each passage. Then consider which answer choice accurately describes these purposes. Choice (C) is the correct answer. Passage 1 focuses on the effects of Bretton Woods, while Passage 2 focuses on the reasons why the international economy may transition to a new global currency.

31. D   Difficulty: Medium

Category: Synthesis

Getting to the Answer: Keep in mind that the correct answer will be a statement that is evident in both passages. The role of the IMF is mentioned prominently in both passages. Therefore, (D) is the correct answer.

Treatment for Paralysis Passage

Suggested Passage Map notes:

> ¶1: six million US people paralyzed; causes of paralysis
> ¶2: patient in Poland became subject of study
> ¶3: spinal cord research on rats, now used to develop treatment
> ¶4: patient responded well to treatment
> ¶5: future benefits of treatment

32. C   Difficulty: Easy

Category: Global

Getting to the Answer: Keep in mind that the correct answer will be supported by all of the information in the text rather than just a few details. The passage is concerned with one experimental treatment that doctors are exploring to help paralyzed patients regain mobility. Choice (C) is the correct answer.

33. D   Difficulty: Medium

Category: Rhetoric

Getting to the Answer: Review the cited lines to determine how the information they present affects the reader's perception of the information that follows in the passage. Just after describing how the treatment of paralytics consists of retraining, the author informs the reader that a cure may be in sight. The description of retraining helps the reader understand that finding a cure is a significant leap forward. Choice (D) is correct.

34. B   Difficulty: Medium

Category: Inference

Getting to the Answer: Consider the main points the author makes throughout the passage. The correct answer will be directly related to these points, even if it is not directly stated in the passage. Choice (B) is the correct answer. It can be inferred that the author feels that increased mobility will have a positive impact on patients suffering from all levels of paralysis.

35. D   Difficulty: Easy

Category: Command of Evidence

Getting to the Answer: Locate each answer choice in the passage. Decide which one provides the best support for the answer to the previous question. In the last line of the passage, the author says that paralyzed patients "can have both their mobility and their hope restored" (lines 68-69). This answer, (D), offers the strongest support for the answer to the previous question.

36. D   Difficulty: Easy

Category: Vocab-in-Context

Getting to the Answer: The correct answer will not only be a synonym for "restricted" but will also make sense in the context of the sentence in the passage. Eliminate answers, such as A, that are synonyms for "restricted" but do not make sense in context. Here, the author is explaining that patients in wheelchairs must learn to prevent complications from restricted movement. In this context, "restricted" most nearly means "limited," answer choice (D).

37. A   Difficulty: Hard

Category: Rhetoric

Getting to the Answer: Locate lines 46-47 in the passage, and then read the paragraph that comes before it. This will help you identify why the author chose "tailor-made" to describe the patient's treatment. The patient received his own cells during the treatment, meaning that the treatment was tailored to his own body. Choice (A) fits this situation and is therefore the correct answer.

38. C   Difficulty: Hard

Category: Inference

Getting to the Answer: Remember that when a question is asking you to infer something, the answer is not stated explicitly in the passage. In paragraph 2, the author explains that the patient who received the experimental treatment had not seen an increase in mobility despite "countless hours" (line 21) of physical therapy. Therefore, it is logical to infer that the patient would not have regained mobility without this experimental treatment. Choice (C) is the correct answer.

39. B   Difficulty: Medium

Category: Command of Evidence

Getting to the Answer: Think about how you selected the correct answer for the previous question. Use that information to help you choose the correct answer to this question. In paragraph 2, the author explains that the patient selected for the experimental treatment had not regained mobility despite intensive physical therapy. This provides the strongest support for the answer to the previous question, so (B) is correct.

40. B   Difficulty: Easy

Category: Vocab-in-Context

Getting to the Answer: Substitute each of the answer choices for "refined." Select the one that makes the most sense in context and does not change the meaning of the sentence. In this context, "refined" most nearly means "improved." Choice (B) is the correct answer.

41. C   Difficulty: Easy

Category: Inference

Getting to the Answer: Skim the passage and look for details about how doctors came to use the treatment described. In paragraph 3, the author explains that the doctors used a technique that was developed during years of research on rats. Therefore, (C) is the correct answer.

42. D   Difficulty: Medium

Category: Connections

Getting to the Answer: Compare and contrast each answer choice with the procedure described in the passage. As in the procedure described in the passage, skin transplants for burn victims involve taking tissue containing healthy cells from one area of the body and using it to repair damage done to another area. Choice (D) is the correct answer.

Mercury in Fish Passage

Suggested Passage Map notes:

¶1: what mercury is, uses for mercury
¶2: causes of mercury pollution

¶3: water affected by mercury, issue for many organisms
¶4: consumption of mercury-laden seafood, risks and benefits
¶5: explanation of safe levels of mercury based on bodyweight and fish type
¶6: nutritionists' recommendations

43. C   Difficulty: Medium

Category: Inference

Getting to the Answer: The correct answer will be directly supported by the evidence in the passage. Avoid answers like A and B that go beyond what can logically be inferred about the author. The author explains how mercury gets into the fish that humans eat and goes on to say that it is possible to eat fish that contain mercury without getting mercury poisoning. Choice (C) is the correct answer because it is directly supported by the evidence in the passage.

44. D   Difficulty: Medium

Category: Command of Evidence

Getting to the Answer: The correct answer will provide direct support for the answer to the previous question. Avoid answers like B that include relevant details but do not provide direct support. In the last paragraph, the author says that nutritionists recommend eating low-mercury fish instead of eliminating fish altogether, adding that an awareness of the issues with mercury can help us make healthy eating choices. This statement supports the answer to the previous question, so (D) is the correct answer.

45. A   Difficulty: Easy

Category: Detail

Getting to the Answer: Review the details provided in the passage about how to determine a safe level of mercury consumption. In paragraph 5, the author explains that humans should consume less than 0.1 microgram of mercury for every kilogram of their own weight. Therefore, (A) is the correct answer.

46. C   Difficulty: Easy

Category: Vocab-in-Context

Getting to the Answer: Eliminate answer choices that are synonyms for "concentration" but do not make sense in context. In this sentence, the author is describing the amount of mercury in the air from power plants. "Concentration" most nearly means "density" in this context, so (C) is the correct answer.

47. A   Difficulty: Medium

Category: Inference

Getting to the Answer: Eliminate any answer choices that are not directly supported by information in the passage. The passage strongly suggests that it is impossible to avoid exposure to mercury completely. Therefore, (A) is the correct answer.

48. B   Difficulty: Easy

Category: Command of Evidence

Getting to the Answer: Locate each of the answer choices in the passage. The correct answer should provide support for the answer to the previous question. In paragraph 1, the author explains that mercury can be found in many places. This supports the conclusion that it is impossible to avoid mercury completely. Choice (B) is the correct answer.

49. C   Difficulty: Hard

Category: Rhetoric

Getting to the Answer: Think about how the process paragraph 3 describes relates to the rest of the passage. Paragraph 3 describes the process by which larger organisms absorb mercury by eating smaller organisms. This information is necessary to understanding why larger fish have the highest mercury levels. Choice (C) is correct.

50. D   Difficulty: Hard

Category: Rhetoric

Getting to the Answer: Consider one of the central ideas of the passage. The correct answer would help provide additional support for this idea. One central idea in the passage is that people can eat fish if they know what mercury levels are safe for human consumption. The author states that scientists have determined safe mercury levels by studying at what point symptoms of mercury poisoning occur. However, the author only provides one example weight of how many micrograms of mercury a person could eat. Therefore, (D) is the correct answer.

51. B   Difficulty: Easy

Category: Vocab-in-Context

Getting to the Answer: Reread the sentence and replace "particulars" with each answer choice. Though the answer choices are similar in meaning to a certain degree, one of them makes the most sense when substituted for "particulars." In this context, "particulars" most nearly means "specifics"; therefore, (B) is the correct answer.

52. D   Difficulty: Hard

Category: Synthesis

Getting to the Answer: Remember that the correct answer will be supported by information in both the passage and the graphic. Refer to the passage to draw conclusions about the information in the graphic. The passage states that it is safe to eat fish that contain mercury as long as certain guidelines are followed regarding daily consumption. The graphic shows that Alaskan pollock has the lowest concentration of mercury of the fish listed. Therefore, (D) is the correct answer; a person can safely eat more Alaskan pollock than black-striped bass in one day.

WRITING AND LANGUAGE TEST

The UN: Promoting World Peace

1. C **Difficulty:** Medium

Category: Punctuation

Getting to the Answer: Examine the passage to determine whether the current punctuation is incorrect. Then consider which set of punctuation marks correctly emphasizes the selected part of the sentence. The dashes provide emphasis for the idea that the UN is a peacekeeping organization; the dashes help set off this part of the sentence from the remaining content. The correct answer is (C).

2. D **Difficulty:** Hard

Category: Development

Getting to the Answer: Review the main points made so far. The correct answer should touch on or summarize previous ideas in the paragraph. Choice (D) is correct. This concluding sentence effectively summarizes the ideas that compose the paragraph's main claim.

3. A **Difficulty:** Medium

Category: Organization

Getting to the Answer: Read the previous paragraph and identify the word or phrase that is the best transition between the two paragraphs. The previous paragraph describes the UN today, and the paragraph beginning with the phrase in question explains the origins of the UN in the 1940s. Choice (A) indicates the correct shift in time period and provides the most effective transition between paragraphs.

4. A **Difficulty:** Medium

Category: Usage

Getting to the Answer: Pay close attention to the context of the previous sentence to help you establish the correct verb tense for this particular sentence. The correct answer is (A). It uses the present tense to logically follow the previous sentence that refers to the UN in the present tense, as well.

5. B **Difficulty:** Easy

Category: Punctuation

Getting to the Answer: Watch out for choices that may create a run-on sentence. The correct choice is (B), which provides a clear separation between one complete sentence and the next.

6. C **Difficulty:** Easy

Category: Effective Language Use

Getting to the Answer: Substitute each choice in the complete paragraph. The correct answer will most appropriately fit within the context of the sentence and the paragraph. The correct answer is (C). The UN encourages, or promotes, environmental protection.

7. A **Difficulty:** Medium

Category: Development

Getting to the Answer: The correct choice should introduce a central idea that is supported by subsequent sentences in the paragraph. The correct answer is (A). The expansion of the UN's budget, goals, and personnel number connects to specific evidence in the rest of the paragraph.

8. C **Difficulty:** Medium

Category: Quantitative

Getting to the Answer: Notice that the graphic gives specific information about the increases and decreases in the UN peacekeeping force over a period of time. Study the answer choices to find the one that best relates to the paragraph while using accurate information from the graphic. The graphic shows data through the year 2010 and does not indicate that personnel levels rose above 100,000. Choice (C) is the correct answer.

9. A   Difficulty: Medium

Category: Effective Language Use

Getting to the Answer: Watch out for unnecessarily wordy choices like B. The correct answer is (A) because it effectively communicates an idea without additional words that distract from the content.

10. C   Difficulty: Easy

Category: Effective Language Use

Getting to the Answer: Look at the context of the sentence in which the word appears as well as the paragraph itself to choose the answer that works best. Choice (C), "noteworthy," is synonymous with "worth mentioning," which clearly fits within the context of the paragraph and the author's intent to highlight the accomplishments of the UN.

11. B   Difficulty: Medium

Category: Development

Getting to the Answer: Read the entire paragraph. Identify the sentence that is least relevant to the paragraph's topic and purpose. The purpose of this paragraph is to sum up the central ideas of the passage. Choice (B) introduces a detail that, while important, does not summarize the central ideas of the passage and therefore detracts from the paragraph's focus.

DNA Analysis in a Day

12. B   Difficulty: Easy

Category: Usage

Getting to the Answer: Read the sentence and notice that the verb in question is in a clause with intervening prepositional phrases that come between the subject and the verb. Check to see what the subject is and whether the verb agrees with the subject. The verb "match" is in a plural form, but the subject is "DNA," not one of the other nouns in the prepositional phrases. "DNA" is singular. Choice (B) is the correct answer because it is the singular form of the verb "to match."

13. A   Difficulty: Medium

Category: Punctuation

Getting to the Answer: Read the sentence to determine whether the two clauses separated by the semicolon are independent or not. If they are both independent, a semicolon is the appropriate punctuation. Be careful of answer choices with inappropriate transition words. A semicolon is the correct way to separate two independent but related clauses, so (A) is the correct answer.

14. B   Difficulty: Easy

Category: Punctuation

Getting to the Answer: Study the words in a series and see where a comma might need to be inserted or eliminated. Choice (B) is correct.

15. B   Difficulty: Hard

Category: Organization

Getting to the Answer: When you see an underlined transition, identify how the sentence relates to the previous one to determine what kind of transition is appropriate. Choice (B) is correct because the sentence to which the transition belongs provides more detail about a general statement that preceded it.

16. D   Difficulty: Easy

Category: Effective Language Use

Getting to the Answer: Imagine that the sentence has a blank where the word in question is. Read the entire paragraph for context and predict what word could complete the blank. Review the answer choices to find the word closest in meaning to your prediction. The paragraph later states that Jane Saunders's goal is to separate the two strands of DNA. Only answer choice (D) has the correct connotation and fits within the context of the sentence.

17. C   **Difficulty:** Medium

Category: Effective Language Use

Getting to the Answer: It is important to combine sentences in order to vary sentence structures. But the correct choice should not only be the most effective way to combine the two sentences; it must also be in parallel construction with the first sentence. Watch out for choices that may have incorrect transition words as well. Choice (C) is the correct answer. It joins the sentences concisely and correctly because the verb "adding" is in parallel construction with the earlier verbs "detaching" and "transferring." The subject in both sentences is the same, "she," so it can be dropped when combining the two sentences.

18. A   **Difficulty:** Medium

Category: Development

Getting to the Answer: Read the entire paragraph and then put each answer choice at the beginning. Choose the one that makes the most sense and is further explained by subsequent details in the paragraph. The paragraph discusses the process of identifying DNA, which is lengthy and involves changing the temperature of the DNA several times. Choice (A) is closest to this summation of what is to follow and is the correct answer.

19. C   **Difficulty:** Easy

Category: Effective Language Use

Getting to the Answer: Watch out for choices that are wordy or redundant. Choice (C) is the most concise and effective way of stating the information in the passage.

20. A   **Difficulty:** Medium

Category: Organization

Getting to the Answer: Consider the function of this sentence. At what point in the paragraph should this function be employed? The sentence is setting the scene, so it should be placed where it is now, at the beginning of the paragraph. To place it later

would make the meaning of the paragraph unclear. Choice (A) is the correct answer.

21. B   **Difficulty:** Easy

Category: Effective Language Use

Getting to the Answer: Think about the connotations of each answer choice, and be sure to pick the one that fits with the context of the sentence. Substitute each answer choice for the word to see which word works best. "Eager" best reflects how the detectives would be feeling while waiting for important test results. They would be eagerly anticipating this important information and would want it as quickly as possible. Choice (B) is the correct answer.

22. C   **Difficulty:** Hard

Category: Development

Getting to the Answer: Decide which sentence sounds like the most appropriate way to conclude the passage. The rhetorical question currently in the passage (choice A) introduces an opinion that the passage never reveals; there is no sign that Jane Saunders would feel this way. Likewise, there is no indication in the passage of how expensive modern DNA analysis is (choice B), nor that Saunders marvels about how far science has come in DNA analysis (choice D). Choice (C) is the correct answer; it presents a fairly natural way for Saunders to feel given her accomplishments for the day.

Will Your Start-Up Succeed?

23. C   **Difficulty:** Medium

Category: Sentence Formation

Getting to the Answer: Check to see whether there are two independent clauses within this sentence. Two independent clauses without punctuation indicate a run-on sentence. As written, this is a run-on sentence. Choice (C) is the correct answer because it separates the two complete but related thoughts with a semicolon.

24. A   Difficulty: Medium

Category: Development

Getting to the Answer: Eliminate answers that might contain details related to the central idea but do not properly express the central idea. This paragraph is mostly about the characteristics of people who are successful entrepreneurs. Choice (A) is the correct answer because it introduces the main idea by summarizing the traits people must have to achieve success as a business owner.

25. B   Difficulty: Hard

Category: Effective Language Use

Getting to the Answer: Eliminate answers such as D that mean nearly the same thing as "grab" but do not clarify the meaning of the sentence. In this context, "derive" best clarifies the meaning of the sentence, which explains how entrepreneurs get ideas for their businesses. Choice (B) is the correct answer.

26. C   Difficulty: Easy

Category: Usage

Getting to the Answer: Read the rest of the paragraph and pay attention to the verb tense used. The verbs in the rest of this paragraph are in past tense. "Graduated" is the past tense of the verb "to graduate"; therefore, (C) is the correct answer.

27. C   Difficulty: Medium

Category: Punctuation

Getting to the Answer: Examine the structure of the whole sentence. Consider whether the punctuation is correct or even necessary. The subject of this sentence is "he," and it is followed by a compound predicate containing the verbs "built" and "founded." When a compound predicate contains only two items, a comma should not separate either verb from the subject. No punctuation is necessary, so (C) is the correct answer.

28. A   Difficulty: Medium

Category: Effective Language Use

Getting to the Answer: Replace the underlined word with each answer choice. Consider which word makes the most sense in context and conveys the clearest meaning. The sentence discusses how Vital began her own business. In this context, "launch" conveys the most precise meaning because it connotes the start of a major endeavor. Choice (A) is the correct answer because no change is needed.

29. D   Difficulty: Easy

Category: Punctuation

Getting to the Answer: This sentence contains a list of items in a series. Think about the rules of punctuation for items in a series. Items in a series should be separated by commas, with a comma following each word except the last item in the series. The word "and" is not an item in the series and, therefore, should not be followed by a comma. Therefore, (D) is the correct answer.

30. D   Difficulty: Easy

Category: Punctuation

Getting to the Answer: Identify the main elements of this sentence, such as the subject, predicate, and any restrictive or nonrestrictive clauses. Remember that a nonrestrictive clause should be set off with a comma. The clause "always seeking a new challenge" is nonrestrictive and should be set off from the rest of the sentence with a comma. Choice (D) is the correct answer.

31. C   Difficulty: Hard

Category: Development

Getting to the Answer: Identify the central idea of the paragraph. Read each answer choice and consider which sentence could be added to the paragraph to provide support for the central idea you identified. This paragraph is mostly about Chris Roth, an entrepreneur who now has several companies. (C) is the correct answer because it provides specific details about one of the companies Roth owns.

32. B   **Difficulty:** Easy

Category: Usage

Getting to the Answer: Read the entire sentence. Identify the subject and determine whether it is plural or singular. Determine the correct verb tense for the sentence. The subject of this sentence is plural (Gomez, Vital, and Roth), so the verb must be plural, as well. (B) is the correct answer because "agree" is the plural present tense of the verb "to agree."

33. B   **Difficulty:** Easy

Category: Usage

Getting to the Answer: Read the entire sentence and identify the antecedent for the underlined pronoun. The correct answer will be the pronoun that is in agreement with the antecedent. In this sentence, the antecedent is "entrepreneurs," which requires a third-person plural pronoun. Therefore, (B) is the correct answer.

Edgard Varèse's Influence

34. C   **Difficulty:** Medium

Category: Sentence Formation

Getting to the Answer: Read the two sentences connected by the underlined portion, and decide which answer choice creates a grammatically correct and logical sentence. Choice (C) is correct. Using the coordinating conjunction "but" with a comma to combine the sentences shows that the second portion, which mentions Varèse as being unique, stands in contrast to the first portion, which mentions many influential artists. The other options, featuring "and" and "or," do not show this necessary contrast.

35. A   **Difficulty:** Hard

Category: Punctuation

Getting to the Answer: Reread the entire sentence to assess how the punctuation in the answer choices affects how each portion of the sentence relates to one another. The correct answer is (A). The semicolon correctly links the two independent clauses that have a direct relationship with one another.

36. D   **Difficulty:** Medium

Category: Effective Language Use

Getting to the Answer: Read the sentence for context clues, and think about the author's intention. Then determine which answer provides the most appropriate word choice. "Employ" is the only word that matches the meaning of the sentence, which states that Varèse did not use traditional melodies. Thus, choice (D) is correct.

37. B   **Difficulty:** Medium

Category: Punctuation

Getting to the Answer: Reread the sentence to determine how each portion relates to the others. Then examine how the punctuation in the answer choices affects these relationships. The portion of the sentence discussing the family's move to Italy is an introductory element and needs a comma to offset it from the rest of the sentence. The portion discussing what Varèse learned in Turin is a parenthetical element and also requires a comma. Therefore, choice (B) is correct.

38. A   **Difficulty:** Medium

Category: Punctuation

Getting to the Answer: Review the sentence for context clues and to assess the subject's ownership of the objects in the sentence. Then determine which form of the possessive noun correctly reflects this ownership. The hands in the sentence belong to a single player using a single theremin; therefore, the correct answer will use the singular possessive noun "player's." Choice (A) is correct.

39. B   Difficulty: Medium

Category: Effective Language Use

Getting to the Answer: Read the sentence for context clues. Decide on the answer choice that makes the sentence's meaning precise and clear. "Conjunction" is the only word that relates to two things occurring at the same time to create a single outcome, which is the intended meaning of the sentence. Choice (B) is correct.

40. A   Difficulty: Hard

Category: Development

Getting to the Answer: Assess the central idea of the introductory sentence in the paragraph, and determine which additional fact noted in the answer choices would have the greatest benefit to the reader. The introductory sentence states that Varèse worked in New York until he secured his first success. Describing the critical reaction to the next event mentioned would help strengthen the idea that the Philadelphia performance was a successful event in Varèse's career. Choice (A) is the correct answer.

41. A   Difficulty: Hard

Category: Usage

Getting to the Answer: Consider what kind of situation the author is presenting here, and decide which tense of the verb "has" creates a grammatically correct sentence that reflects this meaning. Keep in mind the time of the events in the sentence. The sentence imagines a situation in which Varèse had been able to use the Internet, an unrealistic action. The double "had had" is correct; it describes past-tense actions that might have occurred in the past but didn't. Choice (A) is correct.

42. D   Difficulty: Easy

Category: Usage

Getting to the Answer: Read the entire sentence to figure out who is the owner of the burned compositions. Then select the proper personal pronoun for this antecedent. Choice (D) is the correct singular possessive pronoun because the burned compositions belonged to Varèse, one person, and not a group of artists.

43. B   Difficulty: Medium

Category: Quantitative

Getting to the Answer: Study the information in the graphic to determine which answer choice most accurately finishes the sentence. Choice (B) is correct because it accurately reflects information included in the graphic.

44. C   Difficulty: Medium

Category: Development

Getting to the Answer: After reading the final paragraph, examine each answer choice to determine which best summarizes the paragraph's overall message. Choice (C) is correct. It is the one sentence that sets up the idea that Varèse's challenging work has been an inspiration to many later artists, an idea supported by the rest of the paragraph.

MATH—NO CALCULATOR TEST

1. A   Difficulty: Easy

Category: Heart of Algebra / Linear Equations

Getting to the Answer: You could start by cross-multiplying to get rid of the denominators, but simplifying the numerators first will make the calculations easier. Don't forget to distribute the negative to both terms in the parentheses on the right-hand side of the equation.

$$\frac{4(n-2)+5}{2} = \frac{13-(9+4n)}{4}$$

$$\frac{4n-8+5}{2} = \frac{13-9-4n}{4}$$

$$\frac{4n-3}{2} = \frac{4-4n}{4}$$

$$4(4n-3) = 2(4-4n)$$

$$16n-12 = 8-8n$$

$$16n = 20-8n$$

$$24n = 20$$

$$n = \frac{20}{24} = \frac{5}{6}$$

Choice (A) is correct.

2. C   Difficulty: Easy

Category: Passport to Advanced Math / Exponents

Getting to the Answer: Don't be tempted—you can't simply cancel one term when a polynomial is divided by a monomial. You can, however, split the expression into three terms, each with a denominator of $9x^2$, and simplify. You could also use polynomial long division to answer the question. Use whichever method gets you to the answer more quickly on Test Day.

$$\frac{18x^3+9x^2-36x}{9x^2} = \frac{18x^3}{9x^2}+\frac{9x^2}{9x^2}-\frac{36x}{9x^2}$$

$$= 2x+1-\frac{4}{x}$$

Choice (C) is correct.

3. B   Difficulty: Easy

Category: Passport to Advanced Math / Functions

Getting to the Answer: When using function notation, $f(x)$ is simply another way of saying y, so this question is asking you to find the value(s) of x for which $y = 0$, or in other words, where the graph crosses the x-axis. Don't be tempted by the flat parts of the graph—they have a slope of 0, but the function itself does not equal 0 here (it equals -4). The graph crosses the x-axis at the points $(-1, 0)$ and $(1, 0)$, so the values of x for which $f(x) = 0$ are -1 and 1, (B).

4. B   Difficulty: Easy

Category: Passport to Advanced Math / Functions

Getting to the Answer: Your only choice for this question is to compare each statement to the graph. Cross out false statements as you go. A function is decreasing when the slope is negative; it is increasing when the slope is positive. You can see from the graph that the trend is decreasing (going down from left to right), so eliminate A and C. Now, take a closer look to see that there are some time intervals over which the function increases (goes up), so you can't say that the function in decreasing for *all t* such that $1977 < t < 2013$. You can only make a general statement about the nature of the function, like the one in (B). The right-hand side of the graph is lower than the left side, so the function is decreasing overall.

5. C   Difficulty: Medium

Category: Heart of Algebra / Inequalities

Getting to the Answer: You don't need to use algebra to answer this question, and you also don't need to graph each system. Instead, think about how the graphs would look. The only time a system of linear inequalities has no solution is when it consists of two parallel lines shaded in opposite directions. All the inequalities are written in slope-intercept form, so look for parallel lines (two lines that have the same slope but different y-intercepts). The slopes in A are different ($m = 1$ and $m = 2$), so eliminate this choice. The same is true for B ($m = 1$ and $m = -1$) and D ($m = -1$ and $m = 1$). This means (C) must be correct ($m = 1$ and $m = 1$, $b = 1$ and $b = -1$). The graph of the system is shown here:

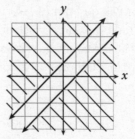

Because the shading never overlaps, the system has no solution.

6. B   **Difficulty:** Medium

Category: Passport to Advanced Math / Quadratics

Getting to the Answer: Although this question asks where the graphs intersect, it is not necessary to actually graph them. The point(s) at which the two graphs intersect are the points where the two equations are equal to each other. So, set the equations equal and use algebra to solve for x. Because the question only asks for the x-values, you don't need to substitute the results back into the equations to solve for y.

$$-2x + 1 = 2x^2 + 5x + 4$$
$$-2x = 2x^2 + 5x + 3$$
$$0 = 2x^2 + 7x + 3$$
$$0 = (2x + 1)(x + 3)$$

Now that the equation is factored, use the Zero-Product Property to solve for x:

$$2x + 1 = 0 \quad \text{and} \quad x + 3 = 0$$
$$2x = -1 \qquad\qquad x = -3$$
$$x = -\frac{1}{2}$$

Choice (B) is correct.

7. D   **Difficulty:** Medium

Category: Heart of Algebra / Linear Equations

Getting to the Answer: You can approach this question conceptually or concretely. When dealing with simple transformations, drawing a quick sketch is most likely the safest approach. You are only concerned about the y-intercept, so keep your focus there. When the graph is reflected over the x-axis, the y-intercept will go from $(0, -1)$ to $(0, 1)$. Next, the line is shifted up 3 units, which adds 3 to the y-coordinates of all the points on the line, making the new y-intercept $(0, 4)$. Choice (D) is correct. A sketch follows:

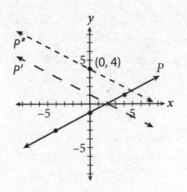

8. D   **Difficulty:** Medium

Category: Passport to Advanced Math / Quadratics

Getting to the Answer: The roots of an equation are the same as its solutions. Take a peek at the answer choices—they contain radicals, which tells you that the equation can't be factored. Instead, either complete the square or solve the equation using the quadratic formula, whichever you are most comfortable with. The equation is already written in the form $y = ax^2 + bx + c$ and the coefficients are fairly small, so using the quadratic formula is probably the quickest method. Jot down the values that you'll need: $a = 3$, $b = -6$, and $c = -5$. Then, substitute these values into the quadratic formula and simplify:

$$x = \frac{-b \pm \sqrt{b^2 - 4ac}}{2a}$$
$$= \frac{-(-6) \pm \sqrt{(-6)^2 - 4(3)(-5)}}{2(3)}$$
$$= \frac{6 \pm \sqrt{36 + 60}}{6}$$
$$= \frac{6 \pm \sqrt{96}}{6}$$

This is not one of the answer choices, so simplify the radical. To do this, look for a perfect square that divides into 96 and take its square root. Then, if possible, cancel any factors that are common to the numerator and the denominator.

$$x = \frac{6 \pm \sqrt{16 \times 6}}{6}$$

$$= \frac{6 \pm 4\sqrt{6}}{6}$$

$$= \frac{\cancel{2}\left(3 \pm 2\sqrt{6}\right)}{\cancel{2}(3)}$$

$$= \frac{3 \pm 2\sqrt{6}}{3}$$

Choice (D) is correct. Be careful—you can't simplify the answer any further because you cannot divide the square root of 6 by 3.

9. A   Difficulty: Medium

Category: Passport to Advanced Math / Exponents

Getting to the Answer: When you write an equation in terms of a specific variable, you are simply solving the equation for that variable. To do this, you'll need to use the property that raising a quantity to the one-fourth power is the same as taking its fourth root and that applying a negative exponent to a quantity is the same as writing its reciprocal. Rewrite the equation using these properties, and then solve for n using inverse operations. Note that the inverse of taking a fourth root of a quantity is raising the quantity to the fourth power.

$$m = \frac{1}{n^{-\frac{1}{4}}}$$

$$m = \frac{\sqrt[4]{n}}{1}$$

$$(m)^4 = \left(\sqrt[4]{n}\right)^4$$

$$m^4 = n$$

Choice (A) is correct.

10. C   Difficulty: Medium

Category: Heart of Algebra / Systems of Linear Equations

Getting to the Answer: When a system consists of two equations already written in terms of y, the quickest way to solve the system is to set the equations equal to each other and then use inverse operations. Don't let the fraction intimidate you—you can write the first equation as a fraction over 1 and use cross-multiplication.

$$\frac{3x - 1}{1} = \frac{5x + 8}{2}$$

$$2(3x - 1) = 5x + 8$$

$$6x - 2 = 5x + 8$$

$$6x = 5x + 10$$

$$x = 10$$

Don't let A fool you—the question is asking for the value of y, not the value of x. To find y, substitute 10 for x in either equation and simplify:

$$y = 3(10) - 1$$

$$= 30 - 1$$

$$= 29$$

Choice (C) is correct.

11. A   Difficulty: Medium

Category: Heart of Algebra / Inequalities

Getting to the Answer: You don't need to separate this compound inequality into pieces. Just remember, whatever you do to one piece, you must do to all three pieces. The fractions in this question make it look more complicated than it really is, so start by clearing them. To do this, multiply everything by the least common denominator, 10.

$$0 < \frac{d}{2} + 1 \le \frac{8}{5}$$

$$10(0) < 10\left(\frac{d}{2} + 1\right) \le \left(\frac{8}{5}\right)10$$

$$0 < 5d + 10 \le 16$$

$$-10 < 5d \le 6$$

$$-2 < d \le \frac{6}{5}$$

Now, read the inequality symbols carefully. The value of d is between -2 and $\frac{6}{5}$, not including -2 because of the $<$ symbol, so (A) is the correct answer. Don't let C fool you—you can't have a 0 *denominator* in a rational expression, but in this expression, the variable is in the numerator, so it *can* equal 0.

12. A   Difficulty: Medium

Category: Additional Topics in Math / Trigonometry

Getting to the Answer: The measure of 40° does not appear on the unit circle, which should give you a clue that there must be a property or relationship on which you can rely to help you answer the question. Complementary angles have a special relationship relative to trig values: The cosine of an acute angle is equal to the sine of the angle's complement and vice versa. Because only one of the answers can be correct, look for the simplest relationship (complementary angles): 50° is complementary to 40°, so $\cos 40° = \sin 50°$, which means (A) is correct.

13. D   Difficulty: Medium

Category: Heart of Algebra / Linear Equations

Getting to the Answer: Assign a variable to the unknown, and then create an equation that represents the scenario. Let n be the number of units the manufacturer sells in a month. Sales must equal expenses for the manufacturer to break even (sales = expenses). The sales are equal to the selling price ($9.50) times the number of units sold (n), so write $9.5n$ on one side of the equal sign. The monthly expenses are the fixed expenses ($11,625) plus the amount paid for the materials needed to produce one unit ($4.85) times the number of units (n), so write $11,625 + 4.85n$ on the other side of the equal sign. Then, solve for n.

$$9.5n = 11,625 + 4.85n$$
$$4.65n = 11,625$$
$$n = 2,500$$

Choice (D) is correct.

14. D   Difficulty: Medium

Category: Heart of Algebra / Linear Equations

Getting to the Answer: There is only one equation given, and it has two variables. This means that you don't have enough information to solve for either variable. Instead, look for the relationship between the left side of the equation and the other expression that you are trying to find. The expression you are trying to find ($6x - 5y$) has the x-term first and then the y-term, so start by reversing the order of the terms on the left side of the given equation. Also, notice that the x term in $6x - 5y$ is not negative, so multiply the equation by -1.

$$\frac{1}{2}y - \frac{3}{5}x = -16 \rightarrow -\frac{3}{5}x + \frac{1}{2}y = -16$$
$$-1\left(-\frac{3}{5}x + \frac{1}{2}y = -16\right) \rightarrow \frac{3}{5}x - \frac{1}{2}y = 16$$

Finally, there are no fractions in the desired expression, so clear the fractions by multiplying both sides of the equation by 10. This yields the expression that you are looking for, so no further work is required— just read the value on the right-hand side of the equation, which is 160.

$$10\left(\frac{3}{5}x - \frac{1}{2}y\right) = 16(10)$$
$$6x - 5y = 160$$

Choice (D) is correct.

15. B   Difficulty: Medium

Category: Passport to Advanced Math / Functions

Getting to the Answer: Understanding the language of functions will make questions that seem complicated much more doable. When you know the output of a function (or in this question, a composition of two functions), you can work backward to find the input. Because $g(x)$ is the inside function for this composition, its output becomes the input for $f(x)$. Unfortunately, you don't have any information about g yet. You do know however that f of some number, $g(2)$, is -1, so set $f(x)$ equal to -1 and solve for x:

$$-1 = x + 1$$
$$-2 = x$$

You now know that $f(-2) = -1$. In the equation for the composition, $g(2)$ represents x, so you also know that $g(2)$ must be -2. Your only option now is to use brute force to determine which equation for g, when evaluated at 2, results in -2.

Choice A: $g(2) = 2 - 6 = -4$ (not -2), so eliminate.

Choice B: $g(2) = 2 - 4 = -2$

You don't need to go any further; (B) is correct.

You could check your answer by working forward, starting with $g(2)$:

$$g(2) = 2 - 4 = -2$$
$$f\big(g(2)\big) = f(-2) = -2 + 1 = -1$$

16. 1/5 or .2   Difficulty: Medium

Category: Heart of Algebra / Linear Equations

Getting to the Answer: There are two variables but only one equation, so you can't actually solve the equation for k. Instead, recall that an equation has infinitely many solutions when the left side is identical to the right side. When this happens, everything cancels out and you get $0 = 0$, which is always true. Start by simplifying the right-hand side of the equation. Don't simplify the left side because k is already in a good position.

$$k(10x - 5) = 2(3 + x) - 7$$
$$k(10x - 5) = 6 + 2x - 7$$
$$k(10x - 5) = 2x - 1$$

Next, compare the left side of the equation to the right side. Rather than distributing the k, notice that $2x$ is a fifth of $10x$ and -1 is a fifth of -5, so if k were $\frac{1}{5}$ (or 0.2), then both sides of the equation would equal $2x - 1$, and it would therefore have infinitely many solutions. Thus, k is $\frac{1}{5}$ or .2.

17. 2   Difficulty: Medium

Category: Additional Topics in Math / Geometry

Getting to the Answer: You could use the Pythagorean theorem to solve this, but it will save valuable time on Test Day if you recognize that this question is testing your knowledge of Pythagorean triples. The triangle is a right triangle with leg lengths of 18 and 24, which, when divided by 6, are in the proportion 3:4. This means that the triangle is a scaled up 3:4:5 right triangle with a scale factor of 6. To keep the same proportion, the hypotenuse must be $5 \times 6 = 30$. For $15n$ to equal 30, n must be 2.

18. 3   Difficulty: Hard

Category: Passport to Advanced Math / Exponents

Getting to the Answer: You need to use rules of exponents to simplify the expression. Before you can do that, you must rewrite the radicals as fraction exponents. Use the phrase "power over root" to help you convert the radicals: $\sqrt{x} = \sqrt[\text{root}\rightarrow 2]{x^{1 \leftarrow \text{power}}} = x^{\frac{1}{2}}$ and $\sqrt[\text{root} \rightarrow 4]{x^{3 \leftarrow \text{power}}} = x^{\frac{3}{4}}$. Then use rules of exponents to simplify the expression. Add the exponents of the factors that are being multiplied and subtract the exponent of the factor that is being divided:

$$\frac{\sqrt{x} \cdot x^{\frac{5}{4}} \cdot x^2}{\sqrt[4]{x^3}} = \frac{x^{\frac{1}{2}} \cdot x^{\frac{5}{4}} \cdot x^{\frac{2}{1}}}{x^{\frac{3}{4}}}$$
$$= x^{\frac{1}{2} + \frac{5}{4} + \frac{2}{1} - \frac{3}{4}}$$
$$= x^{\frac{2}{4} + \frac{5}{4} + \frac{8}{4} - \frac{3}{4}}$$
$$= x^{\frac{12}{4}} = x^3$$

The exponent of the simplified expression is 3.

19. 27   Difficulty: Hard

Category: Additional Topics in Math / Imaginary Numbers

Getting to the Answer: Each of the factors in this product has two terms, so they behave like binomials. This means you can use FOIL to find the product. To avoid messy numbers, simplify the two radicals first using the definition of i. Write each of the numbers under the radicals as a product of -1 and the number, take the square roots, and then FOIL the resulting expressions:

$$\left(3 + \sqrt{-16}\right)\left(1 - \sqrt{-36}\right)$$
$$= \left(3 + \sqrt{16 \times (-1)}\right)\left(1 - \sqrt{36 \times (-1)}\right)$$
$$= (3 + 4i)(1 - 6i)$$
$$= 3 - 18i + 4i - 24i^2$$
$$= 3 - 14i - 24(-1)$$
$$= 3 - 14i + 24$$
$$= 27 - 14i$$

The question asks for the value of a (the real part of the expression), so the correct answer is 27.

20. 6   **Difficulty:** Hard

Category: Passport to Advanced Math / Quadratics

Getting to the Answer: When you are given the graph of a parabola, try to use what you know about intercepts, the vertex, and the axis of symmetry to answer the question. Here, you could try to use points from the graph to find its equation, but this is not necessary because the question only asks for the value of b. As a shortcut, recall that you can find the vertex of a parabola using the formula $x = -\dfrac{b}{2a}$ (the quadratic formula without the radical part). You are given that $a = -1$. Now look at the graph—the vertex of the parabola is (3, 8), so substitute 3 for x, -1 for a, and solve for b.

$$3 = -\frac{b}{2(-1)}$$
$$3 = -\left(\frac{b}{-2}\right)$$
$$3 = \frac{b}{2}$$
$$3(2) = b$$
$$6 = b$$

As an alternate method, you could plug the value of a and the vertex (from the graph) into vertex form of a quadratic equation and simplify:

$$y = a(x - h)^2 + k$$
$$= -1(x - 3)^2 + 8$$
$$= -1(x^2 - 6x + 9) + 8$$
$$= -x^2 + 6x - 9 + 8$$
$$= -x^2 + 6x - 1$$

The coefficient of x is b, so $b = 6$.

MATH—CALCULATOR TEST

1. D   **Difficulty:** Easy

Category: Heart of Algebra / Systems of Linear Equations

Getting to the Answer: A quick examination of the equations in the system will tell you which strategy to use to solve it. Because $4x$ and $-4x$ are opposites of one another, the system is already perfectly set up to solve by elimination (combining the two equations by adding them).

$$\begin{array}{r} \cancel{4x} + y = -5 \\ \underline{-\cancel{4x} - 2y = -2} \\ -y = -7 \\ y = 7 \end{array}$$

Choice (D) is correct.

2. D   **Difficulty:** Easy

Category: Problem Solving and Data Analysis / Scatterplots

Getting to the Answer: Graphically, slope is the ratio of the change in the y-values (rise) to the change in the x-values (run). In a real-world scenario, this is the same as the unit rate. In this context, the rise describes the change in the number of home runs hit in a single season, and the run describes the change in the number of hours a player spends in batting practice. Thus, the unit rate, or slope, represents the estimated increase (since the data trends upward) in the number of single-season home runs hit by a player for each hour he spends in batting practice, (D).

3. B   **Difficulty:** Easy

Category: Heart of Algebra / Linear Equations

Getting to the Answer: Finding an *x*-intercept is easy when you know the equation of the line—it's the value of *x* when *y* is 0. Notice that the answer choices are very close together. This means you shouldn't just estimate visually. Take the time to do the math. Everything you need to write the equation is shown on the graph—just pay careful attention to how the grid-lines are labeled. The *y*-intercept is 10 and the line rises 2 units and runs 1 unit from one point to the next, so the slope is $\frac{2}{1} = 2$. This means the equation of the line, in slope-intercept form, is $y = 2x + 10$. Now, set the equation equal to zero and solve for *x*:

$$0 = 2x + 10$$
$$-10 = 2x$$
$$-5 = x$$

The line will intersect the *x*-axis at −5, which is (B).

4. A   **Difficulty:** Easy

Category: Passport to Advanced Math / Functions

Getting to the Answer: When you see an expression like *f*(*x*), it means to substitute the given value for *x* in the function's equation. When there is more than one function involved, pay careful attention to which function should be evaluated first. You are looking for the value of *f*(*x*) at *x* = 5. Because *f*(*x*) is defined in terms of *g*(*x*), evaluate *g*(5) first by substituting 5 for *x* in the expression *x* + 2.

$$g(5) = 5 + 2 = 7$$
$$f(5) = -3g(5) = -3(7) = -21$$

This means (A) is correct.

5. B   **Difficulty:** Medium

Category: Heart of Algebra / Linear Equations

Getting to the Answer: Write an equation in words first, and then translate from English into math. Keep in mind that the laundry detergent is on sale, but

the dog food is not. The detergent is 30% off, which means Sara only pays 100 − 30 = 70% of the price, or 0.7($8) = $5.60. The dog food is three cans for $4 and she buys 12 cans, which means she buys 4 sets of 3, so she pays 4 × $4 = $16 for the dog food. The total cost equals the detergent price ($5.60) times how many she buys (*x*) plus the total dog food price ($16). This translates as *C* = 5.6*x* + 16, which matches (B). Note that there are variables in the answer choices, so you could also use the Picking Numbers strategy to answer this question.

6. B   **Difficulty:** Medium

Category: Heart of Algebra / Linear Equations

Getting to the Answer: The cost per night in the hospital is the same as the unit rate, which is represented by the slope of the line. Use the grid-lines and the axis labels to count the rise and the run from the *y*-intercept of the line (0, 26,000) to the next point that hits an intersection of two grid-lines, (2, 34,000). Pay careful attention to how the grid-lines are marked (by 2s on the *x*-axis and by 2,000s on the *y*-axis). The line rises 8,000 units and runs 2 units, so the slope is $\frac{8,000}{2}$, which means it costs an average of $4,000 per night to stay in the hospital.

Note that you could also use the slope formula and the two points to find the slope:

$$\frac{34,000 - 26,000}{2 - 0} = \frac{8,000}{2} = 4,000$$

Choice (B) is correct.

7. D   **Difficulty:** Medium

Category: Problem Solving and Data Analysis / Scatterplots

Getting to the Answer: You aren't given much information to go on except the shape of the graph, so you'll need to think about what the shape means. Remember, linear functions increase at a constant rate, exponential functions increase at either an increasing or decreasing rate, gradually at first and then more quickly or vice versa, and quadratics and polynomials reverse direction one or more times. The graph begins by decreasing extremely quickly, but then it almost (but not quite) levels off. Therefore, it can't be linear and because it doesn't change direction, an exponential function, (D), would be the best model for the data.

8. A   Difficulty: Medium

Category: Problem Solving and Data Analysis / Statistics and Probability

Getting to the Answer: This is a science crossover question. Read the first three sentences quickly—they are simply describing the context. The second half of the paragraph poses the question, so read that more carefully. In the sample, 2,800 out of 3,200 acres were free of kudzu after applying the herbicide. This is $\frac{2,800}{3,200} = 0.875 = 87.5\%$ of the area. For the whole region, assuming the same general conditions, 0.875(30,000) = 26,250 acres should be free of the kudzu. Be careful—this is not the answer. The question asks how much of the cropland would *still be covered* by kudzu, so subtract to get 30,000 − 26,250 = 3,750 acres, (A).

9. B   Difficulty: Medium

Category: Passport to Advanced Math / Functions

Getting to the Answer: The notation $g(h(x))$ indicates a composition of two functions, which can be read "g of h of x." It means that the output when x is substituted in $h(x)$ becomes the input for $g(x)$. First, use the top and bottom rows of the table to find that $h(3)$ is 2. This is your new input. Now, use the top and middle rows of the table to find $g(2)$, which is −3, (B).

10. B   Difficulty: Medium

Category: Heart of Algebra / Linear Equations

Getting to the Answer: The key to answering this type of question is determining how many results fit in each category. Here, you need to know how many shots were 3-pointers and how many were 2-pointers. Mae-Ling successfully made 15 shots

total and s were 3-pointers, so the rest, or 15 − s, must have been 2-pointers. Write the expression in words first: points per 3-pointers (3) times number of shots that were 3-pointers (s), plus points per regular goal (2) times number of regular goals (15 − s). Now, translate from English into math: 3s + 2(15 − s). This is not one of the answer choices, so simplify the expression by distributing the 2 and then combining like terms: 3s + 2(15 − s) = 3s + 30 − 2s = s + 30. This matches (B).

11. A   Difficulty: Medium

Category: Problem Solving and Data Analysis / Rates, Ratios, Proportions, and Percentages

Getting to the Answer: Let the units in this question guide you to the answer. You can do one conversion at a time, or all of them at once. Just be sure to line up the units so they'll cancel correctly. The company uses 8 machines, each of which pumps at a rate of 37.5 gallons per minute, so the rate is actually 8 × 37.5 = 300 gallons per minute. Find the total number of gallons needed, and then use the rate to find the time.

$$2,500 \; \cancel{bbl} \times \frac{42 \; \cancel{gal}}{1 \; \cancel{bbl}} \times \frac{1 \; \text{min}}{300 \; \cancel{gal}} = 350 \, \text{min}$$

The answers are given in hours and minutes, so change 350 minutes to 350 ÷ 60 = 5.833 hours, which is 5 hours and 50 minutes, (A).

12. C   Difficulty: Medium

Category: Problem Solving and Data Analysis / Functions

Getting to the Answer: Look for a pattern for the sales of each company. Then apply that pattern to see which one will sell more in the last month of the year. Writing a function that represents each pattern will also help, but you have to be careful that you evaluate the function at the correct input value. Company A's sales can be represented by a linear function because each month the company sells 92 more of the toy than the month before, which is a constant difference. The sales can be represented by the function $f(t) = 92t + 54$, where t is the number of months *after January*. December is 11 months (not 12) after January, so during the last month of the year Company A should sell $f(11) = 92(11) + 54 = 1{,}066$ of the toy. Company B's sales can be represented by an exponential function because the sales are doubling each month, which is a constant ratio (2 for doubling). The function is $g(t) = 15(2)^t$, where t is again the number of months *after January*. In December, Company B should sell $g(11) = 15(2)^{11} = 30{,}720$. This means that in December, Company B should sell $30{,}720 - 1{,}066 = 29{,}654$ more of the toy than Company A. Choice (C) is correct.

13. A   **Difficulty:** Medium

Category: Heart of Algebra / Inequalities

Getting to the Answer: Apply logic to this question first, and then algebra. The dot at the beginning of the shaded portion is an open dot, so -2 is not included in the solution set of the inequality. This means you can eliminate C and D because those symbols *would* include the endpoint. Don't immediately choose B just because the arrow is pointing to the right, which typically indicates *greater than*. When dealing with an inequality, if you multiply or divide by a negative number, you must flip the symbol, so the answer is not necessarily what you might think. Because you were able to eliminate two of the choices, the quickest approach is to pick one of the remaining symbols, plug it in, and see if it works. If it does, choose that answer. If it doesn't, then it must be the other symbol. Try (A):

$$5(x - 2) - 3x < 4x - 6$$
$$5x - 10 - 3x < 4x - 6$$
$$2x - 10 < 4x - 6$$
$$-2x < 4$$
$$x > -2$$

The resulting inequality, $x > -2$, means all the values on the number line greater than (or to the right of) -2, so the initial inequality symbol must have been $<$. Choice (A) is correct.

14. B   **Difficulty:** Easy

Category: Problem Solving and Data Analysis / Rates, Ratios, Proportions, and Percents

Getting to the Answer: When a question involves scale factors, set up a proportion and solve for the missing value.

$$\frac{1}{8} = \frac{x}{19.9}$$
$$8x = 19.9$$
$$x = 2.4875 \approx 2.5$$

Choice (B) is correct.

15. C   **Difficulty:** Easy

Category: Problem Solving and Data Analysis / Rates, Ratios, Proportions, and Percents

Getting to the Answer: Don't make this question harder than it actually is. You don't need to find the new scale factor. Instead, use the length that the student drew the femur and the actual length to set up and solve a new proportion.

$$\frac{\text{drawing of sternum}}{\text{actual sternum}} = \frac{\text{drawing of femur}}{\text{actual femur}}$$
$$\frac{x}{6.7} = \frac{3.5}{19.9}$$
$$23.45 = 19.9x$$
$$1.1783 = x$$
$$x \approx 1.2$$

Choice (C) is correct.

16. B   **Difficulty:** Medium

Category: Heart of Algebra / Linear Equations

Getting to the Answer: Given two points (even when the coordinates are variables), the slope of the line between the points can be found using the formula $m = \dfrac{y_2 - y_1}{x_2 - x_1}$. You are given a numerical value for the slope and a pair of ordered pairs that have variables in them. To find the value of c, plug the points into the slope formula, and then solve for c. Be careful of all the negative signs.

$$m = \frac{y_2 - y_1}{x_2 - x_1}$$

$$\frac{1}{2} = \frac{-8 - 2c}{-c - (4 - c)}$$

$$\frac{1}{2} = \frac{-8 - 2c}{-c - 4 + c}$$

$$\frac{1}{2} = \frac{-8 - 2c}{-4}$$

$$1(-4) = 2(-8 - 2c)$$

$$-4 = -16 - 4c$$

$$12 = -4c$$

$$-3 = c$$

Choice (B) is correct.

17. A   Difficulty: Medium

Category: Problem Solving and Data Analysis / Rates, Ratios, Proportions, and Percents

Getting to the Answer: Questions that involve distance, rate, and time can almost always be solved using the formula Distance = rate × time. Break the question into short steps (first part of trip, second part of trip). Start with the plane from DCA. Use the speed, or rate, of the plane, 338 mph, and its distance from London, 3,718 miles, to determine when it arrived. You don't know the time, so call it t.

$$\text{Distance} = \text{rate} \times \text{time}$$

$$3,718 = 338t$$

$$11 = t$$

It took the DCA flight 11 hours. Now determine how long it took the plane from MIA. You'll need to find the distance for each part of the trip—the question only tells you the total distance. Then, use the formula to find how long the plane flew at 596 mph and how long it flew at 447 mph.

First part of trip: *Second part of trip:*

$$\frac{2}{3} \times 4,470 = 2,980 \, \text{mi} \quad \frac{1}{3} \times 4,470 = 1,490 \, \text{mi}$$

$$2,980 = 596t \qquad 1,490 = 447t$$

$$5 = t \qquad\qquad 3.\overline{3} = t$$

This means it took the MIA flight 5 hours + 3 hours, 20 minutes = 8 hours, 20 minutes. So, the plane from MIA arrived first. It arrived 11 hours − 8 hours, 20 minutes = 2 hours, 40 minutes before the plane from DCA, making (A) correct.

18. D   Difficulty: Medium

Category: Passport to Advanced Math / Quadratics

Getting to the Answer: The graph of every quadratic equation is a parabola, which may or may not cross the x-axis, depending on where its vertex is and which way it opens. When an equation has no solution, its graph does not cross the x-axis, so try to envision the graph of each of the answer choices (or you could graph each one in your graphing calculator, but this will probably take longer). Don't forget—if the equation is written in vertex form, $y = a(x - h)^2 + k$, then the vertex is (h, k) and the value of a tells you which way the parabola opens. When a quadratic equation is written in factored form, the factors tell you the x-intercepts, which means A and B (which are factored) must cross the x-axis, so eliminate them. Now, imagine the graph of the equation in C: The vertex is $(-1, 8)$ and a is negative, so the parabola opens downward and consequently must cross the x-axis. This means (D) must be correct. The vertex is also $(-1, 8)$, but a is positive, so the graph opens up and does not cross the x-axis.

19. D   Difficulty: Medium

Category: Problem Solving and Data Analysis / Statistics and Probability

Getting to the Answer: The two variables are certainly correlated—as one goes up, the other goes up. A linear regression model would fit the data fairly well, so you can eliminate C. The spending is graphed on the x-axis, so it is the independent variable and therefore does not depend on the GDP, graphed on the y-axis, so you can eliminate B as well. The data does show that as spending on students increases, so does the GDP, but this is simply correlation, not causation. Without additional data, no statements can be made about whether spending more on students is the reason for the increased GDP, so (D) is correct.

20. C   **Difficulty:** Easy

Category: Passport to Advanced Math / Exponents

Getting to the Answer: Focus on the question at the very end—it's just asking you to solve the equation for p_2. Multiply both sides by T_2 to get rid of the denominator on the right-hand side of the equation. Then divide by V_2 to isolate p_2.

$$\frac{p_1 V_1}{T_1} = \frac{p_2 V_2}{T_2}$$

$$\frac{p_1 V_1 T_2}{T_1} = p_2 V_2$$

$$\frac{p_1 V_1 T_2}{T_1 V_2} = p_2$$

Stop here! You cannot cancel the V's and T's because the subscripts indicate that they are not the same variable. In math, subscripts do not behave the same way superscripts (exponents) do. Choice (C) is correct.

21. C   **Difficulty:** Medium

Category: Problem Solving and Data Analysis / Rates, Ratios, Proportions, and Percents

Getting to the Answer: The factor-label method (cancelling units) is a great strategy for this question. You're starting with tons, so work from that unit, arranging conversions so that units cancel. To keep units straight, use an E for Earth, an M for Mars, and a J for Jupiter.

$$1.5 \, \cancel{T} \times \frac{2{,}000 \, \cancel{lb(E)}}{1 \, \cancel{T}} \times \frac{0.377 \, lb(M)}{1 \, \cancel{lb(E)}} = 1{,}131 \, lb \, (M)$$

$$1.5 \, \cancel{T} \times \frac{2{,}000 \, \cancel{lb(E)}}{1 \, \cancel{T}} \times \frac{2.364 \, lb(J)}{1 \, \cancel{lb(E)}} = 7{,}092 \, lb \, (J)$$

The object weighs 1,131 pounds on Mars and 7,092 pounds on Jupiter, so it weighs $7{,}092 - 1{,}131 = 5{,}961$ more pounds on Jupiter, (C).

22. C   **Difficulty:** Medium

Category: Problem Solving and Data Analysis / Statistics and Probability

Getting to the Answer: Examine the shape of the data and familiarize yourself with the title and the axis labels on the graph. Data is *symmetric* if it is fairly evenly spread out, and it is *skewed* if it has a long tail on either side. Notice that the data is skewed to the right, so you can immediately eliminate A. Choices B, (C), and D all describe the data as skewed to the right, so you'll need to examine those statements more closely. For B, "adverse reactions" include the last four bars, which represent $89 + 41 + 22 + 8 = 160$ participants total, which is not even close to 50% of 900, so eliminate B. Note that you don't need to add all the bar heights to find that there were 900 participants—the title of the graph tells you that. Now look at C—"failed to have adverse reactions" means "None" or "Mild" (the first three bars), which represent $900 - 160 = 740$ of the 900 participants. 75% of $900 = 675$, and 740 is more than 675, so (C) is correct. For D, the "None" column contains 320 participants, which does not equal approximately 50% of 900, so it too is incorrect.

23. C   **Difficulty:** Medium

Category: Heart of Algebra / Systems of Linear Equations

Getting to the Answer: Use the Kaplan Method for Translating English into Math. Write a system of equations with $p =$ the cost in dollars of the Pennsylvania bar exam and $d =$ the cost of the D.C. bar exam. The Pennsylvania bar exam (p) costs $25 less ($-25$) than 3 times as much ($3d$) as the D.C. bar exam, or $p = 3d - 25$. Together, both bar exams cost \$775, so $d + p = 775$. The system is:

$$\begin{cases} p = 3d - 25 \\ d + p = 775 \end{cases}$$

The top equation is already solved for p, so substitute $3d - 25$ into the second equation for p, and solve for d:

$$d + (3d - 25) = 775$$
$$4d = 800$$
$$d = 200$$

Be careful—that's not the answer. The D.C. bar exam costs $200, which means the Pennsylvania bar exam costs $775 − $200 = $575. This means the D.C. bar exam is $575 − $200 = $375 less expensive than the Pennsylvania bar exam. Choice (C) is correct.

24. B   Difficulty: Medium

Category: Additional Topics in Math / Geometry

Getting to the Answer: The formula for finding the volume of a cylinder is $V = \pi r^2 h$. Leaving the top 5% of the silo empty is another way of saying that the silo should only be filled to 95% of its total height, so multiply the height (60 feet) by 0.95 to get 57 feet and then find the volume. Don't forget to divide the width of the silo (20 feet) by 2 to find the radius:

$$V = \pi r^2 h$$
$$V = \pi (10)^2 (57)$$
$$V = \pi (100)(57)$$
$$V = 5,700\pi$$

Choice (B) is correct.

25. B   Difficulty: Medium

Category: Problem Solving and Data Analysis / Statistics and Probability

Getting to the Answer: Always read the axis labels carefully when a question involves a chart or graph. *Frequency*, which is plotted along the vertical axis, tells you how many students missed the number of questions indicated under each bar. Evaluate each statement as quickly as you can.

Choice A: Add the bar heights (frequencies) that represent students that missed 5 or more questions: 7 + 3 + 3 + 2 = 15. Then, find the total number of students represented, which is the number that missed less than 5 questions plus the 15 you just found: 2 + 3 + 4 + 6 = 15, plus the 15 you already found, for a total of 30 students. The statement is not true because 15 is exactly half (not more than half) of 30.

Choice (B): This calculation will take a bit of time so skip it for now.

Choice C: The tallest bar tells you which number of questions was missed most often, which was 5 questions, not 3 questions, so this statement is not true.

Choice D: The number of students from Mr. Juno's class who took the test that day is the sum of the heights of the bars, which you already know is 30, not 36.

This means (B) must be correct. Mark it and move on to the next question. (In case you're curious, find the mean by multiplying each number of questions missed by the corresponding frequency, adding all the products, and dividing by the total number of students, which you already know is 30:

$$\text{mean} = \frac{2 + 6 + 12 + 24 + 35 + 18 + 21 + 16}{30}$$
$$= \frac{134}{30} = 4.4\overline{6}$$

The mean is indeed between 4 and 5.)

26. C   Difficulty: Hard

Category: Passport to Advanced Math / Quadratics

Getting to the Answer: Writing quadratic equations can be tricky and time-consuming. If you know the roots, you can use factors to write the equation. If you don't know the roots, you need to create a system of equations to find the coefficients of the variable terms. You don't know the roots of this equation, so start with the point that has the nicest values (0, 2) and substitute them into the equation, $y = ax^2 + bx + c$, to get $2 = a(0)^2 + b(0) + c$, or $2 = c$. Now your equation looks like $y = ax^2 + bx + 2$. Next, use the other two points to create a system of two equations in two variables.

$$(-6, -7) \rightarrow -7 = a(-6)^2 + b(-6) + 2 \rightarrow -9 = 36a - 6b$$

$$(8, -14) \rightarrow -14 = a(8)^2 + b(8) + 2 \rightarrow -16 = 64a + 8b$$

You now have a system of equations to solve. If you multiply the top equation by 4 and the bottom equation by 3, and then add the equations, the b terms will eliminate each other.

$$4\big[-9 = 36a - 6b\big] \;\rightarrow\; -36 = 144a - 24b$$
$$3\big[-16 = 64a + 8b\big] \;\rightarrow\; \underline{-48 = 192a + 24b}$$
$$-84 = 336a$$
$$-0.25 = a$$

Now, find b by substituting $a = -0.25$ into either of the original equations. Using the top equation, you get:

$$-9 = 36(-0.25) - 6b$$
$$-9 = -9 - 6b$$
$$0 = 6b$$
$$0 = b$$

The value of $a + b + c$ is $(-0.25) + 0 + 2 = 1.75$, (C).

27. D   Difficulty: Hard

Category: Problem Solving and Data Analysis / Rates, Ratios, Proportions, and Percentages

Getting to the Answer: Read the question, organizing important information as you go. You need to find the ratio of mini muffins to jumbo muffins. You're given two ratios: mini to regular and regular to jumbo. Both of the given ratios contain regular muffin size units, but the regular amounts (2 and 5) are not identical. To directly compare them, find a common multiple (10). Multiply each ratio by the factor that will make the number of regular muffins equal to 10.

Mini to regular: (5:2) × (5:5) = 25:10

Regular to jumbo: (5:4) × (2:2) = 10:8

Now that the number of regular muffins is the same in both ratios (10), you can merge the two ratios to compare mini to jumbo directly: 25:10:8. So, the proper ratio of mini muffins to jumbo muffins is 25:8, which is (D).

28. A   Difficulty: Medium

Category: Heart of Algebra / Systems of Linear Equations

Getting to the Answer: Graphically, a system of linear equations that has no solution indicates two parallel lines, or in other words, two lines that have the same slope. So, write each of the equations in slope-intercept form ($y = mx + b$) and set their slopes (m) equal to each other to solve for k. Before finding the slopes, multiply the top equation by 6 to make it easier to manipulate.

$$6\left(\frac{1}{3}x + \frac{1}{2}y = 5\right) \rightarrow 2x + 3y = 30 \rightarrow y = -\frac{2}{3}x + 10$$

$$kx - 4y = 16 \rightarrow -4y = -kx + 16 \rightarrow y = \frac{k}{4}x - 4$$

The slope of the first line is $-\frac{2}{3}$, and the slope of the second line is $\frac{k}{4}$. Set them equal and solve for k:

$$-\frac{2}{3} = \frac{k}{4}$$
$$-8 = 3k$$
$$-\frac{8}{3} = k$$

Choice (A) is correct.

29. D   Difficulty: Hard

Category: Passport to Advanced Math / Exponents

Getting to the Answer: The numbers in some questions are simply too large to use a calculator (you get an "overflow" error message). Instead, you'll have to rely on rules of exponents. Notice that all of the base numbers have 3 as a factor, so rewrite everything in terms of 3. This will allow you to use the rules of exponents. Because 27 is the cube of 3, you can rewrite 27^{90} as a power of 3.

$$27^{90} = \left(3^3\right)^{90}$$
$$= 3^{3 \times 90}$$
$$= 3^{270}$$

Now the product should read: $3^{90} \times 3^{270}$, which is equal to $3^{90+270} = 3^{360}$. Repeat this process for the quantity that is being divided:

$$\left(\frac{1}{9}\right)^{30} = \left(\frac{1}{3^2}\right)^{30} = \left(3^{-2}\right)^{30} = 3^{-60}$$

Finally, use rules of exponents one more time to simplify the new expression:

$$\frac{3^{360}}{3^{-60}} = 3^{360+60} = 3^{420}$$

All the answer choices are given as powers of 9, so rewrite your answer as a power of 9:

$$3^{420} = 3^{2\times210} = \left(3^2\right)^{210} = 9^{210}$$

Choice (D) is correct.

30. D   **Difficulty:** Hard

Category: Additional Topics in Math / Geometry

Getting to the Answer: If needed, don't forget to check the formulas provided for you at the beginning of each math section. The volume of a right cone is given by $V = \frac{1}{3}\pi r^2 h$. Here, you only know the value of one of the variables, V, so you'll need to use the information in the question to somehow write r and h in terms of just one variable. If the cone is three times as wide at the base as it is tall, then call the diameter $3x$ and the height of the cone one-third of that, or x. The volume formula calls for the radius, which is half the diameter, or $\frac{3x}{2}$. Substitute these values into the formula and solve for x:

$$V = \frac{1}{3}\pi r^2 h$$

$$384\pi = \frac{1}{3}\pi\left(\frac{3}{2}x\right)^2 x$$

$$384 = \left(\frac{1}{3}\right)\left(\frac{9}{4}x^2\right)x$$

$$384 = \frac{3}{4}x^3$$

$$512 = x^3$$

$$\sqrt[3]{512} = x$$

$$8 = x$$

The question asks for the diameter of the base, which is $3x = 3(8) = 24$, choice (D).

31. 1/4 or .25   **Difficulty:** Medium

Category: Heart of Algebra / Inequalities

Getting to the Answer: The question is asking about $\frac{m}{n}$, so think about how fractions work. Large numerators result in larger values ($\frac{3}{2}$, for example, is larger than $\frac{1}{2}$), and smaller denominators result in larger values ($\frac{1}{2}$, for example, is greater than $\frac{1}{4}$). The largest possible value of $\frac{m}{n}$ is found by choosing the largest possible value of m and the smallest possible value for n: $\frac{0.4}{1.6} = \frac{1}{4} = 0.25$.

32. 6   **Difficulty:** Medium

Category: Passport to Advanced Math / Functions

Getting to the Answer: The notation $(f - g)(3)$ means $f(3) - g(3)$. You don't know the equations of the functions, so you'll need to read the values from the graph. Graphically, $f(3)$ means the y-value at $x = 3$ on the graph of f, which is 2. Likewise, $g(3)$ means the y-value at $x = 3$ on the graph of g, which is -4. The difference, $f - g$, is $2 - (-4) = 6$.

33. 85   **Difficulty:** Easy

Category: Problem Solving and Data Analysis / Scatterplots

Getting to the Answer: The *range* of a set of data points is the set of outputs, which correspond to the y-values of the data points on the graph. To find the maximum value in the range of the data, look for the highest point on the graph, which is (250, 85). The y-value is 85, so 85 is the maximum value in the range.

34. 0.06   Difficulty: Medium

Category: Problem Solving and Data Analysis / Statistics and Probability

Getting to the Answer: First, find the probability that the first employee chosen at random will be one who has been with the company for longer than 3 years. The total number of employees who participated in the study is $38 + 30 + 15 + 19 + 54 + 48 = 204$. The total number of both females and males who have been with the company longer (greater) than 3 years is $54 + 48 = 102$. Therefore, the probability of choosing one employee who has been with the company longer than 3 years is: $\frac{102}{204} = \frac{1}{2}$. Because the same employee cannot be randomly selected more than once, the chance that another selected employee will have been with the company more than 3 years is not simply equal to $\frac{1}{2}$. Instead, assuming the first employee chosen at random has been with the company more than 3 years, the chance that a second employee chosen at random will also be is $\frac{(102 - 1)}{(204 - 1)} = \frac{101}{203}$. For a third employee, the chance is $\frac{(102 - 2)}{(204 - 2)} = \frac{100}{202} = \frac{50}{101}$, and for a fourth, the chance is $\frac{(102 - 3)}{(204 - 3)} = \frac{99}{201}$. Thus, to determine the probability that all 4 have been with the company longer than 3 years, multiply all these probabilities together: $\frac{1}{2} \times \frac{101}{203} \times \frac{50}{101} \times \frac{99}{201} \approx 0.06$.

35. 102   Difficulty: Medium

Category: Additional Topics in Math / Geometry

Getting to the Answer: The distance around part of a circle is the same as arc length, so use the relationship $\frac{\text{arc length}}{\text{circumference}} = \frac{\text{central angle}}{360°}$ to answer the question. The unknown in the relationship is the central angle, so call it A. Before you can fill in the rest of the equation, you need to find the circumference of the circle: $C = 2\pi r = 2\pi(840) = 1{,}680\pi$. Now you're ready to solve for A:

$$\frac{\text{arc length}}{\text{circumference}} = \frac{\text{central angle}}{360°}$$

$$\frac{1{,}500}{1{,}680\pi} = \frac{A}{360}$$

$$\frac{1{,}500 \times 360}{1{,}680\pi} = A$$

$$102.314 \approx A$$

Be careful when you enter this expression into your calculator—you need to put $1{,}680\pi$ in parentheses so that the calculator doesn't divide by $1{,}680$ and then multiply by π. If entered correctly, the result is about 102 degrees.

36. 7   Difficulty: Hard

Category: Heart of Algebra / Linear Equations

Getting to the Answer: To write the equation of a line, you need two things: the slope and the y-intercept. Start by finding these, substituting them into slope-intercept form of a line ($y = mx + b$), and then manipulate the equation so that it is written in standard form. Use the given points, $(-4, 1)$ and $(3, -2)$, and the slope formula to find m:

$$m = \frac{y_2 - y_1}{x_2 - x_1} = \frac{-2 - 1}{3 - (-4)} = -\frac{3}{7}$$

Next, find the y-intercept, b, using the slope and one of the points:

$$y = -\frac{3}{7}x + b$$

$$1 = -\frac{3}{7}(-4) + b$$

$$1 = \frac{12}{7} + b$$

$$-\frac{5}{7} = b$$

Write the equation in slope-intercept form: $y = -\frac{3}{7}x - \frac{5}{7}$.

Now, rewrite the equation in the form $Ax + By = C$, making sure that A is a positive integer (a whole number greater than 0):

$$y = -\frac{3}{7}x - \frac{5}{7}$$

$$\frac{3}{7}x + y = -\frac{5}{7}$$

$$7\left(\frac{3}{7}x + y = -\frac{5}{7}\right)7$$

$$3x + 7y = -5$$

The question asks for the value of *B* (the coefficient of *y*), so the correct answer is 7.

37. 380   Difficulty: Medium

Category: Problem Solving and Data Analysis / Rates, Ratios, Proportions, and Percents

Getting to the Answer: You can use the formula Percent × whole = part to solve this problem, but you will first need to think conceptually about what the question is asking. The question is asking for the Dow value *before* the 19.5% decrease to 306. This means that 306 represents 100 − 19.5 = 80.5% of what the stock market was at its record high. Fill these amounts into the equation and solve for the original whole, the record high Dow value.

$$0.805 \times w = 306$$

$$w = \frac{306}{0.805}$$

$$w = 380.124$$

Rounded to the nearest whole point, the record high was approximately 380 points.

38. 25   Difficulty: Hard

Category: Problem Solving and Data Analysis / Rates, Ratios, Proportions, and Percents

Getting to the Answer: Percent change is given by the ratio $\frac{\text{amount of change}}{\text{original amount}}$. To find the total percent change, you'll need to work your way through each of the days, and then use the ratio. Jot down the Dow

value at the end of each day as you go. Do not round until you reach your final answer. First, calculate the value of the Dow at closing on Black Thursday: It opened at 306 and decreased by 2%, which means the value at the end of the day was 100 − 2 = 98% of the starting amount, or 306 × 0.98 = 299.88. Then, it decreased again on Monday by 13% to close at 100 − 13 = 87% of the opening amount, or 299.88 × 0.87 = 260.8956. Finally, it decreased on Tuesday by another 12% to end at 100 − 12 = 88% of the starting amount, or 260.8956 × 0.88 = 229.588. Now use the percent change formula to calculate the percent decrease from opening on Black Thursday (306) to closing on Black Tuesday (229.588):

$$\text{Percent decrease} = \frac{306 - 229.588}{306}$$

$$= \frac{76.412}{306} = 0.2497$$

The Dow had a total percent decrease of approximately 25% between opening on Black Thursday and closing on Black Tuesday.

ESSAY TEST RUBRIC

The Essay Demonstrates ...

4—Advanced	• **(Reading)** A strong ability to comprehend the source text, including its central ideas and important details and how they interrelate; and effectively use evidence (quotations, paraphrases, or both) from the source text. • **(Analysis)** A strong ability to evaluate the author's use of evidence, reasoning, and/or stylistic and persuasive elements, and/or other features of the student's own choosing; make good use of relevant, sufficient, and strategically chosen support for the claims or points made in the student's essay; and focus consistently on features of the source text that are most relevant to addressing the task. • **(Writing)** A strong ability to provide a precise central claim; create an effective organization that includes an introduction and conclusion, as well as a clear progression of ideas; successfully employ a variety of sentence structures; use precise word choice; maintain a formal style and objective tone; and show command of the conventions of standard written English so that the essay is free of errors.
3—Proficient	• **(Reading)** Satisfactory ability to comprehend the source text, including its central ideas and important details and how they interrelate; and use evidence (quotations, paraphrases, or both) from the source text. • **(Analysis)** Satisfactory ability to evaluate the author's use of evidence, reasoning, and/or stylistic and persuasive elements, and/or other features of the student's own choosing; make use of relevant and sufficient support for the claims or points made in the student's essay; and focus primarily on features of the source text that are most relevant to addressing the task. • **(Writing)** Satisfactory ability to provide a central claim; create an organization that includes an introduction and conclusion, as well as a clear progression of ideas; employ a variety of sentence structures; use precise word choice; maintain an appropriate formal style and objective tone; and show control of the conventions of standard written English so that the essay is free of significant errors.
2—Partial	• **(Reading)** Limited ability to comprehend the source text, including its central ideas and important details and how they interrelate; and use evidence (quotations, paraphrases, or both) from the source text. • **(Analysis)** Limited ability to evaluate the author's use of evidence, reasoning, and/or stylistic and persuasive elements, and/or other features of the student's own choosing; make use of support for the claims or points made in the student's essay; and focus on relevant features of the source text. • **(Writing)** Limited ability to provide a central claim; create an effective organization for ideas; employ a variety of sentence structures; use precise word choice; maintain an appropriate style and tone; or show command of the conventions of standard written English, resulting in certain errors that detract from the quality of the writing.

1—Inadequate	• **(Reading)** Little or no ability to comprehend the source text or use evidence from the source text.
	• **(Analysis)** Little or no ability to evaluate the author's use of evidence, reasoning, and/or stylistic and persuasive elements; choose support for claims or points; or focus on relevant features of the source text.
	• **(Writing)** Little or no ability to provide a central claim, organization, or progression of ideas; employ a variety of sentence structures; use precise word choice; maintain an appropriate style and tone; or show command of the conventions of standard written English, resulting in numerous errors that undermine the quality of the writing.

ESSAY RESPONSE #1 (ADVANCED SCORE)

In his speech to the National Union of South African Students in 1966, Robert F. Kennedy makes the claim that the guiding principle of Western societies must be the enhancement of liberty for all individuals. Through appeals to Western values, references to historical evidence, and calls to conscience, Kennedy constructs a powerful and effective argument.

Kennedy begins his speech by praising the core values of Western society—freedom and democracy, and the rights associated with them. In so doing, he both establishes common ground with his South African audience, who viewed themselves as part of Western society, and also highlights the ways in which the repressive government of South Africa in 1966 failed to uphold these values. To Kennedy, the freedom of speech is not merely the right to say whatever one chooses, rather, it allows us to speak up to our governments when they are derelict in their duties, and is a key part of what it means to be an active member of society. Kennedy also insists that the right of individuals to be heard by their government is essential to democracy, because it forces government officials to answer to the people who elected them. Frequently, Kennedy uses heightened language to describe these rights and values, which deepens the impact of his message. The freedom of speech separates us from the "dumb beasts of field and forest." The power to be heard allows people a voice in the decisions that "shape men's lives." Most powerfully, Kennedy states that these rights are "sacred." This kind of elevated language imparts a weight to Kennedy's argument that ordinary language could not.

Kennedy also makes references to historical and current events to bolster his claims. He asserts that the rights he describes are what separate democratic societies from Nazi Germany and Persia, countries known to be extremely repressive. This reference to brutal regimes strengthens his claim that these rights should be the guiding principle of any decent society. He also uses the United States as a model of a society that has been striving for the expansion of liberty and, while failing in some respects, is succeeding overall. Kennedy's father, he says, was barred from many jobs as a young man due to his Irish background, yet several decades later, his son John F. Kennedy became president, proving that conditions can change for the better. Robert Kennedy acknowledges that the United States still has far to go, just like South Africa, yet he cites examples of major progress, such as an African American astronaut and an African American chief justice, as well as Martin Luther King, Jr., who won the Nobel Peace Prize. Kennedy's implication is that the ideals of liberty and justice are worth upholding because they can make a society greater and more inclusive.

Another way Kennedy persuades his audience of the validity of his argument is by making calls to conscience. He states that the most important reason to grant freedom to all is because "it is the right thing to do." He reasons that feelings of compassion are common to all people, as are feelings of outrage when other human beings suffer;

therefore, we should all join together in expanding human rights and lessening the suffering of people everywhere. By calling upon his audience's basic sense of right and wrong, Kennedy gives them a personal lens through which to examine his argument, thus making them more likely to embrace its validity.

Robert F. Kennedy passionately believed in the necessity for all Western societies to make the expansion of liberty their guiding principle. To build and support his argument, Kennedy exalts Western values of democracy and freedom, refers to historical examples in which the promotion of liberty made for a better society, and finally calls upon people's conscience to help them see that the expansion of freedom for all is the right thing to do.

ESSAY RESPONSE #2 (PROFICIENT SCORE)

Robert F. Kennedy's central claim in his speech to the National Union of South African Students is that the guiding principle of Western societies should be the expansion of liberty for all individuals. Kennedy uses several techniques to build his argument, including heightened language, examples of countries that have been improved by the expansion of liberty, and appeals to his audience's sense of right and wrong.

Kennedy was not an ordinary man, nor was he an ordinary writer. His speech contains soaring language that makes his audience feel like they are listening to great literature. When he says that the freedom of speech is what seperates us from "dumb beasts," his vivid language makes that freedom seem even more important. He makes frequent references to God, even calling rights of Western society "sacred." And instead of merely saying that young people must stop racism and injustice, he says that it's there responsibility to "strip the last remnants of that ancient, cruel belief from the civilization of man." This type of language makes the audience feel that they are being called to a higher purpose.

Kennedy also provides examples of ways in which countries that promote liberty fare better than countries that don't. When he contrasts Western societies that value freedom with societies that don't—like Nazi Germany and Persia—he is suggesting that countries that deny people their basic rights eventually fail (in 1966, Nazi Germany and Persia no longer existed, but Western democracies still did). Kennedy then uses America as an example of a country that has been improved by expanding liberties for individuals. He tells a personal anecdote about the prejudice experienced by his Irish father, and acknowledges that the struggle to overcome discrimination can take many years. However he provides evidence that the struggle is worth it as shown by his brother's success in becoming president of the United States, and by the African Americans who at that point had risen to the highest ranks of American society—an astronaut, barristers, and a Nobel Prize winner, Martin Luther King, Jr. These examples support Kennedy's claim that enlarging the liberties of individuals is a worthy goal for Western societies.

Finally, Kennedy appeals to his audience's fundamental sense of right and wrong. He says that expanding liberty is "the right thing to do" and that God commands it. He lists multiple examples of evil in the world—"discrimination in New York, apartheid in South Africa . . ."—and tells his audience of students that they must answer the call to eliminate the suffering of others everywhere in the world. He states that evil is common, therefore it can only be cured by other qualities we all share in common, such as our conscence and determination to make the world a better place.

The argument Kennedy makes in this speech is strengthened by his use of the features mentioned above: heightened language, evidence, and appeals to his audience's sense of what is right and what is wrong.

SAT PRACTICE TEST 8 ANSWER SHEET

Remove (or photocopy) this answer sheet and use it to complete the test. See the answer key following the test when finished.

Start with number 1 for each section. If a section has fewer questions than answer spaces, leave the extra spaces blank.

SECTION 1

1. Ⓐ Ⓑ Ⓒ Ⓓ
2. Ⓐ Ⓑ Ⓒ Ⓓ
3. Ⓐ Ⓑ Ⓒ Ⓓ
4. Ⓐ Ⓑ Ⓒ Ⓓ
5. Ⓐ Ⓑ Ⓒ Ⓓ
6. Ⓐ Ⓑ Ⓒ Ⓓ
7. Ⓐ Ⓑ Ⓒ Ⓓ
8. Ⓐ Ⓑ Ⓒ Ⓓ
9. Ⓐ Ⓑ Ⓒ Ⓓ
10. Ⓐ Ⓑ Ⓒ Ⓓ
11. Ⓐ Ⓑ Ⓒ Ⓓ
12. Ⓐ Ⓑ Ⓒ Ⓓ
13. Ⓐ Ⓑ Ⓒ Ⓓ

14. Ⓐ Ⓑ Ⓒ Ⓓ
15. Ⓐ Ⓑ Ⓒ Ⓓ
16. Ⓐ Ⓑ Ⓒ Ⓓ
17. Ⓐ Ⓑ Ⓒ Ⓓ
18. Ⓐ Ⓑ Ⓒ Ⓓ
19. Ⓐ Ⓑ Ⓒ Ⓓ
20. Ⓐ Ⓑ Ⓒ Ⓓ
21. Ⓐ Ⓑ Ⓒ Ⓓ
22. Ⓐ Ⓑ Ⓒ Ⓓ
23. Ⓐ Ⓑ Ⓒ Ⓓ
24. Ⓐ Ⓑ Ⓒ Ⓓ
25. Ⓐ Ⓑ Ⓒ Ⓓ
26. Ⓐ Ⓑ Ⓒ Ⓓ

27. Ⓐ Ⓑ Ⓒ Ⓓ
28. Ⓐ Ⓑ Ⓒ Ⓓ
29. Ⓐ Ⓑ Ⓒ Ⓓ
30. Ⓐ Ⓑ Ⓒ Ⓓ
31. Ⓐ Ⓑ Ⓒ Ⓓ
32. Ⓐ Ⓑ Ⓒ Ⓓ
33. Ⓐ Ⓑ Ⓒ Ⓓ
34. Ⓐ Ⓑ Ⓒ Ⓓ
35. Ⓐ Ⓑ Ⓒ Ⓓ
36. Ⓐ Ⓑ Ⓒ Ⓓ
37. Ⓐ Ⓑ Ⓒ Ⓓ
38. Ⓐ Ⓑ Ⓒ Ⓓ
39. Ⓐ Ⓑ Ⓒ Ⓓ

40. Ⓐ Ⓑ Ⓒ Ⓓ
41. Ⓐ Ⓑ Ⓒ Ⓓ
42. Ⓐ Ⓑ Ⓒ Ⓓ
43. Ⓐ Ⓑ Ⓒ Ⓓ
44. Ⓐ Ⓑ Ⓒ Ⓓ
45. Ⓐ Ⓑ Ⓒ Ⓓ
46. Ⓐ Ⓑ Ⓒ Ⓓ
47. Ⓐ Ⓑ Ⓒ Ⓓ
48. Ⓐ Ⓑ Ⓒ Ⓓ
49. Ⓐ Ⓑ Ⓒ Ⓓ
50. Ⓐ Ⓑ Ⓒ Ⓓ
51. Ⓐ Ⓑ Ⓒ Ⓓ
52. Ⓐ Ⓑ Ⓒ Ⓓ

☐ # correct in Section 1

☐ # incorrect in Section 1

SECTION 2

1. Ⓐ Ⓑ Ⓒ Ⓓ
2. Ⓐ Ⓑ Ⓒ Ⓓ
3. Ⓐ Ⓑ Ⓒ Ⓓ
4. Ⓐ Ⓑ Ⓒ Ⓓ
5. Ⓐ Ⓑ Ⓒ Ⓓ
6. Ⓐ Ⓑ Ⓒ Ⓓ
7. Ⓐ Ⓑ Ⓒ Ⓓ
8. Ⓐ Ⓑ Ⓒ Ⓓ
9. Ⓐ Ⓑ Ⓒ Ⓓ
10. Ⓐ Ⓑ Ⓒ Ⓓ
11. Ⓐ Ⓑ Ⓒ Ⓓ

12. Ⓐ Ⓑ Ⓒ Ⓓ
13. Ⓐ Ⓑ Ⓒ Ⓓ
14. Ⓐ Ⓑ Ⓒ Ⓓ
15. Ⓐ Ⓑ Ⓒ Ⓓ
16. Ⓐ Ⓑ Ⓒ Ⓓ
17. Ⓐ Ⓑ Ⓒ Ⓓ
18. Ⓐ Ⓑ Ⓒ Ⓓ
19. Ⓐ Ⓑ Ⓒ Ⓓ
20. Ⓐ Ⓑ Ⓒ Ⓓ
21. Ⓐ Ⓑ Ⓒ Ⓓ
22. Ⓐ Ⓑ Ⓒ Ⓓ

23. Ⓐ Ⓑ Ⓒ Ⓓ
24. Ⓐ Ⓑ Ⓒ Ⓓ
25. Ⓐ Ⓑ Ⓒ Ⓓ
26. Ⓐ Ⓑ Ⓒ Ⓓ
27. Ⓐ Ⓑ Ⓒ Ⓓ
28. Ⓐ Ⓑ Ⓒ Ⓓ
29. Ⓐ Ⓑ Ⓒ Ⓓ
30. Ⓐ Ⓑ Ⓒ Ⓓ
31. Ⓐ Ⓑ Ⓒ Ⓓ
32. Ⓐ Ⓑ Ⓒ Ⓓ
33. Ⓐ Ⓑ Ⓒ Ⓓ

34. Ⓐ Ⓑ Ⓒ Ⓓ
35. Ⓐ Ⓑ Ⓒ Ⓓ
36. Ⓐ Ⓑ Ⓒ Ⓓ
37. Ⓐ Ⓑ Ⓒ Ⓓ
38. Ⓐ Ⓑ Ⓒ Ⓓ
39. Ⓐ Ⓑ Ⓒ Ⓓ
40. Ⓐ Ⓑ Ⓒ Ⓓ
41. Ⓐ Ⓑ Ⓒ Ⓓ
42. Ⓐ Ⓑ Ⓒ Ⓓ
43. Ⓐ Ⓑ Ⓒ Ⓓ
44. Ⓐ Ⓑ Ⓒ Ⓓ

☐ # correct in Section 2

☐ # incorrect in Section 2

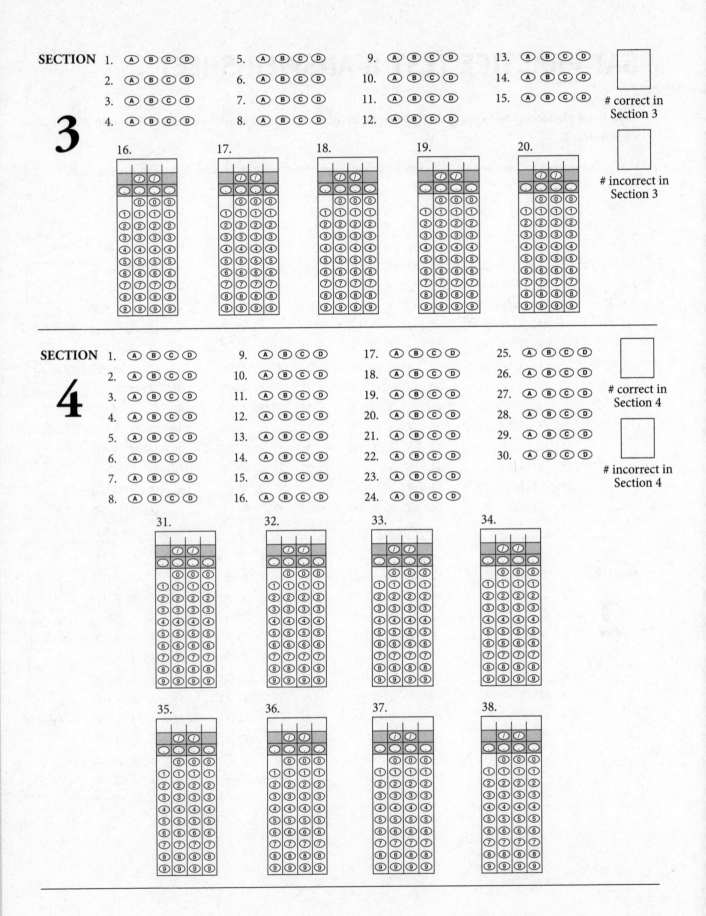

READING TEST

65 Minutes—52 Questions

This section corresponds to Section 1 of your answer sheet.

Directions: Read each passage or pair of passages, then answer the questions that follow. Choose your answers based on what the passage(s) and any accompanying graphics state or imply.

Questions 1-10 are based on the following passage.

This passage is adapted from "Metamorphosis" by Franz Kafka, a famous story that combines elements of fantasy and reality. This excerpt begins with the protagonist realizing he has literally turned into a giant, beetle-like insect.

One morning, when Gregor Samsa woke from troubled dreams, he found himself transformed in his bed into a horrible vermin. He lay on his
Line armor-like back, and if he lifted his head a little
(5) he could see his brown belly, slightly domed and divided by arches into stiff sections. The bedding was hardly able to cover it and seemed ready to slide off any moment. His many legs, pitifully thin compared with the size of the rest of him, waved
(10) about helplessly as he looked.

"What's happened to me?" he thought. It wasn't a dream. His room, a proper human room although a little too small, lay peacefully between its four familiar walls. A collection of textile samples lay
(15) spread out on the table—Samsa was a travelling salesman—and above it there hung a picture that he had recently cut out of an illustrated magazine and housed in a nice, gilded frame. It showed a lady fitted out with a fur hat and fur boa who sat
(20) upright, raising a heavy fur muff that covered the whole of her lower arm towards the viewer.

Gregor then turned to look out the window at the dull weather. Drops of rain could be heard hitting the pane, which made him feel quite sad.
(25) "How about if I sleep a little bit longer and forget all this nonsense," he thought, but that was something he was unable to do because he was used to sleeping on his right, and in his present state couldn't get into that position. However hard he

(30) threw himself onto his right, he always rolled back to where he was. He must have tried it a hundred times, shut his eyes so that he wouldn't have to look at the floundering legs, and only stopped when he began to feel a mild, dull pain there that he had never felt before.

(35) He thought, "What a strenuous career it is that I've chosen! Travelling day in and day out. Doing business like this takes much more effort than doing your own business at home, and on top of that there's the curse of travelling, worries about
(40) making train connections, bad and irregular food, contact with different people all the time so that you can never get to know anyone or become friendly with them." He felt a slight itch up on his belly; pushed himself slowly up on his back
(45) towards the headboard so that he could lift his head better; found where the itch was, and saw that it was covered with lots of little white spots which he didn't know what to make of; and when he tried to feel the place with one of his legs he drew it quickly
(50) back because as soon as he touched it he was overcome by a cold shudder.

He slid back into his former position. "Getting up early all the time," he thought, "it makes you stupid. You've got to get enough sleep. Other
(55) travelling salesmen live a life of luxury. For instance, whenever I go back to the guest house during the morning to copy out the contract, these gentlemen are always still sitting there eating their breakfasts. I ought to just try that with my boss; I'd
(60) get kicked out on the spot. But who knows, maybe that would be the best thing for me. If I didn't have my parents to think about I'd have given in my notice a long time ago, I'd have gone up to the boss and told him just what I think, tell him everything

GO ON TO THE NEXT PAGE ➡

(65) I would, let him know just what I feel. He'd fall right off his desk! And it's a funny sort of business to be sitting up there at your desk, talking down at your subordinates from up there, especially when you have to go right up close because the boss is hard

(70) of hearing. Well, there's still some hope; once I've got the money together to pay off my parents' debt to him—another five or six years I suppose—that's definitely what I'll do. That's when I'll make the big change. First of all though, I've got to get up, my

(75) train leaves at five."

1. According to the passage, Gregor initially believes his transformation is a

   A) curse.

   B) disease.

   C) nightmare.

   D) hoax.

2. As used in line 12, "proper" most nearly means

   A) called for by rules or conventions.

   B) showing politeness.

   C) naturally belonging or peculiar to.

   D) suitably appropriate.

3. The passage most strongly suggests which of the following about Gregor's attitude toward his profession?

   A) He is resentful.

   B) He is diligent.

   C) He is depressed.

   D) He is eager to please.

4. Which choice provides the best evidence for the answer to the previous question?

   A) Lines 14-18 ("A collection . . . gilded frame")

   B) Lines 22-24 ("Gregor then turned . . . quite sad")

   C) Lines 54-60 ("Other . . . the spot")

   D) Lines 66-70 ("And it's . . . hard of hearing")

5. What central idea does the passage communicate through Gregor's experiences?

   A) Imagination is a dangerous thing.

   B) People are fearful of change.

   C) Dreams become our reality.

   D) Humankind is a slave to work.

6. The passage most strongly suggests that which of the following is true of Gregor?

   A) He feels a strong sense of duty toward his family.

   B) He is unable to cope with change.

   C) He excels in his profession.

   D) He is fearful about his transformation.

7. Which choice provides the best evidence for the answer to the previous question?

   A) Lines 11-14 ("What's happened . . . familiar walls")

   B) Lines 22-24 ("Gregor then turned . . . quite sad")

   C) Lines 36-43 ("Doing business . . . with them")

   D) Lines 70-73 ("Well, there's still . . . what I'll do")

GO ON TO THE NEXT PAGE

8. As used in line 33, "floundering" most nearly means

   A) thrashing.

   B) painful.

   C) pitiful.

   D) trembling.

9. The author most likely includes a description of Gregor's itch in lines 43-51 to

   A) remind the reader that Gregor has turned into an insect.

   B) emphasize the disconnect between Gregor's thoughts and his actual situation.

   C) give important details about what Gregor's new body looks like.

   D) show that Gregor's thoughts are focused on the changes to his body.

10. The function of the final sentence of the excerpt ("First of all though, I've got to get up, my train leaves at five") is to

    A) provide a resolution to the conflict Gregor faces.

    B) foreshadow the conflict between Gregor and his boss.

    C) illustrate Gregor's resilience and ability to move on.

    D) emphasize Gregor's extreme sense of duty.

Questions 11-20 are based on the following passage.

This passage is adapted from Hillary Rodham Clinton's speech titled "Women's Rights Are Human Rights," addressed to the U.N. Fourth World Conference on Women in 1995.

If there is one message that echoes forth from this conference, it is that human rights are women's rights. . . . And women's rights are human rights.
Line Let us not forget that among those rights are the
(5) right to speak freely and the right to be heard.

Women must enjoy the right to participate fully in the social and political lives of their countries if we want freedom and democracy to thrive and endure.

It is indefensible that many women in
(10) nongovernmental organizations who wished to participate in this conference have not been able to attend—or have been prohibited from fully taking part.

Let me be clear. Freedom means the right of people to assemble, organize, and debate openly.
(15) It means respecting the views of those who may disagree with the views of their governments. It means not taking citizens away from their loved ones and jailing them, mistreating them, or denying them their freedom or dignity because of
(20) the peaceful expression of their ideas and opinions.

In my country, we recently celebrated the seventy-fifth anniversary of women's suffrage. It took one hundred and fifty years after the signing of our Declaration of Independence for women to
(25) win the right to vote. It took seventy-two years of organized struggle on the part of many courageous women and men.

It was one of America's most divisive philosophical wars. But it was also a bloodless war.
(30) Suffrage was achieved without a shot fired.

We have also been reminded, in V-J Day observances last weekend, of the good that comes when men and women join together to combat the forces of tyranny and build a better world.
(35) We have seen peace prevail in most places for a half century. We have avoided another world war. But we have not solved older, deeply-rooted problems that continue to diminish the potential of half the world's population.
(40) Now it is time to act on behalf of women everywhere.

If we take bold steps to better the lives of women, we will be taking bold steps to better the lives of children and families too. Families rely on mothers and
(45) wives for emotional support and care; families rely on women for labor in the home; and increasingly, families rely on women for income needed to raise healthy children and care for other relatives.

As long as discrimination and inequities remain
(50) so commonplace around the world—as long

GO ON TO THE NEXT PAGE ⇨

as girls and women are valued less, fed less, fed last, overworked, underpaid, not schooled and subjected to violence in and out of their homes— the potential of the human family to create a
(55) peaceful, prosperous world will not be realized.

Let this conference be our—and the world's— call to action.

And let us heed the call so that we can create a world in which every woman is treated with respect
(60) and dignity, every boy and girl is loved and cared for equally, and every family has the hope of a strong and stable future.

11. What is the primary purpose of the passage?

A) To chastise those who have prevented women from attending the conference

B) To argue that women continue to experience discrimination

C) To explain that human rights are of more concern than women's rights

D) To encourage people to think of women's rights as an issue important to all

12. Which choice provides the best evidence for the answer to the previous question?

A) Lines 4-5 ("Let us . . . be heard")

B) Lines 9-12 ("It is indefensible . . . taking part")

C) Lines 37-39 ("But we have . . . population")

D) Lines 44-48 ("Families . . . other relatives")

13. As used in line 28, "divisive" most nearly means

A) conflict-producing.

B) carefully-watched.

C) multi-purpose.

D) time-consuming.

14. Based on the speech, with which statement would Clinton most likely agree?

A) More men should be the primary caregivers of their children in order to provide career opportunities for women.

B) Women do not need the support and cooperation of men as they work toward equality.

C) Solutions for global problems would be found faster if women had more access to power.

D) The American movement for women's suffrage should have been violent in order to achieve success more quickly.

15. Which choice provides the best evidence for the answer to the previous question?

A) Lines 6-8 ("Women . . . endure")

B) Line 30 ("Suffrage . . . shot fired")

C) Lines 44-48 ("Families . . . relatives")

D) Lines 49-55 ("As long . . . realized")

16. As used in line 26, "organized" most nearly means

A) arranged.

B) cooperative.

C) hierarchical.

D) patient.

17. Which claim does Clinton make in her speech?

A) The conference itself is a model of nondis-crimination toward women.

B) Democracy cannot prosper unless women can participate fully in it.

C) Women's rights are restricted globally by the demands on them as parents.

D) Women are being forced to provide income for their families as a result of sexism.

GO ON TO THE NEXT PAGE

18. Clinton uses the example of V-J Day observations to support the argument that

    A) campaigns succeed when they are nonviolent.

    B) historical wrongs against women must be corrected.

    C) many tragedies could have been avoided with more female participation.

    D) cooperation between men and women leads to positive developments.

19. According to lines 35-39, problems that affect women

    A) harm half of the world's women.

    B) are worldwide and long-standing.

    C) could be eliminated in half a century.

    D) are isolated to a few less developed countries.

20. The fifth paragraph (lines 13-20) can be described as

    A) a distillation of the author's main argument.

    B) an acknowledgment of a counterargument.

    C) a veiled criticism of a group.

    D) a defense against an accusation.

Questions 21-31 are based on the following passages and supplementary material.

The following passages discuss the history and traditions associated with tea.

Passage 1

Europe was a coffee-drinking continent before it became a tea-drinking one. Tea was grown in China, thousands of miles away. The opening of trade
Line routes with the Far East in the fifteenth and sixteenth
(5) centuries gave Europeans their first taste of tea.

However, it was an unpromising start for the beverage, because shipments arrived stale, and European tea drinkers miscalculated the steeping time and measurements. This was a far cry from
(10) the Chinese preparation techniques, known as a "tea ceremony," which had strict steps and called for steeping in iron pots at precise temperatures and pouring into porcelain bowls.

China had a monopoly on the tea trade and
(15) kept their tea cultivation techniques secret. Yet as worldwide demand grew, tea caught on in Europe. Some proprietors touted tea as a cure for maladies. Several European tea companies formed, including the English East India Company. In
(20) 1669, it imported 143.5 pounds of tea—very little compared to the 32 million pounds that were imported by 1834.

Europeans looked for ways to circumvent China's monopoly, but their attempts to grow the
(25) tea plant (Latin name *Camellia sinensis*) failed. Some plants perished in transit from the East. But most often the growing climate wasn't right, not even in the equatorial colonies that the British, Dutch, and French controlled. In 1763, the French
(30) Academy of Sciences gave up, declaring the tea plant unique to China and unable to be grown anywhere else. Swedish and English botanists grew tea in botanical gardens, but this was not enough to meet demand.

(35)   After trial and error with a plant variety discovered in the Assam district of India, the British managed to establish a source to meet the growing demands of British tea drinkers. In May 1838, the first batch of India-grown tea shipped
(40) to London. The harvest was a mere 350 pounds and arrived in November. It sold for between 16 and 34 shillings per pound. Perfecting production methods took many years, but ultimately, India became the world's largest tea-producing country.
(45) By the early 1900s, annual production of India tea exceeded 350 million pounds. This voluminous source was a major factor in tea becoming the staple of European households that it is today.

GO ON TO THE NEXT PAGE ⇒

Passage 2

In Europe, there's a long tradition of taking
(50) afternoon tea. Tea time, typically four o'clock,
means not just enjoying a beverage, but taking time
out to gather and socialize. The occasion is not
identical across Europe, though; just about every
culture has its own way of doing things.

(55)   In France, for example, black tea is served
with sugar, milk, or lemon and is almost always
accompanied by a pastry. Rather than sweet
pastries, the French prefer the savory kind, such as
the *gougère*, or puff pastry, infused with cheese.

(60)   Germans, by contrast, put a layer of slowly melting
candy at the bottom of their teacup and top the tea
with cream. German tea culture is strongest in the
eastern part of the country, and during the week tea
is served with cookies, while on the weekend
(65) or for special events, cakes are served. The Germans
think of tea as a good cure for headaches and stress.

Russia also has a unique tea culture, rooted in
the formalism of its aristocratic classes. Loose leaf
black tea is served in a glass held by a *podstakannik*,
(70) an ornate holder with a handle typically made from
silver or chrome—though sometimes it may be
goldplated. Brewed separately, the tea is then diluted
with boiled water and served strong. The strength of
the tea is seen as a measure of the host's hospitality.
(75) Traditionally, tea is taken by the entire family and
served after a large meal with jams and pastries.

Great Britain has a rich tradition of its own.
Prior to the introduction of tea into Britain, the
English had two main meals, breakfast and a sec-
(80) ond, dinner-like meal called "tea," which was held
around noon. However, during the middle of the
eighteenth century, dinner shifted to an evening
meal at a late hour; it was then called "high tea."
That meant the necessary introduction of an after-
(85) noon snack to tide one over, and "low tea" or "tea
time" was introduced by British royalty. In present-
day Britain, your afternoon tea might be served
with scones and jam, small sandwiches, or
cookies (called "biscuits"), depending on whether
(90) you're in Ireland, England, or Scotland.

Wherever they are and however they take it,
Europeans know the value of savoring an afternoon
cup of tea.

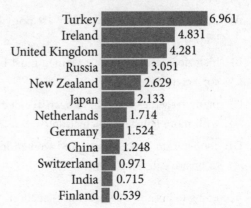

Average Annual Tea Consumption
(Pounds per Person)

Turkey	6.961
Ireland	4.831
United Kingdom	4.281
Russia	3.051
New Zealand	2.629
Japan	2.133
Netherlands	1.714
Germany	1.524
China	1.248
Switzerland	0.971
India	0.715
Finland	0.539

Data from Euromonitor International and World Bank.

21. Based on the information provided in Passage 1, it
can be inferred that

A) European nations tried to grow tea in their
colonies.

B) European tea growers never learned
Chinese cultivation techniques.

C) Europeans' purpose in opening trade routes
with the Far East was to gain access to tea.

D) Europeans believed tea was ineffective as a
treatment against illness.

22. Which choice provides the best evidence for the
answer to the previous question?

A) Lines 6-9 ("However . . . measurements")

B) Lines 17-18 ("Some . . . maladies")

C) Lines 26-29 ("But . . . French controlled")

D) Lines 40-42 ("The harvest . . . per pound")

GO ON TO THE NEXT PAGE

23. Based on the information in Passage 1, what would have been the most likely result if the British had not been able to grow tea in India?

    A) Tea would have decreased in price across Europe.

    B) The British would have learned to grow tea in Europe.

    C) Europeans would have saved their tea for special occasions.

    D) China would have produced more tea for the European market.

24. As used in line 23, "circumvent" most nearly means

    A) destroy.

    B) get around.

    C) ignore.

    D) compete with.

25. It can be inferred from both Passage 1 and the graphic that

    A) English botanical gardens helped make the United Kingdom one of the highest tea-consuming countries in the world.

    B) if the French Academy of Sciences hadn't given up growing tea in 1763, France would be one of the highest tea-consuming countries in the world.

    C) Britain's success at growing tea in India in the 1800s helped make the United Kingdom one of the highest tea-consuming nations in the world.

    D) China's production of tea would be higher if Britain hadn't discovered a way to grow tea in India in the 1800s.

26. It is reasonable to infer, based on Passage 2, that

    A) serving tea is an important part of hosting guests in Russia.

    B) Germans generally avoid medicine for stress.

    C) drinking tea in modern Britain is confined to the upper classes.

    D) the usual hour for drinking tea varies across Europe.

27. Which choice provides the best evidence for the answer to the previous question?

    A) Lines 50-52 ("Tea time . . . socialize")

    B) Lines 65-66 ("The Germans . . . stress")

    C) Lines 73-74 ("The strength . . . hospitality")

    D) Lines 84-86 ("That meant . . . royalty")

28. As used in line 68, "aristocratic" most nearly means

    A) culinary.

    B) political.

    C) rigid.

    D) noble.

29. Compared with France's tradition of tea-drinking, having tea in Germany

    A) is more formal.

    B) involves sweeter food.

    C) requires greater solitude.

    D) is more of a meal than a snack.

GO ON TO THE NEXT PAGE ⟩

30. Which statement is the most effective comparison of the two passages' purposes?

   A) Passage 1's purpose is to describe the early history of tea in Europe, while Passage 2's purpose is to compare European cultural practices relating to tea.

   B) Passage 1's purpose is to argue against the Chinese monopoly of tea, while Passage 2's purpose is to argue that Europeans perfected the art of tea drinking.

   C) Passage 1's purpose is to express admiration for the difficult task of tea cultivation, while Passage 2's purpose is to celebrate the rituals surrounding tea.

   D) Passage 1's purpose is to compare Chinese and European relationships with tea, while Passage 2's purpose is to describe the diffusion of tea culture in Europe.

31. Both passages support which generalization about tea?

   A) Tea drinking in Europe is less ritualized than in China.

   B) Coffee was once more popular in Europe than tea was.

   C) India grows a great deal of tea.

   D) Tea is a staple of European households.

Question 32-42 are based on the following passage.

The following passage is adapted from an article about the Spinosaurus, a theropod dinosaur that lived during the Cretaceous period.

At long last, paleontologists have solved a century-old mystery, piecing together information discovered by scientists from different times and places.

Line   The mystery began when, in 1911, German
(5) paleontologist Ernst Stromer discovered the first evidence of dinosaurs having lived in Egypt. Stromer, who expected to encounter fossils of early mammals, instead found bones that dated back to the Cretaceous period, some 97

(10) to 112 million years prior. His finding consisted of three large bones, which he preserved and transported back to Germany for examination. After careful consideration, he announced that he had discovered a new genus of sauropod, or a
(15) large, four-legged herbivore with a long neck. He called the genus Aegyptosaurus, which is Greek for Egyptian lizard. One of these Aegyptosaurs, he claimed, was the Spinosaurus. Tragically, the fossils that supported his claim were destroyed during
(20) a raid on Munich by the Royal Air Force during World War II. The scientific world was left with Stromer's notes and sketches, but no hard evidence that the Spinosaurus ever existed.

It was not until 2008, when a cardboard box
(25) of bones was delivered to paleontologist Nizar Ibrahim by a nomad in Morocco's Sahara desert, that a clue to solving the mystery was revealed. Intrigued, Ibrahim took the bones to a university in Casablanca for further study. One specific bone
(30) struck him as interesting, as it contained a red line coursing through it. The following year, Ibrahim and his colleagues at Italy's Milan Natural History Museum were looking at bones that resembled the ones delivered the year before. An important
(35) clue was hidden in the cross-section they were examining, as it contained the same red line Ibrahim had seen in Morocco. Against all odds, the Italians were studying bones that belonged to the very same skeleton as the bones Ibrahim received
(40) in the desert. Together, these bones make up the partial skeleton of the very first Spinosaurus that humans have been able to discover since Stromer's fossils were destroyed.

Ibrahim and his colleagues published a study
(45) describing the features of the dinosaur, which point to the Spinosaurus being the first known swimming dinosaur. At 36 feet long, this particular Spinosaurus had long front legs and short back legs, each with a paddle-shaped foot and claws that
(50) suggest a carnivorous diet. These features made the dinosaur a deft swimmer and excellent hunter, able to prey on large river fish.

Scientists also discovered significant aquatic adaptations that made the Spinosaurus unique

GO ON TO THE NEXT PAGE

(55) compared to dinosaurs that lived on land but ate fish. Similar to a crocodile, the Spinosaurus had a long snout, with nostrils positioned so that the dinosaur could breathe while part of its head was submerged in water. Unlike predatory

(60) land dinosaurs, the Spinosaurus had powerful front legs. The weight of these legs would have made walking upright like a Tyrannosaurus Rex impossible, but in water, their strong legs gave the Spinosaurus the power it needed to swim quickly

(65) and hunt fiercely. Most notable, though, was the discovery of the Spinosaurus's massive sail. Made up of dorsal spines, the sail was mostly meant for display.

Ibrahim and his fellow researchers used both

(70) modern digital modeling programs and Stromer's basic sketches to create and mount a life-size replica of the Spinosaurus skeleton. The sketches gave them a starting point, and by arranging and rearranging the excavated fossils they had in their

(75) possession, they were able to use technology to piece together hypothetical bone structures until the mystery of this semiaquatic dinosaur finally emerged from the murky depths of the past.

32. Which of the following best summarizes the central idea of this passage?

A) Paleontologists were able to identify a new species of dinosaur after overcoming a series of obstacles.

B) Most dinosaur fossils are found in pieces and must be reconstructed using the latest technology.

C) The first evidence of the Spinosaurus was uncovered by German paleontologist Ernst Stromer.

D) Fossils of an aquatic dinosaur called the Spinosaurus were first found in Egypt in the early twentieth century.

33. According to the passage, the fossils Stromer found in the Egyptian desert were

A) younger and smaller than he expected.

B) younger and larger than he expected.

C) older and smaller than he expected.

D) older and larger than he expected.

34. Based on the information in the passage, the author would most likely agree that

A) aquatic dinosaurs were more vicious than dinosaurs that lived on land.

B) too much emphasis is placed on creating realistic models of ancient dinosaurs.

C) most mysteries presented by randomly found fossils are unlikely to be solved.

D) the study of fossils and ancient life provides important scientific insights.

35. Which choice provides the best evidence for the answer to the previous question?

A) Lines 13-15 ("After careful . . . long neck")

B) Lines 53-56 ("Scientists also . . . ate fish")

C) Lines 59-61 ("Unlike . . . front legs")

D) Lines 72-78 ("The sketches . . . past")

36. As used in line 37, the phrase "against all odds" most nearly means

A) by contrast.

B) at the exact same time.

C) to their dismay.

D) despite low probability.

GO ON TO THE NEXT PAGE

37. The author uses the phrases "deft swimmer" and "excellent hunter" in line 51 to

    A) produce a clear visual image of the Spinosaurus.

    B) show how the Spinosaurus searched for prey.

    C) create an impression of a graceful but powerful animal.

    D) emphasize the differences between aquatic and land dinosaurs.

38. The information presented in the passage strongly suggests that Ibrahim

    A) chose to go into the field of paleontology after reading Stromer's work.

    B) was familiar with Stromer's work when he found the fossils with the red lines.

    C) did not have the proper training to solve the mystery of the Spinosaurus on his own.

    D) went on to study other aquatic dinosaurs after completing his research on the Spinosaurus.

39. Which choice provides the best evidence for the answer to the previous question?

    A) Lines 24-27 ("It was . . . revealed")

    B) Lines 44-47 ("Ibrahim . . . swimming dinosaur")

    C) Lines 53-56 ("Scientists . . . ate fish")

    D) Lines 69-72 ("Ibrahim and his fellow researchers . . . skeleton")

40. As used in line 76, "hypothetical" most nearly means

    A) imaginary.

    B) actual.

    C) possible.

    D) interesting.

41. Which statement best describes the relationship between Stromer's and Ibrahim's work with fossils?

    A) Stromer's work was dependent on Ibrahim's work.

    B) Stromer's work was contradicted by Ibrahim's work.

    C) Ibrahim's work built on Stromer's work.

    D) Ibrahim's work copied Stromer's work.

42. Which of the following is most similar to the methods used by Ibrahim to create a life-size replica of the Spinosaurus?

    A) An architect using computer software and drawings to create a scale model of a building

    B) A student building a model rocket from a kit in order to demonstrate propulsion

    C) A doctor using a microscope to study microorganisms unable to be seen with the naked eye

    D) A marine biologist creating an artificial reef in an aquarium to study fish

Questions 43-52 are based on the following passage and supplementary material.

The following passage is adapted from an essay about intricacies and implications of laughter.

Today's technology and resources enable people to educate themselves on any topic imaginable, and human health is one of particular interest to all.
Line From diet fads to exercise trends, sleep studies
(5) to nutrition supplements, people strive to adopt healthier lifestyles. And while some people may associate diets and gym memberships with sheer enjoyment, most of the population tends to think of personal healthcare as a necessary but time-consuming,
(10) energy-draining, less-than-fun aspect of daily life.

Yet for centuries, or perhaps for as long as conscious life has existed, sneaking suspicion has

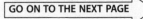 GO ON TO THE NEXT PAGE

suggested that fun, or more accurately, *funniness*, is essential to human health. Finally, in recent years

(15) this notion, often phrased in the adage, "Laughter is the best medicine," has materialized into scientific evidence.

When a person laughs, a chemical reaction in the brain produces hormones called endorphins.

(20) Other known endorphin-producing activities include exercise, physical pain, and certain food choices, but laughter's appearance on this list has drawn increasing empirical interest. Endorphins function as natural opiates for the human body,

(25) causing what are more commonly referred to as "good feelings." A boost of endorphins can thwart lethargy and promote the mental energy and positivity necessary to accomplish challenging tasks. Furthermore, recent data reveal that the

(30) laughter-induced endorphins are therapeutic and stress reducing.

This stress reduction alone indicates significant implications regarding the role of laughter in personal health. However, humor seems to address

(35) many other medical conditions as well. One study from Loma Linda University in California found that the act of laughing induced immediate and significant effects on senior adults' memory capacities. This result was in addition to declines

(40) in the patients' cortisol, or stress hormone, measurements. Another university study found that a mere quarter hour of laughter burns up to 40 calories. Pain tolerance, one group of Oxford researchers noticed, is also strengthened

(45) by laughter—probably due to the release of those same endorphins already described. And a group of Maryland scientists discovered that those who laugh more frequently seem to have stronger protection against heart disease, the illness that

(50) takes more lives annually than any other in America. Studies have shown that stress releases hormones that cause blood vessels to constrict, but laughter, on the other hand, releases chemicals that cause blood vessels to dilate, or expand. This dilation

(55) can have the same positive effects on blood flow as aerobic exercise or drugs that help lower cholesterol.

Already from these reputable studies, empirical data indicates that laughter's health benefits include heart disease prevention, good physical exertion,

(60) memory retention, anxiety reduction, and pain resilience—not to mention laughter's more self-evident effects on social and psychological wellness. Many believe that these findings are only the beginning; these studies pave the way for more

(65) research with even stronger evidence regarding the powerful healing and preventative properties of laughter. As is true for most fields of science, far more can be learned.

As for how laughter is achieved, these studies

(70) used various methods to provoke or measure laughter or humor. Some used comedy films or television clips; others chose humor-gauging questionnaires and social—or group—laughter scenarios. Such variance suggests that the means

(75) by which people incorporate laughter into their daily routine matters less than the fact that they do incorporate it. However, it should be said that humor shared in an uplifting community probably offers greater benefits than that found on a screen.

(80) It is believed that young people begin to laugh less and less as they transition to adulthood. Time-pressed millennials might, in the interest of wellness, choose isolated exercise instead of social- or fun-oriented leisure activities. However,

(85) this growing pool of evidence exposes the reality that amusement, too, can powerfully nourish the health of both mind and body. Humor is no less relevant to well-being than a kale smoothie or track workout. But, then, some combination of

(90) the three might be most enjoyable (and, of course, beneficial) of all.

GO ON TO THE NEXT PAGE ▷

Laughter and Its Effect on Pain

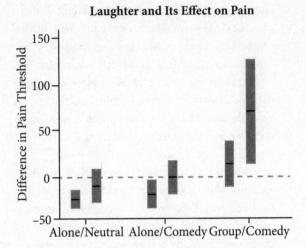

Adapted from I.M. Dunbar, et al., "Social Laughter Is Correlated with an Elevated Pain Threshold." © 2011 by The Royal Society of Biological Sciences.

43. The author would most likely characterize the study findings mentioned in the passage as

A) irrelevant.

B) very promising.

C) inconclusive.

D) mildly interesting.

44. Which choice provides the best evidence for the answer to the previous question?

A) Lines 4-6 ("From diet . . . lifestyles")

B) Lines 14-17 ("Finally, . . . evidence")

C) Lines 18-19 ("When a person . . . endorphins")

D) Lines 74-77 ("Such variance . . . incorporate it")

45. Which statement best explains the relationship between endorphin production and mental outlook?

A) Increasing a person's amount of endorphins encourages a positive state of mind.

B) The act of laughing produces endorphins, which can offer a person protection against heart disease.

C) Research indicates that chemical reactions in the brain produce endorphins.

D) If a person has more endorphins, he or she has a difficult time tolerating pain.

46. As used in line 57, "reputable" most nearly means

A) honorable.

B) distinguished.

C) celebrated.

D) credible.

47. Which of the following statements can be concluded from the passage?

A) Laughing alone or in the company of others benefits people's health equally.

B) There is reason for optimism about future research into laughter's health benefits.

C) Public support for the idea that laughter is healthy is somewhat limited.

D) Physical exercise is sufficient to maintain and improve mental health.

48. Which choice provides the best evidence for the answer to the previous question?

    A) Lines 11-14 ("Yet for centuries, . . . health")

    B) Lines 32-35 ("This stress . . . well")

    C) Lines 63-67 ("Many believe . . . of laughter")

    D) Lines 87-91 ("Humor is . . . of all")

49. Which reason best explains why the author chose to discuss the function of endorphins in lines 23-26 ("Endorphins . . . good feelings")?

    A) To reach a wider audience without a background in physiology

    B) To support the claim that laughter affects an individual's mental state

    C) To show that laughter is one of several endorphin-producing activities

    D) To demonstrate why scientists have an interest in studying laughter

50. As used in line 15, "adage" most nearly means

    A) remark.

    B) comment.

    C) cliché.

    D) proverb.

51. Which value shown on the graph most closely relates to the idea in line 78 that "humor shared in an uplifting community" increases resilience to pain?

    A) −25

    B) 0

    C) 20

    D) 75

52. The information in the passage strongly suggests that

    A) older adults prefer to laugh in a community setting rather than watch funny movies.

    B) adults who laugh less as they age are at greater risk for heart disease.

    C) millennials are in danger of developing heart disease from too much exercise.

    D) soon doctors will be using laughter to treat most diseases.

IF YOU FINISH BEFORE TIME IS CALLED, YOU MAY CHECK YOUR WORK ON THIS SECTION ONLY. DO NOT TURN TO ANY OTHER SECTION IN THE TEST. **STOP**

WRITING AND LANGUAGE TEST

35 Minutes—44 Questions

This section corresponds to Section 2 of your answer sheet.

Directions: Each passage in this section is followed by several questions. Some questions will reference an underlined portion in the passage; others will ask you to consider a part of a passage or the passage as a whole. For each question, choose the answer that reflects the best use of grammar, punctuation, and style. If a passage or question is accompanied by a graphic, take the graphic into account in choosing your response(s). Some questions will have "NO CHANGE" as a possible response. Choose that answer if you think the best choice is to leave the sentence as written.

Questions 1-11 are based on the following passage.

From Here to the Stars

Gene Kranz hadn't slept in ages. **1** The flight director, pacing between rows of monitors in NASA's Mission Control Center, an impossible problem weighing heavy in his weary mind: Three astronauts were operating a crippled spacecraft nearly 200,000 miles from Earth. And time was running out.

Kranz was no stranger to **2** issues. After losing his father at an early age, Kranz turned to the stars for guidance—and found inspiration. His high school thesis was about the possibility of **3** space travel; an idea that prompted Kranz to set a path for the stars. Kranz pursued a degree in aeronautical engineering after high school graduation. After the Wright brothers

1. A) NO CHANGE
   B) The flight director paced
   C) The pacing flight director
   D) The flight director pacing

2. A) NO CHANGE
   B) adversity.
   C) deadlines.
   D) maladies.

3. A) NO CHANGE
   B) space travel: an idea
   C) space travel, an idea
   D) space travel. An idea

GO ON TO THE NEXT PAGE

had pioneered powered, controlled flight only half a century earlier, aviation milestones like breaking the sound barrier changed the future of flight. Aeronautical engineering required a thorough understanding of **4** physics—like lift and drag on wings—as well as proficiency in mathematics to determine maximum weight on an aircraft. After graduating from Saint Louis University's Parks College of Engineering, Aviation, and Technology, Kranz piloted jets for the Air Force Reserve before performing research and development on missiles and rockets. Kranz later joined NASA and directed the successful *Apollo 11* mission to the moon in 1969.

5 Without his unusual vest, no one would have noticed Kranz in the crowd. One year after the launch, the mood had drastically changed; there were no cheers, no celebratory pats on the back or teary-eyed congratulations. Coffee and adrenaline fueled the scientists and engineers communicating with the astronauts on *Apollo 13.* **6** Kranz was easy to spot among the avalanche of moving bodies and shifting papers. He was dressed, as ever, in his signature handmade

4. A) NO CHANGE
    B) physics; like lift and drag on wings, as well as proficiency
    C) physics like lift and drag on wings, as well as proficiency
    D) physics: like lift and drag on wings—as well as proficiency

5. Which sentence would serve as the most effective introduction to the paragraph?
    A) NO CHANGE
    B) During the mission, Kranz stood out as a pillar of strength in the chaos of the command center.
    C) Kranz earned the badges of honor that now adorned his vest.
    D) Kranz possessed more years of experience than anyone in the control center.

6. A) NO CHANGE
    B) Among the avalanche of moving bodies and shifting papers, it is easy to spot Kranz.
    C) Kranz easily spotted the avalanche of moving bodies and shifting papers.
    D) Kranz is easy to spot among the avalanche of moving bodies and shifting papers.

GO ON TO THE NEXT PAGE

vest. **7** The engineers looked to the calm man in the homemade vest.

Kranz's wife, Marta, had begun making vests at his request in the early '60s. **8** Their was power in a uniform, something Kranz understood from his years serving overseas. The vests served not as an authoritative mark or **9** sartorial flair, but a defining symbol for his team to rally behind. During the effort to save the *Apollo 13* crew, Kranz wore his white vest around the clock like perspiration-mottled battle armor.

10 Among meetings and calculations, Kranz and the NASA staff hatched a wild plan. By using the gravitational force of the moon, **11** it could slingshot the injured spacecraft back on an earthbound course. It was a long shot, of course, but also their best and only one. And, due to the tireless efforts of support staff on earth and the intrepid spirit of the *Apollo 13* crew, it worked. Six days after takeoff, all three astronauts splashed down safely in the Pacific Ocean.

Questions 12–22 are based on the following passage.

The UK and the Euro

[1] The United Kingdom is a longstanding member of the European Union (EU), a multinational political organization and economic world leader **12** elected over the course of the past half-century. [2] However, there is

7. Which sentence provides effective evidence to support the main focus of the paragraph?

A) NO CHANGE

B) Many of the men in the Mission Control Center had lengthy military careers.

C) Kranz's thoughts returned to the many tribulations he had experienced.

D) Several engineers joined together as a bastion of calm in a sea of uncertainty.

8. A) NO CHANGE

B) They're was

C) There was

D) They were

9. A) NO CHANGE

B) sanguine

C) military

D) martial

10. A) NO CHANGE

B) In spite of

C) Despite

D) Between

11. A) NO CHANGE

B) he

C) they

D) one

12. A) NO CHANGE

B) determined

C) advanced

D) built

GO ON TO THE NEXT PAGE

one key feature of the EU in which the UK does not **13** participate; the monetary union known as the Eurozone, consisting of countries that share the euro as currency. [3] While the nation's public opinion has remained generally supportive of that decision, evidence suggests that the euro's benefits for the UK might, in fact, outweigh the risks. [4] When the EU first implemented the euro in 1999, intending to strengthen collective economy across the union, Britain was permitted exclusion and continued using the pound instead. [5] This, UK leaders hoped, would shield Britain from financial dangers that the euro might suffer. **14**

Proponents for avoiding the euro point **15** to faltering economies in the Eurozone region throughout the Eurozone. To join a massive, multinational economy would involve surrendering taxable wealth from one's own region to aid impoverished countries that may be some thousands of miles away. If a few economies in the Eurozone suffer, all of the participating nations suffer, too. Other proponents point to details of financial policy such as interest rates and territory responsibilities, fearing loss of agency and political traction. **16** The UK's taxable wealth would decrease if it assisted impoverished countries.

13. A) NO CHANGE
    B) participate: the monetary
    C) participate, the monetary
    D) participate. The monetary

14. To make this paragraph most logical, sentence 3 should be placed
    A) where it is now.
    B) after sentence 1.
    C) after sentence 4.
    D) after sentence 5.

15. Which choice best completes the sentence?
    A) NO CHANGE
    B) to financial dangers that the euro might suffer.
    C) to faltering economies in most if not all Eurozone countries.
    D) to financial dangers and faltering economies in Eurozone countries throughout Europe.

16. Which statement most clearly communicates the main claim of the paragraph?
    A) NO CHANGE
    B) Economic independence from impoverished countries would still be possible.
    C) The UK would take on significant economic risk if it adopted the euro as its currency.
    D) Euro adoption would require subsequent economic assistance on the UK's behalf.

GO ON TO THE NEXT PAGE

But complications loom: the UK's current EU status may be untenable. In recent years, EU leaders seem to intend to transition all members **17** toward the Eurozone, for many reasons, this action appears necessary for protecting nations involved and ensuring the monetary union's long-term success. These conditions may potentially force the UK to choose either the security of its multidecade EU membership, or the pound and all it entails for Britain's economy. Enjoying both may not remain possible. **18** The UK wants to maintain the pound as its currency.

[1] Regarding Britain's intent to be protected from the Eurozone's economic dangers, this hope never quite materialized. [2] The UK saw economic downturns of its own during the euro's problematic years thus far. [3] Many families in the UK still struggle to pay their bills in the face of higher than normal unemployment rates. [4] It seems that regardless of shared currency, the economies of Britain and its Eurozone neighbors are too closely **19** intertwined for one to remain unscathed by another's crises. **20**

Perhaps this question of economic security has been the wrong one. Due to Britain's location and long-standing trade relationships with its neighbors, economies will persist to be somewhat reliant on each other, euro or not. **21** Furthermore, political security, power, and protection bear more significance for the future. If the UK hopes to maintain and expand its

17. A) NO CHANGE
    B) toward the Eurozone. For many reasons,
    C) toward the Eurozone, for many reasons.
    D) toward the Eurozone. For many reasons.

18. Which sentence most effectively concludes the paragraph?
    A) NO CHANGE
    B) All EU members may soon have to accept the euro.
    C) The UK faces a difficult decision regarding its EU membership.
    D) All member nations want to ensure the success of the EU.

19. A) NO CHANGE
    B) disparate
    C) identical
    D) relevant

20. Which sentence is least relevant to the central idea of this paragraph?
    A) Sentence 1
    B) Sentence 2
    C) Sentence 3
    D) Sentence 4

21. A) NO CHANGE
    B) Or,
    C) Also,
    D) However,

GO ON TO THE NEXT PAGE

influential presence in world leadership, its association and close involvement with greater Europe is invaluable. Considering that the euro probably offers a lower risk margin than many have supposed, the benefits of euro **22** <u>adoption: to secure EU membership and strengthen its cause,</u> made Britain carefully reconsider.

Questions 23-33 are based on the following passage.

Coffee: The Buzz on Beans

Americans love coffee. **23** <u>Some</u> days you can find a coffee shop in nearly every American city. But this wasn't always true. How did coffee, which was first grown in Africa over five hundred years ago, come to America?

The coffee plant, from which makers get the "cherries" that **24** <u>is dried and roasted</u> into what we call beans, first appeared in the East African country Ethiopia, in the province of Kaffa. From there, it spread to the Arabian Peninsula, where the coffeehouse, or *qahveh khaneh* in Arabic, was very popular. Like spices and cloth, coffee was traded internationally as European explorers reached far lands and **25** <u>establishing</u> shipping routes. The first European coffeehouse opened in Venice, Italy, in 1683, and not long after London **26** <u>displayed</u> over three hundred coffeehouses.

22. A) NO CHANGE
    B) adoption—to secure EU membership and strengthen its cause—
    C) adoption: to secure EU membership and strengthen its cause—
    D) adoption; to secure EU membership and strengthen its cause,

23. A) NO CHANGE
    B) Many
    C) The
    D) These

24. A) NO CHANGE
    B) are being dried and roasted
    C) are dried and roasted
    D) is being dried and roasted

25. A) NO CHANGE
    B) established
    C) having established
    D) was establishing

26. A) NO CHANGE
    B) bragged
    C) highlighted
    D) boasted

GO ON TO THE NEXT PAGE

There is no record of coffee being amongst the cargo of the *Mayflower*, which reached the New World in 1620. It was not until 1668 that the first written reference to coffee in America was made. The reference described a beverage made from roasted beans and flavored with sugar or honey, and cinnamon. Coffee was then chronicled in the New England colony's official records of 1670. In 1683, William Penn, who lived in a settlement on the Delaware River, wrote of buying supplies of coffee in a **27** New York market, he paid eighteen shillings and nine pence per pound. **28**

Coffeehouses like those in Europe were soon established in American colonies, and as America expanded westward, coffee consumption grew. In their settlement days, **29** Chicago St. Louis and New Orleans each had famous coffeehouses. By the mid-twentieth century, coffeehouses were abundant. In places like New York and San Francisco, they became **30** confused with counterculture, as a place where intellectuals and artists gathered to share ideas. In American homes, coffee was a social lubricant, bringing people together to socialize as afternoon tea had done in English society. With the

27. A) NO CHANGE
    B) New York market and William Penn
    C) New York market so he paid
    D) New York market, paying

28. Which choice best establishes a concluding sentence for the paragraph?
    A) Coffee's appearance in the historical record shows it was becoming more and more established in the New World.
    B) The colonies probably used more tea than coffee because there are records of it being imported from England.
    C) William Penn founded Pennsylvania Colony, which became the state of Pennsylvania after the Revolutionary War with England ended.
    D) The Mayflower did carry a number of items that the colonists needed for settlement, including animals and tools.

29. A) NO CHANGE
    B) Chicago, St. Louis, and New Orleans
    C) Chicago, St. Louis, and, New Orleans
    D) Chicago St. Louis and, New Orleans

30. A) NO CHANGE
    B) related
    C) associated
    D) coupled

GO ON TO THE NEXT PAGE

invention of the electric coffee pot, it became a common courtesy to ask a guest if she wanted "coffee or tea?"

31 There were many coffee shops in New York and in Chicago.

However, by the 1950s, U.S. manufacturing did to coffee what it had done to **32** other foods; produced it cheaply, mass-marketed it, and lowered its quality. Coffee was roasted and ground in manufacturing plants and freeze-dried for a long storage life, which compromised its flavor. An "evangelism" began to bring back the original bracing, dark-roasted taste of coffee, and spread quickly. **33** In every major city of the world, now travelers around the world, expect to be able to grab an uplifting, fresh, and delicious cup of coffee—and they can.

31. Which choice most effectively concludes the paragraph?
    A) NO CHANGE
    B) Electric coffee machines changed how people entertained at home.
    C) Over time, it was clear that coffee had become a part of everyday American life.
    D) People went to coffeehouses to discuss major issues.

32. A) NO CHANGE
    B) other foods produced
    C) other foods, produced
    D) other foods: produced

33. A) NO CHANGE
    B) Now travelers, in every major city of the world, around the world expect to be able to grab an uplifting, fresh, and delicious cup of coffee—and they can.
    C) Now in every major city of the world, travelers around the world expect to be able to grab an uplifting, fresh, and delicious cup of coffee—and they can.
    D) Now travelers around the world expect to be able to grab an uplifting, fresh, and delicious cup of coffee in every major city of the world—and they can.

GO ON TO THE NEXT PAGE

Questions 34-44 are based on the following passage and supplementary material.

Predicting Nature's Light Show

One of the most beautiful of nature's displays is the aurora borealis, commonly known as the Northern Lights. As **34** their informal name suggests, the best place to view this phenomenon **35** is the Northern Hemisphere. How far north one needs to be to witness auroras depends not on conditions here on Earth, but on the sun. **36**

As with hurricane season on Earth, the sun **37** observes a cycle of storm activity, called the solar cycle, which lasts approximately 11 years. Also referred to as the sunspot cycle, this period is caused by the amount of magnetic flux that rises to the surface of the sun, causing sunspots, or areas of intense magnetic activity. The magnetic energy is sometimes so great it causes a storm that explodes away from the sun's surface in a solar flare.

34. A) NO CHANGE
    B) an
    C) its
    D) that

35. A) NO CHANGE
    B) is through the Northern Hemisphere.
    C) is over the Northern Hemisphere.
    D) is in the Northern Hemisphere.

36. Which of the following would most strengthen the passage's introduction?
    A) A statement about the Kp-Index and other necessary tracking tools scientists use
    B) A mention that the National Oceanic and Atmospheric Administration monitors solar flares
    C) An explanation about why conditions on the sun rather than on Earth affect the Northern Lights
    D) A statement about what scientists think people should study before viewing auroras

37. A) NO CHANGE
    B) experiences
    C) perceives
    D) witnesses

These powerful magnetic storms eject high-speed electrons and protons into space. Called a coronal mass ejection, this ejection is far more powerful than the hot gases the sun constantly emits. The speed at which the atoms are shot away from the sun is almost triple that of a normal solar wind. It takes this shot of energy one to three days to arrive at Earth's upper atmosphere. Once it arrives, it is captured by Earth's own magnetic field. It is this newly captured energy that causes the Northern Lights. **38** <u>Scientists and interested amateurs</u> in the Northern Hemisphere **39** <u>use tools readily available to all in order to predict</u> the likelihood of seeing auroras in their location at a specific time. One such tool is the Kp-Index, a number that determines the potential visibility of an aurora. The Kp-Index measures the energy added to Earth's magnetic field from the sun on a scale of 0-9, with 1 representing a solar calm and 5 or more indicating a magnetic storm, or solar flare. The magnetic fluctuations are measured in three-hour intervals (12 AM to 3 AM, 3 AM to 6 AM, and so on) so that deviations can be factored in and accurate data can be presented. **40**

38. A) NO CHANGE
    B) Interested scientists and amateurs
    C) Scientists and amateurs interested
    D) Scientists interested and amateurs

39. A) NO CHANGE
    B) use tools for prediction
    C) use specific tools to predict
    D) use all tools readily available to predict

40. Which of the following, if added to this paragraph, would best support the author's claims?
    A) The speeds of normal solar winds and coronal mass ejections
    B) The strength of Earth's magnetic field
    C) The temperature of normal solar wind
    D) The definition of coronal mass ejection

GO ON TO THE NEXT PAGE

Magnetometers, tools that measure the strength of Earth's magnetic field, are located around the world. When the energy from solar flares reaches Earth, the strength and direction of the energy **41** is recorded by these tools and analyzed by scientists at the National Oceanic and Atmospheric Administration, who calculate the difference between the average strength of the magnetic field and spikes due to solar flares. They plot this information on the Kp-Index and **42** update the public with information on viewing the auroras as well as other impacts solar flares may have on life on Earth. **43** While solar flares can sometimes have negative effects on our communications systems and weather patterns, the most common effect is also the most enchanting: a beautiful light show such as the solar flare that took place from **44** 3 PM to 6 PM on September 11.

Potential Visibility of an Aurora

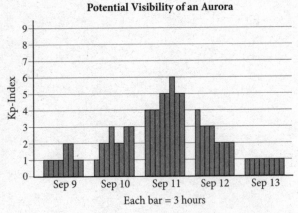

Each bar = 3 hours

Data from National Oceanic and Atmospheric Administration.

41. A) NO CHANGE
    B) are
    C) will be
    D) has been

42. A) NO CHANGE
    B) update aurora viewing information
    C) update information on viewing the auroras
    D) update aurora viewing information for the public

43. A) NO CHANGE
    B) However,
    C) Since
    D) Whereas

44. Which choice completes the sentence with accurate data based on the graphic?
    A) NO CHANGE
    B) 12 AM on September 11 to 3 AM on September 12.
    C) 9 AM on September 10 to 12 PM on September 12.
    D) 9 AM on September 11 to 12 AM on September 12.

MATH TEST

25 Minutes—20 Questions

NO-CALCULATOR SECTION

This section corresponds to Section 3 of your answer sheet.

Directions: For this section, solve each question and select the best answer choice. The available space on each page may be used for scratch work.

Notes:

1. Calculator use is NOT permitted.
2. All numbers used are real numbers, and all variables used represent real numbers, unless otherwise indicated.
3. Figures are drawn to scale and lie in a plane unless otherwise indicated.
4. Unless stated otherwise, the domain of any function f is assumed to be the set of all real numbers x, for which $f(x)$ is a real number.

Information:

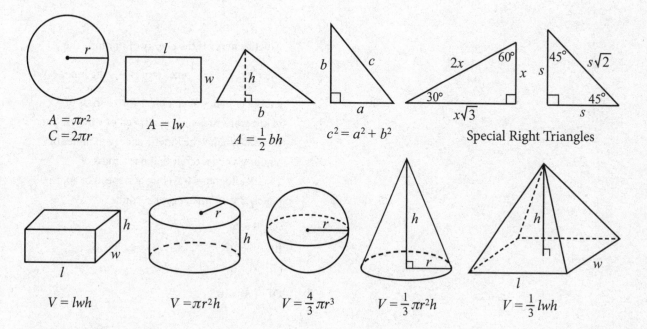

$A = \pi r^2$
$C = 2\pi r$

$A = lw$

$A = \frac{1}{2} bh$

$c^2 = a^2 + b^2$

Special Right Triangles

$V = lwh$

$V = \pi r^2 h$

$V = \frac{4}{3} \pi r^3$

$V = \frac{1}{3} \pi r^2 h$

$V = \frac{1}{3} lwh$

The sum of the degree measures of the angles in a triangle is 180.

The number of degrees of arc in a circle is 360.

The number of radians of arc in a circle is 2π.

GO ON TO THE NEXT PAGE

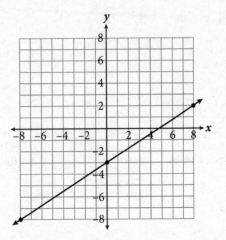

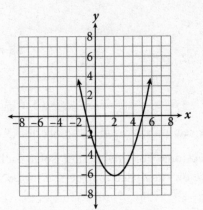

1. What is the average rate of change for the line graphed in the figure above?

   A) $\dfrac{3}{5}$

   B) $\dfrac{5}{8}$

   C) $\dfrac{8}{5}$

   D) $\dfrac{5}{3}$

2. Which of the following could be the factored form of the equation graphed in the figure above?

   A) $y = \dfrac{1}{5}(x - 2)(x + 6)$

   B) $y = \dfrac{1}{5}(x + 2)(x - 6)$

   C) $y = \dfrac{2}{3}(x - 1)(x + 5)$

   D) $y = \dfrac{2}{3}(x + 1)(x - 5)$

3. Kinetic energy is the energy of motion. The equation $E_K = \dfrac{1}{2}mv^2$ represents the kinetic energy in joules of an object with a mass of m kilograms traveling at a speed of v meters per second. What is the kinetic energy in joules of an unmanned aircraft that has a mass of 2×10^3 kilograms traveling at a speed of approximately 3×10^3 meters per second?

   A) 9×5^9

   B) 9×10^8

   C) 9×10^9

   D) 1.8×10^{10}

GO ON TO THE NEXT PAGE

$$\frac{3(k-1)+5}{2} = \frac{17-(8+k)}{4}$$

4. In the equation above, what is the value of k?

A) $\dfrac{9}{13}$

B) $\dfrac{5}{7}$

C) $\dfrac{8}{7}$

D) $\dfrac{8}{5}$

5. An environmental protection group had its members sign a pledge to try to reduce the amount of garbage they throw out by 3% each year. On the year that the pledge was signed, each person threw out an average of 1,800 pounds of garbage. Which exponential function could be used to model the average amount of garbage each person who signed the pledge should throw out each year after signing the pledge?

A) $y = 0.97 \times 1,800^t$

B) $y = 1,800 \times t^{0.97}$

C) $y = 1,800 \times 1.97^t$

D) $y = 1,800 \times 0.97^t$

$$\frac{6x+2}{x+5} - \frac{3x-8}{x+5}$$

6. Which of the following is equivalent to the expression above?

A) $\dfrac{3x-6}{x+5}$

B) $\dfrac{3x+10}{x+5}$

C) $\dfrac{3x-6}{2x+10}$

D) $\dfrac{3x+10}{2x+10}$

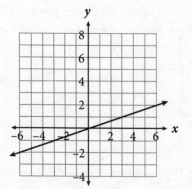

7. If the equation of the line shown in the figure above is written in the form $\dfrac{y}{x} = m$, which of the following could be the value of m?

A) -3

B) $-\dfrac{1}{3}$

C) $\dfrac{1}{3}$

D) 3

8. If $4x^2 + 7x + 1$ is multiplied by $3x + 5$, what is the coefficient of x in the resulting polynomial?

A) 3

B) 12

C) 35

D) 38

GO ON TO THE NEXT PAGE

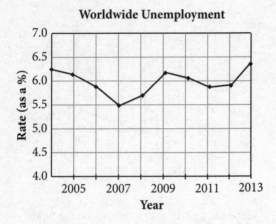

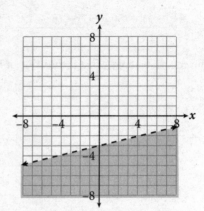

9. The figure above shows worldwide unemployment rates from 2004 to 2013. Which of the following statements is true?

A) The graph is decreasing everywhere.

B) The graph is increasing from 2007 to 2010.

C) The graph is decreasing from 2004 to 2007 and from 2009 to 2011.

D) The graph is increasing from 2007 to 2010 and decreasing from 2011 to 2013.

10. The solution to which inequality is represented in the graph above?

A) $\dfrac{1}{4}x - y > 3$

B) $\dfrac{1}{4}x - y < 3$

C) $\dfrac{1}{4}x + y > -3$

D) $\dfrac{1}{4}x + y < -3$

$$\frac{1}{2}(4a + 10b) = b$$

11. If (a, b) is a solution to the equation above, what is the ratio $\dfrac{b}{a}$, given that $a \neq 0$?

A) -3

B) -2

C) $-\dfrac{1}{2}$

D) $-\dfrac{1}{3}$

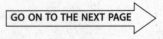
GO ON TO THE NEXT PAGE

$$\begin{cases} \dfrac{1}{3}x + \dfrac{2}{3}y = -8 \\ ax + 6y = 15 \end{cases}$$

12. If the system of linear equations above has no solution, and a is a constant, what is the value of a?

A) $-\dfrac{1}{3}$

B) $\dfrac{1}{3}$

C) $\dfrac{3}{2}$

D) 3

13. A taxi in the city charges \$3.00 for the first $\dfrac{1}{4}$ mile, plus \$0.25 for each additional $\dfrac{1}{8}$ mile. Eric plans to spend no more than \$20 on a taxi ride around the city. Which inequality represents the number of miles, m, that Eric could travel without exceeding his limit?

A) $2.5 + 2m \le 20$

B) $3 + 0.25m \le 20$

C) $3 + 2m \le 20$

D) $12 + 2m \le 20$

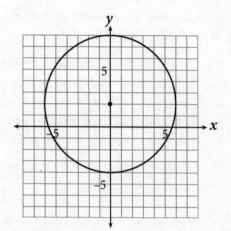

14. If the equation of the circle shown above is written in the form $x^2 + y^2 + ax + by = c$, what is the value of $ab + c$?

A) 6

B) 16

C) 28

D) 32

15. A projectile is any moving object that is thrown near the Earth's surface. The path of the projectile is called the trajectory and can be modeled by a quadratic equation, assuming the only force acting on the motion is gravity (no friction). If a projectile is launched from a platform 8 feet above the ground with an initial velocity of 64 feet per second, then its trajectory can be modeled by the equation $h = -16t^2 + 64t + 8$, where h represents the height of the projectile t seconds after it was launched. Based on this model, what is the maximum height in feet that the projectile will reach?

A) 72

B) 80

C) 92

D) 108

GO ON TO THE NEXT PAGE

Directions: For questions 16-20, enter your responses into the appropriate grid on your answer sheet, in accordance with the following:

1. You will receive credit only if the circles are filled in correctly, but you may write your answers in the boxes above each grid to help you fill in the circles accurately.

2. Don't mark more than one circle per column.

3. None of the questions with grid-in responses will have a negative solution.

4. Only grid in a single answer, even if there is more than one correct answer to a given question.

5. A **mixed number** must be gridded as a decimal or an improper fraction. For example, you would grid $7\frac{1}{2}$ as 7.5 or $\frac{15}{2}$.

   (Were you to grid it as $\boxed{7\ 1\ /\ 2}$, this response would be read as $\frac{71}{2}$.)

6. A **decimal** that has more digits than there are places on the grid may be either rounded or truncated, but every column in the grid must be filled in order to receive credit.

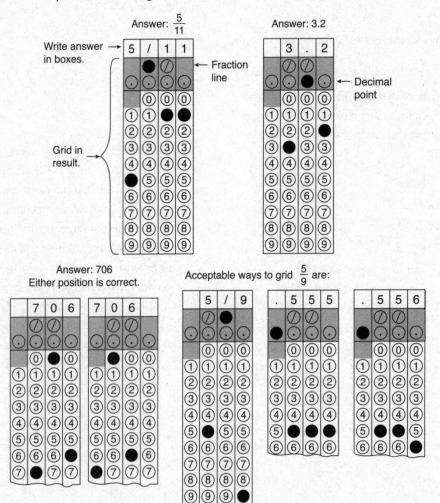

16. If $\frac{3}{4}x + \frac{5}{6}y = 12$, what is the value of $9x + 10y$?

17. How many degrees does the minute hand of an analogue clock rotate from 3:20 PM to 3:45 PM?

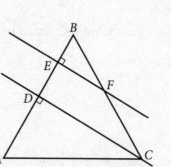

18. Triangle ABC shown above is an equilateral triangle cut by two parallel lines. If the ratio of BF to FC is 3:4 and $EB = 3$, what is the length of DE?

$$\frac{3x^{\frac{3}{2}} \cdot \left(16x^2\right)^3}{8x^{-\frac{1}{2}}}$$

19. What is the exponent on x when the expression above is written in simplest form?

20. An exponential function is given in the form $f(x) = a \cdot b^x$. If $f(0) = 3$ and $f(1) = 15$, what is the value of $f(-2)$?

MATH TEST

55 Minutes—38 Questions

CALCULATOR SECTION

This section corresponds to Section 4 of your answer sheet.

Directions: For this section, solve each question and select the best answer choice. The available space on each page may be used for scratch work.

Notes:

1. Calculator use is permitted.
2. All numbers used are real numbers, and all variables used represent real numbers, unless otherwise indicated.
3. Figures are drawn to scale and lie in a plane unless otherwise indicated.
4. Unless stated otherwise, the domain of any function f is assumed to be the set of all real numbers x, for which $f(x)$ is a real number.

Information:

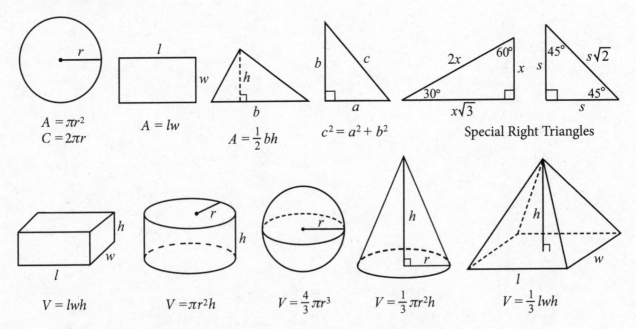

$A = \pi r^2$
$C = 2\pi r$

$A = lw$

$A = \frac{1}{2}bh$

$c^2 = a^2 + b^2$

Special Right Triangles

$V = lwh$

$V = \pi r^2 h$

$V = \frac{4}{3}\pi r^3$

$V = \frac{1}{3}\pi r^2 h$

$V = \frac{1}{3}lwh$

The sum of the degree measures of the angles in a triangle is 180.

The number of degrees of arc in a circle is 360.

The number of radians of arc in a circle is 2π.

GO ON TO THE NEXT PAGE ⇨

1. A home improvement store that sells carpeting charges a flat installation fee and a certain amount per square foot of carpet ordered. If the total cost for f square feet of carpet is given by the function $C(f) = 3.29f + 199$, then the value 3.29 best represents which of the following?

A) The installation fee

B) The cost of one square foot of carpet

C) The number of square feet of carpet ordered

D) The total cost not including the installation fee

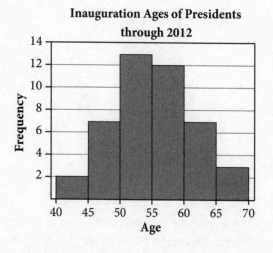

Inauguration Ages of Presidents through 2012

2. The United States Constitution requires that any candidate for the presidency be at least 35 years of age, although no president to date has been that young. The figure above shows the distribution of the ages of the presidents through 2012 at the time they were inaugurated. Based on the information shown, which of the following statements is true?

A) The shape of the data is skewed to the left, so the mean age of the presidents is greater than the median.

B) The shape of the data is fairly symmetric, so the mean age of the presidents is approximately equal to the median.

C) The data has no clear shape, so it is impossible to make a reliable statement comparing the mean and the median.

D) The same number of 55-or-older presidents have been inaugurated as ones who were younger than 55, so the mean age is exactly 55.

$$\frac{1}{3}(5x - 8) = 3x + 4$$

3. Which value of x satisfies the equation above?

A) -5

B) -3

C) -1

D) 1

GO ON TO THE NEXT PAGE

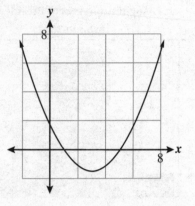

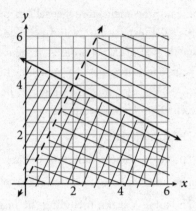

4. The following quadratic equations are all representations of the graph shown above. Which equation could you use to find the minimum value of the function, without doing any additional work?

    A) $y = \dfrac{3}{8}(x - 3)^2 - \dfrac{3}{2}$

    B) $y = \dfrac{3}{8}(x - 1)(x - 5)$

    C) $y - \dfrac{15}{8} = \dfrac{3}{8}x^2 - \dfrac{9}{4}x$

    D) $y = \dfrac{3}{8}x^2 - \dfrac{9}{4}x + \dfrac{15}{8}$

5. The Farmers' Market sells apples by the basket. The market charges $3.00 for the basket itself, plus $1.97 per pound of apples. A 6% sales tax is also applied to the entire purchase. Which equation represents the total cost of p pounds of apples at the Farmers' Market?

    A) $c = (1.97 + 0.06p) + 3$

    B) $c = 1.06(1.97p) + 3$

    C) $c = 1.06(1.97 + 3)p$

    D) $c = 1.06(1.97p + 3)$

6. Which of the following is a solution to the system of inequalities shown in the figure above?

    A) (1, 5)

    B) (2, 6)

    C) (4, 1)

    D) (5, 4)

7. Marion is a city planner. The city she works for recently purchased new property on which it plans to build administrative offices. Marion has been given the task of sizing the lots for new buildings, using the following guidelines:

    • The square footage of each lot should be greater than or equal to 3,000 square feet, but less than or equal to 15,000 square feet.

    • Each lot size should be at least 30% greater in area than the size before it.

    • To simplify tax assessment calculations, the square footage of each lot must be a multiple of 1,000 square feet.

    Which list of lot sizes meets the city guidelines and includes as many lots as possible?

    A) 3,000; 5,000; 10,000; 15,000

    B) 3,000; 4,500; 6,000; 7,500; 10,000; 15,000

    C) 3,000; 4,000; 6,000; 8,000; 11,000; 15,000

    D) 3,000; 3,900; 5,100; 6,600; 8,600; 11,200; 14,600

GO ON TO THE NEXT PAGE

8. One function of the Environmental Protection Agency (EPA) is to reduce air pollution. After implementing several pollution reduction programs in a certain city, EPA calculated that the air pollution should decrease by approximately 8% each year. What kind of function could be used to model the amount of air pollution in this city over the next several years, assuming no other significant changes?

A) A linear function

B) A quadratic function

C) A polynomial function

D) An exponential function

9. Escape velocity is the speed that a traveling object needs to break free of a planet or moon's gravitational field without additional propulsion (for example, without using fuel). The formula used to calculate escape velocity is $v = \sqrt{\dfrac{2Gm}{r}}$, where G represents the universal gravitational constant, m is the mass of the body from which the object is escaping, and r is the distance between the object and the body's center of gravity. Which equation represents the value of r in terms of v, G, and m?

A) $r = \dfrac{2Gm}{v^2}$

B) $r = \dfrac{4G^2m^2}{v^2}$

C) $r = \sqrt{\dfrac{2Gm}{v}}$

D) $r = \sqrt{\dfrac{v}{2Gm}}$

10. A movie rental kiosk dispenses DVDs and Blu-rays. DVDs cost $2.00 per night and Blu-rays cost $3.50 per night. Between 5 PM and 9 PM on Saturday, the kiosk dispensed 209 movies and collected $562.00. Solving which system of equations would yield the number of DVDs, d, and the number of Blu-rays, b, that the kiosk dispensed during the 4-hour period?

A) $\begin{cases} d + b = 209 \\ 2d + 3.5b = \dfrac{562}{4} \end{cases}$

B) $\begin{cases} d + b = 562 \\ 2d + 3.5b = 209 \end{cases}$

C) $\begin{cases} d + b = 562 \\ 2d + 3.5b = 209 \times 4 \end{cases}$

D) $\begin{cases} d + b = 209 \\ 2d + 3.5b = 562 \end{cases}$

11. The United States Senate has two voting members for each of the 50 states. The 113th Congress had a 4:1 male-to-female ratio in the Senate. Forty-five of the male senators were Republican. Only 20 percent of the female senators were Republican. How many senators in the 113th Congress were Republican?

A) 20

B) 49

C) 55

D) 65

GO ON TO THE NEXT PAGE

12. According to the *Project on Student Debt* prepared by The Institute for College Access and Success, 7 out of 10 students graduating in 2012 from a four-year college in the United States had student loan debt. The average amount borrowed per student was $29,400, which is up from $18,750 in 2004. If student debt experiences the same total percent increase over the next eight years, approximately how much will a college student graduating in 2020 owe, assuming she takes out student loans to pay for her education?

A) $40,100

B) $44,300

C) $46,100

D) $48,200

13. Annalisa has 10 beanbags to throw in a game. She gets 7 points if a beanbag lands in the smaller basket and 3 points if it lands in the larger basket. If she gets b beanbags into the larger basket and the rest into the smaller basket, which expression represents her total score?

A) $3b$

B) $3b + 7$

C) $30 + 4b$

D) $70 - 4b$

GO ON TO THE NEXT PAGE

Questions 14 and 15 refer to the following information.

In a 2010 poll, surveyors asked registered voters in four different New York voting districts whether they would consider voting to ban fracking in the state. Hydraulic fracturing, or "fracking," is a mining process that involves splitting rocks underground to remove natural gas. According to ecologists, environmental damage can occur as a result of fracking, including contamination of water. The results of the 2010 survey are shown in the following table.

	In Favor of Ban	**Against Ban**	**No Opinion**	**Total**
District A	23,247	17,106	3,509	43,862
District B	13,024	12,760	2,117	27,901
District C	43,228	49,125	5,891	98,244
District D	30,563	29,771	3,205	63,539
Total	110,062	108,762	14,722	233,546

14. According to the data, which district had the smallest percentage of voters with no opinion on fracking?

A) District A

B) District B

C) District C

D) District D

15. A random follow-up survey was administered to 500 of the respondents in District C. They were asked if they planned to vote in the next election. The follow-up survey results were: 218 said they planned to vote, 174 said they did not plan to vote, and 108 said they were unsure. Based on the data from both the initial survey and the follow-up survey, which of the following is most likely an accurate statement?

A) Approximately 19,000 people in District C who support a ban on fracking can be expected to vote in the next election.

B) Approximately 21,000 people in District C who support a ban on fracking can be expected to vote in the next election.

C) Approximately 43,000 people in District C who support a ban on fracking can be expected to vote in the next election.

D) Approximately 48,000 people in District C who support a ban on fracking can be expected to vote in the next election.

GO ON TO THE NEXT PAGE

$$\begin{cases} 2x + 4y = 13 \\ x - 3y = -11 \end{cases}$$

16. Based on the system of equations above, what is the value of the sum of x and y?

    A) $-\dfrac{1}{2}$

    B) 3

    C) $3\dfrac{1}{2}$

    D) 4

	Bowling Scores		
	Ian	Mae	Jin
Game 1	160	110	120
Game 2	135	160	180
Game 3	185	140	105
Game 4	135	130	160
Game 5	185	110	135
Mean Score	160	130	140
Standard Deviation	22	19	27

17. Ian, Mae, and Jin bowled five games during a bowling tournament. The table above shows their scores. According to the data, which of the following conclusions is correct?

    A) Ian bowled the most consistently because the mean of his scores is the highest.

    B) Mae bowled the least consistently because the standard deviation of her scores is the lowest.

    C) Mae bowled the most consistently because the standard deviation of her scores is the lowest.

    D) Jin bowled the most consistently because the standard deviation of his scores is the highest.

18. Which of the following are solutions to the quadratic equation $(x + 3)^2 = 16$?

    A) $x = -19$ and $x = 13$

    B) $x = -7$ and $x = 1$

    C) $x = -1$ and $x = 1$

    D) $x = -1$ and $x = 7$

19. An architect is building a scale model of the Statue of Liberty. The real statue measures 305 feet, 6 inches from the bottom of the base to the tip of the torch. The architect plans to make her model 26 inches tall. If Lady Liberty's nose on the actual statue is 4 feet, 6 inches long, how long in inches should the nose on the model be?

    A) $\dfrac{1}{26}$

    B) $\dfrac{26}{141}$

    C) $\dfrac{18}{47}$

    D) $\dfrac{13}{27}$

20. If $f(x) = 3x + 5$, what is $f(6) - f(2)$?

    A) 11

    B) 12

    C) 17

    D) 23

GO ON TO THE NEXT PAGE

Northern Spotted Owls
West Oregon, 1994-2014

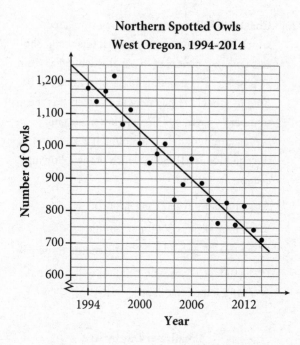

22. The *x*-coordinates of the solutions to a system of equations are −4 and 2. Which of the following could be the system?

A) $\begin{cases} y = 2x - 4 \\ y = (x + 4)^2 \end{cases}$

B) $\begin{cases} y = x - 2 \\ y = (x + 4)^2 + 2 \end{cases}$

C) $\begin{cases} y = x - 2 \\ y = (x - 4)^2 - 16 \end{cases}$

D) $\begin{cases} y = 2x - 4 \\ y = (x + 2)^2 - 16 \end{cases}$

21. The United States Fish and Wildlife Service classifies animals whose populations are at low levels as either threatened or endangered. Endangered species are animals that are currently on the brink of extinction, whereas threatened species have a high probability of being on the brink in the near future. Since 1990, the Northern Spotted Owl has been listed as threatened. The figure above shows the populations of the Northern Spotted Owl in a certain region in Oregon from 1994 to 2014. Based on the line of best fit shown in the figure, which of the following values most accurately reflects the average change per year in the number of Northern Spotted Owls?

A) −25

B) −0.04

C) 0.04

D) 25

Mice Litter Sample Data

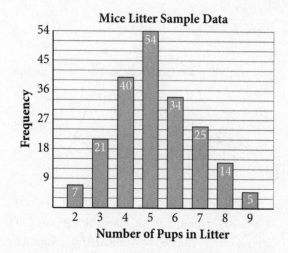

23. The White-footed Mouse, named for its darker body fur and white feet, is primarily found on the east coast of the United States, living in warm, dry forests and brushland. A scientist in Virginia studied a sample of 200 white-footed mice to see how many offspring they had per birth. The results of the study are recorded in the figure above. Based on the data, given a population of 35,000 female white-footed mice living in Virginia, how many would you expect to have a litter of seven or more pups?

A) 3,325

B) 4,375

C) 7,700

D) 15,400

GO ON TO THE NEXT PAGE

24. Human beings have a resting heart rate and an active heart rate. The resting heart rate is the rate at which the heart beats when a person is at rest, engaging in no activity. The active heart rate rises as activity rises. For a fairly active woman in her 20s, eight minutes of moderate exercise results in a heart rate of about 90 beats per minute. After 20 minutes, the same woman's heart rate will be about 117 beats per minute. If the human heart rate increases at a constant rate as the time spent exercising increases, which of the following linear models represents this same woman's heart rate, r, after t minutes of moderate exercise?

A) $r = 0.15t - 5.3$

B) $r = 0.44t - 32$

C) $r = 2.25t + 72$

D) $r = 6.75t + 36$

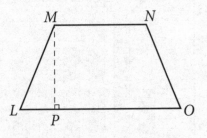

25. What would the percent increase in the area of the isosceles trapezoid shown above be if MN and LO were each multiplied by 4 and MP was reduced by 75%?

A)   0

B)   25

C)   100

D)   400

26. Chantal buys new furniture using store credit, which offers five-year, no-interest financing. She sets up a payment plan to pay the debt off as soon as possible. The function $40x + y = 1,400$ can be used to model her payment plan, where x is the number of payments Chantal has made, and y is the amount of debt remaining. If a solution to the equation is (21, 560), which of the following statements is true?

A) Chantal pays $21 per month.

B) Chantal pays $560 per month.

C) After 21 payments, $560 remains to be paid.

D) After 21 payments, Chantal will have paid off $560 of the debt.

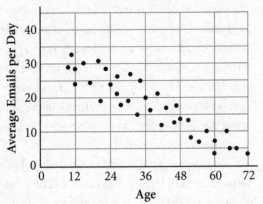

27. Which of the following equations best represents the trend of the data shown in the figure above?

A) $y = -2.4x + 30$

B) $y = -1.2x + 40$

C) $y = -0.8x + 40$

D) $y = -0.4x + 36$

28. The graph of $f(x)$ passes through the point $(5, 1)$. Through which point does the graph of $-f(x + 3) - 2$ pass?

    A) $(-2, -1)$

    B) $(2, -3)$

    C) $(2, 1)$

    D) $(8, -3)$

29. When a certain kitchen appliance store decides to sell a floor model, it marks the retail price of the model down 25% and puts a "Floor Model Sale" sign on it. Every 30 days after that, the price is marked down an additional 10% until it is sold. The store decides to sell a floor model refrigerator on January 15th. If the retail price of the refrigerator was $1,500 and it is sold on April 2nd of the same year, what is the final selling price, not including tax?

    A) $820.13

    B) $825.00

    C) $911.25

    D) $1,012.50

30. When New York City built its 34th Street subway station, which has multiple underground levels, it built an elevator that runs along a diagonal track approximately 170 feet long to connect the upper and lower levels. The angle formed between the elevator track and the bottom level is just under 30 degrees. What is the approximate vertical distance in feet between the upper and lower levels of the subway station?

    A) 85

    B) 98

    C) 120

    D) 147

GO ON TO THE NEXT PAGE ▷

Directions: For questions 31-38, enter your responses into the appropriate grid on your answer sheet, in accordance with the following:

1. You will receive credit only if the circles are filled in correctly, but you may write your answers in the boxes above each grid to help you fill in the circles accurately.

2. Don't mark more than one circle per column.

3. None of the questions with grid-in responses will have a negative solution.

4. Only grid in a single answer, even if there is more than one correct answer to a given question.

5. A **mixed number** must be gridded as a decimal or an improper fraction. For example, you would grid $7\frac{1}{2}$ as 7.5 or $\frac{15}{2}$.

   (Were you to grid it as ⌗, this response would be read as $\frac{71}{2}$.)

6. A **decimal** that has more digits than there are places on the grid may be either rounded or truncated, but every column in the grid must be filled in order to receive credit.

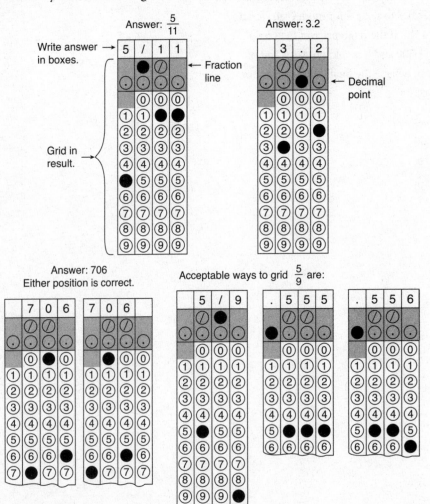

31. If $-\dfrac{3}{2} < 3 - \dfrac{a}{5} < -\dfrac{1}{4}$, what is the maximum possible whole number value of a?

Boeing Jets	Coach	Business	First Class
747-400	310	52	12
767-300	151	26	6
777-200	194	37	16
777-300	227	52	8

32. The table above shows the seating configuration for several commercial airplanes. The day before a particular flight departs, a travel agent books the last seat available for a client. If the seat is on one of the two Boeing 777s, what is the probability that the seat is a Business Class seat, assuming that all seats have an equal chance of being the last one available?

33. Heating water accounts for a good portion of the average home's energy consumption. Tankless water heaters, which run on natural gas, are about 22% more energy efficient on average than electric hot water heaters. However, a tankless hot water heater typically costs significantly more. Suppose one tankless water heater costs $160 more than twice as much as a conventional hot water heater. If both water heaters cost $1,000 together, how many more dollars does the tankless water heater cost than the conventional one?

34. Medically speaking, remission is a period in which the symptoms of a disease or condition subside or, for some diseases, a period during which the condition stops spreading or worsening. In a certain drug trial in which a drug designed to treat cancer was tested, exactly 48% of patients experienced remission while take the drug. What is the fewest number of patients who could have participated in this trial?

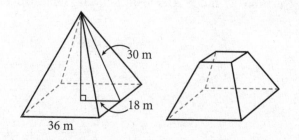

35. When the top of a pyramid (or a cone) is cut off, the remaining bottom part is called a frustum. Suppose the top third (based on the height) of the square pyramid shown above is cut off and discarded. What will be the volume, in cubic meters, of the remaining frustum?

36. After a surface has been cleaned, bacteria begin to regrow. Because bacteria reproduce in all directions, the area covered is usually in the shape of a circle. The diameter of the circle in millimeters can give scientists an idea of how long the bacteria have been growing. For a certain kind of bacteria, the equation $d = 0.015 \times \sqrt{h - 24}$ can be used to find the number of hours, $h \geq 24$, that the bacteria have been growing. If the diameter of a circle of these bacteria is 0.12 millimeters, how many hours have the bacteria been growing?

GO ON TO THE NEXT PAGE

Questions 37 and 38 refer to the following information.

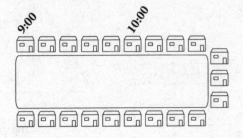

Daniel works for a pest control company and is spraying all the lawns in a neighborhood. The figure above shows the layout of the neighborhood and the times that Daniel started spraying the lawns at two of the houses. Each lawn in the neighborhood is approximately 0.2 acres in size and takes the same amount of time to spray.

37. How many minutes will it take Daniel to spray all of the lawns in the neighborhood?

38. Daniel uses a mobile spray rig that holds 20 gallons of liquid. It takes 1 gallon to spray 2,500 square feet of lawn. How many times, including the first time, will Daniel need to fill the spray rig, assuming he fills it to the very top each time? (1 acre = 43,560 square feet)

ESSAY TEST

50 Minutes

You will be given a passage to read and asked to write an essay analyzing it. As you write, be sure to show that you have read the passage closely. You will be graded on how well you have understood the passage, how clear your analysis is, and how well you express your ideas.

Your essay must be written on the lines in your answer booklet. Anything you write outside the lined space in your answer booklet will not be read by the essay graders. Be sure to write or print in such a way that it will be legible to readers not familiar with your handwriting. Additionally, be sure to address the passage directly. An off-topic essay will not be graded.

As you read the passage, think about the author's use of

- evidence, such as statistics or other facts.

- logic to connect evidence to conclusions and to develop lines of reasoning.

- style, word choice, and appeals to emotion to make the argument more persuasive.

Adapted from Royal Dixon, *The Human Side of Animals*. © 1918 by Frederick A. Stokes Company, New York.

1   The trouble with science is that too often it leaves out feeling. If you agree that we cannot treat men like machines, why should we put animals in that class? Why should we fall into the colossal ignorance and conceit of cataloging every human-like action of animals under the word "instinct"? Man had to battle with animals for untold ages before he domesticated and made servants of them. He is just beginning to learn that they were not created solely to furnish material for stories, or to serve mankind, but that they also have an existence, a life of their own.

2   Man has long claimed dominion over animals and a right to assert that dominion without restraint. This anthropocentric conceit is the same thing that causes one nation to think it should rule the world, that the sun and moon were made only for the laudable purpose of giving light unto a chosen few, and that young lambs playing on a grassy hillside, near a cool spring, are just so much mutton allowed to wander over man's domain until its flavor is improved.

3   It is time to remove the barriers, once believed impassable, which man's egotism has used as a screen to separate him from his lower brothers. Our physical bodies are very similar to theirs except that ours are almost always much inferior. Merely because we have a superior intellect which enables us to rule and enslave the animals, shall we deny them all intellect and all feeling?

GO ON TO THE NEXT PAGE

4   It is possible to explain away all the marvelous things the animals do, but after you have finished, there will still remain something over and above which quite defies all mechanistic interpretation. An old war horse, for instance, lives over and over his battles in his dreams. He neighs and paws, just as he did in real battle . . . This is only one of the plethora of animal phenomena which man does not understand. If you are able to explain these things to humanity, you will be classed as wise indeed. Yet the average scientist explains them away, with the ignorance and empty words of the unwise.

5   By a thorough application of psychological principles, it is possible to show that man himself is merely a machine to be explained in terms of neurons and nervous impulses, heredity and environment and reactions to outside stimuli. But who is there who does not believe that there is more to a man than that?

6   Animals have demonstrated long ago that they not only have as many talents as human beings but that, under the influence of the same environment, they form the same kinds of combinations to defend themselves against enemies, to shelter themselves against heat and cold, to build homes, to lay up a supply of food for the hard seasons. In fact, all through the ages man has been imitating the animals in burrowing through the earth, penetrating the waters, and now, at last, flying through the air.

7   There are also numerous signs, sounds and motions by which animals communicate with each other, though to man these symbols of language may not always be understandable. Dogs give barks indicating surprise, pleasure and all other emotions. Cows will bellow for days when mourning for their dead.

8   In their reading of the weather, animals undoubtedly possess superhuman powers. Even squirrels can predict an unusually long and severe winter and thus make adequate preparations. Some animals act as both barometers and thermometers.

9   There is no limit to the marvelous things animals do. The ape or baboon who puts a stone in the open oyster to prevent it from closing, or lifts stones to crack nuts, or beats other apes with sticks . . . in all these actions is actual reasoning. Indeed, there is nothing which man makes with all his ingenious use of tools and instruments, of which some suggestion may not be seen in animal creation.

Write an essay that analyzes the author's approach in persuading his readers that animals and humans have much in common and humans should treat animals with more respect. Focus on specific features such as the ones listed in the box above the passage and explain how these features strengthen the author's argument. Your essay should discuss the most important rhetorical features of the passage.

Your essay should not focus on your own opinion of the author's conclusion, but rather on how the author persuades his readers.

ANSWER KEY
READING TEST

1. C	14. C	27. C	40. C
2. D	15. D	28. D	41. C
3. A	16. B	29. B	42. A
4. C	17. B	30. A	43. B
5. D	18. D	31. D	44. B
6. A	19. B	32. A	45. A
7. D	20. C	33. D	46. D
8. A	21. A	34. D	47. B
9. B	22. C	35. B	48. C
10. D	23. C	36. D	49. B
11. D	24. B	37. C	50. D
12. D	25. C	38. B	51. D
13. A	26. A	39. D	52. B

WRITING AND LANGUAGE TEST

1. B	12. D	23. D	34. C
2. B	13. B	24. C	35. D
3. C	14. D	25. B	36. C
4. A	15. B	26. D	37. B
5. B	16. C	27. D	38. B
6. A	17. B	28. A	39. C
7. A	18. C	29. B	40. A
8. C	19. A	30. C	41. B
9. A	20. C	31. C	42. B
10. D	21. D	32. D	43. A
11. C	22. B	33. D	44. D

MATH—NO CALCULATOR TEST

1. B	6. B	11. C	16. 144
2. D	7. C	12. D	17. 150
3. C	8. D	13. A	18. 4
4. B	9. C	14. D	19. 8
5. D	10. A	15. A	20. 3/25 or .12

MATH—CALCULATOR TEST

1. B	11. B	21. A	31. 22
2. B	12. C	22. D	32. 1/6 or .166 or .167
3. A	13. D	23. C	33. 440
4. A	14. D	24. C	34. 25
5. D	15. A	25. A	35. 9984
6. C	16. B	26. C	36. 88
7. C	17. C	27. D	37. 252
8. D	18. B	28. B	38. 4
9. A	19. C	29. C	
10. D	20. B	30. A	

ANSWERS AND EXPLANATIONS

READING TEST

"Metamorphosis"

Suggested Passage Map notes:

¶1: Gregor woke up not himself

¶2: description of Gregor's room, job

¶3: thought sleep would make him normal, couldn't roll over

¶4: thought job stress was to blame for how he was

¶5: thinks he needs more sleep, wants more luxury but has to help parents

1. C **Difficulty:** Easy

Category: Detail

Getting to the Answer: Skim the passage to locate Gregor's first reaction to his transformation. The passage states that Gregor woke "from troubled dreams." He only realizes "it wasn't a dream" after he has examined his new body and looked around his room to orient himself. Choice (C) is the correct answer. "Nightmare" describes a dream that is "troubled."

2. D **Difficulty:** Hard

Category: Vocab-in-Context

Getting to the Answer: Use context clues and tone to help determine the meaning of the word. Use the surrounding text to paint a mental picture of descriptive words. Finally, make sure the answer choice does not alter the meaning of the sentence when inserted. The paragraph in which the word appears describes an average room appropriate for a person. Therefore, (D) is the correct answer. "Proper" means "suitably appropriate" in this context.

3. A **Difficulty:** Medium

Category: Inference

Getting to the Answer: Look for Gregor's thoughts and statements about work. Use this as evidence of his attitude. Paragraphs 4 and 5 are essentially rants about Gregor's dissatisfaction with his job. He dislikes travelling, feels that he works much harder than others, and expresses anger toward his boss. Gregor feels that it is unfair that other salesmen have a life of "luxury" while he has to wake up early. Choice (A) is the correct answer. Gregor is resentful and bitter about his job.

4. C **Difficulty:** Medium

Category: Command of Evidence

Getting to the Answer: Review your answer to the previous question. Decide which lines of text give clues to how Gregor feels about his job. Choice (C) offers the best support. These lines describe Gregor's bitterness and the unfairness he perceives. He feels he works much harder than the other salesmen, but that he would be fired if he asked for better treatment or less work.

5. D **Difficulty:** Hard

Category: Global

Getting to the Answer: Ask yourself what purpose the author has in writing the passage. What main point does the majority of the excerpt support? The events in the passage show that despite a dramatic physical transformation, Gregor still plans to go to work. Gregor consistently expresses unhappiness and bitterness about his job but ignores his transformation into an insect because he feels he must still go to work or he will be fired. In this situation, (D) is the correct answer. Gregor's duty to his job overrides reason and sense when he plans to attend work despite the physical transformation that has left him inhuman and helpless.

6. A   Difficulty: Medium

Category: Inference

Getting to the Answer: Reread the text, looking for evidence to support each of the answer choices. Examine Gregor's thoughts and statements for clues about his personality. Based on Gregor's statements about his work, it is clear that he continues to work at a job he dislikes in order to support his parents. He largely ignores his physical transformation, and there is no evidence as to whether he excels at his work. Choice (A) is the correct answer.

7. D   Difficulty: Medium

Category: Command of Evidence

Getting to the Answer: Review your answer to the previous question. Read each choice and figure out which one provides specific support for that answer. Choice (D) provides the best support. These lines show that Gregor thinks it may be best to quit the job he hates, but he will continue to work until he can pay off his parents' debt.

8. A   Difficulty: Medium

Category: Vocab-in-Context

Getting to the Answer: Use context clues from the target sentence and surrounding sentence. Predict the meaning of the word and look for a match in the answer choices. Gregor is attempting to turn over in his bed, but finds his legs and body are useless and unable to turn him over into his preferred position. Choice (A) is the nearest match to the meaning of "floundering" in this context.

9. B   Difficulty: Medium

Category: Rhetoric

Getting to the Answer: Think about where the description of Gregor's itch is placed in the story. Look at the lines before and after it, and consider why the author chose to include it at that particular point in the narrative. The description of the itch comes in the middle of Gregor's thoughts about his job. After

attempting and failing to relieve the itch, Gregor immediately goes back to thinking about his job-related concerns. This shows that Gregor is so preoccupied with his job that he is unable to recognize the seriousness—and absurdity—of his situation. The correct answer is (B).

10. D   Difficulty: Medium

Category: Rhetoric

Getting to the Answer: Contrast Gregor's thoughts with the dark tone of the rest of the excerpt. Think about how this phrase adds to or supports the interpretations you made in previous questions. The author ends the excerpt with Gregor completely disregarding the fact that he is now an insect. Gregor plans to go to work as he always does, and the author draws attention to the absurdity of this decision. Choice (D) is the correct choice. The author uses the matter-of-fact tone in the sentence to emphasize that Gregor will ignore his physical condition and go to work because he has such a strong sense of duty to his family.

Hillary Rodham Clinton Speech

Suggested Passage Map notes:

¶1-3: women are equal and deserve to be treated as such

¶4: what freedom is

¶5-6: history of women fighting for equality

¶7-8: men and women do great things when they work together

¶9-13: must help women in other countries achieve equality and fight discrimination

11. D   Difficulty: Easy

Category: Rhetoric

Getting to the Answer: Consider the word choices Clinton uses throughout her speech. Notice any recurring themes. Choice (D) is the correct answer. Clinton says that working to improve the lives of women will improve others' lives as well.

12. D Difficulty: Medium

Category: Command of Evidence

Getting to the Answer: Beware of answer choices that are only vaguely related to Clinton's point. The correct answer will follow her purpose closely. Clinton indicates that women's rights issues affect more than just women. Choice (D) is the best fit. These lines from the text provide concrete examples of how improving the lives of women improves their families' lives as well.

13. A Difficulty: Medium

Category: Vocab-in-Context

Getting to the Answer: Sometimes you can recognize similarities between the word in question and a more familiar word. "Divisive" is similar to "divide" and "division," both of which have to do with things being split or made separate. Clinton is saying that though suffrage produced great conflict and divided people more than other philosophical wars, it was "bloodless." Choice (A) is correct; "divisive" means "conflict-producing."

14. C Difficulty: Hard

Category: Inference

Getting to the Answer: You're being asked to decide which statement Clinton is most likely to agree with. Because the statement isn't explicitly mentioned in the speech, you must infer, or make a logical guess, based on information in the speech. Clinton states that the world would be improved if women were able to contribute more. She provides specific examples of her vision for an improved world. Choice (C) is correct, as it suggests that if women did not experience discrimination and had more power, the world would be better off.

15. D Difficulty: Medium

Category: Command of Evidence

Getting to the Answer: Try paraphrasing the answer you chose for the previous test item. Then decide which quote from the speech supports this idea. Choice (D) provides the best evidence. This quote notes that women are discriminated against and that it is not just women who suffer from this discrimination; there are global problems that could benefit from women's ideas.

16. B Difficulty: Hard

Category: Vocab-in-Context

Getting to the Answer: A word like "organized" can have several meanings, depending on the context. Beware of choosing the most common meaning, as it may not fit this situation. Choice (B) successfully conveys the idea of the women's suffrage movement being one in which many different people worked together over a long period of time.

17. B Difficulty: Hard

Category: Rhetoric

Getting to the Answer: Be careful to assess not only what topics are mentioned but also how Clinton discusses them. Choice (B) is supported by the passage, which claims that "Women must enjoy the right to participate fully in the social and political lives of their countries if we want freedom and democracy to thrive and endure."

18. D Difficulty: Medium

Category: Rhetoric

Getting to the Answer: Notice how the stem of the question doesn't ask you to find evidence for an argument; it instead gives you the evidence (the example of V-J Day) and then asks you to figure out what argument this evidence supports. Choice (D) is correct. Clinton mentions V-J Day as an example of something that resulted from cooperation between men and women.

19. B   **Difficulty:** Medium

Category: Detail

Getting to the Answer: Pay close attention to the words Clinton uses in the cited lines to describe problems that affect women. Clinton states that the problems that "diminish the potential" (line 38) of women are "older" (line 37) and "deeply-rooted" (line 37), making (B) the correct answer.

20. C   **Difficulty:** Medium

Category: Rhetoric

Getting to the Answer: Notice how the question is asking you to figure out how the paragraph functions in relation to other parts of the speech. Clinton goes into specific detail in this paragraph to provide examples of freedom. She very specifically states what she means by freedom and accuses some of failing to respect others' freedom. Therefore, (C) is the correct answer.

Paired Passages—Tea

Suggested Passage Map notes:

Passage 1

¶1: history of tea, Europe and China

¶2: tea not received well in Europe at first

¶3: China controlled tea production

¶4: Europe wanted to produce tea

¶5: finally had tea growing success in India

Passage 2

¶1: history of tea time in Europe

¶2: tea in France served with savory

¶3: tea in Germany served with sweet

¶4: tea in Russia sign of class

¶5: tea in GB

21. A   **Difficulty:** Medium

Category: Inference

Getting to the Answer: Be careful to choose an answer that is clearly supported by the information in the passage. The passage states that the climate was not right for growing tea "even in the equatorial colonies" (line 28). Choice (A) is the correct answer. Clearly, European tea-drinking nations tried to grow tea in their equatorial colonies; that's how they learned that the climate there wasn't right.

22. C   **Difficulty:** Medium

Category: Command of Evidence

Getting to the Answer: The correct answer will be the reason you were able to make the inference in the previous question. Choice (C) works logically. Europeans knew that tea would not grow well in their colonies; this leads to the conclusion that they tried.

23. C   **Difficulty:** Medium

Category: Inference

Getting to the Answer: When a question refers to only one of the Paired Passages, be sure to focus on the correct passage. Find where Passage 1 discusses Great Britain's attempts to grow tea in India. Eliminate any answer choices that are not supported by information in this section of the passage. The last sentence of Passage 1 states that the large quantities of tea imported from India allowed tea to become a "staple" (line 48) in European households. You can infer that if the British had not succeeded in growing tea in India, Europeans would have had tea less often. Choice (C) is correct.

24. B   **Difficulty:** Medium

Category: Vocab-in-Context

Getting to the Answer: You should be able to replace the original word with the correct answer in the sentence. The passage states that in order to "circumvent" the monopoly, European growers tried growing their own tea. It makes sense that Europeans' attempt at growing their own tea was a way to "get around" the Chinese monopoly. Therefore, (B) is the best choice.

25. C   Difficulty: Hard

Category: Synthesis

Getting to the Answer: Keep in mind that the graphic focuses on tea consumption, not tea production. The last paragraph of Passage 1 describes Britain's great success growing tea in India, which resulted in great increases in the amount of tea arriving in London. Therefore, (C) is a reasonable conclusion that may be drawn by synthesizing information in Passage 1 and the graphic.

26. A   Difficulty: Hard

Category: Inference

Getting to the Answer: Be careful to deduce only information that can reasonably be inferred from the passage. It can logically be inferred that hosting guests in Russia generally involves tea. Passage 2 emphasizes that Russian hosts are judged based on the strength of their tea, and that Russians have elaborate tea-making equipment. Choice (A) is the correct answer.

27. C   Difficulty: Medium

Category: Command of Evidence

Getting to the Answer: Identify the country associated with the correct answer to the previous question and see what evidence fits. The passage states that Russian tea ceremonies are highly formal and that hosts are judged on their tea-making. Choice (C) is the correct answer. The referenced lines support the conclusions about Russia.

28. D   Difficulty: Medium

Category: Vocab-in-Context

Getting to the Answer: Look for other words in this sentence that offer clues to the word's meaning. A noble, or high-ranking, class is likely to have associations with formalism, so (D) is the correct answer.

29. B   Difficulty: Easy

Category: Connections

Getting to the Answer: Make sure to compare only the two countries being asked about. Choice (B) is correct. The passage notes that cookies and cakes are served with tea in Germany, while foods served with tea in France are "savory" and include puff pastry with cheese.

30. A   Difficulty: Easy

Category: Synthesis

Getting to the Answer: Look for true statements about Passage 1. Then do the same for Passage 2. Choice (A) is correct. Passage 1 focuses on an earlier period in European history, while Passage 2 compares different cultures within Europe.

31. D   Difficulty: Medium

Category: Synthesis

Getting to the Answer: For this question, you're looking for a statement that is reflected in both passages. Choice (D) is the only choice supported by both passages.

Spinosaurus Passage

Suggested Passage Map notes:

¶1: Stromer discovered dinosaur fossils in Egypt, new genus, fossils destroyed in WWII, notes and sketches survived

¶2: Ibrahaim rediscovered similar fossils, able to make partial skeleton

¶3: description of spinosaurus

¶4: spino unique - lived on land, hunted in water

¶5: Ibrahaim used digital model and Stromer sketches to create replica

32. A   Difficulty: Easy

Category: Global

Getting to the Answer: Look for the answer choice that describes an important idea that is supported throughout the text rather than a specific detail. The passage is mostly about how the mystery of the Spinosaurus fossils was decoded. Choice (A) is the best summary of the central idea of the passage.

33. D   Difficulty: Medium

Category: Detail

Getting to the Answer: Locate the information about the fossils Stromer expected to find and the fossils he actually found, particularly those fossils' sizes and ages. The passage explains that Stromer expected to find fossils of early mammals, but instead found fossils that "dated back to the Cretaceous period" (line 9). This indicates that the fossils were older than he expected. Eliminate choices A and B. Because the Spinosaurus was larger than any mammal, (D) is correct.

34. D   Difficulty: Medium

Category: Inference

Getting to the Answer: Think about the overall message of the passage and consider why the author would choose to write about this topic. The author's tone, or attitude, toward the topic of the passage demonstrates the point of view that the study of fossils and ancient life has value. Choice (D) is the correct answer. The evidence in the passage supports the idea that the author thinks the study of fossils and ancient life is important.

35. B   Difficulty: Medium

Category: Command of Evidence

Getting to the Answer: Some answer choices may seem important. However, if they don't support your answer to the previous question, they aren't what you should choose. Choice (B) is correct. The author's use of the word "significant" in this quote shows that he or she thinks the study of fossils and ancient life is important.

36. D   Difficulty: Medium

Category: Vocab-in-Context

Getting to the Answer: Though more than one answer choice might seem acceptable, one comes closest to meaning the same as the phrase in question. Earlier in the paragraph, the author explains that two different bones gathered at different times both had a red line coursing through them. This means that the bones were from the same animal. Choice (D) fits best. "Against all odds" most nearly means "despite low probability."

37. C   Difficulty: Medium

Category: Rhetoric

Getting to the Answer: Be careful to avoid answers that don't make sense in the context of the paragraph. These phrases help the author describe the animal in a generally positive way. Choice (C) is the correct answer.

38. B   Difficulty: Hard

Category: Inference

Getting to the Answer: Be careful of answers that make sense but are not implied by the information presented in the passage. Choice (B) is correct. The passage does not explicitly state how Ibrahim became familiar with Stromer's work, but it is implied that he was familiar with Stromer's work when he found the fossils with the red lines and used Stromer's sketches to aid with the modern digital models as mentioned in the last paragraph.

39. D   Difficulty: Hard

Category: Command of Evidence

Getting to the Answer: Eliminate any answer choices that have nothing to do with your answer to the previous question. Choice (D) is correct. It directly supports the inference that Ibrahim was familiar with Stromer's work, showing that he used Stromer's sketches to aid in creating his life-size replica of the Spinosaurus.

40. C   Difficulty: Easy

Category: Vocab-in-Context

Getting to the Answer: Ibrahim and his fellow researchers didn't know how the bones went together. They were making an educated guess with the help of technology and Stromer's sketches. Choice (C) is correct. "Hypothetical" in this sentence means "possible."

41. C   Difficulty: Easy

Category: Connections

Getting to the Answer: Think about the order in which Stromer and Ibrahim's work with the fossils occurred. Choice (C) is correct. Ibrahim used Stromer's sketches to create his models of the Spinosaurus. He built on Stromer's work to complete his own.

42. A   Difficulty: Hard

Category: Connections

Getting to the Answer: Think about the process described in each answer choice and compare it to how Ibrahim went about building his replica of the Spinosaurus. Choice (A) is the right choice. An architect creating a model of a building would use tools and methods similar to those used by Ibrahim, such as drawings and digital technologies.

Laughter Passage

Suggested Passage Map notes:

¶1: people willing to try anything to be healthy

¶2: laughter important part of health

¶3: what happens to body when you laugh

¶4: humor helps many medical conditions, laugh more = better health

¶5: benefits of laughter

¶6: various methods to provoke laughter, best achieved in person, not through watching shows

¶7: laughter decreases with age

43. B   Difficulty: Easy

Category: Rhetoric

Getting to the Answer: When a question asks you about the point of view of an author, look for words and phrases in the passage that hint at the author's feelings or attitude toward the topic. Choice (B) is the correct answer because the author speaks quite positively of the studies throughout the passage.

44. B   Difficulty: Medium

Category: Command of Evidence

Getting to the Answer: Reread each quote in the context of the passage. Consider which one is the best evidence of the author's point of view toward laughter research. The word "finally" in line 14 helps demonstrate that the author finds laughter research worthwhile. Choice (B) is the best answer.

45. A   Difficulty: Medium

Category: Connections

Getting to the Answer: Think about the connection the passage makes between laughter and the ability to accomplish challenging tasks. Choice (A) is correct. The passage notes that endorphin production is associated with "mental energy and positivity" (lines 27-28).

46. D   Difficulty: Medium

Category: Vocab-in-Context

Getting to the Answer: Notice that all of the answer choices are related to the word "reputable," but the correct answer will reflect the specific context in which the word is used. "Reputable" in this case indicates that the studies are official and are based on empirical data (data based on observation and experiment). This makes (D), "credible," the correct choice.

47. B   **Difficulty:** Hard

Category: Inference

Getting to the Answer: Eliminate any answer choices that are not suggested in the passage. Choice (B) is correct because early results of studies into laughter and health all seem to strengthen the relationship between the two.

48. C   **Difficulty:** Medium

Category: Command of Evidence

Getting to the Answer: Avoid answer choices like D that may not support a general conclusion you could take from the passage. Choice (C) is the correct answer. The author expects future research will yield stronger evidence in support of laughter's health benefits.

49. B   **Difficulty:** Hard

Category: Rhetoric

Getting to the Answer: Look at the verbs provided in each of the answer choices. Decide whether the author wanted to "reach," "support," "justify," or "show" by discussing the function of endorphins. After asserting that laughter produces endorphins, the author explains their function in order to help the reader understand why a positive mental state may result. Choice (B) is the correct answer.

50. D   **Difficulty:** Medium

Category: Vocab-in-Context

Getting to the Answer: Look carefully at the paragraph's context to help you decide on the correct answer choice. The phrase "Laughter is the best medicine" (lines 15-16) is an example of an adage, or proverb. Therefore, (D) is correct.

51. D   **Difficulty:** Hard

Category: Synthesis

Getting to the Answer: Decide whether the phrase "uplifting community" is a reference to a person alone or a group of people. Choice (D) is correct. The

graph shows that shared humor with others most significantly increased pain tolerance in individuals.

52. B   **Difficulty:** Medium

Category: Inference

Getting to the Answer: Watch out for answer choices that seem plausible but are not directly supported by information in the passage. The passage states that laughter seems to provide protection from heart disease and that young people laugh less as they get older. You can infer from this information that as young people age, they have less protection from heart disease and are therefore more at risk. Choice (B) is correct.

WRITING AND LANGUAGE TEST

From Here to the Stars

1. B   **Difficulty:** Medium

Category: Sentence Formation

Getting to the Answer: Read the sentence and determine whether it is grammatically complete. To form a grammatically complete sentence, you must have an independent clause prior to a colon. As written, the text that comes before the colon is not grammatically complete because it lacks an independent clause with a subject and predicate. Choice (B) correctly adds a verb to the clause before the comma. It also correctly uses the past tense to match with the tense of "hadn't" in the first sentence of the passage.

2. B   **Difficulty:** Medium

Category: Effective Language Use

Getting to the Answer: Read the sentences surrounding the word to look for context clues. Watch out for near synonyms that are not quite correct. The word "issues" is not precise and does a poor job of conveying the meaning of the sentence. A better word, such as (B), "adversity," more precisely conveys hardship, difficulties, or painful situations.

3. C   **Difficulty:** Medium

Category: Punctuation

Getting to the Answer: Determine whether a clause is independent or dependent to decide between a comma and a semicolon. The clause is dependent, as it contains only a noun ("an idea") and a relative clause to modify it. A semicolon is used to separate two independent clauses, so it cannot be used here. A comma is the appropriate punctuation mark to separate the dependent clause from the independent clause in the sentence. Choice (C) is the correct answer.

4. A   **Difficulty:** Medium

Category: Punctuation

Getting to the Answer: Figure out the role of the underlined phrase in the sentence to find the correct punctuation. "Like lift and drag on wings" is a parenthetical element provided as an example. The sentence is correctly punctuated as written because it uses dashes to set off the parenthetical element. The answer is (A).

5. B   **Difficulty:** Hard

Category: Development

Getting to the Answer: Read the paragraph and summarize the main idea to predict an answer. Then look for an answer that matches your prediction. Choice (B) correctly establishes that Kranz stood out as a leader in a time of crisis.

6. A   **Difficulty:** Easy

Category: Usage

Getting to the Answer: Read the paragraph to establish the correct verb tense for the sentence. Other verbs in the paragraph, such as "were" and "fueled," are past tense and indicate that another past tense verb is needed for this sentence. Choice (A) is correct, because it uses the past tense "was"

and logically transitions into the explanation about Kranz's vest making him easy to spot.

7. A   **Difficulty:** Hard

Category: Development

Getting to the Answer: Quickly summarize the main idea of the paragraph. Eliminate choices that may be accurate but do not support this primary focus. Choice (A) clearly supports the main focus of the paragraph by drawing attention to Kranz's role as a leader in Mission Control.

8. C   **Difficulty:** Easy

Category: Usage

Getting to the Answer: Be careful with homophones. Figure out the part of speech and what the target word refers to if it is a pronoun. "Their" is a possessive pronoun indicating ownership. "There" is a pronoun that replaces a place name. "They're" is a contraction that is short for "they are." Choice (C), "There," is the correct choice.

9. A   **Difficulty:** Hard

Category: Effective Language Use

Getting to the Answer: When faced with unfamiliar words, eliminate clearly incorrect answers first. The paragraph indicates that Kranz did not intend for the vest to be stylish. Kranz wore the vest as a military type of symbol, but the correct answer will need to be in contrast to that idea. Choice (A) is the correct answer. The word "sartorial" means "having to do with clothing."

10. D   **Difficulty:** Medium

Category: Usage

Getting to the Answer: Think about the commonly confused pair between/among. Consider which preposition is usually used to reference two distinct objects. Choice (D) appropriately selects the word "between" because the objects "meetings" and "calculations" are two distinct items. "Among" is used for more than two distinct items.

11. C Difficulty: Medium

Category: Usage

Getting to the Answer: Read the target sentence and the sentence before it. Figure out whom or what the pronoun refers to and make sure it matches the antecedent in number. The plural antecedent is found in the previous sentence ("Kranz and the NASA staff") and is clearly plural. Choice (C) correctly uses a plural pronoun to refer to a plural antecedent.

The UK and the Euro

12. D Difficulty: Medium

Category: Effective Language Use

Getting to the Answer: Read carefully to identify the context of the underlined word. Then, choose the word that best fits the content of the sentence. You're looking for a word that suggests that the organization has developed over time, as is stated in the last part of the sentence. "Built," (D), best fits the context of the sentence.

13. B Difficulty: Medium

Category: Punctuation

Getting to the Answer: Read the entire sentence to get a better sense for which punctuation would be correct. A colon will introduce an explanation of the "key feature," allowing the rest of the sentence to elaborate on the preceding clause. Choice (B) is correct. In this case, the colon prompts the reader to see that the part of the sentence after the colon defines the phrase "key feature."

14. D Difficulty: Medium

Category: Organization

Getting to the Answer: Watch out for any choices that would make the sentence seem out of place. Choice (D) is correct. Sentence 3 offers a transition to a specific discussion of those risks in the next paragraph.

15. B Difficulty: Medium

Category: Effective Language Use

Getting to the Answer: Avoid choices that are redundant, or use more words than necessary to communicate an idea. All of the choices communicate the same idea, but one does so with a greater economy of language. Choice (B) uses a minimal number of well-chosen words to revise the text.

16. C Difficulty: Hard

Category: Development

Getting to the Answer: Watch out for answer choices that correctly identify supporting points but do not explain the main claim. The paragraph contains evidence, including decreased taxable wealth and decreased control over interest rates, to support the main claim. Choice (C) is correct. It expresses the main claim of the paragraph and is supported by the evidence.

17. B Difficulty: Medium

Category: Sentence Formation

Getting to the Answer: Read the text carefully. Notice that the existing structure creates a run-on sentence. Then consider which answer choice will create two complete sentences. Choice (B) revises the run-on sentence to create two grammatically complete sentences.

18. C Difficulty: Medium

Category: Development

Getting to the Answer: Find the main claim in the paragraph and then come back to the question. The statement found in (C) best supports the paragraph statements that maintaining the current status may not be an option and moving to the Eurozone may be in the best interest of the UK.

19. A Difficulty: Easy

Category: Effective Language Use

Getting to the Answer: Watch out for choices that imply little relationship between the EU and the UK. "Intertwined" most accurately reflects the content of the text, because it implies a complex economic relationship between the UK and the Eurozone. Therefore, (A) is correct. No change is necessary.

20. C   Difficulty: Hard

Category: Development

Getting to the Answer: Find the central idea of the paragraph and then come back to the question. The central idea in the paragraph is that economic downturns in the Eurozone also affect the UK. Choice (C) is correct.

21. D   Difficulty: Easy

Category: Organization

Getting to the Answer: Decide which transition word makes the most sense in the context of the sentence by reading each choice in the sentence. The correct choice should connect the two sentences as the text transitions from economic concerns to those of "security, power, and protection." The word "however" is the best transition because it provides a logical contrast between the ideas in the passage. Choice (D) is the correct answer.

22. B   Difficulty: Medium

Category: Punctuation

Getting to the Answer: Consider which punctuation will correctly set off the parenthetical information in this sentence. Dashes are often used to offset parenthetical sentence elements. Choice (B) is correct.

Coffee: The Buzz on Beans

23. D   Difficulty: Easy

Category: Usage

Getting to the Answer: Review each answer choice

and decide which makes the most sense in terms of what the first sentence says. Choice (D) is the correct answer. "These days" contrasts with the next sentence's use of "this wasn't always true."

24. C   Difficulty: Medium

Category: Usage

Getting to the Answer: Make sure that verbs agree with the subject. Check back and figure out what the subject is and then see if it agrees. The word "cherries" requires a plural verb. Choice (C) is the correct answer.

25. B   Difficulty: Medium

Category: Sentence Formation

Getting to the Answer: Read the complete sentence carefully whenever you see a shift in tense or verb form. Decide whether this change is logically correct in the sentence. The verbs in a sentence need to be in parallel form. Choice (B) is in parallel form with the first verb "reached," so it is the correct answer.

26. D   Difficulty: Medium

Category: Effective Language Use

Getting to the Answer: Beware of some answer choices that may have similar meanings but do not fit into the context of this sentence. The word "boasted" is the best fit for the context of the sentence, so (D) is the correct answer.

27. D   Difficulty: Medium

Category: Sentence Formation

Getting to the Answer: Pay close attention to commas to ensure that they do not create run-on sentences. Notice that this sentence contains two complete thoughts. Choice (D) is the correct answer because it combines the two complete thoughts into one sentence in the best way.

28. A   Difficulty: Hard

Category: Development

Getting to the Answer: To find the best conclusion, look for the choice that summarizes the main points of the paragraph and best completes the paragraph. The paragraph begins by talking about the lack of record of coffee as cargo on the Mayflower and then introduces when it was first referenced. Choice (A) does the best job of retelling what the paragraph is about, therefore providing an effective conclusion.

29. B   Difficulty: Easy

Category: Punctuation

Getting to the Answer: Study the words in the series and see where commas might need to be placed or eliminated. Choice (B) is the correct answer.

30. C   Difficulty: Medium

Category: Effective Language Use

Getting to the Answer: Replace the word with the other answer choices. See which word works best in the context of the sentence. One answer choice indicates the correct relationship between coffeehouses and counterculture, and that is (C). "Associated" works best within the context of the sentence.

31. C   Difficulty: Medium

Category: Development

Getting to the Answer: To find the main topic of a paragraph, identify important details and summarize them in a sentence or two. Then find the answer choice that is the closest to your summary. Choice (C) is the correct answer. The sentence best explains the increasing popularity of coffee in American life, the main topic of the paragraph.

32. D   Difficulty: Medium

Category: Punctuation

Getting to the Answer: Determine the relationship between the two parts of this sentence, and

then consider the purpose of the various forms of punctuation. A colon indicates that the rest of the sentence will be a list or an explanation. Choice (D) is the correct answer, as it shows the correct relationship between both parts of the sentence.

33. D   Difficulty: Hard

Category: Sentence Formation

Getting to the Answer: Read the complete sentence carefully and look for sections that do not seem to follow logically. The modifiers need to be in the proper order so the sentence's meaning is clear; choice (D) is correct.

Predicting Nature's Light Show

34. C   Difficulty: Medium

Category: Usage

Getting to the Answer: Recall that a pronoun must agree with its antecedent, or the word to which it refers. Begin by identifying the antecedent of the pronoun. Then, check each choice against the antecedent to find the best match. The antecedent for the pronoun "their" is "this phenomenon," which appears in the main clause. The antecedent and its pronoun do not currently agree as "this phenomenon" is singular and "their" is plural. Although the "s" in "Lights" implies many lights, it is still considered a singular phenomenon and so requires a singular pronoun. Choice (C) is the correct answer.

35. D   Difficulty: Medium

Category: Effective Language Use

Getting to the Answer: Read each answer choice carefully to determine the correct preposition. Choice (D) is the correct answer because it correctly uses the preposition "in".

36. C   Difficulty: Medium

Category: Development

Getting to the Answer: Choice (C) is the correct answer because it provides additional information regarding how people are able to view auroras.

37. B   Difficulty: Hard

Category: Effective Language Use

Getting to the Answer: When choosing the correct verb, note how it alters the relationship between the subject, the "sun," and the stated action, in this case "storm activity." Choice (B) is correct. The verb "experiences" is the only one that states a direct action upon the subject, the sun, rather than the sun "observing" an action occurring externally, as suggested by the other verbs.

38. B   Difficulty: Easy

Category: Effective Language Use

Getting to the Answer: The placement of the adjective has a great effect upon the intention of the noun. Read the sentence carefully to determine where the adjective makes the most sense. By placing the adjective before the nouns, (B) ensures that only those scientists and amateurs interested in the topic at hand use the specific tools mentioned in this passage.

39. C   Difficulty: Hard

Category: Effective Language Use

Getting to the Answer: Generalized statements with inexact definitions that border on opinion have no place in a scientific essay. The tone and style must exhibit a reliance on verifiable statements. Because "readily available" cannot be quantified and implies the author's opinion, using the word "specific" in (C) creates a more exact statement that precedes the information on the precise tools used.

40. A   Difficulty: Medium

Category: Development

Getting to the Answer: Reread the paragraph to understand the author's claims. Which answer

choice provides a fact that would best support these claims? Make sure the answer choice does not digress from the progression of ideas. The speed of the solar flare is referenced as being three times the speed of normal solar winds, but neither exact speed is given. To make a stronger case for the author's statements, both speeds should be stated. Therefore, (A) is the correct answer.

41. B   Difficulty: Medium

Category: Usage

Getting to the Answer: Read closely to find the subject of the verb. Sometimes, the closest noun is not the subject. The subject of the sentence is "strength and direction," not "energy." Choice (B) is the correct answer because it matches the subject in number and maintains a consistent tense with the rest of the passage.

42. B   Difficulty: Hard

Category: Effective Language Use

Getting to the Answer: Eliminate extraneous and redundant information ("the public") and needless prepositions. Then reorder the verb and nouns to achieve the most efficient language possible. Making adjustments to the passage language as shown in (B) results in the most concise phrasing.

43. A   Difficulty: Hard

Category: Sentence Formation

Getting to the Answer: Consider the meanings of each introductory word carefully. Use the context clues in the rest of the sentence to choose the correct word. The context clues in the rest of the sentence reveal that the Northern Lights can create communication and weather problems and yet are still beautiful. Keeping the word "While" makes the most sense in this context, so (A) is the correct answer.

44. D   Difficulty: Hard

Category: Quantitative

Getting to the Answer: Reread paragraph 4 for information that will help you understand how to read the graphic. Use that information to calculate the precise start and end time for the solar flare as indicated in the graphic. The passage states that a solar flare is represented by any Kp-Index of 5 or higher. While there is one three-hour period where the Kp-Index reached 6, there is a consistent period where the chart shows readings of level 5 or higher. Choice (D) is the correct answer. This choice gives the complete time period showing a reading of level 5 or higher, according to the chart.

MATH—NO CALCULATOR TEST

1. B   Difficulty: Easy

Category: Heart of Algebra / Linear Equations

Getting to the Answer: The average rate of change for a linear function is the same as the slope of the line. Find the slope of the line by either using the slope formula or by counting the rise and the run from one point to the next. If you start at $(0, -3)$, the line rises 5 units and runs 8 units to get to $(8, 2)$, so the slope, or average rate of change, is $\dfrac{5}{8}$.

2. D   Difficulty: Easy

Category: Passport to Advanced Math / Quadratics

Getting to the Answer: A root of an equation is an x-value that corresponds to a y-value of 0. The x-intercepts of the graph, and therefore the roots of the equation, are $x = -1$ and $x = 5$. When $x = -1$, the value of $x + 1$ is 0, so one of the factors is $x + 1$. When $x = 5$, the value of $x - 5$ is 0, so the other factor is $x - 5$. The equation in (D) is the only one that contains these factors and is therefore correct.

3. C   Difficulty: Easy

Category: Passport to Advanced Math / Exponents

Getting to the Answer: Substitute the values given in the question into the formula. Then simplify using the rules of exponents. Remember, when raising a power to a power, you multiply the exponents.

$$\begin{aligned}
KE &= \frac{1}{2}\left(2 \times 10^3\right)\left(3 \times 10^3\right)^2 \\
&= \frac{1}{2}\left(2 \times 10^3\right)\left(3^2 \times 10^{3 \times 2}\right) \\
&= \frac{1}{2} \times 2 \times 10^3 \times 9 \times 10^6 \\
&= 9 \times 10^{3+6} \\
&= 9 \times 10^9
\end{aligned}$$

Choice (C) is correct.

4. B   Difficulty: Medium

Category: Heart of Algebra / Linear Equations

Getting to the Answer: Choose the best strategy to answer the question. You could start by cross-multiplying to get rid of the denominators, but simplifying the numerators first will make the calculations easier.

$$\begin{aligned}
\frac{3(k-1)+5}{2} &= \frac{17-(8+k)}{4} \\
\frac{3k-3+5}{2} &= \frac{17-8-k}{4} \\
\frac{3k+2}{2} &= \frac{9-k}{4} \\
4(3k+2) &= 2(9-k) \\
12k+8 &= 18-2k \\
14k &= 10 \\
k &= \frac{10}{14} = \frac{5}{7}
\end{aligned}$$

Choice (B) is correct.

5. D   Difficulty: Medium

Category: Passport to Advanced Math / Functions

Getting to the Answer: Whenever a quantity repeatedly increases or decreases by the same percentage (or fraction) over time, an exponential model can be used to represent the situation. Choice B is not an exponential equation, so you can eliminate it right away. The amount of garbage is decreasing, so the scenario represents exponential decay and you can use the form $y = a \times (1 - r)^t$, where a is the initial amount, r is the rate of decay, and t is time in years. The initial amount is 1,800, the rate is 3%, or 0.03, and t is an unknown quantity, so the correct equation is $y = 1,800 \times (1 - 0.03)^t$, which is equivalent to the equation $y = 1,800 \times 0.97^t$, (D).

6. B   Difficulty: Medium

Category: Passport to Advanced Math / Exponents

Getting to the Answer: The terms in the expression have the same denominator, $x + 5$, so their numerators can be subtracted. Simply combine like terms and keep the denominator the same. Don't forget to distribute the negative to both $3x$ and -8.

$$
\begin{aligned}
\frac{6x + 2}{x + 5} - \frac{3x - 8}{x + 5} &= \frac{6x + 2 - (3x - 8)}{x + 5} \\
&= \frac{6x + 2 - 3x - (-8)}{x + 5} \\
&= \frac{6x - 3x + 2 + 8}{x + 5} \\
&= \frac{3x + 10}{x + 5}
\end{aligned}
$$

Choice (B) is correct.

7. C   Difficulty: Medium

Category: Heart of Algebra / Linear Equations

Getting to the Answer: The slope-intercept form of a line is $y = mx + b$. In this question, the graph passes through the origin, so b is 0. Because b is 0, the equation of this line in slope-intercept form is $y = mx$, which can be rewritten as $\frac{y}{x} = m$. Count

the rise and the run from the origin, $(0, 0)$, to the next point, $(3, 1)$, to get a slope of $m = \frac{1}{3}$. This matches (C).

8. D   Difficulty: Medium

Category: Passport to Advanced Math / Exponents

Getting to the Answer: When multiplying polynomials, carefully multiply each term in the first factor by each term in the second factor. This question doesn't ask for the entire product, so check to make sure you answered the right question (the coefficient of x). After performing the initial multiplication, look for the x terms and add their coefficients. To save time, you do not need to simplify the other terms in the expression.

$$
\begin{aligned}
&\left(4x^2 + 7x + 1\right)(3x + 5) \\
&= 4x^2(3x + 5) + 7x(3x + 5) + 1(3x + 5) \\
&= 12x^3 + 20x^2 + 21x^2 + \underline{35x + 3x} + 5
\end{aligned}
$$

The coefficient of x is $35 + 3 = 38$, which is (D).

9. C   Difficulty: Medium

Category: Passport to Advanced Math / Functions

Getting to the Answer: A graph is *decreasing* when the slope is negative; it is *increasing* when the slope is positive. Eliminate A because there are some segments on the graph that have a positive slope. Eliminate B because the slope is negative, not positive, between 2009 and 2010. Choice (C) is correct because the slope is negative for each segment between 2004 and 2007 and also between 2009 and 2011.

10. A   Difficulty: Medium

Category: Heart of Algebra / Inequalities

Getting to the Answer: Don't answer this question too quickly. The shading is below the line, but that does not necessarily mean that the symbol in the equation will be the less than symbol ($<$). Start by writing the equation of the dashed line shown in the graph in slope-intercept form. Then use the shading to determine the correct inequality symbol. The slope of the line shown in the graph is $\frac{1}{4}$ and the y-intercept is -3, so the equation of the dashed line is $y = \frac{1}{4}x - 3$. The graph is shaded below the boundary line, so use the $<$ symbol. When written in slope-intercept form, the inequality is $y < \frac{1}{4}x - 3$. The inequalities in the answer choices are given in standard form ($Ax + By = C$), so rewrite your answer in this form. Don't forget to reverse the inequality symbol if you multiply or divide by a negative number.

$$y < \frac{1}{4}x - 3$$

$$-\frac{1}{4}x + y < -3$$

$$\frac{1}{4}x - y > 3$$

Choice (A) is correct.

11. C   Difficulty: Medium

Category: Heart of Algebra / Linear Equations

Getting to the Answer: When you're given only one equation but two variables, chances are that you can't actually solve the equation (unless one variable happens to cancel out), but rather that you are going to need to manipulate it to look like the desired expression (which in this question is $\frac{b}{a}$). This type of question can't be planned out step-by-step—instead, start with basic algebraic manipulations and see where they take you. First, distribute the $\frac{1}{2}$ on the left side of the equation to get $2a + 5b = b$. There are two terms that have a b, so subtract $5b$ from both sides to get $2a = -4b$. You're hoping for plain b in the numerator, so divide both sides by -4 to get $\frac{2a}{-4} = b$. Finally, divide both sides by a to move the a into a denominator position under b. The result is $\frac{2}{-4} = \frac{b}{a}$, which means the ratio $\frac{b}{a}$ is $-\frac{2}{4}$, or $-\frac{1}{2}$, making (C) correct.

12. D   Difficulty: Hard

Category: Heart of Algebra / Systems of Linear Equations

Getting to the Answer: Graphically, a system of linear equations that has no solution indicates two parallel lines, or in other words, two lines that have the same slope. So, write each of the equations in slope-intercept form ($y = mx + b$) and set their slopes (m) equal to each other to solve for a. Before finding the slopes, multiply the top equation by 3 to make it easier to manipulate.

$$3\left(\frac{1}{3}x + \frac{2}{3}y = -8\right) \rightarrow x + 2y = -24 \rightarrow y = -\frac{1}{2}x - 12$$

$$ax + 6y = 15 \rightarrow 6y = -ax + 15 \rightarrow y = -\frac{a}{6}x + \frac{15}{6}$$

The slope of the first line is $-\frac{1}{2}$ and the slope of the second line is $-\frac{a}{6}$.

$$-\frac{1}{2} = -\frac{a}{6}$$
$$-6(1) = -a(2)$$
$$-6 = -2a$$
$$3 = a$$

Choice (D) is correct.

13. A   Difficulty: Hard

Category: Heart of Algebra / Inequalities

Getting to the Answer: Pay careful attention to units, particularly when a question involves rates. The taxi charges $3.00 for the first $\frac{1}{4}$ mile, which is a flat fee, so write 3. The additional charge is $0.25 per $\frac{1}{8}$ mile, or 0.25 times 8 = $2.00 per mile. The number of miles after the first $\frac{1}{4}$ mile is $m - \frac{1}{4}$, so the cost of the trip, not including the first $\frac{1}{4}$ mile is $2\left(m - \frac{1}{4}\right)$. This means the cost of the whole trip is $3 + 2\left(m - \frac{1}{4}\right)$. The clue "no more than $20" means that much or less, so use the symbol $\leq$. The inequality is $3 + 2\left(m - \dfrac{1}{4}\right) \leq 20$, which simplifies to $2.5 + 2m \leq 20$, (A).

14. D   Difficulty: Hard

Category: Additional Topics in Math / Geometry

Getting to the Answer: First, find the center and the radius of the circle: Each grid-line represents one unit on the graph, so the center is (0, 2), and the radius is 6. Substitute these values into the equation for a circle, $(x - h)^2 + (y - k)^2 = r^2$, and then simplify until the equation looks like the one given in the question:

$$(x - 0)^2 + (y - 2)^2 = 6^2$$
$$x^2 + (y - 2)^2 = 36$$
$$x^2 + (y - 2)(y - 2) = 36$$
$$x^2 + y^2 - 4y + 4 = 36$$
$$x^2 + y^2 - 4y = 32$$

There is no x term, so $a = 0$. The coefficient of y is -4 and $c = 32$, so $ab + c = (0)(-4) + 32 = 32$, (D).

15. A   Difficulty: Hard

Category: Passport to Advanced Math / Quadratics

Getting to the Answer: The quadratic equation is given in standard form, so use the method of completing the square to rewrite the equation in vertex form. Then, read the value of k to find the maximum height of the projectile.

$$h = -16t^2 + 64t + 8$$
$$= -16\left(t^2 - 4t + \underline{\quad}\right) + 8 - \underline{\quad}$$
$$= -16\left(t^2 - 4t + 4\right) + 8 - (-16 \times 4)$$
$$= -16(t - 2)^2 + 8 - (-64)$$
$$= -16(t - 2)^2 + 72$$

The vertex is (2, 72), so the maximum height is 72 feet, (A).

16. 144   Difficulty: Easy

Category: Heart of Algebra / Linear Equations

Getting to the Answer: There is only one equation given and it has two variables. This means that you don't have enough information to solve for either variable. Instead, look for the relationship between the left side of the equation and the other expression that you are trying to find. Start by clearing the fractions by multiplying both sides of the original equation by 12. This yields the expression that you are looking for, $9x + 10y$, so no further work is required—just read the value on the right-hand side of the equation.

$$\frac{3}{4}x + \frac{5}{6}y = 12$$
$$12\left(\frac{3}{4}x + \frac{5}{6}y\right) = 12(12)$$
$$9x + 10y = 144$$

17. 150   Difficulty: Medium

Category: Additional Topics in Math / Geometry

Getting to the Answer: There are 360° in a circle. You need to figure out how many degrees each minute on the face of a clock represents. There are 60 minutes on the face of an analogue clock. This means that each minute represents $360 \div 60 = 6$ degrees. Between 3:20 and 3:45, 25 minutes go by, so the minute hand rotates $25 \times 6 = 150$ degrees.

18. 4   Difficulty: Medium

Category: Additional Topics in Math / Geometry

Getting to the Answer: Start by marking up the figure with the information you're given. You know the length of EB, which is 3. You also know the triangle is equilateral, which means all three sides are congruent and all three angles are 60°. This means angles A and B are both 60°, which further means that triangles BEF and ADC are 30-60-90 triangles, and therefore similar by the AAA theorem. Now recall that 30-60-90 triangles always have side lengths in the ratio $x : x\sqrt{3} : 2x$, which means if EB is 3, then BF (the hypotenuse) is $2(3) = 6$. Now, because you know the ratio of BF to FC, you can find the length of FC:

$$\frac{3}{4} = \frac{6}{FC}$$
$$3(FC) = 24$$
$$FC = 8$$

Now you can find the length of each side of the original equilateral triangle: $6 + 8 = 14$, which is the length of AC, the hypotenuse of triangle ADC. This means side AD, being the shorter leg of triangle ADC, is $14 \div 2 = 7$. You now have enough information to find the length of DE, which is $AB - (AD + EB) = 14 - (7 + 3) = 4$.

19. 8   Difficulty: Hard

Category: Passport to Advanced Math / Exponents

Getting to the Answer: Read the question carefully to determine what part of the expression you need to simplify and what part you don't. Sometimes, you can work a simpler question and still arrive at the correct answer. The question only asks for the exponent on x, so you do not have to simplify the coefficients. Rewrite the expression without the coefficients and simplify using the rules of exponents.

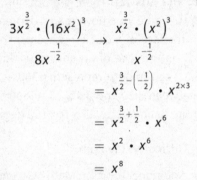

$$\frac{3x^{\frac{3}{2}} \cdot \left(16x^2\right)^3}{8x^{-\frac{1}{2}}} \rightarrow \frac{x^{\frac{3}{2}} \cdot \left(x^2\right)^3}{x^{-\frac{1}{2}}}$$
$$= x^{\frac{3}{2} - \left(-\frac{1}{2}\right)} \cdot x^{2 \times 3}$$
$$= x^{\frac{3}{2} + \frac{1}{2}} \cdot x^6$$
$$= x^2 \cdot x^6$$
$$= x^8$$

The exponent on x is 8.

20. 3/25 or .12   Difficulty: Hard

Category: Passport to Advanced Math / Functions

Getting to the Answer: When a question involving a function provides one or more ordered pairs, substitute them into the function to see what information you can glean. Start with $x = 0$ because doing so often results in the elimination of a variable.

$$f(x) = a \cdot b^x$$
$$f(0) = a \cdot b^0$$
$$3 = a \cdot b^0$$
$$3 = a \cdot 1$$
$$3 = a$$

Now you know the value of a, so the equation looks like $f(x) = 3 \cdot b^x$. Substitute the second pair of values into the new equation:

$$f(x) = 3 \cdot b^x$$
$$f(1) = 3 \cdot b^1$$
$$15 = 3 \cdot b^1$$
$$15 = 3b$$
$$5 = b$$

The exponential function is $f(x) = 3 \cdot 5x$. The final step is to find the value being asked for, $f(-2)$. Substitute -2 for x and simplify:

$$f(-2) = 3 \cdot 5^{-2} = \frac{3}{5^2} = \frac{3}{25}$$

Grid this in as 3/25 or .12.

MATH—CALCULATOR TEST

1. B   Difficulty: Easy

Category: Heart of Algebra / Linear Equations

Getting to the Answer: The total cost consists of a flat installation fee and a price per square foot. The installation fee is a one-time fee that does not depend on the number of feet ordered and therefore should not be multiplied by f. This means that 199 is the installation fee. The other expression in the equation, $3.29f$, represents the cost per square foot (the unit price) times the number of feet, f. Hence, 3.29 must represent the cost of one square foot of carpet, (B).

2. B   Difficulty: Easy

Category: Problem Solving and Data Analysis / Statistics and Probability

Getting to the Answer: Quickly read each answer choice. Cross out false statements as you go. Stop when you arrive at a true statement. There is no long "tail" of data on either side, so the shape is not skewed and you can eliminate A. The shape of the data *is* symmetric because the data is fairly evenly spread out, with about half of the ages above and half below the median. When the shape of a data set is symmetric, the mean is approximately equal to the median so (B) is correct. Don't let D fool you—the *median* is 55, not the *mean*.

3. A   Difficulty: Easy

Category: Heart of Algebra / Linear Equations

Getting to the Answer: Think about the best strategy to answer the question. If you distribute the $\frac{1}{3}$, it creates messy numbers. Instead, clear the fraction by multiplying both sides of the equation by 3. Then use inverse operations to solve for x.

$$\frac{1}{3}(5x - 8) = 3x + 4$$
$$5x - 8 = 3(3x + 4)$$
$$5x - 8 = 9x + 12$$
$$-4x = 20$$
$$x = -5$$

Choice (A) is correct.

4. A   Difficulty: Easy

Category: Passport to Advanced Math / Quadratics

Getting to the Answer: The minimum value of a quadratic function is equal to the y-value of the vertex of its graph, so vertex form, $y = a(x - h)^2 + k$, reveals the minimum without doing any additional work. Choice (A) is the only equation written in this form and therefore must be correct. The minimum value of this function is $-\frac{3}{2}$.

5. D   Difficulty: Easy

Category: Heart of Algebra / Linear Equations

Getting to the Answer: Organize information as you read the question; the total cost includes the per-

pound rate, the cost of the basket, and the 6% tax on the entire purchase. If a customer buys p pounds of apples, the total cost is the per-pound rate, $1.97, multiplied by the number of pounds, p, plus the $3.00 fee for the basket, or $1.97p + 3$. This expression represents the untaxed amount of the purchase. To calculate the amount that includes the 6% tax, multiply the untaxed amount by 1.06. The equation is $c = 1.06(1.97p + 3)$, which is (D).

6. C   Difficulty: Easy

Category: Heart of Algebra / Inequalities

Getting to the Answer: The intersection (overlap) of the two shaded regions is the solution to the system of inequalities. The point (4, 1) lies within the intersection of the two shaded regions, so it is a solution to the system shown in the figure. None of the other points lie within the intersection, so (C) is correct.

7. C   Difficulty: Medium

Category: Problem Solving and Data Analysis / Rates, Ratios, Proportions, and Percentages

Getting to the Answer: Start with the smallest possible lot size, 3,000 square feet. The next lot must be at least 30% larger, so multiply by 1.3 to get 3,900 square feet. Then, round up to the next thousand (which is not necessarily the nearest thousand) to meet the tax assessment requirement. You must always round up because rounding down would make the subsequent lot size less than 30% larger than the one before it. Continue this process until you reach the maximum square footage allowed, 15,000 square feet.

$$3,000 \times 1.3 = 3,900 \rightarrow 4,000$$
$$4,000 \times 1.3 = 5,200 \rightarrow 6,000$$
$$6,000 \times 1.3 = 7,800 \rightarrow 8,000$$
$$8,000 \times 1.3 = 10,400 \rightarrow 11,000$$
$$11,000 \times 1.3 = 14,300 \rightarrow 15,000$$

Choice (C) is correct.

8. D   Difficulty: Medium

Category: Problem Solving and Data Analysis / Functions

Getting to the Answer: Determine whether the change in the amount of pollution is a common difference (linear function) or a common ratio (exponential function), or if it changes direction (quadratic or polynomial function). Each year, the amount of pollution should be $100 - 8 = 92\%$ of the year before. You can write 92% as $\dfrac{92}{100}$, which represents a common ratio from one year to the next. This means that the best model is an exponential function, (D), of the form $y = a \cdot (0.92)^x$.

9. A   Difficulty: Medium

Category: Passport to Advanced Math / Exponents

Getting to the Answer: Don't spend too much time reading the scientific explanation of the equation. Solve for r using inverse operations. First, square both sides of the equation to remove the radical. Then, multiply both sides by r to get the r out of the denominator. Finally, divide both sides by v^2.

$$v = \sqrt{\dfrac{2Gm}{r}}$$
$$v^2 = \dfrac{2Gm}{r}$$
$$v^2 r = 2Gm$$
$$r = \dfrac{2Gm}{v^2}$$

This matches (A).

10. D   Difficulty: Medium

Category: Heart of Algebra / Systems of Linear Equations

Getting to the Answer: One equation should represent the total *number* of rentals, while the other equation represents the *cost* of the rentals. The number of DVDs plus the number of Blu-rays equals the total number of rentals, 209. Therefore, one equation is $d + b = 209$. This means you can eliminate

choices B and C. Now write the cost equation: cost per DVD times number of DVDs ($2d$) plus cost per Blu-ray times number of Blu-rays ($3.5b$) equals the total amount collected (562). The cost equation is $2d + 3.5b = 562$. Don't let A fool you. The question says nothing about the cost *per hour* so there is no reason to divide the cost by 4. Choice (D) is correct.

11. B   Difficulty: Medium

Category: Problem Solving and Data Analysis / Rates, Ratios, Proportions, and Percentages

Getting to the Answer: Break the question into short steps. *Step 1:* Find the number of female senators. *Step 2:* Use that number to find the number of female Republican senators. *Step 3:* Find the total number of Republican senators.

Each of the 50 states gets 2 voting members in the Senate, so there are $50 \times 2 = 100$ senators. The ratio of males to females in the 113th Congress was 4:1, so 4 parts male plus 1 part female equals a total of 100 senators. Write this as $4x + x = 100$, where x represents one part and therefore the number of females. Next, simplify and solve the equation to find that $x = 20$ female senators. To find the number of female senators that were Republican, multiply 20% (or 0.20) times 20 to get 4. Finally, add to get 45 male plus 4 female = 49 Republican senators in the 113th Congress, (B).

12. C   Difficulty: Medium

Category: Problem Solving and Data Analysis / Rates, Ratios, Proportions, and Percentages

Getting to the Answer: Find the percent increase by dividing the amount of change by the original amount. Then apply the same percent increase to the amount for 2012. The amount of increase is $29,400 - 18,750 = 10,650$, so the percent increase is $10,650 \div 18,750 = 0.568 = 56.8\%$ over 8 years. If the total percent increase over the next 8 years is the same, the average student who borrowed money will have loans totaling $29,400 \times 1.568 = 46,099.20$, or about $46,100. Choice (C) is correct.

13. D   Difficulty: Medium

Category: Heart of Algebra / Linear Equations

Getting to the Answer: Write the expression in words first: points per large basket (3) times number of beanbags in large basket (*b*), plus points per small basket (7) times number of beanbags in small basket. If there are 10 beanbags total and *b* go into the larger basket, the rest, or 10 − *b*, must go into the smaller basket. Now, translate the words to numbers, variables, and operations: $3b + 7(10 - b)$. This is not one of the answer choices, so simplify the expression by distributing the 7 and combining like terms: $3b + 7(10 - b) = 3b + 70 - 7b = 70 - 4b$. This matches (D).

14. D   Difficulty: Easy

Category: Problem Solving and Data Analysis / Statistics and Probability

Getting to the Answer: To calculate the percentage of the voters in each district who had no opinion on fracking, divide the number of voters in *that* district who had no opinion by the total number of voters in *that* district. Choice (D) is correct because $3,205 \div 63,539 \approx 0.05 = 5\%$, which is a lower percentage than in the other three districts that were polled (District A = 8%; District B = 7.6%; District C = 6%).

15. A   Difficulty: Medium

Category: Problem Solving and Data Analysis / Statistics and Probability

Getting to the Answer: Scan the answer choices quickly to narrow down the amount of information in the table that you need to analyze. Each choice makes a statement about people from District C who support a ban on fracking that can be expected to vote in the next election. To extrapolate from the follow-up survey sample, multiply the fraction of people from the follow-up survey who plan to vote in the upcoming election $\left(\dfrac{218}{500}\right)$ by the number of people in District C who support a ban on fracking (43,228) to get 18,847.408, or approximately 19,000 people. Choice (A) is correct.

16. B   Difficulty: Medium

Category: Heart of Algebra / Systems of Linear Equations

Getting to the Answer: Solve the system of equations using substitution. Then, check that you answered the right question (find the sum of *x* and *y*). First, solve the second equation for *x* to get $x = 3y - 11$, then substitute this expression into the first equation to find *y*:

$$2x + 4y = 13$$
$$2(3y - 11) + 4y = 13$$
$$6y - 22 + 4y = 13$$
$$10y - 22 = 13$$
$$10y = 35$$
$$y = \frac{7}{2}$$

Now, substitute the result into $x = 3y - 11$ and simplify to find *x*:

$$x = 3\left(\frac{7}{2}\right) - 11$$
$$= \frac{21}{2} - 11$$
$$= -\frac{1}{2}$$

The question asks for the sum, so add *x* and *y* to get $-\dfrac{1}{2} + \dfrac{7}{2} = \dfrac{6}{2} = 3$, which is (B).

17. C   Difficulty: Medium

Category: Problem Solving and Data Analysis / Statistics and Probability

Getting to the Answer: The key word in the answer choices is "consistently," which relates to how spread out a player's scores are. Standard deviation, not mean, is a measure of spread so you can eliminate choice A right away. A lower standard deviation indicates scores that are less spread out and therefore more consistent. Likewise, a higher standard deviation indicates scores that are more spread out and therefore less consistent. Notice the opposite nature of this relationship: lower standard deviation = more consistent; higher standard deviation = less consistent. Choice (C) is correct because the standard deviation of Mae's scores is the lowest, which means she bowled the most consistently.

18. B   Difficulty: Medium

Category: Passport to Advanced Math / Quadratics

Getting to the Answer: Notice the structure of the equation. The expression on the left side of the equation is the square of a quantity, so start by taking the square root of both sides. After taking the square roots, solve the resulting equations. Remember, $4^2 = 16$ and $(-4)^2 = 16$, so there will be *two* equations to solve.

$$(x + 3)^2 = 16$$
$$\sqrt{(x + 3)^2} = \sqrt{16}$$
$$x + 3 = \pm 4$$
$$x + 3 = 4 \rightarrow x = 1$$
$$x + 3 = -4 \rightarrow x = -7$$

Choice (B) is correct.

19. C   Difficulty: Medium

Category: Problem Solving and Data Analysis / Rates, Ratios, Proportions, and Percentages

Getting to the Answer: Pay careful attention to the units. You need to convert all of the dimensions to inches, and then set up and solve a proportion. The real statue's height is $305 \times 12 = 3,660 + 6 = 3,666$ inches; the length of the nose on the real statue is $4 \times 12 = 48 + 6 = 54$ inches; the height of the model statue is 26 inches; the length of the nose on the model is unknown.

$$\frac{3,666}{54} = \frac{26}{x}$$
$$3,666x = 26(54)$$
$$3,666x = 1,404$$
$$x = \frac{1,404}{3,666} = \frac{18}{47}$$

Choice (C) is correct.

20. B   Difficulty: Medium

Category: Passport to Advanced Math / Functions

Getting to the Answer: When evaluating a function, substitute the value inside the parentheses for x in the equation. Evaluate the function at $x = 6$ and at $x = 2$, and then subtract the second output from the first. Note that this is not the same as first subtracting $6 - 2$ and then evaluating the function at $x = 4$.

$$f(6) = 3(6) + 5 = 18 + 5 = 23$$
$$f(2) = 3(2) + 5 = 6 + 5 = 11$$

$$f(6) - f(2) = 23 - 11 = 12$$

Choice (B) is correct.

21. A   Difficulty: Medium

Category: Problem Solving and Data Analysis / Scatterplots

Getting to the Answer: Examine the graph, paying careful attention to units and labels. Here, the years increase by 2 for each grid-line and the number of owls by 25. The average change per year is the same as the slope of the line of best fit. Find the slope of the line of best fit using the slope formula, $m = \dfrac{y_2 - y_1}{x_2 - x_1}$, and any two points that lie on (or very close to) the line. Using the two endpoints of the data, (1994, 1,200) and (2014, 700), the average change per year is $\dfrac{700 - 1,200}{2014 - 1994} = \dfrac{-500}{20} = -25$, which is (A). Pay careful attention to the sign of the answer—the number of owls is decreasing, so the rate of change is negative.

22. D   Difficulty: Medium

Category: Passport to Advanced Math / Quadratics

Getting to the Answer: The solution to a system of equations is the point(s) where their graphs intersect. You could solve this question algebraically, one system at a time, but this is not time efficient. Instead, graph each pair of equations in your graphing calculator and look for the graphs that intersect at $x = -4$ and $x = 2$. The graphs of the equations in A and B don't intersect at all, so you can eliminate them right away. The graphs in C intersect, but both points of intersection have a positive x-coordinate. This means (D) must be correct. The graph looks like:

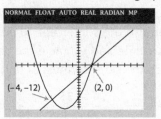

23. C   **Difficulty:** Medium

Category: Problem Solving and Data Analysis / Statistics and Probability

Getting to the Answer: Read the question, identifying parts of the graphic you need—the question asks about litters of 7 or more pups, so you'll only use the heights of the bars for 7, 8, and 9 pups. Start by finding the percent of the mice in the study that had a litter of 7 or more pups. Of the 200 mice in the sample, $25 + 14 + 5 = 44$ had a litter of 7 or more pups. This is $\frac{44}{200} = \frac{22}{100} = 22\%$ of the mice in the study. Given the same general conditions (such as living in the same geographic region), you would expect approximately the same results, so multiply the number of female mice in the whole population by the percent you found: $35{,}000 \times 0.22 = 7{,}700$, (C).

24. C   **Difficulty:** Medium

Category: Heart of Algebra / Linear Equations

Getting to the Answer: You'll need to interpret the information given in the question to write two ordered pairs. Then you can use the ordered pairs to find the slope and the y-intercept of the linear model. In an ordered pair, the independent variable is always written first. Here, the heart rate de-

pends on the amount of exercise, so the ordered pairs should be written in the form (time, heart rate). They are (8, 90) and (20, 117). Use these points in the slope formula, $m = \dfrac{y_2 - y_1}{x_2 - x_1}$, to find that $m = \dfrac{117 - 90}{20 - 8} = \dfrac{27}{12} = 2.25$. Then, substitute the slope (2.25) and either of the points into slope-intercept form and simply to find the y-intercept:

$$90 = 2.25(8) + b$$
$$90 = 18 + b$$
$$72 = b$$

Finally, write the equation using the slope and the y-intercept that you found to get $r = 2.25t + 72$. Note that the only choice with a slope of 2.25 is (C), so you could have eliminated the other three choices before finding the y-intercept and saved yourself a bit of time.

25. A   **Difficulty:** Medium

Category: Additional Topics in Math / Geometry

Getting to the Answer: The formula for finding the area of a trapezoid is $A = \dfrac{1}{2}h(b_1 + b_2)$. This particular formula is not given on the formula page; memorizing it prior to Test Day will save you a bit of time (rather than having to find the sum of the areas of the triangles and the rectangle that make up the trapezoid).

You could pick numbers to represent the lengths of the bases and height, and then find the area of the trapezoid before and after the indicated changes. Or, you might happen to notice that reducing the height by 75% means the new height is $\dfrac{1}{4}$ of the original height, which is likely to cancel nicely with the 4 that the bases are being multiplied by. Using the second strategy, the formula for the area of the new trapezoid becomes $A = \left(\dfrac{1}{2}\right)\left(\dfrac{1}{4}h\right)(4b_1 + 4b_2)$. If you factor 4 out of the bases, you can cancel it with the 4 in the denominator of the new height:

$A = \left(\dfrac{1}{2}\right)\left(\dfrac{\cancel{4}}{\cancel{4}}h\right)\cancel{A}(b_1 + b_2)$. The resulting equation is $A = \dfrac{1}{2}h(b_1 + b_2)$, the same as the original equation, which means the area has not changed, and therefore the percent increase is 0%. Choice (A) is correct.

26. C   Difficulty: Medium

Category: Heart of Algebra / Linear Equations

Getting to the Answer: Pay careful attention to what the question tells you about the variables. The x-value is the number of payments already made, and the y-value is the amount of debt remaining (not how much has been paid). If a solution is (21, 560), the x-value is 21, which means Chantal has made 21 payments already. The y-value is 560, which means $560 is the amount of debt *left to be paid*, making (C) correct.

27. D   Difficulty: Hard

Category: Problem Solving and Data Analysis / Scatterplots

Getting to the Answer: A line that "represents the trend of the data" is another way of saying line of best fit. The trend of the data is clearly linear because the path of the dots does not turn around or curve, so draw a line of best fit on the graph. Remember, about half of the points should be above the line and half below.

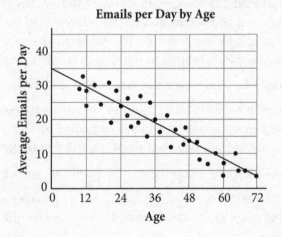

Emails per Day by Age

If you draw your line of best fit all the way to the y-axis, you'll save yourself a step by simply looking at the scatterplot to find the y-intercept. For this graph, it's about 35. This means you can eliminate choices B and C. Next, find the approximate slope using two points that lie on (or very close to) the line. You can use the y-intercept, (0, 35), as one of them to save time and estimate the second, such as (72, 4). Use the slope formula to find the slope:

$$m = \frac{y_2 - y_1}{x_2 - x_1} = \frac{4 - 35}{72 - 0} = \frac{-31}{72} \approx -0.43$$

The equation that has the closest slope and y-intercept is (D). (Note that if you choose different points, your line may have a slightly different slope or y-intercept, but the answer choices will be far enough apart that you should be able to determine which is the *best* fit to the data.)

28. B   Difficulty: Hard

Category: Passport to Advanced Math / Functions

Getting to the Answer: Transformations that are grouped with the x in a function shift the graph horizontally and, therefore, affect the x-coordinates of points on the graph. Transformations that are not grouped with the x shift the graph vertically and, therefore, affect the y-coordinates of points on the graph. Remember, horizontal shifts are always backward of what they look like. Start with $(x + 3)$. This shifts the graph left 3, so subtract 3 from the x-coordinate of the given point: $(5, 1) \to (5 - 3, 1) = (2, 1)$. Next, apply the negative in front of f, which is not grouped with the x, so it makes the y-coordinate negative: $(2, 1) \to (2, -1)$. Finally, -2 is not grouped with x, so subtract 2 from the y-coordinate: $(2, -1 - 2) \to (2, -3)$, which is (B).

29. C   Difficulty: Hard

Category: Problem Solving and Data Analysis / Rates, Ratios, Proportions, and Percentages

Getting to the Answer: Draw a chart or diagram detailing the various price reductions for each 30 days.

Date	% of Most Recent Price	Resulting Price
Jan. 15	100 − 25% = 75%	$1,500 × 0.75 = $1,125
Feb. 15	100 − 10% = 90%	$1,125 × 0.9 = $1,012.50
Mar. 15	100 − 10% = 90%	$1,012.50 × 0.9 = $911.25

You can stop here because the refrigerator was sold on April 2, which is not 30 days after March 15. The final selling price was $911.25, (C).

30. A   Difficulty: Hard

Category: Additional Topics in Math / Geometry

Getting to the Answer: Organize information as you read the question. Here, you'll definitely want to draw and label a sketch.

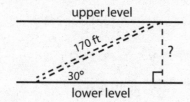

The lower level, the vertical distance between levels, and the diagonal elevator track form a 30-60-90 triangle, where the elevator track is the hypotenuse. The vertical distance is opposite the 30° angle so it is the shortest leg. The rules for 30-60-90 triangles state that the shortest leg is half the length of the hypotenuse, so the vertical distance between levels is approximately 170 ÷ 2 = 85 feet, (A).

31. 22   Difficulty: Medium

Category: Heart of Algebra / Inequalities

Getting to the Answer: You don't need to separate this compound inequality into pieces. Just remember, whatever you do to one piece, you must do to all three pieces. Don't forget to flip the inequality symbols if you multiply or divide by a negative number. Here, the fractions make it look more complicated than it really is, so start by clearing the fractions by multiplying everything by 20.

$$20\left(-\frac{3}{2}\right) < 20\left(3 - \frac{a}{5}\right) < 20\left(-\frac{1}{4}\right)$$
$$-30 < 60 - 4a < -5$$
$$-30 - 60 < 60 - 60 - 4a < -5 - 60$$
$$-90 < -4a < -65$$
$$\frac{-90}{-4} > \frac{-4a}{-4} > \frac{-65}{-4}$$
$$22.5 > a > 16.25$$
$$16.25 < a < 22.5$$

The question asks for the maximum possible whole number value of a, so the correct answer is 22.

32. 1/6 or .166 or .167   Difficulty: Easy

Category: Problem Solving and Data Analysis / Statistics and Probability

Getting to the Answer: This question requires concentration, but no complicated calculations. First, you need to identify the rows that contain information about the seating on the 777s, which are the bottom two rows. To find the probability that the seat is a Business Class seat, find the total number of seats in that category (in only the bottom two rows), and divide by the total number of seats on the planes (in only the bottom two rows):

$$P(\text{Business Class}) = \frac{37 + 52}{194 + 37 + 16 + 227 + 52 + 8}$$
$$= \frac{89}{534} = \frac{1}{6} = 0.1\overline{6}$$

Grid in your answer as 1/6 or .166 or .167.

33. 440   Difficulty: Medium

Category: Heart of Algebra / Systems of Linear Equations

Getting to the Answer: Translate from English into math to write a system of equations with t = the cost of the tankless heater in dollars, and c = the cost of the conventional heater in dollars. First, a tankless heater (t) costs $160 more (+160) than twice as much ($2c$) as the conventional one, or $t = 2c + 160$. Together, a tankless heater (t) and a conventional heater (c) cost $1,000, or $t + c = 1,000$. The system is:

$$\begin{cases} t = 2c + 160 \\ t + c = 1,000 \end{cases}$$

The top equation is already solved for t, so substitute $2c + 160$ into the second equation for t and solve for c:

$$2c + 160 + c = 1,000$$
$$3c + 160 = 1,000$$
$$3c = 840$$
$$c = 280$$

Be careful—that's not the answer! The conventional hot water heater costs $280, so the tankless heater costs $2(280) + 160 = $720. This means the tankless heater costs $720 − $280 = $440 more than the conventional heater.

34. 25   Difficulty: Medium

Category: Problem Solving and Data Analysis / Rates, Ratios, Proportions, and Percentages

Getting to the Answer: The key to answering this question is reading carefully—the word "exactly" is very important because it tells you that there cannot be a portion of a patient, so you are looking for the smallest whole number of which 48% is also a whole number. Every percent can be written as a number over 100 (because *per cent* means *per hundred*), so start by writing 48% as a fraction and reducing it: $\frac{48}{100} = \frac{12}{25}$. The denominator of this fraction (25) gives the least possible number of patients who could have participated in the trial because it is the first number that will cancel when multiplied by the fraction.

35. 9984 Difficulty: Hard

Category: Additional Topics in Math / Geometry

Getting to the Answer: Don't be too quick to answer a question like this. You can't simply find two-thirds of the volume of the pyramid because the top is considerably smaller than the bottom. Instead, you'll need to find the volume of the whole pyramid and subtract the volume of the top piece that is being discarded.

The figure shows a right triangle inside the pyramid. The bottom leg is given as 18 and the slant height, or hypotenuse of the triangle, is given as 30. You might recognize this as a multiple of the Pythagorean triplet, 3-4-5, which is in this case 18-24-30. This means the height of the original pyramid is 24. You now have enough information to find the volume of the original pyramid.

$$V = \frac{1}{3}lwh$$
$$V = \frac{1}{3}(36)(36)(24)$$
$$V = \frac{1}{3}(31,104)$$
$$V = 10,368$$

To determine the dimensions of the top piece that is cut off, use similar triangles.

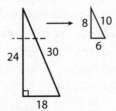

One-third of the original height is $24 \div 3 = 8$, resulting in a 6-8-10 triangle, making the length of the smaller leg 6, which means the length of the whole cutoff pyramid is $6 \times 2 = 12$. Substitute this into the formula for volume again.

$$V = \frac{1}{3}lwh$$
$$V = \frac{1}{3}(12)(12)(8)$$
$$V = \frac{1}{3}(1,152)$$
$$V = 384$$

Thus, the volume of the frustum is $10,368 - 384 = 9,984$ cubic meters.

36. 88   Difficulty: Hard

Category: Passport to Advanced Math / Exponents

Getting to the Answer: When you're asked to solve an equation that has two variables, the question usually gives you the value of one of the variables. Read carefully to see which variable is given and which one you're solving for. You are given the diameter (0.12), so substitute this value for d in the equation and then solve for the other variable, h. Before dealing with the radical, divide both sides of the equation by 0.015.

$$0.12 = 0.015 \times \sqrt{h - 24}$$
$$8 = \sqrt{h - 24}$$
$$8^2 = \left(\sqrt{h - 24}\right)^2$$
$$64 = h - 24$$
$$88 = h$$

37. 252   Difficulty: Medium

Category: Problem Solving and Data Analysis / Rates, Ratios, Proportions, and Percentages

Getting to the Answer: Break the question into steps. First, find how long it took Daniel to spray one lawn, and then use that amount to find how long it took him to spray all the lawns. According to the figure, he started the first house at 9:00 and the sixth house at 10:00, so it took him 1 hour, or 60 minutes, to spray 5 houses. This gives a unit rate of $60 \div 5 = 12$ minutes per house. Count the houses in the figure—there are 21. Multiply the unit rate by the number of houses to get $12 \times 21 = 252$ minutes to spray all the lawns.

38. 4   Difficulty: Hard

Category: Problem Solving and Data Analysis / Rates, Ratios, Proportions, and Percentages

Getting to the Answer: This part of the question contains several steps. Think about the units given in the question and what you need to convert so that you can get to the answer. The total acreage of all the lawns in the neighborhood is $21 \times 0.2 = 4.2$ acres. This is equivalent to $4.2 \times 43,560 = 182,952$ square feet. Each gallon of spray covers 2,500 square feet so divide to find that Daniel needs $182,952 \div 2,500 = 73.1808$ gallons to spray all the lawns. The spray rig holds 20 gallons, so Daniel will need to fill it 4 times. After he fills it the fourth time and finishes all the lawns, there will be some spray left over.

ESSAY TEST RUBRIC

The Essay Demonstrates ...

4—Advanced	• **(Reading)** A strong ability to comprehend the source text, including its central ideas and important details and how they interrelate; and effectively use evidence (quotations, paraphrases, or both) from the source text.
	• **(Analysis)** A strong ability to evaluate the author's use of evidence, reasoning, and/or stylistic and persuasive elements, and/or other features of the student's own choosing; make good use of relevant, sufficient, and strategically chosen support for the claims or points made in the student's essay; and focus consistently on features of the source text that are most relevant to addressing the task.
	• **(Writing)** A strong ability to provide a precise central claim; create an effective organization that includes an introduction and conclusion, as well as a clear progression of ideas; successfully employ a variety of sentence structures; use precise word choice; maintain a formal style and objective tone; and show command of the conventions of standard written English so that the essay is free of errors.
3—Proficient	• **(Reading)** Satisfactory ability to comprehend the source text, including its central ideas and important details and how they interrelate; and use evidence (quotations, paraphrases, or both) from the source text.
	• **(Analysis)** Satisfactory ability to evaluate the author's use of evidence, reasoning, and/or stylistic and persuasive elements, and/or other features of the student's own choosing; make use of relevant and sufficient support for the claims or points made in the student's essay; and focus primarily on features of the source text that are most relevant to addressing the task.
	• **(Writing)** Satisfactory ability to provide a central claim; create an organization that includes an introduction and conclusion, as well as a clear progression of ideas; employ a variety of sentence structures; use precise word choice; maintain an appropriate formal style and objective tone; and show control of the conventions of standard written English so that the essay is free of significant errors.
2—Partial	• **(Reading)** Limited ability to comprehend the source text, including its central ideas and important details and how they interrelate; and use evidence (quotations, paraphrases, or both) from the source text.
	• **(Analysis)** Limited ability to evaluate the author's use of evidence, reasoning, and/or stylistic and persuasive elements, and/or other features of the student's own choosing; make use of support for the claims or points made in the student's essay; and focus on relevant features of the source text.
	• **(Writing)** Limited ability to provide a central claim; create an effective organization for ideas; employ a variety of sentence structures; use precise word choice; maintain an appropriate style and tone; or show command of the conventions of standard written English, resulting in certain errors that detract from the quality of the writing.

1—Inadequate	• **(Reading)** Little or no ability to comprehend the source text or use evidence from the source text.
	• **(Analysis)** Little or no ability to evaluate the author's use of evidence, reasoning, and/ or stylistic and persuasive elements; choose support for claims or points; or focus on relevant features of the source text.
	• **(Writing)** Little or no ability to provide a central claim, organization, or progression of ideas; employ a variety of sentence structures; use precise word choice; maintain an appropriate style and tone; or show command of the conventions of standard written English, resulting in numerous errors that undermine the quality of the writing.

ESSAY RESPONSE #1 (ADVANCED SCORE)

In "The Human Side of Animals," Royal Dixon makes the argument that animals are complex beings with thoughts and feelings that deserve the same respect as humans. When Dixon first makes his argument, he probably realizes that he faces an uphill climb. Most people are meat-eaters, and it is likely that much of Dixon's audience consists of people whose lifestyle depends on the domination and consumption of animals. In order to build a strong argument in the face of such opposition, Dixon effectively uses persuasive techniques that include emotional language and imagery, appeals to his audience's intelligence, and persuasive reasoning and evidence.

Dixon uses emotionally laden language and imagery to persuade his audience of the humanity of animals. First, he conjures the heartwarming image of "young lambs playing on a grassy hillside," only to give his audience an unpleasant jolt when he abruptly turns the lambs into cold, impersonal "mutton." Dixon uses a similarly emotional image later in the passage when he describes cows "[bellowing] for days when mourning for their dead." By including these powerful images that are likely to upset people, Dixon makes it difficult for his audience to maintain the position that humans should have no feeling for animals.

Dixon also uses appeals to his audience's intelligence to sway them to his side. In the first paragraph, he asks the rhetorical question, "Why should we fall into the colossal ignorance and conceit of cataloging every human-like action of animals [as] instinct?" By associating disrespect of animals with ignorance, Dixon leads his audience, who wants to feel intelligent, into agreeing with his views. In the second paragraph, Dixon uses the analogies of fascism and primitive religion to compare dominion over animals to other misguided ideas. Later, he labels the views of the average scientist as ignorant and "empty," encouraging his audience to align themselves with his views instead.

Dixon, however, relies on more than just stylistic elements and emotional appeals to make his case. He also uses persuasive reasoning and evidence to support his point that animals are worthy of the same respect as humans. To critics who would argue that animals' abilities are due to instinct and neurological impulses, Dixon counters that humans, too, are ruled by the same forces, and yet we allow a level of compassion and feeling for humans that we deny to animals. He also makes the point that physically, humans and animals are very similar to each other, and in fact, animals are physically superior to humans in most cases. The major difference, he says, is that we have a superior intellect. By pointing out how much we have in common with animals, Dixon removes the barrier between us and them, making it harder for his opposition to argue that animals have neither intellect nor feeling.

He continues this line of reasoning by pointing out that human and animal behaviors are similar, and that "man has been imitating the animals" by flying, tunneling, and exploring Earth's waters. Dixon uses a variety of examples to provide evidence for his case: animals organizing themselves against enemies, building shelter, storing food, and making and using tools, just like humans. He also cites animal communication as a marker of intelligence and different emotional states, even if humans don't understand what they are hearing. An especially vivid piece of evidence is the example of a dreaming war horse who "lives over and over his battles," just as humans re-live their exploits in their dreams. Time and again, Dixon proves humans and animals share common experiences, and are therefore worthy of mutual respect.

By presenting the evidence of commonalities between humans and animals, as well as evidence of animals' feeling and intellect, Dixon makes an effective case that we should cease our dominion over them. He bolsters his case with appeals to his audience's intelligence and emotional imagery, both of which make his audience less resistant to his claims. While Dixon may not persuade every member of his audience that animals are worthy of respect, his use of these features makes his argument much more effective than it would be without them.

ESSAY RESPONSE #2 (PROFICIENT SCORE)

Royal Dixon makes the argument in "The Human Side of Animals" that animals and humans should be treated with the same respect. He uses appeals to emotion, rhetorical questions, and evidence of animals' thoughts and feelings to make his case.

Knowing that most people who eat meat would disagree with his claims, Dixon uses emotional language to break down their resistance. It is hard to argue that animals have no feelings when Dixon describes cows mourning for days for their dead. Dixon gives other examples of animals having strong emotions, like when a war horse acts out its former battles in its sleep. These examples remind people of themselves; which is Dixon's goal: to break down the barriers between animals and humans.

He also uses rhetorical questions to persuade his audience to agree with ideas that may be new to them. In the first paragraph he asks, "If you agree that we cannot treat men like machines, why should we put animals in that class?" Since most people would agree with the first part of the statement, they are more likely to agree with the second part as well. The next rhetorical question in the paragraph asks people if they want to "fall into the colossal ignorance" of thinking that all animal behavior is due to instinct, the answer is obviously no. By carefully constructing these questions, Dixon puts his audience in a position in which they will be more likely to agree with his claims.

For readers who still may doubt that animals and humans have much in common, Dixon offers many examples of how animal behavior is like human behavior. Animals build shelter, make tools, and do other things that are just like the things humans do. With these examples, and others, Dixon shows that animals and humans are so similar that it makes no sense for one to dominate the other. In fact, he points out, some animal abilities are superhuman, like their ability to predict the weather. By giving examples of animals' traits and abilities that are similar to and even better than ours, Dixon causes the audience to feel respect for animals.

In conclusion, Dixon uses different ways of getting his audience to agree that animals are worthy of respect in "The Human Side of Animals." The use of emotional appeals, rhetorical questions, and evidence of animals' "humanity" helps him to persuade an audience that may be resistent at first to hearing his ideas.